Organ and Tissue Transplantation

The International Library of Medicine, Ethics and Law
Series Editor: Michael D. Freeman

Organ and Tissue Transplantation

Edited by

David Price

De Montfort University, UK

ASHGATE

Published by
Ashgate Publishing Limited
Gower House
Croft Road
Aldershot
Hampshire GU11 3HR
England

Ashgate Publishing Company
Suite 420
101 Cherry Street
Burlington, VT 05401-4405
USA

Ashgate website: http://www.ashgate.com

British Library Cataloguing in Publication Data

Organ and tissue transplantation. – (The international
    library of medicine, ethics and law)
    1. Transplantation of organs, tissues, etc. – Moral and
    ethical aspects 2. Transplantation of organs, tissues, etc.
    – Law and legislation 3. Death – Proof and certification
    4. Consent (Law)
    I. Price, David
    174.2'97954

Library of Congress Control Number: 2006931596

ISBN 0 7546 2539 7
ISBN 978-0-7546-2539-1

Printed in Great Britain by TJ International Ltd, Padstow, Cornwall

Contents

PART V   LIVING DONOR TRANSPLANTATION

PART VI   SPECIFIC CLASSES OF DONORS

PART VII ORGAN ALLOCATION

PART VIII XENOTRANSPLANTATION

Acknowledgements

The editor and publishers wish to thank the following for permission to use copyright material.

Blackwell Publishing for the essays: Carl Becker (1999), 'Money Talks, Money Kills – The Economics of Transplantation in Japan and China', *Bioethics*, **13**, pp. 236–43. Copyright © 1999 Blackwell Publishing; Donna Dickenson and Guy Widdershoven (2001), 'Ethical Issues in Limb Transplants', *Bioethics*, **15**, pp. 110–24. Copyright © 2001 Blackwell Publishing.

British Medical Journal for the essays: Charles A. Erin and John Harris (1999), 'Presumed Consent or Contracting Out', *Journal of Medical Ethics*, **25**, pp. 365–66; Stephanie Eaton (1998), 'The Subtle Politics of Organ Donation: A Proposal', *Journal of Medical Ethics*, **24**, pp. 166–70.

Cambridge University Press for the essays: Susan E. Herz (1999), 'Two Steps to Three Choices: A New Approach to Mandated Choice', *Cambridge Quarterly of Healthcare Ethics*, **8**, pp. 340–47. Copyright © 1999 Cambridge University Press; Ryan Sauder and Lisa S. Parker (2001), 'Autonomy's Limits: Living Donation and Health-Related Harm', *Cambridge Quarterly of Healthcare Ethics*, **10**, pp. 399–407. Copyright © 2001 Cambridge University Press; Robert A. Crouch and Carl Elliott (1999), 'Moral Agency and the Family: The Case of Living Related Organ Transplantation', *Cambridge Quarterly of Healthcare Ethics*, **8**, pp. 275–87. Copyright © 1999 Cambridge University Press. James F. Childress (2001), 'Putting Patients First in Organ Allocation: An Ethical Analysis of the U.S. Debate', *Cambridge Quarterly of Healthcare Ethics*, **10**, pp. 365–76. Copyright © 2001 Cambridge University Press; Rachel A. Ankeny (2001), 'The Moral Status of Preferences for Directed Donation: Who Should Decide Who Gets Transplantable Organs?', *Cambridge Quarterly of Healthcare Ethics*, **10**, pp. 387–98. Copyright © 2001 Cambridge University Press.

Columbia Law Review Association for the essays: John A. Robertson (1976), 'Organ Donations by Incompetents and the Substituted Judgment Doctrine', *Columbia Law Review*, **76**, pp. 48–78; Jay A. Friedman (1990), 'Taking the Camel by the Nose: The Anencephalic as a Source for Pediatric Organ Transplants', *Columbia Law Review*, **90**, pp. 917–78.

Copyright Clearance Center for the essay: Jerry Menikoff (2002), 'The Importance of Being Dead: Non-Heart-Beating Organ Donation', *Issues in Law and Medicine*, **18**, pp. 3–20.

Elsevier for the essays: B. Hoffmaster (1985), 'Freedom to Choose and Freedom to Lose: The Procurement of Cadaver Organs for Transplantation', *Transplantation Proceedings*, **17**, pp. 24–30; P.T. Menzel (1992), 'The Moral Duty to Contribute and Its Implications for Organ Procurement Policy', *Transplantation Proceedings*, **24**, pp. 2175–78; C. Cohen (1992), 'The Case for Presumed Consent to Transplant Human Organs After Death', *Transplantation*

Series Preface

Few academic disciplines have developed with such pace in recent years as bioethics. And because the subject crosses so many disciplines important writing is to be found in a range of books and journals, access to the whole of which is likely to elude all but the most committed of scholars. The International Library of Medicine, Ethics and Law is designed to assist the scholarly endeavour by providing in accessible volumes a compendium of basic materials drawn from the most significant periodical literature. Each volume contains essays of central theoretical importance in its subject area, and each throws light on important bioethical questions in the world today. The series as a whole – there will be fifteen volumes – makes available an extensive range of valuable material (the standard 'classics' and the not-so-standard) and should prove of inestimable value to those involved in the research, teaching and study of medicine, ethics and law. The fifteen volumes together – each with introductions and bibliographies – are a library in themselves – an indispensable resource in a world in which even the best-stocked library is unlikely to cover the range of materials contained within these volumes.

It remains for me to thank the editors who have pursued their task with commitment, insight and enthusiasm, to thank also the hard-working staff at Ashgate – theirs is a mammoth enterprise – and to thank my secretary, Anita Garfoot for the enormous assistance she has given me in bringing the series from idea to reality.

MICHAEL FREEMAN
Series Editor
Faculty of Laws
University College London

Introduction

The Meaning of Death

There has been a recent proliferation in the number of non-heart-beating donor protocols in Europe and the United States, currently for generating kidneys and livers for transplantation, and possibly in the future even for hearts. These protocols utilize traditional notions of death based on cardiopulmonary cessation and often provide for organ procurement or organ preservation methods (for example, cooling and perfusion techniques) to be instituted very soon after cardiac and respiratory function ceases. This has generated claims that such individuals may not in fact be dead at the relevant point in time. Under English law it is clear that patients who satisfy the criteria for brain stem death are legally dead, but the status of patients whose respiration and circulation has ceased per se is currently uncertain. In the large majority of US states which have statutes based on the Uniform Determination of Death Act, it is explicitly stated that death may be declared on the basis of either whole brain death *or* the irreversible cessation of circulatory functions. Whilst non-heart-beating donor protocols place reliance on this alternative legal foundation in the United States, Jerry Menikoff (Chapter 2) nevertheless highlights that this is problematic because, among other things, the individual who is declared dead may still retain brain function, possibly including some higher brain function. He contends that such statutes should not be read formalistically and that, even in the United States, there is only one condition properly recognized as constituting death – namely, brain death – although there are two sets of *criteria* which may alternatively be used to establish that condition. If this were not the case, we would be endorsing 'differing categories of deadness'.

Menikoff notes that the dead donor rule, under which patients must not be killed by the removal of organs, is a universal and central element of moral and legal frameworks relating to organ procurement. He suggests, however, that, although there is potential for the definition of death to be gerrymandered in the context of certain non-heart-beating protocols because certain individuals are typically moribund and very willing organ donors, this may be justified on the basis of the benefits of such a policy and the absence of any real harms.

Suggestions that the dead donor rule should be either modified or abandoned and replaced with reliance on the concept of informed consent to guard against abuse have emanated from various quarters (see for example, Arnold and Youngner, 1993). However, Robert Truog's essay (Chapter 1) not only develops this theme, but also contains trenchant criticisms of the concept of brain death itself and its *deleterious* effects on the supply of organs for transplantation. Truog alleges that patients declared brain dead have not in fact suffered a permanent cessation of the whole brain (and thus do not satisfy the legal test for brain death in the United States – a stumbling block obviated to a degree in the UK by reliance on brain *stem* death instead), and that this concept has been designed solely to serve the project of organ procurement. He suggests that the organ donor pool may be increased by shifting the ethical foundations to principles of non-maleficence and consent and that, paradoxically, the concept of brain death hinders procurement because it is counterintuitive to regard respiring (pink and hydrated) patients as dead. He advocates amending policies (as well as laws) so that they permit organ procurement, with the consent of the donor or appropriate surrogate, where this would not harm the donor – in other words, legitimizing such practices as a form of justified killing. The concept of brain death would then be rendered obsolete, and questions of organ donation would be separated from the life–death dichotomy. This controversial proposal challenges our views as to the proper principles underpinning organ procurement, and raises the question whether different moral frameworks for living and cadaveric donation are appropriate. It might also permit latitude to allow the operation of *individual* conceptions of death and to view death as occurring at different points in time for different ends.

The Body as Property

Very many issues relating to organ and tissue donation are influenced by perspectives of the relationship between the self and the body, and whether we own our bodies either before or after the severance of body parts. This issue has generated diverse views and considerable policy ambiguity around the world. There are many potential applications and uses of human tissue and it may be that a property rights-based framework is more plausible or desirable in certain contexts than in others. In Chapter 3 Margaret Swain and Randy Marusyk propose a model in which transplantable human tissue entails no property rights but in which such rights may be generated by the investment of labour in creating new forms of tissue. They identify three tiers: that of the person and persona; that of the functional bodily unit; and that of the production of something else from human material, such as a cell line. Whilst it is still an integral part of the body, tissue forms part of the first tier and is beyond property, but once it has been removed it falls within the second tier. It is at this second stage that transplantable human materials are now able to be individually identified. Swain and Marusyk propose that such materials should be regarded as *res nullius* prior to being transplanted into another person. Clinicians would be 'possessors in trust' for the benefit of the ultimate recipient. Thus, it would be impossible for such tissue, which is only *temporarily* removed from the human body, to become a marketable commodity. However, if tissue is permanently removed it falls within the third tier and is *res communes omnium* and is thus capable of generating property rights in cases where something is produced from it. This proposition relies on Lockean labour theory – that is, merging one's labour with 'common property' creates private property interests.

According to Swain and Marusyk's thesis, John Moore's spleen tissue would be categorized as falling within this third tier and would be capable of being the catalyst for property rights, although the *patient* would be denied any rights over the tissue. However, in Chapter 4 Bernard Dickens reminds us that the California Supreme Court in *Moore* v. *Regents of the University of California* was motivated principally by the need to free biomedical researchers from undue constraints and disincentives, and consequently denied Moore's property claim for *these*, although not for all, purposes. Dickens notes that similar instrumental reasoning in the transplantation context may be applied to achieve *different* conclusions. He emphasizes the need for legal control over such transplantable material following removal but prior to transplantation of organs donated *inter vivos*. He suggests such organs are *not res nullius* or abandoned at this point and that granting living organ donors property rights during this period may ensure the proper handling and usage of such organs in the interim. He considers *Moore* to be distinguishable by virtue of the biotechnological processes applied to his tissues.

Commerce in Organ Procurement

The possibility of commercial dealings in transplantable material seems to require that it be capable *a priori* of being property. Indeed, some commentators and even various statutes (including the recently enacted Human Tissue Act 2004, which is applicable to England, Wales and Northern Ireland) conflate property with market alienability. Whilst trading in organs generally elicits an overwhelmingly negative response, this has frequently been a gut, or intuitive, reaction of distaste. Objections based on coercion, exploitation, commodification and harmfulness have not only tended to be taken at face value, but the 'altruistic' system of organ procurement currently utilized around the world is also universally failing to provide sufficient organs to meet the need – a situation that is relentlessly worsening. Janet Radcliffe-Richards (Chapter 5) not only reveals the lack of cogency and evidence supporting many of these objections, and their largely rhetorical character, but also more broadly analyses the merits and limitations of emotional responses as a proper ethical guide. She insists that, insofar as restrictions are constraints on liberty, the burden of proof should fall on the objectors to establish their case and argues persuasively that they have so far failed to do this. Indeed, she shows that sometimes policies advocated in this sphere have the very reverse effect that objectors allege and that there is a serious danger that paternalism and the mere protection of *our own* sensibilities is at play here. Poverty is its own harm and is not, per se, a reason for rejecting organ sales viewed from an autonomy perspective.

In Chapter 6 Robert Veatch shifts the debate away from the issue of autonomous decision-making and the voluntariness of consent and coercion, which are typical of the analytical framework adopted, and moves the focus to justice as the dominant principle. Poverty may not constitute coercion sufficient to undermine legitimate consent, but the seller may be 'exploited' by having other less extreme options unreasonably denied to them. In other words, it is the manipulation of the neediest, and the *justice* concerns which this raises, that are the real ethical difficulty here – even for liberals. However, he argues that in the United States successive administrations have proved unwilling over the decades to ensure the basic necessities to all and submits that, in this light, liberals should cease to oppose financial incentives for organ procurement, albeit with a sense of shame. Instead, they should view this as the lesser moral evil.

Most of the above discussion has focused on living organ sellers. As most commentators consider that paying relatives to donate dead relatives' organs is unable to be countenanced, proposals relating to deceased persons have either focused on modest contributions to funeral expenses only (as in Pennsylvania) or have advocated some form of futures market. Lloyd Cohen (Chapter 7) has set out the most sophisticated and comprehensive futures market proposal. An economist as well as a lawyer, he has suggested that individuals should be able to contract for the sale of their body tissue after death. Around $5000 would be paid for major organs and lesser amounts for minor tissues, which would be paid to the deceased person's estate or his designee. This would, *inter alia*, prevent next of kin from trading their decedents' remains. His preferred model is the payment of a fee only where the organs or tissues are actually harvested as this would avoid very much higher transaction costs, and, in this, he differs from earlier proposals put forward by Schwindt and Vining, and Hansmann. Cohen's proposal seeks to overcome the inevitable existing psychological and religious barriers to organ donation by providing economic incentives and it has inevitably provoked criticism from those who believe that the body should not generally be perceived as a financial asset or commodity. Moreover, in the absence of any pilot scheme, it is difficult to know whether such a scheme would adversely reduce organ *donation*, thus obviating the potential benefits. The US AMA Council on Ethical and Judicial Affairs Committee has, however, stated its willingness to support such a pilot scheme. The specific form of futures market proposed by Cohen has also been criticized as being wholly unrealistic and as having drastically underestimated how high the fees would have to be to cover organ buyers' transaction costs and still retain adequate incentives to contract. Crespi (1994) recommends instead that prices should be left to be determined by market forces. None of these proposals, however, addresses the issue of organ allocation or who the organ buyers might be. In the UK the role could be taken up by the NHS which would act as a monopsonistic purchaser, allowing organs to continue to be distributed in the way in which they currently are – that is, according to predominantly clinical criteria.

Commercial *influences* in organ procurement, over and above issues relating to payment to donors or their families, are pervasive. Organ and tissue transplantation can, quite legitimately, be a lucrative business in some spheres and regions. In Chapter 8 Carl Becker examines systemic economic influences in both Japan and China. He analyses the Japanese law reforms of the 1990s, emphasizing that the brain death criteria which were adopted for the first time are only able to be utilized in the context of a potential transplant. This not only generates discrepancies in the concept of death between different contexts and patients, but also serves to ensure that individuals are not to be taken off life-support systems unless a transplant is in prospect, thus guaranteeing continued income to hospitals from such patients as well as subtle pressure to donate organs. As regards China, which refuses to officially accept the notion of brain death in any situation, the revenue-generating capability of organ transplantation has resulted in executed criminals having organs removed for such purposes. Becker contends that the imposition of the death penalty (for instance, capital punishment for petty crimes) and the method of execution have been manipulated for profit.

Cadaveric Organ and Tissue Donation

Turning to organ donation, as opposed to organ selling, and initially considering cadaveric donors, Hoffmaster (Chapter 9) notes that the organ donation scheme and policy adopted within a particular region is principally a product of the society's underlying social and political philosophy, including, in particular, the respect accorded to individual autonomy. He notes that not only is there no *a priori* necessity to give overriding effect to individual consent, but that the type of consent regime adopted (explicit or presumed, and permutations thereof) is not an issue to which there can be any 'right' ethical or legal conclusion. Communitarian societies are likely, therefore, to have rather different regimes to those where a policy of individual liberalism holds sway, and we can see contrasts between the laws in Anglo-American jurisdictions and many continental European jurisdictions (the latter more generally favouring presumed consent). Indeed, in Chapter 10 Menzel argues that organ donation should not be viewed as 'gifting' at all, but should rather be seen as a concomitant of the duty of easy rescue. Thus, consent should not be regarded as an essential prerequisite to legitimate organ procurement.

Even so, Menzel would allow deceased persons to veto procurement by way of objection before death, and indeed all jurisdictions currently require at least an absence of such an objection. This is, however, the essence of presumed consent regimes where organs may be removed unless an objection has previously been made: in some cases, either the deceased or next of kin may object and, in others – Austria, for example – only the former. Whether a lack of objection can properly be viewed as a form of (implicit) consent is a hotly debated issue. In Chapter 11 Carl Cohen notes that all schemes ought to reliably reflect the will of the deceased person and that, with regard to the deceased's wishes, 'error' is a feature of *all* donation systems, although in explicit consent systems the error is on the side of *non*-donation. Indeed, presumed consent systems, which on the whole tend to have higher rates of organ procurement, give *greater* weight to the wishes of the deceased rather than to the deceased's family and are often alleged to be ethically preferable on that account. However, in opposition, Charles Erin and John Harris (Chapter 12) contend (although without any necessary derogatory connotation) that there is no consent at all under such regimes and that, in reality, organs are merely 'taken' by the state for the greater good, and that we simply ought to be honest about this fact.

James Childress (Chapter 13) advises that rationalistic policies aimed at increasing organ supply may fail to properly take into account the symbolic and emotional aspects of the process and the beliefs that people hold. He counsels that unduly legalistic and individualistic policies may be counterproductive. In particular, he observes that, regardless of the precise legal scheme, social *practices* in the United States (and also in most other jurisdictions) are primarily communitarian, reflecting the views of the family as a whole. He states that '[a]s a matter of social practice, the default mechanism of the family has become the primary mechanism …' (p. 206). He further emphasizes that society should primarily express, rather than impose, community, which may 'grate' with some conceptions of the inherent character of presumed consent laws. Societies should seek to reduce actual and perceived risks, costs and burdens of donating. Nevertheless, a principal obstacle to organ procurement at present is the failure of individuals to make decisions as to whether they wish to donate organs before they die. One strategy proposed to remedy this difficulty is mandated choice, which has a number of variants but which has at its crux a requirement that individuals express a choice in the matter one way or other at various intervals prior to their death. Even if the requirement to express a choice is coerced, *what* choice is made is not, and it might be permissible for the choice to be made that the decision should be left for the family (as in the Texas model). Susan Herz, however, argues in Chapter 14 that, in any event, no choice *is* already a 'choice' under the present system – that is, to let the family decide. Whilst we do generally allow individuals not to make explicit decisions, the benefits of requiring such a choice arguably outweigh any such incursion on freedom.

So far, the emphasis has been on organ, as opposed to tissue, donation for transplantation. However, many of the innovative developments over the last few years have been in relation to the latter – procedures which enhance quality of life rather than being life saving, a factor which has been argued to alter the overall risk–benefit equation (especially in view of the substantial ongoing immunosuppression therapy and consequent susceptibility to major diseases, attendant on any such transplantation). In Chapter 15 Donna Dickenson and

Guy Widdershoven allude to this ethical obstacle in relation to limb allografting and the inadequacies of conventional principlist bioethical models in this field. They go on to look at alternative considerations relating to bodily integrity and identity and the crucial features and significance of hand transplants for the recipient – in particular, whether hands represent one's personal identity in a way that other human tissue, including internal organs, may not. They conclude that although the arguments as a whole do not show that limb transplants are wrong per se, they highlight their problematic character and the need for close ethical and individual consideration.

Even nearer to the (literal) cutting edge of cadaveric transplantation is facial transplantation – a procedure that is currently situated at the transitional point between scientific research and clinical application. This is, once again, a procedure that carries substantial potential benefits in terms of quality of life, but also entails significant risks associated with the effects of potential graft failure and the toxicity of immunosuppressant therapy, as well as other less well-defined risks. In Chapter 16 Osborne Wiggins and his colleagues appraise these risks and also apply Francis Moore's long-standing criteria for innovative applications in transplantation, including the broad exposure of the subject to scrutiny within the professional community and to the general public. The authors conclude that progression to the clinical phase in patients can now be supported, although they concede that there is uncertainty attached to some of the psychological and psychosocial aspects of the procedure, including the fact that the (new) face may be even more integrally and intimately associated with a person's sense of personal and social identity than a transplanted hand.

Living Donor Transplantation

Although cadaveric donation is the typically perceived standard form of organ and tissue donation, this was not the case at the dawn of solid organ transplantation, and even today it is frequently supplemented to a substantial, if not indispensable, extent by the living donation of non-vital organs and certain forms of tissue such as bone marrow. However, by dint of the fact that living donation is generally a non-therapeutic procedure for the donor it has always been ethically and legally controversial and contentious. Not only are there issues relating to the maximum degree of risk to which a donor may be submitted at the hands of a clinician, but there are also incongruities with paradigmatic notions of informed, voluntary consent which have led to allegations that a valid consent is not possible in this context. Ryan Sauder's and Lisa Parker's essay (Chapter 17) alludes to both of these issues in relation to the offer by a prisoner of his second and remaining kidney to his daughter. They suggest that, assuming a proper consent could be given and certain other conditions satisfied (including that there are no other less drastic alternatives available to achieve the same outcome), it may be appropriate to respect his autonomous choice. Whilst his health-related interests may be compromised by donation, his psychological and social interests might very understandably motivate such an offer. They counsel against an overly 'medico-centric perspective'. In order for the consent to be valid the donor would need to understand the implications of such a decision and, in the case of a prisoner, there should be no unrealistic expectation of additional benefits as a consequence. For some, the family context and the daughter's immediate need constrain autonomous choice per se, but Sauder and Parker suggest that the donor's relation to others should be understood as unavoidably part of the *context* of the decision. Moreover, the immediacy of decision-making, prior to full knowledge of all the foreseeable risks and benefits, and the emotional character of the decision, should not be seen to undermine informed consent, as this would be to adhere to the letter, rather than the spirit, of the doctrine.

Building on these themes, Robert Crouch and Carl Elliott (Chapter 18) examine consent and moral agency in the family context, including parent-to-(minor)child and sibling-to-sibling scenarios. The pressure on a parent to donate part of a liver to their ailing child may be great, generated partly by need and partly by beliefs as to appropriate role behaviours, but these authors argue that agency should not be regarded as being synonymous with independence and an absence of emotional bonds or ties. Such constraints, the authors maintain, are not coercive but, rather, a part of ordinary everyday life, and in this they counter the views of certain other commentators in this sphere. As regards donation of kidneys between minor siblings, the best-interests principle has assumed primary importance in judicial decisions in the United States (and would be equally determinative in the UK). Crouch and Elliott suggest that this is to insist on identifying best interests with *self*-interests; but because individuals are necessarily *connected* to families and other intimate collectivities, the notion of best interests distorts the reality behind such decision-making. They advance a model of family benefit and consider whether it is permissible to impose burdens on some individuals for the benefit of collective (family) interests. Of course, this does then raise questions as to how one determines the maximum permissible burden, if net individual benefit is to be rejected as the standard.

In Chapter 19 John Robertson considers organ donation by adults lacking decision-making capacity, and examines the notion of benefit. He argues that the benefits rule evidences respect for persons, but that respect for persons does not necessitate benefit in every situation, whether involving competent or incompetent individuals. He suggests that, as regards the latter, the benefit rule must be subservient to the wishes of the incompetent person and that the substituted judgement standard should apply here, allowing the possibility of a course of action which would involve maximizing the welfare of others. This may be problematic in respect of those who have never possessed autonomy, and even in respect of those who have in that genuine differences of opinion will remain as to how *far* the person would wish to have gone to further the interests of others – in other words, the question remains as to what risks such a person may be exposed to. Nevertheless, this approach attempts to penetrate behind the objectivity and veneer of the best-interests standard.

Specific Classes of Donors

Shortages of organs for transplantation have led to the procurement of organs from certain specific classes of donors, and this often raises its own specific legal and ethical issues. The shortage of paediatric organs for transplant, especially hearts, has led some centres, principally in the United States, to develop strategies for removing organs from anencephalic infants. Difficulties emanate from the fact that although such a child's anticipated lifespan can typically be calculated in days, rather than even weeks, they do not satisfy conventional criteria for death during this time as a consequence of their still functioning brain stems. Their permanently insentient state has, however, stimulated proposals to either harvest organs prior to the traditionally accepted moment of death or at least to apply aggressive measures (such as artificial ventilation) solely to preserve organs prior to death. In Chapter 20 Jay Friedman considers the legal impediments to utilizing anencephalics as donors and proposes measures that might be introduced to facilitate this. These measures are supported by reliance on a theory of personhood which would deny rights to anencephalics despite their humanity. Sharon Sytsma (Chapter 21), on the other hand, questions whether, even accepting such a moral theory of personhood, *only persons* have moral status. She notes those who support using anencephalics as donors emphasize the absolute 'uniqueness' of the condition, but points to the existence of other catastrophic neurological defects that are destined to result in imminent death and the slippery-slope implications of such utilitarian-driven thinking.

In terms of transplantation using foetal material, it is currently tissue, rather than organs, that are potentially the most valuable, notably pancreatic and brain tissue transplants, the latter being used for neurological diseases such as Parkinson's. In Chapter 22 John Robertson appraises the arguments for and against their use, bearing in mind that most foetal tissue becomes available following abortion. He not only evaluates those situations where tissue may become available after abortion, but also abortions carried out with the purpose of obtaining tissue for transplantation. Whilst recognizing that, instinctively, many immediately reject the latter practice on ethical grounds, he nevertheless finds it acceptable to use such tissue for transplantation whether or not the foetus was initially conceived with this objective in mind and assuming that the abortion occurred at a stage when the foetus was not yet sufficiently developed to experience harm. In the UK the Polkinghorne Code of Practice mandates a need for 'separateness' of both decision-making and personnel in respect of such tissue resulting from an abortion, which limits the applicability of the latter course of conduct. However, this practice now conflicts with the general contemporary perception that individuals should give explicit consent to the use of tissue for therapy or research, although there may be a compelling distinction between knowledge of a general use and the *specific* use of that particular material.

As noted at the outset, the limited numbers of heart-beating (that is, artificially ventilated brain-dead) donors has led to a re-emergence of the non-heart-beating donor on the transplant scene (the 'typical' donors at the beginning of the transplant era). David Price, in Chapter 23, broadly considers notions of 'harm' with regard to non-heart-beating donors, in contexts where their organs are cooled and perfused to ensure their viability for transplantation but where no consent has yet been obtained, and also, in the context of a practice which has become known as 'elective ventilation', in which an insentient individual who is certain to die imminently is ventilated purely to ensure the viability of the donor organs. With regard to the former practice, the question arises as to whether one can harm the dead. In the latter scenario, in the absence of consent and because it would not be in the best interests of the 'patient', it would legally constitute a battery (as a consequence of which the practice was quickly aborted in the UK), although it has frequently been asserted that it is an entirely appropriate practice *ethically* as no harm can accrue to the individual. Price's essay explores various perceptions and accounts of 'harm' in evaluating both practices. In certain jurisdictions there is now explicit statutory support for minimally invasive measures to preserve organs *after* death, such as in the Netherlands and under the Human Tissue Act 2004 which will become law in England, Wales and Northern Ireland in 2006.

In the final essay in Part VI, a non-affiliated expert group, the International Forum for Transplant Ethics (Hoffenberg *et al.*), considers the legitimacy of taking organs from patients in a permanent vegetative state (PVS), prior to their death, in order to ensure the optimal condition of their organs, which would be unusable if they were removed only following death from withdrawal of treatment. They suggest that if death by such means is acceptable, why not death brought about by the administration of a lethal drug, where no distress can occur? Closing the full circle of discussion in this section, they appreciate the congruity of many of the issues in such cases with those pertaining to anencephalic neonates.

Organ Allocation

The crucial link between organ procurement and organ allocation has been emphasized most strongly by James Childress. If allocation practices and criteria are unfair this will potentially have an impact on organ procurement, especially amongst certain groups. In Chapter 25 Childress notes that issues concerning equitable access and equitable allocation of organs are tied to issues surrounding who 'owns' donated organs. Is the owner the retrieving team or institution or society as a whole, or merely a region thereof? In order to ensure justice and transparency he asserts the need for the public to be at least involved in designing policies of organ allocation, with such organs being subject to *community* ownership. According to Childress, organs are not owned by transplant teams; they are owned by the national, rather than the local, community. This, he maintains, avoids 'accidents of geography' in terms of who receives organs, even though, in some specific instances, for logistical or other reasons some organs may be distributed locally first. He then examines other morally legitimate criteria for generating priority in organ allocation, including need, probability of success and so on.

Numerous factors are potentially relevant, in some degree or other, to the prioritization for organ allocation. These often implicate a tension between considerations of utility and good likely outcomes, and justice, involving medical need. Different commentators and societies accord different moral and practical weight to these criteria. Further, the weighting of factors may vary with regard to the particular organ involved. In Chapter 26 Stephanie Eaton, in an attempt to deal with the 'free rider' – the person willing to receive but not give – adds another factor to the mix. She advocates a scheme under which likely clinical outcome is the principal factor but, where clinical outcomes are neutral as between recipients, willingness to give (that is, desert) should be considered. She advances this alongside an opting-out scheme to highlight the essential interdependence of organ recipient and organ donor. This is a 'softer' recognition of such reality in comparison with Jarvis's earlier proposal that organs should not be made available at all to those who have not previously consented to becoming donors after death (Jarvis, 1995). However, Gillon (1995) has noted the difficulties of introducing notions of assumed moral blameworthiness into this arena, despite the fact that some commentators regard this as a relevant criterion – for example, where a liver transplant is required due to excessive alcohol consumption.

If cadaveric organs are a community (typically national) or societal resource, and organs are allocated according to previously agreed criteria founded essentially on clinical factors, does this imply that donors are unable to decide who should, or indeed should not, be entitled to an organ post-mortem? In Chapter 27 Rachel Ankeny considers the notion of *directed* donation and the tension and conflict between values of justice and the right of self-determination. There are various forms of directed donation, despite the tendency not to distinguish between them. In the UK there was universal condemnation of an attempt to place a ban on recipients based on their race – in other words, a class-based restriction – but what if one simply wishes to benefit one's sick nephew after death?

Xenotransplantation

Xenotransplantation offers the prospect of an unlimited supply of organs for transplantation, thus obviating shortages at a stroke. This future possibility is quickly becoming a clinical reality with genetically modified animals (pigs) being experimentally bred with the aim of avoiding the worst excesses of interspecies (hyperacute) rejection. This is, however, merely the tip of the iceberg in terms of ethical dilemmas generated by such a potential therapy. The clinical obstacles have gradually given way to the broader ethical and legal ramifications of such a practice. In the UK, during the 1990s, two important Working Party Reports were published, first by the Nuffield Council on Bioethics (1995) and then by the Department of Health's Advisory Group on the Ethics of Xenotransplantation (1997). Both reports supported these general developments although they counselled caution. In Chapter 28 Will Cartwright considers the Nuffield report, *Animal-to-Human Transplants* (1995), arguing that, provided its central ethical premise is accepted, it is a supportable and sensible document – that is, it is justifiable, as an undesirable and unavoidable necessity, to use non-human animals to improve health and alleviate suffering in humans. He maintains that the report implicitly endorses the view that animals matter morally although less so than humans, and argues that not only is this view widely shared within society but that it is also intellectually defensible. He observes that, viewed from a rights and/or interests perspective, if one seeks to identify characteristics associated with being human then we will necessarily find that these are all shared, to a certain extent, by very many animals, whereas some humans (for example, anencephalics, patients in a PVS and so on) may partially or wholly lack such characteristics. However, he contends that, as we are unable to transcend the human point of view, we predictably and properly matter more than animals. This view, of course, contrasts sharply with accounts that suggest that use of animals for such ends amounts to speciesism.

But xenotransplantation generates a plethora of concerns apart from the moral status and permissible uses of animals. Interspecies transplantation carries the capacity for disease transmission affecting not just the organ recipient but society as a whole, thus requiring a societal response to the practice. If xenotransplants are acceptable, then specific and extensive safeguards will need to be instituted and enforced. In the final chapter of this volume Patrik Florencio and Erik Ramanathan consider alternative legal strategies for managing, minimizing, containing and responding to the threat of disease and emphasize the substantial inherent difficulties in terms of human rights and enforceability. They advocate the creation of xenotransplantation-specific legislation in this sphere and believe that existing mechanisms by way of consent law, contract law and existing public health law are inadequate due to inherent constraints.

References

Advisory Group on the Ethics of Xenotransplantation (1997), *Animal Tissue into Humans*, London: Department of Health.

Arnold, R. and Youngner, S. (1993), 'The Dead Donor Rule: Should We Stretch It, Bend It, or Abandon It?', *Kennedy Institute of Ethics Journal*, 3(2), p. 263.

Crespi, G. (1994), 'Overcoming the Legal Obstacles to the Creation of a Futures Market in Bodily Organs', *Ohio State Law Journal*, 55(1), p. 1.

Gillon, R. (1995), 'On Giving Preference to Prior Volunteers When Allocating Organs for Transplantation', *Journal of Medical Ethics*, **21**, p. 195.

Hansmann, H. (1989), 'The Economics and Ethics of Markets for Human Organs', *Journal of Health Politics, Law and Policy*, **14**, p. 57.

Jarvis, R. (1995), 'Join the Club: A Modest Proposal to Increase Availability of Donor Organs', *Journal of Medical Ethics*, **21**, p. 199.

Nuffield Council on Bioethics (1995), *Animal-to-Human Transplants: The Ethics of Xenotransplantation*, London: Nuffield Council.

Schwindt, R. and Vining, A. (1986), 'Proposal for a Future Delivery Market for Transplant Organs', *Journal of Health Politics, Law and Policy*, **11**, p. 483.

Further Reading

Books

Andrews, L. and Nelkin, D. (2001), *The Body Bazaar*, New York: Crown Publishers.

Arnold, R., Youngner, S., Shapiro, R. and Mason Spicer, C. (eds) (1995), *Procuring Organs by Transplant: The Debate Over Non-Heart-Beating Cadaver Protocols*, Baltimore, MD: Johns Hopkins University Press.

Australian Law Reform Commission (1977), *Human Tissue Transplants,* Report No. 7, Canberra: ALRC.

Chapman, J., Deierhoi, M. and Wight, C. (eds) (1997), *Organ and Tissue Donation for Transplantation*, London: Arnold.

Collins, G., Dubernard, J., Land, W. and Persijn, G. (eds) (1997), *Procurement, Preservation and Allocation of Vascularised Organs*, Dordrecht: Kluwer.

De Charro, F., Hessing, D. and Akveld, J. (eds) (1992), *Systems of Donor Recruitment*, Deventer: Kluwer.

Donnelly, P. and Price, D. (eds) (1995), *Questioning Attitudes to Living Donor Transplantation*, EUROTOLD Project Report to the European Commission, Leicester: The Project Management Group, EUROTOLD.

Englert, Y. (ed.) (1995), *Organ and Tissue Transplantation in the European Union*, Dordrecht: Martinus Nijhoff.

Fox, R. and Swazey, J. (1974), *The Courage to Fail*, Chicago: University of Chicago Press.

Fox, R. and Swazey, J. (1992), *Spare Parts: Organ Replacement in American Society*, New York: Oxford University Press.

Garwood-Gowers, A. (1999), *Living Donor Organ Transplantation: Key Legal and Ethical Issues*, Aldershot: Ashgate.

Gaston, R. and Wadstrom, J. (eds) (2005), *Living Donor Kidney Transplantation: Current Practices, Emerging Trends and Evolving Challenges*, London: Taylor & Francis.

Gervais, K.G. (1986), *Redefining Death*, New Haven, CT: Yale University Press.

Institute of Medicine (1997), *Non-Heart-Beating Organ Transplantation: Medical and Ethical Issues in Procurement*, Washington, DC: Institute of Medicine, National Academy Press.

Gutmann, T., Daar, A., Sells, R. and Land, W. (eds) (2004), *Ethical, Legal, and Social Issues in Organ Transplantation*, Lengerich: Pabst Science.

Jones, D. (2000), *Speaking for the Dead*, Aldershot: Ashgate.

Kjellstrand, C. and Dossetor, J. (eds) (1992), *Ethical Problems in Dialysis and Transplantation*, Dordrecht: Kluwer.

King's Fund Institute Working Party (1994), *A Question of Give and Take*, Research Report No. 18, London: King's Fund.

Lamb, D. (1985), *Death, Brain Death and Ethics*, Albany, NY: State University of New York.

Lamb, D. (1990), *Organ Transplants and Ethics*, London: Routledge.

Land, W. and Dossetor, J. (eds) (1991), *Organ Replacement Therapy: Ethics, Justice, Commerce*, Berlin: Springer-Verlag.

Law Reform Commission of Canada (1992), *Procurement and Transfer of Human Tissues and Organs*, Working Paper No. 66, Minister of Supply and Services.

Lock, M. (2002), *Twice Dead: Organ Transplants and the Reinvention of Death*, Berkeley, University of California Press.

Machado, N. (1998), *Using the Bodies of the Dead*, Aldershot: Ashgate.

Mathieu, D. (1988), *Organ Substitution Technology: Ethical, Legal and Public Policy Issues*, Boulder: Westview Press.

McCullagh, P. (1987), *The Foetus as Transplant Donor: Scientific, Social and Ethical Perspectives*, Chichester: John Wiley.

McCullagh, P. (1993), *Brain Dead, Brain Absent, Brain Donors*, Chichester: John Wiley.

Nuffield Council on Bioethics (1995), *Human Tissue: Legal and Ethical Issues*, London: Nuffield Council.

Palmer, L. (ed.) (1999), *Organ Transplants from Executed Prisoners*, Jefferson, NC: McFarland & Co.

Price, D. and Akveld, J. (eds) (1996), *Living Organ Donation in the Nineties: European Medico-Legal Perspectives*, Leicester: EUROTOLD.

Price, D. (2000), *Legal and Ethical Aspects of Organ Transplantation*, Cambridge: Cambridge University Press.

Richardson, R. (1989), *Death, Dissection and the Destitute*, London: Penguin.

Ross, L.F. (1998), *Children, Families, and Health Care Decision-Making*, Oxford: Clarendon Press.

Scott, R. (1981), *The Body as Property*, New York: Viking Press.

Shanteau, J. and Jackson, Harris R. (eds) (1991), *Organ Donation and Transplantation*, Washington, DC: American Psychological Association.

Spielman, B. (ed.) (1997), *Organ and Tissue Donation: Ethical, Legal and Policy Issues*, Carbondale: Southern Illinois University Press.

Stark, T. (1996), *A Knife to the Heart*, London: Macmillan.

Stern, K. and Walsh, P. (eds) (1997), *Property Rights in the Human Body*, Occasional Papers Series No. 2, London: King's College.

Ten Have, H., Welie, J. and Spicker, S. (eds) (1998), *Ownership of the Human Body*, Dordrecht: Kluwer.

Veatch, R. (2000), *Transplantation Ethics*, Washington, DC: Georgetown University Press.

Wilkinson, S. (2003), *Bodies for Sale: Ethics and Exploitation in the Human Body Trade*, London: Routledge.

Wolstenholme, G. and O'Connor, M. (eds) (1966), *Ethics in Medical Progress*, CIBA Foundation Symposium, London: J. & A. Churchill Ltd.

Youngner, S., Anderson, M. and Shapiro, R. (eds) (2004), *Transplanting Human Tissue: Ethics, Policy and Practice*, New York: Oxford University Press.

Youngner, S., Arnold, R. and Shapiro, R. (eds) (1999), *The Definition of Death: Contemporary Perspectives*, Baltimore, MD: Johns Hopkins University Press.

Youngner, S., Fox, R. and O'Connell, L. (eds) (1996), *Organ Transplantation: Meanings and Realities*, Madison, WI: University of Wisconsin Press.

Articles

Boulier, W. (1995), 'Sperm, Spleens, and Other Valuables: The Need to Recognize Property Rights in Human Body Parts', *Hofstra Law Review*, **23**, p. 693.

Calabresi, G. (1991), 'Do We Own Our Bodies?', *Health Matrix*, **1**(5), p. 5.

Cooper, S. (1985), 'Consent and Organ Donation', *Rutgers Computer and Technology Law Journal*, **11**, p. 559.

Crothers, D. and Uglem, C. (1992), 'A Proposal for a Presumed Consent Organ Donation Policy in North Dakota', *North Dakota Law Review*, **68**, p. 637.

Dickens, B. (1977), 'The Control of Living Body Materials', *University of Toronto Law Journal*, **27**, p. 142.

Dukeminier, J. (1970), 'Supplying Organs for Transplantation', *Michigan Law Review*, **68**, p. 811.

Dworkin, G. (1970), 'The Law Relating to Organ Transplantation in England', *Modern Law Review*, **33**, p. 353.

Dworkin, G. and Kennedy, I. (1993), 'Human Tissue: Rights in the Body and its Parts', *Medical Law Review*, **1**, p. 29.

English, V. and Sommerville, A. (2003), 'Presumed Consent for Transplantation: A Dead Issue after Alder Hey?', *Journal of Medical Ethics*, **29**(3), p. 147.

Evans, M. (1989), 'Organ Donation Should Not Be Restricted to Relatives', *Journal of Medical Ethics*, **15**, p. 17.

Gimbel, R., Strosberg, M., Lehrman, S., Gefenas, E. and Taft, F. (2003), 'Presumed Consent and Other Predictors of Cadaveric Organ Donation in Europe', *Progress in Transplantation*, **13**(1), p. 17.

Grubb, A. (1998), '"I, Me, Mine": Bodies, Parts and Property', *Medical Law International*, **3**, p. 299.

Hazony, O. (1993), 'Increasing the Supply of Cadaver Organs for Transplantation: Recognising that the Real Problem is Psychological, not Legal', *Health Matrix*, **3**, p. 219.

Hoffmaster, B. (1985), 'Freedom to Choose and Freedom to Lose: The Procurement of Cadaver Organs for Transplantation', *Transplantation Proceedings*, **17**(6), Supplement 4, p. 24.

Hoffmaster, B. (1992), 'Between the Sacred and the Profane: Bodies, Property, and Patents in the *Moore* Case', *Intellectual Property Journal*, **7**, p. 116.

Joralemon, D. and Cox, P. (2003), 'Body Values: The Case Against Compensating for Transplant Organs', *Hastings Center Report*, **33**(1), p. 27.

Keown, J. (1993), 'The Polkinghorne Report on Foetal Research: Nice Recommendations, Shame about the Reasoning', *Journal of Medical Ethics*, **19**, p. 114.

Lanham, D. (1971), 'Transplants and the Human Tissue Act 1961', *Medicine, Science and the Law*, **11**, p. 16.

Lizza, J. (1993), 'Persons and Death: What's Metaphysically Wrong with our Current Statutory Definition of Death?', *Journal of Medicine and Philosophy*, **18**, p. 351.

McHale, J. (1995), 'Elective Ventilation – Pragmatic Solution or Ethical Minefield?', *Professional Negligence*, **2**, p. 23.

Murray, T. (1987), 'On the Human Body as Property: The Meaning of Embodiment, Markets, and the Meaning of Strangers', *Journal of Law Reform*, **20**(4), p. 1055.

Norrie, K. (1985), 'Human Tissue Transplants: Legal Liability in Different Jurisdictions', *International and Comparative Law Quarterly*, **34**, p. 442.

Nowenstein, G. (2004), 'Organ Procurement Rates: Does Presumed Consent Legislation Really Make a Difference?', *Law, Social Justice & Global Development Journal* at: http://elj.warwick.ac.uk/global/04-1/nowenstein.htm.

Price, D. and Mackay, R. (1991), 'The Trade in Human Organs: Part I', *New Law Journal*, **141**, p. 1272.

Price, D. and Mackay, R. (1991), 'The Trade in Human Organs: Part II', *New Law Journal*, **141**, p. 1307.

Price, D. and Garwood-Gowers, A. (1995), 'Transplantation from Minors: Are Children Other People's Medicine?', *Contemporary Issues in Law*, **1**, p. 1.

Price, D. (1996), 'Contemporary Transplantation Initiatives: Where's the Harm in Them?', *Journal of Law, Medicine and Ethics*, **24**, p. 139.

Price, D. (1997), 'Organ Transplant Initiatives: The Twilight Zone', *Journal of Medical Ethics*, **23**, p. 170.

Price, D. and Akveld, J. (1998), 'Living Donor Organ Transplantation in Europe: Re-evaluating its Role', *European Journal of Health Law*, **5**(1), p. 19.

Price, D. (2004), 'From Cosmos and Damien to Van Velzen: The Human Tissue Saga Continues', *Medical Law Review*, **11**, p. 1.

Price, D. (2005), 'The Human Tissue Act 2004', *Modern Law Review*, **68**, pp. 798.

Quay, P. (1984), 'Utilizing the Bodies of the Dead', *Saint Louis University Law Journal*, **28**, p. 889.

Radcliffe-Richards, J. et al. (1998), 'The Case for Allowing Kidney Sales', *The Lancet*, **351**, p. 1950.

Skegg P. (1974), 'Liability for the Unauthorized Removal of Cadaveric Transplant Material', *Medicine, Science and the Law*, **14**, p. 53.

Skegg, P. (1976), 'Human Tissue Act 1961', *Medicine, Science and the Law*, **16**, p. 197.

Skegg, P. (1977), 'Liability for the Unauthorized Removal of Cadaveric Transplant Material: Some Further Comments', *Medicine, Science and the Law*, **17**, p. 123.

Smith, G.P. II (1993), 'Market and Non-Market Mechanisms for Procuring Human and Cadaveric Organs: When the Price is Right', *Medical Law International*, **1**(1), p. 17.

Wilkinson, S. and Garrard, E. (1996), 'Bodily Integrity and the Sale of Human Organs', *Journal of Medical Ethics*, **22**, p. 334.

Part I
Meaning of Death

Is It Time to Abandon Brain Death?

by Robert D. Truog

Despite its familiarity and widespread acceptance, the concept of "brain death" remains incoherent in theory and confused in practice. Moreover, the only purpose served by the concept is to facilitate the procurement of transplantable organs. By abandoning the concept of brain death and adopting different criteria for organ procurement, we may be able to increase both the supply of transplantable organs and clarity in our understanding of death.

O ver the past several decades, the concept of brain death has become well entrenched within the practice of medicine. At a practical level, this concept has been successful in delineating widely accepted ethical and legal boundaries for the procurement of vital organs for transplantation. Despite this success, however, there have been persistent concerns over whether the concept is theoretically coherent and internally consistent.[1] Indeed, some have concluded that the concept is fundamentally flawed, and that it represents only a "superficial and fragile consensus."[2] In this analysis I will identify the sources of these inconsistencies, and suggest that the best resolution to these issues may be to abandon the concept of brain death altogether.

Definitions, Concepts, and Tests

In its seminal work "Defining Death," the President's Commission for the Study of Ethical Problems in

Robert D. Truog, "Is it Time to Abandon Brain Death?" *Hastings Center Report* 27, no. 1 (1997): 29-37.

Medicine and Biomedical and Behavioral Research articulated a formulation of brain death that has come to be known as the "whole-brain standard."[3] In the Uniform Determination of Death Act, the President's Commission specified two criteria for determining death: (1) irreversible cessation of circulatory and respiratory functions, or (2) irreversible cessation of all functions of the entire brain, including the brainstem."

Neurologist James Bernat has been influential in defending and refining this standard. Along with others, he has recognized that analysis of the concept of brain death must begin by differentiating between three distinct levels. At the most general level, the concept must involve a *definition*. Next, *criteria* must be specified to determine when the definition has been fulfilled. Finally, *tests* must be available for evaluating whether the criteria have been satisfied.[4] As clarified by Bernat and colleagues, therefore, the concept of death under the whole-brain formulation can be outlined as follows:[5]

Definition of Death: The "permanent cessation of functioning of the organism as a whole."

Criterion for Death: The "permanent cessation of functioning of the entire brain."

Tests for death: Two distinct sets of tests are available and acceptable for determining that the criterion is fulfilled:

(1) The cardiorespiratory standard is the traditional approach for determining death and relies upon documenting the prolonged absence of circulation or respiration. These tests fulfill the criterion, according to Bernat, since the prolonged absence of these vital signs is diagnostic for the permanent loss of all brain function.

(2) The neurological standard consists of a battery of tests and procedures, including establishment of an etiology sufficient to account for the loss of all brain functions, diagnosing the presence of coma, documenting apnea and the absence of brainstem reflexes, excluding reversible conditions, and showing the persistence of these findings over a sufficient period of time.[6]

Critique of the Current Formulation of Brain Death

Is this a coherent account of the concept of brain death? To answer this question, one must determine whether each level of analysis is consistent with the others. In other words, individuals who fulfill the tests must also fulfill the criterion, and those who satisfy the criterion must also satisfy the definition.[7]

First, regarding the tests-criterion relationship, there is evidence that many individuals who fulfill all of the tests for brain death do not have the "permanent cessation of functioning of the entire brain." In particular, many of these individuals retain clear evidence of integrated brain function at the level of the brainstem and midbrain, and may have evidence of cortical function.

For example, many patients who fulfill the tests for the diagnosis of brain death continue to exhibit intact neurohumoral function. Between 22 percent and 100 percent of brain-dead patients in different series have

Hastings Center Report, January-February 1997

been found to retain free-water homeostasis through the neurologically mediated secretion of arginine vasopressin, as evidenced by serum hormonal levels and the absence of diabetes insipidus.[8] Since the brain is the only source of the regulated secretion of arginine vasopressin, patients without diabetes insipidus do not have the loss of all brain function. Neurologically regulated secretion of other hormones is also quite common.[9]

In addition, the tests for the diagnosis of brain death require the patient not to be hypothermic.[10] This caveat is a particularly confusing Catch 22, since the absence of hypothermia generally indicates the continuation of neurologically mediated temperature homeostasis. The circularity of this reasoning can be clinically problematic, since hypothermic patients cannot be diagnosed as brain-dead but the absence of hypothermia is itself evidence of brain function.

Furthermore, studies have shown that many patients (20 percent in one series) who fulfill the tests for brain death continue to show electrical activity on their electroencephalograms.[11] While there is no way to determine how often this electrical activity represents true "function" (which would be incompatible with the criterion for brain death), in at least some cases the activity observed seems fully compatible with function.[12]

Finally, clinicians have observed that patients who fulfill the tests for brain death frequently respond to surgical incision at the time of organ procurement with a significant rise in both heart rate and blood pressure. This suggests that integrated neurological function at a supraspinal level may be present in at least some patients diagnosed as brain-dead.[13] This evidence points to the conclusion that there is a significant disparity between the standard tests used to make the diagnosis of brain death and the criterion these tests are purported to fulfill. Faced with these facts, even supporters of the current statutes acknowledge that the criterion of "whole-brain" death is only an "approximation."[14]

If the tests for determining brain death are incompatible with the current criterion, then one way of solving the problem would be to require tests that always correlate with the "permanent cessation of functioning of the entire brain." Two options have been considered in this regard. The first would require tests that correlate with the actual destruction of the brain, since complete destruction would, of course, be incompatible with any degree of brain function. Only by satisfying these tests, some have argued, could we be assured that all functions of the entire brain have totally and permanently ceased.[15] But is there a constellation of clinical and laboratory tests that correlate with this degree of destruction? Unfortunately, a study of over 500 patients with both coma and apnea (including 146 autopsies for neuropathologic correlation) showed that "it was not possible to verify that a diagnosis made prior to cardiac arrest by any set or subset of criteria would invariably correlate with a diffusely destroyed brain."[16] On the basis of these data, a definition that required total brain destruction could only be confirmed at autopsy. Clearly, a condition that could only be determined after death could never be a requirement for declaring death.

Another way of modifying the tests to conform with the criterion would be to rely solely upon the cardiorespiratory standard for determining death. This standard would certainly identify the permanent cessation of all brain function (thereby fulfilling the criterion), since it is well established by common knowledge that prolonged absence of circulation and respiration results in the death of the entire brain (and every other organ). In addition, fulfillment of these tests would also convincingly demonstrate the cessation of function of the organism as a whole (thereby fulfilling the definition). Unfortunately, this approach for resolving the problem would also make it virtually impossible to obtain vital organs in a viable condition for transplantation, since under current laws it is generally necessary for these organs to be removed from a heart-beating donor.

These inconsistencies between the tests and the criterion are therefore not easily resolvable. In addition to these problems, there are also inconsistencies between the criterion and the definition. As outlined above, the whole-brain concept assumes that the "permanent cessation of functioning of the entire brain" (the criterion) necessarily implies the "permanent cessation of functioning of the organism as a whole" (the definition). Conceptually, this relationship assumes the principle that the brain is responsible for maintaining the body's homeostasis, and that without brain function the organism rapidly disintegrates. In the past, this relationship was demonstrated by showing that individuals who fulfilled the tests for the diagnosis of brain death inevitably had a cardiac arrest within a short period of time, even if they were provided with mechanical ventilation and intensive care.[17] Indeed, this assumption had been considered one of the linchpins in the ethical justification for the concept of brain death.[18] For example, in the largest empirical study of brain death ever performed, a collaborative group working under the auspices of the National Institutes of Health sought to specify the necessary tests for diagnosing brain death by attempting to identify a constellation of neurological findings that would inevitably predict the development of a cardiac arrest within three months, regardless of the level or intensity of support provided.[19]

This approach to defining brain death in terms of neurological findings that predict the development of cardiac arrest is plagued by both logical and scientific problems, however. First, it confuses a prognosis with a diagnosis. Demonstrating that a certain class of patients will suffer a cardiac arrest within a defined period of time certainly proves that they are *dying*, but it says nothing about whether they are *dead*.[20] This conceptual mistake can be clearly appreciated if one considers individuals who are dying of conditions not associated with severe neurological impairment. If a constellation of tests could identify a subgroup of patients with metastatic cancer who invariably suffered a cardiac arrest within a short period of time, for example, we would certainly be comfortable in concluding that they were dying, but we clearly could not claim that they were already dead.

Second, this view relies upon the intuitive notion that the brain is the principal organ of the body, the "in-

Hastings Center Report, January-February 1997

tegrating" organ whose functions cannot be replaced by any other organ or by artificial means. Up through the early 1980s, this view was supported by numerous studies showing that almost all patients who fulfilled the usual battery of tests for brain death suffered a cardiac arrest within several weeks.[21]

The loss of homeostatic equilibrium that is empirically observed in brain-dead patients is almost certainly the result of their progressive loss of integrated neurohumoral and autonomic function. Over the past several decades, however, intensive care units (ICUs) have become increasingly sophisticated "surrogate brainstems," replacing both the respiratory functions as well as the hormonal and other regulatory activities of the damaged neuraxis.[22] This technology is presently utilized in those tragic cases in which a pregnant woman is diagnosed as brain-dead and an attempt is made to maintain her somatic existence until the fetus reaches a viable gestation, as well as for prolonging the organ viability of brain-dead patients awaiting organ procurement.[23] Although the functions of the brainstem are considerably more complex than those of the heart or the lungs, in theory (and increasingly in practice) they are entirely replaceable by modern technology. In terms of maintaining homeostatic functions, therefore, the brain is no more irreplaceable than any of the other vital organs. A definition of death predicated upon the "inevitable" development of a cardiac arrest within a short period of time is therefore inadequate, since this empirical "fact" is no longer true. In other words, cardiac arrest is inevitable only if it is allowed to occur, just as respiratory arrest in brain-dead patients is inevitable only if they are not provided with mechanical ventilation. This gradual development in technical expertise has unwittingly undermined one of the central ethical justifications for the whole-brain criterion of death.

In summary, then, the whole-brain concept is plagued by internal inconsistencies in both the tests-criterion and the criterion-definition relationships, and these problems cannot be easily solved. In addition, there is evidence that this lack of conceptual clarity has contributed to misunderstandings about the concept among both clinicians and laypersons. For example, Stuart Youngner and colleagues found that only 35 percent of physicians and nurses who were likely to be involved in organ procurement for transplantation correctly identified the legal and medical criteria for determining death.[24] Indeed, most of the respondents used inconsistent concepts of death, and a substantial minority misunderstood the criterion to be the permanent loss of consciousness, which the President's Commission had specifically rejected, in part because it would have classified anencephalic newborns and patients in a vegetative state as dead. In other words, medical professionals who were otherwise knowledgeable and sophisticated were generally confused about the concept of brain death. In an editorial accompanying this study, Dan Wikler and Alan Weisbard claimed that this confusion was "appropriate," given the lack of philosophical coherence in the concept itself.[25] In another study, a survey of Swedes found that laypersons were more willing to consent to autopsies than to organ donation for themselves or a close relative. In seeking an explanation for these findings, the authors reported that "the fear of not being dead during the removal of organs, reported by 22 percent of those undecided toward organ donation, was related to the uncertainty surrounding brain death."[26]

On one hand, these difficulties with the concept might be deemed to be so esoteric and theoretical that they should play no role in driving the policy debate about how to define death and procure organs for transplantation. This has certainly been the predominant view up to now. In many other circumstances, theoretical issues have taken a back seat to practical matters when it comes to deter-

> Only 35 percent of physicians and nurses who were likely to be involved in organ procurement for transplantation correctly identified the legal and medical criteria for determining death.

mining public policy. For example, the question of whether tomatoes should be considered a vegetable or a fruit for purposes of taxation was said to hinge little upon the biological facts of the matter, but to turn primarily upon the political and economic issues at stake.[27] If this view is applied to the concept of brain death, then the best public policy would be that which best served the public's interest, regardless of theoretical concerns.

On the other hand, medicine has a long and respected history of continually seeking to refine the theoretical and conceptual underpinnings of its practice. While the impact of scientific and philosophical views upon social policy and public perception must be taken seriously, they cannot be the sole forces driving the debate. Given the evidence demonstrating a lack of coherence in the whole-brain death formulation and the confusion that is apparent among medical professionals, there is ample reason to prompt a look at alternatives to our current approach.

Alternative Approaches to the Whole-Brain Formulation

Alternatives to the whole-brain death formulation fall into two general categories. One approach is to emphasize the overriding importance

Hastings Center Report, January-February 1997

of those functions of the brain that support the phenomenon of consciousness and to claim that individuals who have permanently suffered the loss of all consciousness are dead. This is known as the "higher-brain" criterion. The other approach is to return to the traditional tests for deter-

from moral as well as ontological perspectives.[29] In addition, this view correlates very well with many commonsense opinions about personal identity. To take a stock philosophical illustration, for example, consider the typical reaction of a person who has undergone a hypothetical "brain

rently possible. This would be an especially important issue in the context of diagnosing death, where false positive diagnoses would be particularly problematic.[31] Similarly, while the Medical Task Force on Anencephaly has concluded that most cases of anencephaly can be diagnosed by a competent clinician without significant uncertainty, others have emphasized the ambiguities inherent in evaluating this condition.[32]

Most people find it counterintuitive to perceive a breathing patient as "dead."

---

mining death, that is, the permanent loss of circulation and respiration. As noted above, this latter strategy could fit well with Bernat's formulation of the definition of death, since adoption of the cardiorespiratory standard as the test for determining death is consistent with both the criterion and the definition. The problem with this potential solution is that it would virtually eliminate the possibility of procuring vital organs from heart-beating donors under our present system of law and ethics, since current requirements insist that organs be removed only from individuals who have been declared dead (the "dead-donor rule").[28] Consideration of this latter view would therefore be feasible only if it could be linked to fundamental changes in the permissible limits of organ procurement.

The Higher-Brain Formulation. The higher-brain criterion for death holds that maintaining the potential for consciousness is the critical function of the brain relevant to questions of life and death. Under this definition, all individuals who are permanently unconscious would be considered to be dead. Included in this category would be (1) patients who fulfill the cardiorespiratory standard, (2) those who fulfill the current tests for whole-brain death, (3) those diagnosed as being in a permanent vegetative state, and (4) newborns with anencephaly. Various versions of this view have been defended by many philosophers, and arguments have been advanced

switch" procedure, where one's brain is transplanted into another's body, and vice versa. Virtually anyone presented with this scenario will say that "what matters" for their existence now resides in the new body, even though an outside observer would insist that it is the person's old body that "appears" to be the original person. Thought experiments like this one illustrate that we typically identify ourselves with our experience of consciousness, and this observation forms the basis of the claim that the permanent absence of consciousness should be seen as representing the death of the person.

Implementation of this standard would present certain problems, however. First, is it possible to diagnose the state of permanent unconsciousness with the high level of certainty required for the determination of death? More specifically, is it currently possible to definitively diagnose the permanent vegetative state and anencephaly? A Multi-Society Task Force recently outlined guidelines for diagnosis of permanent vegetative state and claimed that sufficient data are now available to make the diagnosis of permanent vegetative state in appropriate patients with a high degree of certainty.[30] On the other hand, case reports of patients who met these criteria but who later recovered a higher degree of neurological functioning suggest that use of the term "permanent" may be overstating the degree of diagnostic certainty that is cur-

Another line of criticism is that the higher-brain approach assumes the definition of death should reflect the death of the *person*, rather than the death of the *organism*.[33] By focusing on the person, this theory does not account for what is common to the death of all organisms, such as humans, frogs, or trees. Since we do not know what it would mean to talk about the permanent loss of consciousness of frogs or trees, then this approach to death may appear to be idiosyncratic. In response, higher-brain theorists believe that it is critical to define death within the context of the specific subject under consideration. For example, we may speak of the death of an ancient civilization, the death of a species, or the death of a particular system of belief. In each case, the definition of death will be different, and must be appropriate to the subject in order for the concept to make any sense. Following this line of reasoning, the higher-brain approach is correct precisely because it seeks to identify what is uniquely relevant to the death of a person.

Aside from these diagnostic and philosophical concerns, however, perhaps the greatest objections to the higher brain formulation emerge from the implications of treating breathing patients as if they are dead. For example, if patients in a permanent vegetative state were considered to be dead, then they should logically be considered suitable for burial. Yet all of these patients breathe, and some of them "live" for many years.[34] The thought of burying or cremating a breathing individual, even if unconscious, would be unthinkable for many people, creating a significant barrier to acceptance of this view into public policy.[35]

One way of avoiding this implication would be to utilize a "lethal in-

Hastings Center Report, January-February 1997

jection" before cremation or burial to terminate cardiac and respiratory function. This would not be euthanasia, since the individual would be declared dead before the injection. The purpose of the injection would be purely "aesthetic." This practice could even be viewed as simply an extension of our current protocols, where the vital functions of patients diagnosed as brain-dead are terminated prior to burial, either by discontinuing mechanical ventilation or by removing their heart and/or lungs during the process of organ procurement. While this line of argumentation has a certain logical persuasiveness, it nevertheless fails to address the central fact that most people find it counterintuitive to perceive a breathing patient as "dead." Wikler has suggested that this attitude is likely to change over time, and that eventually society will come to accept that the body of a patient in a permanent vegetative state is simply that person's "living remains."[36] This optimism about higher-brain death is reminiscent of the comments by the President's Commission regarding whole-brain death: "Although undeniably disconcerting for many people, the confusion created in personal perception by a determination of 'brain death' does not . . . provide a basis for an ethical objection to discontinuing medical measures on these dead bodies any more than on other dead bodies."[37] Nevertheless, at the present time any inclination toward a higher-brain death standard remains primarily in the realm of philosophers and not policymakers.

Return to the Traditional Cardiorespiratory Standard. In contrast to the higher-brain concept of death, the other main alternative to our current approach would involve moving in the opposite direction and abandoning the diagnosis of brain death altogether. This would involve returning to the traditional approach to determining death, that is, the cardiorespiratory standard. In evaluating the wisdom of "turning back the clock," it is helpful to retrace the development of the concept of brain death back to 1968 and the conclusions of the Ad Hoc Committee that developed the Harvard Criteria for the diagnosis of brain death. They began by claiming:

There are two reasons why there is need for a definition [of brain death]: (1) Improvements in resuscitative and supportive measures have led to increased efforts to save those who are desperately injured. Sometimes these efforts have only partial success so that the result is an individual whose heart continues to beat but whose brain is irreversibly damaged. The burden is great on patients who suffer permanent loss of intellect, on their families, and on those in need of hospital beds already occupied by these comatose patients. (2) Obsolete criteria for the definition of death can lead to controversy in obtaining organs for transplantation.[38]

These two issues can be subdivided into at least four distinct questions:
1) When is it permissible to withdraw life support from patients with irreversible neurological damage for the benefit of the patient?
2) When is it permissible to withdraw life support from patients with irreversible neurological damage for the benefit of society, where the benefit is either in the form of economic savings or to make an ICU bed available for someone with a better prognosis?
3) When is it permissible to remove organs from a patient for transplantation?
4) When is a patient ready to be cremated or buried?
The Harvard Committee chose to address all of these questions with a single answer, that is, the determination of brain death. Each of these questions involves unique theoretical issues, however, and each raises a different set of concerns. By analyzing the concept of brain death in terms of the separate questions that led to its development, alternatives to brain death may be considered.

Withdrawal of life support. The Harvard Committee clearly viewed the diagnosis of brain death as a necessary condition for the withdrawal of life support: "It should be emphasized that we recommend the patient be declared dead before any effort is made to take him off a respirator . . . [since] otherwise, the physicians would be turning off the respirator

on a person who is, in the present strict, technical application of law, still alive" (p. 339).

The ethical and legal mandates that surround the withdrawal of life support have changed dramatically since the recommendations of the Harvard Committee. Numerous court decisions and consensus statements have emphasized the rights of patients or their surrogates to demand the withdrawal of life-sustaining treatments, including mechanical ventilation. In the practice of critical care medicine today, patients are rarely diagnosed as brain-dead solely for the purpose of discontinuing mechanical ventilation. When patients are not candidates for organ transplantation, either because of medical contraindications or lack of consent, families are informed of the dismal prognosis, and artificial ventilation is withdrawn. While the diagnosis of brain death was once critical in allowing physicians to discontinue life-sustaining treatments, decisionmaking about these important questions is now appropriately centered around the patient's previously stated wishes and judgments about the patient's best interest. Questions about the definition of death have become virtually irrelevant to these deliberations.

Allocation of scarce resources. The Harvard Committee alluded to its concerns about having patients with a hopeless prognosis occupying ICU beds. In the years since that report, this issue has become even more pressing. The diagnosis of brain death, however, is of little significance in helping to resolve these issues. Even considering the unusual cases where families refuse to have the ventilator removed from a brain-dead patient, the overall impact of the diagnosis of brain death upon scarce ICU resources is minimal. Much more important to the current debate over the just allocation of ICU resources are patients with less severe degrees of neurological dysfunction, such as patients in a permanent vegetative state or individuals with advanced dementia. Again, the diagnosis of brain death is of little relevance to this central concern of the Harvard Committee.

Organ transplantation. Without question, the most important reason for the continued use of brain death cri-

Hastings Center Report, January-February 1997

teria is the need for transplantable organs. Yet even here, the requirement for brain death may be doing more harm than good. The need for organs is expanding at an ever-increasing rate, while the number of available organs has essentially plateaued. In an effort to expand the limited pool of organs, several attempts have been made to circumvent the usual restrictions of brain death on organ procurement.

At the University of Pittsburgh, for example, a new protocol allows critically ill patients or their surrogates to offer their organs for donation after the withdrawal of life-support, even though the patients never meet brain death criteria.[39] Suitable patients are taken to the operating room, where intravascular monitors are placed and the patient is "prepped and draped" for surgical incision. Life-support is then withdrawn, and the patient is monitored for the development of cardiac arrest. Assuming this occurs within a short period of time, the attending physician waits until there has been two minutes of pulselessness, and then pronounces the patient dead. The transplant team then enters the operating room and immediately removes the organs for transplantation.

This novel approach has a number of problems when viewed from within the traditional framework. For example, after the patient is pronounced dead, why should the team rush to remove the organs? If the Pittsburgh team truly believes that the patient is dead, why not begin chest compressions and mechanical ventilation, insert cannulae to place the patient on full cardiopulmonary bypass, and remove the organs in a more controlled fashion? Presumably, this is not done because two minutes of pulselessness is almost certainly not long enough to ensure the development of brain death.[40] It is even conceivable that patients managed in this way could regain consciousness during the process of organ procurement while supported with cardiopulmonary bypass, despite having already been diagnosed as "dead." In other words, the reluctance of the Pittsburgh team to extend their protocol in ways that would be acceptable for dead patients could be an indication that the patients may really not be dead after all.

A similar attempt to circumvent the usual restrictions on organ procurement was recently attempted with anencephalic newborns at Loma Linda University. Again, the protocol involved manipulation of the dying process, with mechanical ventilation being instituted and maintained solely for the purpose of preserving the organs until criteria for brain death could be documented. The results were disappointing, and the investigators concluded that "it is usually not feasible, with the restrictions of current law, to procure solid organs for transplantation from anencephalic infants."[41]

Why do these protocols strike many commentators as contrived and even somewhat bizarre? The motives of the individuals involved are certainly commendable: they want to offer the benefits of transplantable organs to individuals who desperately need them. In addition, they are seeking to obtain organs only from individuals who cannot be harmed by the procurement and only in those situations where the patient or a surrogate requests the donation. The problem with these protocols lies not with the motive, but with the method and justification. By manipulating both the process and the definition of death, these protocols give the appearance that the physicians involved are only too willing to draw the boundary between life and death wherever it happens to maximize the chances for organ procurement.

How can the legitimate desire to increase the supply of transplantable organs be reconciled with the need to maintain a clear and simple distinction between the living and the dead? One way would be to abandon the requirement for the death of the donor prior to organ procurement and, instead, focus upon alternative and perhaps more fundamental ethical criteria to constrain the procurement of organs, such as the principles of consent and nonmaleficence.[42]

For example, policies could be changed such that organ procurement would be permitted only with the consent of the donor or appropriate surrogate and only when doing so would not harm the donor. Individuals who could not be harmed by the procedure would include those

who are permanently and irreversibly unconscious (patients in a persistent vegetative state or newborns with anencephaly) and those who are imminently and irreversibly dying.

The American Medical Association's Council on Ethical and Judicial Affairs recently proposed (but has subsequently retracted) a position consistent with this approach.[43] The council stated that, "It is ethically permissible to consider the anencephalic as a potential organ donor, although still alive under the current definition of death," if, among other requirements, the diagnosis is certain and the parents give their permission. The council concluded, "It is normally required that the donor be legally dead before removal of their life-necessary organs . . . The use of the anencephalic neonate as a live donor is a limited exception to the general standard because of the fact that the infant has never experienced, and will never experience, consciousness" (pp. 1617-18).

This alternative approach to organ procurement would require substantial changes in the law. The process of organ procurement would have to be legitimated as a form of justified killing, rather than just as the dissection of a corpse. There is certainly precedent in the law for recognizing instances of justified killing. The concept is also not an anathema to the public, as evidenced by the growing support for euthanasia, another practice that would have to be legally construed as a form of justified killing. Even now, surveys show that one-third of physicians and nurses do not believe brain-dead patients are actually dead, but feel comfortable with the process of organ procurement because the patients are permanently unconscious and/or imminently dying.[44] In other words, many clinicians already seem to justify their actions on the basis of nonmaleficence and consent, rather than with the belief that the patients are actually dead.

This alternative approach would also eliminate the need for protocols like the one being used at the University of Pittsburgh, with its contrived and perhaps questionable approach to declaring death prior to organ procurement. Under the proposed system, qualified individuals who had

Hastings Center Report, January-February 1997

given their consent could simply have their organs removed under general anesthesia, without first undergoing an orchestrated withdrawal of life support. Anencephalic newborns whose parents requested organ donation could likewise have the organs removed under general anesthesia, without the need to wait for the diagnosis of brain death.

The diagnosis of death. Seen in this light, the concept of brain death may have become obsolete. Certainly the diagnosis of brain death has been extremely useful during the last several decades, as society has struggled with a myriad of issues that were never encountered before the era of mechanical ventilation and organ transplantation. As society emerges from this transitional period, and as many of these issues are more clearly understood as questions that are inherently unrelated to the distinction between life and death, then the concept of brain death may no longer be useful or relevant. If this is the case, then it may be preferable to return to the traditional standard and limit tests for he determination of death to those based solely upon the permanent cessation of respiration and circulation. Even today we uniformly regard the cessation of respiration and circulation as the standard for determining when patients are ready to be cremated or buried.

Another advantage of a return to the traditional approach is that it would represent a "common denominator" in the definition of death that virtually all cultural groups and religious traditions would find acceptable.[45] Recently both New Jersey and New York have enacted statutes that recognize the objections of particular religious views to the concept of brain death. In New Jersey, physicians are prohibited from declaring brain death in persons who come from religious traditions that do not accept the concept.[46] Return to a cardiorespiratory standard would eliminate problems with these objections.

Linda Emanuel recently proposed a "bounded zone" definition of death that shares some features with the approach outlined here.[47] Her proposal would adopt the cardiorespiratory standard as a "lower bound" for determining death that would apply to

all cases, but would allow individuals to choose a definition of death that encompassed neurologic dysfunction up to the level of the permanent vegetative state (the "higher bound"). The practical implications of such a policy would be similar to some of those discussed here, in that it would (1) allow patients and surrogates to request organ donation when and if the patients were diagnosed with whole-brain death, permanent vegetative state, or anencephaly, and (2) it would permit rejection of the diagnosis of brain death by patients and surrogates opposed to the concept. Emanuel's proposal would not permit organ donation from terminal and imminently dying patients, however, prior to the diagnosis of death.

Despite these similarities, these two proposals differ markedly in the justifications used to support their conclusions. Emanuel follows the President's Commission in seeking to address several separate questions by reference to the diagnosis of death, whereas the approach suggested here would adopt a single and uniform definition of death, and then seek to resolve questions around organ donation on a different ethical and legal foundation.

Emanuel's proposal also provides another illustration of the problems encountered when a variety of diverse issues all hinge upon the definition of death. Under her scheme, some individuals would undoubtedly opt for a definition of death based on the "higher bound" of the permanent vegetative state in order to permit the donation of their vital organs if they should develop this condition. How-

ever, few of these individuals would probably agree to being cremated while still breathing, even if they were vegetative. Most likely, they would not want to be cremated until after they had sustained a cardiorespiratory arrest. Once again, this creates the awk-

---

> The most difficult challenge for this proposal would be to gain acceptance of the view that killing may sometimes be a justifiable necessity for procuring transplantable organs.

---

ward and confusing necessity of diagnosing death for one purpose (organ donation) but not for another (cremation). Only by abandoning the concept of brain death is it possible to adopt a definition of death that is valid for all purposes, while separating questions of organ donation from dependence upon the life/death dichotomy.

Turning Back

The tension between the need to maintain workable and practical standards for the procurement of transplantable organs and our desire to have a conceptually coherent account of death is an issue that must be given serious attention. Resolving these inconsistencies by moving toward a higher-brain definition of death would most likely create additional practical problems regarding accurate diagnosis as well as introduce concepts that are highly counterintuitive to the general public. Uncoupling the link between organ transplantation and brain death, on the other hand, offers a number of advantages. By shifting the ethical foundations for organ donation to the principles of nonmaleficence and consent, the pool of potential donors may be substantially increased. In addition, by reverting to a simpler and more traditional definition of death, the long-standing

Hastings Center Report, January-February 1997

debate over fundamental inconsistencies in the concept of brain death may finally be resolved.

The most difficult challenge for this proposal would be to gain acceptance of the view that killing may sometimes be a justifiable necessity for procuring transplantable organs. Careful attention to the principles of consent and nonmaleficence should provide an adequate bulwark against slippery slope concerns that this practice would be extended in unforeseen and unacceptable ways. Just as the euthanasia debate often seems to turn less upon abstract theoretical concerns and more upon the empirical question of whether guidelines for assisted dying would be abused, so the success of this proposal could also rest upon factual questions of societal acceptance and whether this approach would erode respect for human life and the integrity of clinicians. While the answers to these questions are not known, the potential benefits of this proposal make it worthy of continued discussion and debate.

Acknowledgments

The author thanks numerous friends and colleagues for critical readings of the manuscript, with special acknowledgments to Dan Wikler and Linda Emanuel.

References

1. Some of the more notable critiques include Robert M. Veatch, "The Whole-Brain-Oriented Concept of Death. An Outmoded Philosophical Formulation," *Journal of Thanatology* 3 (1975): 13-30; Michael B. Green and Daniel Wikler, "Brain Death and Personal Identity," *Philosophy and Public Affairs* 9 (1980): 105-33; Stuart J. Youngner and Edward T. Bartlett, "Human Death and High Technology: The Failure of the Whole-Brain Formulations," *Annals of Internal Medicine* 99 (1983): 252-58; Amir Halevy and Baruch Brody, "Brain Death: Reconciling Definitions, Criteria, and Tests," *Annals of Internal Medicine* 119 (1993): 519-25.

2. Stuart J. Youngner, "Defining Death: A Superficial and Fragile Consensus," *Archives of Neurology* 49 (1992): 570-72.

3. President's Commission for the Study of Ethical Problems in Medicine and Biomedical and Behavioral Research, *Defining Death* (Washington, D.C.: Government Printing Office, 1981).

4. Karen Gervais has been especially articulate in defining these levels. See Karen G. Gervais, *Redefining Death* (New Haven:

Yale University Press, 1986); "Advancing the Definition of Death: A Philosophical Essay," *Medical Humanities Review* 3, no. 2 (1989): 7-19.

5. James L. Bernat, Charles M. Culver, and Bernard Gert, "On the Definition and Criterion of Death," *Annals of Internal Medicine* 94 (1981): 389-94; James L. Bernat, "How Much of the Brain Must Die in Brain Death?" *Journal of Clinical Ethics* 3 (1992): 21-26.

6. Report of the Medical Consultants on the Diagnosis of Death, "Guidelines for the Determination of Death," *JAMA* 246 (1981): 2184-86.

7. Aspects of this analysis have been explored previously in, Robert D. Truog and James C. Fackler, "Rethinking Brain Death," *Critical Care Medicine* 20 (1992): 1705-13; Halevy and Brody, "Brain Death."

8. H. Schrader et al., "Changes of Pituitary Hormones in Brain Death," *Acta Neurochirurgica* 52 (1980): 239-48; Kristen M. Outwater and Mark A. Rockoff, "Diabetes Insipidus Accompanying Brain Death in Children," *Neurology* 34 (1984): 1243-46; James C. Fackler, Juan C. Troncoso, and Frank R. Gioia, "Age-Specific Characteristics of Brain Death in Children," *American Journal of Diseases of Childhood* 142 (1988): 999-1003.

9. Schrader et al., "Changes of Pituitary Hormones in Brain Death"; H. J. Gramm et al., "Acute Endocrine Failure after Brain Death," *Transplantation* 54 (1992): 851-57.

10. Report of Medical Consultants on the Diagnosis of Death, "Guidelines for the Determination of Death," p. 339.

11. Madeleine M. Grigg et al., "Electroencephalographic Activity after Brain Death," *Archives of Neurology* 44 (1987): 948-54; A. Earl Walker, *Cerebral Death*, 2nd ed. (Baltimore: Urban & Schwarzenberg, 1981), pp. 89-90; and Christopher Pallis, "ABC of Brain Stem Death. The Arguments about the EEG," *British Medical Journal [Clinical Research]* 286 (1983): 284-87.

12. Ernst Rodin et al., "Brainstem Death," *Clinical Electroencephalography* 16 (1985): 63-71.

13. Randall C. Wetzel et al., "Hemodynamic Responses in Brain Dead Organ Donor Patients," *Anesthesia and Analgesia* 64 (1985): 125-28; S. H. Pennefather, J. H. Dark, and R. E. Bullock, "Haemodynamic Responses to Surgery in Brain-Dead Organ Donors," *Anaesthesia* 48 (1993): 1034-38; and D. J. Hill, R. Munglani, and D. Sapsford, "Haemodynamic Responses to Surgery in Brain-Dead Organ Donors," *Anaesthesia* 49 (1994): 835-36.

14. Bernat, "How Much of the Brain Must Die in Brain Death?"

15. Paul A. Byrne, Sean O'Reilly, and Paul M. Quay, "Brain Death—An Opposing Viewpoint," *JAMA* 242 (1979): 1985-90.

16. Gaetano F. Molinari, "The NINCDS Collaborative Study of Brain Death: A Historical Perspective," in U.S. Department of Health and Human Services, *NINCDS monograph No. 24. NIH publication No. 81-2286* (1980): 1-32.

17. Pallis, "ABC of Brain Stem Death," pp. 123-24; Bryan Jennett and Catherine Hessett, "Brain Death in Britain as Reflected in Renal Donors," *British Medical Journal* 283 (1981): 359-62; Peter M. Black, "Brain Death (first of two parts)," *NEJM* 299 (1978): 338-44.

18. President's Commission, *Defining Death*.

19. "An Appraisal of the Criteria of Cerebral Death, A Summary Statement: A Collaborative Study," *JAMA* 237 (1977): 982-86.

20. Green and Wikler, "Brain Death and Personal Identity."

21. President's Commission, *Defining Death*.

22. Green and Wikler, "Brain Death and Personal Identity"; Daniel Wikler, "Brain Death: A Durable Consensus?" *Bioethics* 7 (1993): 239-46.

23. David R. Field et al., "Maternal Brain Death During Pregnancy: Medical and Ethical issues," *JAMA* 260 (1988): 816-22; Masanobu Washida et al., "Beneficial Effect of Combined 3,5,3'-Triiodothyronine and Vasopressin Administration or Hepatic Energy Status and Systemic Hemodynamics after Brain Death," *Transplantation* 54 (1992): 44-49.

24. Stuart J. Youngner et al., "'Brain Death' and Organ Retrieval: A Cross-Sectional Survey of Knowledge and Concepts among Health Professionals," *JAMA* 261 (1989): 2205-10.

25. Daniel Wikler and Alan J. Weisbard, "Appropriate Confusion over 'Brain Death,'" *JAMA* 261 (1989): 2246.

26. Margareta Sanner, "A Comparison of Public Attitudes toward Autopsy, Organ Donation, and Anatomic Dissection: A Swedish Survey," *JAMA* 271 (1994): 284-88, at 287.

27. Green and Wikler, "Brain Death and Personal Identity."

28. Robert M. Arnold and Stuart J. Youngner, "The Dead Donor Rule: Should We Stretch It, Bend It, or Abandon It?" *Kennedy Institute of Ethics Journal* 3 (1993): 263-78.

29. Some of the many works defending this view include: Green and Wikler, "Brain Death and Personal Identity"; Gervais, *Redefining Death*; Truog and Fackler, "Rethinking Brain Death"; and Robert M. Veatch, *Death, Dying, and the Biological Revolution* (New Haven: Yale University Press, 1989).

30. The Multi-Society Task Force on PVS, "Medical Aspects of the Persistent Vegetative State," *NEJM* 330 (1994): 1499-

Hastings Center Report, January-February 1997

1508 and 1572-79; D. Alan Shewmon, "Anencephaly: Selected Medical Aspects," *Hastings Center Report* 18, no. 5 (1988): 11-19.

31. Nancy L. Childs and Walt N. Mercer, "Brief Report: Late Improvement in Consciousness after Post-Traumatic Vegetative State," *NEJM* 334 (1996): 24-25; James L. Bernat, "The Boundaries of the Persistent Vegetative State," *Journal of Clinical Ethics* 3 (1992): 176-80.

32. Medical Task Force on Anencephaly, "The Infant with Anencephaly," *NEJM* 322 (1990): 669-74; Shewmon, "Anencephaly: Selected Medical Aspects."

33. Jeffrey R. Botkin and Stephen G. Post, "Confusion in the Determination of Death: Distinguishing Philosophy from Physiology," *Perspectives in Biology and Medicine* 36 (1993): 129-38.

34. The Multi-Society Task Force on PVS, "Medical Aspects of the Persistent Vegetative State."

35. Marcia Angell, "After Quinlan: The Dilemma of the Persistent Vegetative State," *NEJM* 330 (1994): 1524-25.

36. Wikler, "Brain Death: A Durable Consensus?"

37. President's Commission, *Defining Death*, p. 84.

38. Report of the Ad Hoc Committee of the Harvard Medical School to Examine the Definition of Brain Death, "A Definition of Irreversible Coma," *JAMA* 205 (1968): 337-40.

39. "University of Pittsburgh Medical Center Policy and Procedure Manual: Management of Terminally Ill Patients Who May Become Organ Donors after Death," *Kennedy Institute of Ethics Journal* 3 (1993): A1-A15; Stuart Youngner and Robert Arnold, "Ethical, Psychosocial, and Public Policy Implications of Procuring Organs from Non-Heart-Beating Cadaver Donors," *JAMA* 269 (1993): 2769-74. Of note, the June 1993 issue of the *Kennedy Institute of Ethics Journal* is devoted to this topic in its entirety.

40. Joanne Lynn, "Are the Patients Who Become Organ Donors Under the Pittsburgh Protocol for 'Non-Heart-Beating Donors' Really Dead?" *Kennedy Institute of Ethics Journal* 3 (1993): 167-78.

41. Joyce L. Peabody, Janet R. Emery, and Stephen Ashwal, "Experience with Anencephalic Infants as Prospective Organ Donors," *NEJM* 321 (1989): 344-50.

42. See for example, Norman Fost, "The New Body Snatchers: On Scott's 'The Body as Property,'" *American Bar Foundation Research Journal* 3 (1983): 718-32; John A. Robertson, "Relaxing the Death Standard for Organ Donation in Pediatric Situations," in *Organ Substitution Technology: Ethical, Legal, and Public Policy Issues*, ed. D. Mathieu (Boulder, Col.: Westview Press, 1988), pp. 69-76; Arnold and Youngner, "The Dead Donor Rule."

43. AMA Council on Ethical and Judicial Affairs, "The Use of Anencephalic Neonates as Organ Donors," *JAMA* 273 (1995): 1614-18. After extensive debate among AMA members, the Council retracted this position statement. See Charles W. Plows, "Reconsideration of AMA Opinion on Anencephalic Neonates as Organ Donors," *JAMA* 275 (1996): 443-44.

44. Youngner et al., "'Brain Death' and Organ Retrieval."

45. Jiro Nudeshima, "Obstacles to Brain Death and Organ Transplantation in Japan," *Lancet* 338 (1991): 1063-64.

46. Robert S. Olick, "Brain Death, Religious Freedom, and Public Policy: New Jersey's Landmark Legislative Initiative," *Kennedy Institute of Ethics Journal* 1 (1991): 275-88.

47. Linda L. Emanuel, "Reexamining Death: The Asymptotic Model and a Bounded Zone Definition," *Hastings Center Report* 25, no. 4 (1995): 27-35.

❖

[2]

The Importance of Being Dead: Non-Heart-Beating Organ Donation

Jerry Menikoff, M.D., J.D.*

ABSTRACT: There is no definitive answer to the question of how long one must wait, after a person's heart stops beating, before concluding that the person meets the heart-lung criteria for death. This question has assumed new importance with attempts to remove transplantable organs from people declared dead using those criteria. An examination of the legal definition of death suggests that organs are indeed being procured from some of these people prior to their being legally dead. Moreover, the fact that the donors have consented to these procedures does not eliminate reason for concern regarding this state of affairs, since patient autonomy must at times be overridden in pursuance of important social goals.

Few can dispute that there is a shortage of transplantable organs. Thousands of people die each year, waiting for an organ that did not arrive in time. A variety of proposals are being pursued in an effort to remedy this unfortunate situation. One of the more controversial proposals involves the use of a new class of possible donors: people who die in the "usual" manner, when they stop breathing and their hearts stop beating. This article discusses several issues raised by the use of these so-called "non-heart-beating" organ donors. In particular, it will explore whether organs are being removed from such donors prior to the time when they are legally dead, and why we should be concerned about this.

The great majority of the transplantable organs that are removed from people after they have died are currently taken from people who have been declared "brain

---

* Associate Professor of Law, Ethics and Medicine, Department of History and Philosophy of Medicine, The University of Kansas Medical Center, Kansas City, Kansas; M.D., Washington University, 1986; J.D., Harvard Law School, 1977.

dead."[1] The concept of brain death initially received prominence in the late 1960's as the result of a report by a committee at the Harvard Medical School,[2] and in the ensuing years it has become part of the legal definition of death in virtually every state, either by the passage of a law, or through a court's adoption of such a rule.[3] A person who meets the criteria for brain death has suffered the irreversible cessation of function of all of the brain: both the "higher" brain, responsible for thinking and feeling, and the "lower" brain, responsible for many of the housekeeping chores that keep the rest of the body functioning (such as breathing and maintaining a constant temperature).[4] Such a person's heart is usually still beating, although the body needs to be hooked up to a ventilator, which effectively breathes for that person. Because oxygenated blood is still circulating through the person's body, the organs remain healthy for some period of time after the person is declared dead, and are thus useful for transplantation purposes.[5]

In general, relatively few people die in a manner that allows them to meet the brain death criteria.[6] There usually needs to be an interruption in the blood flow to the brain (for example, due to a hemorrhage in the brain that increases intra-cranial pressure) under circumstances where blood flow to the rest of the body continues

---

[1] Such organ donations are described as "cadaveric" donations, to distinguish them from organs that are donated while someone is still alive. Over a third of current organ donations come from living donors. *See* U.S. DEPARTMENT OF HEALTH AND HUMAN SERVICES, REPORT TO CONGRESS ON THE SCIENTIFIC AND CLINICAL STATUS OF ORGAN TRANSPLANTATION 1 (1999). Such donors cannot, however, donate an organ that is necessary for maintaining life (a so-called unpaired "vital" organ), since, as discussed further herein, the physicians removing that organ would in most cases be committing homicide. Thus, among the organs donated by these living donors are a single kidney, a lung, or a portion of a liver. In contrast, a living donor would not be permitted to donate her heart.

[2] *See generally Report of the Ad Hoc Committee of the Harvard Medical School to Examine the Definition of Brain Death, A Definition of Irreversible Coma*, 205 JAMA 337 (1968).

[3] *See, e.g.*, In re Bowman, 617 P.2d 731 (Wash. 1980); INSTITUTE OF MEDICINE, NON-HEART-BEATING ORGAN TRANSPLANTATION: MEDICAL AND ETHICAL ISSUES IN PROCUREMENT 21 (1997) (hereinafter INST. MED. REP. I); BARRY R. FURROW ET AL., HEALTH LAW 806-08 (2d ed. 2000); JERRY MENIKOFF, LAW AND BIOETHICS: AN INTRODUCTION 443-55 (2001).

In those states in which a law has been enacted defining brain death, the law is usually some version of the Uniform Determination of Death Act, 12 U.L.A. 340 (Supp. 1991) (hereinafter "UDDA"), which is discussed in detail later in this article. This Act is one of the many model laws drafted by the National Conference of Commissioners on Uniform State Laws, an independent organization that drafts a variety of model laws and then circulates these drafts to state legislatures and others with the hope that states will then adopt versions of such laws. In this way, state laws concerning particular topics may end up exhibiting a remarkable degree of similarity from state to state. Copies of all the model acts drafted by this organization, including the Uniform Determination of Death Act, can be found on the web at http://www.law.upenn.edu/bll/ulc/ulc_frame.htm (accessed on Oct. 4, 2001).

[4] *See, e.g.*, In re Bowman, 617 P.2d 731 (Wash. 1980).

[5] *See, e.g.*, MARK A. HALL, ET AL., HEALTH CARE LAW AND ETHICS IN A NUTSHELL 279-82 (2d ed. 1999).

[6] *See* INST. MED. REP. I, *supra* note 3, at 14-15. ("Today most deaths in the United States are determined by application of the traditional heart-lung definition of death."); Prefatory Note to the UDDA, *supra* note 3, at § 1 ("The overwhelming majority of cases will continue to be determined according to [the heart-lung] criteria."). *See also* FURROW, *supra* note 3, at 806.

(or, at least, is restarted before substantial damage occurs to the heart and other organs). Thus, the supply of organs for transplantation that come from brain dead donors is of necessity limited.[7]

Given the disparity between the large number of people who could benefit from an organ transplant, and the much smaller number of currently available transplantable organs, policy makers have been seeking ways to shrink this gap.[8] One obvious thought relates to possibly obtaining organs from those of us who will not die in a way that meets the brain death criteria, but rather in the "usual" way: our heart stops beating, or we stop breathing. In either of these two cases, as a result of the loss of oxygen (since no oxygenated blood is flowing through the body) all of the body's organs (including the heart, lungs and brain) will shortly thereafter be so damaged that they permanently stop functioning.

In formal terms, this set of events is referred to in the Uniform Determination of Death Act (UDDA),[9] the model statute whose language has been adopted by most states in their legal definitions of death, as "irreversible cessation of circulatory and respiratory functions." This is referred to as being declared dead under "heart-lung" or "cardio-pulmonary" criteria. Since this is the way most of us will indeed die[10]—for example, we will have a severe heart attack, our heart stops beating, blood flow stops, and the above-mentioned cascade of cell death proceeds throughout our body—a reader might think that it is very straightforward to determine death under this standard. Indeed, supporters of the use of non-heart-beating organ donation will at times claim that since this form of organ donation involves the traditional definition of death, it really should be viewed as less controversial than even removing organs from people who are declared dead under brain death criteria.[11]

That point of view ignores one crucial element of non-heart-beating organ donation: the *timing* issue. As noted above, when a person is declared dead under brain death criteria, oxygenated blood is still circulating through that person's body. Thus, there is no particular hurry in removing organs, since that blood flow will

---

[7] *See* INST. MED. REP. I, *supra* note 3, at 14-15.

[8] *See id.* at 14-15; U.S. DEPARTMENT OF HEALTH AND HUMAN SERVICES, *supra* note 1, at 2-3; Roger Herdman et al., *The Institute of Medicine's Report on Non-Heart-Beating Organ Transplantation*, 8 KENNEDY INST. ETHICS J. 83, 86-87 (1998).

[9] UDDA, *supra*, note 3, at § 1. The relevant portion of this Act reads: "An individual who has sustained either (1) irreversible cessation of circulatory and respiratory functions, or (2) irreversible cessation of all functions of the entire brain, including the brain stem, is dead." Clause (1) describes the heart-lung criteria for determining death, while clause (2) describes the criteria for determining "brain death." *Id.*

[10] *See* INST. MED. REP. I, UDDA, and FURROW, *supra* note 6.

[11] Personnel involved in organ procurement at various institutions have informally told the author of instances in which these arguments have been prominently employed in encouraging them to adopt a non-heart-beating donor protocol at their institutions.

keep the organs healthy for at least days, if not longer.[12] In contrast, when a person is declared dead under the heart-lung criteria, there is no oxygenated blood circulating, and the organs we wish to use for transplantation purposes immediately begin to deteriorate. There is a great deal of dispute regarding how long an organ can go without oxygen and still be useful for transplantation purposes, and much research is being done on this question.[13] The answers vary from organ to organ. Nonetheless, in terms of current practices regarding which organs are viewed as acceptable, the effective answer to this question is in the range of minutes, as opposed to hours.[14] In other words, there is a need to declare a person dead relatively soon after the event that causes the flow of oxygenated blood to stop.[15]

Imagine that you are in the room with someone at the very moment when that person's heart stops beating. The person had previously indicated they did not want any measures taken to revive them, such as cardiopulmonary resuscitation.[16] When, we might ask, is this person dead? Is it the very moment the heart stops beating? Is it seconds or minutes later? At what point in time has the legal standard of "irreversible cessation of circulatory and respiratory functions" been met?

Somewhat surprisingly, this question has never been adequately answered![17] The primary reason is that until recently—until, in particular, the attempts to remove organs from non-heart-beating donors—there never was any particular need to "rush" the process of declaring death. If the hypothetical person described above was found in a hospital room by a nurse, not breathing and pulseless, then the nurse would call a member of the medical staff to come and pronounce the person dead. This procedure did not require any particular haste, and it would be of no special importance if the person were pronounced dead five minutes, fifteen minutes, or even an hour or more after the heart had stopped beating.

---

[12] Indeed, recent evidence indicates that the bodies of brain dead persons can be kept alive for surprisingly long periods of time, leading to such (somewhat inaccurate) terminology as "chronic" or "persistent" brain death. *See, e.g.,* D. Alan Shewmon, *Chronic "Brain Death": Meta-analysis and Conceptual Consequences,* 51 NEUROLOGY 1538 (1998). *See generally* Ronald Cranford, *Even the Dead Are Not Terminally Ill Anymore,* 51 NEUROLOGY 1530 (1998).

[13] *See, e.g.,* INST. MED. REP. I, *supra* note 3, at 24. *See generally* Yong W. Cho et al., *Transplantation of Kidneys From Donors Whose Hearts Have Stopped Beating,* 338 NEW ENG. J. MED. 221 (1998); K.P. Platz et al., *Influence of Warm Ischemia Time on Initial Graft Function in Human Liver Transplantation,* 29 TRANSPLANTATION PROC. 3458 (1997); Jeffrey T. Cope et al., *Intravenous Phenylephrine Preconditioning of Cardiac Grafts from Non-Heart-Beating Donors,* 63 ANN. THORACIC SURG. 1664 (1997).

[14] *See, e.g.,* INST. MED. REP. I, *supra* note 3, at 23-24.

[15] *See id.* at 26 (describing "intense pressure" for having a "short interval to" declaring death).

[16] More formally, if the patient were an in-patient in a hospital, then a "do not resuscitate" or DNR order should have been entered in the chart, consistent with that person's wishes. There are many reasons this might be the case. For example, that person might have determined that her current quality of life was not acceptable, and thus wished to be allowed to die under such circumstances.

[17] "Unfortunately, no scientific studies allow a definite conclusion on how long this interval [from when the heart stops to when circulation has irreversibly ceased] might be. Protocols and practices in the United States and other countries vary significantly in defining this interval, which reflects the lack of scientific certainty." INST. MED. REP. I, *supra* note 3, at 58.

Thus, even today, if you look in almost any major textbook on internal medicine, emergency medicine, or physical diagnosis, you may perhaps find a complicated and detailed protocol that discusses how to declare someone dead using "brain death" criteria; that protocol is likely to be based on the initial recommendations of the Harvard Committee discussed above.[18] But with regard to declaring someone dead under the "heart-lung" criteria—the standard by which the vast majority of us will be declared dead—the textbook is likely to say very little or even nothing.[19] In particular, it will likely not address the issue of how long one needs to wait after a person's heart has stopped.

The fact that the "heart-lung" criteria are the traditional way for determining death, used for hundreds of years, in no way helps resolve this issue. Certainly, there is no reason to think that someone from, say, the Middle Ages—even a medical expert from that time period—would be comfortable in declaring someone dead only a few minutes after the person's heart had stopped beating. Indeed, during much of the prior millennium, there was occasional concern about people being inadvertently buried alive, and devices were created to make sure that, even in the coffin, a resumption of breathing would be detected.[20] Thus, while the "heart-lung" basis for determining death does indeed have a long and illustrious history, that history by itself in no way resolves the timing issue presented by the use of non-heart-beating organ donors.

Why We Care About Determinations of Death

Before more directly delving into the timing issue, it is appropriate to first address the question of why we care about whether or not a person is dead. Only an answer to that initial question can help us then decide what is at stake in concluding that a person is dead a particular number of minutes after that person's heart has stopped beating.

The dividing line between life and death serves a number of legal purposes. Many of these are relatively mundane matters, primarily concerned with the affairs of the survivors of the recently deceased person: for example, health insurance and

---

[18] The criteria for diagnosing brain death still generate a great deal of attention, as demonstrated by a recent article and accompanying editorial in the *New England Journal of Medicine. See generally* Alexander Morgan Capron, *Brain Death: Well Settled Yet Still Unresolved,* 344 New Eng. J. Med. 1244 (2001); Eelco F.M. Wijdicks, *The Diagnosis of Brain Death,* 344 New Eng. J. Med. 1215 (2001).

[19] A 1968 article surveyed fifty then-current textbooks on physical diagnosis, and found only one, published in 1926, which discussed how to diagnose death. *See* J.D. Arnold et al., *Public Attitudes and the Diagnosis of Death,* 206 JAMA 1949, 1951 (1968). This author's very informal survey of the books at my institution's library suggests things have not changed during the last 33 years. Indeed, the only book I found that had any significant discussion of this issue also included the following comment: "Edwin V. Mott, M.D., a resident on our service, called the authors' attention to the dearth of instructions on this subject in books on diagnosis." E.L. DeGowin & R.L. DeGowin, Bedside Diagnostic Examination 843 (4th ed. 1981).

[20] *See, e.g.,* Kenneth V. Iserson, Death to Dust: What Happens to Dead Bodies? 34-38 (1994).

Issues in Law & Medicine, Volume 18, Number 1, 2002

social security payments cease, life insurance payments become payable, and the assets of the deceased person pass to the heirs.[21] But these legal consequences, and a host of similar legal events, are representative of a broader, more significant change: the human being in question has gone from being a *person* in the eyes of the law, to now being a *non-person*. And the United States Constitution, many state constitutions, and thousands of laws enacted pursuant to these documents, grant a variety of rights to human beings who are accorded the status of being "persons." When a human being dies, their transition to non-personhood means that they are no longer subject to the legal protections of being a person.

We are possibly more familiar with discussions of this issue not in the context of people dying, but rather in a very different context: the *forward* transition from non-personhood to personhood that takes place when someone is born. The United States Supreme Court addressed this circumstance in *Roe v. Wade*:

> The Constitution does not define 'person' in so many words. Section 1 of the Fourteenth Amendment contains three references to 'person.' The first, in defining 'citizens,' speaks of 'persons born or naturalized in the United States.' The word also appears both in the Due Process Clause and in the Equal Protection Clause. 'Person' is used in other places in the Constitution . . . . But in nearly all these instances, the use of the word is such that it has application only postnatally. None indicates, with any assurance, that it has any possible pre-natal application.[22]

It appears equally clear that the term person has no "post-death" application, even though the U.S. Supreme Court has not directly addressed this issue. As the Florida Supreme Court has said, citing *Roe v. Wade*, "we begin with the premise that a person's constitutional rights terminate at death."[23]

What are the consequences of this change in legal protections? Again, the analogy to the events surrounding the birth of a child is helpful. After the moment of birth, an infant attains personhood, and the full set of legal rights accompanying that status. The infant thus has rights that are equivalent to those of other persons. In particular, in disputes that pit the interests of the infant against those of other

---

[21] *See* PRESIDENT'S COMMISSION FOR THE STUDY OF ETHICAL PROBLEMS IN MEDICINE AND BIOMEDICAL AND BEHAVIORAL RESEARCH, DEFINING DEATH, A REPORT ON THE MEDICAL, LEGAL AND ETHICAL ISSUES IN THE DETERMINATION OF DEATH 60 (1981) (hereinafter PRESIDENT'S COMM. REP.).

[22] 410 U.S. 113, 157 (1973).

[23] State v. Powell, 497 So. 2d 1188, 1190 (Fla. 1986). Of course, through a variety of specific laws, such as the laws relating to inheritance, society may take cognizance of a dead person's pre-mortem wishes. As to the specific issue of what can be done with a dead body, in most states relatives of the deceased are considered to have what is commonly called a "quasi-property" interest in the corpse: they can control its disposition (including burial), but do not really "own" it or have any rights other than that narrow decisionmaking authority. *But cf.* Whaley v. County of Tuscola, 58 F.3d 111 (6th Cir. 1995) (next of kin's rights relating to a deceased relative's body may raise due process claims under the Fourteenth Amendment to the U.S. Constitution). For more on these complicated and still-evolving issues, *see, e.g.*, Radhika Rao, *Property, Privacy, and the Human Body*, 80 B.U. L. REV. 359 (2000).

persons, there is an initial assumption that the law will be even-handed in protecting the interests of both parties.

This can be contrasted with the situation that exists merely a few moments
before the birth of the child. The pregnant woman is a person, while the fetus has
not yet been accorded the protections of personhood. While the Supreme Court in
Roe v. Wade and its progeny acknowledged that states may, if they wish, protect the
interests of the fetus, those protections must nonetheless recognize that the interests of the fetus are less than those of a person.[24] Thus, for example, if the pregnancy is imposing any risks on the health of the woman, then she may choose to
terminate the existence of the fetus by electing to have an abortion. This right is
fully protected by the Constitution, even in the case of a near-term fetus. This conclusion follows a relatively straightforward balancing: the well-being of a person
(the woman) trumps that of a non-person (the fetus).

Thus, it matters a great deal, from the viewpoint of the law, whether someone
is or is not considered a person. And just as the moment of birth provides a relatively well-demarcated line to help us recognize the acquisition of personhood, the
moment of death must similarly provide an ascertainable way of determining when
a human being has lost the legal protections that come from personhood. It would
not be acceptable to have a highly blurred line, in which we are often uncertain
whether the person is alive or dead, for then we would similarly be uncertain of the
legal protections to be accorded that person. This straightforward proposition has
been recognized for nearly two decades, and was affirmed in the landmark report
on the definition of death by the President's Commission for the Study of Ethical
Problems in Medicine and Biomedical and Behavioral Research: "The Commission
concurs in the view that 'death' should be viewed *not as a process but as the event* that
separates the process of dying from the process of disintegration."[25] Thus, attempts
by some to identify a "zone of uncertainty" in which a person's status would be
classified as neither fully dead nor fully alive, but rather indeterminate, with the
law treating such a person as if they were dead, should be viewed with more than a
little skepticism: in effect, these efforts do nothing more than deny the not-yet-
fully-dead person the legal protections to which they should be entitled.

The Commission goes on to further specify the changes in treatment of the
now-deceased person that accompany this moment of transition:

> A determination of death immediately changes the attitudes and behavior of the
> living toward the body that has gone from being a person to being a corpse. Dis-
> continuation of medical care, mourning and burial are examples of customary
> behavior; people usually provide intimate care for living persons and identify with
> them, while withdrawing from contact with the dead. In ordinary circumstances,

---

[24] *See, e.g.*, Planned Parenthood of Southeastern Pennsylvania v. Casey, 505 U.S. 833 (1992); Roe
v. Wade, 410 U.S. 113 (1973).

[25] PRESIDENT'S COMM. REP., *supra* note 21, at 77 (emphasis added).

10 *Issues in Law & Medicine, Volume 18, Number 1, 2002*

the time at which medical diagnosis causes a change in legal status should be synchronous with the time that social behaviors naturally change.[26]

The Limits Of Voluntariness

Let us now apply to non-heart-beating organ donation these concepts relating to how our society distinguishes between the treatment of living persons and non-persons (for our purposes, dead persons). Assume that a hypothetical candidate for non-heart-beating organ donation will soon be dead, and that the impending death will take place either (a) because even with appropriate medical treatment, it is not possible to significantly delay the death, or (b) the donor has chosen to refuse the life-sustaining treatment that might otherwise keep him alive. Moreover, as previously noted, the person's choice to donate his organs has been voluntarily made.

One might well surmise that since everything we are hypothesizing is being done *with the consent of the donor*—i.e., completely voluntarily—then there is certainly no possibility that any of the proposed events involved in effectuating the donation could violate any legal or moral rules. To the contrary, quite the opposite is the case. To understand that conclusion, we need to explore two situations in which such rules are specifically designed to override a person's autonomy, either to protect that person from his own possibly poor judgments, or to preserve certain values of our society, regardless of the interests of that autonomous individual.

The first such rule is the *law of homicide*. In every state in this country, it is a crime for someone to murder another person. And, in particular, the consent of the person being murdered does not change this circumstance. In other words, *a person cannot consent to his own murder*.[27] Sometimes this scenario is dealt with under specific criminal statutes dealing with assisted suicide, but the underlying result is similar to what would otherwise take place under homicide law.

On the other hand, we must distinguish the situation of a person who refuses medical care, and thereby "causes," in some sense, his own death. That is not considered homicide, because the person is exercising an important legal right, the right not to be subjected to a battery: having things done to your body against your will, even if these things are medical treatments that will keep you alive, is considered a legal (and moral) wrong. Indeed, the United States Supreme Court, in *Cruzan*[28] and the physician-assisted suicide cases,[29] suggested that this right might even be embodied in the Constitution.

Thus, on the one hand, it is perfectly acceptable for a person to require a doctor to turn off a ventilator, and thus "cause" the person's death. In contrast, it

---

[26] *Id.*

[27] *See, e.g.,* David Orentlicher, *The Alleged Distinction Between Euthanasia and the Withdrawal of Life-Sustaining Treatment: Conceptually Incoherent and Impossible to Maintain,* 1998 U. Ill. L. Rev. 837, 849-850.

[28] Cruzan v. Director, Missouri Dep't of Health, 497 U.S. 261 (1990).

[29] Washington v. Glucksberg, 521 U.S. 702 (1997); Vacco v. Quill, 521 U.S. 793 (1997).

would be homicide (or the more specific but related crime, assisted suicide) for the doctor, following the request of the patient, to either hand the patient a deadly dose of pills for him to swallow,[30] or to directly inject into the patient's bloodstream a deadly compound. Although this distinction—letting some patients end their lives by ordering the withdrawal of life-sustaining care, while making it a crime for others, not dependent on such care, to similarly effectuate their own deaths—may seem a tenuous one,[31] it is well recognized by legal (and, to a lesser extent, ethical) doctrine. Indeed, the Supreme Court fully supported the rationality of this form of line-drawing in its paired decisions upholding the authority of states to continue to implement this very system of rules.[32]

In the physician-assisted suicide opinions, the Supreme Court noted that there are a variety of justifications for the existing distinction. It noted that states have an "unqualified interest in the preservation of life," an interest which is "symbolic and aspirational as well as practical."[33] Quoting from the New York State Task Force on Life and the Law, it noted:

> While suicide is no longer prohibited or penalized, the ban against assisted suicide and euthanasia shores up the notion of limits in human relationships. It reflects the gravity with which we view the decision to take one's own life or the life of another, and our reluctance to encourage or promote these decisions.[34]

This concept goes beyond protecting the interests of a particular person in whether or not that person wishes to remain alive. It reaffirms a societal interest in preserving life, regardless of the desires of the particular patient.

The Supreme Court also favorably noted society's interest in "protecting vulnerable groups—including the poor, the elderly, and disabled persons—from abuse, neglect, and mistakes."[35] It went on to state:

> The State's interest here goes beyond protecting the vulnerable from coercion; it extends to protecting disabled and terminally ill people from prejudice, negative and inaccurate stereotypes, and "societal indifference." The State's assisted-suicide ban reflects and reinforces its policy that the lives of terminally ill, disabled and elderly people must be no less valued than the lives of the young and healthy, and that a seriously disabled person's suicidal impulses should be interpreted and treated the same way as anyone else's.[36]

---

[30] There is an exception to this in Oregon, which allows this to take place under certain circumstances. Oregon Death With Dignity Act, OR. REV. STAT. §§ 127.800-.897. Thus far, no other state has modified its laws to permit any form of physician-assisted suicide.

[31] *See, e.g.,* James Rachels, *Active and Passive Euthanasia*, 292 NEW ENG. J. MED. 79 (1975).

[32] *See Glucksberg* and *Quill, supra* note 29.

[33] *Glucksberg, supra* note 29, at 728-29, quoting from the majority opinion in *Cruzan.*

[34] *Id.* at 729.

[35] *Id.* at 731.

[36] *Id.* at 732.

Again, we see a reason, based on societal needs, that argues in favor of overriding an autonomous patient's decision in favor of a particular course of action. As the Supreme Court further noted, changing the laws to liberalize assisted suicide might lead to a slippery slope in which we find ourselves ending the lives of people who really did not want to die[37]—thus shattering the illusion that this policy is merely the effectuation of a person's right to autonomy.

The second rule we must address is a much narrower one, but one which specifically relates to organ donation: the so-called *dead donor rule*. This "unwritten" rule, which has effectively become mandatory practice among those practicing in organ transplantation, states that if organs are to be removed from a person after that person's death, the actual removal of the organs should not begin prior to the person being declared dead.[38] One can clearly see in this rule echoes of the same reasons that justify the laws against physician-assisted suicide. Even if we could obtain a few more organs by beginning organ removal prior to a person's death, there is a certain aura of ghoulishness about rushing to remove the organs without even permitting the person to die in peace. Granted that some patients would consent to this, this is perhaps not something we should permit them to consent to: our society might be better off for not having allowed this practice to take place.

Finally, there is an additional, pragmatic justification for the dead donor rule. If it were the case that organs might in some cases be removed during the dying process, and not only after death, then some persons who currently agree to donate organs might choose not to do so. They might worry that, in such a regime, doctors would be so eager to remove the organs that they end up removing them at a time when it was quite possible the patient would otherwise have been able to live. Allowing pre-death removal of organs might thus create additional suspicion in a patient and his family about whether he is receiving all appropriate care, and that suspicion might well adversely impact organ donation, which depends critically on the support of those who choose to donate. The dead donor rule, rigidly applied, allows the organ donation community to better quash any such concerns, telling patients that organs will never be removed prior to their deaths.[39]

The Legal and Ethical Criteria for Determining Death

With these considerations about how our society treats differently persons (the living) and non-persons (the dead) now firmly in hand, let us return to our

---

[37] *Id.* at 732-35.

[38] *See, e.g.*, Robert M. Arnold & Stuart J. Youngner, *The Dead Donor Rule: Should We Stretch It, Bend It, Or Abandon It?* 3 KENNEDY INST. ETHICS J. 263 (1993).

[39] If one further explores the reasoning behind this rule, one concludes that it is less protective than it might seem. Presumably the medical personnel can still undertreat the patient, and thus accelerate that patient's death (even if the patient wanted maximal life-sustaining care), in order to more quickly gain access to the organs. Nonetheless, many in the transplantation community believe that adhering to the dead donor rules does indeed instill at least some additional confidence in the public regarding the integrity of the organ donation process.

initial problem, that of drawing a line between life and death in the case of persons who die as a result of the cessation of heart and lung function. As noted, it has not heretofore been necessary to answer the question about how long one must wait, after a person's heart has stopped beating, in order to determine that the person is dead, consistent with legal and ethical understandings of that concept. Even if we were declaring some people dead a few minutes before they were "really" dead, it really did not matter, since nothing inconsistent with their being alive happened during those few minutes.[40]

But the use of non-heart-beating organ donation squarely poses this question in a manner that does raise legitimate concerns. The desire to maximize the utility of the donated organs means that there is a pressure to minimize the time between the cessation of cardiac function and removal of the organs.[41] And removing organs from a person while that person is still alive, as we shall discuss, raises issues under both of the two previously mentioned rules: homicide laws[42] and the dead donor rule.[43]

The "leading" criteria for determining when a possible non-heart-beating donor is dead are those promulgated by the Institute of Medicine, a prestigious non-profit group that advises the federal government on important medical issues. In April, 1997, after a report on the CBS newsmagazine *60 Minutes* suggested that organs were being removed from some people before they were actually dead, the general counsel of the federal Department of Health and Human Services commissioned the Institute to determine "the alternative medical approaches that can be used to maximize the availability of organs from [a non-heart-beating] donor without violating prevailing ethical norms regarding the rights and welfare of donors."[44]

The Institute initially wrote a report that came out at the end of 1997, determining that a person could be declared dead five minutes after the person's heart had stopped beating.[45] The five-minute rule was based on scientific evidence that by such a point in time, the heart was virtually certain not to begin beating again on

---

[40] The situation I am referring to involves, as described earlier in the text, a person who had refused resuscitative measures (was "do not resuscitate" according to the person's own wishes), and was found pulseless and not breathing in a hospital bed. That person might immediately be declared dead by a passing physician. Had the patient's heart stopped only seconds earlier, then in fact, under an appropriate interpretation of the relevant law, it is likely that the person should not be considered to have truly met the criteria for death for another several minutes (as discussed *infra*). In most cases, this premature pronouncement of death has little ethical or practical impact: if the declaration of death occurs a few minutes prematurely, then the only difference is the official time of the declaration of death. In either event, the body would be lying in the bed, with nothing being done to it differently in terms of attempting to revive the person.

[41] INST. MED. REP. I, *supra* note 3, at 26.

[42] *See* text at notes 27-37, *supra*.

[43] *See* text at notes 38-39, *supra*.

[44] INST. MED. REP. I, *supra* note 3, at 73.

[45] *See id.* at 59-61.

its own.[46] As a result, the Institute determined that the appropriate standard for determining cardio-pulmonary death—the irreversible cessation of heart and lung function—had then been met. In a subsequent report designed to help organ transplant programs implement the earlier report, the Institute again reaffirmed its confidence in this rule.[47]

The Institute's rule raises concerns regarding two facts that might suggest the person is still alive (and thus is perhaps to still be accorded the rights of personhood discussed earlier). The first fact is that at the five-minute point, even though the person is then being declared dead, the person's heart may well still be capable of being restarted through external means (e.g., by defibrilation, applying an electrical shock to the heart).[48] Thus, some might question whether the "irreversibility" element of the criteria had been met.[49] The Institute determined that this possibility of reversal was not relevant in determining the time of death, since the donor had indicated that he did not want the heart restarted.[50] "The point made is that the dying individual's wishes (in this case, a family acting as surrogate) justifies, in fact *requires*, not attempting to resuscitate after five minutes."[51] In other words, the Institute claimed, since it would violate the dying person's legal and moral rights to restart the heart, then the possibility of restarting the heart should not be relevant in determining irreversibility.

The second relevant fact is that at the time that the individual is declared dead, it is quite possible that substantial portions of that person's brain (including the higher brain, responsible for thoughts and emotions) have not yet permanently ceased to function.[52] If one, for example, were to restart pulmonary and cardiac function in that person, the brain (including the higher brain) might then be brought back to some degree of function. The Institute concluded that since the person is

---

[46] *Id.* The Institute of Medicine Report did not cite specific evidence, but it noted that its adoption of the five-minute mark was "[b]ased on expert information and advice from its senior special experts." *Id.* at 59.

[47] INSTITUTE OF MEDICINE, NON-HEART-BEATING ORGAN TRANSPLANTATION: PRACTICES AND PROTOCOLS (2000).

[48] The Institute of Medicine itself recognized this possibility, noting that "[w]ithdrawal of life support undoubtedly leads to cessation of circulatory function that, even if the possibility of spontaneous return of effective heartbeat is left aside, might sometimes be reversed if life support were restored or other resuscitative measures were initiated." INST. MED. REP. I, *supra* note 3, at 58.

[49] *See, e.g.,* Alexander Morgan Capron, *The Bifurcated Legal Standard for Determining Death: Does it Work?* in THE DEFINITION OF DEATH: CONTEMPORARY CONTROVERSIES 132-33 (Stuart J. Youngner et al., eds. 1999).

[50] INST. MED. REP. I, *supra* note 3, at 58.

[51] John T. Potts, Jr. et al., *Commentary: Clear Thinking and Open Discussion Guide IOM's Report on Organ Donation,* 26 J. L. MED. & ETHICS 166, 167 (1998).

[52] The Institute of Medicine claimed only that there would be some degree of "irreversible brain damage" at the five-minute mark it recommended as the time for declaring death. In making this claim, it cited a paper that apparently demonstrated that following loss of blood circulation for periods of from five to twenty minutes, a brain would suffer "various degrees of permanent multifocal" damage. INST. MED. REP. I, *supra* note 3, at 59.

being declared dead under the heart-lung criteria for determining death (as opposed to the brain death criteria), the status of brain function—and, in particular, whether the brain has irreversibly ceased functioning—does not matter. In the Institute's words, the actual amount of brain damage "is not relevant to a determination of death."[53]

Each of these points merits further scrutiny. With regard to the irreversibility issue, is it consistent with our purposes in distinguishing persons from non-persons to have the determination of whether a person is dead turn not on scientific irreversibility, but rather on the person's intent to disallow resuscitation? As a starting point, note that we live in a world in which, sad as it may be, a person's desires often are not transformed into reality. In spite of a person's request that life-sustaining treatment be withheld, it might be the case that this treatment ends up being reinstituted, against that person's will. Such a circumstance might take place through mere inadvertence (e.g., the mistake of one of the health care providers), or perhaps through someone's intentional wrongdoing. In either case, one is left with the curious circumstance that a person who was declared dead may subsequently end up being very much (and incontrovertibly) alive. This possibility suggests that there is something seriously wrong in declaring a person dead when there is a real-world possibility that the "cause" of their death may indeed be reversed.[54]

As we saw in the preceding discussion, our society currently places various restrictions on the extent to which a person's desire to end his life will be effectuated; refusal of life-sustaining treatments are acceptable, whereas "active" measures, such as an injection of a lethal drug, are not.[55] The person who is suffering horribly, dying of an untreatable cancer, is not currently permitted, merely because he is on an inevitable path to death within days, to have that journey shortened by such an active intervention.[56]

Given these distinctions, it would seem doubly inappropriate to conclude that a person whose heart *could* be restarted is dead, and thus as a result a doctor could "actively" remove major organs. In effect, by doing so, we would be denying

---

[53] *Id.* at 58.

[54] One proponent of non-heart-beating organ donation has argued in favor of recognizing a reversible "state of death." *See* James M. DuBois, *Non-Heart-Beating Organ Donation: A Defense of the Required Determination of Death,* 27 J. L. MED. & ETHICS 126, 130 (1999). Thus, for example, presumably the soul might have left the person's body, but the intervention of health care providers might lead to "reanimation" of the body and a return to life. However valid this concept might be from a philosophic or religious viewpoint, nothing in the applicable legal standard contemplates distinguishing "reversibly dead" people from "irreversibly dead" people. As noted previously, death occurs for legal purposes when the applicable conditions—in the case under discussion, cessation of heart and lung function—have *irreversibly* ceased. *See* text at note 9, *supra.*

[55] *See* text at notes 27-37, *supra.*

[56] The only possible current exception is in the State of Oregon, where certain types of active measures (in particular, providing a prescription for a lethal drug dose) are permitted. *See* Oregon Death With Dignity Act, *supra* note 30.

the person whose heart is capable of being restarted exactly those protections that we provide other "living" persons. Most particularly, they would be denied the protection against active measures being taken to end their lives, a protection no one is allowed to "waive." Such a course of action smacks of more than a little hypocrisy: the suffering cancer patient is prevented from more quickly ending his life, when all he wants to do is eliminate his own suffering, yet when the dying person conveniently becomes the source of valuable organs, we suddenly find no problem in taking the *active* step of removing organs at a time when there is still a great deal of life left in that person's body. One cannot help thinking that the declaration that such a person is dead was motivated more by the desire to claim that they removed useable organs without violating the dead donor rule, than by the application of the careful logic and science underlying the determination of death.

Turning to the second issue, should it matter whether or not all of the brain has irreversibly ceased functioning when a person is declared dead? The Institute is certainly correct based on the wording of the statute, since under the heart-lung criteria in the Uniform Determination of Death Act, nothing at all is mentioned about brain function.[57] On the other hand, even a cursory review of both the history of this Act, and the history of ethical thinking about the meaning of death, suggests that the Institute view is flawed.

Most significantly, the history of the Act indicates a consistent understanding that both prongs—cardio-pulmonary death and brain death—are considered to be merely two sets of criteria that prove the existence of a *single* condition we understand as being dead.[58] Indeed, the very first statute that defined brain death, a Kansas law, was subsequently criticized and rejected in large part because it failed to demonstrate how the new brain death criteria were related to the pre-existing concepts of what it meant to be dead.[59] The subsequent revisions of state laws that led to the UDDA noted that declaring someone brain dead was really nothing new, since the irreversible death of the entire brain was in effect what we had always been testing for—whether we knew it or not—even when we were traditionally applying heart-lung tests for determining death.

Indeed, if we do not accept this view, then we are interpreting the UDDA in a way that creates exactly the problem that led to condemnation of the early Kansas law. If we declare someone dead under the cardio-pulmonary standard at a time when there are portions of the person's brain that have not irreversibly stopped functioning, that person would then *not* meet the criteria for being brain dead.[60]

---

[57] UDDA, *supra* note 3, at § 1.

[58] *See* Jerry Menikoff, *Doubts About Death: The Silence of the Institute of Medicine*, 26 J. L. Med. & Ethics 157 (1998).

[59] *See* Alexander M. Capron & Leon R. Kass, *A Statutory Definition of the Standards for Determining Human Death: An Appraisal and a Proposal*, 121 U. Pa. L. Rev. 87 (1972).

[60] The brain death clause of the UDDA is satisfied only when there is "irreversible cessation of all functions of the entire brain, including the brain stem." *See* UDDA, *supra* notes 9-10.

Thus, that person is clearly "less dead" than if we waited the several extra minutes until the entire brain had irreversibly ceased functioning. We are back to the rejected scenario in which the two prongs of the UDDA create differing categories of deadness. Contrary to the claims of those who defend the use of non-heart-beating donors as non-controversial since it involves the "traditional" definition of death,[61] that traditional definition appears to have been warped in a way that makes these people less dead than people declared dead under brain death criteria.

These issues are not new. As early as 1978, in an editorial that defended the then-new criteria for declaring people brain dead, the *New England Journal of Medicine* editorialized as follows: "Indeed, it is clear that a person is not dead unless his brain is dead. The time-honored criteria of stoppage of the heartbeat and circulation are indicative of death only when they persist long enough for the brain to die."[62] This conclusion, fully representative of the thinking at the time, and, indeed, what has remained the thinking supporting the two-pronged structure of the UDDA, is squarely and incontrovertibly inconsistent with the definition of death currently being promulgated by the supporters of non-heart-beating organ donation.[63] Yet those supporters fail to give any arguments as to why commentary such as this was (or is) wrong—indeed, they do not even bother to mention it in their writings.[64] Doing so might force them to acknowledge that their interpretation of the heart-lung criteria is motivated not by reasoning consistent with that behind the UDDA, but rather a pragmatic desire to allow the use of non-heart-beating donors, regardless of whether or not they really are dead at the time organ harvesting begins.

What Can Be Done Pre-Mortem

The discussion thus far—noting the inappropriateness of drawing the life-death dividing line at a place that wrongly places some very alive people on the "death" side of that line and thus denies them (and society) appropriate legal protections—should *not* be viewed as a death knell for the possibility of removing organs from non-heart-beating donors. To the contrary, all it means is that we need to appropriately analyze the steps we are taking in removing such organs. Based on such an analysis, it may well work out that we conclude that there are conditions under which such donors can indeed be a useful source of organs. But in any event, that analysis should be *consistent* with the way similar issues are evaluated.

As was noted earlier, actively removing organs from a person while that person is still alive may constitute homicide, and would certainly violate the dead donor rule.[65] Nonetheless, given that in many non-heart-beating donation scenarios

---

[61] *See* comment, *supra* note 11.

[62] W.H. Sweet, *Brain Death*, 299 NEW ENG. J. MED. 410, 410 (1978).

[63] *See* text at notes 52-53, *supra* (acknowledgment by Institute of Medicine that portions of a person's brain may still not have been irreversibly destroyed at the time of declaration of death under its proposed standard).

[64] *See, e.g.*, John T. Potts, Jr., et al., *supra* note 51, at 166 (1998).

[65] *See* text at notes 27-39, *supra*.

18   *Issues in Law & Medicine, Volume 18, Number 1, 2002*

the person in question has voluntarily chosen to die, and will in any event likely be dead in a few minutes even if the organs were not actively removed, it is perhaps appropriate to enact changes to the homicide laws which would permit removal of organs from such persons. Similarly, it might perhaps be determined that the dead donor rule should not apply to these scenarios. In both instances, however, these changes require debate and analysis relating to whether or not they inappropriately alter the welfare of the donors, or otherwise create an adverse impact on society (e.g., by creating a slippery slope which may cause society to similarly discount the interests of other classes of people, such as those who are severely retarded, persons with advanced Alzheimer's disease, infants with anencephaly, and persons in a persistent vegetative state).

A good example of how we might further evaluate the issue of pre-death organ removal is provided by comparing it to the use of "organ-preserving" drugs during non-heart-beating organ donation. Anticoagulants (e.g., heparin) and vasodilators (e.g., phentolamine) are sometimes given to a donor shortly before the person's death in order to "improve" the quality of the donated organs.[66] These drugs are not beneficial to the patient, however, and in fact may be harmful. In some circumstances, they may even hasten the death of the patient.

The argument in favor of allowing the use of such drugs has been based on a religious doctrine known as the "doctrine of double effect" that has been adopted to some extent in secular bioethics. This complicated rule, in very simplified terms, allows one to pursue a course of action that has both a good and bad effect if one intends only the good effect, the bad effect is not the cause of the good effect, and the good effect outweighs the bad effect.[67] The Institute of Medicine's analysis of this issue led it to conclude that even under this rule, these drugs could *not* be used if they would actually harm the patient.[68]

As the Institute noted, even the patient's consent to the use of these drugs would not be sufficient to justify that use: "informed consent by itself does not allow or excuse interventions that are injurious or actively life-shortening."[69] The Institute thus determined that even though the patient almost certainly would be dead in a few minutes (e.g., due to discontinuance of life support, consistent with

---

[66] INST. MED. REP. I, *supra* note 3, at 51-53.

[67] *See, e.g.,* NEW YORK STATE TASK FORCE ON LIFE AND THE LAW, WHEN DEATH IS SOUGHT: ASSISTED SUICIDE AND EUTHANASIA IN THE MEDICAL CONTEXT 163 (1994).

[68] INST. MED. REP. I, *supra* note 3, at 51-52.

[69] *Id.*

the patient's wishes),[70] that fact was not sufficient to allow the use of a harmful drug, even when the patient is consenting to its use.[71]

If indeed we accept that line of reasoning, then it is necessary to come up with appropriate arguments that distinguish the scenario of removing organs from a person while that person is still alive from that of injecting that person with a harmful drug. At first glance, it appears that both situations are quite similar: if we are going to impose rules that forbid active measures that harm a person, regardless of whether the person will be dead in a few minutes, and regardless of whether the person consented to these measures, then such rules would appear to forbid both courses of action. Of course, we might well conclude that the initial analysis relating to the use of "organ-preserving" drugs is itself wrong, and that such drugs can indeed be used under these circumstances. If that conclusion were reached, then it would be much easier to conclude that pre-death removal of organs is also acceptable.

These arguments are merely designed to demonstrate that a great deal more analysis needs to be done in order to justify removing organs from people while they are still alive. And, most importantly, that analysis must not be arbitrary, but rather needs to be consistent with our analysis of similar situations.

Conclusion

One might well conclude that the definition of death currently being employed in non-heart-beating organ donor protocols represents a knowing gerrymandering of the existing legal definition. In order to make it more convenient to get organs out of non-heart-beating donors, a less-than-well-reasoned modification of the definition has taken place, which conveniently puts a certain group of people on the "dead" side of the live-versus-dead dividing line.

Some might say this is no big deal, since after all, these people are otherwise dying, and very much wanted to donate their organs. On the other hand, as this article attempts to demonstrate, the protections given to living persons are important protections for all members of society, since they determine what kind of society we live in. These protections often, for good reason, do not permit a person to waive certain rights. We do not generally allow a person to "consent" to being

---

[70] One possible qualification might be to note that unlike the person whose heart has already stopped beating, we cannot be so certain that the person will indeed be dead in a few minutes, and, lacking that certainty, the drug would indeed be producing a real harm. But in many situations, for example, a person who is known to be ventilator-dependent (due to neurological damage, for example), and who has requested that the machine be turned off, the patient's forthcoming death is indeed quite certain, absent, in the Institute's own words, the "moral and legal wrong" that would take place if we failed to follow the patient's command that the ventilator be turned off. Yet nothing in the Institute's analysis suggests it would permit the injection of a "harmful" dose of organ-preserving drugs even in this situation.

[71] INST. MED. REP. I, *supra* note 3, at 51-52.

injected with a life-threatening medication (or to having his life ended by surgical removal of vital organs). Presumably, such a rule should apply not just to a healthy person, but to a dying person—even one who will otherwise be dead in a few minutes. As Mary Ellen Waithe said to Mike Wallace in the *60 Minutes* segment on non-heart-beating donation:

WALLACE: Look, these people are on their way to death.

PROF. WAITHE: Yes. . . .

WALLACE: . . . They're going to die. . . .

PROF. WAITHE: So is this a philosopher splitting hairs? You bet. . . . I'm splitting hairs because "as good as dead" is not "dead." And it's not up to physicians. It's up to the legislature of the state of Ohio and the separate states to determine what our legal criteria of death are.[72]

Perhaps it would indeed be a good policy to remove organs from donors using the five-minute rule. Perhaps doing so would not involve much of a "bending" of the rules that protect living persons. But the appropriate debate preceding such a change cannot take place if we sidestep this issue by inappropriately declaring the donors dead too soon. And if we find such a move acceptable in this instance, we might well in the future be similarly motivated to "cut corners" when it comes to procuring organs from vulnerable members of society, members who are less able to speak up for themselves.

---

[72] *Not Quite Dead,* 60 Minutes, CBS Television, Apr. 13, 1997.

Part II
The Body as Property

[3]

Recent developments in biotechnology involving human tissue are sweeping our interactions with this material well beyond the boundaries of existing law. Some of these developments allow profit-oriented companies to use human tissue to generate lucrative products such as drugs, diagnostic tests, and human proteins. The profits obtained elevate the monetary worth of certain types of human tissue, which until very recently has had little or no monetary value, to incalculable levels.[1] Such changes require a society to reassess the present and future status of human tissue within the legal system.

As a free market society, we believe in the general principle of economic justice and attempt to render all individuals their economic due. Based on this general principle, some have argued for recognizing a limited form of property rights in human tissue, such that the profits can be shared amongst all who contribute to the development of the product, including the donor of the tissue.[2] Still others have called for full recognition of property rights in human tissue such that organs and other tissues can be sold as a source of revenue for the donor.[3]

This article investigates whether current ethical standards prohibiting a commercial market in transplantable organs and tissues can be maintained in a legal structure within which human tissue can also be used as a source to generate enormous profit. It is generally considered that the only options available are to recognize or not recognize property rights in human tissue.[4] We propose instead a legal structure in which transplantable human tissue entails no property rights, but in which such rights can be created in new forms of tissue through the investment of labor. This structure will be applied to the facts of *Moore v. The Regents of the University of California* to illustrate how a claim based upon

Margaret S. Swain is completing her PhD in neuroscience at the University of Montreal and is currently enrolled in McGill University's Faculty of Law, Montreal, Canada; Randy W. Marusyk is a student-at-law with Macera & Jarzyna, Ottawa, Canada.

An Alternative To Property Rights in Human Tissue

by Margaret S. Swain and Randy W. Marusyk

A three-tiered legal structure of the substances constitutive of human beings can accommodate property rights in new products created by the investment of labor in human tissue.

the recognition of property rights in human tissue would be decided.[5]

Property Rights and the Body

Modern legal systems have consistently held that no property rights attach to the human body.[6] This standard has been affirmed regardless of whether the human body was alive or not. However, the courts have recognized that a temporary right of possession may exist in a dead body in favor of an executor until proper disposal of the body has occurred. In *Pierce v. Proprietors of Swan Point Cemetery*, the Rhode Island Supreme Court held:

Although...the body is not property in the usually recognized sense of the word, yet we may consider it as a sort of *quasi* property, to which certain persons may

have rights, as they have duties to perform towards it, arising out of our common humanity. But the person having charge of it cannot be considered as the owner of it in any sense whatever; he holds it only as a sacred trust for the benefit of all who may from family or friendship have an interest in it...[7]

This supposed "right" is not only a very limited possessory right (for purposes of a proper burial, etc.), exercisable only by the executor of an estate, but is recognized for a limited time; the "right" is extinguished upon burial or cremation.

Courts have also consistently refused to recognize any form of property rights in a living human body. This reflects society's moral abhorrence toward any form of slavery. When faced with a plaintiff seeking the recognition of property rights in his or her body, the courts have classified the action as a tort and analyzed the matter through this legal framework.[8] Specific legislation, such as Congress's *National Organ Transplant Act*, builds upon this policy by explicitly prohibiting the *inter vivos* sale of many human organs.[9]

Nevertheless, developments in biotechnology hold great promise for both the advancement of scientific knowledge and the improvement of human health, and this eventually requires the use of human tissue in research. Private industry will typically participate only in research from which it can generate profit to recoup its investment of time and money. However, to generate profit, it must be able to claim property rights in its research products. Thus, when private industry develops a commercial product—regardless if such products were generated through direct or indirect utilization of human tissue—it demands some form of proprietary protection (patents or trade secrets) for these products. Given society's ethical standard of forbidding the recognition of property rights in human tissue, the question is how these standards can be maintained while allowing private industry to secure property rights in their inventions that directly or indirectly involve human tissue.

We can identify three distinct levels to classify the substance that makes up the whole human being. The first

Hastings Center Report, September/October 1990

level is that of the person and persona.[10] The second is that of a functional bodily unit, such as blood, an organ, or cell, which can be transplanted into another person and carry out its function in the same capacity it did in its originator. At a third level, something must be produced from the human material, such as a cell line or cloned genetic material for it to become useful. It is through the labor of cultivating the tissue that the laborer could claim property rights in the final product.

The Level of Person

According to Kantian philosophy, it is imperative that a legal system distinguish natural persons from things. The concept of free will differentiates human beings from mere objects, and dictates that human beings receive nothing less than full human dignity. If free will is recognized as the basis of moral rights, then it is this free will that allows humans to exercise control over objects.

The legal recognition of property rights in the pecuniary value of one's name, voice, appearance, and personal features may appear contrary to this basic philosophy. However, these "rights of publicity" are property rights that attach to *the concept* of a human entity and not directly to the human body itself.[11] Such rights disappear upon the death of the natural person though the corpse may continue to exist, as exemplified in *Lugosi v. Universal Pictures* where it was questioned whether the persona of a movie actor—a proprietary right—could be passed on to his heirs. The court held that there did exist a right in an actor's name and likeness but that this right did not survive the actor.[12]

In this first level, then, the legal structure should view the human body in its entirety, including the persona. This level represents the most complex sum of the parts (that is, organs, tissue, proteins, genetic material, etc.) and could not be attained by any one of the parts independently. Although each of the parts are very similar, if not identical, from person to person, the *sum total collection* of these parts creates a unique individual. As long as the parts

remain within that person, they serve the function of that total and hence fall under the classification of property rights for that total, viz., the "rights of publicity." However, once a part is removed from the total in such a way that it no longer functionally serves its original possessor, it would fall within the second level of the legal structure.

Res Nullius

The second level is constituted by functional bodily units capable of being transplanted. Upon removal from a person, human bodily material would be statutorily or judicially deemed *res nullius;* it would become a corporeal moveable owned by no one. If tissue is removed for transplantation into another person, the tissue would lose its *res nullius* status once the transplant was complete. Additionally, by having extracted tissue pass through the *res nullius* categorization, a donor would be prohibited from legally reclaiming rights in his transplanted tissue at some later date.

Under the classical definition of *res nullius*, ownership would be acquired by the first person who took possession of the tissue. However, for the purpose of transplantation, the legal system could deem those in possession of the excised tissue—physicians, nurses, or tissue transporters—as being possessors "in trust" of the tissue until the transplant was complete. During this period, the tissue would be classified as *trust res nullius;* a thing owned by nobody but held in trust for a recipient.[13]

A categorical distinction must be made regarding tissue that is permanently removed from the body as opposed to tissue that is temporarily removed with the intention of having it subsequently become part of the same person. A temporary removal may come about by an unintentional event such as the accidental amputation of a limb or by an intentional act such as the storage of blood for use in future surgery. In these situations, the patient would be both the donor and the recipient; the person in possession during the interim would be the trustee.

Some companies, such as those

that concentrate bone marrow or blood factors, may be concerned that their products would fall under the second level of classification, prohibiting them from being able to protect their products for lack of property rights. These products are types of human tissue that have been temporarily removed with the intention of transplantation into another body. Furthermore, such products are composed of tissue maintained in its original form. However, these products could be protected through other means, such as the doctrine of unjust enrichments arising for a service performed.

The benefit of declaring a functional unit of bodily material *res nullius* is that this material will continue to serve humankind (for example, organ transplant and blood transfusion) under a traditional altruistic spirit without becoming a marketable commodity, as could occur if property rights were to be recognized in it. Furthermore, isolating human transplantable tissue within its own classification would serve to protect its status in the future where the unknowns of technological development might threaten its status. Tissue that is *permanently* removed from a body, however, would fall under a third level of classification.

Res Communes Omnium

A third level would deem permanently removed human tissue as *res communes omnium:* things that by natural law are the common property of all humans.[14] This classification would allow human material to be used in conjunction with high technology to generate property rights in the product. However, only after something is produced from tissue deemed *res communes omnium* could property rights be created in that thing. A key distinction between matter deemed *res communes omnium* and *res nullius* is that the latter need not be transformed in any way to be useful to humankind: it functions in much its original form.

This view of property reflects the philosophical justification of property expounded by John Locke's labor theory. Locke's justification rested upon two basic assumptions: A

Hastings Center Report, September/October 1990

person has the right to maintain his life; and, God has provided us with the means to carry out this maintenance. The entire world is a common resource given by God to all persons to maintain themselves. These resources are the raw materials from which useful things are made through a person's labor. Since the labor is part of the person himself, as soon as the person mixes his labor with these raw materials to create a new product, he creates something that belongs only to him and nobody else. Locke stated that:

It being by him removed from the common state Nature placed it in, it hath by this labour something annexed to it that excludes the common right of other men. For this labour being the unquestionable property of the labourer, no man but he can have a right to what that is once joined to…[15]

Thus the creation of a new thing through merging that thing with one's labor results in property that that person alone has the right to own; this is the case regardless if the labor is performed directly by the person, a servant under that person's control, or an animal (or machine) under that person's ownership.

How would this Lockean justification for the creation of property rights through labor apply to tissue permanently removed from the human body? Perhaps the following analogy will help us answer this question.

No one can claim exclusive property rights in information that is found in a common state, as this information is free for all to discover and utilize. This concept is expounded in the U.S. Supreme Court's decision of *International News Service v. The Associated Press:*

The general rule of law is, that the noblest of human productions—knowledge, truths ascertained, conceptions and ideas—become, after voluntary communication to others, free as the air to common use. Upon these incorporeal productions the attribute of property is continued after such communication only in certain classes of cases where public policy has seemed to demand it. These exceptions are confined to productions which, in some degree, involve creation, invention, or discovery. But by no means all such are endowed with this attribute of property.[16]

Such information can be used to create property through the cultivation of this information into a report. This occurs every day within the business of news reporting. News can be recognized as having a dual character: the substance and the actual report. The substance of the information contained in the production is not the creation of the reporter, rather, as the court states, if it is a thing of "common property, so that none can make use of it, it is said to be *publici juris,* as in the case of light, air and public water."[17] However, property rights are created when a person transforms this common information into a report; the particular collocation of words in which the reporter has communicated the information is where property rights are created by virtue of the *Copyright Act.*[18]

Many parallels can be drawn between the information contained within a news report, and the utility contained within human matter, such as a cell line or particular sequence of genetic material. First, *res communes omnium* has been defined as "things incapable of appropriation, such as light or air."[19] The judicial pronouncement that the substance of a news report is *publici juris* parallels the proposal that permanently excised human substance be deemed *res communes omnium,* as both these substances belong to a common state.

Secondly, scientists could justify a claim for ownership in a cell line, and products generated therefrom, much in the same way that a news gathering agency claims rights in the news that it has collected and collocated. As stated in *International News Service:*

Not only do the acquisition and transmission of news require elaborate organization and a large expenditure of money, skill, and effort; not only has it an exchange value to the gatherer, dependent chiefly upon its novelty and freshness, the regularity of the service, its reputed reliability and thoroughness, and its adaptability to the public needs; but also, as is evident, the news has an exchange value to one who can misappropriate it.[20]

Thus, the transformation of this information into a news report or the transformation of a cell's genetic material into a viable product (for example, via cloning) would, through

labor, produce a new thing capable of being owned. The newspaper article is property under the *Copyright Act,* whereas the new genetic material would enjoy property rights under the *Patent Act* or trade secret law.

Additional support for *res communes omnium* can be found in case law. In *Funk Brothers Seed Co. v. Kalo Inoculant Co.,* the court held that unmodified cells found in nature are free for all to use:

…these bacteria, like the heat of the sun, electricity, or the qualities of metals, are part of the storehouse of knowledge of all men. They are manifestations of laws of nature, free to all men and reserved exclusively to none.[21]

Furthermore, a series of cases, commonly referred to as the *Sears-Compco* doctrine, state that if a thing cannot be the subject of a patent in its current form, then such a thing is free to use by all (that is, is within "the common state of Nature").[22] It follows then, as unmodified human tissue cannot be patented, once it has been permanently removed from the body it is free for anyone to use; this use, however, is always subject to our legal, moral, and ethical standards.

Thus, case law exists that supports the proposal to classify human tissue permanently removed from the body as *res communes omnium.* In addition, Locke's theory for the creation of property through labor supports the concept of allowing human material to be used in conjunction with skill and effort to create property rights in the product.

DNA in the Legal Structure

The advent of a DNA fingerprint technology has allowed for the exact identification of an individual from a very small sample of tissue.[23] Given that a DNA fingerprint is unique for a particular person, how can the three-tiered structure claim that the information contained in an individual's genetic code is common to all humankind and thus *res communes omnium?* This apparent paradox is resolved by acknowledging that a major distinction exists between the uniqueness created by the organization of the total genetic material versus the nonuniqueness of components of the genetic material. A

Hastings Center Report, September/October 1990

DNA fingerprint is an expression of a particular pattern of genetic material; nonetheless, each gene is common to humankind. In other words, though the parts are all the same, the way in which they are collected together makes the sum total unique.

The actual original strand of genetic material obtained from a donor is also problematic. Who owns this material? The third level dictates that substances contained within human tissue permanently removed from the body be deemed *res communes omnium* and are thus themselves incapable of becoming property. The original strand of genetic material would act as the initial template from which the laborer's property would be generated. Newly formed strands of genetic material would, in turn, act as the template for successive generations of the product. Thus, the laborer would own everything produced except the original genetic material, which would continue to belong to nobody. If a human gene is cloned into a million copies of that gene, the laborer would own only the million copies but not the original gene. The same scenario would apply to human cell cultures. The original cell that initiated the culture could never be owned, though all copies of the cell would be owned by the laborer.

The *Moore* Case

How might this structure be applied to the facts of *Moore*, a case involving nonconsensual use of the plaintiff's cancerous spleen cells to develop lucrative pharmaceutical products? The crux of this dispute concerned whether the plaintiff held personal property rights in the tissue and substances of his body and, if so, whether these rights were breached when the defendant converted this tissue for commercial profit.

The first level of the structure is not applicable to the facts of *Moore*. A persona attaches to the whole person; these proprietary rights would not apply to a mere part of a person such as a cell or a strand of DNA. The second level pertains to tissue destined for transplantation and is also not applicable to the facts of the *Moore* case.

As Moore's spleen and blood were removed with the intention of being permanently removed, this tissue would be classified as *res communes omnium*. This classification would not recognize the existence of property rights in human tissue, yet it would allow laborers to generate property rights through work—justified by a Lockean analysis. This would deny Moore any form of remuneration based upon property rights in his tissue. However, it would not deny the plaintiff the right to seek recourse through causes of actions independent of the need to have property rights in the human body.

Legally classifying the substances that make up humans into three distinct levels as we have suggested would thus allow us to preserve society's present ethical standards with regard to the transplantation of human tissue as an altruistic donation while at the same time allowing laborers to secure property rights in their inventions. Such a classification would, moreover, allow the legal system expressly to address our intuitive sense that while we each partake of universals of physiology, as unique personae we are more than the mere aggregation of our interchangeable parts.

References

1 Thomas P. Dillon, "Source Compensation for Tissue and Cells Used in Biotechnical Research: Why a Source Shouldn't Share in the Profits," *Notre Dame Law Review* 64 (1989), 628-45, at 630.

2 Roy Hardiman, "Towards the Rights of Commerciality: Recognizing Property Rights in the Commercial Value of Human Tissue," *UCLA Law Review* 34 (1986), 207-64; Mary T. Danforth, "Cells, Sales, and Royalties: The Patient's Right to a Portion of the Profits," *Yale Law and Policy Review* 6 (1988), 179-202.

3 Lori B. Andrews, "My Body, My Property," *Hastings Center Report* 16:5 (1986), 28-38; Ellen F. Paul, "Natural Rights and Property Rights," *Harvard Journal of Law and Public Policy* 13 (1990), 10-16.

4 For discussion addressing why property rights should not be recognized in human tissue, see Allen B. Wagner, "Human Tissue Research : Who Owns the Results," *Journal of the Patent and Trademark Office Society* 69 (1987), 329-52; and Dillon, "Source Compensation for Tissue and Cells."

5 249 Cal. Rptr. 494 (1988) (Cal.C.A.); File "S006987" (July 9, 1990) (Cal.Sup.Ct.).

6 In fact, the Supreme Court of California verified this position in its recent ruling in *Moore*. However, some jurisdictions have created statutory exception for such regen-

erative tissue as hair, blood, and semen. The monetary consideration involved in such transactions, however, can be explained as service charges; see the *Uniform Commercial Code*, the American Law Institute and National Conference of Commissioners on Uniform State Laws (Official Text—1978).

7 14. Am. Rep. 667 at 681 (R.I.Sup. Ct 1872).

8 *Morky v. University of Texas Health Center at Dallas* 529 S.W. 2d 802 (1975) (Texas Ct. of Civ. App.); *Browning v. Norton Children's Hospital* 504 S.W. 2d 713 (1974) (Ky. C.A.).

9 *National Organ Transplant Act*, Public Law 98-507; Additionally a state's version of the *Uniform Anatomical Gift Act* or the *Uniform Commercial Code* usually classify the paid transfer of nonvital regenerative tissue as a service rather than a sale.

10 This right is a recognized and accepted form of incorporeal property; see *Brown Chemical Co. v. Meyer* 139 U.S. 540 (1891).

11 *Price v. Hal Roach Studies Inc.* 400 F.Supp. 836 (1975) (S.D.N.Y.).

12 *Lugosi v. Universal Pictures* 603 P.2d 425 (1979) (Cal.Sup.Ct.) However, in 1984, the California legislature enacted §.990 *California Civil Code* which permitted limited rights in the personality to be passed to the heirs of the deceased (50 years post-death); furthermore, some other states have held the right of publicity to be descendible; see *Estate of Presley v. Russen* 513 F.Supp. 1339 (1981).

13 A subclassification of *res nullius* may better serve this function such as *hereditas iacens*— a thing belonging to nobody but part of a deceased's estate prior to its acquisition by an heir, or perhaps *res divini iuris*—things under divine law, thus making them non-negotiable and excluded from any legal transactions; Adolf Berger, ed., *Transactions of the American Philosophical Society: Encyclopedic Dictionary of Roman Law* 43:2 (Philadelphia: The American Philosophical Society, 1953), 486, 677.

14 Berger, *Transactions*, at 677.

15 John Locke, *The Second Treatise of Civil Government: A Letter Concerning Toleration*, ed. J.W. Gough (Oxford: Basil Blackwell, 1946), 15.

16 *International News Service v. The Associated Press* 248 U.S. 215 (1918), at 235.

17 *International News Service*, 221.

18 *International News Service*, 239.

19 J. Burke, *Jowitt's Dictionary of English Law*, 2nd ed. (London: Sweet & Maxwell Ltd., 1977), at 1556.

20 *International News Service*, at 221.

21 333 U.S. 127 (1948), at 130.

22 *Sears, Roebuck & Co. v. Stiffel Co.* 376 U.S. 225 (1964); *Compco Corp. v. Day-Brite Lighting Inc.* 376 U.S. 234 (1964); Also William D. Noonan, "Ownership of Biological Tissue," *Journal of the Patent and Trademark Office Society* 72 (1990), 109-113.

23 Andrew G. Uitterlinden *et al.*, "Two-dimensional DNA Fingerprinting of Human Individuals" *Proceedings of the National Academy of Science* 86 (1989), 2742-46; Paivi Helminen *et al.*, "Application of DNA 'Fingerprints' to Paternity Determinations" *The Lancet*, 21 March 1988, 574-76.

[4]

LIVING TISSUE AND ORGAN DONORS AND PROPERTY LAW: MORE ON *MOORE*

*Bernard M. Dickens**

I. INTRODUCTION

John Moore's claim that his medical mistreatment[1] justified the award of the three billion dollars he sought was likely to attract attention, but the amount of compensation for which he sued was not as extraordinary as the basis of his claim in property law. Moore first visited the University of California's Medical Center at Los Angeles after learning that he had hairy-cell leukemia. Samples were taken of his blood, bone marrow, and other body substances to confirm the diagnosis. The defendant physicians became aware that certain of Moore's blood products and components were of great value to commercial and scientific enterprises and access to his blood afforded "competitive, commercial, and scientific advantages."[2] Upon recommendations, Moore consented to the removal of his spleen, which occurred in October 1976. Until September 1983, he regularly went to UCLA Medical Center from his home in Seattle in order to donate samples of blood, blood serum, skin, bone marrow, and sperm.

Moore stated that while he was under treatment by the defendant physicians, he was advised that the splenectomy and later donations of body substances were required for his health and well-being. He further complained that the physicians concealed both research on his cells and their plans to exploit financially their exclusive access to Moore as derived from the physician-patient relationship. By mid-1979, the physicians developed a cell line from Moore's blood cells for which a patent was sought by the Regents of the University of California in January 1981. The patent application listed Moore's physicians as inventors and was approved in March 1984. The patent covered various methods of using the cell line to achieve biotechnological products for which commercial firms in the industry had predicted a potential market of over three billion dollars by 1990. With the Regents' assist-

---

* Ph.D., LL.D., Professor of Law, Faculty of Law, Faculty of Medicine and Centre for Bioethics, University of Toronto, Toronto, Ontario.
    1. *See* Moore v. Regents of the Univ. of Cal., 793 P.2d 479 (Cal. 1990), *cert. denied*, 111 S. Ct. 1388 (1991).
    2. *Id.* at 481.

ance, the physician-inventors negotiated for and procured 75,000 shares of common stock in a biotechnology company and payments of at least $330,000.[3]

Moore sued for conversion of his property. He also stated an additional twelve causes of action, namely lack of informed consent, breach of fiduciary duty, fraud and deceit, unjust enrichment, quasi-contract, bad faith breach of the implied covenant of good faith and fair dealing, intentional infliction of emotional distress, negligent misrepresentation, intentional interference with prospective advantageous economic relationships, slander of title, accounting, and declaratory relief.[4]

At trial, the superior court reasoned that the twelve additional claims were incorporated into the claim of conversion and expressly considered only that cause of action. In dismissing the claim, the court concluded that Moore had not stated a valid cause of action for conversion of his property. The court's decision reflected the historic "no property" rule, which provides that there are no property interests that individuals can apply prospectively to their own remains.[5] Additionally, an individual's survivors can only assert a so-called quasi-property right of burial or cremation.[6] On appeal, however, the California Court of Appeal held that Moore had stated a valid cause of action for conversion and remanded the case back to the superior court to decide that claim and the remaining causes of action on which no express ruling had been given. The defendants appealed the court of appeal's decision to the Supreme Court of California.

II.   DECISION OF THE SUPREME COURT OF CALIFORNIA

The majority of the Supreme Court of California based its approach on the available causes of action for breach of fiduciary duty and lack of informed consent to satisfy and redress any complaint that John Moore could establish on the facts. Accordingly, the court remanded the case to the court of appeal with instructions to direct the superior court to try Moore's case regarding fiduciary duty and informed consent and sustain the superior court's rejection of the claim for conversion. The majority stated that, "the law already recognizes that a reasonable patient would want to know whether a physician has an economic interest that might affect the physi-

---

3. *Id.* at 482.

4. *Id.* at 482 & n.4.

5. *See* Paul Matthews, *Whose Body? People as Property*, 36 CURRENT LEGAL PROBS. 193, 193 (1983); *see also* Margaret J. Radin, *Market-Inalienability*, 100 HARV. L. REV. 1849, 1850 (1987).

6. Matthews, *supra* note 5, at 193.

cian's professional judgment."[7] The court cited an earlier observation by the California Court of Appeal that, "a sick patient deserves to be free of any reasonable suspicion that his doctor's judgment is influenced by a profit motive."[8]

Relying on legislation regarding physicians' commercial investments in clinical laboratories and other health auxiliary services, the majority found that physicians' conflicts of interest with their patients can be resolved by prior and due disclosure to potential patients.[9] While an alternative to prior and due disclosure of conflicts of interest is complete prohibition,[10] the court modified this prohibition and analogized to California's Business and Professions Code, which prohibits a physician from charging a patient on behalf of, or referring a patient to, any organization in which the physician "has a significant beneficial interest, unless [the physician] first discloses in writing to the patient, that there is such an interest and advises the patient that the patient may choose any organization for the purpose of obtaining the services ordered or requested by [the physician]."[11]

The court noted a similar duty of disclosing plans to conduct medical experiments under California's Health and Safety Code.[12] It emphasized, however, that "no law prohibits a physician from conducting research in the same area in which he practices. Progress in medicine often depends upon physicians, such as those practicing at the university hospital where Moore received treatment, who conduct research while caring for their patients."[13] Although this observation does not in itself address whether such physicians may lawfully engage their own patients as research subjects without the patient's knowledge, the court found that this would be permissible if prior disclosure revealed any research interests which may be opposed to any interests of the patients. The court held that, "a physician who is seeking a patient's consent for a medical procedure must, in order to satisfy his fiduciary duty and to obtain the patient's informed consent, disclose personal interests unrelated to the patient's health, whether research or economic, that may affect his medical judgment."[14]

The qualified solicitude the majority showed to medical researchers and

---

7. *Moore*, 793 P.2d at 483.

8. Magan Medical Clinic v. California State Bd. of Medical Examiners, 249 Cal. App. 2d 124, 132 (Dist. Ct. App. 1967), *cited in Moore*, 793 P.2d at 483.

9. *Moore*, 793 P.2d at 483-84.

10. *See* John K. Iglehart, *Congress Moves to Regulate Self-Referral and Physicians' Ownership of Clinical Laboratories*, 322 NEW ENG. J. MED. 1682, 1682 (1990).

11. CAL. BUS. & PROF. CODE § 654.2(a) (West 1990).

12. CAL. HEALTH & SAFETY CODE § 24173 (West 1984).

13. *Moore*, 793 P.2d at 484.

14. *Id.* at 485.

biotechnological researchers influenced its treatment of Moore's claim of conversion of property. The court first addressed the conversion claim under existing law and observed that if the claim could not be sustained according to prevailing precedents or principles, then extending the jurisprudence that did exist would cover or absorb Moore's novel assertion of liability.[15] Next, the court questioned whether Moore could show an actual interference with his ownership or his right of possession of his cells, which is necessary to establish conversion.[16] Because Moore had donated his cells to his physicians, the court found that he clearly did not expect to retain possession. Furthermore, no precedents existed to support Moore's claim of ownership of his voluntarily donated tissues either directly or indirectly,[17] and California's statutory law was strictly interpreted to limit patients' control over excised cells. Indeed, the Health and Safety Code superseded other state legislation in providing, "Notwithstanding any other provision of law, recognizable anatomical parts, human tissues, anatomical human remains, or infectious waste following conclusion of scientific use shall be disposed of by interment, incineration, or any other method determined by the state department [of health services] to protect public health and safety."[18]

This health and safety provision did not necessarily preclude Moore's ownership of the cells since its primary purpose was only to ensure the safe handling of potentially hazardous biological waste materials. Similarly, the provision did not necessarily establish a competing claim of ownership in the defendants, even though their possession of the virus infected cells derived from the plaintiff and conformed to the required level of containment set for such potentially biohazardous materials.[19] Nonetheless, the majority found,

> the statute's practical effect is to limit, drastically, a patient's control over excised cells. By restricting how excised cells may be used and requiring their eventual destruction, the statute eliminates so many of the rights ordinarily attached to property that one cannot simply assume that what is left amounts to "property" or "ownership" for purposes of conversion law.[20]

---

15. *Id.* at 493-97.

16. Del E. Webb Corp. v. Structural Materials Co., 123 Cal. App. 3d 593, 610 (Dist. Ct. App. 1981).

17. For a discussion of the possibility of retaining an inchoate right of ownership in tissues involuntarily severed from one's own body, see Bernard M. Dickens, *The Control of Living Body Materials*, 27 U. TORONTO L.J. 142, 180-83 (1977).

18. CAL. HEALTH & SAFETY CODE § 7054.4 (West Supp. 1992).

19. *See* AMERICAN TYPE CULTURE COLLECTION, CATALOGUE OF CELL LINES AND HYBRIDOMAS 176 (Robert Hay et al. eds., 6th ed. 1988).

20. Moore v. Regents of the Univ. of Cal., 793 P.2d 479, 492 (Cal. 1990), *cert. denied*, 111 S. Ct. 1388 (1991).

The majority acknowledged the distinction between physical control of the cells, which Moore did not seek, and control of the commercial exploitation of their scientific use, which was the basis of Moore's claim of ownership and ultimate control. The judges considered, however, that the plaintiff's ownership rights were suitably accommodated through his claims for breach of fiduciary duty and negligence in failing to obtain his adequately informed consent to donate tissue. Accordingly, the court directed that the case be remitted for trial primarily on the basis of those claims.

The majority summarily dealt with the suggestion that Moore could claim an ownership interest in the Regents' patent over the cell line and the products derived from it. The patented cell line was found to be both factually and legally distinct from the cells surrendered by Moore. The cell line was amenable to patent protection because it was a useful product of "human ingenuity," whereas naturally occurring organisms are not patentable.[21] Granting the Regents' patent constituted an authoritative determination that the cell line was a product of invention since patent law rewards not only the discovery of materials that are of natural origin but also inventive efforts that make materials what they would not otherwise naturally become.

Having dismissed Moore's property claim under prevailing law, the majority then addressed whether the court should extend the existing scope of property law to accommodate Moore's action for conversion. In their review of existing law, the judges noted that legislation was promulgated for public policy purposes. They observed that it is necessary to regulate the disposition of such things as human tissues, transplantable organs, blood, fetuses, pituitary glands, corneal tissue, and dead bodies to achieve policy goals rather than abandon them to the general law of personal property.[22]

Two reasons were given for the majority's refusal to extend the existing law of conversion to Moore's tissues. First, this extension was not needed to protect his rights since there were alternative actions based on theories of fiduciary duty and informed consent. Specifically, the court found that a fair balancing of the relevant policy considerations weighed against extending principles of property law and the tort of conversion to developers of cell lines and their users.[23] Second, as in the disposition of other body materials, specialized legislation was considered the preferable medium rather than judge-developed law.[24]

The majority did not claim that human cells could never be the subject of

---

21. *See* Diamond v. Chakrabarty, 447 U.S. 303, 309 (1980).
22. *Moore*, 793 P.2d at 489.
23. *Id*. at 493.
24. *Id*. at 493, 496.

a property claim. On the contrary, the judges specifically stated that, "we do not purport to hold that excised cells can never be property for any purpose whatsoever . . . ."[25] Concluding that Moore's claim of ownership of his excised tissues should not be accommodated in property law, the judges considered it an important utilitarian matter, stating the importance of not threatening "innocent parties who are engaged in socially useful activities, such as researchers who have no reason to believe that their use of a particular cell sample is, or may be, against a donor's wishes."[26]

The 1987 report to Congress by the Office of Technology Assessment[27] reinforced sensitivity to the restrictive effects on biomedical research of the potential for cell donor litigation. The report emphasized the uncertainty about legally resolving any dispute that might arise between tissue donors and subsequent users, which could impair the activities of both academic researchers and the infant biotechnology industry.[28] Because of the way in which cell lines are developed among teams of related researchers and research facilities and often used by biotechnologically-equipped laboratories and enterprises, products of an individual donor's cells are likely to be widely distributed and employed over a considerable period of time. If researchers and laboratories were forced to account to the donor, both would be hindered by either legal or financial liability. Furthermore, the insurance costs to laboratories could prevent research and industrial development from being economically viable because insurance companies must ensure that adequate funds are available to meet high compensation awards, as demonstrated by John Moore's suit for three billion dollars.

The Office of Technology Assessment Report urged resolution of the uncertainty regarding ownership of cells and cell lines. Because this undecided factor was hampering the biotechnology industry, any resolution would be a benefit to progress.[29] However, the majority in *Moore* had to make an arbitrary choice as to whether the donor possessed legal rights. If a donor had been deceived or abused by nondisclosure of material information in the acquisition of his cells, then actions based on theories of fiduciary duty and informed consent protected the donor's legal rights to privacy and autonomy. The critical unfairness and dysfunction of a conversion claim is that it

---

25. *Id.* at 493.

26. *Id.*

27. U.S. Cong., Office of Technology Assessment, New Developments in Biotechnology: Ownership of Human Tissues and Cells—Special Report, OTA-BA-337 (Washington, D.C., U.S. Government Printing Office, Mar. 1987).

28. *Id.* at 27.

29. *Id.*

invokes a theory of strict liability in tort[30] in which a defendant's innocence
in acquiring cells and conscientious care of the patient is no defense. Because an action in conversion would not discriminate between wrongful and
innocent holders of a donor's cells and its resulting products, the majority
concluded that conversion law should not be extended to Moore's claim.[31]
The majority was inspired by not only protecting innocent parties but also
liberating them from the burden of ensuring that the original donors consented before acquiring and using their cells, cell lines, or other biotechnological products derived from their cells. The court stated,

> Research on human cells plays a critical role in medical research.
> This is so because researchers are increasingly able to isolate natu-
> rally occurring, medically useful biological substances and to pro-
> duce useful quantities of such substances through genetic
> engineering. These efforts are beginning to bear fruit. Products
> developed through biotechnology that have already been approved
> for marketing in this country include treatments and tests for leu-
> kemia, cancer, diabetes, dwarfism, hepatitis-B, kidney transplant
> rejection, emphysema, osteoporosis, ulcers, anemia, infertility, and
> gynecological tumors, to name but a few . . . .
> The extension of conversion law into this area will hinder re-
> search by restricting access to the necessary raw materials.[32]

The majority also noted that the patent office requires holders of patents on
cell lines to make samples available to anyone, and cell lines are routinely
copied and distributed to other researchers for experimental purposes, usually without charge.[33] Therefore, the court held that this beneficial degree of
access and exchange would be compromised if each cell sample became the
potential subject matter of property litigation.[34]

California case law was reviewed to discern the impact that expanded tort
liability had "on activities that are important to society, such as research."[35]
The court recalled a judgment in which drug manufacturers had been held
immune from strict liability lest they be reluctant to market or even develop
beneficial products for fear of large damage awards for injuries not occa-
sioned by their fault.[36] Analogizing this case to *Moore*, the court found that,

---

30. *See generally* Byer v. Canadian Bank of Commerce, 65 P.2d 67, 68 (Cal. 1937) (holding a bailee strictly liable for conversion of property despite innocent mistake).
31. Moore v. Regents of the Univ. of Cal., 793 P.2d 479, 494 (Cal. 1990) (citations omitted), *cert. denied*, 111 S. Ct. 1388 (1991).
32. *Id.* (citations omitted).
33. *Id.* at 495 & n.39 (citations omitted).
34. *Id.* at 495 & n.40 (citations omitted).
35. *Id.* at 495.
36. *See* Brown v. Superior Court, 751 P.2d 470, 477 (Cal. 1988), *cited in Moore*, 793 P.2d
at 495.

"the theory of liability that *Moore* urges us to endorse threatens to destroy the economic incentive to conduct important medical research."[37] In promoting research interests and protecting Moore's rights to pursue remedies for breach of fiduciary duty and lack of informed consent, the majority[38] denied that Moore could assert a property right through an action for conversion.

III. Tissues and Organs for Transplantation

The development of products from human cells for therapeutic implantation into patients is a biotechnologically sophisticated procedure by which human tissues and organs are directly transferred from a human donor, whether or not alive, to a human recipient. The recognition that the California Supreme Court gave biotechnological medical research and cell line development in the *Moore* case might be applicable *a priori* to transplantation research and, even more so, recognized transplantation therapies. Accordingly, the instrumental reasoning on property law and conversion liability that the court applied in *Moore* might inspire similar reasoning regarding direct transplantation to achieve the same goals of facilitating research and achieving medical therapies for patients.

A legal distinction has been commonly drawn between tissues and organs. Tissues are taken to mean bodily substances that are replaceable by natural regeneration, such as blood and bone marrow; organs are understood to be more discretely located structural arrangements of tissues that the body does not regenerate,[39] such as kidneys. The distinction between regenerative and nonregenerative body materials continues to be insightful for a number of purposes, particularly in distinguishing materials that may lawfully be removed from child donors on the basis of a parent's or guardian's decision. For example, blood and bone marrow may be lawfully removed, while solid organs such as kidneys may not be removed regardless of parent or guardian authorization.[40]

The distinction has become blurred, however, by legislation that relies not on a generic division of tissues and organs but rather on specific categorizations. For instance, the U.S. National Organ Transplantation Act defines human organ as including bone marrow.[41] The distinction is naturally con-

---

37. *Moore*, 793 P.2d at 495.

38. For a discussion of the dissenting opinions, see Laura M. Ivey, Comment, *Moore v. Regents of the University of California: Insufficient Protection of Patients' Rights in the Biotechnological Market*, 25 Ga. L. Rev. 489 (1991).

39. *See* Human Organ Transplants Act, 1989, ch. 31, § 7(2) (Eng.).

40. *See, e.g.*, Ontario Human Tissue Gift Act, R.S.O., ch. H-20 (1990) (Can.).

41. 42 U.S.C. § 274e(c)(1) (1988).

founded, moreover, by the realization that small areas of skin and slivers of bone regenerate, whereas greater surfaces of skin and lengths of bone do not. In fact, recent developments have shown that carefully defined liver segments regenerate spontaneously, although the liver, as a whole organ, does not.[42] Accordingly, the distinction between tissues and organs tends to be specific to individual legal instruments and jurisdictions, since what may be classified as tissue in one may be considered an organ in another.

A sharper distinction may be drawn between living and posthumous, or cadaveric, donors. Recognizing a neurological or brain death criterion for the end of human life has widened the potential for recovering, or "harvesting," of transplantable organs immediately upon determination of death.[43] Confusion occurs when legislation treats fetal tissues as if they are not derived from the gestating woman but from the fetus itself. For instance, the Uniform Anatomical Gift Act deals only with *post mortem*, as opposed to *inter vivos*, recovery of transplantable materials, but includes fetal tissues.[44] While the legal personhood of previable and viable fetuses raises sensitive questions, the placenta produced following successful childbirth is considered a valuable fetal tissue since it is used for pharmaceutical research of whether drugs cross the placental barrier.

The application of *Moore*'s rationale to transplantation of tissues and organs is clearly demonstrated in reference to living, adult, mentally competent donors. Blood donations, like semen donations, tend to be given without designating an individual recipient. When donations are offered,[45] the donor may be subject to human immunodeficiency virus (HIV) testing and, thereafter, the donation may be delivered to a clinic or tissue bank rather than to any individual consumer. However, individuals may specifically designate that their blood be stored in anticipation of an autologous blood transfusion either during or following surgery, or that their sperm or ova be stored for their own diagnostic or reproductive use. On the other

---

42. See Whitington et al., *Living Donor Nonrenal Organ Transplantation: A Focus on Living Related Orthotopic Liver Transplantation, in* ORGAN REPLACEMENT THERAPY: ETHICS, JUSTICE, COMMERCE 117 (W. Land & J. Dossetor eds., 1991).

43. See U.S. PRESIDENT'S COMM'N FOR THE STUDY OF ETHICAL PROBLEMS IN MEDICINE AND BIOMEDICAL AND BEHAVIORAL RESEARCH, DEFINING DEATH: A REPORT ON THE MEDICAL, LEGAL AND ETHICAL ISSUES IN THE DETERMINATION OF DEATH 23 (1981).

44. The Uniform Anatomical Gift Act (UAGA) defines decedent to mean "a deceased individual and includes a still born infant or fetus." UNIF. ANATOMICAL GIFT ACT § 1(b), 8A U.L.A. 30 (1983). The UAGA has been adopted, with minor variations, in all 50 states and the District of Columbia. 2 PHILLIP G. WILLIAMS, LIFE FROM DEATH: THE ORGAN AND TISSUE DONATION AND TRANSPLANTATION SOURCE BOOK WITH FORMS 9 (1989).

45. For a discussion of the aqcuisition of living body materials through gifts, sales, and gratuitous services, see Dickens, *supra* note 17, at 163, 166-71.

hand, solid organs that living donors make available are almost invariably intended for the benefit of specified recipients, such as close relatives. If an individual receives no legally enforceable assurance that tissues or organs that she may give from her living body will be employed only for her own use or the benefit of a particularly designated recipient, then she may decline to make such donations.

Individuals who provide for posthumous donation of their body materials tend to donate them randomly or otherwise identify a recipient institution such as a hospital or university. Similarly, those who exercise a dispositive legal power over the tissues and organs of dead bodies, usually the deceased's relatives, tend to dedicate them to institutions rather than specifically designated recipients. For instance, there is a practical difficulty in finding well matched cadaveric kidneys for transplantation into African Americans, which is further aggravated by the disproportionately low rate of donation by such people.[46] Programs have been designed which recommend that African Americans direct posthumous donation of their kidneys to other people of the same race.[47] Such proposals and the general legislation on posthumous donation of body materials affect the operation of the common law principle that there are no property rights in a dead body,[48] except the "quasi-property" interest regarding burial or cremation.[49] The common law rule and current legislation fail to address the issue raised by *Moore* of an individual living donor's legal interests in the tissues and organs he may make available for transplantation into designated recipients. The primary issue is legal control over tissues and organs, such as bone marrow, kidneys, and liver segments, from the time they are released or removed from the donor's body until they are implanted in designated recipients.

IV. *MOORE* AND THE RIGHTS OF LIVING DONORS

To extrapolate the rationale in *Moore* to tissue and organ gifts made to designated recipients by living donors would presuppose that the priority reflected in the court's approach to biotechnological development and progress in medical research would also be accorded to *inter vivos* tissue and organ transplantation. However, grounds exist to disfavor gifts from living donors and give priority to donations that take effect *post mortem*. In 1991,

---

46. *See* C.O. Callender, *Organ Donation in Blacks: A Community Approach*, 19 TRANSPLANTATION PROCEEDINGS 1551, 1551 (1987).

47. *See* Wayne B. Arnason, *Directed Donation: The Relevance of Race*, HASTINGS CENTER REP., Nov.-Dec. 1991, at 13, 13.

48. P.D.G. Skegg, *Human Corpses, Medical Specimens and the Law of Property*, 4 ANGLO-AM. L. REV. 412, 412 (1975).

49. For an historical critique of the "no property" rule, see Matthews, *supra* note 5.

the World Health Organization proposed Guiding Principles on Human Organ Transplantation that included terms "intended to emphasize the importance of developing cadaveric donation programmes in countries where this is culturally acceptable, and to discourage donations from living, genetically unrelated donors, except for transplantation of bone marrow and of other acceptable regenerative tissues."[50]

Under a mandate from the World Health Assembly, the World Health Organization proposed the Guiding Principles to consider provisions designed to contain "the trade for profit in human organs among living human beings."[51] Courts are wary of deliberately or inadvertently facilitating living donors to traffic their tissues or organs and rendering individuals susceptible to financial inducements to enter a market of human body materials. When donors are unrelated to designated recipients genetically, by marriage, or by long-standing affinity, suspicions may arise that unsavory commercial incentives motivate the will to donate. In contrast, an individual's willingness to donate tissues or organs to others she knows is considered noble, altruistic, and honorably self-sacrificing according to the law. Legislation and practice widely accommodate designated tissue and organ donations by relatives to intended recipients, thereby offering legal protection.

The California Supreme Court resolved Moore's property claim with the express purpose of liberating commercial development of potentially therapeutic products and protecting "the economic incentive to conduct important medical research."[52] For this reason, it seems the court would have been equally protective of altruistic incentives to contribute to important medical therapy, which many tissue and organ transplantations are considered to be. The court applied instrumental reasoning in declining to extend liability for conversion to Moore's cells, in order to enhance prospects of medical benefit for all patients. If the evidence had shown that prospective tissue and organ donors would more likely donate upon being assured that they could invoke concepts of property law through claims for conversion and give legal effect to their purposes, then the judges might recognize such claims. The court preserved this prospect when it carefully observed that "we do not purport to hold that excised cells can never be property for any

---

50. *Guiding Principles on Human Organ Transplantation*, Res. 40.13, World Health Assembly (May 1987), *reprinted in Human Organ Transplantation: A Report on Developments Under the Auspices of WHO (1987-1991)*, 42 INT'L DIG. HEALTH LEGIS. 389, 395 (1991) [hereinafter *WHO Report*].

51. *Id.* at 390.

52. Moore v. Regents of the Univ. of Cal., 793 P.2d 479, 495 (Cal. 1990), *cert. denied*, 111 S. Ct. 1388 (1991).

purpose whatsoever . . . ."[53]

There are few recorded instances when body materials donated for transplantation into designated recipients were not properly used or were rendered unuseable by negligence. In *York v. Jones,*[54] heard by the District Court for the Eastern District of Virginia, a married couple had given gametes to the Jones Institute for Reproductive Medicine in Norfolk, Virginia to combine them *in vitro* to create a pre-embryo[55] and store it by cryopreservation for eventual implantation in the wife. The couple moved to Los Angeles and asked the Institute to transfer the frozen pre-embryo to a local hospital for thawing and implantation. The Institute declined the transfer because it purportedly fell outside the options agreed to in its contract with the plaintiffs and because the transfer was not permitted by the research protocol under which the Institute operated its *in vitro* fertilization clinic. However, the court interpreted the language of the contract as affording the plaintiffs the right they claimed.

While the contract referred to property rights in pre-embryos created *in vitro*, the plaintiffs reinforced their contractual claim with an independent claim in detinue to recover their improperly retained property. This court observed,

> The requisite elements of a detinue action in Virginia are as follows: (1) plaintiff must have a property interest in the thing sought to be recovered; (2) the right to immediate possession; (3) the property is capable of identification; (4) the property must be of some value; and (5) defendant must have had possession at some time prior to the institution of the act. Moreover, if the property is in the possession of a bailee, an action in detinue accrues upon demand and refusal to return the property or upon a violation of the bailment contract by an act of conversion.
>
> After review of plaintiffs' Complaint, the Court finds that plaintiffs have properly alleged a cause of action in detinue.[56]

The court's willingness to treat a pre-embryo, which has the biological potential to develop naturally into a human being, as property indicates that lesser cells such as tissues and organs which lack that natural potential may also be treated as property.

In *Moore*, the court first asked whether Moore's removed cells were property under prevailing law and concluded that they were not. Second, the

---

53. *Id.* at 493.

54. 717 F. Supp. 421 (E.D. Va. 1989).

55. For a philosophical contribution on the appropriateness of this expression, see Richard A. McCormick, *Who or What is the Preembryo?*, 1 KENNEDY INST. ETHICS J. 1 (1991).

56. *York*, 717 F. Supp. at 427 (citations omitted).

court asked whether existing categories of legal property should be extended to cover them and concluded that they should not. However, the court in *York v. Jones* treated the pre-embryo as property according to prevailing law. In view of the unresolved moral status of a pre-embryo *in vitro*, the awareness of its inherent potential for human development, and the fact that strongly held religious views believe that the pre-embryo is a person,[57] the court's application of principles of property law in *York* is striking. The judgment indicates *a fortiori* that transplantable tissues and organs, whose moral status is not contentious and that have never been of inherent spiritual significance, are property too. Nonetheless, *Moore* rejected the applicability of property law because of California's Health and Safety Code provisions on disposal of anatomical waste following scientific use[58] and the lack of precedents establishing a property interest. While *York*'s impact on property law remains to be seen, the provisions on waste disposal which were applicable in *Moore* are clearly not relevant to healthy tissues and organs removed for the sole purpose of transplantation.

In determining instrumentally whether property law concepts should be applied to the cells in question, the *Moore* court fashioned its rationale on a long and reputable tradition of jurisprudence. In fact, ideas about the relation of persons to things are traceable to classical Greek philosophy, including the discourse of Plato and Aristotle on the proper role of common and private property in civil life. The evolution of modern concepts of the proper role of property law has followed several paths,[59] although it appears that contemporary legal scholars generally subscribe to a utilitarian or instrumental approach. Furthermore, one scholar has observed that "[p]roperty, as a creature of law, is only justifiable (like all law) by utilitarian considerations."[60] This approach, however, is not unchallenged and the juridical nature of property remains an issue of vigorous and varied contention.

Present analytical jurisprudence dictates that the term "property" refers

---

57. *See* Davis v. Davis, 15 Fam. L. Rep. (BNA) 2097 (Tenn. Cir. Ct. 1989) (treating pre-embryos as the equivalent of born children), *rev'd*, 16 Fam. L. Rep. (BNA) 1535 (Tenn. Ct. App. 1990). *See generally* Bernard M. Dickens, *Comparative Judicial Embryology: Judges' Approaches to Unborn Human Life*, 9 CAN. J. FAM. L. 180 (1990) (addressing the implications of recent decisions which held that pre-embryos are human beings whose control is governed by principles of child custody law).

58. *See supra* notes 17-19 and accompanying text.

59. For a historical review of modern concepts of property law, see Boudewijn Bouckaert, *What is Property?*, 13 HARV. J.L. & PUB. POL'Y 775 (1990).

60. Francis S. Philbrick, *Changing Conceptions of Property in Law*, 86 U. PA. L. REV. 691, 730 (1938).

to the "bundle of rights" a person possesses in a thing or an interest, rather than simply the tangible thing or interest itself. Furthermore,

> [t]he term "property" is sufficiently comprehensive to include every species of estate, real and personal, and everything which one person can own and transfer to another. It extends to every species of right and interest capable of being enjoyed as such upon which it is practicable to place a money value.[61]

The broad and abstract concept of property is molded by legislation and common law declared by the courts in accordance with pragmatic and policy reasons. Although the *Moore* majority chose to reject the plaintiff's assertion of a property right, it left room to hold differently in appropriate circumstances.[62]

The dissenting judge in *Moore*, Justice Broussard, proposed such circumstances and found that the cells in issue were property according to prevailing law. He observed,

> In the transplantation context, for example, it is common for a living donor to designate the specific donee—often a relative—who is to receive a donated organ. If a hospital, after removing an organ from such a donor, decided on its own to give the organ to a different donee, no one would deny that the hospital had violated the legal right of the donor by its unauthorized use of the donated organ. Accordingly, it is clear under California law that a patient has the right, prior to the removal of an organ, to control the use to which the organ will be put after removal.
>
> It is also clear, under traditional common law principles, that this right of a patient to control the future use of his organ is protected by the law of conversion.[63]

Justice Broussard's conclusion, however, is flawed because a contrast exists between Moore's cells and an organ donated for transplantation. Specifically, Moore's cells were without value and required the application of sophisticated biotechnological techniques to realize their commercial utility, while an organ is of imminent utility once preserved and prepared for transplantation. In other words, Moore's cells had to be extensively processed and refined before their potential could be extracted, whereas a donated organ is transferred to its designated recipient fundamentally intact. Additionally, the organ directly performs functions in the recipient that are virtually identical to those performed in the donor; cell line products, in contrast,

---

61. Yuba River Power Co. v. Nevada Irrigation Dist., 279 P. 128, 129 (Cal. 1929).

62. *See* Moore v. Regents of the Univ. of Cal., 793 P.2d 479, 493 (Cal. 1990), *cert. denied*, 111 S. Ct. 1388 (1991).

63. *Id.* at 502.

depend on the artificial development of qualities in primary cells that they do not normally possess.[64] Lastly, an organ donor's control over the deployment of the organ is more feasible and immediate than a cell donor's control over cells that are of no use in themselves but, if subjected to advanced scientific processes, may form the basis of a biotechnologically engineered product.

Justice Broussard's proposition is not entirely incompatible with the majority decision. In fact, the majority did not have to reject his conclusion concerning property rights over organs for transplantation in order to assert the absence of property rights over John Moore's extracted cells. Where Justice Broussard found that prevailing law recognizes property interests in transplantable organs, the majority was never forced to address or agree that property law should be extended to such organs because the second issue would have been preempted by Justice Broussard's original finding. The majority's discussion of the benefits of organ transplantation suggests that they, too, would extend concepts of property law to transplantable organs. The court recognized that organ donations offered direct health benefits to recipients which were immediately implemented through transplantation. Further, the court suggested that potential donors may be encouraged to donate if given legal certainty that, through recourse to principles of property law, their designated purposes will be respected upon clinical assessment of the suitability of their organs and the medical status of intended recipients.

V. Donors' Alternatives to Property Law

The question remains whether a remedy for lack of informed consent or breach of fiduciary duty would serve a transplantation donor better than, or as well as, a property claim. In *Moore*, the defendant physicians allegedly concealed the full purposes for which they sought consent for access to the plaintiff's cells. In reviewing basic principles of patient autonomy and informed consent,[65] the court found that,

> [t]hese principles lead to the following conclusions: (1) a physician must disclose personal interests unrelated to the patient's health, whether research or economic, that may affect the physician's professional judgment; and (2) a physician's failure to disclose such interests may give rise to a cause of action for performing medical procedures without informed consent or [for] breach of fiduciary

---

64. *Id.* at 482 n.2.

65. The court offered three well established principles: 1) an adult of sound mind has the autonomy to choose whether to submit to medical treatment; 2) a patient's consent to treatment must be an informed consent; and 3) a physician has a duty to disclose all material information to the patient's decision. *Id.* at 483.

88   *Journal of Contemporary Health Law and Policy*   [Vol. 8:73

duty.[66]

In this case, John Moore initiated his relationship with the defendants for therapeutic purposes, specifically the removal of his spleen to retard the progress of his hairy-cell leukemia. The physician performing the procedure, however, was already aware that Moore's cells had unusual potential. The court observed that the physician "had an undisclosed research interest in Moore's cells at the time he sought Moore's consent to the splenectomy. Accordingly, Moore has stated a cause of action for breach of fiduciary duty, or lack of informed consent, based upon the disclosures accompanying that medical procedure."[67]

In theory, physicians who ask to remove body materials for transplantation may have similarly undisclosed purposes of their own. However, donors are more concerned with being reassured that, once organs or other materials have been excised or otherwise procured, they will not be so negligently mishandled that the purpose of transplantation will be frustrated. In contrasting remedies for negligent mishandling under property concepts with those under alternative principles of law, informed consent and fiduciary duty principles will have little to offer if they center on physicians' intentions that are undisclosed prior to acquiring the body materials.

When the risk of inadvertent or deliberate mismanagement is foreseen, contractual terms may be proposed with those likely to be at fault. However, this offers limited protection to donors because intermediate handlers of tissues or organs and those responsible for their implantation, both of whom are essential to the enterprise, may decline to enter into contractual agreements with donors. Similarly, when designated recipients or third parties pay the costs, donors are unlikely to have contract claims for the due performance of agreements, and thus no remedies for violation. Furthermore, donors may lack an insurable interest in transfer of their donations. Physicians who manage donations are unlikely to underwrite the performance of subsequent handlers. Nonetheless, the physicians' liability may arise if they accepted responsibility for choosing them expressly or by implication and were negligent in making or advising selections.

Liability for a physician's negligent damage to body materials in removing or transfering them may be sought when a legal duty of care to the donor exists either through a contract or the general tort law applicable to the doctor-patient relation. Breach of duty may also be found due to the physician's negligent failure to conform to the legally required standard of care. However, if medical personnel are paid by, or on behalf of, the intended

---

66. *Id.*
67. *Id.* at 485.

recipient, then the legal duty to preserve and transfer the material may be owed primarily to the intended recipient rather than the donor. If payment for the transfer service is by neither the donor nor the intended recipient, then the beneficiary of primary legal duties of care in preserving the material may be more difficult to establish. On the other hand, even when the legal duty is clearly owed to the donor, she may not successfully sue for damages if the removal procedure is completed before the intention of her gratuitous donation becomes frustrated. In this case, the donor suffers no personal injury, although the donor may pursue a remedy for negligent or deliberate infliction of emotional or psychic harm,[68] the latter of which permits punitive damages. The donor's success may depend upon the peculiar characteristics of his personality and circumstances[69] and the intermediate handlers' awareness that the tissues or organ they process comes from a live, as opposed to a cadaveric, donor. Another consideration is whether the article transplanted is destined for a designated or anonymous recipient. However, it is unlikely that intermediate handlers are legally bound to inquire about matters of this nature, although extended duties may arise if they are given appropriate notice that both the live donor and the designated recipient anticipate effective delivery of the material for transplantation.[70]

Among his thirteen causes of action, John Moore's claim for negligence was interwoven with his claim of lack of informed consent to treatment,[71] although the former claim was based on alleged premeditation and deliberation rather than the defendants' oversight. In addition, Moore filed claims for negligent misrepresentation, fraud, and deceit, which similarly depend on intentions alleged to have occurred prior to the induced donation of body materials. His other claims included slander of title deriving from his assertion of a property right, and unjust enrichment, which derived from the riches the defendants had already negotiated to receive. However, this claim would not avail a plaintiff when a defendant who rendered materials unsuitable for transplantation was not enriched.

---

68. For a comprehensive and detailed statement supporting recovery for negligently inflicted psychic harm, see Peter A. Bell, *The Bell Tolls: Toward Full Tort Recovery for Psychic Injury*, 36 U. FLA. L. REV. 333 (1984); *cf.* Richard N. Pearson, *Liability for Negligently Inflicted Psychic Harm: A Response to Professor Bell*, 36 U. FLA. L. REV. 413 (1984).

69. *See* Carel J.J.M. Stolker, *The Unconscious Plaintiff: Consciousness as a Prerequisite for Compensation for Non-Pecuniary Loss*, 39 INT'L & COMP. L.Q. 82, 96-100 (1990).

70. For a discussion of the potential liability of a doctor for refusing to transplant an organ into a needy recipient until consent is obtained from the patient's next of kin, see Daniel G. Jardine, Comment, *Liability Issues Arising Out of Hospitals' and Organ Procurement Organizations' Rejection of Valid Anatomical Gifts: The Truth and Consequences*, 1990 WIS. L. REV. 1655.

71. *See* Cobbs v. Grant, 502 P.2d 1, 8 (Cal. 1972).

90 *Journal of Contemporary Health Law and Policy* [Vol. 8:73

VI. The Merit of Property Law

Principles of property law as applied to tissues and organs donated *inter vivos* for transplantation raise questions about when the designated recipient takes possession and at what point the tissues and organs lose their status as the donor's property and become integrated with the recipient. Before the tissues or organs become wholly integrated but after they leave the donor's body, they are not necessarily *res nullius* or abandoned. With respect to pathological, diagnostic, and waste body materials, the Maryland Court of Special Appeals found that, as a matter of law, anyone who consents to surgery does not abandon all removed tissue.[72] However, the court also stated that, "when a person does nothing and says nothing to indicate an intent to assert his right of ownership, possession, or control over such material [as comes from his body], the only rational inference is that he intends to abandon the material."[73] Following this logic, when a person makes clear her intention that the material should be transplanted into a designated recipient, that person asserts a right of ownership and control until the transplantation takes place, even though possession may pass to others in the interim. The observation based on body waste materials receives greater weight when it concerns healthy organs or tissues intended for transplantation.

Property law, including such incidents as bailment of goods and liability for conversion, affords those who directly procure materials for transplantation, specifically the intermediate handlers and the medical staff serving the intended recipient, the knowledge that they are accountable to the donor for their use and misuse of that material. Those who control property can lawfully direct not only its use but also its return or deliberate destruction. However, the principle remains that materials separated from the body cannot be used except in accordance with either the donor's pre-release directions or subsequent adequately informed consent, particularly when dealing with reproductive tissues. When couples deposit their gametes for *in vitro* fertilization, they intend exclusive use for themselves and possess the legal power to forbid any other reproductive use. If statutory or regulatory provisions regarding human reproduction or research do not ensure exclusive control over the materials and it is not explicitly stated in an agreement,[74] then this exclusivity nevertheless arises as an incident of property law.[75]

While legal title does not exclude abandonment in particular circum-

---

72. Venner v. Maryland, 354 A.2d 483, 498 (Md. Ct. Spec. App. 1976).

73. *Id.* at 499.

74. *See generally* York v. Jones, 717 F. Supp. 421 (E.D. Va. 1989) (questioning whether a Virginia human research statute precludes parents from exercising exclusive control over their frozen prezygote).

75. *See* Derek J. Jones, *Artificial Procreation, Societal Reconceptions: Legal Insight from*

stances, it operates more positively to facilitate transfer of ownership to tissue or organ banks, thereby confirming the legal title in the many tissue and organ banks that exist worldwide. In the United States, for instance, regional tissue banks, acting in conjunction with the American Association of Tissue Banks, are indispensable in arranging over 300,000 musculoskeletal grafts each year.[76] In Western Europe, Czechoslovakia, Poland, and Russia, tissue banking has been established for over three decades.[77] Multitissue banks now operate effectively in Thailand, China, Myanmar, the Philippines, and Vietnam.[78] It can scarcely be contended that the level of activity of these agencies, particularly in legally regulated environments, is maintained without identifiable property rights over the materials they receive, process, and transfer.

Resistance to the recognition of property rights in transplantable tissues and organs stems in large measure from the fear that such rights would inevitably lead to unsavory and exploitative commerce, including donors' sales to the highest bidder and the poor, induced by money, offering the substance of their being to trade. Likewise, John Moore's property claim may have been prejudiced because he too sought a profit from the use of his property.[79] Voluminous literature opposes the commercialization of human body parts from both living and cadaveric donors; however, emerging literature extols the virtues of the marketplace in increasing access to transplantable tissues and safeguarding personal integrity and tissue quality. The World Health Organization has stated that commerce in property rights in transplantable human organs can be restricted.[80] Furthermore, the California Court of Appeal, which upheld John Moore's property claim but was reversed by the California Supreme Court, carefully emphasized that, "[t]o the extent that unacceptable consequences, which can now only be the subject of speculation, do follow, legislative solutions are possible and likely."[81]

An encouraging feature of the opposing bodies of literature is that protagonists and commentators throughout the spectrum offer feasible suggestions

---

France, 36 AM. J. COMP. L. 525 (1988) (analyzing the impact of a French case in which a depository was ordered to return a deceased sperm depositor's sample to his widow).

76. Glyn O. Phillips, *Conference: Tissue Banks in Europe*, 338 LANCET 1514, 1514 (1991).

77. *Id.*

78. *Id.* at 1515.

79. *See* Moore v. Regents of the Univ. of Cal., 793 P.2d 479, 497 (Cal. 1990) (Arabian, J., concurring), *cert. denied*, 111 S. Ct. 1388 (1991).

80. *See WHO Report, supra* note 50, at 396.

81. Moore v. Regents of the Univ. of Cal., 249 Cal. Rptr. 494, 509 (Ct. App. 1988), *aff'd in part and rev'd in part*, 793 P.2d 479 (Cal. 1990), *cert. denied*, 111 S. Ct. 1388 (1991). In agreement with the California Court of Appeal, the California state legislature promulgated a law which prohibits donors from receiving any "valuable consideration" for donation. CAL. HEALTH & SAFETY CODE § 7155(a) (West Supp. 1992).

92   *Journal of Contemporary Health Law and Policy*   [Vol. 8:73

for legal elimination of commerce,[82] many of which do not depend on the denial of property rights. Indeed, denial of property rights may itself lead to commercial exploitation in the regulation of tissue and organ transfers. Recognition of living donors' property rights may forestall the emergence of an unsavory and exploitative growth of payments for services associated with acquiring tissues and organs, such as finders' fees and brokerage charges. If living donors' property rights exist, then subsequent handlers may fear liability for conversion. Thus, they will ensure legal and proper management of tissue and organ acquisition. However, this principle applies to tissues and organs that retain their inherent qualities and are directly traceable to a living donor. This does not contradict the *Moore* judgment because the *Moore* decision applies to cells subjected to biotechnological processes when traceability of cells is no longer convenient.

However, it may be asserted that, despite the application of biotechnological processes, John Moore's cells were traceable because the cell line was named the Mo cell line[83] and because the defendants knew from whom the cells were taken. The law must determine when property rights may be recognized in cells that are subject to biotechnological development as well as in tissues and organs given by living donors for transplantation into designated recipients. The instrumental reasoning of the Supreme Court of California in *Moore* provides a starting point. The defendants certainly faced the incongruity of claiming that while John Moore cannot legally own his cells, they can.[84] Here the court draws a distinction between the cells when they were extracted from Moore, at which point they had no use or value and therefore were not property, and the cells when they were developed in the possession of the defendants, whereupon they had patentable value. This distinction raises the questions of the cells' value during their interim status and whether John Moore's property interest in the cells was limited to prohibition of use but not approval of use. A satisfactory response may be found through the legal development of inchoate rights in these cells.[85]

VII. CONCLUSION

The majority in *Moore* approached the question of property rights in cells extracted from a living person's body primarily in terms of public or social

---

82. *See, e.g.*, Nancy E. Field, Note, *Evolving Conceptualizations of Property: A Proposal to De-Commercialize the Value of Fetal Tissue*, 99 YALE L.J. 169, 185-86 (1989) (arguing for federal legislation prohibiting the sale of fetal tissue but permitting the acquisition of fetal tissue strictly through donative transfers).

83. *See Moore*, 793 P.2d at 510.

84. *See id.* at 492.

85. *See* Dickens, *supra* note 17, at 193.

policy. The majority took this approach because of the absence of a prevailing jurisprudence on whether or not property rights were already established; accordingly, they drew inferences from state legislation hostile to such rights. However, the dissenting justices in *Moore* invoked an applicable jurisprudence and found that state legislation did not oppose it but rather prohibits or could prohibit objectionable commerce of tissues and organs. Nothing in the *Moore* decision suggests that living persons who intend to donate tissues or organs for almost direct transplantation into designated recipients may not invoke their property rights in such materials to advance their own objectives. A body of case law exists that supports this contention. Nonetheless, if this case law is not considered persuasive, then property law should be extended to protect such donors' interests consistently with the reasoning applied in *Moore*.

Courts are concerned that beneficial enterprises in medical advances and individuals' health care not be obstructed. This concern would be served by living donors being able to enjoy the certainty that, through principles of property law, they could compel medical and related intermediaries to comply with their altruistic intentions and make them aware of their continuing interests in their donated materials. The *Moore* majority expressly drew back from a claim that "excised cells can never be property."[86] The speed and scope of biotechnological processing of human cells into therapeutically useful products cannot be reliably predicted, although it is anticipated that tissue and organ donations from living persons will remain significant to therapy. Accordingly, tissue and organ donations will continue to warrant the law's instrumental protection through legal recognition of donors' claims to control the destination and use of their *in vitro* body materials.

---

86. *Moore*, 793 P.2d at 493.

Part III
Commerce in Organ Procurement

[5]

NEPHRARIOUS GOINGS ON
Kidney Sales and Moral Arguments[1]

JANET RADCLIFFE RICHARDS

ABSTRACT. From all points of the political compass, from widely different groups, have come indignant outcries against the trade in human organs from live vendors. Opponents contend that such practices constitute a morally outrageous and gross exploitation of the poor, inherently coercive and obviously intolerable in any civilized society. This article examines the arguments typically offered in defense of these claims, and finds serious problems with all of them. The prohibition of organ sales is derived not from the principles and argument usually invoked in support of prohibition, but rather, from strong feelings of repugnance which exert an invisible but powerful influence on the debate, distorting the arguments [and working] to the detriment of the [very] people most in need of protection.

Key Words: organ sales, organ transplantation

PART ONE – *THE TRADITIONAL ARGUMENTS*

I. THE SITUATION AND THE RESPONSE

When evidence of the trade in transplant organs from live vendors first filtered through to Western attention a few years ago, the most remarkable aspect of the immediate response was its unanimity. From all points of the political compass, from widely different groups who were normally hard pressed to agree about anything, there came indignant denunciations of the whole business. It was a moral outrage; a gross exploitation of the poor by the rich, who were now taking the very bodies of those from whom there was nothing else left to take, and obviously intolerable in any civilized society.

It is significant that this indignation was not, in the first instance, directed at the supplementary horrors of which media-fuelled rumors soon began to grow. Stories about kidneys stolen

Janet Radcliffe Richards, Ph.D., Department of Philosophy, Open University, Milton Keynes, United Kingdom.

during other operations, failure afterwards to pay the agreed price, flagrant profiteering, and even abduction and murder, later inflamed the outrage, but the trade in organs from live vendors was almost universally denounced as a moral scandal quite independently of any such embellishments, and such remarkable concord must suggest that the moral case for prohibition is unequivocal.

Nevertheless, the matter is nothing like as clear as it may seem. The case has some curious features that suggest a different explanation for this unusual meeting of minds, and shows the problem of organ sales in a rather different light.

I shall limit the discussion to kidneys – which, in being both paired and non-renewable, come in some sense midway between hearts on the one hand, and livers and blood on the other – and to the problem of live vendors. Conclusions reached about laws and policies appropriate to this case will not necessarily transfer to the sale of organs or tissues of other kinds and in other circumstances, but this case raises matters of principle that are central to all, and, indeed, to most other areas of medical ethics.

II. THE BURDEN OF PROOF

Perhaps the most striking curiosity comes right at the beginning, in the way the situation is typically described. To hear the organ trade characterized in terms of the greedy rich and the exploited poor, you might think that the rich, tired of gold plating their bathrooms and surfeited with larks' tongues, had now idly turned to collecting kidneys to display with their Fabergé eggs and Leonardo drawings. But the rich in question here are *dying*, and desperately trying to save their lives; or, at the very least, to escape the crushing miseries of chronic illness and perpetual dialysis.[2] Most critics of the trade in organs would do all they could to find similar amounts of money if private medicine offered their only chance of escaping death or disability, and would not, in doing so, expect to be regarded as paradigm cases of greed. There is, if anything, less greed involved in spending money to save your life or to achieve your freedom than in keeping it to spend on luxuries before you become ill.

And the attitude shown to the poor who are selling the organs is even odder. Consider, for instance, the case of the young Turkish father swept to everyone's television screen by the surge of outrage that followed the first revelations.[3] He was trying to meet the expense of urgent hospital treatment for his daughter. Presumably the prospect of selling his kidney was, to say the least, no more attractive to him than it seems to us, but he nevertheless judged this to be his best available option. As we rush to intervene, therefore, saying how dreadful it is that he should be exploited in this way, we are taking away what he regards as his best option and leaving him in a situation he thinks even worse than the loss of a kidney. The same applies to other "desperate individuals" who advertise kidneys and even eyes in newspapers, or write to surgeons offering to sell them, "often for care of an ill relative" (Council of the Transplantation Society, 1985, pp. 715–716). The worse we think it is to sell a kidney or an eye, the worse we should think the situation in which we leave these people when we remove that option. Our indignation on behalf of the exploited poor seems to take the curious form of wanting to make them worse off still.

So, as we contemplate with satisfaction our rapid moves to thwart greed and protect the poor, we leave behind one trail of people dying who might have been saved, and another of people desperate enough to offer their organs thrust back into the wretchedness they were hoping to alleviate. And, furthermore, in a surprising contravention of our usual ideas about individual liberty, we prevent adults from entering freely into contracts from which both sides expect to benefit, and with no obvious harm to anyone else. Our intervention, in other words, seems in direct conflict with all our usual concerns for life, liberty, and the pursuit of happiness.

It is irrelevant to respond indignantly, as many people do, that no one should be in these desperate situations. Of course they should not; but even if there were any moral point in making rules for the world as we should like it to be rather than as it is, that would still provide no justification for prohibition. If we could eliminate poverty to the extent of removing all temptation for anyone to sell organs, prohibition would have nothing to do; and, conversely, as long as it has anything to do, some people must be at whatever level of desperation makes them see organ selling as their best option. Whatever the state of the world, prohibition either causes these harms or has no point at all.

Of course this is a long way from the end of the matter. The claim so far is that prohibition seems to cause various harms or to be undesirable in other ways;[4] but a hundred times a day we make choices that have some bad aspects, because we nevertheless judge the options that involve them to be best, all things considered.[5] To accept that some aspects of prohibition are intrinsically undesirable is compatible with claiming that it is still, all things considered, justified.

Nevertheless, when some course of action seems to involve positive harms, that does at least provide a clear direction of burden of proof. If you knew nothing more about some practice than that it involved sticking needles into children, your presumption, pending further evidence, would be that it should be stopped. You would (probably) withdraw your objections when you saw that nothing more sinister was going on than vaccination or the administration of anaesthesia, whose benefits far outweighed the intrinsic harm, but you would want the evidence first. The same applies here. Even if the conclusion can be reached that organ sales should be prohibited, the starting presumption must be the other way. Anyone wanting to forbid organ sales, therefore, must do one (or both) of two things: either show that there is something wrong with this account of the matter, and that prohibition does not involve any or all of these harms, or argue that they are outweighed by more important considerations on the other side.

It is difficult to separate these two elements in the debate, since the usual arguments against organ sales are not offered as replies to this particular challenge. Arguments that would, if successful, show that organ selling did not involve the evils alleged, are usually presented simply as arguments for prohibition. However, I shall use the distinction to determine the order of what follows. Sections III and IV contain discussions of arguments that would, if successful, undermine the claim that prohibition was a constriction of individual liberty and harmful to vendors and recipients. Section V analyses arguments which attempt to show that prohibition is justified in spite of such harms. Part 2 (sections VI–VIII) considers more generally what is shown by the way the debate has gone, and draws conclusions for the conduct of moral enquiry in this and other contexts.

III. AUTONOMY AND CONSENT

Consider first the claim that prohibition prevents free contracts between consenting adults. Most people involved in the organs debate accept the fundamental tenet of Western liberalism that people should be allowed to control their own destinies as far as possible, but many claim that there can be no genuine, free consent to the sale of organs, and therefore (in effect) that there is no curtailment of liberty in preventing it. Since it is also claimed that genuine consent is an absolute requirement for any surgical procedure, the alleged impossibility of obtaining such consent under these circumstances is offered not merely as the removal of a *prima facie* objection to prohibition, but as a positive reason for demanding it. Several different arguments are produced to defend the claim that apparent consent to the sale of organs is not genuine. I shall discuss the three most familiar.

A. *Incompetence through ignorance.* The most obvious way to argue that would-be organ vendors are not choosing freely is to claim that there is something about the people themselves that prevents their making genuinely autonomous choices. Enlightened Westerners will hesitate to suggest that Turkish and Indian peasants must be prevented from making their own decisions just because they are poor or foreign, but they may well argue that "since paid organ donors will always be relatively poor, and may be underprivileged and undereducated, the donor's full understanding of [the] risks cannot be guaranteed" (Sells, 1993, pp. 2983–2984). The requisite informed consent is impossible, and therefore organ sales should not be allowed.

This line of argument does get off to a reasonably promising start. It is plausible, though by no means uncontroversial, to claim that if people do not understand the implications of the various options open to them, the choices they make are in some sense not genuinely autonomous. It is probably also reasonable to think that people poor enough to be tempted by organ selling are likely to know little about the implications of the procedure. But even if both these matters were beyond controversy, there would still remain the question of how their conjunction with a commitment to the value of autonomy – to the intrinsic desirability of allowing rational beings to make their own choices about what happens to them – is supposed to support the conclusion that organ sales should be prohibited; and this is where the problems arise.

In the first place, no one committed to the value of autonomy would rush to institute a prohibition that would limit the freedom of *everyone*, just on the grounds that some, or even most, of the people most likely to be involved were incapable of making autonomous choices. At the very least, the first impulse should be to try to discriminate between people, and to interfere only with the ones who really are incapable of doing so. To justify a general prohibition it would be necessary to argue both that this could not be done, and that it would be worse to risk allowing the incompetent to choose than to curtail the freedom of the competent. I am not aware of anyone's having tried to make out such a case.

Second, ignorance as such is not an irremediable state. If ignorance is the obstacle to genuine choice, anyone concerned about autonomy will try to remove the ignorance before starting to foreclose options. In other contexts where we think it important that people should make considered decisions about risky and complicated matters (as in the case of other surgery, or abortion, or AIDS testing) we typically insist on counselling, both to check for ignorance and to provide information. Anyone who opposed giving the ignorant the chance to become informed would hardly be regarded as a respecter of autonomy.

And third, even if counselling were likely to be impracticable, or the ignorance of prospective organ sellers irremediable,[6] another problem would still remain. Respect for autonomy lies in the idea that *if* people are capable of genuine choice there is a presumption in favor of allowing their choices, but that implies nothing about what should happen if they are not. That is a quite separate question,[7] to which considerations of autonomy are *ex hypothesi* irrelevant.

Commitment to the intrinsic value of self-determination and fear that rational decisions about organ selling must be impossible for anyone who might be tempted by it, therefore, however unexceptionable in themselves, come nowhere near supporting the conclusion that organ sales should be prohibited. But even if the argument did work, it would still not do what is required in this context, because it would equally rule out a great many things that most objectors to organ sales have no intention of ruling out. In particular, it would preclude unpaid organ donation, at least in any population where kidney selling might be a temptation, since genuine consent would be impossible for the same reasons.[8] Whatever moral merits there may be in the giving of an organ, it can hardly be claimed as a miraculous remover of whatever intractable ignorance would have made genuine consent to its sale impossible, let alone one that works by backward causation.

This double criticism of the argument from ignorance – that its premises, even if plausible in themselves, do not support the conclusion that organ sales should be forbidden, and that even if they did they would equally support the unwanted conclusion of ruling out the unpaid donation of organs – sets a pattern that will soon be familiar.

B. *Coercion by poverty.* Arguments about ignorance and incompetence concern what might be called internalities: characteristics of agents themselves that are supposed to make them incompetent to choose properly among whatever options are open to them. The most familiar arguments about autonomy and consent in the organs debate, however, are of a different kind. Most depend on the idea that would-be vendors are coerced by external circumstances, and that a coerced choice cannot count as genuine.

The commonest agent of alleged coercion is poverty. "Surely abject poverty . . . can have no equal when it comes to coercion of individuals to do things – take risks – which their affluent fellow-citizens would not want to take? Can decisions taken under the influence of this terrifying coercion be considered autonomous? Surely not . . . " (Dossetor and Manickavel, 1992, p. 63).[9] And, it is implied, since coerced consent is not genuine, the choice should not be allowed.

Once again, it is easy to see how this idea gets going. The poor would not be selling organs but for their poverty, so it may be reasonable to say that the poverty is coercing them into the sale. It is also widely taken for granted that decisions and agreements made under duress should not count, and it is easy to think of cases that support this idea. If some dealer in organs kidnaps me and threatens to take out one of my kidneys in some rat-infested cellar, without anaesthetic, unless I sign a document authorizing you to do the job properly in your modern hospital, of course I sign it; but equally of course, when I am delivered already anaesthetized to your operating theatre, and you are presented with this surprising document, you rightly suspect nefarious goings on and disregard my authorization. And when you do, nobody is likely to accuse you of gratuitously interfering with my decisions about how to run my life.

Nevertheless, illustrations like this are misleading, as can be shown by a slight change of scenario. Suppose the kidnapping went as before, but you knew that if you did not perform the operation the kidnapper could easily get me back and carry out his original intention. My consent would be just as coerced as before, but it would be preposterous for you to claim that respect for my autonomy obliged you to refuse to operate and leave me to the other fate. Coercion as such, therefore, cannot justify the disregarding of stated preferences.

This may seem surprising, but the matter becomes clear if, instead of going off into the metaphysics of true consent, we ask directly what it is about coercion that makes a defender of autonomy regard it as intrinsically undesirable. Coercion is a matter of reducing the range of options there would otherwise be. Deliberate coercers come and take away options until the best available is what they want you to choose; circumstances like poverty can, by extension, be regarded as coercive because they are also constrictors of options that make you choose what you otherwise would not.[10] This shows what it is about the first of the kidnapping cases that makes it right for anyone concerned about autonomy to ignore the coerced choice. The relevant point is not that my original consent was coerced, but that, having got me into your hands and away from the kidnapper, you are in a position to *remove the coercion* by restoring my original range of options. In the second case, by contrast, you cannot remove the coercion because the kidnapper can get me back, and if you disregard my wishes you will (in the extended sense that allows poverty as a kind of coercion) coerce me yet further, by precluding the best option even among the horribly limited range the original coercer has left me.

This is why it is quite wrong to say that the poor should be protected from selling their kidneys, "preferably, of course, by being lifted out of poverty" (Dossetor and Manickavel, p. 63), but otherwise by the complete prevention of sales. It implies that prohibition and "lifting out of poverty" are unequally desirable variations on the same general theme, whereas the foregoing argument shows them to be, in the relevant sense, direct opposites. Protecting the poor from kidney selling by removing poverty works by increasing the options until something more attractive is available; prevention of sales, in itself, only closes a miserable range of options still further. To the coercion of poverty is added the coercion of the supposed protector, who comes and takes away (what the prospective vendor sees as) the best that poverty has left. This cannot be justified by a concern for freedom and autonomy.

What has happened, once again, is that an argument starting from intuitively acceptable beginnings – the idea that poverty is a kind of coercion, and that anyone concerned with freedom and autonomy should regard coercion as intrinsically undesirable – has veered off into confusion. The idea that coercion precludes proper consent depends on a confusion between the possession of a limited range of options and an inability to choose properly between whatever options there are. Anyone concerned with autonomy and liberty must be concerned about both of these individually, but must also take care not to run them together. If having a narrow range of choices (coercion, in this extended sense) is mistaken for incompetence to choose among the existing range (absence of true consent), and the coerced choice is prevented for that reason, the effect is to produce *exactly the opposite* of what *each* concern requires. The competent are prevented from making their own choices, and the already circumscribed are constricted still further.[11] The plausible premises are actually at odds with the conclusion they are supposed to support.

And, once again, even if the argument did work it could still make no distinction between sales and donations. If vendors can be said to be coerced by circumstances, then, for the same reasons, so can donors. If losing a kidney is intrinsically undesirable, it is just as undesirable for a donor as for a vendor, and chosen only because constricted circumstances have made it the best option all things considered. If coercion is a reason for not allowing organ sales, and poverty counts as a kind of coercion, coercion by threat of the death of a relative – quite a heavy kind of coercion, you would think – should equally rule out donation.[12] The logic is the same.

C. Coercion by unrefusable offers. A different kind of argument is that tempting someone like the Turkish peasant with a payment of several hundred times his annual income amounts to making him an offer he cannot refuse, and coercing him in that way. Sells, for instance, objecting to any "externally applied constriction of an individual's right to choose not to donate," includes in this category "all cases where a person sells one of his organs during life," because "here the financial benefits have such an impact on the life of the donor and his family as to be irresistible: the element of voluntariness of donation must be at least compromised, or, in extreme cases, abolished" (Sells, 1991, p. 20).

It is once again easy to see how this idea might arise. The irresistible offer, like poverty, has the effect of making the intrinsically
unattractive prospect of losing an organ part of the best all-things-
considered option, and may therefore seem coercive in the same
way. And, furthermore, there is a significant difference between
this and coercion by poverty. You cannot improve the situation of
the poor by cutting off the organ-selling option, because what
needs to be removed is the poverty that is doing the coercing, not
the best option poverty has left. But the irresistible offer is quite
different, because it is itself the source of the alleged coercion. It
may seem, therefore, that in this case ending the trade removes
what is doing the coercing, and is genuinely liberating.

This argument, however, fails at a different point. The second
premise is wrong: the unrefusable offer is not a form of coercion. It
does indeed change the situation until the all-things-considered best
option includes the intrinsically undesirable element of kidney loss,
but it does so, not through the narrowing of options that is characteristic of coercion, but through a broadening of them. The original
options are all still there, and if you choose the new one you presumably regard it as better, all things considered, than any you had
before; and, furthermore, the more irresistible you find it, the more
decisive your preference. Removing it is yet again a constriction of
options, not an elimination of coercion, and therefore cannot be
justified by arguments based on ideals of freedom and autonomy.

It is also worth noticing that a corollary of this argument, if it
worked, would be that the less you offered – the more resistible
the potential vendor found your offer – the less coercion you
would be applying. It would be convenient to be able to show
consideration for the poor by paying less for what they had to sell.

This is not the end of the arguments about coercion. It is also
objected that organ selling can be indirectly coercive, in exposing
people to coercion by relatives: if the option to sell organs is there,
people may be put under pressure to take it. This is important, but
it raises rather different issues. It will be discussed later (section
V.E, below).

IV. PROBLEMS FOR PATERNALISTS

A. Harm to the vendor. It seems to be taken for granted, in this
debate, that if it is impossible to get informed, autonomous

consent for nephrectomy, that is enough to rule it out. This is what underlies all the attempts to justify prohibition by way of arguments that genuine consent is unobtainable. The assumption is, however, a rather surprising one, since it is quite at odds with our usual attitudes to consent in medical contexts. If a rational agent *withholds* informed consent that is usually thought to settle the matter, but if someone is incapable of giving consent for consent-requiring procedures such as surgery we do not automatically say that these cannot go ahead; we usually say instead that some guardian should make the decision. Even if we could show that some would-be organ vendors were incapable of deciding for themselves, therefore, that would justify only our taking the decision out of their hands. It would not, in itself, justify our deciding one way rather than another.

To take the next step, and say that a competent guardian must decide against the sale of organs, is to claim that this is what is best for the would-be vendor. This amounts, in effect, to disputing another of the apparent harms of prohibition: that it takes away the best option of the badly off. Someone who claims, for instance, that "state paternalism grounded in social beneficence dictates that the abject poor should be protected from selling parts of their bodies to help their sad lot in life" (Dossetor and Manickavel, p. 63) needs to explain why the poor are misguided in their judgment that organ selling is in their best interests.

The issue the paternalist has to settle is one of rational risk taking. The potential harm of losing a kidney must be weighed against the potential benefits of whatever payment is received, and assessed against the probabilities that these harms and benefits will actually come about. This is obviously not easy. Probabilities are difficult to estimate and differ considerably between cases, and individuals have different views about the comparative merits of different outcomes. There is also great variation in individuals' willingness to take risks.

In spite of these difficulties, however, one conclusion does seem clear. Most prospective paternalists have no hope of claiming plausibly that the poor who want to sell their kidneys are obviously wrong about what is in their interests, because they cheerfully countenance, in other contexts, the running of risks that are quite objectively much less rational than this one. The dangers of hang gliding or rock climbing, or diving from North Sea oil rigs, are much greater than those of nephrectomy;[13] and even though it is impossible to generalize about the benefits of particular sums of money to individuals, it is plausible to say that the expected benefits will be much greater to the desperately poor, who see in selling a kidney the only hope of making anything of their wretched lives and perhaps even of surviving, than to the relatively rich.[14] If the rich who take risks for pleasure or danger money are not misguided, it is difficult to see why the poor, who propose to take lower risks for higher returns, should be regarded as so manifestly irrational as to need saving from themselves. You might rather think, *contra* Dossetor and Mackinavel, that the poorer you were the more rational it would be to risk selling a kidney.

And once again, even if we could reach the general conclusion that kidney selling was bad for the vendors, the argument would apply equally to donors. If any aspect of organ selling is against the interests of the vendor, it is not (though this obvious fact seems to be overlooked most of the time) the getting of money but the loss of a kidney, and this is in principle identical for donor and vendor. There is no reason to presume that whatever the money is wanted for must matter less to the vendor than saving the life of a relative must to a donor; it all depends on how much the relative is valued and what the money is for.[15] Even if we discount the people who want to save sick relatives, and think only of the ones bent on paying off debts or educating children or finding dowries for sisters (see, e.g., Reddy, 1991, p. 176),[16] they may well be much more anxious to do these things than many a downtrodden wife has been to save her husband's life. The exchange of money is not even an indicator, let alone a determinant, of what is from the point of view of the vendor (and therefore the paternalist) the difference between reasonable and unreasonable risk.

B. Harm to the purchaser. Given the way the organ selling issue is usually presented, you would expect the third claimed disadvantage of prohibition – harm to the prospective purchaser – to go uncontested. If what is complained about is the unfair advantage of the greedy rich, obviously the complainer wants to put a stop to that advantage.

It is therefore worth noticing for the sake of completeness, and for evidence of the scrambling that goes on in this debate, that the purchasers sometimes find themselves transformed from exploiters into the victims of unscrupulous middlemen, of substandard and profiteering clinics (Abouna *et al.*, 1991, p. 167), and even – in what would in less serious circumstances be an entertaining reversal of the original position – of the poor themselves, who are likely to be suffering from all kinds of dreadful diseases, and who, in their eagerness to get their hands on the money, will probably lie about their health and infect the hapless recipient with hepatitis or AIDS (Broyer, 1991, pp. 198–9). It has also been alleged that the purchasers, like the vendors, cannot be said to have given the proper consent required for treatment, because the lack of donors in their own country leaves them with no real choice (Abouna *et al.*, 1991, p. 166).

However, the foregoing arguments about the poor show by implication the mistakes in both these lines of argument. Even though many of the claims about exploitative and careless clinics and less than candid vendors may be true, the question here is not of whether the purchasers are less well served than they ought to be, but of whether they would be better off without the trade at all. Clearly many, if not most, would not. Even if treatment carries a significant risk of disease, the alternative for most of the patients is certain death. And, furthermore, even if the risk were not worth taking in the present circumstances, that would still be an objection only to inadequacy of control, rather than to the trade as such.

The other claim, that the purchasers have not really given voluntary consent, is yet another case in which having a narrow range of choice is confused with an inability to make a fully informed choice among the options there are. Once again, you cannot show respect for people's autonomy by preventing them from taking the best option in a range you are arguing is already too narrow. If, on the other hand, the problem is an inability to make an informed choice because of inadequate information, that is a reason for supplying the information rather than for removing the option altogether.

V. OVERRIDING OBJECTIONS

The conclusion of the arguments so far, then, is that the original account of the situation must stand. Prohibition does interfere with the choices of competent adults, and it does typically harm would-be vendors and purchasers. If the case for prohibition is to be made out, therefore, it must be shown that these intrinsic dis-

advantages are outweighed by considerations of greater importance. Since opponents of organ sales have not on the whole even
reached the stage of recognizing that prohibition has any disadvantages, not many arguments are presented as actually setting
out to do this. There are, however, several in the field that might
be offered for the purpose. This section considers an assortment of
the most familiar.

A. Collateral damage. The most obvious kind of objection to look
for, if the vendors and purchasers themselves must on the whole
be regarded as beneficiaries of the trade, is counterbalancing harm
elsewhere. A first glance at possibilities, however, looks unpromis-
ing. Anecdotes and statistics are offered about harm to the principals that may have repercussions for their families; but if on the
whole the principals can expect to benefit, so, typically, can their
families. Help for the family is often the purpose of the sale.
Increased wealth to individuals presumably also tends to benefit
the surrounding community, and the process in general involves a
transfer of wealth from the rich to the poor. And, indeed, *unless*
the trade can be shown to be wrong – the point presently at issue –
even depriving the despised middlemen and operators of clinics
of their socially useful niche in lands of few opportunities must
count as an unjustifiable harm. If anything, the first foray into the
area of collateral harm suggests that even more harm is done by
prohibition than appeared at first.

Perhaps that is why the dark predictions are usually about
dangers less tangible and more amorphous, such as the corruption
of sensibilities and general moral decline.[17] Rhetoric, however, is
not enough to counterbalance such positive harms as death and
destitution. It is necessary to be clear about exactly which evils are
threatened, what evidence there is that that they would come
about, and how bad it would be if they did. Most of the threats
turn out to be ill equipped to withstand this kind of scrutiny.

For instance, there is the allegation that the trade is wrong
because it commodifies the body. In this case the claim is clear
enough – the trade involves treating parts of the body as a pur-
chasable commodity – and since this is precisely what the trade is,
rather than anything it does, the question of evidence does not
arise. But so far this is just a restatement of the point at issue, not
an argument for objecting to it, and the question remains of what
the harm is supposed to be. "Commodification" carries deroga-

tory overtones, of course, which is why it is used; but without further explanation the pejorative term simply begs the question. This one takes its force from our outrage at the idea of treating people themselves as commodities, but before the moral implications can be dragged over – before we approve the loaded word "commodification" in this context – we need to see whether the moral suggestion is justified; and obviously it is not. Treating people as commodities, with no say in their own destiny, is just about as different as it could be from letting them decide for themselves what to do with their own bodies, which is what is at issue here and might reasonably be regarded as the most fundamental issue of autonomy there was.

Commodification is also alleged to cause further harms. "It depreciates some of the fundamental professional and moral values of society by demeaning the dignity and autonomy of the human individual" (Abouna *et al.*, p. 170); "By commodifying the body, mutual respect for all persons will be slowly eroded" (Dossetor and Manickavel, p. 66). Those certainly sound like harms; but now there is the problem of evidence. Autonomy is not infringed by the trade, as has already been argued at length. And even though it may be degrading to be in a state where organ selling is the best option left, that does not imply that actually going through with the sale increases the degradation (as is usually thought about prostitution, for instance). On the contrary, Reddy claims that for many vendors a positive motive is given by the duties of Hindu ethics, and that respect and self-respect increase because of a duty done (Reddy, p. 176). And even in Western cultures, if some of the unemployed could get a large sum of money and start again, supporting their families instead of living on the dole, would there be anything but a huge increase in their self respect, and the respect of others? This is an empirical question, but I defy any caviller to produce any evidence the other way, or even evidence of having looked for any.

It is also said that the trade "invites social and economic corruption . . . and even criminal dealings in the acquisition of organs for profit" (Abouna *et al.*, p. 171). That too is a clear harm, but again there is the question of evidence. It is well known that when a commodity is in demand it is the illegality of trade that produces corruption, as happened during Prohibition in the United States. Many people now defend the legalization of drugs and prostitution on just these grounds.

Another idea is that the trade has adverse effects on the transplant programme itself. One claim is that if purchase is a possibility, related donors are more reluctant to come forward.[18] But if it is
being claimed as a harm of the trade that vendors rather than
donors are used, that once again begs the question at issue. *Unless*
there is a reason for objecting to the trade it does not matter intrinsically that organs should come from vendors rather than from
donors. If, on the other hand, the concern is that transplants from
related donors are likely to be more successful than from vendors,
the question arises of what the evidence is that the harm would
occur. If relatives knew that their kidney would probably do better
than a stranger's, that would presumably be a significant element
in their calculations.

It is also said that if organs can be bought from living vendors
there will be no incentive to overcome public resistance to a
cadaver programme (Broyer, p. 199). That would indeed be a
drawback, since nobody doubts that it is desirable (other things
being equal) to make as much possible use of the dead before
resorting to the living, but there is the question of evidence again.
The availability of purchased organs is certainly not the only or
main reason for the shortage of cadaver organs, since there is a
shortage where they are not available. It is said that people in
positions of power will have no incentive to press for the programme if they can go and buy kidneys; but it might equally well
be claimed that since these very people are the ones who respond
with such disgust to the trade, its continuation might induce them
to press even harder for change. This is a possibility, but in the
absence of any proper research, nothing more; and, in the meantime, nobody who is seriously concerned about the supply of
organs will rush to cut off one source of supply without positive
evidence that doing so will open up better ones.

And so it goes on. Nearly all the objections that appeal to claims
about harms caused by organ selling either beg the question, or
treat mere possibilities as actual, or fly in the face of positive evidence. It is still possible that trade causes collateral harms substantial enough to outweigh the harms done by prohibition, but
that has yet to be shown; and in the meantime the burden of proof
continues to lie against prohibition.

B. *Exploitation.* An objection of a different kind is that the trade
must be ended because it involves exploitation. Poverty may not

make people irrational, it may be agreed, but it does make them vulnerable to exploitation, and the vulnerable must be protected. The trade should therefore be stopped.

The problem about this argument lies in the way exploitation works, and, once again, in the crucial difference between coercion and inducement to do what is intrinsically unattractive. Coercion works by the removal of other options until the unattractive one is the best left; and in such cases it is possible, as already argued, to protect the victim by putting a stop to the coercer's activities. But exploitation does not take this form. It works the opposite way, by adding inducements until they just tip the balance, and the intrinsically unattractive option becomes part of a package that is, all things considered, the best available. What is bad about exploitation, and makes it different from the offering of inducements that is a normal part of buying and hiring, is that the exploiter seeks out people who are so badly off that even a tiny inducement can improve on their best option, and in that way can get away with paying less than would be necessary to someone who had more options available. (If this is exploitation, of course, it looks suspiciously like free market capitalism; there is nothing new in that idea.) But the fact remains that it works by inducement, and the logic of inducements still applies. Nobody can improve your position by removing an effective inducement, however small, because to do so is to take away your all-things-considered best option.[19]

Once again, in other words, we have an argument with unexceptionable premises – that the poor are vulnerable to exploitation, and that they should be protected – but whose conclusion does not follow. Although we can stop the exploitation by stopping the trade, to do so would be like ending the miseries of slum dwelling by bulldozing slums, or solving the problem of ingrowing toenails by chopping off feet. We put an end to that particular evil, but only at the cost of making things even worse for the sufferers. If our aim is the protection of the poor rather than just the thwarting of the exploiters,[20] and we lack either the will or the power to remove the poverty that makes them exploitable in the first place, the next best thing is (once again) to subject the trade to stringent controls. That is the only way of ending the exploitation that also protects the poor.

C. *Altruism.* Another kind of argument still is presented, like the voluntarism requirement, as a moral absolute overriding all weighings of harms and benefits. Financial inducements, it is said, are to be ruled out because they preclude altruism, and an absolute requirement of organ donation is that it should be altruistic.

Since this requirement is usually asserted rather than argued for, it is presumably taken to be self-evident. Nevertheless, it is surprising. At least the other arguments discussed so far have started with plausible moral concerns about such things as coercion and exploitation, and have foundered only in the transition between these and their conclusions. But in this case the principle itself, for all its supposed self evidence, seems positively at odds with all our usual attitudes. The world is, after all, full of transactions which the transactors see as being to their mutual benefit, and to which in principle we have not the slightest objection. We may particularly admire their one-way equivalents, when goods and services are given that would otherwise have to be bought, but it normally does not occur to us that unless some transaction can be guaranteed to be of this one-way kind it should not take place at all. It would normally be regarded as astonishing, and in the absence of explanation absurd,[21] to claim that it would actually be better that neither side should benefit than that both should.

Even if we accepted the principle, however, it would still have the usual problem of not supporting the required conclusion. Selling is not in itself at odds with altruism; it all depends on what the money is wanted for. It does not even matter exactly what definition of altruism is accepted. For any action that an opponent of sales would count as altruistic, it is easy to imagine a case of selling that would be altruistic by the same standards. If a father who gives a kidney to save his daughter's life is acting altruistically, then so, by the same criterion, is one who sells his kidney to pay to save his daughter's life; if it is altruistic to work long hours to earn money for your family, it is altruistic to sell your kidney for the same purpose.

And yet again, if a demand for altruism could form any part of an argument to rule out sales – if, for instance, it were claimed that organ sales should be prohibited because they *might* not be altruistic – it would rule out donations as well. For any gift or service that would count as non-altruistic in other contexts, an equivalent can be imagined for the donation of organs. If your hope of inheriting money deprives your visits to your rich great-aunt of altruistic content, it does the same for your similarly-motivated kidney donation. The distinction between the altruistic and the non-altru-istic, however defined, is unrelated to the distinction between organ giving and organ selling.

D. *Slavery*. Another common line of objection works by appealing to other practices that most people would agree were intolerable, and attempts to derive an objection to kidney selling from a linking of the two. Slavery is the commonest of these. "It is some-times argued that an individual should be free to sell his organs just as he sells his labor, and why should there be any objection? This argument, if taken to its conclusion, may easily be used to justify a return to allowing individuals to sell themselves into slavery, which is clearly unacceptable" (Abouna *et al.*, p. 169). Similar lines of argument suggest that if kidneys can be sold, there can be no objection to the selling of vital organs such as hearts.

Arguments like this are not always clear, and particular versions may need spelling out before detailed replies can be given. But the usual intention seems to be to produce a *reductio ad absurdum*: anyone who thinks kidney sales are acceptable is committed to thinking slavery (or, as it may be, heart selling) is also acceptable; but since slavery is manifestly wrong, kidney sales must be wrong as well.

If this is the idea, the quotation above shows by implication where this strategy goes wrong. The argument does not show that the acceptability of kidney selling entails the acceptability of slavery, but only that *one particular justification* someone might offer for condoning organ sales – that people should be free to sell what-ever is theirs – also entails the acceptability of slavery. The argu-ment therefore works only *ad hominem*, against someone who offers that particular defence. Acceptance of one practice can never, in itself, logically commit anyone to acceptance of some other: it always depends on what the reasons are. The line of argument being developed here, for instance – depending on the claim that prohibition does definite harms, and therefore that there is a pre-sumption against it until good arguments in its favor are produced – does not depend on the principle that people have an entitlement to sell what is their own, and is immune to this particular attack.[22]

Arguments of this kind exemplify yet again the now-familiar pattern. Most people are likely to agree that to allow slavery or the selling of hearts would obviously be wrong, but those premises are not enough to support the conclusion that kidney sales must therefore be wrong as well. And anyway, such an argument could not make the necessary distinction between sales and donations. People are not allowed to *give* themselves into slavery or give away their hearts, either, so if the argument did work we should have to conclude that the unpaid donation of kidneys should also be forbidden.

E. Higher-level preferences. This by no means exhausts the arguments, but the sound of barrel scraping increases with every new attempt, and enough of the familiar ground has been covered for the purposes of this essay. There is, however, one other kind of argument that should be mentioned, because although it hardly ever appears in the current debate – at least in a recognizable form – it is of an important general kind, and has a potential for success lacked by the candidates considered so far.

This is the possibility that lurks behind the idea that organ sales should be stopped because of the danger of pressure from relatives.[23] As it stands, this argument is as hopeless as the rest of the repertoire, and for much the same reasons. If the risk of pressure to choose some option were enough on its own to justify the removal of that option altogether, it would lead to the conclusion that no one should have any options at all. (People should not be allowed to choose whom to marry, in case they were morally bullied into making an unwelcome choice.) And, in particular, it would rule out organ donations, since if the possibility of donations exists, so does the possibility of pressure to donate.

Nevertheless a potentially good kind of argument can be developed from these beginnings, which raises the possibility of bridging legitimately the gap between ideals of freedom and self determination, on the one hand, and conclusions that options should be restricted, on the other. This can be spelt out as a reply to the earlier arguments about coercion by unrefusable offers. The essence of the point is that it is too simple to presume that giving people a new opportunity must necessarily count as an extension of their options in any relevant way. What looks superficially like a straightforward addition to some range of choices, leaving all previous options intact, may really be nothing so simple. The addition may subtly change the existing range, removing possibilities that were there before; and if that happens, the choice of the new option is not enough to prove that it is preferred to anything previously available.

The pressure argument can be recast, schematically, in this form. As long as kidney selling is not a possibility you can keep at once your kidney, a clear conscience and family harmony. If a market develops you may feel you are being selfish for not taking the opportunity to benefit the family, or they may start dropping hints about how useful the money would be, and then your original option will have gone, and you will have to choose between keeping the kidney and satisfying the family. If you would have preferred the old situation to any of the options available in the new one, your range of choice has been *lessened* by the new one in the relevant sense of its having deprived you of a better option than it has introduced. Deciding in advance whether some new option is to be welcomed is once again a matter of deciding which risks should be taken. If you think the new option offers more dangers than benefits, and if in consequence you would prefer the present range of options to the new possibilities that would be opened up by the market in kidneys, anyone concerned for your freedom and autonomy would prefer to satisfy your higher-level preference to be without the new one.

This kind of recasting is important, because it shows how an argument starting with principles about the importance of autonomy might reach a conclusion that options should be curtailed, and explains how it might be rational to prefer to be without some option, even though it would have been chosen if it had been available. It also has another great advantage conspicuously lacked by other arguments considered so far, which is the potential for distinguishing between sales and donations. There may be good reasons for preferring to have one option open, but not the other. It depends on how the risks and benefits of each are assessed.

And, furthermore, this way of looking at the matter extends the range of possibly effective arguments for prohibition still further, because it shows that the risk of coercion is not the only reason there might be for preferring to be without a particular option. We have all kinds of reasons for preferring to be without options, many familiar from everyday life,[24] and others might arise in this context too.

One other possibility particularly worth mentioning is proposed (as part of a separate thesis, rather than as part of the organs debate) by the economist Robert Frank (1985, chapter 10). He

argues that individuals are more concerned than is generally recognized about their relative, as opposed to absolute, position in
the possession of various goods, and that one consequence of this
is their agreeing to restrain competitions that would use considerable effort and resources, but leave relative positions much as they
had been before.[25] He thinks this accounts for ways in which societies try to limit the role of money, and in particular for prohibitions on the sale of bodily parts. Although you can get ahead
temporarily by selling yours, so can everyone else by selling
theirs; and everyone will end up in the same relative position but
with jeopardized health.

Frank presents this idea rather ambiguously between an *explanation* of why societies do this, and a *justification* of their doing it.
The question here is about justification, and from this point of
view the proposal is interesting for various reasons. It is like the
foregoing argument about pressures in offering a justification in
terms of higher-level preferences for removing a lower-level
option, but it is different in several significant ways. One
difference is that it contains, much more obviously than the pressure argument, the potential for distinguishing between sales
and donations: organ giving does not offer a way for people
to improve their social positions that could lead to a self-defeating competition, whereas organ selling might. But a more
fundamental one is that it defends the conclusion that *everyone*
in a particular society should be deprived of the option in question.

If the pressure argument considered earlier works, it is important that it works *for individuals*: any individual may decide, irrespective of what any others decide, that the danger of pressure to
use some option may make it better to be without it. But it is the
essence of the kind of case just considered that it is always a
potential disadvantage to any individual, considered alone, to be
without the option in question. It makes sense to want to be
without it *only if you can get everyone else to agree to do the same*, and,
it may be added, if the only way to get them to agree is for you to
agree as well. (The best of all, from your own point of view, is to
deprive everyone else, but not yourself, of the option.)[26] This difference has considerable implications for social policy, since in the
first kind of case anyone concerned with individual liberty will
try, as far as possible, to devise ways of giving different people
their individual preferences, while in the second kind it is essen-

tial that the restriction should apply to whole communities. This possibility is therefore important for the question of which general prohibitions are compatible with concerns for freedom and autonomy.

However, it is essential to stress that, interesting as such possibilities are, they are still only possibilities. This is a kind of argument that *could* work, but only *if* it is actually the case that people do, or at least rationally should, have higher-level preferences to be without particular options, and so far none of the arguments seems compelling. Even the Frank proposal – the most interesting contender so far, and the only one I am aware of that actually recognizes the form of the problem and addresses it in that way – depends on accepting that most of the goods people want are for their positional rather than their absolute value, and that organ selling has the potential for runaway competition that would benefit nobody.[27] It seems far from clear that either of these is true. Even in affluent societies by no means all goods are wanted for their positional value, and in poor societies – the source of the vendors – even fewer of them must be. There is nothing in the least positional about the Turkish man's wish to save his daughter, nor in the desire of the abjectly poor to have the prospect of something other than a miserable grind for the whole of their short lives. Nor does organ selling have the runaway potential of the paradigm cases cited by Frank, since there is a fairly low limit to the number of kidneys that can be sold.

It is also significant that this line of argument works only from the point of view of potential vendors, and entirely overlooks the interests of recipients. People trying to decide whether it would be rational to be bound by rules of this kind would have to take into consideration the possibility not only that they might be tempted to sell organs, but also that they might need to buy them.

So although there are possibilities in arguments of this general form, no successful one seems yet to have been produced; and possibilities are not enough, because here is another context in which there seems to be a clear direction of onus of proof. A curtailment of options is just that, and must be presumed by anyone concerned with liberty an unjustifiable restriction of liberty until proved otherwise. Until a properly worked out argument is produced, the prohibition of organ sales remains without justification.

398   *Janet Radcliffe Richards*

PART TWO – *THE IMPLICATIONS FOR MORAL ENQUIRY*

VI. A SERIES OF SHOW TRIALS

The claim so far has been that the prohibition of organ sales seems to involve real harms of various sorts, and that none of the arguments offered by its defenders has succeeded in showing either that these are illusory, or that allowing the trade would cause even greater harms, or that there are overriding moral reasons of other kinds for concluding that they must be put up with. The conclusion at this stage must therefore be that there is no justification for prohibition, but only for trying to lessen whatever incidental harms are now involved in the practice.

The form the arguments have taken shows that this conclusion is only provisional. Someone may yet come along with good enough reasons to overcome the presumption in favor of organ sales; and, for what it is worth, I have a sneaking hope that this will happen, since I find the whole business as intuitively repugnant as does everybody else. But even if it does happen that will not affect the significance of the foregoing arguments, because the primary purpose of this paper is not to defend organ sales. Its purpose is to draw wider conclusions about the form of the debate; and to explain this it is necessary to go back and reconsider what has been going on so far.

A. The form of the arguments. An outsider, hearing that some essay had presented a defence of kidney selling, would probably presume that the argument was based on controversial libertarian principles about free trade and the rights of people to do what they liked with their own bodies, and – if unsympathetic – start raising moral or empirical objections to principles of that kind. But not only have the arguments offered here not depended on such principles; what is more significant is that they have not depended on controversial premises at all, either moral or empirical. They have depended almost entirely on logic and analysis, and have tried to show that the traditional arguments against organ sales fail not by the standards of some outside critic, but in their proponents' own terms.

There is, for instance, no sign that any opponent of organ sales would dispute the minimal moral starting point of this paper. There is nothing arcane about the idea that death, suffering, and the lessening of people's control over their own destinies are intrinsically undesirable and not to be tolerated without good reason. The fact that most opponents of organ sales accept this is shown by their attempts to prove that it is organ selling, rather than its prohibition, that results in such harms.

Conversely, hardly any of my own objections to the familiar arguments against organ sales have disputed the moral premises on which the arguments are based. I have not denied, for instance, that freedom and autonomy are good things, or that people should be protected from exploitation, or that it is dreadful for anyone to be driven by poverty into organ selling. Nearly all the criticisms made have been about the impossibility of reaching the conclusion that organ sales should be forbidden *given* the principles invoked by their proponents. The only principle that has been challenged is the altruism requirement, and even in that case the argument is based on the incompatibility of the requirement with what its proponents would accept in other contexts.

The criticisms have also not depended on controversial empirical claims. Most of them (about why unrefusable offers are not forms of coercion, for instance, or why the harm of exploitation cannot be prevented by the removal of the exploiters) have had nothing at all to do with empirical matters. But even in the exceptions, the arguments have not depended on positive empirical claims of my own, but on the negative claim that the arguments against organ sales themselves depend on empirical claims (for instance, about harmful consequences of the trade) for which their proponents have no evidence, or even, in some cases (as with the idea that legalization is likely to lead to corruption), have positive evidence against. Mere possibilities are being treated as facts, which is particularly unacceptable when the onus of proof goes the other way, and which nobody would regard as acceptable in an opponent's arguments.

The usual run of arguments against organ sales, therefore, fails not by the standards of some external critic who is producing rival empirical claims or offering different bases for moral judgment, but in terms of the very standards recommended by the proponents of the arguments themselves. The conclusions do not follow from the principles invoked in their support, either because the logic goes wrong or because the inference depends on invented facts. And it is worth noticing that this point is relevant to the familiar, last resort, all-purpose escape route of people driven into unwelcome corners by argument, which is the claim that logic must not be placed above moral intuitions. This line of argument cannot get off the ground because what logic demonstrates in cases like these is conflicts *of intuitions* (between, for instance, the importance of autonomy and impermissibility of organ selling) which the familiar arguments try to hide by presenting them as compatible or even necessarily connected. If there really is a conflict, so that one or the other must be given up or made subordinate to the other, it is *morally essential* that this should be faced.[28] Flailing at logic is not an appeal to a higher morality, but a refusal to attend to moral questions at all.

B. *The significance of the failures.* The next significant point about the failures of the usual arguments is that they are not of an obscure kind, discoverable only by deep philosophical analysis, but mistakes that no one would be in any danger of making in less fraught contexts. This becomes apparent as soon as they are suitably transposed.

It is claimed, for instance, that concern for the vendor's autonomy demands the prohibition of organ sales, because the trade involves coercion by poverty or unrefusable offers, and true consent is therefore impossible. But if you reluctantly came to the conclusion that you must sell your great-grandmother's portrait, either because you were poor and threatened with eviction (coercion) or because Sotheby's had predicted it would fetch a million pounds at auction (unrefusable offer), no one would think it anything but a joke if friends expressing concern for your autonomy proposed to rush in to stop you on the grounds of coercion's precluding your true consent.[29]

Much the same applies to the rest of the arguments. It is argued that organ sales must be stopped because of exploitation and shoddy practices; but if the only shop in a neighborhood has been getting away with exploitatively high prices, or the only hospital with substandard treatment, it does not occur to anyone that simply closing them down, and leaving no services at all, is a useful way to protect the local population. Or it is argued that organ giving must be altruistic; but although we admire altruism, and are full of approval when aging parents are looked after by their children for love, we are not usually tempted to infer from this that people who have no relatives, or who are not loved by them, should do without care altogether rather than pay for it. Or it is said that organ selling involves unreasonable risks for the poor, but (as already argued) no one thinks twice about leaving well-off people to their own devices when they take greater risks for lower returns. And so on. In neutral contexts, these arguments would not deceive anyone for a moment.

This shows what is really going on. The familiar arguments against organ sales are rationalizations, and flagrant ones at that, of something already believed for other reasons. No one starting innocently from the beginnings of these arguments could possibly arrive at the conclusions to which they are supposed to lead. They seem to work only because their proponents are already, independently, convinced of their truth.

This is also suggested by many other aspects of the debate. It appears, for instance, in the speed of public reaction to the discovery of the trade, and the terms in which it was immediately condemned. If people had really been trying to work out whether this quite new activity was justified or not, they could hardly have overlooked so completely the obvious *prima facie* harms of prohibition, and would have been agonizing over the complexities of the problem rather than rushing into action. It appears in the way every demolished argument is immediately replaced by another, with ever weaker ones recruited to the cause as the early contenders fail. If the conclusion had been reached *by means of* some argument, refutation of that argument would be recognized as removing the reasons for accepting the conclusion. It also shows in the way assorted arguments of quite different and often incompatible kinds are heaped up together,[30] and in the flagrant invention of convenient facts. Both of these typically occur when deeply held convictions are being anxiously defended.

It is probably this deep conviction, furthermore, that underlies the ready characterizations (by people who probably know nothing of the matter) of all the surgeons and clinic organizers and middlemen involved as villains. There are horror stories about all these groups; but there are horror stories about most areas of commerce, and this does not tempt us to assume that all dealers must be scoundrels or all trade profiteering, or even to express outrage (as opposed to disquiet) in other contexts where vast profits are made from the practice of medicine. If it is assumed that anything earned through organ sales must be tainted, that suggests the trade is regarded as inherently, not merely incidentally, corrupt.

The moral of these arguments, therefore, is not just that the arguments offered for prohibition do not work, though that is important in itself. What is more significant is that there obviously exists a deep intuition about the unacceptability of organ sales, quite independent of, and fuelling, the curiously bad arguments pressed into its defence. That is why, even if a good argument for prohibition does appear later, it will not undermine the significance of the failure of the familiar set. The form of that failure proves the verdict of guilty to have been pronounced in advance, and the supposed debate merely a series of show trials.

VII. REPUGNANCE AS A MORAL GUIDE

The fact that the intuitive resistance to organ sales exists quite independently of the arguments normally invoked to justify prohibition does not in itself prove that the intuition is misguided. Organ selling might still be something intrinsically evil, defying justification in terms of anything more fundamental. We do think there are such things; we must, if we think ethics is to get off the ground at all. Perhaps, then, all that can ultimately be said about the matter is caught by our rapid characterization of the whole business as *repugnant* – a word we tend to use when we are deeply averse to something, but find our feelings difficult to explain in terms of more obvious kinds of good and evil.

It is often said that such deep intuitions should be our ultimate moral authority: that "it is the emotional conviction which ultimately should determine where one makes one's stand" (Dossetor and Manickavel, p. 71). But nobody seriously believes that all strong feelings of a moral kind are reliable guides to action. We are not even tempted to think so except in the case of our own; intuitions we do not share are seen as manifestations of irrationality and bigotry. And we should have doubts even about our own when we consider how passionately people may feel about matters that detached reflection suggests must be morally neutral, such as particular forms of the treatment of the dead,[31] or how many traditional reactions of deep repugnance to such things as interracial marriage, unfeminine women and homosexuality are now widely regarded as themselves repugnant. Mere strength of feeling cannot be taken to prove that moral bedrock has been reached.

How, then, can the moral reliability of this particular strong feeling be tested? If the idea is that whatever causes it is a fundamental evil in its own right, it is obviously irrelevant to test that claim by seeing whether it can be shown to be wrong in other terms. But anyone who is inclined to accept it as a moral guide can start by checking carefully exactly what circumstances prompt its appearance. Just as people are inclined to justify their wish to prohibit organ selling in terms of other kinds of moral concern, so, for obviously related reasons, they are inclined to explain their emotional response as arising in response to exploitation, or inequality, or some other morally plausible generator of strong feelings. To test such claims, what is needed is a series of thought experiments. Organ sales and these other causes of moral concern can be imagined away from each other, to discover what really gives rise to the feelings of disgust. When that has been identified, it will be possible to look whatever it is squarely in the eye, and see whether reflection can endorse the idea that it is a fundamental evil.

So, for instance, it may be said that we find the trade repugnant because of the harm it does to the vendors; but if that were true, we should find the idea of making their situation worse by stopping the trade more repugnant still (worse that the Turkish father should be forced to keep his kidney and watch his daughter die than that he should sell it and save her); and we should find donations repugnant in exactly the same way, since they do the same kind of harm.

We may claim to be disgusted that organs should be sacrificed for any other reason than love, or with less than complete willingness; but then we should find it no more repugnant that a father should sell his kidney to save his daughter than that he should give it to her directly, and we should feel just the same kind of repugnance at the thought that some reluctant relative should feel the heavy pressure of duty, or fear, and donate an organ without love.

We may say that what we find most repugnant about the trade is the abuse and exploitation; but in that case we should feel just as much disgust, of the same kind, about equal exploitation and abuse in other areas, and even more when these are worse (as, for instance, with the slave labor that produces cheap luxury goods for the affluent world). And, conversely, if the abuses were ended, and the trade properly regulated, the feelings of revulsion should go.

We may say that the disgust arises from the idea of cutting into, and damaging, a healthy body. If so, we should feel as much disgust about donations as about sales; and since no harm can be done by cutting into a dead body, there should be no disgust at the prospect of selling organs from the dead.[32]

We may claim that the source of the disgust is the unfairness of distribution: "wealthy people obtaining services not available to others" (Land and Dossetor, p. 231). If so, we should feel the same repugnance about any kind of private medicine (and, indeed about state-financed triple bypasses for citizens of the rich world whose cost would save thousands of lives elsewhere), and none if public agencies were to buy organs for general distribution.

Or we may say that the disgust is aroused by the desperate situation of the poor, and their being forced by circumstances to make such terrible decisions. If so, we should feel the same kind of disgust when desperation forces them to sell their labor at appallingly low prices (and more still if they can find no one to buy at any price and cannot alleviate their situation at all), and none at the idea that some reasonably well off person from a rich society might sell a kidney to achieve some non-necessary personal project, like travelling round the world or learning to fly.

Thought experiments like these make it clear to most people that when suffering and exploitation are imagined separately from the element of selling, the *peculiar kind of horror* aroused by the trade in organs does not appear. There may be other feelings of moral outrage, but not this one. And they also make it clear that in most cases – and probably, for most people, all cases[33] – the converse is also true. Take away these other elements that are claimed as the source of the disgust – consider organ selling in altruistic, non-exploitative, well-regulated circumstances – and the disgust obstinately remains. It really does seem to be the business of exchanging money for parts of the body, in itself and for no further reason, that catches our feelings in this distinctive way.

It is perhaps worth commenting that an indirect confirmation of this conclusion seems to lie in the only solution I have been able to think of to the mystery of the altruism requirement. There are many familiar contexts in which the contrast between giving and selling is described as between doing things for love – altruistically – and doing them for money. If this kind of contrast is (mistakenly) thought of as paradigmatic, the demand for altruism may get its apparent force from seeming to coincide with the absence of payment, while at the same time giving the appearance of offering justification because nobody doubts that altruism is a good thing. The altruism requirement, in other words, looks suspiciously like a mere restatement of the non-selling requirement, with spurious moral knobs on.[34]

If all this is true, and the emotional reaction really is to organ sales as such, irrespective of circumstances and consequences, is it possible to endorse it as a moral guide? Can the wrongness of organ sales be accepted as a ground-level moral fact, and one of such importance as to outweigh all our usual concens about death, destitution and loss of liberty whenever they come into conflict?

When the matter is put as starkly as this it is hard to see how anyone could see it as a fundamental moral fact at all, let alone one of such overriding importance. Most people who react with repugnance to organ sales see nothing wrong in the exchange of money for goods in other circumstances, and see the donation of organs as positively commendable. Is it plausible that the combination of the two, in itself and for no further reason, can nevertheless be self-evidently and invariably evil? Can a sacrifice made with love and altruism be turned into a moral outrage just because payment comes somewhere into the matter, while an equal sacrifice made reluctantly or through vested interests is acceptable because it does not? Can the mere exchange of money transmute something inherently good into a transaction so appalling that it might even be better, as Broyer suggests (Broyer, 1991, p. 198), to risk losing genuinely unpaid donations (and allow people to die in consequence) than allow even the *possibility* that payment might be involved? Presumably the feelings of repugnance can in principle be explained (perhaps in terms of Frank-type reasons), but it is hard to see how anyone could endorse them as moral guides.[35]

And as a matter of fact, it seems that nobody really does. Even if these arguments did not make it obvious that the prevention of organ selling *could* not plausibly be regarded as morally fundamental, it is nevertheless clear that it *is* not so regarded, because all the familiar arguments against organ sales try to explain its wrongness in other terms. Nobody says that it just is more important to prevent organ selling than any more obvious sort of harm, and leaves the matter there. Prohibition, it seems, must be justified, even if the only way to do it is to fudge connections and compatibilities with the very moral concerns that it overrides.

In fact, another thing that seems implied by the fragility of the familiar arguments is that the extreme strength of feeling underlying the resistance to organ sales runs with a recognition that it needs some defending. People do not resort to arguments as bad as these unless they think arguments are badly needed.

VIII. THE NEW FORM OF THE PROBLEM

The situation then is this. When states enact laws forbidding the exchange of money for organs, or professional bodies pronounce their anathemas against it, they present their conclusions as arising from plausible moral concerns about autonomy, exploitation, and the interests of the poor. If my arguments have been right, however, this is not at all what is going on. In fact there is a strong, widely held and quite independent conviction that organ sales must be wrong, into whose defence has been pressed a motley array of arguments that could not have begun to persuade anyone who was really trying to work out the rights and wrongs of the issue from scratch. The prohibition of organ sales is derived not from the principles usually invoked in its support, but from a powerful feeling of repugnance that apparently numbs ordinary moral sensitivities and anaesthetizes the intellect, making invisible the obvious harms of prohibition, giving plausibility to arguments whose inadequacy would in less fraught contexts proclaim itself from the rooftops, and, in doing both these things, hiding the extraordinary force of its own influence.

And, furthermore, it exerts this force in a particularly sinister way. If we allow the feeling to direct our actions, the effect will be that we will try to get rid of whatever causes it. If it is not reliably connected to anything that ought, morally, to be eliminated, the *only* systematic benefit of removing its cause will be the elimination of the feeling as an end in itself. This is, of course, a great advantage to all those sensitive Westerners who suffer from it. Prohibition may make things worse for the Turkish father and other desperate people who advertise their kidneys, as well as for the sick who will die for lack of them; but at least these people will despair and die quietly, in ways less offensive to the affluent and healthy, and the poor will not force their misery on our attention by engaging in the strikingly repulsive business of selling parts of themselves to repair the deficiencies of the rich. But to place our own squeamish sensibilities above this real death or despair seems about as thoroughgoing an exploitation of the poor by the rich as any that has yet been discussed. If that is to be avoided, the influence of the feeling of repugnance must be eliminated from the analysis.

This is not, unfortunately, something that can be simply resolved on and done. It has been shown how thoroughly the deep opposition to organ sales can distort the arguments, and how invisible its influence can be even in the relatively straightforward cases discussed earlier. In complicated arguments about risks and probabilities, or individual preferences and social policies, it is inherently difficult for even the most unprejudiced enquirer to reach objective conclusions, and therefore all too easy to go through the motions of analysis and make the conclusion come out where the emotions have already determined that they should. On the other hand, once the problem and its manifestations have been recognized, there are various ways in which the danger may be lessened.

In the first place, if the failed arguments really do involve mistakes that would not be made in neutral contexts, one remedy is to be much more critical about the analysis of arguments in general, asking firmly of any candidate what we should think of its merits if we were really starting from the premises and asking, without any preconceptions, whether they supported the conclusion. Another technique is to use analogous arguments from other contexts as checks (as in the beginning of VI.B, above). Yet another is to regard with particular suspicion arguments whose conclusions come out the way we want them to.

It is also worth remembering that a favorite hiding place of old prejudices is in modified versions of absolute constraints. For instance, Dossetor and Manickavel (reluctantly) concede that there may sometimes be adequate justification for organ selling, but want to allow it only among certain populations, and even then hedged round with qualifications and restrictions. "For ethical acceptability potential kidney sellers must justify their desire on the grounds of 'indirect altruism' and potential buyers must be considered for the additional social obligation of 'mandated philanthropy' [essentially a tax to pay for transplants for members of the class from which the vendor came] – the decision being taken by a panel of society representatives" (Dossetor and Manickavel, 1992, p. 68).[36] Because dogma is being loosened and good causes supported this may sound liberal and benevolent, but the fact remains that purchasers and vendors are to be put through a series of hoops for which no justification is offered, and that the ones who stumble are left with the same unjustified harms as before. Why should vendors be made to prove altruistic intentions, rather than be allowed to judge their own best interests? Why should there be a tax on this surgical procedure, and this trade, but not others? Pretty obviously, there is still lurking in the background an assumption that the whole business is inherently shady, and that if it has to be allowed at all it must be severely restricted and purified by being forced to do other kinds of good. The feelings of repugnance are still working as hard as ever to distort the analysis, and the apparent concessions only slight lessenings of unjustified harm.

It is not only the details of the arguments, however, that have been distorted by the feelings of repugnance. More fundamentally, their influence has extended to the way the whole problem has been presented. The issue is usually seen as a "for and against" question, with two opposing sides. There is certainly an *against* side, in the sense that most of the opponents of organ sales seem to accept, as a moral absolute, the idea that organ sales are always and obviously wrong. But if you reject this idea – if you agree that the appearance of an absolute can be traced to a feeling of repugnance with highly dubious credentials – that does not mean you are *for* organ sales in the sense of supporting a corresponding absolute in favor of them, let alone in favor of an unfettered trade. To reject the absolute is, in itself, only to remove a constraint on the kind of answer that can be given to the wider question of how we can most acceptably procure organs for transplant, thereby opening the question up, and turning it (it has to be admitted) into the the kind of messy calculation of pros and cons that characterizes most moral decisions about public policy. And once the problem is recognized as taking this form, it becomes clear that there is no reason to expect a single answer to it, or to think of fixed and opposing sides at all.

In the first place, the answer may depend on all kinds of contingencies: on how many organs are needed, how many people are disposed to bequeath or donate them, the state of technology, the definition of death, social attitudes, the practicability of controls, the possibility of xenografting, and innumerable other matters. Changing circumstances may make prohibition desirable at some times but not at others.

Second, different answers may be appropriate in different places, even at a single time. Even if prohibition were thought desirable for one social group, it need not be for all. If (say) India came to a different conclusion from Britain – as an argument along the Frank lines might well imply, if one could be made to work – it would be a mistake to see that as a matter of India's accepting second class ethics (see e.g. Abouna *et al.*, p. 170). Quite the contrary; if poor countries were put (or put themselves) under pressure to adopt policies appropriate only for richer ones, that would amount to yet another kind of oppression of the poor by the rich.[37] (This danger seems to lurk everywhere in this debate except where it is expected.)

And third, whether the purchase of organs can be justified may depend not only on what the current circumstances are, but also on what arrangements we can devise within them. We might well decide that organ sales should be allowed if they could be arranged in certain ways (for instance with proper controls), but not in others (unbridled free enterprise). And when this is recognized, the issue of organ procurement changes its character completely, because instead of a simple question about whether this or that should be allowed, what appears is a choice between indefinitely many competing alternative policies. Total prohibition is only one option, to be compared with various kinds of local or temporary prohibitions, and every imaginable kind of arrangement for the controlling of sales. The question becomes permanently the general one of whether we can think of *better ways of arranging matters than at present*.

That, as it stands, leaves entirely open the question of the permissibility of organ sales. However, the fact also remains that nothing has yet dislodged the claim that the prohibition of organ sales harms both vendors and purchasers, and involves interventions in personal liberty. Nobody setting out in an unprejudiced way to improve some situation rushes to cause harm or restrict liberty. If there are abuses and dangers in the present trade, as there certainly are, the obvious way to improve the situation is to try to remove those. Only in circumstances where that turns out to be impossible, *and* there is good reason to think that the harms of organ trading outweigh the benefits, can prohibition be justified. Since the second has not been demonstrated, or the first even tried in any systematic way, the presumption must still be against prohibition.

410   *Janet Radcliffe Richards*

There is also one further, positive, reason for keeping the trade in organs, which sounds perverse but is actually offered here more than half seriously. This is the very fact that most people do find it so profoundly shocking and distressing. It certainly is shocking; it is dreadful that people should be forced by distress and destitution into selling parts of themselves. Nevertheless, the fact remains that we seem quite capable of putting up with even worse distress as long as it is not forced on our attention in this peculiarly distasteful way. Many a Turkish peasant is now presumably worse off than before we banned the trade, and the potential recipients of their kidneys may be dead; but we are not clamouring about these desperate lives and untimely deaths in the way we did about the evils of the trade. If we can be so unpleasantly reminded of the way things really are we may begin to take the despair of the poor and the dying more seriously: to make comparable outcries about the terms of third world trade, and give money to Oxfam, and leave kidneys to whoever needs them.

The sale of organs may perhaps be, as Broyer says, "a visible and intolerable symptom of the exploitation of the poor by the rich" (Broyer, 1991, p. 199), but if so that is a reason for allowing it to continue. If we are forced to suffer the intolerable symptoms, we shall less easily forget the disease.

NOTES

[1] An earlier version of some of these arguments appeared in Radcliffe Richards, 1991. I am grateful to members of the International Transplant Ethics Forum for helpful discussions of the present version.

[2] Most sufferers from ESRD cannot be saved by dialysis, sometimes for physiological reasons, but in most cases because dialysis is simply unavailable. In India, for example, it is estimated that over 90% of sufferers die (see, e.g., Reddy et al., 1990), and the ones who buy kidneys in Bombay clinics would otherwise be among them; in Britain it is estimated that 2,000 patients a year die because of the unavailability of dialysis. Dialysis is also far more expensive than transplantation, in Britain costing about £25,000 *per year*, as opposed to a single cost of about £8,000 for a transplant (*The Sunday Times*, 30 July 1995). However much money were available for treatment, therefore, transplantation could save many times more lives than dialysis. Since there is an enormous shortage of organs available for transplant it must be presumed, in the absence of evidence to the contrary, that the purchase of organs does save lives and would, if more widely allowed, save many more.

Dialysis is also incomparably less satisfactory from the point of view of quality of life. The patient in the *Sunday Times* report "felt as if his life had stopped" when renal disease forced him to give up his work and go on to dialysis. He found the experience "incredibly stressful," and expressed surprise that suicide was not more common among dialysis patients.

3 This happened in Britain in January 1989. The case was reported and discussed in all national newspapers between mid-January and early February, e.g., in *The Independent*, January 18.

4 This way of expressing the matter is meant to show that the argument is neutral between consequentialist and non-consequentialist approaches to ethics. Irrespective of whether interfering with people's choices about their own destinies is thought to *do them harm*, for instance, or to *deny their* prima facie *rights*, there is still a presumption against doing it, and a need for justification if it is to be done. Because nothing in the argument is affected by this distinction I shall ignore it from now on, and 'doing harm' should be taken as standing in for any kind of concern that provides a presumption against a particular action or policy.

5 The distinction between the claim that something is *intrinsically* bad (harmful or otherwise undesirable), and the quite different claim that it is bad *all things considered* and should not happen, will be crucial throughout this essay. It will not be practicable to hammer the point home on every occasion where their confusion would lead to misunderstanding.

6 See, e.g., Broyer, 1991, p. 199: "It is far from sure that the donor would be able to understand fully the information about the sequelae of nephrectomy."

7 See the beginning of section IV, below.

8 Some people object to the use of live donors altogether, but for them the separate question of payment does not arise. This paper is specifically about whether the exchange of money can make unacceptable something that would otherwise have been acceptable. Anyone who has a general objection to the use of live donors can still consider the case of cadaveric organs, and the acceptability of payment for those. The arguments of this paper apply also to that problem, even though it is not directly discussed.

9 See also Abouna *et al.*, 1991, p. 166: "A truly voluntary and noncoerced consent is also unlikely. . . . the desperate financial need of the donor is an obvious and clear economic coercion."

10 This is how coercion differs from direct force: it depends on getting the person being coerced to make a choice. This is true even in extreme cases, although it may sound paradoxical. Before the kidnapper holds a gun to your child's head you can, technically, choose to keep your money and your child, or only the child (by giving away the money), or only the money (by abandoning the child). You do not think of these as a set of options only because it is so obvious which to choose, but they are all there. The kidnapper removes the first (best) option, leaving you to choose between the other two. This is also why it may be plausible to count poverty as a kind of coercion, even though there is no coercer trying to bring about a particular result: there are fewer choices than there would be if

412   *Janet Radcliffe Richards*

there were no poverty, so different choices are made. Note, however, that if this extended sense of the word is accepted it follows that we are coerced by circumstances whenever we do anything we find intrinsically undesirable, like paying the gas bill or having to work for a living. This makes coercion a matter of degree, and its complete absence impossible.

[11] Note, however, a limiting case that may be the cause of some confusion: coercion may sometimes be so extreme as to remove the possibility of rational judgment. This is not a general truth about coercion, but it can happen (through torture or other extreme suffering). This may be partly what Dossetor and Manickavel have in mind. In cases where this can be established (and it certainly cannot be presumed true for all or even most organ vendors), the problem becomes the one discussed in the preceding section, of competence to consent.

[12] Note also that this kind of coercion increases if other sources of organs are not available. Any curtailment of sales increases pressure on relatives to donate.

[13] It may be said that there are great dangers at the moment, because the trade is inadequately controlled. But if so the problem lies in the lack of control, not in the trade itself.

[14] It is also alleged that the sudden rush of wealth will do the poor no good at all: that they are just at the mercy of friends and relatives who will rush in to scoop up whatever pickings they can, and will squander their substance in riotous living (see, e.g., Mani, 1991, p. 165). But to the extent that this is a significant danger that is a reason for recommending counselling, or perhaps payment by instalments, rather than for saying that the poor would be better off without the money.

[15] The issue here is specifically the interests of vendors, not the objective value of a life.

[16] See, e.g., Reddy (1991) p. 176.

[17] See, e.g., Dossetor and Manickavel, 1992, p. 66; Broyer, 1991, p. 199; Abouna *et al.*, 1991, p. 169.

[18] See, e.g., Abouna *et al.*, 1991, p. 167; Broyer, 1991, p. 199. It might also be added that this argument comes oddly from people who are anxious to establish the "true willingness" of people who volunteer organs for transplant. If there is a difficulty in finding donors when vendors are available (see e.g., Broyer, p. 199), that suggests something less than true willingness on the part of the donors.

[19] People may be *deluded* into thinking that some inducement is in their interest, of course, but that is a different matter. Exploitation is often accompanied by deceit by the exploiter or misjudgment by the exploited, but it need not be.

[20] Note, however, that according to this account the moral position of the so-called exploiters depends on their own means. If you are poor yourself, and cannot afford more than you offer, you are not exploiting. The higher the payment to the vendor, the richer the purchaser needs to be. A poor person suffering from kidney failure might non-exploitatively make a low offer for a kidney, but its not being exploitative would not help the vendor.

[21] There are some contexts where payment is unacceptable because of the possibility of corruption, but these are quite unlike this case.

[22] It may be replied that it is nevertheless vulnerable to a different attack of the same kind, since if slavery were the best option of the poor, there would, on the basis of this line of argument, have to be a presumption in its favor as well. That is true: if slavery really were someone's best option, *and* there were no overriding reasons to prohibit it, it would, by these arguments, have to be allowed. But this still would not show that there was anything wrong with allowing kidney sales. In the first place, if such an argument could be produced, it would show not that kidney selling must be rejected, but that slavery should be accepted. And anyway, second, the fact that it is proving difficult to find cogent objections to the trade in kidneys does not in the least suggest that it would be equally difficult in the case of slavery. One obvious difference between the two cases, for instance, is that if slavery is banned, employers who want laborers will have to hire the people they would otherwise have enslaved, whereas if kidney selling is banned the purchasers will have no reason at all to give money to the vendors. Organ selling also saves the lives of the purchasers; slavery has no correponding benefits. And there may be comparable differences between the cases of vital and non-vital organs, which make it possible to find justifications for prohibition in the case of hearts but not of kidneys. The arguments discussed in section V.E are relevant to the matter of making distinctions of this kind; the overall line of argument being developed here leaves entirely open the extent to which it can be achieved.

[23] This line of argument arises in many contexts, most familiarly in the case of voluntary euthanasia. It is also sometimes used against unpaid organ donation from live donors (see, e.g., *The Sunday Times*, 30 July 1995 [or back ref. to note 2]). The analysis given here applies to all issues of the same general kind.

[24] For instance, some people would rather genetic counselling and amiocentesis were not available, so that they did not have to face decisions about starting families or terminating pregnancies. Game theorists also recognize the deliberate limiting of options as a strategic or bargaining ploy, in e.g., trade union negotations or Cold War strategy (see, e.g., Schelling, 1960, 1980, p. 37 *et passim*).

[25] This is most familiar as the idea underlying arms control agreements, but Frank extends it to many unexpected areas of social life.

[26] In other words, this is a characteristic solution to a problem of the Prisoner's Dilemma type.

[27] This criticism of the Frank thesis applies only to its justificatory mode. It may still be correct as an explanation. Some evidence in favor of this seems to be offered by the fact that it is in the richer countries, and among the rich in the poorer countries – where positional goods are most important – that there is most opposition to organ selling. The poor do not seem to oppose it.

[28] Dossetor and Manickavel (p. 71) say we should go by "reason informed by emotion." I should put it the other way round.

[29] It is irrelevant to argue here that heirlooms are less important than organs. Even if they are (which presumably depends on the organ, the heirloom, and the values of the owner) this point concerns only the issue of autonomy, not the general advisability of doing either of these things.

[30] As, for instance, when it is complained that vendors are exploited (paid too little), coerced by unrefusable offers (paid too much), and anyway should be altruistic (not paid at all); or when it is said that sales must be banned both because if people want to be paid that shows they must be less than fully willing (so failing to meet the voluntariness requirement), and because if organs can be bought relatives may be less willing to come forward to donate (in which case the relatives do not meet the requirement, and should be unacceptable on the same grounds).

[31] As shown over 2,500 years ago by the well-known story from Herodotus, of Darius's experimental attempts to induce groups of Greeks, who buried their dead, and Callatians, who ate theirs, to treat their dead according to the other's customs. They both regarded the proposals with horror, and said no amount of money would induce them to do it.

[32] If it is protested that the harm is to the people who have to sell their relatives' organs, rather than to the dead, the question changes to one of the earlier kind, about harm to the vendors themselves.

One of the most significant indications that harm to the vendor is not the real source of most people's feelings is that the idea of exchanging money even for the organs of the dead seems to arouse disgust of much the same kind. It may be worth noting in passing that at the conference where an earlier version of some of these arguments was presented there was also a paper on the possibility of payment for organs from the dead (Cohen, 1991). This was extremely well argued, but (I think it is true to say) pretty well ignored.

[33] Since experiments like these are intended as self-diagnosis procedures, rather than arguments about justification, there is no reason to think everyone will come up with the same response. Some people may, for instance, find that their feelings of repugnance lessen, or perhaps even disappear, if the surrounding causes of disquiet are thought away. They may feel less disgust if organs are sold by the rich or bought for the poor, or if exploitation and carelessness are prevented. As long as the feelings do not appear in response to inequality or exploitation on their own, however, the selling is still the root cause of the disgust, even though that disgust may be lessened or removed by other mitigating circumstances.

Some people, of course, may find that their responses of disgust are not correlated either way with organ selling; but these will not be the people who joined in the immediate cry for prohibition.

[34] A variant on this phenomenon comes in the claim that organ sales must be prohibited because they are incompatible with true voluntariness. This idea trades on an equivocation between "voluntary" as meaning on the one hand something like "willing," and on the other "unpaid." If the two meanings are

coalesced the willingness requirement seems to coincide with the non-payment requirement. See, for example, Sells's "altruistic voluntarism" (Sells, 1991, p. 22) as a requirement for organ donation.

[35] It may seem that the modified version of the feeling, which appears only when selling is combined with other grounds for moral disquiet, is not open to these objections. But that is an illusion resulting from the distracting impression that the response is to the other grounds for concern. The impulse it supports is still *to prohibit organ sales*, even if only in some cases rather than all, rather than to remove these other causes of disquiet. Furthermore, although the reaction may be to the worst cases, treating the feeling as a *guide to action* may often lead to harming the worst off rather than the better off. If organ selling by the poor, but not the rich, arouses this horror, the impulse will be to allow the rich to sell their organs to increase their pleasures, while intervening between the poor and their only hope. This is, in fact, a particularly dangerous form of the intuition, because its correlation with obvious causes of moral concern masks even more effectively what is really going on. That is why it is necessary to assess feelings of moral revulsion as guides to action, rather than more vaguely as expressions of moral concern.

[36] Contrast this proposal with other things that such panels might do, such as checking for informed consent and proper conditions of sale and treatment, offering financial advice, and so on.

[37] Note that this possibility does not depend on ideas of cultural relativism, or even on the lesser idea that societies ought to be allowed to decide for themselves. The point here is just that different circumstances may give rise to different rational conclusions; and although one element in those circumstances is people's actual beliefs and preferences, a simple difference of economic circumstances might be sufficient to bring about a difference of conclusion.

REFERENCES

Abouna, G.M., Sabawi, M.M., Kumar, M.S.A., and Samhan, M.: 1991, 'The negative impact of paid organ donation,' in W. Land and J.B. Dossetor (eds.), *Organ Replacement Therapy: Ethics, Justice, Commerce*, Springer-Verlag, Berlin, New York, pp. 164–172.

Broyer, M.: 1991, 'Living organ donation; the fight against commercialism,' in W. Land and J.B. Dossetor (eds.), *Organ Replacement Therapy: Ethics, Justice, Commerce*, Springer-Verlag, Berlin, New York, pp. 197–199.

Cohen, L.R.: 1991, 'The ethical virtues of a futures market in cadaveric organs,' in W. Land and J.B. Dossetor (eds.), *Organ Replacement Therapy: Ethics, Justice, Commerce*, Springer-Verlag, Berlin, New York, pp. 302ff.

Council of the Transplantation Society: 1985, 'Commercialization in transplantation: The problems and some guidelines for practice,' *The Lancet*, September 28, pp. 715–716.

416   Janet Radcliffe Richards

Dossetor, John B. and Manickavel, V.: 1992, 'Commercialization: The buying and selling of kidneys,' in C.M. Kjellstrand and J.B. Dossetor (eds.), *Ethical Problems in Dialysis and Transplantation*, Kluwer Academic Publishers, Dordrecht, pp. 61–71.

Frank, R.: 1985, *On Choosing the Right Pond*, Oxford University Press, Oxford.

Kjellstrand, Carl M., and Dossetor, John B. (eds.): 1992, *Ethical Problems in Dialysis and Transplantation*, Kluwer Academic Publishers, Dordrecht.

Land, W., and Dossetor, J.B. (eds.): 1991, *Organ Replacement Therapy: Ethics, Justice, Commerce*, Springer-Verlag, Berlin, New York.

Mani, M.K.: 1992, 'The argument against the unrelated live donor,' in C.M. Kjellstrand and J.B. Dossetor (eds.), *Ethical Problems in Dialysis and Transplantation*, Kluwer Academic Publishers, Dordrecht, pp. 163–168.

Radcliffe Richards, J.: 1991, 'From him that hath not,' in W. Land and J.B. Dossetor (eds.) *Organ Replacement Therapy: Ethics, Justice, Commerce*, Springer-Verlag, Berlin, New York; reprinted in C.M. Kjellstrand and J.B. Dossetor (eds.), *Ethical Problems in Dialysis and Transplantation*, Kluwer Academic Publishers, Dordrecht, 1992, pp. 53–60.

Reddy, K.C.: 1991, 'Organ donation for consideration,' in W. Land and J.B. Dossetor (eds.), *Organ Replacement Therapy: Ethics, Justice, Commerce*, Springer-Verlag, Berlin, New York, pp. 173–180.

Reddy, K.C., Thiagarajan, C.M., Shunmugasundaran, D., et al.: 1990, Unconventional renal transplantation in India: To buy or let die. Transplant Proceedings 22: 910.

Schelling, Thomas C.: 1960, 1980, *The Strategy of Conflict*, Harvard University Press, Cambridge.

Sells, R.A.: 1991, 'Voluntarism of consent,' in W. Land and J.B. Dossetor (eds.), *Organ Replacement Therapy: Ethics, Justice, Commerce*, Springer-Verlag, Berlin, New York, pp. 18–24.

Sells, R.A.: 1993, 'Resolving the conflict in traditional ethics which arises from our demand for organs,' *Transplantation Proceedings* 25 (6), December, pp. 2983–2984.

[6]

Why Liberals Should Accept Financial Incentives for Organ Procurement

Robert M. Veatch

ABSTRACT. Free-market libertarians have long supported incentives to increase organ procurement, but those oriented to justice traditionally have opposed them. This paper presents the reasons why those worried about justice should reconsider financial incentives and tolerate them as a lesser moral evil. After considering concerns about discrimination and coercion and setting them aside, it is suggested that the real moral concern should be manipulation of the neediest. The one offering the incentive (the government) has the resources to eliminate the basic needs that pressure the poor into a willingness to sell. It is unethically manipulative to withhold those resources and then offer payment for organs. Nevertheless, the poor have been left without basic necessities for 20 years since the passage of the prohibition on incentives. As long as the government continues to withhold a decent minimum of welfare, liberals should, with shame, cease opposing financial incentives for organ procurement.

Liberals and others oriented to justice in health care traditionally have had a problem with proposals to increase the supply of organs for transplant by offering financial payments or other incentives to the one supplying the organ. The debate generally has followed a pattern in which libertarians and other defenders of a free-market have endorsed payments of whatever the market would bear (Peters 1991; Williams 1984). Their position has seemed clear enough, no matter how controversial.

Those approaching the question from the left, however, have supported a more complicated position. On the one hand, these people often have been strong defenders of individual liberty, especially in the medical sphere (Caplan 1983, 1984a & b). On the other hand, they have worried that offers of money in exchange for organs would put pressure primarily on the poor

KENNEDY INSTITUTE OF ETHICS JOURNAL • MARCH 2003

who thus would become the source of organs while, depending on the plan, the wealthy might become the recipients of them (Guttmann 1991, 1992). Finding this repulsive, they have supported bans on markets in organs.

One tactic to respond to these concerns has been to substitute more subtle incentives for more blatant money payments. Even with a more nuanced incentive scheme, however, resistance among those who focus on justice in health care has been both strong and persistent. After examining the moral arguments surrounding the proposals for substituting indirect incentives, I review the traditional arguments against permitting more explicit payment for organs. I suggest that the argument based on concern for discrimination against the poor is more complex than is often realized. I then argue that, even if some version of the argument from justice has enough plausibility to have supported the prohibition on markets in organs over the past two decades, it is time to abandon it—at least if the society continues to refuse to provide a decent minimum of health and welfare services for its most needy citizens.

In this paper, I speak generally about financial and nonfinancial incentives—both for the sale of organs from living people and for the procurement of permission from families to remove organs from the deceased. I do not address the obvious fact that, even if people have the legal authority to sell their own organs or those of their deceased relatives, it may be an unwise decision. There is increasing evidence, particularly for procurement of kidneys from living people, that the medical effects of living donation may give someone pause and even the financial benefits may not be sufficient to warrant a decision to sell (Rothman 2002; Goyal et al. 2002).

PROPOSALS TO SUBSTITUTE INDIRECT AND NONFINANCIAL INCENTIVES

One type of response to the concern about the unjust discrimination or coercion that is perceived to be associated with the use of market mechanisms to increase organ procurement has been to shift to more subtle or indirect incentives. Although these incentives have been proposed in countless forms, they generally have taken one of two forms: nonfinancial incentives or indirect financial payments.

Nonfinancial Incentives

If the worry is that money puts undue pressure on the poor to become the society's supplier of organs, one response is to shift from financial to nonfinancial incentives. These are sometimes called "moral" incentives.

They include proposals to award those who donate organs commemorative certificates or plaques expressing the appreciation of the people, the legislature, or the head of state. Similarly, the creation of a donor's memorial on which names could be listed would provide a mechanism for praising donors for their altruistic actions and expressing the gratitude of the public for the life-saving gifts that those individuals have given. Such a memorial currently is being planned at the United Network for Organ Sharing's offices in Richmond, Virginia.[1]

Such tokens of appreciation can be called "moral" incentives because, rather than providing monetary reward, they merely express the moral approval of the population. Since they are not monetary and all people generally appreciate moral approval, these incentives might not be as discriminatory in their impact.

The problem with moral incentives is usually a pragmatic one. There is doubt that they would work to increase the supply of organs sufficiently. About 4,400 people a year in the United States die while waiting for an organ. Many more kidney patients suffer for prolonged periods on dialysis while they await transplants. The number of people added to the waiting list each year is presently three-and-a-half times the number of organs that could be transplanted (depending on the organ).[2] Would more public recognition of cadaver or living donation of organs provide enough of an incentive to make much difference? It seems unlikely. Although there is no obvious moral objection to nonfinancial incentives, there is real doubt that they will be sufficient to produce the number of organs needed. This does not mean that such moral rewards should be opposed; merely that they probably will not work to solve the critical supply problem.

Indirect Financial Incentives

There is more reason to hope that explicit monetary payments might sufficiently increase the supply of organs for transplant. Nevertheless, many people find the idea of a direct payment to a "donor" or to the surviving family members crass or unseemly.

First, it is linguistically unseemly since, once the organ is supplied in response to payment, it is hard to continue to refer to the organ source as a "donor." He or she becomes a "vendor," one who is paid for a product. In what appears to be a desperate effort to hold on to the attractive metaphor of gift giving and donation, some have even proposed the concept of "rewarded gifting" (Alexander 1992; Daar 1992; Dosseter 1992; Kahan

KENNEDY INSTITUTE OF ETHICS JOURNAL • MARCH 2003

1992; cf. Murray 1992). Under this plan organs could not be sold. If, however, someone, makes a gift of an organ, something of monetary value would be provided to the "donor" in exchange.

Giving monetary rewards in exchange for the gift of organs seems to be a blatant corruption of the language. The term "rewarded gifting" seems to be proposed only because liberal western societies are so strongly committed to the gift model that it is attractive to try to make sales sound like gifts. Regardless of whether payment of financial incentives turns out to be acceptable, calling something a "gift" when it is really a "sale" seems to be an unethical deception. It is a corruption of the obvious meaning of the terms. If one entertains monetary incentives for increasing organ procurement, one should at least be honest enough to call a payment what it is. The transfer of money is not a "reward;" it is a payment. The transaction would be a "sale."

Even if one corrects the language to avoid this linguistic problem, however, many still would find payments discomforting. In order to respond to that discomfort, proposals have been put forward to avoid payments of cash to the vendor either by providing something of monetary value that is not a direct payment or even by making a payment to the donor's favorite charity (American Medical Association 1995, p. 582; Dewhurst 1987; Banks 1995, p. 78). The exact plan depends on whether the payment is to be made to the one who is the source of the organ or to a surviving relative. It also depends on whether the payment is to be made, in advance, while the organ source is still alive or after that individual is deceased.

Proposals have been put forward to make payments to those who eventually might become the source of organs. The funds either could be committed while the organ source is still alive—e.g., an insurance policy that would pay the beneficiary if and only if organs ultimately are procured— or take the form of a token payment to the potential organ source for a commitment to provide organs upon death (such as a discount on one's driver's license if one checks the organ "donor" box).

Such financial commitments made well in advance of procurement present some problems, however. With the proposed insurance policy, the payout would occur only if organs are procured (or only if they actually are used). This raises serious practical problems. Would those who supply many organs get larger payments than those who supply only one? What about those who willingly commit to providing all organs but turn out to have diseased hearts or livers that are not usable for transplant? If someone had signed up who turns out to have a marginal organ, could a surviving beneficiary have a tort action against a surgeon or an OPO that refused to offer the organ to anyone on the waiting list?

Similar problems arise with the offer of a token payment for merely signing a card (no longer a "donor" card, but something else—perhaps a "vendor" card). Should larger payments be made for signing up to provide many organs? Should people who appear to have prime organs get larger payments? Since the quality of the organs would not be apparent until after the death of the organ source, it would be virtually impossible to provide fair compensation based on organ quality at the time a commitment is made. What should happen if someone signs up to provide usable organs, but his or her organs become medically unsuitable before the time to procure them? Would it make a difference if they become medically unsuitable because of life-style choices of the one committing the organs? Similar problems arise if those who sign up are later permitted to change their minds about providing organs. By then, the payment would have been spent, and expecting the individual to repay in order to have the right to change his or her mind seems impractical.

A more plausible alternative to advance payments or financial commitments is to pay only if the organs are procured (or utilized). The payment could go to the next-of-kin of a newly deceased individual who turns out to have usable organs. It could also go to an individual who provides certain organs while he or she is alive: a kidney and perhaps even a liver or lung lobe. However, this approach also poses some problems. For any scheme that pays to beneficiaries only if organs are procured, should the beneficiary of those with marginal organs have a right of action if the procurement agency rejects the card as providing unacceptable organs?

In order to create some distance between the decision to provide organs and the economic benefit of doing so, some have proposed that the payment be indirect. Instead of paying cash to the next-of-kin, one could pay funeral expenses—up to, say, $3000—or pay a survivor's expenses related to the death of the individual—e.g., hotel, transportation, and meals. Such a proposal was enacted in the state of Pennsylvania (Pennsylvania Act 1994-102 (S.B. 1662), codified as amended in 20 Pa. Cons. Stat. 8601 *et seq.*). The law permits the state of Pennsylvania to begin a pilot program that would pay up to $3000 in hospital and other medical expenses, funeral expenses, and incidental expenses incurred by the donor or donor's family in connection with making a vital organ donation.[3]

There is a problem, however. If the payments are really to be for expenses for funerals or travel or meals, it seems only reasonable that the payments should cover real costs. Someone who dies suddenly and is committed to a very inexpensive cremation might leave relatives with no significant medical or funeral expenses, whereas other families may incur significant costs. Some mechanism must exist for documenting who is entitled to how much.

One might, of course, commit to the payment of some flat amount—$3000—in lieu of documenting expenses. That, however, makes the payment look more and more like a payment for the organs, rather than a compensation for costs incurred. Furthermore, assuming that the relatives who receive the payment are the same ones who are the beneficiaries of the deceased individual's will, the bottom-line cash position of the relatives will be exactly the same regardless of whether the state pays them directly for the organs or, instead, pays for the funeral and medical expenses that would otherwise have been paid from the estate of the deceased. If the payment covers the funeral expenses, the estate will be larger by that amount, and the beneficiaries will be made richer by the same amount.

The only case where this would not occur is that in which the next-of-kin with organ procurement decision-making authority turns out not to be the beneficiary of the will of the deceased. In that case, however, it seems odd indeed that beneficiary rather than the decision maker would receive the payment. At the very least, the situation would tend to neutralize the incentive to consent to procurement.

I am left with the conclusion that indirect incentives—whether moral or monetary—either will not work or are immorally deceptive in the pretense that there is no payment of cash to the decision maker when, in effect, there is. I therefore generally have opposed all efforts to provide planned systematic "rewards" for "gifts" or to provide payment of end-of-life medical or burial expenses. Such plans are really gimmicks to avoid the reality that financial incentives are being paid for the organs provided.

TRADITIONAL LIBERAL OPPOSITION TO ORGAN MARKETS

If such fictions as rewarded gifting and indirect incentives do not provide a basis for legitimating payments for organs and there is still a desperate need for more organs, what other options exist? There are some limited alternatives within the donation model. For years I have endorsed a strategy that I call "required response" (Veatch 1991). We know that not everyone who presently is willing in principle to donate organs has indicated the desire to do so (The Gallup Organization, Inc. 1993). Inertia simply precludes taking all the actions humans would be willing to take. Hence, many individuals never have gotten around to preparing economic wills or advance directives for medical treatments even though they indicate that they support the concepts in principle. Fifty-five percent of the population indicates the willingness to donate organs, while only 28 percent of the group has actually done so (The Gallup Organization, Inc. 1993).

To overcome this inertia, federal laws now require that the next-of-kin of deceased persons who are potential sources for organs be asked if they wish to donate (Omnibus Reconciliation Act 1986). Still, this strategy is only marginally successful. In some cases family members are unwilling to make the decision to donate on behalf of a loved one, especially if they do not know what the individual would have chosen. Moreover, even if family members are induced to donate on behalf of a deceased relative, this is, at best, a second choice option. The goal of the donation model is to give individuals rather than their relatives the opportunity to decide to donate. In a liberal society, it is the individual who is deemed to have the first priority for making decisions about his or her own body. The family member's surrogate choice is an inferior substitute.

One strategy for facilitating individual decision making while one is competent and capable of making a choice is to ask for a donation *and require the individual to respond*. This could be done on admission to a hospital or as part of the work-up in a physician's office (although these private transactions probably do not provide a legitimate basis for making response a requirement). Another option would be to make the question a part of the driver's license application and renewal, much as it presently is except that a state could require that the question be answered. A much better strategy is to make the question a part of the annual income tax return. Refusal to answer would constitute an incomplete return and it would be rejected just like an unsigned return is today. In order to avoid encouraging people to answer the question in the negative, an "I don't know" response should be offered. Anyone making that choice would be treated, just as they are now. The next-of-kin would have to act as a surrogate.

The income tax return has many advantages. It is completed by virtually all adults. It is already entered into a computerized data base. The IRS officials are well-prepared to protect confidentiality. The result would be a single national database with annual updates. Amitai Etzioni has argued persuasively elsewhere in this issue of the *Journal* that such requests for donation should not be presented neutrally, as if society did not care whether one donated. Rather the message should be that a good citizen will donate unless he or she has some principled reason not to do so.

KENNEDY INSTITUTE OF ETHICS JOURNAL • MARCH 2003

Other techniques for extending the donation model may add further to the numbers of organs potentially available. Nevertheless, there is good reason to suspect that, even with required response and a presumption that a donation is an act of good citizenship, many people will fail to donate, including some who are not strongly opposed to organ procurement. Some further incentive to have people address the difficult and complex issue of being an organ source seems to be in order. Hence, many free-market libertarians have proposed direct payment of some type of incentive.

I am not concerned about the details of the incentive. Rather, I want to focus on the traditional resistance to such proposals by justice-oriented liberals who variously worry that positive incentives are either discriminatory against the poor or coercive against them.

The Discrimination Argument

It seems plausible that the poor—those in desperate need of money for the basic necessities of life for themselves and their loved ones—would be more likely to respond to financial incentives.[4] Assuming that the poor are, in fact, more influenced by economic offers as a device for encouraging organ transfer, would such a practice constitute discrimination and, if so, is it unethical discrimination?

Discrimination refers to the act of differentiation. In ethics, it refers to treating people or groups of people differently, usually without morally justifiable reason. Thus, if the poor perceive more incentive to consent to organ procurement when financial incentives are offered, it would be consistent with English usage to say that they are treated in a discriminatory way, at least in the morally neutral sense of being treated differently. Many years ago out of concern for this problem, while writing on the use of incentives for controlling family size, I proposed that financial incentives should be "negative," that is they should be in the form of fees rather than rewards so that larger fees could be charged for higher income people in order to make the psychological effect on all income groups more equal (Veatch 1977). In the case of incentives for organ procurement, however, this would require purchasing a license to *avoid* having one's organs procured—a terribly implausible model for the use of incentives even if the size of the fee could be manipulated to generate as much pressure on the wealthy as on the poor.

The real question is whether the different level of perceived force from a positive financial incentive makes such incentives unethical. Those most committed to a radical egalitarian interpretation of a principle of justice perhaps may be inclined to hold that any financial offer that moves the poor more effectively to act than it moves the wealthy is unethically discriminatory because of its differential effect. I admit to certain sympathy with that view.

One who adopts that position, however, must realize how radical the position is. Virtually any financial transaction would seem to have effects that differentiate based on income level. Most tellingly, offers to hire laborers for unpleasant or risky work would seem to move the poor much more persuasively than the wealthy. Yet, all but the most radical egalitarian communists and Christian socialists act as if they believe that some differential impact of economic offers is tolerable. One may feel uncomfortable recognizing that minimum wage is sufficient to attract some poor people to accept jobs as collectors of garbage and performers of menial and boring tasks. Most people, however, do not hold to the view that all people should be situated so as to perceive the incentive of economic offers equally. Depending on how one defines the term, one can hold either that this is discrimination that is tolerable, or, alternatively, that it should not be called discrimination at all because it is not necessarily unethical.

The Coercion Argument

The real problem with economic incentives to induce offers to procure organs actually may not be that the offers are discriminatory. Rather, it may be that they are perceived as "coercive" when the offer is made to people who are destitute, who desperately need food, clothing, or medical care for themselves or members of their family. Something seems wrong when some people would perceive an offer to sell a kidney for $5000 as irresistibly powerful while others would not be moved in the slightest. Figuring out exactly what is wrong, however, may take considerable work. This brings us squarely into the complex philosophical realm of the ethics of coercion, pressure, inducements, and irresistible offers.

Many of the best philosophical scholars working on the concept of *coercion* would appear to hold that, whatever the ethics of financial incentives to consent to organ procurement, it does not constitute coercion (Faden and Beauchamp 1986, pp. 337–73). Coercion is defined more appropriately as the use of force or the threat of force to compel someone to engage in an action against his or her will. Holding a gun to someone's head to force him to sign a "donor" card would be coercion. So would drugging the individual and removing her kidney while she was unconscious (assuming that were done against her will). Merely offering an

KENNEDY INSTITUTE OF ETHICS JOURNAL • MARCH 2003

inducement to motivate someone to choose to engage in a behavior is not, by this definition, coercion. It adds an additional option to the array of options previously available. In some cases, the additional option may so fit with the goals of the person that that option is preferred above all those previously available.

An offer to hire a skilled worker away from his present employer, especially if it is at a much higher wage for similar working conditions, may be an offer that is very attractive, even irresistibly attractive, but one would not normally say that the person was "coerced" into taking the new job. Unless "coerced" means merely "presented with an option that is so much more attractive than any other that it is irresistible," such offers are not coercion. One could call such offers "irresistibly attractive" but not "coercive." Attractive offers may be perceived as offers that exert pressure or inducement, but they are neither coercive nor unethical offers simply because they are very attractive. In fact, offers are not necessarily unethical even if they are perceived as *irresistibly* attractive. Unless one is prepared to claim that all offers that are perceived as differentially attractive are automatically unethical, something more must be said to demonstrate that even an irresistibly attractive offer is unethical. The question, then, is when does an attractive offer become unethical?

The Worry about Unethical Offers

Much of the moral opposition to financial incentives to induce consent to organ procurement seems to stem from the fact that the offer may be perceived as irresistible to the poor while it is easily resistible to the wealthy. The problem is why offers to induce consent to procure organs that are irresistible only to the poor are deemed unethical while offers of jobs and offers of basic necessities are not.

I suggest that the ethical problem with irresistibly attractive offers is not at all related to the fact that they may be irresistibly attractive compared to the alternatives available. Rather, the ethical problem must be understood in terms of the options available to the one making the offer. The case we are concerned about is one in which one party, say a poor person, is desperately in need of something possessed by another, say funds to buy basic necessities such as food for his or her children. If the wealthier party makes an irresistibly attractive offer, such as an offer to pay a financial incentive if consent is given to permit procuring an organ, the morally critical issue is whether the one making the offer has the option of addressing the desperate need in some other way. If that person could respond to the desperate need and provide food, for example, without taking advantage of the poor person's desperate need, then intentionally withholding the food in order to create the situation in which the offer of money is irresistibly attractive is an unethical manipulation of the options of the poor person. If, on the other hand, the one making the offer has no other options, then the offer is not necessarily unethical.

Consider a closely related analogous case. Imagine a transplant surgeon who is caring for a child in liver failure and is discussing options with a parent of the child. The surgeon can offer the parent the opportunity to donate a liver lobe that has the potential to save the child's life while posing only moderate risk to the parent. The parent's liver will regenerate while the child will have sufficient liver function from the lobe to save his life while the liver grows to provide normal function. Although the surgery poses only moderate risk, it still is potentially dangerous and is undertaken only in serious cases in which no cadaver liver is available. The mortality of the procedure for the donor is uncertain, but is often given as being around 1 percent (Surman 2002).

It is plausible to view the offer of the surgeon to procure a liver lobe from the parent in order to save the child's life as an irresistibly attractive offer. I suggest, however, that it is not immoral merely because it is irresistibly attractive. If the surgeon has no other alternative available to save the child, the mere fact that the parent is so desperate to save her child is not a reason to conclude that the surgeon's offer to perform the surgery is immoral. (By that logic, such an offer would become moral in the case of the parent who really does not care too much whether his or her child lives or dies.)

If, however, the surgeon had ready access to a cadaver liver that was suitable for the child and withheld that option from the parent because the surgeon wanted to practice performing an adult liver lobe retrieval, that action certainly would be unconscionably immoral. The offer is no less resistible in the first case than the second. The moral difference is that, in the second case, the one making the offer had another option for addressing the parent's desperate concern and intentionally withheld that option in order to force the consent of the parent to the liver lobe procurement. It is the fact that the one making the offer had access to an alternative means of addressing the parent's serious concern that would make the offer to procure the liver immoral.[5]

That distinction goes far to explain why some of us have, until now, opposed markets in procuring organs. In 1983, I testified before the Sen-

KENNEDY INSTITUTE OF ETHICS JOURNAL • MARCH 2003

ate Subcommittee for Investigations and Oversight of the Committee on Science and Technology in its hearings on "Procurement and Allocation of Human Organs for Transplantation" (Veatch 1984). These hearings led to the passage of the National Organ Transplantation Act, including its title III on the "Prohibition of Organ Purchases," which states that it is unlawful for any person to knowingly acquire, receive, or otherwise transfer any human organ for valuable consideration for use in human transplantation" if the transfer affects interstate commerce (National Organ Transplant Act 1984). In that hearing, I, and almost everyone else involved, endorsed the prohibition on marketing of organs in the United States. Part of the motivation was the testimony of a physician named Barry Jacobs who was proposing to become a broker in human organs who would connect, for a fee, those who wanted to sell and those who wanted to buy. The impression he left was one of the worst imaginable. Even those who came into the sessions open to the possibility of some kind of financially-based incentive system to encourage organ procurement left appalled at the possibility that organs might be marketed to the highest bidder like deodorant or potato chips. Any possibility of a more sophisticated and regulated market seemed lost in the huckster-quality of his presentation. More recent proposals, for example, to separate the use of markets in the procurement of organs from their use in allocating organs (Cohen 1989, p. 33; Hansmann 1989, p. 62; Gill and Sade 2002, p. 19) were not yet on the horizon. Under these proposals, economic incentives would be used to encourage people to provide organs to a national, governmental organ procurement agency while that agency would use medical criteria to allocate the organs independent of recipients' ability to pay. The financial incentive would be designed to overcome inertia and presumably would increase supply while not permitting ability to pay to influence who ended up with the organs.

In the 1983 hearings, I stated that I was, for the time, opposed to permitting economic transactions even in the procurement of organs. My opposition was based on the belief that it would be the very poor who would differentially feel pressured to consent to selling their organs, either while alive or after their deaths. What was unethical, I suggested, was that the ones contemplating the authorization of economic incentives to procure organs—i.e., the United States Congress—had at their disposal the means to address the desperate situations of the very poor in the United States. They could rather easily have raised the minimum wage, offered a guaranteed annual income, provided a minimally decent standard of living for all in the United States, or undertaken some other plan to address the desperation of the poorest of the poor. It was the fact that the decision makers , in effect, would be forcing the poor to sell their organs by withholding alternative means of addressing their problems that made an American policy of legalizing a market in organs unethical.

I was aware at the time and have stated publicly since then that the same reasons for banning a market in organs might not apply in some other cultures (Veatch 2000, p. 152). A Bombay physician, K. C. Reddy, has conducted such a market, functioning as broker in what appears to be a reputable alternative to an uncontrolled back-alley system outside of medical supervision (Reddy 1992). I have met with Dr. Reddy and found his case for such a market in Bombay credible. I came away with an acute sense that I, as a Westerner, did not have adequate knowledge to assess whether the Indian government and the elites of Bombay had the resources necessary to address in some other manner the desperation of those selling their kidneys through Dr. Reddy.[6] My judgment in 1983 and still today is limited to the relatively wealthy United States in which I remain convinced that the needs of the very poor could be met by some other means thus removing the concern that any resident of the United States would find the offer of an incentive to part with his or her organs irresistibly attractive. It was the fact that the legislators considering whether to ban markets in organs had the resources to address in other ways the needs of those who might find a market irresistibly attractive that led me to testify against legalization of a market.

IS IT TIME TO REASSESS?

At the time I testified in 1983 against legalization of a market in organs I said that it was with ambivalence that I endorsed a law that would block the access of the very poor to a means of addressing their desperation. I said at the time that, if the United States continued to refuse to provide a decent minimum standard of living, the issue would have to be reexamined. In particular, I said that, if the problem was not addressed in the next 20 years, we as a society would have to re-think the prohibition on marketing organs.

That 20 years has now passed. It is clear that, although the standard of living of some of the very worst off members of our society has improved at least marginally, others still are being forced to live at intolerably low standards of living. Single parents are raising large numbers of children on irresponsibly low levels of resources. People are still homeless, chronically unemployed, and without basic medical care. We have had more

KENNEDY INSTITUTE OF ETHICS JOURNAL • MARCH 2003

than one opportunity to pass universal health insurance, provide a minimally decent standard of living, and guarantee a job to everyone who is willing and able to work. We have not done so.

There are still people desperate to provide the most basic necessities for themselves and their families. The kidney in their body may be their most valuable and marketable possession. They might be quite willing to adjust their values and their priorities to consent to either cadaveric or live organ procurement in exchange for an economic payment.

The ethical situation is similar to that of 1983 with one exception. We now have a situation in which a wealthy society still has the capacity to meet the basic needs of all residents, but now has demonstrated that it is unwilling to do so. An offer to the poorest of the poor to permit them to sell their organs might still be irresistibly attractive. It is still an immoral offer provided those making the offer have the resources to address those needs in some other way.

What then is the critical difference? Our society now has demonstrated a moral weakness of the will to address those needs by some other means. If it is immoral to make an offer to buy organs from someone who is desperate because those making the offer refuse to make available the alternative solutions, it must be even more immoral to continue under these circumstances to withhold the right of the desperate to market the one valuable commodity they possess. If we are a society that deliberately and systematically turns its back on the poor, we must confess our indifference to the poor and lift the prohibition on the one means they have to address their problems themselves.

It is thus with shame and some bitterness that I propose that the time has come to lift the ban on marketing organs. There has never been any serious moral problem with permitting financial incentives to nudge middle and upper class people to think about their willingness to consent to organ procurement. The offer has never been irresistible to them. For those who do find such an offer irresistible, it is that very desperation that requires that, if we are going to intentionally withhold the alternative solutions, we must at least get out of the way and let them address the problem themselves in the best way that they can. In a strange twist, the very same reason that made a market in organs unethical 20 years ago, today makes it a moral necessity, at least if we continue to live in a society in which desperate poverty is tolerated amidst affluence. The time has come to admit defeat, join with the conservatives who have always accepted monetizing of the body, and legalize financial incentives to encourage

VEATCH • WHY LIBERALS SHOULD ACCEPT FINANCIAL INCENTIVES

consent to procure organs from both cadaveric and living sources. They will no longer be donors, they will be vendors selling their bodies because the alternatives are all foreclosed to them.

NOTES

1. The memorial is described at the UNOS web site under the heading "UNOS National Donor Memorial Plans Take Shape." The full account can be located on the UNOS site (*http://www.unos.org/frame_Default.asp? Category=Newsroom*) and scrolling down to the story dated 18 July 2002.
2. In 1999, 36,952 organ transplant candidates were added to the waiting list while only 10,659 organs were donated.
3. Apparently, the present policy is to pay a maximum of $300 per donor and to limit payments to family expenses related to the death of the one who is the source of the organs.
4. One might argue to the contrary that in many cases the better educated and higher income members of the population are actually less opposed to organ procurement and therefore more susceptible to the power of incentives to overcome inertia. Many who are poorly educated may be more influenced by fundamentalist religious factors, alienation from the medical establishment, and unexamined psychological revulsion than are the higher socioeconomic strata (Callender 1996). Someone who believes that God will provide a bodily resurrection and worries about being resurrected without all his or her organs may be totally immune from economic incentives to provide organs. For someone with religious objections, what may be needed is a more sophisticated theological education. At least within Christianity, concern about the state of the body has been a worry since the Middle Ages. Sophisticated orthodox Christians affirm a resurrection of the "new and perfect" body—sort of a completely fixed copy of one's present earthly body. This doctrine was a great comfort to medieval Christians who worried about a loved one whose body was consumed in a fire or was damaged in a crushing accident. However, getting poorly educated fundamentalists either to understand this doctrine or to adopt a more secular skepticism about any form of bodily resurrection is a complex undertaking.
5. This analysis, which rests on whether the one making the offer could make other options available, follows closely my discussion years ago of the Krugman Willowbrook experiments in which a researcher wanting to study hepatitis went to a facility for the mentally retarded in which hepatitis was endemic and offered parents of newly arriving children the option of a clean, safe, hepatitis-free ward if only they would volunteer to permit him to ad-

KENNEDY INSTITUTE OF ETHICS JOURNAL • MARCH 2003

minister hepatitis intentionally for the purposes of testing his vaccine. He relied on the fact that the children were going to get hepatitis anyway to justify his administering hepatitis to them for research purposes. My claim was that, if the researcher had the power to use his medical skills and administrative authority to clean up the standard wards, it would be immoral to refuse to clean up those wards and to take advantage of the parents' desperate desire for a clean ward to obtain parental permission to intentionally give the children hepatitis. If, however, cleaning up the standard wards was beyond the researcher's ability, then his offer might be more justified (see Veatch 1974).

6. I also am aware that recent evidence suggests that the poor who have sold their organs in India may not have come out as medically or financially well off as expected and that many have reported that they would not engage in the sale if they had it to do over again (Goyal et al. 2002). I am in no way suggesting that a market in organs—particularly a market in organs procured from the living—is a prudent policy, merely that the traditional moral arguments about discrimination and coercion against the poor may not stand up to moral scrutiny.

REFERENCES

Alexander, J. Wesley. 1992. Pro: Rewarded Gifting Should Be Tried. *Transplantation & Immunology Letter* 8 (1): 4, 6.

American Medical Association. Council on Ethical and Judicial Affairs. 1995. Financial Incentives for Organ Donation. *Archives of Internal Medicine* 155: 581–89.

Banks, Gloria J. 1995. Legal & Ethical Safeguards: Protection of Society's Most Vulnerable Participants in a Commercialized Organ Transplantation System. *American Journal of Law & Medicine* 21: 45–110.

Callender, Clive. 1996. Testimony of Group 13. Presented at Increasing Organ Donation Liver Allocation, 10–12 December, Natcher Center, National Institutes of Health, Bethesda, MD.

Caplan, Arthur. 1983. Organ Transplants Must Not Be Put on Highest-Bidder Basis. *Atlanta Constitution* (2 October): 23–32.

———. 1984a. Ethical and Policy Issues in the Procurement of Cadaver Organs for Transplantation. *New England Journal of Medicine* 311: 981–83.

———. 1984b. Ethical Issues in the Sale of Human Organs for Transplantation. *Bioethics Reporter* (January): 6–8.

Cohen, Lloyd R. 1989. Increasing the Supply of Transplant Organs: The Virtues of a Futures Market. *George Washington Law Review* 58: 1–51.

VEATCH • WHY LIBERALS SHOULD ACCEPT FINANCIAL INCENTIVES

Daar, A. S. 1992. Rewarded Gifting. *Transplantation Proceedings* 24: 2207–11.

Dewhurst, F. W. 1987. A Computerized Kidney Donorship Register. *Journal of Medical Systems* 11: 381–88.

Dosseter, J. B. 1992. Rewarded Gifting: Is It Ever Ethically Acceptable? *Transplantation Proceedings* 24: 2092–94.

Faden, Ruth, and Beauchamp, Tom L., in collaboration with Nancy N. P. King. 1986. *A History and Theory of Informed Consent.* New York: Oxford University Press.

Gill, Michael B., and Sade, Robert M. 2002. Paying for Kidneys: The Case against Prohibition. *Kennedy Institute of Ethics Journal* 12: 17–45.

Goyal, Madhav; Mehta, Ravindra L.; Schneiderman, Lawrence J.; and Sehgal, Ashwini R. 2002. Economic and Health Consequences of Selling a Kidney in India. *Journal of American Medical Association* 288: 1589–93.

Guttman, Ronald D. 1991. The Meaning of "The Economics and Ethics of Alternative Cadaveric Organ Procurement Policies." *Yale Journal on Regulation* 8: 453–62.

———. 1992. Future Markets: Claims and Meanings. *Transplantation Proceedings* 24: 2203.

Hansmann, Henry. 1989. The Economics and Ethics of Markets for Human Organs. *Journal of Health Politics, Policy, and Law* 14: 57–85.

Kahan, Barry D. 1992. Rewarded Gifting—PRO and CON: Bringing the Arguments Into Focus. *Transplantation & Immunology Letter* 8 (1): 3.

Murray, Thomas H. 1992. The Moral Repugnance of Rewarded Gifting. *Transplantation & Immunology Letter* 8 (1): 5, 7.

Peters, Tom G. 1991. Life or Death: The Issue of Payment in Cadaveric Organ Donation. *Journal of the American Medical Association* 265: 1302–5.

Reddy, K. C. 1992. A Perspective on Reality. In *Ethical Problems in Dialysis and Transplantation*, ed. Carl M. Kjellstrand and John B. Dossetor, pp. 155–61. Boston: Kluwer Academic.

Rothman, David J. 2002. Ethical and Social Consequences of Selling a Kidney. *Journal of American Medical Association* 13: 1640–41.

Surman, Owen S. 2002. The Ethics of Partial-Liver Donation. *New England Journal of Medicine* 346: 1038.

The Gallup Organization, Inc. 1993. Survey prepared for the Partnership for Organ Donation and Harvard School of Public Health, 25–26 March. Available at: *http://www.transweb.org/reference/articles/gallup_survey/gallup_index.html*. Accessed 8 August 2002.

Veatch, Robert M. 1974. Human Experimentation: The Crucial Choices Ahead. *Prism* (July): 58, 61, 71.

————. 1977. Governmental Population Incentives: Ethical Issues at Stake. *Studies in Family Planning* 9: 100–108.

————. 1984. Statement Before the Subcommittee for Investigations and Oversight of the Committee on Science and Technology. In *Procurement and Allocation of Human Organs for Transplantation: Hearings before the Subcommittee on Investigations and Oversight of the Committee on Science and Technology*, pp. 343–53. U.S. House of Representatives, Ninety-Eighth Congress, 7, 9 November. Washington, DC: U.S. Government Printing Office.

————. 1991. Routine Inquiry About Organ Donation—An Alternative to Presumed Consent. *New England Journal of Medicine* 325: 1246–49.

————. 2000. *Transplantation Ethics*. Washington, DC: Georgetown University Press.

Williams, Walter. 1984. Vital Organs—Let the Market Decide. *Washington Times* (19 April): C1.

[7]

Increasing the Supply of Transplant Organs: The Virtues of a Futures Market

Lloyd R. Cohen*

Introduction

There is no mere scarcity of transplant organs, but a severe and tragic shortage. Because price is not used 1) to bring more organs to the market, and 2) to ration those organs among the potential recipients, the quantity demanded at a zero price far exceeds the quantity supplied. The central focus of this Article is a call to create a market in transplantable organs and to use price for the first, if not for the second, of these purposes.[1]

---

* John M. Olin Research Fellow in Law and Economics, University of Chicago Law School; Associate Professor, California Western School of Law (on leave). B.A. 1968, Harpur College; Ph.D. 1976, State University of New York at Binghamton; J.D. 1983, Emory University.

1. I am not the first to suggest that the market may be a useful tool for increasing the supply of transplantable organs to the market. *See, e.g,* Andrews, *My Body, My Property,* HASTINGS CENTER REP., Oct. 1986, at 28; Brams, *Transplantable Human Organs: Should Their Sale Be Authorized by State Statutes?,* 3 AM. J.L. & MED. 183 (1977); Buc & Bernstein, *Buying and Selling Human Organs is Worth a Harder Look,* HEALTH SCAN, Oct. 1984, at 3; Hansmann, *The Economics and Ethics of Markets for Human Organs,* 14 J. HEALTH POL. POL'Y & L. 57 (1989); Mavrodes, *The Morality of Selling Human Organs,* in 38 ETHICS, HUMANISM & MED. 133 (M. Basson ed. 1980); Perry, *Human Organs and the Open Market,* 91 ETHICS 63 (1980); Rottenberg, *The Production and Exchange of Used Body Parts,* in 2 TOWARD LIBERTY 322 (1971); Schwindt & Vining, *Proposal for a Future Delivery Market for Transplant Organs,* 11 J. HEALTH POL. POL'Y & L. 483 (1986); Comment, *Retailing Human Organs Under the Uniform Commercial Code,* 16 J. MARSHALL L. REV. 393 (1983); Note, *The Sale of Human Body Parts,* 72 MICH. L. REV. 1182 (1974); Note, *Regulating the Sale of Human Organs,* 71 VA. L. REV. 1015 (1985).

My proposed solution is a futures market in which healthy individuals would be given the opportunity to contract for the sale of their body tissue for delivery after their death. If the vendor's organs are harvested and transplanted, a payment in the range of $5000 for each major organ and lesser amounts for minor tissue would be made to his estate or designee. The hospital in which the vendor dies, as any bailee entrusted with valuable property, would have the legal duty to preserve his cadaver in a manner suitable for organ harvesting and to notify the purchasing agency of the decedent's condition so that it may harvest his organs. The proposal speaks only to increasing the supply of organs, not to allocating them. Consistent with my proposal, the harvested organs may be purchased by a state agency, an unregulated private entrepreneur, or something in-between, and may be allocated by the market, doctors, a lottery, or any other conceivable means.

In order to be more than an intellectual exercise, a proposed market must garner legislative approval and popular support, and to do that it must be ethically acceptable. The futures market I propose avoids three potential ethical and political pitfalls. First, because there will be no acquisition of organs from live donors, it does not raise the spectre of exploiting the poor. Second, because the market need not be used to allocate the harvested organs, the rich need have no greater access than the poor. Finally, because people will be selling their own organs, their next of kin will not be required to traffic in the decedents' remains.

In addition to being ethically acceptable, a futures market is a robust solution. Unlike other proposed reforms, it will successfully respond to a wide variety of potential causes of the organ shortage. It provides powerful incentives to donors, doctors, and hospitals to participate in and to next of kin to acquiesce in the process of organ retrieval. Beyond that, a market solution is efficient in two senses. First, it imposes fewer additional costs on society or the particular individuals concerned than on its rivals. Second, much like the difference between regulating water pollution with effluent taxes rather than by rules and prohibitions, a cash incentive to deliver organs to the market is more subtle, balanced, and sensitive when compared with the alternatives.

The presentation of the proposal and an expansion of this all too cryptic summary of the advantages of a market solution are the substance of this Article. Before detailing the proposal and its advantages, however, I will review the medical nature and magnitude of the organ shortage (Section I), present the current state of the law (Section II), explore the psychological and religious barriers to organ donation (Section III), criticize rival approaches to organ retrieval (Section IV), and discuss the ethical barriers that must be overcome in designing an acceptable organ market (Section V). A more detailed exposition of the proposed market solution is next (Section VI), followed by a brief discussion of other supply issues

Increasing the Supply of Transplant Organs
THE GEORGE WASHINGTON LAW REVIEW

(Section VII), and a reflection on the ethical virtues of using the market to allocate the harvested organs (Section VIII).

I. The Organ Shortage

We are witnessing an evolving medical miracle. The improvement in technique, the invention of the ventilator and respirator, and the development and refinement of immuno-suppressant drugs—particularly the introduction of cyclosporin-A in 1980 and prednisone more recently—have combined to make the transplantation of human tissue almost routine.[2] At least twenty-five different body parts and fluids have now been transplanted in human beings, including parts of the inner ear, a variety of glands (pancreas, pituitary, thyroid, parthyroid, and adrenal), blood vessels, tendons, cartilage, muscles (including the heart), testicles, ovaries, fallopian tubes, nerves, skin, fat, bone marrow, blood, livers, kidneys, and corneas.[3]

The recently improved success rate of organ transplantation has exacerbated what was recognized as a serious problem twenty years ago: the shortage of available transplant organs.[4] Additionally, other valuable medical uses of cadavers, such as the traditional uses for autopsy, study of anatomy, research, and experimentation, and newer uses, such as employing human tissue in the preparation of therapeutic extracts, create a large and increasing demand for cadavers. For non-transplantation purposes, however, corpses at later stages of decomposition and those having expired from a variety of

---

2. Although the successful transplantation of human organs, *i.e.*, bones, began in 1878, it was only when the process of rejection began to be understood during World War II that real progress could be made. The first major and vital organ to be transplanted successfully was the kidney in 1951. By the late 1960s, with the improvement in technique and the availability of immuno-suppressant drugs, the procedure was successfully extended to large-scale transplantation from unrelated cadavers. *See* Bergan, *History of Renal Transplant Registry*, in U.S. KIDNEY TRANSPLANT FACT BOOK, at v, 10 (1972) (United States Department of Health, Education, and Welfare Publication Number (NIH) 73-335). By 1976 there were 301 kidney transplant teams operating throughout the world, and over 25,000 kidneys had been transplanted. In the mid- and late 1960s, the transplantation of livers and hearts began, but only in the 1970s was the technique perfected to a degree that allowed for widespread use.

The one-year transplant survival rates reached the following levels by 1985: kidneys 92-95%, hearts 75-85%, livers 60-70%, pancreas 75-80%, and heart-lung combinations 50%. *See* TASK FORCE ON ORGAN TRANSPLANTATION, ORGAN TRANSPLANTATION: ISSUES AND RECOMMENDATIONS 17 (1986) [hereinafter TASK FORCE REPORT]. With improved survival rates has come an enormous increase in the frequency of organ transplants. Between 1981 and 1983, kidney transplant operations in the United States increased 40%, heart transplants 700%, and liver transplants 1100%. White, *Update: A Review of Organ Transplantation Policy*, HEALTH AFFAIRS, Winter 1985, at 109. In 1986 there were 8960 kidneys, 1368 hearts, 924 livers, and 45 heart-lung combinations transplanted in the United States. N.Y. Times, Sept. 6, 1987, § 1, at 26, col. 1.

3. R. SCOTT, THE BODY AS PROPERTY 19 (1981).

4. *See, e.g.*, Dukeminier, *Supplying Organs for Transplantation*, 68 MICH. L. REV. 811 (1970).

causes are equally suitable. While those on the demand side of this market would undoubtedly prefer to have more, better, and cheaper cadavers available, there is no dramatic evidence that medical education or research is being materially retarded because of current availability.[5]

In the case of cadavers suitable for organ harvesting, however, there is a severe shortage. These cadavers must be maintained on a respirator and ventilator, contain relatively healthy major organs, and preferably have died as a result of either a cerebral hemorrhage or an injury to the head. The shortage created by the failure to harvest more than a fraction of the organs potentially available from this class of cadavers has become acute and visibly tragic in its consequences over the last two decades. Tens of thousands of individuals are suffering and dying while the organs that could restore them to health are disposed of like carrion.

The key questions are: How large is the demand for transplant organs; and if all the salvageable organs that are now buried and burned were harvested, would it satisfy that demand? Judging from the waiting lists for organ transplants, the demand for organs is very modest. As of September 1987 the waiting lists for transplants were: kidney—10,000; heart—450; liver—300; heart/lungs—91.[6] The demand represented by the waiting lists is artificially low, however, because the lists employ an endogenous and arbitrary definition of clinical suitability. As of 1985 there were 80,000 people on dialysis.[7] While a large proportion of them would probably have benefited from a kidney transplant if one were available, it is understood that there is a limited supply of available kidneys and that most of those on dialysis have little chance of receiving one; thus their names never appear on the waiting list.

At the other extreme, looking at those who die of organ failure, the potential demand for transplant organs is immense, far exceeding any conceivable domestic supply. For example, over 700,000 Americans die each year from heart disease.[8] If those people could be identified prior to their death and if heart transplantation were a thoroughly safe and reliable procedure, all of them would benefit from a heart replacement. For now and the foreseeable future that level of medical expertise is the stuff of science-fiction novels, not of medical practice. At the current level of medical knowledge and technique, approximately 15,000 Americans could benefit from a

---

5. The shortage of cadavers for medical applications is not an entirely new phenomenon. During the 18th and early 19th centuries in England, the illegal disinterment of corpses by "resurrectionists" for sale to medical schools and practitioners was common. This practice was completely eliminated by the Anatomy Act of 1832, which provided for the orderly donation of bodies to medical schools by those in lawful custody. An Act for Regulating Schools of Anatomy, 1832, 2 & 3 Will. 4, ch. 75, § 12.

6. N.Y. Times, Sept. 6, 1987, § 1, at 26, col. 1.

7. Annas, *Regulating Heart and Liver Transplantation*, 25 JURIMETRICS J. 249, 254 (1985) [hereinafter Annas, *Regulating Transplantation*]. The number of people on dialysis as of 1989 is in the range of 110,000. Interview with Dr. Christopher E. Broelsch, Professor of Surgery at the University of Chicago Medical Center, in Chicago (Apr. 1989).

8. R. SCOTT, *supra* note 3, at 45.

Increasing the Supply of Transplant Organs
THE GEORGE WASHINGTON LAW REVIEW

heart transplant, 22,500 from a kidney transplant, and 5000 each from a liver or pancreas transplant.[9]

How many cadavers suitable for organ harvesting are potentially available to meet that demand?[10] The most desirable cadavers, though not the only ones suitable for transplantation, come from people who die of accidental causes. Each year approximately 60,000 people die in automobile accidents alone. The Center for Disease Control estimates that 12,000 to 27,000 of these people die in a hospital. Thus at a minimum something on the order of 12,000 hearts and livers and 24,000 kidneys are potentially available for transplantation.[11] This is six times the approximately 4000 cadaver kidneys donated in 1983.[12] Were those 12,000 hearts and livers, and 24,000 kidneys available, they would be more than sufficient to satisfy the demand for tissue as defined by the current waiting lists and current definitions of clinical suitability. In addition, there would be more than enough to satisfy the demand of all categories of potential transplant patients, other than heart patients, even under the most liberal definition of clinical suitability.

---

9. Callender, *Legal and Ethical Issues Surrounding Transplantation: The Transplant Team Perspective*, in HUMAN ORGAN TRANSPLANTATION 50 (1987); Evans, Manninen, Garrison & Maier, *Donor Availability as the Primary Determinant of the Future of Heart Transplantation*, 255 J. A.M.A. 1892, 1892 (1986) [hereinafter *Donor Availability*]; R. Evans, The Present and Future Need for and Supply of Organs for Transplantation, Update No. 33 to NATIONAL HEART TRANSPLANTATION STUDY (June 15, 1983) (Prepared for the Surgeon General's Workshop on Solid Organ Procurement for Transplantation: Educating the Physician and Public) (copy on file at the *George Washington Law Review*).

10. Note that live donors are a substitute for cadavers as a source of some tissue. The tail of the pancreas, one kidney, and regenerative fluids such as bone marrow and blood may be removed from a donor without causing severe injury or death. Ascher, Bolman & Sutherland, *Multiple Organ Donation from a Cadaver*, in MANUAL OF VASCULAR ACCESS, ORGAN DONATION, AND TRANSPLANTATION 105 (1984) [hereinafter MANUAL]. It is likely that during the fall of 1989 doctors at the University of Chicago Medical Center will remove part of a liver from an adult and transplant it into a related child. Interview with Dr. Christoph E. Broelsch, Professor of Surgery at the University of Chicago Medical Center, in Chicago (Apr. 1989).

11. Cooper, *Survey of Development, Current Status, and Future Prospects for Organ Transplantation*, in HUMAN ORGAN TRANSPLANTATION 18, 22-23 (1987); *see also* S. REP. No. 382, 98th Cong., 2d Sess. 2, *reprinted in* 1984 U.S. CODE CONG. & ADMIN. NEWS 3975, 3976 (stating that "up to 120,000 people die annually under circumstances that would make them suitable organ donors").

Other more optimistic figures of 20,000 usable cadavers per year have been suggested. See Callender, *supra* note 9, at 46. And even those estimates are perhaps too conservative. Extrapolating from a 1972 study of deaths and demands for organs in Milwaukee, Wisconsin in 1966, it appears that as many as 107,000 livers suitable for transplantation are potentially available each year in this country, as well as presumably similar numbers of other organs. See R. SCOTT, *supra* note 3, at 83.

Note also that the clinical criteria for organ suitability differ from organ to organ and are more restrictive for the heart than for other major organs such as the kidney. Hence a somewhat smaller proportion of hearts will be salvageable than of livers or kidneys. *See Donor Availability, supra* note 9, at 1894.

12. Cooper, *supra* note 11, at 19.

The current waiting lists as well as the enlarged waiting lists incorporating an expanded definition of clinical suitability are stocks, not flows. If an increased number of organs were available, the expanded waiting lists would all contain large backlogs of past unsatisfied demand. Therefore, even if in the first year not everyone on the list could receive a replacement organ, after a few years during which the backlog is reduced through death and transplantation, the newly available organs would exceed the newly added potential recipients, and the backlog would be eliminated. So, although with more significant advances in medical science the demand for transplant organs may come to exceed the number of people dying with usable organs, the current untapped supply of cadavers appears to be more than adequate to meet the current demand of all organs, with the possible but doubtful exception of the heart.

II. *The Law of Organ Donation*

Because organ transplantation as a routinely successful medical procedure is a relatively recent phenomenon, no statutory provision for organ donation existed in this country prior to World War II.[13] In 1947 California became the first state to adopt laws regulating the bequeathal of organs. It authorized citizens to donate their organs through any written instrument and provided that the heirs and executors of the decedent's estate were obligated to abide by the bequeathal. During the next decade most other states followed California's lead in addressing the question. The laws they passed varied in their provisions, some displaying little understanding of the urgency with which organs had to be harvested.[14]

In 1968 the Commissioners on Uniform State Laws announced the Uniform Anatomical Gift Act. By 1973 all fifty states and the District of Columbia had adopted it with minor amendments.[15] The principal provisions are as follows:

> 1. Any individual of sound mind and eighteen years of age or more may give all or any part of his body . . . the gift to take effect upon death.
> 2. In the absence of a gift by the deceased, and of any objection by the deceased, his or her relatives, in a stated order of priority (spouses, adult children, parents, adult brothers and sisters, etc.) have the power to give the body or any of its contents.
> 3. The recipients of a gift are restricted to hospitals, doctors, medical and dental schools, universities, tissue banks, and a specified individual in need of treatment. The purposes are restricted to

---

13. Prior to the 19th century a person had no power to direct the disposition of his body at death; the right of disposal was in the next of kin. Beginning in the 19th century statutes were enacted to give effect to the decedent's wishes as to place of burial or means of disposal. For a summary of the history of the prior law on the disposal of cadavers, see, Note, *The Sale of Human Body Parts*, 72 MICH. L. REV. 1182, 1241-46 (1974).

14. *See generally*, R. SCOTT, *supra* note 3, at 66-70 (discussing both state and national efforts to legislate organ donation).

15. *See* 2 P. WILLIAMS, LIFE FROM DEATH (1989) (listing a current compendium of the various state and federal statutes bearing on organ retrieval).

Increasing the Supply of Transplant Organs
THE GEORGE WASHINGTON LAW REVIEW

transplantation, therapy, research, education, and the advancement of medical or dental science.

4. A gift may be made by will (to be effective immediately upon death without waiting for probate), or by a card or other document. If the donor is too sick or incapable of signing, it can be signed for him if two witnesses are present. A gift made by a relative can be made by document, or by telegraph or a recorded telephone message or other recorded message.

5. A gift may be revoked at any time.

6. A donee may accept or reject a gift.[16]

The Act provides immunity from civil or criminal proceedings to any person acting in good faith in accordance with its terms. As should be expected in such a sensitive area, the Act has been the subject of substantial criticism. Two sources of criticism stand as markers for outlining the subject of this essay: 1) the statute's failure to mention commerce in organs, which has been widely interpreted as implying the illegality of organ sales at least to the extent of making unenforceable contracts for sale;[17] and 2) the priority the statute assigns to the disposition of the body, except in the case of legally required autopsies, to the decedent himself and then to his family rather than to the state or medical authorities.[18] These two characteristics create a regime that permits donation, but neither requires it nor permits incentives to induce it.[19] Thus far the statute has been judged a failure at procuring the organs of those who have no substantial objection to organ donation.[20]

For a very brief period between 1968 and 1973, some American jurisdictions permitted limited commerce in human organs. Nevada, Delaware, Hawaii, New York, and Oklahoma, while banning payment to living individuals for the promise of the delivery of their body parts after death, did permit contingent sales by the decedent as well as sales by next of kin. I have no evidence that any such commerce ever took place. All but one statute permitting sale were

---

16. R. SCOTT, *supra* note 3, at 71-72.

17. The chairmen of the committee that drafted the Act, however, did not intend that it preclude payment for organs. *See* Stason, *The Uniform Anatomical Gift Act*, 23 BUS. LAW. 919, 927-28 (1968).

18. It has also been criticized for even permitting the next of kin to donate the decedent's organs without the permission of the decedent. *See* Quay, *Utilizing the Bodies of the Dead*, 28 ST. LOUIS U.L.J. 889, 894 (1984).

19. Colorado requires those applying for a driver's license to specify whether or not they wish to permit the harvesting of their organs in the event of their death. *See* COLO. REV. STAT. § 42-2-106(5) (1981). Sixty percent of those who apply for a license have opted to be potential donors. *See* Overcast, Evans, Bowen, Hoe & Livak, *Problems in the Identification of Potential Organ Donors*, 251 J. A.M.A. 1559, 1560 (1984).

20. *See, e.g.,* Weissman, *Why the Uniform Anatomical Gift Act Has Failed*, 116 TR. & EST. 264, 266 (1977).

effectively abolished by the universal adoption and subsequent interpretation of the Uniform Anatomical Gift Act.[21] Mississippi is the one jurisdiction that still authorizes its citizens to sell their body parts to hospitals to be delivered after their death.[22]

Although organ donation and transplantation have traditionally been the exclusive province of state law, in October, 1984, the President signed the National Organ Transplant Act.[23] Its primary provisions are 1) the creation of a 25-man committee to make recommendations to and through the office of the Secretary of Health and Human Services;[24] (2) the authorization to the Secretary to make grants to qualified organ procurement agencies,[25] an expenditure of some $70,000,000 annually;[26] and 3) the creation of a National Organ Procurement and Transplantation Network to match organ donors with those who need transplants.[27] The one substantive provision prohibits and criminalizes the purchase of all transplant tissue, with the exception of blood.[28] If the absence of specific statutory provision in the Uniform Anatomical Gift Act left any ambiguity on the question of sale, that uncertainty is now at an end. The law of the United States prohibits the purchase of human organs for transplantation, at least to the extent that it "affects interstate commerce," and specifies a punishment of a fine of $50,000, or five years in jail, or both.[29] Given the Supreme Court's broad reading of the Commerce Clause, it is doubtful that intra-state sales would escape federal jurisdiction.

More recently the federal government has gone further in its efforts to encourage organ harvesting. As of October 1, 1987, pursuant to a provision of the 1986 Omnibus Budget Reconciliation Act, hospitals may not participate in Medicare and Medicaid unless they establish "written protocols for the identification of potential organ donors."[30] The protocols must embody procedures by which families of potential donors are informed in a "discret[e] and sensitiv[e]" manner of their option to donate organs.[31] It is too early and the law is too ambiguous in its mandate to know whether it will have a substantial impact on the amount of organs harvested.

III. *Psychological and Religious Barriers to Organ Donation*

The human body is a peculiar thing. At the moment of death, it is

---

21. *See* R. SCOTT, *supra* note 3, at 190.
22. *See* MISS. CODE ANN. § 41-39-9 (1972 & Supp. 1988).
23. Pub. L. No. 98-507, 98 Stat. 2339 (codified as amended at 42 U.S.C. §§ 273-274e (Supp. IV 1986)).
24. 42 U.S.C. § 273 note (Supp. IV 1986).
25. *Id.* § 273(a).
26. *See* H.R. REP. No. 769, 98th Cong., 2d Sess. 3 (1984) (stating that in 1984, "the federal government spen[t] in excess of $70 million per year to fund 110 separate organ procurement agencies").
27. 42 U.S.C. § 274(b)(2) (Supp. IV 1986).
28. *Id.* § 274e.
29. *Id.* § 274e(b).
30. *Id.* § 1320b-8(a)(1)(A).
31. *Id.* § 1320b-8(a)(1)(A)(ii). *See generally* 2 P. WILLIAMS, *supra* note 15.

transformed from the exalted state of the corporeal incarnation of the human spirit to the irreversible status of a cadaver. It is understandably difficult for people to immediately recognize and accept such an awesome transformation. If an unwillingness to acknowledge this incomprehensible change were widely and deeply held, it is doubtful that any voluntary system of organ acquisition would be very successful. Disregarding for a moment the question of the weight of such quasi-religious concerns, it is clear that they are present. Even atheists do not usually divorce themselves from the symbolic recognition of the sanctity of the human body; few will that their physical remains be treated as mere carrion.

The question though is not whether there are barriers to organ donation but what is the strength of those barriers. Empirical evidence suggests that aesthetic/ethical/religious barriers to organ donation are not very powerful. In Colorado, where acquiring a driver's license requires that the applicant state whether he is willing to be an organ donor, sixty percent of the population answer in the affirmative.[32] A 1985 Gallup poll estimated that seventy-five percent of all American adults approved of the concept of organ donation and transplantation. Nevertheless, only twenty-seven percent were willing to donate their own organs in the event of their death, and only seventeen percent claimed to have signed organ donor cards. Those who refused to be organ donors cited the following reasons: (1) a fear that their death would be hastened by over-eager doctors; (2) aesthetic or religious objections to being dismembered; and (3) an unwillingness to think about their own mortality.[33]

While all of the proferred reasons seem plausible, none is of a character that precludes organ donation in the face of some reasonably strong incentive. The fear of over-eager doctors is not irrational. That there are procedural safeguards in place to prevent just such abuse is itself evidence of some real possibility of its occurrence. Those safeguards as well as the ethical and other constraints on physicians seem to be effective. I have come across no evidence that anyone has ever been prematurely declared dead as a result of agreeing to be an organ donor. Although unsupported by any empirical evidence, the fear is undoubtedly real. It is unlikely, however, absent the publication of actual occurrences, that this fear is a serious barrier to organ donation.[34]

---

32. *See* sources cited *supra* note 19.

33. MATHIEU, *Introduction*, in ORGAN SUBSTITUTION TECHNOLOGY 34 (D. Mathieu ed. 1988). *See also* TASK FORCE REPORT, *supra* note 2, at 37 ("[A] large majority of [Americans] are supportive of organ donation and consider it praiseworthy.").

34. The fear of the premature declaration of one's death appears to have been both more common and more reasonable in earlier eras. In the 19th century there were a number of widely publicized stories of apparently dead individuals regaining consciousness as their coffins were about to be lowered into the grave. From 1868 to 1925, 22

If the second category of objections, religious and aesthetic concerns, were strongly and universally held by those unwilling to donate their organs, it would be doubtful that any market solution would provide a marked increase in organ donation. At the same time it is equally doubtful that any non-voluntary legal solution would either have much chance of legislative approval or be very effective. The only prospect of a legislative solution to the problem rather than a social, psychological, or religious evolution is that the religious and aesthetic objections to donating one's organs are not strongly and universally held.

Both the results of the Gallup poll and the response of Colorado drivers suggests that these objections are indeed weak. As the Gallup poll reveals, seventy-five percent express no objection in theory to organ donation. Their unwillingness to donate is personal rather than doctrinal. All of the major Eastern and Western religions recognize a modern exception to the rule of dignified disposal of the physical remains of the deceased when there is a valuable medical use for the cadaver. The willingness of people to permit such a use of their own or their relatives' bodies varies depending on religious affiliation and fervor, and most importantly, on the purpose for which the body is to be employed. Transplantation is a particularly favored use of the remains even by those who have religious objections to other uses of the cadaver. Orthodox Jews, for example, who in Israel have periodically fought politically with physicians and physically with police over the question of the use of cadavers for medical research and teaching, are willing to permit transplantation.[35]

The final reason for not donating cited by those participating in the Gallup poll, an unwillingness to think about their own mortality, is probably the most important barrier to organ donation. In his treatise on death, Ernest Becker argues that the fear of death is universal and "haunts the human animal like nothing else; it is a mainspring of human activity—activity designed largely to avoid the fatality of death, to overcome it by denying in some way that it is the final destiny of man."[36] And Freud has said:

> Our own death is indeed unimaginable, and whenever we make the attempt to imagine it we can perceive that we really survive as spectators. Hence . . . at bottom no one believes in his own death,

---

separate inventions were patented in the United States to permit a mistakenly buried person to notify the world that he was alive. R. SCOTT, *supra* note 3, at 148-49.

  Such mistaken premature burial is not entirely a thing of the past. In August, 1988, a representative of a funeral parlor was summoned to a nursing home to remove the body of a 90 year-old woman who had died during the night. By mistake he removed her semi-comatose roommate. The error was discovered by a nursing home attendant before the lady was laid to permanent rest. *The Continuing Crisis*, 22 AM. SPECTATOR, Jan. 1989, at 8.

  35. *See* N. Rabinovitch, *What is the Halakhah [Jewish Law] for Organ Transplants?*, in JEWISH BIOETHICS 351 (F. Rosner & J. Bleich eds. 1979); Rosner, *Organ Transplants: The Jewish Viewpoint*, 3 J. THANATOLOGY 233 (1975). For a discussion of the doctrinal roots of the Jewish objection to autopsy, see Lauterbach, *The Jewish Attitude Toward Autopsy*, 35 CENT. CONF. AM. RABBIS Y.B. 130, 132 (1925).

  36. E. BECKER, THE DENIAL OF DEATH, at ix (1973).

or to put the same thing in another way, in the unconscious every one of us is convinced of his own immortality.[37]

Death comes inevitably to all, painfully to most, and suddenly to many. Being asked when healthy to volunteer to be dismembered at the time of one's death compels the recognition of both the inevitability of one's mortality and its temporal uncertainty. To actually make the donation is to unequivocally affirm that recognition. Most of us would, for better or worse, prefer to remain oblivious to the angel of death resting on our shoulders. That eighty percent of Americans die without a will is suggestive that even when there are compensating personal benefits, we are reluctant to come to grips with our own mortality.[38]

All of the reasons given by the respondents to the Gallup poll appear authentic, and thus in a sense the barriers to organ donations are indeed medical, psychological, religious, social, and aesthetic. Delving too deeply into the root causes of the barriers to organ donation, however, obscures the problem with too much detail. Although social, religious, medical, and psychological issues are at play, the uneasiness generated over donating one's organs does not operationally distinguish it from a host of other activities in which individuals engage despite deep-seated antipathies to the contrary. I would rather not serve on committees, grade exams, or clean public toilets. While extensive discussion with a psychiatrist might reveal the psychological or ontological root of my aversions and even eliminate them, that is hardly the most efficient way of overcoming them. I perform the first two noxious activities despite my antipathy because I am compensated for doing so, and if sufficiently compensated I would even overcome my deep-rooted neurotic aversion to human excrement and perform the third task as well. In the same spirit, all of the objections given by the respondents to the Gallup poll are costs that prospective donors must incur. The respondents were unwilling to donate because they were being asked to assume costs without being offered a sufficient compensating benefit.

IV. Rival Approaches to Organ Retrieval

The system of organ procurement that prevailed in this country until 1987, donation, and its three rivals, escheatage, sale, and the post-1987 required request, have much in common as they are all

---

37. S. FREUD, *Our Attitude Towards Death*, in 4 COLLECTED PAPERS 304-05 (1956).
38. Hoffmaster, *Freedom to Choose and Freedom to Lose: The Procurement of Cadaver Organs for Transplantation*, 17 TRANSPLANTATION PROC. 24, 29 (Supp. IV 1985). One must keep in mind, however, that there are costs to making a will, and for many people there are no compensating benefits.

motivated by similar values. Each seeks to preserve life and reduce suffering, and at the same time to honor the autonomy of the individual and respect the property right that he and his family have in his body. They differ in the balance they strike between these competing goals and the hostility that three of the systems have toward the use of the market. What follows is a discussion and critique of donation, escheatage, and required request.

A. Donation[39]

The pure donation system focused on a presumed unwillingness of people to donate. The public was informed in various ways of the virtuous nature of organ donation and was asked to sign donor cards at a time when they were in otherwise excellent health. When a signed organ donor card was not found, and often even if it was, medical professionals acting as agents of those who could make good use of the body parts of the deceased, observing due care to prevent a conflict of interest and to avoid badgering the next of kin, were expected to inform them of the option of donating the organs.[40] The only financial inducement they were, and still are, permitted to offer was payment for any future expenses attendant to the organ harvesting procedure.[41]

The singular failing of this approach was that it only succeeded in recovering a tiny proportion of the available organs. Considering the many valuable, even vital, uses for human remains and the absence of strong moral or aesthetic reasons not to use them, it was scandalous that perhaps ninety percent of the usable bodies went to waste.[42] Despite extensive campaigns only a trivial number of people signed organ donor cards,[43] and only a small number of next of kin were successfully approached for organ donation.

The cause of this failure was fundamentally economic. The healthy individual being asked to make a prospective donation of his own organs, the heirs of the decedent, and most importantly, the medical professional who must take the initiative and the hospital in which he practiced, all lacked sufficient incentive to carry out their

---

39. Although this section is written in the past tense, most of the characteristics, costs, and benefits of donation have been retained in the current system of required request, to be discussed in Section C, *infra*.

40. Although there is some statutory confusion as to who actually has the right to dispose of the cadaver, the next of kin are normally granted custody and control. *See* R. SCOTT, *supra* note 3, at 69-71.

41. *See* MANUAL, *supra* note 10, at 107.

42. Blood donation, though not directly comparable in that it entails some degree of physical and psychological discomfort to the donor, is similar to organ donation because it is a gift of something uniquely human. Despite the many campaigns to encourage individuals to donate this "gift of life," it attracts but 6% to 8% of the suitable donors. *Fear of AIDS Creating a Market in Blood*, Wall St. J., Sept. 4, 1986, at 26, col. 1.

43. Despite the 10,000,000 organ donor cards issued in this country as of 1972, and many more since, the number of signed cards found on the person of accident victims at the time of death has been negligible. *See* R. SCOTT, *supra* note 3, at 83-87. In the early 1970's, after an extensive radio, television, and newspaper campaign in the Minneapolis-St. Paul area directed at 566,000 individuals, only 3100 signed cards were received. *Id.* at 89.

Increasing the Supply of Transplant Organs
THE GEORGE WASHINGTON LAW REVIEW

assigned tasks in shifting these vital organs from those who no longer required them to those who had a vital need for them.

For the healthy individual asked to sign an organ donor card, the costs were largely psychological, but nonetheless real. He was asked to make a precious gift that would become effective when he would be as impoverished as anyone could be; he would have suddenly lost that which was most valuable to him: his life. In making such a gift he had to confront his own mortality in the particularly vexing form of an invitation to assent to his own dismemberment.

Nor did the hospital administrators have any incentive to establish policies and provide staff and equipment to facilitate organ transplantation.[44] Such services were often an uncompensated gratuity. Despite much hortatory rhetoric about the virtue of transplantation, there was usually no standard mechanism for reimbursing the hospital for the expenses of maintaining and transferring a cadaver.[45]

For the medical professionals, the psychological costs of this process were substantial. For the doctor, who only moments before was caring for an injured young man, to approach the man's mother and suggest that she donate her son's liver was and still is an onerous task.[46] Even when the decedent had expressed his desire to donate his organs, the doctor in charge, perhaps fearing adverse publicity and litigation if he harvested the organs without consulting the next of kin,[47] would frequently either not harvest the organs or approach the nearest relative first and ask for permission.[48] This request could not be made after time and circumstance had allowed

---

44. *See* Skelley, *Practical Issues in Obtaining Organs for Transplantation*, in HUMAN ORGAN TRANSPLANTATION 261, 262-64 (1987).

45. *See* ONTARIO MINISTRY OF HEALTH, ORGAN DONATION IN THE EIGHTIES: THE MINISTER'S TASK FORCE ON KIDNEY DONATION 91 (1985).

46. As one commentator has said:

> It is hard to imagine a physician reaching for a telephone and saying: "Mrs. Smith, I deeply regret having to inform you that your husband Thomas had a car accident on Interstate 5. He was admitted here in a dying condition and he died five minutes ago. We very much need his kidneys for transplantation. Will you give us permission to remove them?" This approach seems callous and uncivilized . . . .

Dukeminier, *supra* note 4, at 831.

47. MANITOBA LAW REFORM COMMISSION, REPORT ON THE HUMAN TISSUE ACT 26 (1986). Their fears are not entirely unwarranted. On occasion suit is brought by the next of kin or the administrator of the estate alleging negligence, battery, premature declaration of death, and a host of other causes of action. *See e.g.*, Williams v. Hofman, 266 Wis.2d 145, 223 N.W.2d 844 (1974). No physician, however, has ever successfully sued because of his participation in organ transplantation. Prottas, *The Rules for Asking and Answering: The Role of Law in Organ Donation*, 63 U. DET. L. REV. 183, 190 (1985).

48. Physicians may be wary of brain death declarations, even in states that explicitly allow it, may resent the implication that the patient is unsalvageable, may be concerned about supposed legal liabilities, may wish to avoid extraordinary involvement with the family, or may feel that investing more time with a terminal patient is impractical.

the open wound of terrible loss to heal even minimally. Because of the need to preserve the organs, the request had to be made while the cadaver was being maintained by "life" support systems and still appeared to house a sentient human being.[49] Maintaining the cadaver as a living-dead person was in itself a psychological burden for the medical professionals.[50] It is now generally recognized that for all of these reasons the primary roadblock to organ retrieval was and remains the reluctance of medical professionals to, on the one hand, harvest the organs without consulting the next of kin, or on the other hand, to approach the next of kin with such a request.[51]

For the family members confronted by such a request, the psychological costs were often equally great. When asked to donate her son's liver a mother would often respond, at least initially, with hostility and anger.[52] At the very moment of her greatest loss, she expected to receive charity rather than to be asked to bestow it. One woman who received a request to donate her husband's kidneys wrote:

> In my state of acute shock, distress and grief, there suddenly came this totally unexpected question—I was astounded and utterly appalled at such a complete lack of feeling. . . . To make such a decision for oneself is hard enough but to be asked to make it on behalf of another, while one is so shocked and grief-stricken, is both harrowing and cruel.
>
> . . . Never could I want any close relative to suffer as I had done in making such an agonizing decision during the worst moment of a life time.[53]

Nevertheless, while it was rare that any relative volunteered to donate the organs of his dead loved one, it is estimated that as many as seventy percent of the requests made by a medical professional were

---

Skelley, *supra* note 44, at 263. *See also* Mathieu, *supra* note 33, at 34 (stating that physicians require family consent because of the fear of legal liability, adverse publicity, and appearing disrespectful of the family).

49. The organ donor must of course be declared legally dead before organ harvesting can take place. This has been facilitated by the widespread adoption by the states of the Uniform Brain Death Act, § 1, 12 U.L.A. 17 (1978), and the Uniform Determination of Death Act, § 1, 12 U.L.A. 312 (1980). No controlling state court that has considered the standard has rejected it. *See, e.g.,* Lovato v. District Court, 601 P.2d 1072 (Colo. 1979); State v. Shaffer, 223 Kan. 244, 574 P.2d 205 (1977).

Some body parts, including the pituitary, the cornea, bones, joints, parts of the inner ear, and the skin can be harvested and preserved well after the heart has stopped beating. MANITOBA LAW REFORM COMMISSION, *supra* note 47, at 37. The major organs, however, will quickly degenerate and become useless if they are permitted to remain at room temperature without receiving oxygenated blood. The technology that forestalls the degeneration of harvested organs varies in effectiveness across organs. A kidney can be preserved in cold storage for 48 hours, a pancreas for up to 24 hours, a liver for as long as 12 hours, and a heart for only three to four hours. In harvesting each of these organs, it is always best if the cadaver can be kept on a respirator and a ventilator after the decedent is brain dead. *See* MANUAL, *supra* note 10, at 110, 174, 203-04; R. SCOTT, *supra* note 3, at 88.

50. *See* Skelley, *supra* note 44, at 264.

51. *See* Prottas, *Structure and Effectiveness of American Organ Procurement System,* 22 INQUIRY 365, 374 (1985); TASK FORCE REPORT *supra* note 2, at 43.

52. Callender, *supra* note 9, at 47.

53. Demetrius, *Transplantation: The Relatives' View,* J. MED. ETHICS 71 (1975).

granted.[54] In conclusion, although the costs to the decedent, his family, his physician, and his hospital were trivial compared to the gain to the recipient, those costs were substantial compared to the compensation for those who must bear the costs.[55]

B. *Escheatage*

In response to the desperate state of the organ shortage, some commentators have suggested, and a number of nations have mandated, that if the decedent has not specified his desires to the contrary his body will escheat to the state.[56] The state then delegates the right to physicians to harvest the organs and allocate them. An escheatage, "presumed consent," or "opting out" system has been adopted by at least fourteen European countries.[57]

This attempt at a solution is viewed by some as a moral outrage. In their view, even if this system were far more successful at harvesting organs than the current one, it would still be unacceptable because it grants to the state a property right in that quintessentially private thing, the human body.[58] This quasi-libertarian antipathy to escheatage is rooted in powerful analogies and metaphors. It calls

---

54. MANITOBA LAW REFORM COMMISSION, *supra* note 47, at 28. Other studies, however, have shown less willingness of next of kin to agree to organ donation. *See, e.g.,* Matas, Arras, Muyskens, Tellis, & Veith, *A Proposal for Cadaver Organ Procurement: Routine Removal with Right of Informed Refusal,* 10 J. HEALTH POL. POL'Y & L. 231, 235 (1985) [hereinafter *Routine Removal*] (stating that "only 47% of families gave consent"). Nor is the willingness to donate uniform across the population. Blacks in particular have been relatively unwilling to donate. This has created a particularly severe shortage of kidneys for black patients. Blacks have a predisposition to hypertension, and hypertension is a leading cause of renal problems; thus blacks are disproportionately in need of kidneys. At the same time because whites are genetically closer to other whites than to blacks, a better tissue match for a kidney from a white donor will usually be with a white recipient.

55. The reasons given by commentators from other countries for why people fail to donate either their own or their relative's organs and why doctors fail to accede to the wishes of the deceased are virtually identical to American explanations. *See, e.g.,* MANITOBA LAW REFORM COMMISSION, *supra* note 47, at 23-29.

56. *See* Z. COWEN, REFLECTIONS ON MEDICINE, BIOTECHNOLOGY AND THE LAW 19-20 (1986); R. SCOTT *supra* note 3, at 260; *Routine Removal, supra* note 54, at 235; Note, *Consent and Organ Donation,* 11 RUTGERS COMPUTER & TECH. L.J. 559 (1985).

An even more radical system of compulsory tissue removal regardless of the wishes of the decedent has been discussed though ultimately rejected in the transplant literature. *See, e.g.,* MANITOBA LAW REFORM COMMISSION, *supra* note 47, at 30-31; Weissman, *supra* note 20, at 267;

57. These are Austria, Czechoslovakia, Denmark, Finland, France, Greece, Hungary, Italy, Norway, Poland, Spain, Sweden, Switzerland, and West Germany. *See* Cantaluppi, Scalamogna, & Ponticelli, *Legal Aspects of Organ Procurement in Different Countries,* 16 TRANSPLANTATION PROC. 102, 103 (1984). *See also* Norrie, *Human Tissue Transplants: Legal Liability in Different Jurisdictions,* 34 INT'L & COMP. L.Q. 442, 460-61 (1985).

58. Some commentators even find the voluntary donation by next of kin morally objectionable and thus are opposed to the Uniform Anatomical Gift Act. *See, e.g.,* Quay, *supra* note 18. *See also* ANNUAL REPORT, ALBERTA HUMAN TISSUE PROCUREMENT TASK FORCE 18 (1983/1984); ONTARIO MINISTER'S TASK FORCE ON KIDNEY DONATION, PRELIMINARY REPORT OF THE DONATION PROCESS SUBCOMMITTEE 9, 11 (December 1984).

forth historical analogies to slavery and contemporary ones to totalitarianism. Even when perceived more benignly, as justified by the belief that bigger and better government will improve the lot of mankind, it should rightly give one pause.

At a time when the great flowering of liberty in the 18th and 19th centuries seems to be eclipsed by an ever more powerful state, and entire political systems are grounded in a view of private property as an atavistic remnant of a bygone era, it is hardly surprising that so visceral an attack on the right to one's body is viewed with suspicion and hostility. Nor need we resort to the wider legal and political culture to draw offensive analogies to escheatage; medicine provides enough of its own. Agents of the state and philanthropic institutions when permitted to take a proprietary interest in the bodies of helpless individuals have not always displayed a selfless concern with their welfare. Instead at times, in the name of medical science, they have wantonly endangered the lives and well-being of their subjects.[59] It is understandable therefore, but premature, to react with strong antipathy to escheatage. While persuasive, these metaphors and analogies are fundamentally misleading and inapposite.

Ideologically, escheatage and sale appear to be on opposite ends of the spectrum. But this is indeed more appearance than reality. It is true that an escheatage system can be generated by an ideology that is hostile to the market and the libertarian impulses that underly it. It is also true that escheatage seeks to diminish a person's property rights in his own body by giving the state the position of the remainderman, and that in contrast a futures market would expand those property rights by allowing people to dispose of their bodies for cash after their death. Despite these differences, however, it is also true that an escheatage system can be generated and justified by the same quasi-libertarian motivations that underly a sales system.

Even extreme libertarian property rights enthusiasts recognize that all private property rights are, and should be, limited. For example, if I light a match on my property it will emit photons that will invade my neighbor's land. Yet, no one would suggest that I should have to obtain his permission before I light the match or must pay damages if I do not. The shared appreciation of the mutual gains that accrue from recognizing a limited right of invasion is so obvious and powerful that rather than incurring the exorbitant transaction costs of negotiating for such rights, we recognize them as existing as exceptions in the property itself, and thus these invasions do not

---

59. For example in Hyman v. Jewish Chronic Disease Hospital, 21 A.D.2d 495, 251 N.Y.S.2d 818 (1964), 22 elderly patients were, without their consent, injected with cancer cells to determine how quickly rejection would take place. In another New York case in 1964 and 1965, mentally retarded children were injected with hepatitis virus. Perhaps the most famous American case is that of 600 black men from Alabama who were deprived of treatment for syphilis in order to track the progress of the disease. *See* R. Scott, *supra* note 3, at 125-26.

constitute trespass.[60] In the same spirit, when deciding whether a law that grants someone the right to possess and dispose of a cadaver is morally correct, we must make a judgment, either explicit or implicit, as to what property rights serve our *ex ante* self-interest, or what amounts to much the same thing, what is social wealth maximizing.

All forms of property must be owned either communally, privately, or collectively. The last category implies a collective political decision as to use and disposition. Every political system and its defenders recognize some of each form of property. The differences are merely as to proportion and specific content in each category, which is more than enough to drive men to the barricades. Nonetheless, with the exception of a few anarchists, everyone recognizes a role for each of these property rights forms.

When a particular property rights regime works reasonably well, it seems to those who live under it to have the moral force of natural law or God's will. If, however, changes in technology, tastes, market forces, or some other factor cause it to become significantly less efficient than an alternative, the moral justification of the former natural property right will collapse.[61] Arguably just such a transformation of a natural right is occurring with respect to the human cadaver. As long as a dead body was merely a nuisance for the rest of the community, specification of property rights in the body was relatively unimportant. All anyone wanted to do was dispose of it, and so the next of kin were given the limited right to choose the method of disposal. Now that valuable uses exist for our all too mortal flesh, and the current quasi-private, quasi-collective property rights regime fails miserably in moving it to its most highly valued use, the old regime begins to lose its moral force and we are driven to redefine property rights in cadavers. But in which direction should we move? Should we create more private property in the form of a

---

60. I borrow this example from D. FRIEDMAN, THE MACHINERY OF FREEDOM ch. 41 (2d ed. 1989) (forthcoming).

61. Examples of this are infrequent, but dramatic when they occur. The Labrador indians provide a striking illustration. Prior to the arrival of the white man, the indians did not have a system of private property rights in their hunting grounds. After a few French traders arrived the indians developed such a system. Why?

The advent of the fur trade both increased the demand for animals and changed its elasticity from close to zero to close to infinity. As a result, communal property rights in land led to significant overtrapping. The move to an institution of private property was social wealth increasing because it internalized the externality of overtrapping. Because the changes in relative costs and benefits made everyone *ex ante* much better off under a system of private property rights, the communal right system lost its moral force. *See* Demsetz, *Toward a Theory of Property Rights*, 57 AM. ECON. REV. 347 (1967).

I have argued elsewhere that our intuitive moral sense of where rights lie is intimately tied to social wealth maximization; that is, we demand of a broad class of moral law that it serve our *ex ante* self-interest. *See* Cohen, *A Justification of Social Wealth Maximization as a Rights-Based Ethical Theory*, 10 HARV. J.L. & PUB. POL'Y 411 (1987).

market for organs, or more collective property in the form of escheatage?

If, as some observers believe, the public's reluctance to donate is rooted either in religion or fear of over-eager doctors,[62] escheatage will be largely ineffective in making more cadavers available for harvesting because it provides no inducement for the decedent to collaborate and his next of kin to acquiesce in the process. Most people will simply opt out of the system. The private property alternative of a futures market would be more effective because it would provide positive incentives for people to relinquish their organs.

On the other hand, if the primary reason people do not now donate is a reluctance to come to terms with their own mortality, then a strong argument can be made that escheatage is Pareto superior to a futures market, that is, that it will make some people better off and nobody worse off. Permitting people to sell their cadaver merely compensates them for incurring the transaction cost of thinking about their own death.[63] The escheatage system could in theory make at least as many organs available without the transaction-cost loss of requiring people to confront their own mortality, and like a futures market, it would also eliminate painful confrontations between doctors and next of kin. Even if people's motivations are not so singular and universal, and escheatage is not theoretically Pareto superior to the market, escheatage may come close enough in its efficiency implications to be a worthy rival, and thus need not be seen as the exclusive project of totalitarians but can appeal to a wider audience with an appreciation of the diversity of tastes and a deep affection for personal liberty.

Can the theoretical efficiencies of escheatage be realized in practice, and if so, under what circumstances? We must examine more closely the relationship between the morality, politics, and economics of escheatage. These are not three unrelated categories. If a property rights regime is viewed as morally illegitimate, it will have scant chance of gaining legislative approval, and even if enacted it will not garner the willing and active participation and support of the citizenry.

Escheatage is widely viewed as immoral. The National Organ Transplant Task Force reports that

> [a]lthough there are recurring proposals to extend presumed consent from corneas to other tissues and vascularized organs, both consensus derived from experts in the field and public opinion polls show that there is little support for this mechanism as a way

---

62. *See* Childress, *Some Moral Connections Between Organ Procurement and Organ Distribution,* 3 J. CONTEMP. HEALTH L. & POL'Y 85, 93-94 (1987).

63. There are those who believe that it is all to the good that people confront their own mortality. Various mystical traditions teach that enlightened self-realization can be achieved, if at all, only if life is lived in the conscious shadow of death. *See, e.g.,* Castaneda, *Death is an Advisor,* in JOURNEY TO IXTLAN 46 (1972). Under such a view, these putative social costs are in fact a social benefit. The approach employed in this text, however, is the traditional economic one of methodological individualism. It treats social cost as the sum of private costs as perceived by each individual at the time he must incur it.

Increasing the Supply of Transplant Organs
THE GEORGE WASHINGTON LAW REVIEW

of increasing the availability of donor organs. It is clear that potential organ donors and their families want to continue to be the
primary decisionmakers. Thus, the Task Force believes that present efforts should focus on enhancing the current voluntary system rather than on reducing the role of actual consent.[64]

When all is said and done, escheatage is still a diminution of the
individual's legal rights in what most Americans believe is quintessentially something to which he has a natural right, his body. The
hostility to escheatage is rooted in an ethical presumption, albeit
rebuttable, in favor of either communal or private property as opposed to collective property. Communal rights to cadavers is an obviously absurd alternative. Private property rights in a person's
dead body, as in his live one, seems the natural choice. Unless and
until that presumption has been rebutted by showing the private
property alternative to be either too costly or a failure, escheatage
will find little support either legislatively or in implementation. The
private property alternative will not be seen as a failure until it has
been tried. Therefore, even if escheatage is ultimately the better
system, it will have to wait its turn before it becomes ethically
acceptable.

The hypothesis that the lack of public approval of escheatage will
adversely affect organ harvesting is not mere theoretical speculation; it is supported by empirical evidence. While it might seem obvious that escheatage would result in significantly greater numbers
of harvested organs, experience has been to the contrary. In
France, escheatage has failed to result in a significant increase in the
supply of organs.[65]

The root of the failure of escheatage is twofold. First, it misiden-
tifies the major roadblock to organ retrieval. The problem is not
people's unwillingness to donate organs, but doctors' reluctance to
take the initiative. Second, escheatage fails to adequately address
the critical moral problem, the obligation that doctors feel to obtain
the consent of the decedent, his next of kin, or both. Though the
law has assigned to doctors the legal right to harvest the organs
without anyone's express consent, it has neither succeeded in assigning them the moral right, nor has it provided them with sufficient incentive to exercise that right. Because many physicians
continue to feel a moral obligation to ask the next of kin for permission, and that is an onerous task without sufficient compensation,
they remain largely unaffected by the law. If even in France, which

---

64. TASK FORCE REPORT, *supra* note 2, at 30-31.
65. *See* Caplan, *Beg, Borrow, or Steal: The Ethics of Solid Organ Procurement*, in ORGAN
SUBSTITUTION TECHNOLOGY 59, 64 (D. Mathieu ed. 1988); Gerson, *Refining the Law of
Organ Donation: Lessons from the French Law of Presumed Consent*, 19 N.Y.U. J. INT'L L. & POL.
1013, 1024-25 (1987); Prottas, *The Rules for Asking and Answering: The Role of Law in Organ
Donation*, 63 U. DET. L. REV. 183, 187-88 (1985).

was quick to enact an escheatage system, doctors do not harvest many more organs than they did in the past, how much more or less successful will we be if we enact the same law?

As in many areas of regulatory law, the initial attempt at regulation fails to correctly identify the problem and anticipate all the difficulties. The typical response is to enact more regulation to solve the previously unrecognized problem. Consider the case of agricultural policy. The initial goal of raising the income of farmers was accomplished by instituting a system of federal price supports. The farmers responded by growing more grain that the government had to store. The government responded by paying the farmers to take land out of production. The farmers responded by putting virgin land into production in order to be paid by the government to take it out of production, and so on.

Similarly, one can anticipate that at the next step down the escheatage road an effort will be made to induce or compel physicians to harvest and deliver all suitable organs. This could be accomplished by giving doctors an actual property right in the cadaver, specifically the right to sell the harvested organs. That solution, at least in its naked form, is undoubtedly ethically unacceptable. The more likely legislative response is the enactment of an expanded set of administrative rules and prohibitions. No set of rules, orders, directives, prohibitions, or guidelines, however, could hope to match the efficiency, subtlety, and sensitivity of a private property regime. Unlike a futures market that would make available all and only those organs suitable for transplantation, the regulatory mechanism is bound to encourage undesired activity, discourage desired activity, and generate a new set of problems and costs.

Escheatage suffers other defects as well. It provides no positive incentive to people to permit either their own or their loved one's organs to be harvested. Thus some potential suppliers will opt out of the system rather than permit donation, and some relatives will seek to prevent harvesting. A more subtle defect is that it will result in the accidental, but nonetheless tragic, dismemberment of the bodies of unwilling decedents. Each system of organ procurement, whether by donation, sale, or escheatage, requires that someone determine whether the decedent has made a choice. Has he chosen to donate, sell, or opt out of the system? While in most cases the correct determination will be made, some errors are inevitable. Two different mistakes are possible: incorrect determinations that one has made an affirmative decision to donate, sell, or opt out; and incorrect determinations that one has not made an affirmative decision. The frequency of the two types of error will sharply differ.

If I have not chosen to exercise the option available in whatever system is in force, that is to sell, bury, or donate my body, a check of the computer files is unlikely to mistakenly find another Lloyd Cohen with the same vital statistics. On the other hand, if I have chosen the available option, but at some stage in the process there is a misspelled name, a misentered digit, or a lost file, Lloyd Cohen will disappear from the records, and my choice will not be discovered. A futures market and an escheatage system will generate symmetrical errors but with very different effects. The market will result in more cases of the failure to harvest organs from people who chose to sell them, while escheatage will result in more cases of people's bodies being dismembered when they specifically chose to preserve them intact. Given the great respect that we accord to a person's desire to be buried whole and given that both systems if successful will result in a large increase in the number of available organs and therefore a substantial fall in the value of the marginal organ, unwanted dismembering seems clearly the more costly failure.

C. Required Request

In 1984 Arthur Caplan first proposed the less radical reform proposal of "required request."[66] It would mandate that physicians ask the next of kin if they wish to donate the organs of the deceased. After a number of states adopted it, the federal government mandated that as of October, 1987, hospitals put in place some form of required request in order to be eligible to participate in Medicare and Medicaid.[67]

The results of required request have been promising. The National Kidney Foundation reports a fifty percent increase in organ donations in those states that have the longest history of such a policy,[68] and Oh and Uniewski report a 300% increase in a pilot study at a major medical center.[69] The Oh and Uniweski findings are interesting for two very different reasons. They are encouraging in that they provide strong evidence of how large and price elastic the supply is that can be tapped. On the other hand, the difference in the results between the pilot study and the statewide figures highlights how difficult it is to adopt and put into operation such a policy for an entire society.

Absent either positive or negative incentives imposed on doctors or hospitals, the legislative requirement of required request will merely be hortatory language having little impact. Doctors fail to ask not because they are forgetful or thoughtless. Asking the family of the victim whose life has just ended to donate his organs is an

---

66. Caplan, *Organ Procurement: It's Not in the Cards,* 14 HASTINGS CENTER REP. 9 (1984).

67. *See supra* note 30 and accompanying text.

68. NATIONAL KIDNEY FOUNDATION, GIVING THE GIFT OF LIFE (1987). There has been an increase of 50% nationally in the number of kidneys recovered from 5070 in 1982 to 7750 in 1986. Prottas, *The Organization of Organ Procurement,* 14 J. HEALTH POL. POL'Y & L. 41, 46 (1989).

69. Oh & Uniewski, *Enhancing Organ Recovery by Initiation of Required Request Within a Major Medical Center,* 18 TRANSPLANTATION PROC. 426 (1986).

onerous task.[70] Therefore, in order to be effective, such a system must offer physicians incentives to overcome the significant costs they must bear.[71] At the same time, because the request itself, even when made with sensitivity, often imposes emotional costs on the deceased's family, care must be taken to craft incentives for hospitals and their personnel. Those incentives should not over-induce organ donation requests in the sense of encouraging hospital personnel to inflict excess distress on the heirs of the decedent by badgering them to donate.[72] The Oh and Uniewski study suggests that such a problem may have arisen in the pilot project they examined. They report that "[c]onsents were denied in three cases, even after exhaustive efforts from personnel involved in the care of the potential donors."[73] Those requesting donation were apparently unwilling to take "no" for an answer.

Even more than in the case of escheatage, what is desired of the doctors is a subtle and sensitive act. They must ask the next of kin of suitable decedents for permission to harvest the organs in a way that both encourages a positive response and does not impose distress on the survivors. How can such a requirement be effected? No conceivable set of rules can be subtle enough to induce those who make the request to achieve the individuated knife-edge balance that encourages donation without imposing additional suffering on the next of kin. Some commentators suspect "that some states that adopted required reqest laws may have been implementing them in ways that created a backlash among potential organ donors."[74]

As an example of the problems in monitoring and crafting incentives for those who must ask for organ donations, consider the following. Under the 1984 National Organ Transplant Act, qualified Organ Procurement Organizations (OPO's) receive substantial grants from the federal government.[75] The recertification rules of the Department of Health and Human Services for OPO's require that they secure twenty-three cadaveric kidneys per million population in their service area.[76] How sensitive do you suppose OPO personnel will be to the feelings of family members when the year is

---

70. *See supra* notes 46-51 and accompanying text.

71. *See, e.g.*, Caplan, *Obtaining and Allocating Organs for Transplantation*, in Human Organ Tranplantation 5, 15 (1987).

It has been suggested that paying doctors a finder's fee of $250 would induce greater cooperation in organ retrieval. *See* Somerville, *"Procurement" vs "Donation"—Access to Tissues and Organs for Transplantation: Should "Contracting Out" Legislation Be Adopted?*, 17 Transplantation Proc. 53, 66 (Supp. IV 1985) [hereinafter *"Procurement" vs "Donation"*].

72. For example, in the case of *Strachan v. John F. Kennedy Memorial Hospital*, 209 N.J. Super. 300, 507 A.2d 718 (App. Div. 1986), a brain-dead 20 year-old suicide victim was kept on life support for two and a half days despite his parents' desires to the contrary after they refused to permit organ harvesting, and the hospital did not have policies in place to cover such an eventuality.

73. Oh & Uniewski, *supra* note 69, at 428.

74. Schuck, *Government Funding for Organ Transplants*, 14 J. Health Pol. Pol'y, & L. 169, 171 n.7 (1989).

75. 42 U.S.C. §§ 273-274e (Supp. IV 1986).

76. 53 Fed. Reg. 6526, 6551 (1988) (to be codified at 42 C.F.R. § 405.306).

Increasing the Supply of Transplant Organs
THE GEORGE WASHINGTON LAW REVIEW

drawing to a close and they are several organs short?[77]

While being sensitive to the dangers of over-inducing requests, one must not lose track of the overriding goal of inducing more requests from reluctant doctors. Arthur Caplan proposes that the law mandate that no one on a respirator may be declared dead, and the respirator may not be turned off until an organ donation request has been made of the next of kin.[78] Such a bright-line rule would be necessary to eliminate the discretion that doctors now have and insure that all appropriate requests are made. Nevertheless, it would be a rule that is grossly overinclusive, and somewhat underinclusive. Because the majority of people on respirators do not have major organs suitable for donation, it would require the physician to make an intrusive request and impose a moral dilemma on millions of people for no real purpose. There is something bizarre and offensive in compelling doctors to confront relatives of a newly deceased person and ask them if they are willing to donate his organs when the doctors already know that the organs are unsuitable for transplantation. As callous and uncivilized as is the request for organ donation, and as horrifying and shocking as its receipt when usable organs may be harvested, how much more callous and horrifying is it when no organs could be harvested.[79] In addition, the rule is underinclusive in that some organ harvesting, particularly of the cornea, the pituitary, the skin, and bone, can take place even if the deceased is not on a respirator.[80]

The required request proposal has a Rube Goldberg quality about it. It seeks to do something very simple in a very indirect and complicated fashion. The reason for the complication is that the goal of obtaining more transplant organs is channeled between two constricting barriers. On the one hand, respect for a person's disposition of his own or his loved one's remains is to be retained. In contrast to escheatage, the state will exercise no affirmative property rights over the body of the decedent. On the other hand, the rights of the individual and his relatives to his body are severely circumscribed with no positive incentives permitted to induce the decedent or his family to donate his vital organs. So the reformers instead seek to apply negative incentives on the doctors and hospitals in the form of a mechanical legal rule that results in the macabre maintainance of dead people in a state mimicking life while relatives

77. Some critics contend that "a policy of required request creates conflicts of interest at the clinical, psychological and social/economic levels that produce considerable disvalue." Martyn, Wright, & Clark, *Required Request for Organ Donation: Moral, Clinical, and Legal Problems,* 18 HASTINGS CENTER REP. 27 (Apr.-May 1988).

78. *See* Caplan, *Sounding Board: Ethical and Policy Issues in the Procurement of Cadaver Organs for Transplantation,* in HUMAN ORGAN TRANSPLANTATION 272, 275 (1987).

79. See *supra* notes 46-53 and accompanying text.

80. *See* MANUAL, *supra* note 10.

are contacted and mechanically asked what might or might not be an honest question about their willingness to donate the decedent's organs. While required request will probably generate more organ retrieval, the improvement will be gained by imposing a large and unnecesssary cost on a great many people.

V. Overcoming Ethical Barriers to an Organ Market

A cash market in transplantable organs would prevent much needless death and suffering. Yet the law does not permit such a market. There are many public policy questions on which the law is opposed to the social interest. In most of those cases one can point to an entrenched and politically potent special interest that is well served by the current law.[81] While restricting the market for transplantable organs is in principle no different, I do not believe that a special interest is the ultimate source of the opposition to a market in transplant organs.[82] Rather, it is a widely felt repugnance to the notion of trafficking in human flesh that is at the root of this pernicious policy. Even if there is a special interest that gains from the current law, their influence on public policy has taken the form of marshalling public sentiment by employing rhetoric that feeds on and is consistent with the beliefs and values of a broader slice of the

---

81. International trade regulation is a typical example of this phenomenon. Import competing industries, such as steel, autos, and textiles, succeed in persuading Congress to pass laws that cost the American people billions of dollars in order to provide only millions of dollars to those in the affected industries.

82. It has been suggested that health insurance companies that provide transplant coverage gain from the limitation on the supply of tranplant organs. *See "Procurement" vs "Donation," supra* note 71, at 56. This seems unlikely. Were there a large increase in the supply of organs and the frequency of transplant operations, insurance companies could and would adjust their coverage, premiums, and reimbursement schedules.

A more plausible special interest explanation is that while *potential* transplant surgeons lose, *current* transplant surgeons gain by reducing both the cost and the supply of that essential input, transplant organs. Although the current means of acquiring organs ensures that they are less costly than they otherwise would be, the quantity supplied is but a tiny fraction of what would be available at even a very low price. Thus, if there were an increased supply of transplantable organs there could be many more transplant operations, and many more transplant surgeons earning high incomes as a result. Potential transplant surgeons, however, are an unorganized group, and thus, incapable of focusing political pressure.

Current transplant surgeons present an entirely different case. They are a discrete, highly organized group. To the extent that they have an adequate supply of organs to keep them well employed, restricting supply not only provides them with a necessary input at a lower price, but also, by indirectly limiting the potential supply of transplant services, gives them a measure of monopoly power. Although some transplant doctors express a willingness to transplant organs from paid donors, *see* ETHICS, HUMANISM, AND MEDICINE 127-46 (M. Basson ed. 1980), three medical transplant associations have adopted a resolution calling for the expulsion of any member who participates in a commercial organ market. The three associations are the American Society of Transplant Surgeons, the American Society of Transplant Physicians, and the International Transplantation Society. *See Procurement and Allocation of Human Organs for Transplantation: Hearings on H.R. 5580 Before the Subcomm. on Investigation and Oversight of the House Comm. on Science and Technology,* 98th Cong., 1st Sess. 271 (1983) (testimony of Oscar Salvatierra, M.D., president of the American Society of Transplant Surgeons).

In suggesting that the policy views of transplant surgeons might have knavish motives at their root, the author, perhaps like the reader, was forced to overcome a naive faith in the beneficence of physicians. For support for the proposition of the less-than-saintly motivations of transplant surgeons, see R. DWORKIN, *infra* note 136.

Increasing the Supply of Transplant Organs
THE GEORGE WASHINGTON LAW REVIEW

public. Therefore, it is the set of widely shared beliefs and values hostile to trafficking in human body parts and the misleading and outdated ethical metaphors and analogies on which they rest that are the ultimate barriers to realizing a market in transplant organs.

To an economist, the problem of valuable organs going to waste cries out for a market solution. When goods are worth more to one person than another, and there are no substantial externalities, the market is a wonderfully efficient mechanism to induce transfer from the latter to the former. The problem in the instant case is that the legal institutions that prevent the operation of the market are not the creation of some bizarre sovereign with an obscure view of the proper role of markets. Rather, they are a reflection of a deeply felt antipathy to the sale of human body parts. Consider for example the following statement by Arthur Caplan: "There is a real *danger* that unless something is done to improve the efficacy of the voluntary system, advocates of a free-market solution will attempt to create a for-profit system to meet the large demand for organs."[83] Caplan's hostility to the market is so strong that he implies that a market solution would be a cure worse than the disease of thousands of individuals suffering and dying for the lack of an adequate supply of transplant organs. He considers the moral shortcomings of a market solution to this tragic problem so obvious that it requires no explication but merely an invocation.

The reason that markets are usually uncontroversial and work so well is that there is a widely shared notion of property rights that includes concepts of alienability. That is, we believe that individuals are entitled to certain property and that they have a right to dispose of it for value. Most of us feel neither guilt nor shame when we sell or purchase goods or services. Nor do we disapprove or resent when others do so. Although this is the general rule, there are exceptions.[84] Certain transactions, although voluntary and between consenting adults, are nevertheless viewed as illegitimate, degrading, or wealth reducing. What are the categories and characteristics of these transactions, and to what degree must or may organ sales fall into these suspect categories?

I have identified four broad categories of transactions that might render a market morally unacceptable to either potential participants or third parties: (1) the degrading sale; (2) the rich man's purchase; (3) the sale of what is not yours; and (4) the sale of what cannot be sold.[85] In the first category, while both the buyer and

83. Caplan, *supra* note 78, at 274 (emphasis added).
84. *See, e.g.*, Epstein, *Why Restrain Alienation?*, 85 COLUM. L. REV. 970 (1985).
85. For a discussion of alternative taxonomies of suspect market exchanges, see M. WALZER, SPHERES OF JUSTICE 100-03 (1983); Radin, *Market-Inalienability*, 100 HARV. L. REV. 1849 (1987).

seller may be willing, the seller is selling something so precious that
no man should part with it. He may be viewed as foolish, in which
case others, out of paternalism, seek to block the sale. Or, he may
be viewed as desperate, in which the sale would reveal a level of
impoverishment of some within our society that we wish to conceal
and deny. For either or both of these reasons, some people would
not permit others to sell parts of their bodies. It is in the same spirit
that we do not permit people to sell themselves into slavery.[86]

The second category of objection, the rich man's purchase, is like
the first in that it rests on an uneasiness about wealth distribution
and its consequences. Many believe that certain basic and bare necessities of life and health—housing, food, and medical care—
should be available to all regardless of ability and willingness to pay.
If there is an insufficient quantity for all to obtain the minimum,
then allocation should not be on the basis of purchasing power.
They are loath to permit rich people to purchase kidneys that poor
people cannot afford. It is in the spirit of this objection that we no
longer allow draftees to purchase substitutes.

The third category of objection, selling what is not yours, views
profiting from the sale of something when you have a custodial or
status right, but not a full-fledged private property right, as immoral. You may not sell what is not yours. The ethical disapproval
is that much greater if the vendor is expected to have a strong feeling of love and devotion towards the person whose property they
hold. For example, consider the disapproval of selling children. A
mother may exercise extreme and onerous control over her child,
but her right of custody and control does not imply ownership. If
there is no ownership then sale is illegitimate. Therefore, even if
permitting the sale of unwanted children would result in transferring them to parents who would given them the care and love that
the current parents are unwilling to provide, those engaging in such
sales would still be treated with disdain.[87] As applied to the transplant organ market, this moral objection surfaces in response to the
suggestion that the next of kin sell the organs of the deceased.
Since a mother does not own her son's liver, she has no moral right
to sell it.

The final morally problematic category is the sale of that which
cannot be sold. Some would assert that one *may* not purport to sell
what *cannot* be sold, for in the very process of sale that which is purportedly sold is transformed and its value is destroyed or diminished. For example, if this evening you wished to make love to your
wife and she were disinclined, were you to offer her cash remuneration for her acquiesence, it is hardly likely to improve your marriage.

---

86. *See* Calabresi & Melamed, *Property Rules, Liability Rules, and Inalienability: One View of the Cathedral,* 85 HARV. L. REV. 1089, 1112 (1972) (discussing prohibitions against both slavery and organ sales from this perspective).

87. *But see* Landes & Posner, *The Economics of the Baby Shortage,* 7 J. LEGAL STUD. 323 (1978). Perhaps if the unattractive metaphor of "baby selling" were abandoned and the language of assignment and delegation were substituted, such transactions would be more acceptable.

Increasing the Supply of Transplant Organs
THE GEORGE WASHINGTON LAW REVIEW

It is generally recognized that sexual union between loving spouses precludes the exchange of money. To offer payment for the act would imply a spiritual distance inconsistent with the marital bond, thereby destroying the meaning your wife wishes to attach to the act. Another example that I recall from my youth is a child saying, "if you share your potato chips with me I'll be your best friend." The instinctive and correct reaction to such an offer is that friendship is the sort of thing that cannot be bought, and offering to sell it makes transparent that it is not there to be purchased.

This last category of suspect exchanges, unlike the others, does not have a natural and necessary public policy aspect. Prohibiting the exchange of money for sex between spouses would be like killing the bearer of bad tidings. If you and your wife exchange money for sex, it is merely the outward manifestation of the degraded spiritual character of your marriage. That spiritual character will not be elevated by prohibiting this transaction. Therefore, it is difficult to see why the state or anyone else should object.

On the other hand, perhaps there is some sort of tenuous externality at play, as though the demonstration of the vacuous character of your marriage were a virus that might infect my marriage. But even if that were true, it is difficult to see how outlawing the exchange of sex for money between spouses would have any but a trivial effect on arresting the spread of the virus of loveless marriages. The loveless marriage will give evidence of itself in a thousand other ways.

Even if a case could be made for prohibiting the sale of sex between spouses, the underlying moral objection, that is, one may not sell what cannot be sold, has no application to an organ market, and a fortiori no comprehensible public policy aspect. Were George to sell rather than give his kidney to Martha she would receive the identical physical object, and while it is true that the awareness of a charitable impulse is missing in the former case, that seems a trivial loss.[88] It is, after all, the same loss that we suffer by permitting the sale of food, clothing, shelter, and medical care rather than insisting that they may only be transferred by charitable donation.

In the case of human organs and fluids, rather than destroying or

---

88. A concern with fostering altruism apparently bulks large in the consideration of the Task Force on Organ Transplantation. They believe that organ donation is to be favored because it "promot[es] a sense of community through acts of generosity," and they attach great " 'value [to] social practices that enhance and strengthen altruism and our sense of community.' " TASK FORCE REPORT, *supra* note 2, at 28 (quoting THE HASTINGS CENTER, ETHICAL, LEGAL AND POLICY ISSUES PERTAINING TO SOLID ORGAN PROCUREMENT: A REPORT OF THE PROJECT ON ORGAN TRANSPLANTATION 2 (1985)).

diminishing the value of what is offered, the vendor for cash provides the purchaser with more than the altruistic donor precisely because he demands cash payment. In the artificial insemination market, for example, those who donate for cash are less likely to have as strong an interest in what becomes of the offspring they sire; they thereby pose fewer potential problems for the recipient couple. Similarly, in inter vivos kidney transplants, psychological examination of the donor is required to weed out those who wish to donate for reasons that portend future difficulties for the donor or his relationship to the recipient.[89] Donating your kidney for money rather than out of love, guilt, or the desire to inspire guilt, will be less problematic for the recipient.

Even if we accept the notion that the donation of organs should be encouraged simply because charity in all its forms is a good thing, it hardly follows that sale should be prohibited. Permitting sale does not mandate it. Charitable donation of organs not only remains possible but in fact becomes a more noble act when sale is permitted. Prohibiting sale only encourages charity to the extent that it diminishes its character. It is hardly an act of great generosity to donate that which you cannot use and may not sell.[90]

The first two moral objections to markets, the degrading sale and the rich man's purchase, are of a single stripe in that they rest on the consequences of unequal distribution of wealth. Were third parties not so important in executing the transfer of transplant organs, these two objections would be less serious barriers to an organ market. Aesthetic and moral objections to the current distribution of wealth or its consequences are far from universally shared. While some of us believe "from each according to his ability, to each according to his needs," more believe "from each according to his willingness to sell, to each according to his willingness to purchase," and still more believe in the variety of positions between these two

---

89. *See* R. Fox & J. Swazey, The Courage to Fail 25-27 (2d ed. 1978).

90. While I can make no sense of this objection as applied to an organ market, it perhaps underlies otherwise incomprehensible arguments. Consider the following:

> That which cannot be bought and sold is by definition priceless. By removing human life and health from the marketplace, we affirm this principle which underlies much contemporary thinking about ethics: the intrinsic, ineliminable, ineluctable value of human life and health. This affirmation is itself a process which can and should be constantly repeated without ever exhausting its point.

Freedman, *The Ethical Continuity of Transplantation,* 17 Transplantation Proc. 17, 23 (Supp. IV 1985). *See also* Lee, *The Organ Supply Dilemma: Acute Responses to a Chronic Shortage,* 20 Colum. J.L. Soc. Probs. 363, 401-02 (1986) (arguing that financial incentives may undermine the altruistic motive for organ donation and fail to increase the supply).

What does it mean to say that life and health are priceless? Does Freedman mean that it is of a nature that it cannot be priced, or, alternatively, that it is of infinite value? If life and health are priceless in the first sense and should not have their sacred spiritual purity soiled by contact with the profane market, one wonders why Freedman does not argue for outlawing the remuneration of physicians, nurses, pharmacists, hospitals, etc. On the other hand, if it is priceless in the second sense, should not he argue for a prohibition of all discretionary spending not related to the preservation of life and health so that all of society's resources could be directed to that singular and incomparably important goal?

Increasing the Supply of Transplant Organs
THE GEORGE WASHINGTON LAW REVIEW

extremes. More importantly, these wealth-based objections make their presence felt as the preferences of third parties. Were George to sell his kidney to Martha, neither of them would object to the exchange on the grounds that George is foolish for selling or that a poorer person than Martha should have received the kidney in exchange for less money. Thus, much like gambling, prostitution, and drug use, wealth-based moral objections to organ sales are neither universal nor internalized by the participants in the suspect activity. Were not so many third parties necessary for the transaction, organ sales would likely take place in spite of such objections.

Were it necessary to overcome these wealth distribution objections in order to realize an organ market, sellers could be subjected to substantial criticism for being arbitrarily selective. It is hard to see how kidney sales from living donors differ in more than degree, if even in that, from a host of other unpleasant, degrading, and dangerous, but legal activities, such as boxing, coal mining, lumbering, cleaning toilets, or collecting garbage, that people engage in because of the remuneration. Nor can transplant tissue, especially bone marrow, be sharply distinguished from blood, the sale of which is exempt from legal and moral opprobrium. I believe, ironically, the explanation for the anomaly of blood is its enormous value—its dramatic and widespread ability to prevent death. The law and public morality will indulge prejudice, cant, and hypocrisy when those who would benefit from reform are few in number and far from here. It is precisely because all of us have been so potentially dependent on a secure supply of blood for so long that resorting to the market system is accepted. In contrast, transplants were a rarity until very recently; hence the prohibition against trafficking in transplant tissue resulted in the death of only a relative handful of strangers. Now, when the prospect of needing a replacement organ at some point is more real, the need to abandon laws having as their only support a selective distaste for the consequences of unequal distribution of wealth will be more widely appreciated.[91]

---

91. Note also that some of the practical shortcomings of a cash market for blood will not be present in the cadaver market. Richard Titmuss has argued that a cash market in blood is inferior to donation because the former results in a greater frequency of blood carried diseases in the blood supply. *See* R. TITMUSS, THE GIFT RELATIONSHIP 157 (1971). For a variety of reasons, this reduced quality of the sold versus the donated product is not likely to be present to nearly the same degree or to pose the same problems with cadaver organs. First, in cadavers unlike in blood, there is no disproportionality problem. While some of us may sell or donate our blood many more times than others, each of us, even cowards, die but once. Second, in the case of cadavers, unlike blood, the altruistic donor is more likely to unknowingly donate defective organs. The decision to permit one's organs to be harvested, whether gratuitously or for value, will normally take place well in advance of death; disease and injury to the organs that occur later will not be anticipated. Third, it is more cost effective in the case of organ harvesting than blood donation to screen out inferior tissue. Not only is there far more benefit

I will not explore and criticize these wealth distribution objections to an organ market any further, for whether or not they have any real moral force, the battle need not be fought. The objections need not be overcome, but instead can be avoided at little cost. In the hope that my proposal when properly understood will be remarkably uncontroversial, I will state once more, and repeat later, that I am proposing neither the purchase of organs from living donors, nor that organs be allocated on the basis of the willingness to pay.

The answer to the first wealth-based objection is that by only harvesting organs from the dead exploitation of the poor is precluded.[92] For in the cadaver market the vendors are neither rich nor poor, merely dead. No one will be forced by the desperation of poverty to sacrifice their dignity or health, or undergo great suffering. At present organ donors are more likely to be rich, white, and well-educated.[93] If donation of one's organs is not now considered an indignity when undertaken by the rich, why would it become so for the poor merely because they receive payment for the organs?

The answer to the second objection is that the proposal speaks only to the question of organ acquisition, not organ allocation. The organs can be acquired by a government agency or licensee and then allocated according to any conceivable criteria. Though there will be an efficiency loss in not using a market to allocate the organs,

---

to doing extensive testing given the greater marginal value of the organs, but it is much cheaper to do so when the cadaver lies exposed in the hospital treatment room.

92. Proposals by academics and attempts by entrepreneurs, potential buyers, and sellers to create a market in which people sell transplant tissue for delivery while the donor is still alive are frequent. *See* Brams, *supra* note 1, at 187 n.13. In the spring of 1989, the relatives of a 13-year-old San Diego boy dying of leukemia placed newspaper advertisements offering $5000 for the bone marrow of a compatible donor. The ads were withdrawn when the family learned that the transaction they were proposing was illegal. *Transplant Reward Offer Raises Furor*, N.Y. Times, June 23, 1989, at A1, col.1. Even if allowed to proceed, the effort would almost certainly have proven futile. Because of graft versus host disease, immuno-suppressant drugs are not effective in bone marrow transplants. Therefore a very close match is required between the donor and recipient. The possibility of a randomly chosen individual matching the unfortunate boy is about 1 in 60,000. *See infra* notes 148-49 and accompanying text.

On the other side of the potential market, every week several people contact transplant organ coordinating agencies and offer to sell a kidney, for prices usually less than $25,000. One Georgia woman, born with three kidneys, has repeatedly offered to sell one of her kidneys to the Medical College of Georgia for $50,000. The intermediaries who acquire and allocate donated organs have consistently rebuffed their efforts. Unlike bone marrow, these kidneys could readily find buyers if the market were permitted to function. Markets in transplant organs surface more successfully elsewhere. Rich Arabs and others from the third world in need of kidney transplants have been known to arrive at London hospitals with "donors" in tow. *See* R. Scott, *supra* note 3, at 1.

As interesting as a live organ donor market might be, it has several substantial shortcomings. First, it raises the distressing prospect of the poor selling organs in desperation. Second, such sales would effectively be limited to kidneys and bone marrow since all the other major organs are necessary for life. *But see* note 10, *supra*. Finally, if the ethical barriers to purchasing organs from live donors can be overcome, then surely the barriers to purchasing cadaver organs will prove far easier to surmount, and because of the much lower value of a kidney to a dead person than a live one, a cash market in cadaver organs would permit exchanges at prices well below the reservation price of virtually all potential live donors.

93. *See* R. Scott, *supra* note 3, at 89.

Increasing the Supply of Transplant Organs
THE GEORGE WASHINGTON LAW REVIEW

it should be considerably less for organs than for other goods and services. The demand for transplant organs is highly inelastic at low prices. While lowering the price of edible chicken livers to zero will induce many people who do not really care for liver to acquire and consume more, lowering the price of human livers for transplantation to zero will not induce a healthy person to replace his liver or acquire an additional one for good measure.

Another important function of a cash market for a heterogeneous good, like human livers, is to enable a sorting out based on the particular characteristics of each liver and each recipient (tissue matching). When the market for other heterogeneous goods is not permitted to operate freely, such as the housing market under rent control, efficient sorting and matching often does not take place. The man in Brooklyn who would prefer to move to Manhattan, and the woman in Manhattan who would prefer to move to Brooklyn, retain apartments that do not serve their needs very well because there is no mechanism by which they can exchange them for others.

While it is conceivable that the failure to use price to allocate transplant organs could generate a similar problem, there is no evidence of a severe misallocation problem under the current regime. Indeed rather than too little weight being given to matching organs with potential recipients and all organs being allocated regardless of whether or not there is a good match, some critics claim that there is a severe wastage of organs because of the inability to find a suitable match for the decedent's organs when such matches are available.[94] This may be the result of the market only being driven at one end. Only those who seek organs have an incentive to search, those who have custody of cadavers do not. I am optimistic that in conjunction with a futures market for acquiring organs, something like the current method of allocation would still do a reasonable, albeit imperfect, job of assigning organs to highly compatible recipients.

The third moral objection, sale of what is not yours to sell, is more serious because it is more deeply and universally held than base concerns about wealth distribution. As the ancient Greeks so eloquently said, the human body is the temple of the soul. When the soul departs, religious fealty reflecting a symbolic awareness of the significance of the event requires that those with custody of the body dispose of it with all the dignity consistent with its former exalted role.[95] They can donate the organs, but because they have

---

94. *See* Prottas, *Organ Procurement in Europe and the United States*, 63 MILLBANK MEMORIAL FUND Q. 94 (1985).

95. A long held and deeply rooted belief in the appropriateness of burying the dead is certainly an aspect of the problem. Lord Coke, employing a questionable etymology, claimed that "cadaver" is an acronym of the Latin "caro data vernibus" ("flesh given to worms"). *See* R. SCOTT, *supra* note 3, at 186.

custody and not title they may not sell it.[96] Some might suggest as a solution to the organ shortage reforming the law to permit the heirs of the decedent to sell his organs on the open market.[97] Such a solution is unsatisfactory not merely because it would face enormous difficulty in gaining legislative approval, but more importantly because it is highly unlikely to result in a substantial increase in the quantity of organs supplied.

The motivation for the legal prohibition is a widely felt religious and ethical repugnance at the thought of mothers treating their sons' livers as a commodity.[98] Mothers of young men killed in motorcycle accidents are likely to share in this ethical proscription at least as strongly as the rest of society. Regardless of what property rights in cadavers the law purportedly granted to the next of kin, few mothers will sell their sons' livers.

The solution to the problem of finding a morally acceptable means of substantially increasing the number of organs supplied for transplantation is the creation of a futures market in which individuals sell their own organs for delivery at death. There is a long history of the legal and widespread sale by people of their blood, semen, hair, and saliva. Unlike your mother, you do have a moral claim to a property right in your body and therefore may sell parts of it.

VI.   *A Futures Market in Organs*

Although it is possible to conceive of the occasional severely injured person moments before his death prospectively and conditionally selling his liver, kidneys, etc., this is hardly a satisfactory solution in the general case. Given the emotional and physical agony of the vendor, discussing such matters would be unseemly and in most cases the soon to be deceased will be be incapable of expressing his desire. The major organs of those who die of disease are usually unsuitable for transplantation. The best organs come from victims of traumatic head injuries and cerebral hemorrhage.[99] By the time these people arrive at the hospital they are usually in a state of permanent unconsciousness. The futures market therefore

---

96. Because the common law of England recognized no title to the body of the decedent in the heirs, and a fortiori none in anyone else, " 'stealing the corpse itself, which has no owner (though a matter of great indecency), [was] no felony.' " R. Scott, *supra* note 3, at 7 (quoting W. Blackstone, Commentaries).
  "Although an anatomy school could have no right of property or ownership in [a stolen corpse in its possession], neither could anyone else, and the only persons who had any kind of a claim at all were executors and close family members asserting not ownership but the right or duty of burial."
Id. See also R. Veatch, Death, Dying, and the Biological Revolution 221-22 (rev. ed. 1989) (listing the duties of the family of the deceased with respect to the corpse).
97. At least one economist has made such a suggestion. *See* Rottenberg, *supra* note 1, at 333.
98. Freedman states that, in reference to transplant organs, "contemporary society makes a considered judgment in a variety of contexts that not everything should be bought and sold." Freedman, *supra* note 90, at 21.
99. The ideal donor cadaver is brain dead but still maintains blood perfusion through the major organs. *See* Manual, *supra* note 10, at 105.

Increasing the Supply of Transplant Organs
THE GEORGE WASHINGTON LAW REVIEW

requires that the decedent make a prospective contingent sale of his own organs at a time when he is in good health.

In its appearance, the proposed market would be but a slight variation on the current system of contingent organ donation. People could be offered the opportunity to sign organ sales contracts when they receive their driver's licences, buy insurance, stand on street corners, or are solicited through the mail. The only substantial difference from the current system is that the vendor will be promised remuneration in return. Pertinent information, such as name, sex, date of birth, social security number, beneficiary, and limitations on which organs may be harvested, would be placed in a computer file that could be accessed by telephone. In that respect it would function much like the National Organ Procurement and Transplantation Network.[100]

Theoretically the remuneration could take three different forms. First, the seller could be paid a fee at the time of signing an organ sales contract for any or all of his organs in the event of his death.[101] Second, the contract between the purchaser and the vendor could be executory for both parties, and the estate or designee of the seller could be paid a fixed fee for his cadaver whether or not any usable organs were harvested. Third, the estate or designee could be paid a fee only for those organs that are actually harvested from the decedent's body.[102]

Payment at death only for successfully harvested organs is probably the most efficient choice. Excluding transaction costs all three would offer the same expected return to the seller. Transaction costs, though, for a variety of reasons, would be much higher for the first two forms of the market. First, given the small probability that one will die with usable organs, the first two plans would require at least fifty times as many financial transactions as the third plan. Second, if competition among organ procurement agencies is permitted, the first two forms of the market would result in the otherwise unnecessary costs of determining the appropriate differential payments to members of various risk categories: should men get more than women, blacks more than whites, the young more than the old, motorcyclists more than automobile drivers, etc. Third, if payment occurs at the time of contracting, much more monitoring would be necessary to insure that individuals did not contract away the same body several times. Fourth, with a system of payment at the time of contracting especially, and even with payment regardless of whether

---

100. *See supra* note 27 and accompanying text.

101. This is the plan advocated by Professor Hansmann. *See* Hansmann, *supra* note 1, at 62.

102. One entrepreneur has proposed essentially this plan. *See* Goodman, *Life for Sale,* Wash. Post, Oct. 1, 1983, at A15, col. 1.

organs are harvested, the next of kin would have a strong incentive to void the contract, and thus bypass the futures market and either sell the organs or bury the body whole.

The law should treat the decedent's body like any other valuable piece of property that belonged to him and was devised or transferred in a will or other instrument. In order to create the appropriate incentives for hospital personnel to take the required action in the event of the death or impending death of a patient, such as maintaining him on life support, determining that he has signed an organ sales contract, and informing the organ purchasing agency of his condition, a cause of action for negligence should be established on behalf of the estate and/or the organ purchasing agency against the hospital for the financial value of the loss. It is important to distinguish this cause of action from a medical malpractice claim. The hospital and doctors will not be expected to perform any arcane, heroic, or specialized medical procedures. In fact, their primary duties will be administrative rather than medical. The hospital will in effect be treated as a bailee of the decedent's body, and will be required to take as much care with it as with his wallet and watch. That is, to preserve it and to deliver it to the proper party.

A few successful court actions against hospitals for negligently failing to take the appropriate steps should prove sufficient to ensure that they put in place standard procedures for the routine harvesting of organs from those who have agreed to sell. Should some doctors still feel inclined to ask the relatives of the deceased for permission, and acquiesce in a negative response, they will receive a sharp blow to their wallet when they are successfully sued by another relative who is the named beneficiary under the organ sales contract; such requests for permission will quickly become extinct. The preservation of the body and the harvesting of the organs without consulting the next of kin will thereby become institutionalized. The purpose and effect of this tort liability will be not merely to align the hospitals' and doctors' financial incentives with an efficient system of organ procurement, but also to reinforce the moral canon that a person's body is in the first instance his private property and that, like other property, he has a right to provide for its disposition after his death.

A futures market is a robust solution to the organ shortage problem. Not only does it directly attack the problem of insufficient incentives for people to donate and for their next of kin to acquiesce, it also indirectly and powerfully attacks the more pressing problem of providing incentives for hospitals and medical professionals to facilitate the process. It is like clearing a clogged pipe with a constant high pressure blast of water rather than replacing the suspected clogged section. Wherever the blockage, now or in the future, the financial incentive will flush it out. Whether the problem is people's reluctance to confront their own mortality, relatives' reluctance to authorize the dismemberment of their loved ones, doctors' reluctance to harvest organs without the approval of relatives, or hospitals' reluctance to establish appropriate procedures, the creation and legal enforcement of property rights in the decedent's body will bring all the incentives into line.

How large a fee will be paid to the decedent's estate for the harvested organs? This could either be left to the market or imposed legislatively. If the former, price will be determined at the point where the supply and demand curves cross. If the latter, it must be a politically acceptable price, in the sense that it is generous enough to bring to the market those who are in the relatively price elastic portion of the supply curve, and yet not so generous as to seriously increase the cost of organ transplantation. I doubt that there would be much difference between the outcomes of the market and a reasonable political process. What might that outcome be? Acknowledging that we are reasoning in the dark and this is but the bare outline of a proposal, I will offer some ballpark estimates: $5000 for each major organ such as the liver, kidney, or heart, and substantially lesser amounts for other tissue such as blood, pituitary glands, skin, bone marrow, and corneas.

After a period of time for the public to get accustomed to the notion, I believe most potential donors would readily sign on to provide their family with what is in effect an uncertain supplementary life insurance policy with a payoff of as much as $30,000. The payoff is most likely to be realized in precisely the circumstances when such a supplementary payment would be appreciated, that is when death comes suddenly and accidentally. It is in just those circumstances that life insurance policies frequently contain a double indemnity provision.

While $5000 per organ may seem like a small fortune to many potential donors, it would be only a trivial addition to the costs of transplants.[103] The one-year cost for a liver transplant is $230,000 to $340,000 and for a heart transplant is $170,000 to $200,000.[104] Five thousand dollars plus additional administrative costs of perhaps $1000 for each heart would represent a small fraction of the

---

103. Such additional costs would be of a magnitude similar to cost differences resulting from the location of the donor. When hearts are harvested from patients in southern California and transported by plane to Stanford Medical Center, it adds between $3000 to 5000 to the cost of the transplant procedure as compared to harvesting the organ at Stanford. *Anatomical Transplant Comm. Hearing, Senate Select Comm. on Anatomical Transplants*, California Legislature (Nov. 4, 1983) (testimony of Dr. Lewis Wexler).

104. Annas, *Regulating Transplantation, supra* note 7, at 250-51. These figures are among the highest estimates offered in the literature. For lower estimates, *see* Cooper, *supra*, note 11, at 22. Transplants of minor tissue and even other major organs are markedly less expensive. A pancreas transplant, for example, costs in the neighborhood of $30,000 to $50,000. *Id.*; Caplan, *supra* note 71, at 5. All estimates of cost in this area are crude and inaccurate. Transplant centers are not free-standing medical facilities, but are rather small parts of large hospital operations. Allocation of fixed costs, therefore, is somewhat arbitrary.

total cost of the transplant operation and further treatment expenses.

In addition to being effective, robust, and morally acceptable, such an organ market would be efficient; that is, it would both generate more organs and cost less than the alternatives. What would it cost? While it would be naive and erroneous, particularly in this case, to treat cost as synonymous with budgetary expenditures, let us begin there. If as many as 20,000 cadavers are harvested each year at an average payment to the estate of $15,000 plus another $2000 for administrative costs unique to a futures market, the entire expenditure will be $340,000,000 per year. That figure, however, greatly overstates the social costs. If the same amount of money were spent each year in some alternative attempt to increase organ donation, such as by educating and informing the public and the medical profession, it would entail the consumption of real resources equal to the entire expenditure, and thus represent a true social cost. When it is paid to the estate of the decedent, in contrast, only the marginal person will have exhausted totally his expected payment as a compensation for enduring the psychological pain of thinking about and acknowledging his mortality. The total of these psychological costs for all those who sign on to the plan will depend on the elasticity of the supply curve of cadaver sales and is likely to be considerably less than the $300,000,000 portion of the expenditure that goes to the decedents' estates. This of course assumes that the psychological cost of confronting one's own mortality should be treated as a social cost.[105] If not, then arguably the entire $300,000,000 paid to the decedents' estates is a mere transfer payment rather than a social cost. Even if some portion of the $15,000 payment to the estate is properly treated as an opportunity cost, in that it compensates the decedent for acknowledging his own mortality in this particularly vexing fashion, all payments above the opportunity costs are a mere transfer payment or producer's surplus. Thus the remuneration could be increased tenfold to $50,000 per major organ or more without increasing the social cost.

Donation, escheatage, and required request are not only much less effective at procuring organs than a market would be, but generate additional real social costs as well. Though clearly substantial, those social costs, such as psychologically painful confrontations between doctors and next of kin, do not translate well into dollars.

VII. Other Supply Issues

A. The "Natural" Gatekeeper?

Organ transplant operations are among the most expensive medical procedures, perhaps so expensive that their benefits are

---

105. *See supra* note 63.

Increasing the Supply of Transplant Organs
THE GEORGE WASHINGTON LAW REVIEW

swamped by their costs. If so, how can the number of such operations be limited? It has become increasingly difficult for government institutions to explicitly acknowledge that they will not expend resources when to do so will save lives. If the public understood that the primary barrier to organ transplantation was an unwillingness to shift resources from other uses, it would become politically difficult or impossible to limit government funding.[106] On the other hand if the impression can be created that the barrier to organ transplantation is a natural or social phenomenon outside public control, an "organ shortage," then the number of social-wealth reducing operations can be reduced in a politically acceptable fashion. Is this a valid rationale for restricting the sale of transplant organs?

At least in the case of the kidney, which represents seventy-five percent of all transplant operations, the central premise of the argument is incorrect. Long term dialysis is a more costly treatment than transplantation for end stage renal disease.[107] Since 1978 the federal government, through the Medicare administered End Stage Renal Disease Program, has undertaken to assume virtually all of those costs.[108] Thus bringing more kidneys to the market would reduce medical costs overall and to the federal government in particular.[109] This cost reduction is of course a gross underestimate of the social benefit of such operations, as it fails to include the value of the transplant operation to the patient, his family, and society from the greater productivity and happiness of a healthy

---

106. Increased proportions of the cost of transplantation are being assumed by the federal government. Two recent changes are the Omnibus Reconciliation Act of 1986, 42 U.S.C. § 1395x note (Supp. IV 1986), which authorized Medicare to pay 100% of the cost of immuno-suppressant drugs for one year after a transplant operation; and as of October 17, 1986, the U.S. Health Care Financing Administration authorized Medicare coverage for heart transplant operations, including the payment for transplant organs. *See* Criteria for Medicare Coverage of Heart Transplants, 52 Fed. Reg. 10,935 (1987).

107. *See infra* note 109.

108. 42 U.S.C. § 426-1 (1982).

109. Estimating the magnitude of the cost savings is difficult and subject to significant changes with medical advances. The entire End Stage Renal Disease Program has a total cost for both transplantation and dialysis of approximately $2.8 billion per year and that is therefore the upper limit to any potential cost saving. Eggers, *Analyzing the Cost Effectiveness of Kidney Transplantation*, in PROCEEDINGS OF THE NINETEENTH NATIONAL MEETING OF THE PUBLIC HEALTH CONFERENCE ON RECORDS AND STATISTICS 216 (National Center for Health Statistics, Hyattsville, Md.) (1983). In 1978 Stange and Sumner estimated that over a 10 year period, providing kidney transplants to 1000 patients who would otherwise be on facility dialysis would result in a cost saving of between $279 and $300 million. Stange and Sumner, *Predicting Treatment Costs and Life Expectancy for End Stage Renal Disease*, 298 NEW ENG. J. MED. 372, 375 (1978); *See also* R. SCOTT, *supra* note 3, at 55-56, 73. More recently the Department of Health and Human Services has estimated a cost saving from cadaver transplants vis-à-vis dialysis of $62,000 per patient over a five-year period. OFFICE OF ANALYSIS AND INSPECTIONS, OFFICE OF INSPECTOR GENERAL, DEP'T OF HEALTH AND HUMAN SERVS., THE ACCESS OF FOREIGN NATIONALS TO U.S. CADAVER ORGANS 10 (1986). Eggers has estimated a much more modest cost savings of perhaps several million dollars per thousand patients over a 10 year span. Eggers, *supra*, at 218.

recipient.[110]

Heart and liver transplants are in a different class. The cost per year of life saved is probably higher for these operations than for any other major medical procedure. While it is beyond the scope of this Article to address the social costs and benefits of such transplants, there are a number of relevant observations that can be made.[111] One can say with some confidence that the costs of transplantation will decline over time and that the decline will be substantially accelerated by a successful organ sales plan.[112] The greater supply of organs would lower the per unit cost of organ transplantation in a variety of ways. First, it would allow transplant teams to move more quickly along the learning curve and become more efficient at performing the procedure. Second, it would allow the human and physical capital costs of transplantation to be spread over a greater number of patients. Third, because most of the costs of transplantation are not for the operation itself, but for postoperative care, including immuno-suppressant drugs and the treatment of infection brought on by the use of those drugs, the greater availability of organs would lead to better matching of donors and recipients and therefore diminish the use of immuno-suppressants.[113] Fourth, it would reduce screening costs per successful operation because fewer patients need to be screened out.[114] In addition, it is likely that there will be unforeseen medical innovations that will make the procedure more successful, less expensive, or both.

If the economics of transplant operations follow the pattern of dialysis treatment, the decline in costs should be impressive indeed. Between 1972 and 1983 the payment level for outpatient dialysis treatment remained nominally constant with no evident decline in supply. During this period the general medical care input price index rose 250%, implying a seventy-two percent fall in the real price of dialysis.[115] In 1983 when the nominal price was reduced further, there was still no evidence of a fall in the quantity supplied.[116] The data on kidney transplants show a similar decline in cost. The average Medicare reimbursement fell from $45,284 in 1981 to $40,252 in 1985.[117] This decline was in current dollars; thus, adjusting for inflation would reveal a more dramatic decline.

---

110. Long term dialysis treatment, though it keeps the patient alive, is not a cheery substitute to a transplant for those suffering renal failure. "Suicide rates among dialysis patients are over 100 times that in the rest of the population." Ethics, Humanism, and Medicine 131 (M. Basson, ed. 1980) *See also* U.S. Dep't of Health and Human Servs., Findings from the National Kidney Dialysis and Kidney Transplant Study (1987).

111. For a discussion of the cost-benefit analysis of organ transplantation, see Centerwall, *Cost-Benefit Analysis and Heart Transplantation*, 304 New Eng. J. Med. 901 (1981).

112. *See* Healy, *Organ Transplantation: Future Directions for Federal Policy*, in Human Organ Transplantation 193, 199 (1987).

113. *See infra* note 146.

114. *See generally* Roberts, *The Economics of Organ Transplants*, 25 Jurimetrics J. 256, 259-67 (1985) (analyzing the costs of organ transplantation).

115. Pauly, *Equity and Costs*, in Human Organ Transplantation 251, 225 (1987).

116. *Id.*

117. Schuck, *supra* note 74, at 171.

Increasing the Supply of Transplant Organs
THE GEORGE WASHINGTON LAW REVIEW

What if the costs of heart and liver transplants do not decline, however, and we can successfully harvest 12,000 of each organ a year; what will be the total cost of transplanting these major organs?[118] Assuming a cost of $200,000 for each heart transplant and $300,000 for each liver transplant, and 12,000 heart and 5000 liver transplants a year, the cost of heart transplants will be $2.4 billion, and the cost of liver transplants will be $1.5 billion per year.[119] If at the same time we can successfully harvest 24,000 kidneys and transplant them into the 22,500 people expected to demand them, assuming an increase of 16,000 over current levels, and that the cost saving is approximately $62,000 per patient over a five year period, then the total cost saving as compared to dialysis will be approximately $1 billion.[120] All of these figures are rather crude and are offered only to give a ballpark estimate of the costs. In addition, they give no hint of the countervailing benefits that will result.

Even if heart and liver transplants are not cost justified procedures and costs do not fall enough to make them so for all those who could clinically benefit, the use of an artificial shortage of organs as a gatekeeper to curtail a hypothetical future public expense would be a most unseemly and invidious strategy. It condemns to death and suffering those who could make use of other cadaver organs such as the kidney for which the costs are less than the benefits. It also severely reduces the supply of a variety of minor tissue, such as pituitary glands used to prevent dwarfism, corneas to restore sight, and skin used to prevent the death and aid the recovery of burn victims.[121] These procedures are not particularly costly, and the required tissue could be harvested as a byproduct of a more general organ retrieval procedure. In addition, by reducing the available supply of hearts, livers, and kidneys, it limits those who are approved for transplants to a smaller choice of available organs and therefore a poorer tissue match. Finally, the artificial barrier of organ availability not only limits those transplant operations that would be financed publicly, but those that would be financed privately as well. It thereby makes it impossible for someone to save his own or his child's life with his own resources, because to do so allows us with greater ease and less embarrassment to restrict others from drawing on the public fisc.[122]

---

118. For the derivation of the figure of 12,000 hearts and livers, see *supra* note 11 and accompanying text.

119. *See supra* note 104 and accompanying text.

120. *See supra* note 109 and accompanying text.

121. *See* Weissman, *supra* note 20, at 265.

122. Much the same argument was raised in response to the Massachusetts Task Force Report on Organ Transplantation.

> My understanding of the Task Force's recommendations is that they would prohibit a person who lives in Massachusetts from buying a transplant [out

Calabresi and Bobbitt argue that a subterfuge, such as pretending that the limitation on organ transplant operations is the result of a natural and immutable scarcity, cannot ultimately survive in a society that values honesty and candor unless it serves some other ancillary purpose.[123] Whether or not the prohibition on organ sales was a subterfuge intended to provide the illusion of a natural barrier to costly organ transplants, this Article, and those that have preceded it arguing for other solutions, lay bare the lie behind the subterfuge. The pretense can no longer be maintained that you cannot receive a new heart because they are simply not available. They are unavailable because of a law of man, not one of nature.[124]

B. Suicide

A futures market in organs, offering as it does the prospect of a significantly greater remuneration to one's heirs, might exacerbate a moral hazard problem. Some may take their own lives in order to provide a financial windfall to their families. How great is this danger? Because of the relatively small remuneration for harvested organs and uncertainty about the organs being successfully preserved and transplanted, an organ market provides only a minimal incentive to commit suicide. Thus the number of induced suicides should be quite small.

If even that small increased incentive is unacceptable, it can be eliminated by voiding these contingent contracts in the event of suicide. The costs of voiding the sale, however, probably outweigh the benefits. The vast majority of suicides will not be generated by the expectation of remuneration to the decedent's estate for his organs. In addition, suicide victims generally have healthier organs than those who die of other causes. Therefore, unless some substitute mechanism were put in place for the state to exercise dominion over the organs, voiding the sales contracts of suicide victims would result in the waste of many of the most valuable organs for little gain. In addition, although this may sound heartless and ghoulish, it is all to the good if those who commit suicide can be induced to do so in a manner designed to preserve their organs for others to use.

C. Murder

People are often killed for money. Selling the victim's body is as

---

of his own pocket]. In effect the Task Force finds objectionable a family's decision that it is willing to sacrifice other things it might consume in order to prolong the life of one of its members.

Pauly, *supra* note 115, at 253.

123. *See* G. CALABRESI & P. BOBBITT, TRAGIC CHOICES 78-79 (1978).

124. Choices among patients that seem to condemn some to death and give others an opportunity to survive will always be tragic. Society has developed a number of mechanisms to make such decisions more acceptable by camouflaging them. In an era of scarce resources and conscious cost containment, such mechanisms will become public, and they will be usable only if they are fair and efficient.

Annas, *The Prostitute, the Playboy, and the Poet: Rationing Schemes for Organ Transplantation*, 75 AM. J. PUB. HEALTH 187, 189 (1985) [hereinafter Annas, *Rationing Schemes*].

Increasing the Supply of Transplant Organs
THE GEORGE WASHINGTON LAW REVIEW

good a motive for murder as any other. In eighteenth and nineteenth century Britain a number of ghoulish murders were committed for just that purpose.[125] Would a futures market in body parts
result in a materially increased number of murders?

While it is true that a cash market in bodies will, at the margin,
increase the incentive to murder and thus the number of murders,
both the incentive and the response should be modest in this case.
Although the financial return to organ harvesting is in principle no
different than any other incentive, there are a variety of powerful
reasons why murder is a much less likely prospect in response to a
market in cadavers now than in the nineteenth century. First, under
the organ sales plan the victim must have named the perpetrator as
a beneficiary. Because the vendor need inform no one that he has
signed a sales contract or whom he has chosen as beneficiary, and
people will usually not choose their prospective murderer, it is unlikely that someone contemplating murder can have much expectation of being named the beneficiary. Second, most vendors will
designate their close relatives as beneficiaries. Those designees will
have an insurable interest in the deceased and will therefore be able
to purchase a life insurance policy on the victim as a more secure
and lucrative means of cashing in on his murder. Such an insurance
policy could be for a substantially greater amount of money than an
organ sales contract and would not be contingent on successful organ harvesting. Finally, organ harvesting requires that the body be
presented at the hospital while the victim is still alive, thereby (1)
creating some risk of recovery; (2) restricting the method of murder;
and (3) providing the cadaver itself as evidence of the crime. Still, I
am sure that from time to time it will be reported that someone has
committed murder for the ostensible reason of collecting as a beneficiary under an organ sale agreement. While this would make a
very dramatic headline, it does not represent a very significant
problem.

D. Stillborns, Infants, Children, and Executed Convicts

Permitting voluntary contingent sales of one's own organs still
leaves the serious problem of acquiring organs from those who are
incapable of forming such contracts, for example stillborns, infants,
and children. In these cases the organs are likely to be healthier and

---

125. The most famous of these were the Edinborough murders committed by Burke
and Hare, who sold some 16 cadavers to medical schools for dissection. *See* W.
ROUGHEAD, KNAVE'S LOOKING GLASS 291-326 (1935).

stronger than adult organs.[126] In addition, the potential recipients are infants and children who are too small to make use of adult organs.[127]

The solution to the problem requires that we find a morally acceptable way for the parents to sell the organs. Standing alone such a sale, even if contingent and prospective, would appear mercenary. If the contingent sale of the child's organs, however, were coupled with a contingent sale of the parents', it could be cleansed of any intimation that the parents were dealing with their child's organs in an opportunistic manner. Their willingness to dispose of their own remains under the same terms and subject to the same contingencies will satisfy the ethical demand that parents show the appropriate degree of love and concern for their offspring. As a practical matter this might be handled by a family contingent sales form.

If the child dies as a result of abuse at the hands of his parents, the sales contract should be voided. Voluntarily aborted fetuses, though far more frequent than children murdered by their parents, present a less severe problem. The organs of aborted fetuses are too immature to be transplanted. There are, however, other medical uses for fetal tissue. Given the questionable ethical propriety of abortion, it is unseemly that the mother who chooses to abort her fetus should be able to profit from this procedure. At the same time it would be a terrible waste of valuable human tissue to simply bury or cremate aborted fetuses and murdered children. Therefore I propose that the state or federal government take custody of the cadaver and sell the organs for its own fiscal benefit. A similar principle could apply to executed criminals.[128]

E. Secondary Markets

The proposed futures market will provide a sufficient incentive to attract those who (1) are currently unwilling to incur the costs of considering and affirming their own mortality by donating their organs unless compensated; but (2) are concerned enough with the financial welfare of their heirs that they consider a substantial yet contingent life insurance payment sufficient compensation. This still leaves open the problem of those who satisfy the first criterion but not the second: those whose concern for the welfare of their heirs or potential organ recipients is insufficient to overcome their reluctance to confront their own mortality.

This subset of potential suppliers could perhaps be induced to sell the right to the proceeds from the sale of their organs to a firm that specializes in purchasing such contingencies for a current cash

---

126. The survival rate of kidney transplant recipients is significantly higher if the donor organ comes from a 6-15 year-old than from a 56-70 year-old. U.S. KIDNEY TRANSPLANT FACT BOOK 21 (1972) (United States Department of Health, Education, and Welfare Publication Number (NIH) 73-335).

127. *See* MANUAL, *supra* note 10, at 324.

128. *See* Lee, *supra* note 90, at 397; Note, *Medical Breakthroughs in Human Fetal Tissue Transplantation: Time to Reevaluate Legislative Restrictions on Fetal Research*, 13 VT. L. REV. 373 (1988).

payment. The small likelihood that a particular individual's organs will actually be used, the additional monitoring costs of insuring that he sells his body only once, the possibility of litigation brought by heirs who object, and the increased transaction costs are all significant barriers to the success of such a secondary market. On the other hand, such a market might function tolerably well when addressed to some discrete segment of the population, groups such as the Hell's Angels, made up of disaffected, violent young males who care little about their estates and have relatively high death rates from causes that leave many healthy, valuable organs intact.

F. Regulating the Market

Every market requires regulation in the sense of procedural and substantive rules establishing how transactions are to take place.[129] Some of the rules for an organ futures market may simply be extended from current practice. Organ donations now are not costless; costs are incurred in maintaining, harvesting, preserving, delivering, and transplanting the organs. Any additional costs generated by a futures market could be subject to the same sorts of rules, and paid by the same party that pays for the transplantation.[130] Other questions peculiar to a futures market, such as who shall be authorized to purchase the organs from the original vendor, under what circumstances will further transfer take place, and when rights to payment on the one hand and to the organs on the other will vest, can be answered in a variety of ways consistent with the overriding goal of increasing the supply of organ donors.[131]

VIII. The Demand Side

I have thus far only addressed the supply side of the problem. The enormous number and proportion of useful organs that needlessly go to waste compels such an emphasis. The demand side of the problem, that is, to whom and by what mechanism those organs are allocated among the potential recipients, though of vital importance to those in the pool, is dwarfed in social significance by what should be the central focus of public policy reform increasing the quantity of organs supplied to the market.

In addition, avoiding the issue of how the supply of organs should be allocated may be prudent because whatever mechanism one chooses it will be controversial. While not logically required for

---

129. For a discussion of the regulatory issues under the current regime, see Spencer, *Maximizing Use of a Scarce National Resource: An Analysis of Alternatives for Establishing Uniform Standards of Conduct for Organ Procurement Agencies*, 42 FOOD DRUG COSM. L.J. 430 (1987).

130. On occasion, whether out of bureaucratic error or otherwise, the donor gets billed for services attendant to harvesting his organs. *See* R. SCOTT, *supra* note 3, at 262.

131. Many of the relevant questions have been addressed in Comment, *supra* note 1.

consistency, employing the price mechanism to allocate transplant organs might appear to be the natural corollary to using it to acquire the organs, and the price mechanism is for many a particularly controversial and offensive solution. Allocating life-saving medical treatment by willingness to pay exemplifies what some would regard as the inequities and not merely inequalities of a market economy.[132] While I do not fear controversy, I seek a policy change and do not wish to distract attention from the major proposal around which I believe a consensus can be achieved. Therefore, before proceeding I reiterate that the supply side proposals are central to this Article and are consistent with virtually any means of allocation. That said, it is of some interest to discuss the moral virtues of using the market to allocate the harvested organs.[133]

A. Rationing

It is possible, indeed likely, that for the forseeable future the increased supply generated by the creation of a futures market will fully satisfy the demand for transplant organs even at a zero price.[134] If that is so, then while there may be those who would object to the wealth transfers generated by the market, they could not object to the rationing, for there need be none. If, however, a sufficient supply of livers, kidneys, or hearts were not available to satisfy the demand at a zero price, rationing must take place, and some institutional mechanism employing some rationing criterion must be created to allocate the available organs among the various potential recipients.

Supply side reform will do much to relieve the psychological burden of this rationing decision. When there are but nine livers available, however, they are allocated, the tenth person in line will be someone capable of living a long and full life had he not been denied that life-saving liver. When there are 9999 livers available the 10,000th person in line is less likely to be able to make good use of it. Nevertheless, as long as there is someone waiting in line who must be denied a liver, rationing must take place, and the gut-wrenching decision of who shall receive a life-saving liver and who shall die in his stead cannot be avoided.

If price is used as a rationing device, the rich may be able to purchase advantages of health that are foreclosed to the poor, and that may seem to some a particularly invidious outcome. Price, of course, need not be used to ration. Consistent with my supply side proposal, one could limit payments to the procurement agency, and from the procurement agency to the original vendor, to legislatively

---

132. *See* Caplan, *supra* note 78, at 274.
133. Markets, of course, have substantial economic virtues. Those allocational virtues are somewhat reduced in the case of transplant organs. The demand for transplant organs is so inelastic at the prices discussed in this Article that price need not be used to exclude from the market those who would receive little marginal benefit from the organ. I am hopeful that price will not be necessary to sort and match organs and recipients on the basis of tissue compatibility. *See supra* text following note 92.
134. *See supra* notes 6-12 and accompanying text.

fixed fees, and have those fees paid by the government. If rationing is not on the basis of willingness to pay, then some other criterion must be employed.

There are three polar forms of rationing: the lottery, allocation by a judgment of deservability, and the market.[135] Each represents a uniquely different way of responding to the demand that the system be fair. Organ allocation, like every other element of a liberal social order must, in order that it be just or fair, embody some notion of equality.[136] Each of these organ transplant allocation schemes is egalitarian in a different sense of that term.

The lottery is egalitarian in that it places everyone who would like a liver on an equal footing. Their names would simply be chosen at random from a common pool. A lottery, however, suffers the vice of its virtue. In choosing between potential recipients it gives no weight to the strength of their desire, the likely medical value of the liver to them, their ability to share the burden of paying for the liver transplant, or their value to the community. Thus an elderly, indigent, solitary criminal, who is almost indifferent to the prospect of receiving the liver, is as likely to receive it as a wealthy young scientist with family responsibilities who could and would surrender a great deal of his wealth in exchange for the liver.

The "deservability" of the candidate is egalitarian in a different sense. It reflects the principle that although equals should be treated equally, unequals should be treated unequally. Deservability seeks to give appropriate weight to the various dimensions of inequality among candidates in deciding claims to the liver. Deservability is the criterion most often employed to allocate life saving medical care. This says little, however, as there are an infinite number of form and content variations of this method. One variation, employed in the past, was the public committee of laymen applying an ad hoc, eclectic, subjective standard. Before dialysis machines became widely available, Seattle, Washington, along with a number of other localities, employed such a committee to decide who would gain access to these devices and who would not.[137] That committee was free to consider any characteristic of the candidate. When certain committee members revealed the criteria they employed, social worth in particular, they were subjected to harsh

---

135. For a discussion and criticism of the various possible rationing schemes, see J. KATZ & A. CAPRON, CATASTROPHIC DISEASES: WHO DECIDES WHAT? 184-95 (1975); Bayer, *Justice and Health Care in an Era of Cost Containment*, in 9 SOCIAL RESPONSIBILITY: JOURNALISM, LAW, AND MEDICINE 37, 38-42 (L. Hodges ed. 1983).

136. *See* R. DWORKIN, TAKING RIGHTS SERIOUSLY 273 (1977).

137. *See* Sanders & Dukeminier, *Medical Advance and Legal Lag: Hemodialysis and Kidney Transplantation*, 15 UCLA L. REV. 357, 371 (1968).

criticism.[138]

The current approach to kidney transplants differs from the earlier Seattle approach to dialysis in two important respects.[139] First, as rationing has become more commonplace, it has also become less public. Individual doctors and transplant teams decide who shall be placed on waiting lists and who shall be chosen from those lists. Second, the criteria employed do not ostensibly give weight to the social worth of the recipient. Instead the procedure and standards employed are a continually evolving eclectic hodgepodge of considerations that speak to the medical value that the recipient is likely to obtain from the organ, referred to as "clinical suitability." The factors considered are, in part objective, for example, age; in part subjective, for example, psychological suitability; in part purely medical, for example, likelihood of surviving the operation; and in part social and economic, for example, does the patient have the financial and family support necessary for successful aftercare.[140] The public is only dimly aware of the standards employed and is led to believe that the cutoff points are clear, constant, and exogenous, rather than fuzzy, fluid, and endogenous. One commentator has observed:

> [T]here are . . . 80,000 individuals on dialysis in the United States today, yet only about 7,000, or less than 10 percent, are on waiting lists for kidney transplants. Because of the shortage of available organs, physicians have determined that more than 90 percent of all possible kidney transplant candidates are not 'clinically suitable.'[141]

As Bismarck said of making sausage and laws, so perhaps too with allocating life saving medical procedures, we would be sickened if we understood the process too well. Whatever standard is employed, and whatever weight it gives to various factors, the question can always be asked why a particular factor was included or excluded and given so much or so little weight. If the operative criteria are obscured by the heading "clinical suitability," then the public is less likely to be outraged by the outcome. Many of those who understand the system well, however, believe that "the present mechanisms for rationing access to needed transplants—subtle, surreptitious, not publicly discussed—are ethically wrong."[142]

---

138. *Cf. id.* at 378 (stating that selecting patients by ad hoc comparisons of social worth is objectionable).

139. Access to and allocation of transplant operations for other major organs differs from the kidney. Transplantation of the liver is not, and transplantation of the heart prior to 1987 was not, paid for by the federal government. As a result "[t]here are a number of medical centers in the United States which simply will not admit someone to their waiting list for a transplant unless he or she has the financial resources to pay for the procedure." Caplan, *supra* note 71, at 6.

140. *See* Annas, *Allocation of Artificial Hearts in the Year 2002:* Minerva v. National Health Agency, 3 AM. J. L. & MED. 59, 67 (1977); Annas, *Rationing Schemes, supra* note 124, at 188; Bayer, *supra* note 135, at 38-42 ; Evans & Yagi, *Social and Medical Considerations Affecting Selection of Transplant Recipients: The Case of Heart Transplantation,* in HUMAN ORGAN TRANSPLANTATION 27, 30 (1987).

141. Annas, *Regulating Transplantation, supra* note 7, at 254.

142. Caplan, *supra* note 71, at 8. I am assuming that the allocation decision is made in

Increasing the Supply of Transplant Organs
THE GEORGE WASHINGTON LAW REVIEW

It is a mistake to suppose that these are only teething problems and that there is some set of criteria that could be established that would be generally acceptable and uncontroversial. The impenetrable core of the problem with the "deservability" approach is that it runs into the brick wall of fairness.[143] While an individual is normally free to dispose of his property in a manner consistent with his self-interest, a public body is not. It does not even have the normative category of self-interest available as a criterion of allocation. The public body must allocate the organs to serve some social interest, and in doing so must treat each potential recipient fairly.[144] Further, some formulations of fairness, such as equal distribution, are simply unavailable. Edible chicken livers can be divided up equally, transplanted human livers cannot. Either you will get the next liver and have a chance at life, and I will not, or vice versa.

Because each person's desire to carry on his life figures so prominently in the values that our society seeks to serve, and no higher order scale with which to weigh one person's desire against another's is compelling, we face an insoluble dilemma. Why should George's desire to live be given precedence over Martha's? No set of criteria and weights that would be viewed as fair and just from behind the veil of ignorance is available to answer such questions. Making a convincing case that a particular allocation formula is fair becomes even more difficult when the arguments are addressed to those for whom the veil has been lifted. When it is your daughter who is suffering from end-stage renal failure, what possible argument could convince you that it is more just, because it serves some social end, that a stranger receive the kidney that would save your child's life?

A market solution to the problem of organ allocation is egalitarian in a different sense of the term. It does not treat kidneys as a good that the government must distribute equally, fairly, or justly, but instead as something that we all have an equal right to acquire from the owner through voluntary transactions. As with other life preserving commodities such as food, clothing, or shelter, so too with

---

good faith. It should be recognized, however, that the more open ended and amorphous the criteria, the greater the possibility and likelihood that they will be ignored in favor of a narrower, more private motive. "Numerous reports have appeared in the popular press concerning favoritism shown to those persons who can make significant contributions, either monetary or in terms of favorable publicity, that will benefit the medical centers where transplants are performed." *Id.* at 7.

143. For an example of how commentators have struggled with the question of fairness in allocating medical resources, see Brock, *Ethical Issues in Recipient Selection for Organ Transplantation,* in ORGAN SUBSTITUTION TECHNOLOGY 86 (D. Mathieu ed. 1988); Roberts, *supra* note 114, at 258;

144. *See generally* TASK FORCE REPORT, *supra* note 2 (adopting the view that donated organs should be viewed as scarce public resources to be allocated in accord with standards of justice).

human organs, the vendor is neither expected nor required to be fair. Indeed, it is hard to see how the category applies. The question of fairness can thus be avoided rather than answered.

In addition, the market implicitly responds to the same set of fairness concerns that would motivate a public body, and may even measure them more accurately. The price that an individual will be willing to pay for a particular organ will be a function of the likelihood that that organ will add substantially to the quality and quantity of life he can expect to receive. Thus, between two candidates of approximately equal wealth, the one who would be willing to pay more will usually be the one who can make best use of it. There is also the matter of the social value of the potential recipient. Despite the criticism heaped on the Seattle Committee, it is not obvious that it was ethically incorrect in assigning substantial weight to social worth in its dialysis access decisions. The value that others place on a potential recipient continuing his life seems an eminently reasonable concern. A market approach gives real weight to the intensity of the desire of both the recipient and others that the recipient's life continue. More than moral posturing or presidential appeals, willingness to pay is powerful evidence of that desire.[145]

B. *Price Gouging*

Because the potential recipient is desperate for the organ and the selling agency has it in its power to withhold the supply, if private businesses purchase the organs and sell them at the market price will it result in egregious price gouging? No; merely because a good or service is a necessity of life does not imply that its price will be exorbitant. As in the case of such necessities as food, clothing, and shelter, so too with livers, if there is competition among the providers, market price will reflect the marginal cost to the provider rather than the reservation price of the purchaser.

In the event that a single vendor owns the only tissue suitable for a particular individual, however, competition will be non-existent, and price gouging, *i.e.*, charging the recipient his reservation price, may arise. This will be rarer than one would suppose from all the talk of tissue matching and transplant rejection. Most human organs such as kidneys, hearts, and livers elicit an immune reaction.[146] Therefore, tissue rejection is a major concern in transplants. More effective matching of donor and recipient is one conceivable path to

---

145. Not everyone would agree that permitting the allocation of organs or transplant operations by willingness to pay is equitable in any sense of the word.

> Rationing by financial ability says that we do not believe in equality and that we do believe that a price can and should be placed on human life and that it should be paid by the individual whose life is at stake. Neither belief is tolerable in a society in which income is inequitably distributed.

Excerpts from the Report of the Massachusetts Task Force on Organ Transplantation, in HUMAN ORGAN TRANSPLANTATION 211, 233 (1987).

146. Note, however, that the immune response varies markedly among organs. There is a weaker immune reaction to a transplanted liver than to other major organs and a still weaker reaction to the cornea and some other minor tissue. *See* R. SCOTT, *supra* note 3, at 48-51.

Increasing the Supply of Transplant Organs
THE GEORGE WASHINGTON LAW REVIEW

greater transplant success. The increased transplant success of the last decade, however, had its origin elsewhere. Tissue matching has not become more effective, but rather, less important. The development of immuno-suppressant drugs has made it possible for a given recipient to make use of organs from a variety of individuals.[147] Thus competition among suppliers will generally be an effective constraint on price.[148]

In the case of some tissue, however, immuno-suppressant drugs are not yet effective. Transplanting bone marrow, for example, because of a medical phenomenon known as graft versus host disease, in which the normal problem of the recipient rejecting the transplant is exacerbated by the transplant rejecting the recipient, requires a very close tissue match in order to be successful. Finding a good match for a bone marrow recipient in the general population is about a one in 60,000 probability. A harvesting agency with a good tissue match would indeed have the recipient over a barrel, and being a repeat player in the market would have a reputational interest in playing hardball. If a family member fell victim to certain severe illnesses one might have to pay the greater of $7000 or one's entire estate for suitable transplant tissue.[149] Such a prospect would both create enormous anxiety and could potentially reduce the incentive to accumulate large amounts of wealth. A restrained version of the unconscionability doctrine might usefully be employed to

---

147. *See supra* note 2.

148. Immuno-suppressants, like most extraordinarily powerful drugs, have vicious side-effects, the most serious being an increased susceptibility to infection. Many transplant patients die of those infections, as well as suffering an increased proclivity to cancer. Some scientists believe that superior tissue matching will eventually yield better results without the intensive use of immuno-suppressants.

The most promising areas of research for superior matching of donors and recipients are in histocompatibility antigens (HL-A) and mixed lymphocyte culture antigens. Thus far HL-A matching has been the more successful, but its victories are small, in part because not all the antigens have been discovered. As more are discovered, however, and as the salutory effects of finding a good match are increased, the probability of finding a match between donor and recipient are decreased. The chance at present of making a good match of a major organ among unrelated individuals is one in one thousand. Arehart-Treichel, *Organ Transplants: What Hope for Patients?*, 106 SCI. NEWS 314, 314-15 (1974).

Should an organ market come to fruition and more organs become available, the isolated exceptionally good match will be found more frequently. This may mean that more vendors will be well positioned for hard bargaining. It is important to keep in mind, however, that despite that danger, reducing the need for immuno-suppressants must be seen as a major net potential gain of an organ market.

149. Both the possibility of price gouging and the side effects of immuno-suppressants may, before too long, be eliminated by technological change. Monoclonal antibodies (mabs) are being developed to reduce the incidence of rejection and graft versus host disease with only minimal side effects. A mab designated as Campath-1 has been tested for use in bone marow transplants and has met with some success. *See New Organs for Old*, 295 ECONOMIST, June 8, 1985, at 78-79.

limit the price paid to the estate of the decedent and to the harvesting agency to a level that corresponded to a point on the supply curve where elasticity has approached but not reached zero. Such a limitation would likely be *ex ante* utility maximizing, in that it would not reduce by much the amount of tissue supplied but would considerably reduce uncertainty about one's future wealth.

The problem of price gouging and visions of individuals paying their entire personal estate of several million dollars for a liver should be placed in proper perspective. In comparison with the current method of tissue acquisition and allocation, it would still be a vast improvement for the recipient. Consider the case of Robert McFall, who in 1978 discovered that he had aplastic anaemia. His only hope was a bone marrow transplant. His cousin, David Shrimp, was discovered to be a compatible doner. Shrimp, however, under pressure from his wife, refused to donate. McFall's suit seeking that the court compel donation was denied and he died shortly afterward.[150] Surely the market can do no worse than that.

C.   Are There No Graveyards?

This discussion of permitting free reign to the market on the demand side of the equation, while hopefully of some interest, is neither a central nor even a necessary part of my main thesis. I have buried it near the end of the Article so as not to distract the reader. The vision of desperate parents seeing their child die because they cannot afford a liver will hardly endear the market to any but Ebenezer Scrooge—"Are there no graveyards?" Although I believe that such a vision is a distortion of the likely result of a full-fledged market, the argument is barely worth the effort. It has already taken us too far away from the main job of demonstrating that a substantially increased supply of organs can be brought to the market cheaply and without unduly offending our sense of moral propriety.

Conclusion

There has been a scandalous wastage of life-saving organs under the donative system of organ retrieval. If the failure to harvest these organs were rooted in a respect for the strong religious values of the decedent that his body not be dismembered, it would not be amenable to legislative remedy. The problem, however, is not at bottom psychological and religious; it is economic. The Gallup survey, the high proportion of assents to request for donation, and the vigorous legislative activity all demonstrate that people are willing to donate organs. At the same time, they do not wish to think about it and will not take the initiative. In addition, doctors and hospitals, though certainly not opposed to organ harvesting, are not willing to gratuitously play their assigned and difficult roles.

The solution to this tragic problem is neither overly difficult, nor

---

150. *See* R. Scott, *supra* note 3, at 127-39.

does it require a moral revolution. Instead of diminishing people's property rights in their bodies, we need to expand those rights and to allow individuals to make prospective sales of their organs in exchange for substantial payments to their estates. This market solution is more effective, more efficient, and more robust than the alternatives of donation, escheatage, and required request.

There are those who will view this Article as the ravings of a ghoulish law and economics fanatic. They blanche at the thought of creating any sort of market in so precious and sacred a thing as the human body, even a cadaver. But I urge you not to be overly delicate and prissy in considering these questions. We must take man as he is, not as we would like him to be. Man is neither an entirely selfish, profane, private-wealth maximizer, nor a saintly, social-wealth maximizer. He is not indifferent to his moral obligation to others, but he does not love his neighbor as himself. Were he either of these, organs would not go to waste. Were he saintly, all organs would be donated. Were he entirely profane and selfish, there would be no legal prohibition against the sale by next of kin, and even in the face of a prohibition sales would occur. It is because man is part saint and part sinner that we have the tragedy of many thousands of people needlessly suffering and dying each year while the precious organs that could restore them to health are fed to worms.

[8]

MONEY TALKS, MONEY KILLS — THE ECONOMICS OF TRANSPLANTATION IN JAPAN AND CHINA

CARL BECKER

ABSTRACT

Japan and China have long resisted the Western trend of organ transplantation from brain-dead patients, based on a 'Confucian' respect for integrity of ancestors' bodies. While their general publics continue to harbor grave doubts about such practices, their medical and political elites are hastening towards the road of organ-harvesting and organ-marketing, largely for economic reasons. This report illustrates the ways that economics is motivating brain-death legislation in Japan and criminal executions in China.

JAPANESE BRAIN DEATH AND TRANSPLANTATION

Prior to 1997, Japan had no brain death laws. In 1968, Sapporo University's Dr. Wada failed in an illegal heart-transplant procedure, killing both donor and recipient. Wada was acquitted for lack of testimony — an indication of the difficulty of whistle-blowing in Japanese society.[1] Despite the lack of brain-death laws, thousands of kidneys were transplanted from live donors (some of them judged brain-dead) in the 1980's and 1990's, resulting in at least a dozen lawsuits by the mid '90's.[2] At the same time, Japanese were proposing to pay Philippine kidney donors $30,000 per kidney.[3] Dr. Kazuo Ota (Tokyo Women's Medical School), Head of the Japan Society for Transplantation, confessed to having personally performed 'at least' 13 liver

---

[1] Jiro Nudeshima, 'Obstacles to brain death and organ transplantation In Japan,' *Lancet* 338: 8774; (26 Oct., 1991): p. 1063.

[2] *Yomiuri Shinbun*, 4 June, 1994, p. 31, and 19 June, 1994, p. 31.

[3] *Ibid.*

ECONOMICS OF TRANSPLANTATION IN JAPAN AND CHINA   237

transplants using old diseased livers rejected for age and hepatitis by the American transplant network UNOS.[4] Although LDP Prime Ministers have formed *ad hoc* committees to oversee such matters, they are notoriously paternalistic and unconcerned with public opinion.[5] While opinion polls show over 50% of Japanese people acquiescent to brain-death criteria, some of these polls include the tell-tale but practically unimaginable proviso, 'if everyone else in the family agrees,' while other polls indicate that less than 12% of respondents even know the meaning of the brain death to which they are acquiescing.[6]

The driving force behind Japan's brain-death laws is not popular opinion. On the contrary, it tends to be the JMA, especially foreign-educated surgeons, hospital CEOs, and the LDP politicians whom they back, such as Taro Nakayama. With the strong support of the JMA and the LDP, Japan's brain-death law passed the Lower House of the Diet on April 24, 1997 and the Upper House on the eve of its adjournment, October 16, 1997. A compromise hammered out in late-night political negotiations, the bill contains a number of problematically ambiguous phrasings that we shall not examine individually here. More striking are its two major features: (1) that brain death is inextricably intertwined with organ transplantation, and (2) the double standard that two bodies in absolutely identical physical states may receive opposite diagnoses.

In brief, the law defines the criteria for brain death as (1) that the body meets standard brain-death criteria for six hours, (2) that a valid organ donor card for the patient has been confirmed, (3) that there are no objections to organ transplantation by family members, and presupposes (4) that the hospital is qualified to conduct such transplantation. In other words, it enjoins, 'First, see if the patient is clinically brain dead. If she is brain dead, then try to locate a valid organ donor card for her, and ask her relatives what they think. If you can find her valid donor card, and if her relatives agree to harvesting her organs, then she is legally dead. If her relatives do not want her body cut, or if you cannot find a valid donor card for her, then she is not dead.'[7] In other words, although two people may be in the very same medical condition of brain death, one can be legally

---

[4] C. Ross, 'Towards acceptance of organ transplantation?' *Lancet*, 346 (1 July, 1995), pp. 41–42.

[5] Nudeshima, *loc.cit.*

[6] Carl Becker, *Mainichi Shinbun*, 10 October, 1997 (?).

[7] Steven Butler, 'Dead When You Say You're Dead.' *U.S. News and World Report.* 122, 25 (June 30, 1997): 42.

pronounced dead if his relatives want him dead and a valid donor card can be found, while another must be maintained by machines because a card cannot be found, or because some relative doesn't want to acknowledge her death yet, or because the hospital is not prepared to conduct such an organ transplant.

Compare this Japanese stance with that of brain-death laws everywhere else in the world. Most brain death laws are discrete from laws governing transplantation. They are designed to free terminal patients from tubes and respirators, allowing a more natural death — the Japanese law does not. They free doctors from liability for terminating brain-dead patients, and free hospital resources for use by other patients — the Japanese law does not. They reduce costs to society and insurance companies — the Japanese law does not. They accord with the popular will that brain dead patients need not be prolonged. The Japanese law is not grounded upon any popular understanding. It refuses to recognize as brain dead anyone but organ donors. What is the motivation here?

Prima facie, the Japanese law lets patients and their families choose whether they admit that they are dead, based on feeling rather than on medical criteria. Yet families cannot choose to allow their tube-supported, respirated relative to die naturally unless they agree to organ donation. Seen from the economics of hospital management, this is a blatant attempt to derive as much income as possible from the patients' families and insurance. Keeping a patient alive mechanically costs great sums every day. In other countries, when people are found to be brain dead, they are taken off life-support systems, and the hospital 'loses' that source of income. In Japan, however, they cannot be taken off life-support systems, so the hospital never loses that income. The only time the machines can be stopped is if everyone concerned agrees to organ donation, which produces even more money for the hospital.

So, full of contradictions, this Japanese 'brain death' law is welcomed by Japanese hospitals and ridiculed by other countries. It does not respect Japanese people's desire to die naturally, nor Japanese people's desire to reduce the tax burden for indefinite prolongation of brain-dead patients. It opens the door to legal organ transplantation from warm pulsing cadavers. External second opinions and whistle-blowing are still unthinkable in the Japanese hospital context, but this law provides no safeguards against the Japanese fears that donors may be prematurely pronounced brain-dead. It does, however, grandfather protection for those Japanese doctors who procured kidneys

ECONOMICS OF TRANSPLANTATION IN JAPAN AND CHINA   239

from consenting brain-dead patients before the brain-death law
had been passed.

In sum, Japanese doctors' (and politicians') desire to
maximize hospital incomes brought them to a simple dilemma.
Many want to conduct transplantation for the high fees that it will
bring (not for the patients that it will save, as shown by the many
cases of transplants they already conduct with old contaminated
organs and almost zero chance of success). But if they admit
world-wide brain death criteria, then they would have to remove
thousands of mechanically-sustained Japanese patients from life-
support systems, losing precious income.

Their political solution was to allow termination of life-support
only when hospitals gain even greater income through
transplantation. This has not satisfied the Japanese minority
who wanted brain death criteria to enable death with dignity. Nor
has it pleased the majority who still fear unscrupulous
transplantation.[8] It has only placed Japanese doctors in a win-
win situation, regardless of the rights and will of the people. It
guarantees that public insurance funds for life-support will
continue to pour into hospitals' coffers, protecting doctors and
hospital administrators at the expense of the taxpayers, unless
even greater income is procurable for transplantation.

The Japanese double-standard brain-death law was a product
of economic incentives in the JMA and the conservative LDP.
Ethically, it violates the will of the people, by denying termination
of life-support when desired, and by urging transplantation from
those who are not yet even sure of the meaning of brain death.
Yet in Japan, economics only rarely results in the death of
patients, when patients are terminated in order to harvest their
organs, or when non-viable organs are transplanted into
recipients. The situation in China is even more alarming.

CHINESE BRAIN DEATH AND TRANSPLANTATION

Hard on the heels of the discovery of cyclosporine (the
immunosuppressant which facilitated organ transplants) in
1983,[9] China announced its first 'Strike Hard' campaign allowing
the death penalty for common criminals,[10] and in 1984, the

---

[8] Sheryl WuDunn, 'In Japan, Use of Dead Has the Living Uneasy (Organs
from the Brain-Dead Patient)' *New York Times*, 146 s.1, (May 11, 1997): 1.

[9] Ikels, C. 'Kidney Failure and Transplantation in China.' *Social Science and
Medicine*, 44, 9 (May, 1997): 1271–83.

[10] Burns, John P. 'When Peking Fights Crime, News is On the Wall,' *New
York Times*, 135 (Jan 2S, 1986): 6, A2.

240   CARL BECKER

follow-up law, 'Rules for the Use of Corpses.' While the masses of Chinese were still Confucian enough to reject organ reception as well as donation, elite members of the communist party began receiving organs from executed prisoners. The number of common-criminal executions increased, and their timing was often scheduled for the convenience of senior party officials or their family connections.[11]

China's 'Rules Concerning the Utilization of Corpses or Organs from Corpses from Executed Criminals,' specify that organs can be used from any prisoner who consents to organ use. It is preposterous that a shackled and doomed prisoner could give meaningful free consent — or free refusal. And once a prisoner is executed, it is the state's word against anyone else's. Human Rights Watch has documented that prisoners are rarely even informed that their organs will be transplanted.[12] The rules also say that 'use of corpses or organs of executed prisoners must be kept strictly secret, and attention paid to avoiding negative repercussions.'[13] In a country where hardly anyone will donate their bodies for science or organs, this underscores that most of China's organ donors are executed prisoners.[14]

Another reason for this high secrecy is that legally speaking, China does not recognize brain death. Since many organs must be transplanted before the heart stops beating — this means that many prisoners have their organs removed before they are dead.[15] Even official Chinese law texts describe how to deliberately botch executions so as to keep organs alive longer, and describe cases of removing organs before the official executions(!)[16]

For example, a young lady teaching middle school in Jiangxi in the 1970's was found guilty of possessing politically incorrect manuscripts written by a colleague. Her blood type was determined, she was condemned and shot in the head twice, but even before she died, her kidneys were removed and

[11] John P. Burns, 'Peking Focuses on Execution of Three Officials' Sons,' *New York Times*, 135 (Feb 25, 1986): 8, A11.

[12] Asia Watch Committee, Human Rights Watch. 'China: Organ Procurement and Judicial Execution in China,' *Human Rights Watch*, 6, 9 (August, 1994): 42.

[13] Translated and quoted by Robin Munro in David Rothman, 'Body Shop: Chinats Booming Trade in Organs for Transplant.' *Sciences*, 37 (1997): 17.

[14] Barbara Basler, 'Kidney Transplants in China Raise Concern About Source.' *New York Times*, 140 (June 3, 1991): A1.

[15] Paul Lewis, 'China Executes Dissidents in Secret (Amnesty International Reports).' *New York Times*, 138 (Aug. 31, 1989): A3.

[16] Asia Watch Committee, *loc. cit.*

ECONOMICS OF TRANSPLANTATION IN JAPAN AND CHINA   241

transplanted to the son of the military officer who arranged the operation.[17]

Thousands of prisoners are executed every year in order to provide fresh organs for transplantation in the times and places where they are most needed. First prisoners are shot through the back of their heads,[18] but drugged, IV'd, and occasionally even respirated so that their hearts will keep beating until they are adjacent to the organ recipients. Then the doctors cut the functioning organs out of the prisoners and transplant them to the waiting patients — often either high-paying foreigners or members of the communist elite. Since brain death is not recognized in China, prisoners' organs are usually removed while they are technically alive, and there is no concern for the pain or death which this causes the prisoner. In this situation, doctors cooperate with executioners, not only to 'save' life, but to take it away.[19]

Reports indicate that this is closer to the rule than the exception: executions are located and scheduled for the convenience of the recipients. American physicians — who have been invited to China to oversee transplants, have been assured that the proper types of donors can be arranged in the proper locations to suit their convenience, as is often the case for wealthy recipients coming from Hong Kong or Singapore.[20]

Growing evidence indicates that this state execution machine is driven increasingly by motives of economic rather than criminal justice or law enforcement. In 1996, a new 'Strike Hard' death penalty campaign was instituted, and documented death sentences rose from some 3000 in 1995 to over 6100 in 1996, three times more than the executions of the entire rest of the world put together, including African and Islamic police states.[21] The death sentence can be imposed for more than 70 crimes including hooliganism, bribery and political deviance.[22] Of course, the levying of the death penalty is very selective; not every hooligan or deviant is killed.[23] In 1996, two Shanghai men

---

[17] quoted in Rothman.

[18] Paul Lewis, 'Method of Execution: A Stark Tradition.' *New York Times*, 138 (Thurs. June 22, 1989): A6, A10.

[19] David P. Hamilton, 'China Uses Prisoners for Transplants (Human Rights Watch Asia Report).' *Wall Street Journal*, (Aug. 29, 1994): A6–A7.

[20] Rothman, *loc. cit.*

[21] Dmitry Balburov, 'China's Chechnya.' *Moscow News*, (May 22, 1997).

[22] Stacy Mosher, 'Ultimate Response (Execution of Smugglers in China).' *Far Eastern Economic Review*, 155, 1 (June 8, 1992): 9.

[23] Donald C. Clarke, 'The Execution of Civil Judgments in China.' *China Quarterly*, 141 (March, 1995): 65.

242 CARL BECKER

were executed for stealing badminton rackets and ballpoint pens from powerful officials, and another Sichuan farmer for selling a stone Buddha head he had found. Dozens of Tibetans and hundreds of Xinjiang separatists have been executed annually.[24] However, even legal specialists in China itself acknowledge that these death penalties do not deter crime — rather they are directly related to the demand for organ sales.[25] Both the timing and the choice of which prisoners to be sentenced is as much influenced by their organ donation as by their crimes. In other words, whether a young protestor is let off with a warning or shot and harvested for organs depends more on her blood type and organ demand in her region than on the public danger of her crime.

In the early 1990's, thousands of wealthy clients from Hong Kong, Singapore, and surrounding countries, went to China to receive lung, heart, kidney, and liver transplants. The cost of a transplant is usually between US. $15,000 and $25,000 — less than a third of what it might cost in the West — but the value of that same foreign currency within China is more than three times what it would be worth outside of China.[26] Moreover, in the 1990's, Chinese hospitals have fallen on economic hard times and often resort to medicine sales and overcharging patients in order to avoid bankruptcy.[27] So a single prisoner's organ transplantation to a foreign recipient can keep a hospital economically solvent, even after appropriate payoffs to concerned officials. This may help to explain the caprice in the Chinese law enforcement — that petty criminals can be executed if they have the right organs and blood type at the right time and place, whereas much more heinous criminals may get off lightly if they are old, alcoholic, or their organs are otherwise in low demand.[28]

Recently many governments have become critical of China's unethical organ trade: Singapore has charged Chinese doctors with responsibility for the death of Singaporeans;[29] America has

---

[24] Keith B. Richburg, 'China Executes Hundreds in Crackdown.' *Washington Post*, 119 (Sat., July 6, 1996): A1.

[25] *Economist*, 339, 7970 (June 15, 1996) 4; 'Three Embezzlers Executed in South China,' *Beijing Review*, 37, 32 (Aug. 8, 1994): 6.

[26] Rothman, *loc. cit.*

[27] S. Hillier, & X. Zheng, 'Reforms of the Chinese Health Care System: the Jiangxi Study.' *Social Science and Medicine*, 41, 8 (Oct. 1995): 1058.

[28] Clarke, 'Execution,' 65.

[29] Barbara Crossette, 'Singapore Ties Seven Deaths to China Kidney Transplants,' *New York Times*, 137 (Sun., Feb. 7, 1988): 9, 20.

ECONOMICS OF TRANSPLANTATION IN JAPAN AND CHINA   243

refused to return suspects to Hong Kong for fear that they may be summarily executed for organ harvest;[30] and German pharmaceutical companies have left China over this issue.[31] Despite American Senate Hearings condemning these practices,[32] America continues to grant China a most favored nation status for economic reasons.

We should grant China the right to non-Western views of crime and crime control.[33] Yet the ethical problems in China's death sentencing for organ transplantation are legion. The utter disregard for human rights of prisoners and their families, the vagaries of trial and sentencing procedures, the cruel and unusual methods of removing organs from heart-beating and sometimes conscious convicts, and the doctors' participation in the execution of prisoners, all give serious pause. But the critique of this report is that the economics of organ sales and transplants itself influences and motivates China's inordinately high rate of capital punishment for petty crimes.

SUMMARY

In Japan's much subtler case, medical economics has overridden Asian desires for dignified death, and a medical elite is trying to push Japanese people into organ donation. In China's case, medical economics is in fact a killing machine of prisoner execution, based less on justice than on supply and demand. Of course supply and demand economics poses troubling ethical problems in the West as well. The difference is that these issues are open to public debate, open to third party review, and open to international critique. The closed circles of Japanese hospitals, and the strict secrecy cloaking Chinese executions for transplant sales, raise fundamental ethical questions of the price of freedom of choice — and the price of human life.

Kyoto University

---

[30] David E. Rovella, 'No Extradition to Hong Kong'. *National Law Journal*, 19, 21 (Jan 20, 1997): A6; and see Christopher Drew. 'US Says Two Chinese Offered Organs from the Executed,' *New York Times*, 147 (24 Feb. 1998): A1.

[31] Edmund L. Andrews, 'German Company to Leave China Over Sales of Organs,' *New York Times*, 147 (March 7, 1998): A5.

[32] United States Senate Committee on Foreign Relations. 'China: Illegal Trade in Human Body Parts,' *Hearings*, 104th Congress, 1st Session, (May 4, 1995): 104–126.

[33] Troyer, Ronald J. *Chinese Thinking About Crime and Social Control.* Society for the Study of Social Problems, 1988.

Part IV
Cadaveric Organ and Tissue Donation

[9]

Freedom to Choose and Freedom to Lose: The Procurement of Cadaver Organs for Transplantation

B. Hoffmaster

THE ETHICAL ISSUES that surround organ transplantation are protean. As the xenograft performed on Baby Fae illustrates, the main question enveloping any form of transplantation, in its early stages, is how realistic the expected therapeutic benefit must be before a patient is subjected to an experimental procedure. But as technology advances and experience is acquired, the moral questions change along with the increasing success of the procedure. Today, the main moral issues that arise with respect to kidney transplantation concern the extent to which the demand for organs exceeds the supply, the concomitant need to ration organs among the pool of potential recipients,[1] and the allocation of finite health care dollars to this expensive medical technology. It is impossible to deal with all three here, so I shall concentrate on the one that makes transplantation possible: the procurement of organs.[2] For ethical reasons I shall narrow my focus even further to the acquisition of cadaver organs. Richard McCormick suggested, in pre-cyclosporine (CsA) days, that there should be a thrust away from using living donors and that such use should be regarded as transitional only.[3] The promising results of CsA have changed the clinical picture dramatically and have strengthened, if not yet confirmed, McCormick's view. Thomas Starzl recently reported that, as of 1 year after surgery, "the results for cadaver and intrafamily transplants have become competitive"; this evidence leads him

to suggest that "soon, if current trends continue, it may be hard to justify using living donors."[4] These serious moral reservations about the use of living donors, combined with the shortage of cadaver organs, make the need to assess competing policies for acquiring cadaver organs quite pressing.

The first point that needs to be made in a moral assessment of organ procurement policies is that there is no *a priori* necessity for a policy that gives overriding effect to individual consent. The determination of a policy for organ acquisition is largely a function of a society's underlying social and political philosophy, and different philosophies assign different degrees of importance to the value of individual freedom. A conception of society as a collection of independent, autonomous individuals, or "Godlets,"[5] as one writer has aptly dubbed them, entails that organ donation be entirely a matter of free choice. Autonomous individuals have no obligations to persons, especially strangers, that are not voluntarily self-imposed, so organ donation could not be morally demanded or required of them. A donation, whether inter vivos or postmortem, would have to be a gift, a free expression of the will of an autonomous being. A more communitarian vision of society, however, does not make the moral permissibility of every act depend upon the free choices of individuals. By "communitarian" I do not mean a society in which the members are subordinated to the whole. Rather, communitarian refers to the nature of the relationships that exist between individual members of the society. A communitarian society takes seriously the notion of obligations to determinate others, even if these obligations are not voluntarily incurred. With this conception of society, organ donation could be recognized as a responsibility. One has a responsibility to do good for other members of society when the opportunity

From the Department of Philosophy, University of Western Ontario, London, Ontario.

Address reprint requests to Barry Hoffmaster, Associate Professor and Director, Graduate Program in Biomedical Ethics, Department of Philosophy, University of Western Ontario, London, Ontario N6A 3K7.

© 1985 by Grune & Stratton, Inc.

0041–1345/85/1706–4006$03.00/0

presents itself and there is no great cost involved. One has a responsibility, in other words, to be a Good Samaritan. But because the indivivual is not subjugated to others, because a balance between interests has to be struck, the responsibility is defeasible, not absolute. In recognition of the diversity of values that exist within even relatively homogeneous societies and the importance of respecting a person's strongly held values when he or she is not consonant with those of the majority, individuals are permitted to exempt themselves from this responsibility. In a communitarian society, then, after death one's organs could be used routinely for transplantation unless one has exempted oneself from this responsibility by registering a prior objection. The differences between these two approaches are illustrated in Table 1.

It is no accident that in North America, where a philosophy of liberal individualism reigns supreme, autonomy and freedom are the paramount values and an opt-in policy for organ donation exists. The President of the National Kidney Foundation in the United States, a physician, has said the following:

> Most of the people I've spoken to ... feel that presumed consent is not quite the American way. It is relatively coercive, compared to the more classical freedom of choice that characterizes our way of life. Consent should be positive, not implied. Those who are very anxious for more organs are tempted by such ideas.[6]

Although an opt-in policy is not accidental given the ideology behind "the American way," it is not necessary, either. In Europe and other parts of the world where the philosophical tradition is not similarly fixated on the notion of individual freedom, a number of countries have adopted an opt-out policy. As

of late 1979, a survey in which 28 of 40 countries responded revealed that 13 countries used presumed consent as the basis for removing organs for transplantation.[7] In six of these 13 countries, physicians still approached the families to see whether they objected, but in the other seven countries physicians proceeded with organ salvage in the absence of prior objection by the decedent or his or her family. To support the claim about the relationship between political philosophy and an organ procurement policy, it should be noted that all of the English-speaking countries that responded had opt-in policies.

Can the classical "freedom of choice" characteristic of "the American way" be defended when lives and significant improvement in the quality of life are at stake? That is the central moral question here. Affirmations of an opt-in policy invariably take the inviolability of individual freedom and consent for granted.[8] An opt-out policy is seen as transparently wrong because it does not respect the individual freedom which is the cornerstone of Anglo-American political philosophy. Engelhardt's view is typical:

> The more one presumes that organs are not societal property, the more difficult it is to justify shifting the burden to individuals to show that they do not want their organs used. If sufficient numbers of organs are not available, it will be unfortunate, but from the point of view of general secular morality, not unfair. Free individuals will have valued other goals (eg, having an intact body for burial) more highly than the support of transplantation.[9]

The issue, however, is precisely *why* the free choices of individuals should be dispositive here. Engelhardt's answer appeals to considerations such as taking seriously the notion of respect for persons and the nature of a free,

Table 1. Implications of Social Philosophy for Organ Procurement

Social Philosophy	Perceived Nature of Organ Donation	Organ Procurement Policy
Individualism	A gift	Explicit voluntarism (Opt-in)
Communitarianism	A defeasible responsibility	Presumed altruism (Opt-out)

secular, pluralist society. As he says, most illuminatingly, ". . . free societies are characterized by the commitment to live with the tragedies that result from the decisions of free individuals not to participate in the beneficent endeavors of others."[9] But these consideratons simply reflect a philosophy of liberal individualism; they do not justify it.

To return to the central moral question: Why is individual freedom so important that a person's organs, when they no longer are of use to that person, cannot be taken without that person's prior consent or the consent of a relative to save the life of someone else or to improve significantly the quality of life of someone else? What significant costs would be incurred by recognizing a responsibility to others in this respect? Why must the tragedies that result from the exercise of individual freedom be accepted here? To pose the question in terms of the two visions of society, would one, knowing the fragility of the human condition, rather live in a society of independent, free choosers or in a society of Good Samaritans? The ideal, of course, would be a society in which voluntary altruism were widespread. But short of that, one needs to decide whether, with respect to transplantation and the benefits it offers, society should be oriented primarily along the lines of freedom and consent or along the lines of communal responsibility.

A number of arguments have been taken to provide a "philosophical and humanistic" basis for an organ procurement policy based on consent.[10] The most commonly cited argument comes from Paul Ramsey, who favors the "organized giving" over the "routine salvaging" of cadaver organs for the following reasons:

> A society will be a better human community in which giving and receiving is the rule, not taking for the sake of good to come. The civilizing task of mankind is the fostering, the achievement, or the shoring up of *consensual community* in general, and not only in regard to the advancement of medical science and the availability of cadaver organs in efforts to save the lives of others. Civilization means living our consensual communities, not living in communities in which consent and refusal go on, just as surely as we live our bodies, not in them. The positive consent called for by Gift Acts, answering the need for gifts by encouraging real givers, meets the measure of authentic community among men. The routine taking of organs would deprive individuals of the exercise of the virtue of generosity.[11]

The sentiments in this passage are nobly expressed but, again, undefended. What criteria are to be used to assess the relative goodness of human communities? On what grounds is "civilization" to be defined in terms of a *consensual* community? Why isn't a community in which individuals possess responsibilities to others morally superior to and more civilized than a community in which individuals do only what they freely choose to do, presumably for whatever reasons they find persuasive? Most importantly, why is fostering the exercise of the virtue of generosity more important than saving lives or improving the quality of lives? This is the key value judgment, and Ramsey, to his credit, proceeds to make it, albeit somewhat hesitatingly:

> The moral sequels that might flow from education and action in line with the proposed Gift Acts *may be* of far more importance than prolonging lives routinely. The moral history of mankind is of more importance than its medical advancement, unless the latter can be joined with the former in a community of affirmative consent.[11]

Ramsey is a pioneer in the movement towards a more humane, morally sensitive approach to the delivery of health care, but one wonders what attitude toward the value of life is implicit in the phrase "prolonging lives routinely." One is not talking here about zealous, aggressive efforts to prolong for a limited period the existence of seriously ill persons who have a dim prospective quality of life. One is talking about persons who can be restored to a relatively normal level of functioning for a substantial time. It is difficult to understand what can be more valuable than this tangible good, especially when it is produced "routinely." In addition, Ramsey's argument now, if not at the time it was written, misconceives what is at issue. It is not respect for consent, or in his terms, the moral history of mankind versus medical advancement; rather it is consent versus saving lives and improving the quality of lives. How can either of these be antithetical to the moral history of mankind? Finally, one would think that the actual example of prolonging lives routinely would be a more effective educational strategy for eliciting consent than the legal imprimatur of a Human Tissue Gift Act. Ramsey's arguments, therefore, are not persuasive. If opt-in and opt-out policies were equally effective in generating supplies of cadaver organs, his considerations might tip the moral balance in favor of an opt-in policy. But when an opt-in policy results in a serious shortage of organs and an opt-out policy is likely to increase the supply, his reasons are not conclusive. Ramsey's preference for consensual community and fostering the virtue of generosity over the routine prolonging of lives simply cannot be accepted.[11,12]

A second challenge to an opt-out policy questions the nature of the good that the routine salvaging of cadaver organs is intended to produce. Writing about the ethical issues involved in experimentation on human subjects, Hans Jonas says the following:

> We concede, as a matter of course, to the common good some pragmatically determined measure of precedence over the individual good. In terms of rights, we let some of the basic rights of the individual be overruled by the acknowledged rights of society.... But in making that concession, we require a careful clarification of what the needs, interests, and rights of society are, for society—as distinct from any plurality of individuals—is an abstract and as such is subject to our definition, while the individual is the primary concrete, prior to all definition, and his basic good is more or less known.[13]

Regardless of how cogent this objection is to experimentation with human subjects, it lacks any force for organ transplantation. The good procured by a transplant is not the common good or the public good—it is not something analogous to national defence, clean air, or a provincial park; rather, it is a definite, specifiable, concrete, individual good. It is not amor-phous, abstruse, or mystical; nor is it speculative, uncertain, or far in the future as the proposed benefits of medical research often are. Thus, the "careful clarification" that Jonas demands before sacrifices of the individual good can be justified is met by the benefits likely to accrue to a recipient of an organ transplant.

A third objection involves the possible erosion of trust in the health care system that might be caused by an opt-out policy. William May, for example, says the following:

> While the procedure of routine salvaging may, in the short run, furnish more organs for transplants, in the long run, its systemic effect on the institutions of medical care would seem to be depressing and corrosive of that trust upon which the arts of healing depend.[8]

It is exceedingly difficult to assess such long-range projections of dire consequences. The required causal assumptions are manifold and poorly understood. Do we know what engenders trust between patient and physician and what destroys it? And if one is concerned about trust in the medical system, isn't it precisely the kinds of successes that organ transplantation and other technological advancements represent that produce trust? The phenomenon of transplantation gives people hope that if they become seriously ill, medical science might be able to do something for them. And how can one have trust without hope?

What worries May, though, is that a policy of routine salvaging of organs would change the image of the hospital from that of "a place of healing and recuperation for the sick and wounded" to that of a "devourer":

> The healing mission of the hospital is obscured . . . if the hospital itself becomes the arch-symbol of a world that devours. Categorical salvaging of organs suggests that eventually and ultimately the process of consumption that dominates the outer world must now be consummated in the hospital. One's very vitals must be inventoried, extracted, and distributed by the state on behalf of the social order. What is left over is utterly unusable husk.[8]

This criticism is objectionable because it associates transplantation with "devouring." One can try to score moral points through the use of emotionally charged labels. The crucial question is whether the application of the label is justified. Here it is not. Only atavistic sentimentality could lead one to equate transplantation with "devouring."[12]

A less dramatic but more pervasive illustration of this moral labelling is the frequent characterization of an organ donation as a gift. To call it a gift emphasizes that it must be freely given from a motive of genuine self-sacrifice and altruism. As with exchanges between lovers and relatives, a gift is not primarily valuable in itself, but rather because of what it symbolizes about the relationship between giver and receiver. To insist that organ donation be a gift is more apt in the context of living related donors, therefore, and helps explain the concern that such a donation be truly voluntary. But there is no comparable relationship between a cadaver donor and a recipient. In this context "donor" refers simply to the source of the organ, and the primary value of the donation resides in the organ itself, not what the exchange symbolizes about a relationship. Thus, the notion of organ donation as a gift does not support the same kind of concern with voluntary consent from prospective cadaver donors as it does from living related donors.

So where are we? We need to recognize, first of all, the fundamental nature of the moral issue posed by alternative policies for organ procurement. As Ramsey has pointed out, we can begin with the judgment that neither the giving nor the taking of cadaver organs is intrinsically wrong.[11] The moral conflict is between the interests of potential recipients and the freedom of potential donors. I have maintained that the sweeping deference our current opt-in policy gives to individual freedom is a reflection of our underlying political philosophy. The moral significance of organ transplantation is that it raises a serious challenge to the values embodied in this philosophy. I also have maintained that the arguments given to meet this challenge are woefully inadequate. All of this has been an attempt to undermine the support for

an opt-in policy. To strengthen the support for an opt-out policy, one can raise the question of how morally different a policy of giving and receiving and a policy of taking and getting really are. The answer, surprisingly, is not very different. As Ramsey also has pointed out, the essential difference is in terms of who has the burden of action.[11]

A policy of giving and receiving, of opting-in, puts the burden on those who want to donate their organs. A policy of taking and getting, of opting-out, puts the burden on those who do not want to donate their organs. Although an opt-out policy gives less scope to "classical" individual freedom, it does not eliminate it. Nobody is unwillingly conscripted into donating an organ. Individuals remain free to *choose* not to *lose* their organs after death. The diminished freedom that would exist under an opt-out policy therefore is marginal. Moreover, the Human Tissue Gift Act has been in force for more than 10 years, so the policy of giving and receiving has received a fair trial[8] and it has failed. As Caplan has observed, organ procurement is not in the cards,[14] and it's not in the drivers' licences, either.

There are other arguments that can be adduced on behalf of an opt-out policy. The claim that an opt-in policy is preferable because it respects individual autonomy might, in fact, be turned around. Caplan has argued that families cannot make truly autonomous decisions in "an emotional climate of sudden death, grief, and vulnerability."[15] The basic ingredients of a voluntary choice—the ability to comprehend information, a suitable decision-making environment, time to reflect, and the absence of pressure or coercion—often can be absent in the circumstances surrounding an unexpected death. It might be objected that these worries are irrelevant because they pertain to the family of the donor, rather than the donor himself or herself. But despite the authority of the Human Tissue Gift Act, health care professionals still seek the consent of relatives for cadaver donations, so their capacity to make autonomous decisions is relevant to the moral assessment of a general social policy. Moreover, as we shall see shortly, an opt-in policy also can threaten the autonomy of an individual donor.

The autonomy argument can be taken even further. It might be that an opt-out policy would promote individual autonomy even more than an opt-in policy. Public opinion polls reveal that, although a large proportion of the people surveyed are willing to donate their organs after death, only a small proportion sign donor cards.[16] How are these apparently inconsistent results to be reconciled? On the one hand, it could be suggested that it is too psychologically tempting to give an altruistic answer to a faceless pollster, so the signing of a donor card, which is a much more significant event, is a truer indication of a person's real desires.[7] On the other hand, it could be pointed out that less than 20% of all decedents leave wills.[7] This suggests that the failure to take affirmative steps to implement the desire to donate has more to do with the general inertia that surrounds decisions related to one's death, not that the desire is not genuine. And if the desire is genuine and as widespread as the polls indicate, the prevailing opt-in policy is, for whatever reason, largely frustrating that desire.

Thus, even on an opt-in policy's own grounds where individual freedom occupies its morally exalted position, an opt-out policy might be superior. In addition, an opt-out policy would not require the significant costs of continuous advertising and education campaigns, directed at both the general public and health care professionals.[15]

It has been objected, however, that the public would not accept an opt-out policy and any attempt at law reform in this direction "could attract opprobrium to transplantation" that would set back the recent increase in supplies of cadaver organs.[17] The answer to this criticism is easy—we simply don't know that. As Thomas Starzl has observed:

> The ease and uniformity with which cadaveric organ donation under conditions of brain death was accepted by society came as a great surprise to transplant surgeons of two decades ago who did not

appreciate the wisdom and altruism of the public at large. The mistake could be made again by assuming that implied consent statutes would create controversy and a public outcry.[18]

The issue is too important to be decided by speculation rooted in an entrenched conservatism.

CONCLUSION

I have three concluding comments. First, regardless of which policy prevails, mistakes will be made. I recently had the opportunity to discuss ethical issues in family medicine with a group of family doctors. Following the session one family physician asked me whether there were any ethical issues in organ transplantation. After I assured him there were, he said that he wanted to donate his organs when he died, but his wife refused to discuss the matter. In such circumstances the affirmative requirement of consent can be an impediment to implementing the desire to donate. This doctor may never consent to donate because he cannot discuss the matter with his wife. And if his wife will not even discuss the matter with him, what are the chances of her consenting upon his death? Paradoxically, an opt-in policy is likely to thwart this physician's exercise of his personal autonomy. Here an opt-in policy could lead to the loss of organs that should not be lost. That would be a mistake. On the other hand, an opt-out policy undoubtedly would lead to the salvaging of organs from persons who would not wish to donate. That, also, would be a mistake. But unless one can show that taking an organ that was not meant to be taken is an immeasurably greater harm than not using an organ that was meant to be used, the possibility of mistakes with an opt-out policy is not a conclusive objection to it.

Second, this paper has discussed only moral issues surrounding the procurement of cadaver organs. Despite the lack of any insuperable ethical obstacles to an opt-out policy, there could be empirical reasons against it. It has been suggested, for example, that the supply of organs for transplantation would not be significantly increased by moving to an opt-out policy.[17] It is, in this view, possible to get in touch with relatives of potential donors, and there is a high rate of acceptance of organ donation by relatives. In the experience of this unit, 94% of relatives do not object.[7,17] So the major impediment to an adequate supply of cadaver organs, it is claimed, is the attitude of health care professionals. It is their reluctance to refer dead patients with functioning organs or to approach relatives at the time of death that is primarily responsible for the shortage.

The reserve and reticence of health care professionals are a problem for both opt-in and opt-out policies, however. Even those countries with presumed consent statutes have sizable waiting lists for renal transplantation:

> Presumed consent laws increase the likelihood of kidney salvage after a potential donor has been identified, but they do little or nothing to stimulate hospital-based nurses and physicians to aid in that identification.... The problem of enlisting the interest and support of hospitals distant from or unfamiliar with the transplant centers is a serious one for countries with and without presumed consent laws, but countries with presumed consent seem to come closer to meeting their needs for transplant kidneys.[7]

One way of dealing with this problem is through what Caplan has called a "required request" policy, that is, a policy that would mandate, at the time of death, that a person not connected with the determination of death (but obviously a health care professional) ask family members about the possibility of organ donation.[14] Such a policy would infringe the individual freedom of health care professionals; but if an opt-out policy for potential donors is morally permissible, a required request policy for health care professionals is certainly morally permissible.

Finally, one might think that in Canada, where the political tradition is different from that of the United States, a philosophy of liberal individualism is not as rampant, so there is some hope for an opt-out policy. Until recently, that view would have been plausible. But with the advent of our Charter of Rights and Freedoms, Canadians are becoming increasingly enchanted with the rhetoric of rights and the liberal individualism that this rhetoric embodies. Consequently, I am not sanguine about the adoption of an opt-out policy in this country.

REFERENCES

1. Annas GJ: Amer J Pub Health 75:187, 1985

2. Mass Task Force Report: Law Med Health Care 13:8, 1985

3. McCormick RA: In Encyclopedia of Bioethics (vol 3). New York, Free Press, 1978, 1172

4. Starzl TE: Hastings Cent Rep 15:5, 1985

5. Leff AA: Duke Law J 1979:1229, 1979

6. Ogdon DA: Hastings Cent Rep 13:28, 1983

7. Stuart FP: Transplantation 31:238, 1981

8. May W: Hastings Cent Rep 1:10, 1973

9. Engelhardt HT Jr: N Engl J Med 311:70, 1984

10. Sadler AM Jr, Sadler BL: Hastings Cent Studies 14:8, 1984

11. Ramsey P: The Patient as Person. New Haven, Yale University Press, 1970, p 210

12. Feinberg J: Proc and Addresses Amer Philosoph Assn 56:33, 1982

13. Jonas H: Daedalus 98:221, 1969

14. Caplan AL: Hastings Cent Rep 14:9, 1984

15. Caplan AL: Hastings Cent Rep 13:27, 1983

16. John Q Public on Organ Donation: Hastings Cent Rep 13:23, 1983

17. Sells RA: J Med Ethics 5:168, 1979

18. Starzl TE: JAMA 251:1592, 1984

[10]

The Moral Duty to Contribute and Its Implications for Organ Procurement Policy

P.T. Menzel

THE language we commonly use to discuss transplant organs is loaded. For example, we commonly use donor to refer to the person whose organs are used for transplant, regardless of whether the genesis of the transplantation is that person's own consent, the survivors' postmortem agreement, or society's prerogative to remove usable organs regardless. Donor implies a donation, and the paradigm of donation is a conscious act of giving. Thus the language in which the organ procurement discussion has been commonly couched inclines us to assume that what we are doing when we contribute our or our loved one's organ is charity. Giving, after all, is not a legal or even moral duty, but a good thing for good people to do (or as philosophers would say, not duty but "supererogation"). If, then, donating organs for transplant is beyond the call of even moral, much less legal, duty, of course society should leave it to individuals to make private, personal decisions about whether to donate. We are properly wary of trying to make people into saints, heroes, or heroines by social pressure.

I want to challenge this whole way of thinking about organ contribution. I argue first that contributing cadaver organs is not a matter of charitable goodness but instead normally an instance of the moral duty of easy rescue. This will lead me to reject the allegedly more "voluntaristic" policy of consenting in cases where no organs may be used unless contributors competently consent, and defend instead a policy of objecting out where removal is permitted unless the potential contributor objects. I will contend, furthermore, that if they are correctly formed, objecting out policies respect individual autonomy at least as well as consenting in policies do. Finally, I will comment both on whether it is the state that carries the burden of searching out objections or the individual who carries the burden of registering them. I will not comment here on the further question of whether the proper party to object (or consent) is the predeceased person or the family and survivors, although in general my analysis will seem more at home with the assumption that the predeceased person's objection or consent is the proper primary focus.

MORAL DUTY

Besides our language about donation, another immediate conceptual barrier to thinking in terms of a moral duty to contribute is that we do not think everyone ought to donate their organs. There are those who religiously or conscientiously object, for example. Since we tend to think of judgments concerning moral duty as holding more universally than judgments that people ought to perform a given

kind of charitable act, we infer that contributing one's organs must be an optional, charitable thing to do. Yet that conclusion simply does not follow. In times of military conscription, for example, we acknowledge that not everyone has a duty, legal or moral, to serve in the military (eg, conscientious objectors), yet we do not regard military service as only something people charitably donate, eg, we may conscript people. Moral and legal duties can be duties and still have firmly honored exceptions.

More positively though, what can we say about the conditions for the presence of moral duty? The very clearest cases occur when three conditions are met. (1) The behavior makes a great difference to someone else, it prevents a great harm or provides some very significant benefit. (2) It must not be so difficult to perform that one cannot realistically and easily carry it out. If we have a duty to rescue, for example, it is a duty to relatively easy rescue. (3) Some expectation or understanding we have helped to foster creates a special relationship with the person to whom we owe the duty.

The clearest examples of acts that we ought to do but which lie beyond the call of duty occur when the last two conditions are missing. Some people go much out of their way to visit other persons and cheer them up, for example, having previously given them no expectation whatever that they would.

Now note how for most people, contributing one's cadaver organs clearly meets the first two conditions for moral duty. Transplantable organs often confer huge benefits on their recipients, and unless one has religious or ethical objections against contribution, contributing is a very easy thing to do in terms of time, effort, life plans, and effects on one's other duties.[1] If, for example, the reason I do not contribute by signing the back of my driver's license is that I just do not like to think about my possible death, am I any different from the proverbial bystander who, enjoying a newspaper on the park bench, lets a blind person walk off a cliff? People who desperately need my cadaver organs are admittedly not identifiable at the time of prior contribution as the blind pedestrian is when the bystander fails to warn. But what kind of an excuse for not contributing my organs is that? It remains entirely clear that if I (or my survivors) fail to contribute, someone will

From the Department of Philosophy, Pacific Lutheran University, Tacoma, Washington.

Address reprint requests to Paul T. Menzel, PhD, Professor of Philosophy, Pacific Lutheran University, Tacoma, WA 98447.

probably die who would otherwise live. If contributing my organs is then also an exceedingly easy thing to do, how can it be any less my moral duty than shouting a word of warning to the blind pedestrian?

So the first two conditions of moral duty are met. It is then commonly noted, however, that for organ contribution the third condition is missing, previous understanding or "special relationship." Failure to meet this condition is also at the heart of the classic examples used to reject a legal duty to rescue strangers. Again that proverbial blind man: enjoying myself on a park bench 10 feet away, I utter not one word of warning as he walks off a cliff to his demise. Almost certainly I am not legally liable. Should I be? Perhaps not, either.[2] (Note also two exceptions in state law on easy rescue. Vermont and Minnesota have had easy rescue statutes since 1968 and 1971; Vermont Statutes Annotated, Title 12, Sec. 519, Supp. 1971, and Minnesota Statutes Annotated, v. 38, sec. 604.05 [West, 1985]). Note, however, that in pursuing such an argument about what the law should be, we all seem to agree at the start that I would have a moral duty to warn.

Right here we are apt to make an important mistake when we shift the discussion back to organ procurement: seldom does any special relationship exist between organ contributor and recipient, so we think that the case for any policy less "voluntaristic" than consenting in faces the same major difficulties as any argument for a legal duty of easy rescue. But the case for less voluntaristic policies need not carry that same burden at all. Appropriately shaped objecting out policies do not impose a legal duty to contribute. They only give to society an initial legal prerogative, not any right to coerce. In an objecting out arrangement, people can still be allowed to object with absolutely no burden of justifying their objection. It is simply a mistake to charge that kind of objecting out policy with legal moralism, forcing people to do what they ideally ought to do.

Although objecting out policies need not constitute any legal duty to contribute, there may be a way to argue that they virtually meet that difficult, third, special relationship condition anyway. At first sight the context of the normal organ contribution, contributing for anyone who happens to need our organs, seems not to involve any special relationship. We thus mistakenly assume that the use of a moral duty of easy rescue to shape organ procurement policy amounts to making altruism into some sort of requirement. Duties to rescue, however, can be based on tacit agreements of mutual self-interest, not altruism: if we are talking about easy rescues of great benefit, it would seem to be in everybody's mutual interest to at least morally bind themselves to a universal practice of easy rescue.[3]

Thus, a moral viewpoint much less idealistic than general altruism underlies duties of easy rescue. Whether or not that holds for legal duties of easy rescue, it certainly holds for moral duties. In cases of easy rescue we confront an implicit, mutual, rationally self-interested, contractual relationship among human beings. Admittedly this is not what we normally mean by special relationship, certainly not the one I have with my 80-year-old aunt, for example, for whom I have done the grocery shopping the last 10 years. But it does constitute a sufficiently close cousin of that third condition to create a moral duty.

Note also that taking the second condition of duty seriously, that a duty must be relatively easy to perform, can strongly influence the specific shape of an objecting out policy. Allowing anyone with serious objections to opt out just reflects taking the easy limitation on the duty to rescue seriously: anyone with serious objections cannot easily contribute. In practice, objecting out policies can be more generous yet: any objection that people are willing to state counts, with no need to justify that objection in any way. We are led to such an open and easy-to-object out policy by the difficulty of devising and implementing any "reasons" test on what will count as legitimate objection. Some modification does not indicate we are backing away from the belief that people have a moral duty to contribute. They do, unless they seriously object. If they object but their objection is not serious, they still have a moral duty to contribute. However, then we run into another problem: because of the difficulty of determining sufficiently serious reasons, we would probably be wise not to enforce their moral duty in public policy.

In any case, the central point remains: we should stop talking and thinking of contributing transplantable organs as a charitable donation. Although perhaps we should not legally require removal, we should think about organ contribution in terms of moral duty. We should do that even if the contribution of transplantable organs does not meet the strong special relationship condition that may hold for making contribution a legal duty.

OBJECTION, NOT CONSENT

As long, then, as an objecting out policy for organ procurement protects the right of unchallenged objection, it meets the necessary conditions for a moral duty of easy rescue. Despite that fact, however, some critics will claim that any form of objecting out policy is cavalier in handling the dead bodies of free persons. Only voluntaristic consenting in, it will be said, completely respects people's autonomy. Should we not be looking for positive approval, not just the absence of objection? No, I argue, in terms of respecting individuals and their autonomy, not at all.

Asking potential contributors, "Do you consent?" is, of course, an importantly different query than "Do you object?" Imagine generally changing the language of patient consent forms: "Do you object to our taking out half your small intestine?" A query about objection is much more likely to presume that the inquiring party is not just neutral. In a therapeutic context the patient is already subordinate in knowledge and power to health care providers, and it is important not to exacerbate that subordination further. In therapeutic settings there is thus every reason to ask whether people consent, and not whether they object.

Prospectively contributing cadaveric organs, however, is very different. One is not likely to be in the same disadvantageous position vis-à-vis a representative of society asking about organ contribution as one usually finds oneself in when confronted by one's physician. What is the risk in objecting to what some officer behind a driver's license application desk may seem to suppose by the question asked? Why would the officer take any objection one might choose to express as an affront? By contrast, we naturally expect that a provider might feel affronted by a patient's refusal to accept carefully suggested therapy.

Furthermore, we must remember here that unless one has some objection, contributing one's organs is easy and therefore one's moral duty. This provides the most important argument of all for making objection, not consent, the focus of public policy. If the stakes of one's decision for transplant recipients are as high as they usually are, failure to consent is not at all the right thing on which to focus in carving out exceptions to one's duty. Why should one not have to object, not merely fail to consent, to escape the moral duty of easy rescue? Does one not owe at least that to desperate potential recipients?

It is easy to understand why objectors themselves may overlook this connection of organ procurement policy with the usual moral duty to contribute. After all, being objectors, they would then not have any duty to contribute. Occupying that position can unfortunately lead objectors to forget that if they did not have any serious objection, they would indeed have a duty to contribute. But see what this means: were objectors to take that contingency to heart (the fact that *if* they had no objection, they would be morally required to allow their organs to be used), would they not be willing to carry some small burdens to make it clear that they do in fact object? Wouldn't they admit their responsibility to express any real objections they have instead of totally controlling a life-saving situation by mere default?

This also clarifies how an objecting out policy can handle the case of people who do not know when they are queried about possible objection. On the one hand, an "I don't know" response indicates a hesitation that makes us reluctant to remove organs without further consent. But on the other hand, isn't that response sufficient to justify removal when society has provided such a clear opportunity to object? If people really do regard their ambivalence as reason enough to block society's use of their organs, why should they not carry the burden of expressing that ambivalence as an objection? Perhaps the case where "I don't know" really is an objection can be brought out rather easily by a follow-up query: "Does that mean that you would rather not have any of your needed organs removed for transplant?" If after that people still say "I don't know," why should we think we have taken away some part of their freedom of choice if we later remove their organs?

We need to be frank about this. To claim that any and all absence of positive consent should control the use of a person's organs suggests that our notions of moral responsibility and self-determination are incredibly weak. Do rights of self-determination and the moral principle of "autonomy" warrant the freedom to follow our views no matter how passively we hold or uncourageously we express them? Do the internal workings of self-determination ask absolutely no price from us before moral rights of autonomy kick in? Our negative answers to these rhetorical questions, combined with the existence of a moral duty to contribute unless one objects, compels us to focus on the absence of objection and not the presence of consent in shaping public policy on organ procurement.

PLACING THE BURDEN OF EXPRESSION

None of this settles another different matter; who should carry the official burden of stating or recording any objection? The normal moral duty to contribute determines that absence of objection and not presence of consent is the proper requisite state of a contributor's mind, but the locus of the burden of expressing that objection is another matter. Who should initiate and record whatever state of mind we decide is properly dispositional?

A very strong view of responsibility would place on people the responsibility to record any objection they might have. At the other extreme, the very weakest view would hold not only that consent, not objection, is the proper query, but that no one should even raise the issue of organ donation with people for fear of pressuring them or invading their "privacy." Between these extremes, arrangements might be made for representatives of society to ask as many people as possible whether they object, or to ask as many as possible whether they consent.

People usually think of objecting out rather narrowly, as a policy in which it is entirely up to individuals to record their own objection. If that is the kind of objecting out arrangement under discussion, and we want to argue for it in terms respectful of individual autonomy, we would have to defend the legitimacy of presuming that when people have not registered any objection, they would not have objected had they been asked. In certain circumstances, presumption of people's agreement is legitimate, but it is not whenever actually consulting them is easy.[4] And in fact, consulting people in the organ contribution case would seem to be relatively easy. We can devise inexpensive arrangements for asking most people whether they object to removal of the organs of their dead body. We might ask everyone who applies for a driver's license, for example, or at whatever other convenient occasions could be added to give people the widest opportunity for easy objection. We could also have a qualifying policy of not removing organs when there is any reason to suspect that people did not have the opportunity for easy objection. We have a wide spectrum of arrangements here from which to choose. (It is interesting to note the varying burdens on

2178   MENZEL

providers who remove corneas in states that have some sort of routine-removal/objecting-out statute for corneal tissue in particular. Arizona, Colorado, and Utah require "reasonable search" for the donor's objection and still have to import corneal tissue from other states, whereas Florida, Georgia, Maryland, Michigan, and Texas require only that there be "no known objection" and collect more than they use.[5])

So the moral duty to contribute that makes a policy of objecting out preferable to one of consenting in may still leave the burden of inquiry with the society instead of the burden of expression on the individual.

CONCLUSIONS

In summary, people have a moral duty to contribute their transplantable cadaveric organs unless they object. Objecting out policies reflect and communicate that duty better than consenting in policies do, and they respect individual autonomy at least as well if they place no reasons test on valid objection. To be received as impec-

cably respectful of individuals' freedom and their control of their bodies, however, society in adopting an objecting out arrangement should still carry the burden of discovering whether people object to contributing their organs. The best next step in organ procurement needs to be a policy that both emphasizes this contribution as not just an "optional" matter and yet respects the beliefs of individuals about their bodies. (Much of this article is derived from chapter 10 of Menzel.[4] I owe a considerable debt to David Peters, PhD [University of Wisconsin, River Falls], whose views brought me a long way toward the position developed here.)

REFERENCES

1. Peters DA: J Med Human Bioeth 7:106, 1986
2. Feinberg J: The Moral Limits of the Criminal Law. Vol. I: Harm to Others. Oxford: Oxford University Press, p 126
3. Lipkin RJ: UCLA Law Rev 31:252, 1983
4. Menzel PT: Strong Medicine: The Ethical Rationing of Health Care. Oxford: Oxford University Press, 1990, p 29
5. Lambertson MA: Colorado Lawyer 13:615, 1984

[11]

The Case for Presumed Consent to Transplant Human Organs After Death

C. Cohen

A NECESSARY condition for the lifesaving uses of the organs of a human body after death is the permission of those who have rightful authority over the body in question. Each of us is the possessor, master, of our own body, and therefore (it is almost universally agreed) we have wide moral authority to give or withhold permission for the use of our body after death.

Just rules for the disposition of human bodily remains therefore must respect individual autonomy in that disposition. Autonomous expressions of will regarding the posthumous disposition of one's organs are most often not made while alive, and therefore a decedent's autonomous judgments are rarely known with certainty. After death, authority over the body is commonly thought to rest with the decedent's family, who are likely to represent best the true will of the decedent. But even they cannot exercise the decedent's autonomy, since no one can do that.

PRESUMED CONSENT

A great change in our national system of organ procurement, a change grounded in the moral foundation of human autonomy, is now called for. Current American practice tacitly assumes that, absent specific notification to the contrary, decedents are best protected if we act as though they had autonomously willed that their organs not be donated for transplantation. Organ procurement therefore now relies utterly upon consent expressly given (by the decedent before death, or by his family after death) that rebuts this presumption. I argue that this system of rules, formal and informal, ought to be wholly reformed; the underlying assumption that ought to be made is the very opposite of the one now made. To protect the autonomous wishes of decedents we ought to assume that they did will or would have willed their organs for beneficent medical uses. Expectations would be reversed under the reformed system; the normal pattern would be one in which lifesaving transplants of cadaveric organs proceed as a matter of course unless consent for such uses had been expressly refused. Absent express refusal, no permission for the donation of organs need be sought from any party, no discussion of any kind being required save that called for by purely medical considerations. Presumed consent is the name commonly given to the system here proposed.[1]

This is certainly not a new idea; it was first brought to wide attention by Dukenminier and Sanders in 1968,[2] and has since been entertained by a number of others, sometimes only halfheartedly or as a possible recourse to which our need for cadaver organs unhappily drives us.[1,3–6] I submit, however, that a system in which consent is presumed is not merely expedient or advantageous; it is also just. Such a system is good because it maximizes benefits for all concerned. Because it best protects the autonomy of decedents it is also right, more right than the system now employed.

NEEDS AND GOODS

What is good for society is largely a function of what its members need. We need a great many more organs for transplant than are presently procured. The gravity of that need, and the likelihood that it will increase as the years go on, I take to have been established by others, at this conference and elsewhere. Therefore, the existing system of organ procurement depending utterly upon express consent, almost always sought from the decedent's family at the time of the loved one's death, is not very good and certainly is not good enough.

The enlargement of organ supply required to meet these compelling needs does not appear feasible within the current framework of express consent, whether that consent be sought voluntarily or the request for consent be required by law. Whatever the reasons for this—the failure of young persons to express their judgment while healthy, the psychological stress upon families at the time of the dying of a loved one, the reluctance or awkwardness of physicians and administrators in making donation requests as patients are dying, or others—long experience teaches that circumstances commonly conspire to block the needed express consent for the donation of the organs of a decedent. In sum, the need for organs is great and will increase, while the present system of procurement through express consent fails and almost certainly will continue to fail to meet that need.

We may conclude without serious doubt that overall human well-being will be substantially improved if some way were found, within the boundaries of morally right conduct, to increase greatly the supply of human cadaver organs for transplantation. A system of presumed consent would very probably increase the supply of needed organs vastly. This is the outcome one would expect, and it is confirmed by experience with presumed consent in other countries,[4] although even where presumed consent is

From the School of Medicine, University of Michigan, Ann Arbor, Michigan.

Address reprint requests to Carl Cohen, PhD, Professor of Philosophy, University of Michigan, School of Medicine, M7330 Medical Science Building I, Ann Arbor, MI 48109-0624.

operative the needs for cadaver organs are not fully met.[7] The disadvantages of presuming consent are minimal, nearly nil. On balance, therefore, an organ procurement system founded upon presumed consent is almost certainly good.

WHAT IS RIGHT TO PRESUME?

For utilitarian moralists, therefore, the justifiability of the proposed reform is plain. But for those of us whose deepest moral principles are not grounded in utility, serious moral questions remain. Is the presumption of consent right? Principles of right conduct ought not be sacrificed to improve the balance of results. Can a system of presumed consent be fully reconciled with the autonomous disposition of human organs by those having rightful authority over them? The answer is yes.

Putting the question in that way, however, suggests that there is some difficulty in the reconciliation. Suppose the critical question were posed in this way: How can we most fully realize most persons' autonomous wishes concerning the disposition of the organs of their own bodies after their death? While healthy, most persons do not confront the matter; while dying most cannot decently be asked their preferences; when dead all are silent. In the great run of cases, therefore, we do not learn what we would most like to know at the time we need to know it: the actual desires of persons whose body organs are at issue. Therefore, under any system whatever, we are forced to make some very general presumptions concerning the wishes of persons about the uses of their organs after their deaths. And under any system we must receive and implement autonomous expressions of preference that do not conform to the general presumption.

That is the form of what we do now, but the present substance is problematic. We presume now for all persons that there was a will not to donate; then under some circumstances we seek express consent to do what we had presumed would not have been wanted. That express consent we most often seek from the family of the decedent, there being no other resource.

The consequences of presuming in this pattern are often gravely unfortunate; familial distress is commonly caused by the mere request for consent, and the refusal of it often results in the loss of human lives that might otherwise have been saved. But in addition to its unfortunate results, the present system is wrong, wrong because it undermines in practice the very principle upon which it was supposed to have been built. As it must, it incorporates into law and practice a presumption about what people generally want to happen to the organs of their bodies after death, but the presumption thus incorporated is one now known to be inconsistent with the actual wishes of most persons, at least, of most persons in these times in the United States. We honestly aim to protect autonomy, but by our current practice we commonly vitiate it.

The majority of people now heartily support the concept of organ donation. Most persons, when asked, express without qualification their willingness to donate their own organs after death. As early as 1968, support in the United States for organ transplantation from cadavers was shown to be strong and widespread.[8] By 1975, still an early date from the perspective of organ transplantation, a majority of those even in rural and relatively unsophisticated areas expressed positive support for organ transplantation.[9] In regions more sophisticated, in Los Angeles County, for example,[10] and in Houston,[11] those supporting organ donation (even back in 1975) were more than three fourths the whole. In Liverpool in 1979 that figure was 93%.[12]

Some who support transplantation are nevertheless uneasy with the vision of the donation of their own organs. Every person conscious of his own will has some difficulty in picturing his own death. But what most Americans would say in their most rational moments, and (if they were in a position to be asked) would most likely say about the lifesaving uses of their own bodily remains, is clear: Yes, our organs may be used by others, if this will save lives. The present system, depending entirely upon the express consent of the decedent's family after death, thus errs in its empirical underpinning, and by that error promotes a great moral mistake.

All too frequently the spouses and children of dying patients respond negatively to the request for donation. But families are thus being obliged to answer a question terrible, at the moment it is being asked, for the very reason it must then be asked. And they are being asked at that moment to override what is widely presumed. Under such circumstances the responses of families often do not reliably reflect the autonomous wishes of decedents. We ask the wrong persons, at the worst possible times, what they should never have been asked at all.

As a matter of morality, our weightiest obligation here is to decedents, about whose wishes we (usually) must make some presumption. To best realize their autonomy we should presume what we have strong empirical reason to believe was in fact their wish, that if their organs might be used to save another life, they ought to be so used.

Presuming general consent to organ donation is therefore the right thing to do; that is the chief reason, and a very powerful reason, to turn the present system right side up. At the moral core of this matter lies autonomy, of which consent in the disposition of one's body is one manifestation; presuming consent for beneficent transplantation of organs is the best, imperfect but still the best, realization of autonomy in any population like ours that strongly favors the donation of cadaveric organs.

OTHER GOOD CONSEQUENCES OF PRESUMED CONSENT

By this morally right presumption we may improve and prolong the lives of persons who would otherwise have died. But other great goods also ensue. Grieving families are given enormous relief. Many people who, when rational and calm, would donate their own organs without qualm, want not to think about the matter when not obliged to do so, and when forced to make that decision for others at moments of despair and stress, are agonized. At the very moment when the removal of a loved one's vital organs is most dreadful to contemplate, when feelings of guilt or helplessness are most likely to distort calm judgment, grieving families need not confront the matter. Moreover, this resolution of the matter by an earlier, and universally understood presumption, would be a service not only to the bereaved, but also to physicians and nurses who are relieved of the need to ask questions laden with pain and doom, as grief-ridden families are relieved of the need to answer them.

PROTECTING THOSE WHO OBJECT

The operational details of a system of presumed consent would be important, of course, but they present no insuperable difficulties. Some persons do not wish to have their organs removed for any purpose, even to save lives after their deaths. To them it must be said, without hesitation or rancor, "as you wish." Giving to every person the opportunity, while alive, freely to opt out of the system of general donation is a social obligation entailed by respect for individual autonomy, and an obligation readily fulfilled. Any individuals, *for any reason or without reason*, must have and will have the right and the fullest opportunity to cancel the presumption in their own case, and that simply by registering this wish, without need for justification or argument or delay, or for any other judgment by any other person.

Once the system of presumed consent has become widely understood (and probably even when first introduced) those who opt out will be a minority, and the interests of that minority must be carefully respected. A national computerized registry will be required, to which there will be appropriate access by authorized individuals and by hospitals, so that those who do object may record their wishes in ways that will protect the autonomy of their judgments. In short: any person's exercise of the option to demur, for any reason whatever, must settle the matter for that person's remains. No one else need ever be asked anything.

TRANSITIONAL MATTERS

The transformation of the present system of organ procurement into one of presumed consent (with ready option out) must take place in ways that will not result in surprise or disadvantage. Of no one may it later be said that objections would have been registered if only the rules had been known. Wide public education must therefore precede the reversing reform, and the revised presumption must be openly and clearly expressed in ways that all may fully grasp. That is surely within our power. The twice-annual shift from standard to daylight saving time and back is infuriating to many, and more coercive than the shift proposed here, but (I observe) very few are they who, the very next day, do not know the correct time. When there is a widespread understanding that human organs are an absolutely priceless resource, wasted only at the cost of life, most persons will be proud of this shift. But for those who remain troubled by it the fullest opportunity to opt out must be given, their recourse made simple, convenient, and always revocable. In less time than we now may think, I hazard, most will wonder how ever it could have been any other way. Did once people need to give express permission in order that another's life be saved by what would otherwise soon rot? Did once people commonly presume that some must die because others were in psychological distress? It was that way once, but that was back in unenlightened times.

AUTONOMY AND THE FAMILY

Until the presumption of consent has become widely understood and assimilated, objections to the donation of organs by the decedent's next-of-kin will have to be respected. This family veto is likely to reduce the supply of needed organs at first, but authorizing it will smooth passage into the new system. Eventually, I believe, we will come to regard the authority of the family to block donation as more a burden to the decedent's autonomous will than a safeguard of it.

On the other hand, if any individuals while competent register an affirmative expression of their will that their organs be donated if they prove usable after death, by this act converting a presumed consent into consent expressly given, the will so expressed ought not to be subject to contravention by the will of any others, even that of family members.

Presumed consent has been criticized by some as insensitive to the ethical demands of bereaved families,[13] but this complaint misconceives the ethical issue. The psychological well-being of bereaved families must be safeguarded, of course, and will be. But at bottom the moral authority for consent to donate organs lies only with the person whose organs they are, or were. Families properly enter, in this as in other proxy contexts, to represent the will of those who cannot speak for themselves; however good their motivation, family members ought not to be permitted to contravene the wills of those with genuine moral authority in the matter.

In spirit and in detail an organ procurement system should aim to realize the will of the donor while alive, and to preclude the frustration of that will. With very few exceptions, imposed in special circumstances, we are properly sovereign over our own bodies while alive, and our wishes concerning the uses of our organs after death deserve continuing respect. Autonomy ought to be the ruling principle in this sphere; under a system of presumed consent it will be, and if not perfectly realized at least autonomy will be more fully realized then than it is now.

OBJECTIONS AND REPLIES

Objections of three kinds have been registered to systems of presumed consent. Some are mechanical, some sociologic, some moral; all fail.

1. Mechanical or technical objections are raised to the workings of the system. The registry of those opting out would become too complicated, it is said, or some might fail to get ready access to it, and so on.[14] Others are troubled by the fact that maintaining uniformity across state boundaries will present a problem.[15] Such objections are essentially insignificant. If a change to presumed consent is fundamentally wise we can surely make it work, and we can devise the needed machinery to smooth its operation in practice. Occasional breakdowns there will be under any system, of course; in a few cases, especially at the outset, the presumption of consent may result in some organs being used that should not have been. But when the common presumption made is consonant with the common will on the matter, misfire is much less likely than when (as under the present system) it is dissonant. Moreover, while the lifesaving use of organs that ought not to have been used cannot be right, it is at least a wrong more tolerable than the wrong of not using organs that should have been used. In choosing between the two approaches, each subject to some operational failure, it is surely wise to implement the one whose failures are likely to be fewer and whose results are certain to be better.

2. What I call "sociologic" objections are rooted in the fear of attitudes or practices that the new system will (allegedly) promote. The fears are various:

A. That organ farms or other macabre fantasies will be encouraged by a system of presumed consent.

B. That the spirit of voluntarism will be undermined.[14]

C. That the distrust of physicians will be increased because, as the routine harvesters of organs, they will come to be viewed as persons in whose hands a very sick person cannot be safe. Or that hospitals will by this change be transformed in the popular imagination into places of bodily mutilation and brutality. May[16] writes:

> "While the procedure of routine salvaging may, in the short run, furnish more organs for transplants, in the long run, its systemic effect on the institutions of medical care would seem to be depressing and corrosive of that trust upon which acts of healing depend."

Such dismal speculations, and others like them, and the objections to which they give rise, have no good empirical foundation. Anecdotal horror stories, in a context of antipathy toward medical researchers and hospitals, are magnified by imagination into what may be called anticipatory speculative condemnation. Anxiety and mistrust of the same sort long accompanied the development of recombinant DNA technology, we will recall, and commonly arise when changes in old ways are proposed. The real empirical consequences of presuming consent, of which we cannot now be certain of course, are in fact as likely to support humane care as to undermine it. The life-enhancing possibilities of organ transplantation, the change of focus from those dying to those who may yet live, may bring a fuller appreciation of the gratitude of organ recipients and their families, and may prove a great boon for humanity, celebrating as it does the most wholesome and productive of human values. Widespread recognition of the goods achieved by organ transplantation may do more to enhance the spirit of voluntarism than to erode it. All such claims are speculative; the fears have as little foundation as the hopes. We ought not to treat ungrounded speculations as rational objections to a presumption about the common will that we know to be correctly applicable to most people.

Those who find the removal of organs from a cadaver to be frightening, or self-seeking, or otherwise unscrupulous, will of course attack any system that promotes organ transplantation as brutal. Those who make of physicians common objects of abuse will feel threatened by any proposal appearing to enlarge their authority. Ghastly misbehaviors in the handling of dead bodies are of course possible under any system whatever. Avoiding the ugly, the abusive, and the insensitive is a matter of wise and intelligent administration. Wisdom and intelligence may on occasion prove wanting, but their want is in no case likely to be the consequence of the presumption made about the will of decedents. And what is most insensitive after all, even macabre, is watching persons die whose lives could and should have been saved, but were not.

3. Finally, account must be taken of two genuinely moral objections:

A. The first is based on the moral conviction that the process of harvesting human organs is intrinsically wrong. Some (but not all) Orthodox Jews, seeking to respect Divine command, and some who hope for a resurrection of their bodies in the afterlife have this conviction. The religiosity of such objectors we must respect, but their convictions cannot be allowed to block an otherwise justifiable change in the presumption of consent, so long as these persons and all others are clearly free to reject the presumption of consent effectively in their own case, and are unhindered in doing so. With those who hold such views no contest is in order, nor any effort to persuade or bring pressure. Convictions about the history of the body after death, or other supernatural beliefs causing organ removal to be thought unacceptable, are not the business of the community at large. We may all believe what we please, and all must be free to work our own will regarding our own organs, without objection or obstruction.

B. A second moral objection rests upon what is claimed to be a critical difference between consenting and not objecting. If we rely upon express consent we realize autonomy (this critic holds), but if we rely only upon the absence of objection we may fail to do so. Hence a procurement system built upon express consent is always morally sound even if clumsy, while one built upon the presumption of consent could not be reliably sound even if it were expeditious.

Wrong. There is a difference between express consent and not objecting, but that difference cannot guide us in a moral choice between the one presumption and the other. If persons do in reality object to the use of their organs (but never register that objection) a system that requires express consent will protect his autonomy more surely than the revised system here defended. But with the presumption reversed, the very same point can be made in reverse: if one does in reality consent to the use of one's organs (as most of us do, although never registering that consent) a system that presumes *consent* will protect his autonomy more surely than the present system can.

The difference in focus here is that between positive acts (expressly consenting or expressly refusing consent) and negative acts (refraining from refusing or refraining from consenting). This is an operational difference, not a moral one. It can have moral consequences, but the merit of proceeding in the one way or the other depends largely upon what we believe to be the general inclination of those about whom one of those presumptions must be made. If we knew that only 1 or 2 persons in 10 would autonomously donate their organs, a system that presumed consent, protecting 10% automatically but obliging the other 90% to register their objections to make their will effective, would be unfair. But if we have good reasons to believe that 7 or 8 of 10, or even 6 of 10, would in fact choose to donate their own organs for lifesaving uses after death, a system that presumes the absence of consent (what we have now) similarly protects a minority and obliges the majority to register their views expressly, and it is then unfair.[6]

Whether we require consent to be expressed, or require refusal to be expressed, should depend upon what we believe the majority would have done in fact, if all had registered their views. We may presume one way, or presume the other, but presume we must. Either way we place a heavier load upon those for whom the presumption made is incorrect. Moral principles by themselves give no indication which presumption is the fairer. Acting justly requires respect for the autonomous judgments people would actually have made, or (if we are unsure of that) what we may most reasonably suppose they would have made. That reasonable supposition we can reliably make. Therefore, presuming that consent would have been given is in fact fairer, more protective, and more likely to realize autonomy than presuming (as we do now) that it would not have been given.

REFERENCES

1. Matas AJ, Veith FJ: Theor Med 5:155, 1984

2. Dukenminier J, Sanders D: N Engl J Med 179:413, 1968

3. Caplan AL: Hastings Cent Rep 13:23, 1983

4. Hull AR: Nephrol News Issues October:28, 1990

5. Matas A, Arras J, Muyskens J: J Health Polit Policy Law 10:231, 1985

6. Menzel PT: Strong Medicine. Oxford University Press, 1990, p 171

7. Childress J: Hearings before the Subcommittee on Investigations and Oversight of the Committee on Science and Technology, US House of Representatives, 1983, 281

8. Gallup G: The Gallup Report. Princeton, NJ: Gallup, January 17, 1968

9. Kidney Foundation of Eastern Missouri, Assessment of Public and Professional Attitudes Regarding Organ Transplantation, St Louis, Mo, 1975

10. Transplantation Council of Southern California, Public Opinion and Attitudes about Medical Transplantation Among Los Angeles County Residents, Los Angeles, 1975

11. Cleveland SE: Psychosom Med 37:306, 1975

12. Sells RA: J Royal Soc Med 72:109, 1979

13. Mahoney J: J Med Ethics I:67, 1975

14. Sadler AM, Sadler BL: Hastings Cent Rep, October:6, 1984

15. Prottas J: Hearings Before the Subcommittee on Investigations and Oversight of the Committee on Science and Technology, US House of Representatives, 1983, 745

16. May W: Hastings Cent Rep I:6, 1973

[12]

Presumed consent or contracting out

Charles A Erin and John Harris *University of Manchester, Manchester*

In the United Kingdom, we have become habituated to an opting-in system of cadaveric organ procurement. It is becoming of increasing concern that this system is failing to meet the demand for organs for transplantation, with 5,349 people on waiting lists for solid organ transplants at the end of 1998.[1] Manifestly, such a tragic statistic alarms us all, and calls for urgent attention, and, perhaps, for radical action. And, at one level, this is what we have witnessed in the British Medical Association's (BMA) recent reversal of its historical opposition to a system of so-called presumed consent for the procurement of cadaver organs.[2][3] The BMA's overwhelming vote in favour of changing to an opt-out system at its annual conference in early July followed, almost immediately, publication of the results of a government survey which showed a lack of public support for such a system,[4] and it thus came as no great surprise that the government later rejected the BMA's proposal.[5][6] Bad timing perhaps, but, whilst any necessary change in legislation might be minimal, if the United Kingdom was to adopt a system of cadaveric organ donation based on presumed consent, this would clearly represent a major overhaul of social policy in this area, and an overnight tidal change in public opinion is hardly to be expected.

For the sake of argument, let us accept the general view that presumed consent legislation does increase the yield of cadaver organs for transplantation.[7][8] However, there is more than efficiency to consider, and here we will be concerned with arguments from moral principle, not from statistics.[9]

Presumed consent is a fiction

The first point to note is that presumed consent is a fiction. Without the *actual* consent of the individual, there is *no* consent. This is an important point in the context of cadaver organ procurement, particularly in the face of legal instruments adopted in various jurisdictions to increase the number of cadaver organs available for transplantation.

Many see presumed consent as synonymous with contracting out.[10] And it is, of course, intuitively attractive to do so. The underpinning message of the system to which the conflation of these terms refers is something like this: "unless you make it clear during your lifetime that you would refuse to donate organs on death, we will presume that you consent to organ removal, even though you do not actually consent". Even ignoring the question of whether presumed consent represents a contradiction in terms, there is a significant and worthwhile distinction to be drawn between the notion of presumed consent and contracting or opting out, and the distinction speaks to what is at the basis of social policy in this area, and how that policy sells itself, and is interpreted.

Are we not, in adopting the language of *consent*, attempting to disguise what we are actually doing in a way which, however well motivated, appeals to the now well recognised principle of respect for individual autonomy? In reality, by *presuming* consent, we are acting against that principle; we are being disrespectful of individual autonomy. However it might be perceived, in formalising a contracting-out approach for the removal of organs from cadavers, we are, in essence, articulating a particular society's view of what it is morally supportable to do with the body of a dead person,[11] where that person has not consented prior to death[12] to such treatment of her body after death. Effectively, we are saying: "where citizens do not explicitly make known their refusal to donate organs when dead, we feel that it is morally justifiable to remove them in order to improve the quality of life of living citizens and to save lives". It seems that, however we care to represent it, if we are prepared to remove organs from the dead in the absence of prior consent, we do so simply because we believe it is the right thing to do; and we believe that it is the right thing to do because we know it is in the best interests of those patients in need of an organ, and that not to remove these organs would be to harm those patients and to respect no values of moral significance comparable to respect for the lives that are at risk.[13][14]

Two final points seem apposite. Presuming consent is an affront to the moral principle that is the foundation of consent itself. That said, as fictions go, this is a very popular fiction, having the support of, for example, the Declaration of Helsinki, and the Council for International Organisations of Medical Sciences (CIOMS) guidelines.[15][16] Nevertheless if we are to presume anything, we should presume that people would wish to do the morally right thing in the particular situation. In the case of cadaver organs this is certainly to make them available for life-saving or life-enhancing use.

We must also remember that while people talk of their ownership of their own organs and their rights to dispose of them as they wish, the normal incidents of ownership are lacking in the case of cadaver transplantation. There is no one who gets to keep the organs. If they don't go for donation, the worms or the fire, or sometimes the coroner, will have them. Of course there are such things as wills for disposal of property after death, but there are also such things as death duties. Perhaps best of all would be to think of cadaver donation in such terms, as a duty the dead owe to the living, which costs them little or nothing to pay and which does huge amounts of good.

Acknowledgement

We are indebted to Phil Dyer and John Evans for useful discussion of the statistics mentioned in reference 1.

Charles A Erin, BSc (Wales), MSc (London), MSc and PhD (Manchester), is Head of the Centre for Social Ethics and Policy, and Senior Lecturer in Applied Philosophy at the University of Manchester, and a Fellow of the Institute of Medicine, Law and Bioethics. John Harris, BA (Kent), DPhil (Oxford), is Sir David Alliance Professor of Bioethics and a Director of the Institute of Medicine, Law and Bioethics at the University of Manchester. Address for correspondence: Dr Charles A Erin, Institute of Medicine, Law and Bioethics, University of Manchester, Oxford Road, Manchester M13 9PL, United Kingdom. Tel/fax: + 44 161 275 3468 / 3473. E-mail: Charles.Erin@man.ac.uk

References and notes

1 United Kindom Transplant Support Service Authority (UKTSSA) figures, taken from http://www.argonet.co.uk/users/body/DoH.html. The figure of 5,349 represents the active waiting list; including the suspended figure, the total is 6,502. And this is despite there having been 2,694 solid organ transplants from cadavers during 1998.
2 Anonymous. Doctors back organ donation reform. *BBC News Online.* http://news.bbc.co.uk/hi/english/health/newsid_389000/389043.stm posted 8 July, 1999.
3 Beecham L. BMA wants presumed consent for organ donors. *British Medical Journal* 1999;319:141.
4 Department of Health. Press release 1999/0405. Survey shows that public prefers existing organ donor scheme. 2 Jul 1999.
5 Anonymous. Opposition to changing organ donor scheme. *BBC News Online.* http://news.bbc.co.uk/hi/english/health/newsid_384000/384401.stm posted 3 July, 1999.
6 Anonymous. Organ donor reform rejected. *BBC News Online.* http://news.bbc.co.uk/hi/english/health/newsid%5F396000/396430.stm posted 16 July, 1999.
7 Compare with: Sells RA. Radical options for improving the supply of cadaveric organs, presented at *Multi-cultural ethical issues in transplantation.* International Conference, Institute of Medicine, Law and Bioethics (IMLAB), University of Manchester, and University of Tel Aviv, Manchester, 21-22 February, 1999 (unpublished observations).
8 Though, as Michielsen warns, we should be careful in comparing national statistics. See Michielsen P. Informed or presumed consent legislative models. In Chapman JR, Deierhoi M and Wright C, eds. *Organ and tissue donation for transplantation.* London: Arnold, 1997:349-354, esp. 349.
9 For what it is worth, however, the successful Spanish experience suggests that a change of law alone is insufficient, and, whether we are to go this route or not, it seems that greater resourcing for transplant co-ordinators, for example, is called for.
10 For example, see reference 8:344.
11 A dead person? There is something self-contradictory about this.
12 That is, where an express consent was not obtained, and there is no relevant, reliable advance directive, whether in the form of a living will, or a record on the National Organ Donor Register, or an organ donor card.
13 Compare with Harris J. Research, transplantation and the duty to others. (unpublished observations).
14 We assume the moral and causal symmetry of acts and omissions. See Harris J. *Violence and responsibility.* London: Routledge & Kegan Paul, 1980.
15 World Medical Association. *Declaration of Helsinki,* as amended by the 48th General Assembly, October 1996: basic principle 11.
16 Council for International Organisations of Medical Sciences (CIOMS) in collaboration with the World Health Organization (WHO). *International ethics guidelines for biomedical research involving human subjects.* CIOMS and WHO: Geneva, 1993: guideline 1.

[13]

The Failure to Give: Reducing Barriers to Organ Donation

James F. Childress

ABSTRACT. Moral frameworks for evaluating non-donation strategies to increase the supply of cadaveric human organs for transplantation and ways to overcome barriers to organ donation are explored. Organ transplantation is a very complex area, because the human body evokes various beliefs, symbols, sentiments, and emotions as well as various rituals and social practices. From a rationalistic standpoint, some policies to increase the supply of transplantable organs may appear to be quite defensible but then turn out to be ineffective and perhaps even counterproductive because of inadequate attention to these rich and complex features of human body parts. Excessively *rationalistic* policies neglect deep beliefs, symbols, sentiments, and emotions and the like, and that deficiency marks many actual and proposed policies. In addition, policies are often too *individualistic* and too *legalistic*.

MOST ETHICAL ANALYSES of possible ways to increase the supply of cadaveric human organs for transplantation focus on the gift of life through organ donation. I will focus on moral frameworks for evaluating non-donation strategies and ways to overcome barriers to organ donation. My starting point is the persistent, chronic shortage of organs for transplantation, and the relative stagnation of cadaveric organ donation for the last several years, at least in the United States.

The stagnation in organ procurement in the U.S. has resulted in part from a decline in the potential donor pool, especially because of the success of seat-belt laws, and the limited growth that has occurred in procurement is the result, to a great extent, of changes in the criteria for donor eligibility—e.g., accepting organs from older donors.

In discussing the failure to give and ways to overcome this failure, I will make two assumptions: (1) that we need to increase the supply of

KENNEDY INSTITUTE OF ETHICS JOURNAL • MARCH 2001

organs in order to save lives and/or to enhance the quality of life and (2) that our societal efforts to increase the supply of transplantable organs should remain within certain ethical boundaries. Each of these assumptions is somewhat controversial: the first, because of challenges to organ transplantation in general as an overvalued enterprise relative to its benefits and its costs; the second, because of uncertainties about the appropriate ethical boundaries. I will ignore the controversy about the first assumption and only address the second through indirect efforts to clarify what I believe to be important ethical constraints on societal efforts to increase the number of transplantable organs.

Organ transplantation is a very complex area, because the human body evokes various beliefs, symbols, sentiments, and emotions as well as various rituals and social practices. From a rationalistic standpoint, some policies to increase the supply of transplantable organs may appear to be quite defensible but then turn out to be ineffective and perhaps even counterproductive, because of inadequate attention to these rich and complex features of human body parts. Excessively *rationalistic* policies neglect deep beliefs, symbols, sentiments, and emotions and the like–these various psychosocial factors–and that deficiency marks many actual and proposed policies. In addition, policies are often too *individualistic* and too *legalistic*. Those are three charges I will level against several efforts in the U.S. to increase the number of available organs. Much of my argument will hinge on how one characterizes the failure to give or to donate organs.

A CASE OF ORGAN DONATION

I will focus on an actual case in order to identify different frameworks of moral discourse that affect how we view failures to donate (or, if that language is too strong, acts of non-donation):

In early June, 1995, a popular, athletic Texan in his twenties, who was undecided about what he wanted to be and do, died unexpectedly from an aneurysm. "In death," as a sports section in a newspaper noted, "he gave half a dozen people their futures, among them a truck driver, a farm manager, a backwoods-resort operator and an American legend named Mickey Mantle" (Dallas Morning News 1995). All six operations occurred at about the same time at Baylor University Medical Center in Dallas.

Newspaper reporters later managed to identify the source of the organs, but, at the family's request, they did not disclose his identity in their reports or to the recipients. His mother explained the family's decision to donate: "Once his soul and spirit is gone, nothing is left. His body is of use to somebody else only in this way. It never even crossed my mind not to donate. To me, it's the decent thing to do. It's the thing we should do." In addition, she noted, "We thought we might as well make something good come out of our tragedy." Hence, as soon as the doctors asked her, she responded, "Yes, definitely." She made this decision even though her son had never discussed organ donation with her. However, his Texas driver's license indicated "donor" (Dallas Morning News 1995).

Contrast the mother's comment about why she donated her son's organs with various media reports about organ donation. With specific reference to this case, the media underlined the "sacrifice" of organ donors and praised their "heroic" actions. Others have called such cadaveric organ donations "extraordinary," a term that could refer to their relative infrequency or to their exceptional normative status—that is, beyond duty and obligation.

I will raise a few questions about this case and then examine two frameworks of moral discourse that are often used to evaluate such cases. First, what criteria must be met before we can appropriately refer to someone as a *donor*? As obvious as this question sounds, it is far from obvious. By the term "donor," we sometimes refer to the decision maker about donation–i.e., the one who decides to donate organs–and sometimes to the cadaveric source of the organs. Obviously, the two may be the same. However, the decision maker may not be the source of the organs, and the source may never have been competent to make a decision about donation—perhaps an anencephalic newborn, a child, or a mentally retarded person—or, if competent, may never have made a decision to donate. For instance, a dead child may be the source of organs, the one who provides organs, but cannot be the donor, that is, the one who makes the donation. Furthermore, someone who sells his or her human biological materials is not a donor, but a vendor or seller. For a long time, I have protested the promiscuous use of the terms "donor," "donation," "giver," and "gift." Their loose usage inappropriately extends a moral aura that is overrated but nonetheless important; hence, we need to be more precise in our language.

Second, who was the donor in this case? From the brief report in the newspapers, it appears that the mother viewed herself as the donor–i.e., the decision maker–and her son as the source or provider of the organs. She said: "It never even crossed my mind not to donate." However, in view of the fact that the young man had checked "donor" on his driver's license, he could have legitimately been viewed as the decision maker about donation. By signing a document of gift, he was the donor as well

[3]

as the source, and, from one standpoint, his mother then merely conveyed or expressed his wishes. She simply implemented his prior donation.

Even if the young man had never indicated his decision to donate, his mother still could have argued that donation is what he would have wanted because of his fundamental values and commitments. She could even have appealed to his specific recent actions as indicative of those values and commitments. A week before his death this young man, a former life-guard, was at a lake when a swimmer attempting to reach an island started to go under; he swam out a long distance and pulled the floundering swimmer safely to shore. Thus, his mother perhaps could have constructed his willingness to donate from the way he lived—she could have taken his recent heroic rescue as indicative of the kind of moral character that would seek to save others, even at some risk.

Third, it is not surprising that the mother and newspaper reports viewed her as actual "donor"–i.e., decision maker about the donation–of her dead son's organs, in view of the laws and social practices that have evolved in the U.S. The legal structure for organ donation appears in state versions of the Uniform Anatomical Gift Act, as formulated in the late 1960s and then rapidly adopted by all 50 states and the District of Columbia. Within that "gift" framework, competent individuals can determine what will be done with their organs after their deaths. In the absence of a valid expression of the decedent's prior wishes, the family can decide whether to donate his or her organs.

As a matter of social practice, the default mechanism of the family has become the primary mechanism—individuals rarely sign donor cards, or-gan procurement teams rarely find them, and, in occasional cases of con-flict between the decedent's expressed wish to donate and the family's opposition, procurement teams generally yield to the family for mistaken legal reasons and understandable ethical reasons. The legal concerns are misplaced because the Uniform Anatomical Gift Act, as implemented by the states, provides immunity from criminal and civil liability for good faith actions on the basis of a signed document of gift. The moral con-cerns focus on harm to the grieving family and, ultimately, on risks to organ donation as a result of bad publicity.

In the U.S., then, the transfer of solid organs generally occurs through express donation by the individual or by the family. The law is primarily individualistic while social practice is primarily communitarian, that is, it views the deceased individual as part of a family. One ethical and practical problem is bringing the two together for educational and other purposes.

Social practices around the world are more similar than different, regardless of their specific legal context (Prottas 1994). Whether the legal structure is express donation or presumed donation, procurement teams still generally consult family members. Debates persist about whether these practices reflect moral wisdom or professional bias and thus whether they should be maintained or altered.

In this context, we should not neglect the moral and practical importance of not blocking donations in the U.S. Even if the individual while alive did not explicitly or expressly donate, it is important that he or she not block donation by the family by saying "no." Checking "no" on the donor card blocks any subsequent action by the family, while in practice the family may block the decedent's "yes" because, as previously noted, procurement teams rarely override the family's rejection of donation. (Even though some state laws are being changed to emphasize the legal priority of the decedent's express decision to donate, even against familial objections, it is too early to determine how they will work out in practice.) Not blocking donation can itself express benevolence or altruism. It is passive benevolence or passive altruism that does not assert one's legal or social-practice rights. For example, when an individual has expressly indicated his/her wish to donate, it is morally important that the family not take advantage of social practice and block the donative transfer. There is good reason to affirm in law, as the amended UAGA proposes and some state laws now affirm, the primacy of an individual's decision over the family's decision, but practical difficulties may limit enforcement (National Conference 1987).

FRAMEWORKS OF MORAL DISCOURSE ABOUT ORGAN DONATION

Two frameworks of moral discourse appear in discussions of the Texas mother's act of donation (and other such cases): morality of *aspiration* and morality of *duty*; *supererogation* and *obligation*; *ideal* and *right*; *praiseworthiness* and *blameworthiness*. The paired categories are not totally separate; the lines between them are not always clear; and we move back and forth between them. The mother's framework, which stressed that her action was "the decent thing to do . . . the thing we should do," appears to be one of obligation, duty, and right action. By contrast, commentators often used the language of aspiration, supererogation, ideals, and good actions to describe and praise acts of donation of cadaveric organs. These two frameworks of moral discourse produce different descriptions of and responses to non-donation or the failure to donate.

[5]

KENNEDY INSTITUTE OF ETHICS JOURNAL • MARCH 2001

Within a morality of aspiration or supererogation, the failure to donate does not produce guilt–although it might produce shame if an agent has committed himself/herself to living up to certain ideals. Others may not be indignant or complain about the agent's failure to donate. Instead, when donation does occur, praise and gratitude are appropriate responses. By contrast, within a morality of duty or obligation, the failure to donate does, or should, produce a feeling of guilt; others may be indignant and complain; and praise and gratitude are inappropriate—after all, the donor just did his or her duty.

Both patterns of moral discourse play significant roles in our social-moral practices relating to organ donation. It is tempting to say that one perspective is *internal*, not only to individuals but also to families, as in the case of the Texas mother—and perhaps to a small community, such as a religious community—while the other is *external*, the perspective that observers and spectators must take, as in the case of reporters, legislators, courts, and society at large.

But could we establish an obligation of beneficence, or obligatory beneficence, versus ideal or supererogatory beneficence? In *Principles of Biomedical Ethics*, Tom Beauchamp and I describe a continuum between obligation and supererogation, with few bright lines to separate them. We note that it is "extremely difficult to pin down and discharge obligations of beneficence. We bounce back and forth between viewing actions as charitable and as obligatory; and we sometimes feel guilty for not doing more, at the same time doubting that we are obligated to do more" (Beauchamp and Childress 1994, p. 268). "Strongly recommended" is possible intermediate language. A framework of obligation may include both general beneficence and specific beneficence, and specific beneficence may include both a duty to rescue and role-related beneficence. If there is a duty to donate cadaveric organs, it largely falls under the duty to rescue.

It is plausible to argue from liberal, secular premises for such a (moral) duty of rescue: Apart from special moral relationships, such as contracts, a person D has a determinate obligation of beneficence toward person R if and only if each of the following conditions is satisfied (assuming that D is aware of the relevant factors). (D stands for potential donor, while R stands for potential recipient.)

(1) R is at risk of significant loss or damage to life or health or some other major interest;
(2) D's action is needed (singly or in concert with others) to prevent this loss or damage;

(3) D's action (singly or in concern with others) has a high probability of preventing that loss or damage;

(4) D's action would not present significant risks, costs, or burdens to D [or to others];

(5) the benefit that R can be expected to gain outweighs any harms, costs, or burdens that D is likely to incur [or that others are likely to incur as a result].

We could increase the stringency of D's obligation by increasing the benefit, that is, by increasing the probability and magnitude of a positive outcome for R (conditions 1-3), with impact on the fifth condition. We could also decrease the risk, cost, or burden to D (condition 4), again with an impact on the fifth condition.

Both moral frameworks are important: (1) cadaveric organ donation as supererogatory, and (2) cadaveric organ donation as obligatory. Nevertheless, the moral discourse of the larger society, apart from particular communities, must, I believe, remain within the framework of heroic, even sacrificial action, that earns societal praise and gratitude.

A strong obligation to donate cadaveric organs also emerges in Judaism and Christianity, among other religious traditions, and it converges with a duty to rescue in liberal, secular morality. However, this "overlapping consensus" does not provide a warrant for society to accept an enforceable legal obligation to donate. As I will argue, in this context, the society should primarily *express community*, not *impose community*.

In the common law tradition, Good Samaritan laws tend to work this way. A few states in the U.S. do impose a legal obligation to act to rescue someone in trouble—usually a failure to do so is a misdemeanor punishable by a modest fine. However, most Good Samaritan laws do not obligate but rather facilitate actions. They facilitate beneficent actions by reducing risks or perceived risks. For example, they may reduce risks to the Good Samaritan by protecting him or her from legal liability for good faith actions. Such laws may point a direction for society's interventions—through both policies and education—to increase cadaveric organ donation.

FACILITATING ORGAN DONATION

I will consider four main ways the society could facilitate cadaveric organ donation by making it more reasonable for individuals and/or families to choose to donate. The first two focus on the value of organs to rights-holders and to potential recipients; the second two focus on the risks and benefits of acts of donation. They are not mutually exclusive and may be combined in various ways.

[7]

KENNEDY INSTITUTE OF ETHICS JOURNAL • MARCH 2001

First, we could try to increase the perceived value of donated organs to the potential recipients and the society. In principle this approach could be useful in both obligation and supererogation models. And it has been widely used, particularly through attention to the needs of potential transplant recipients, especially children, and to successful outcomes. In commenting on mandated choice, the American Medical Association Council on Judicial and Ethical Affairs stresses: "To be effective, information on the importance of organ donation and the success of organ transplantation must be provided when the donation decision is made" (AMA Council 1994, p. 812). Although such information is necessary, merely attempting to increase the perceived value of donated organs fails to address what is really crucial for many individual and familial decisions to donate, viz., the perceived risks, costs and burdens of acts of donation.

Second, we could try to reduce the perceived value of the organs to the initial rights holders. The mother who donated her son's organs in Texas insisted that they had no value, except insofar as they could be useful to others. We might view organs as "spare parts" that will go to "waste" if not used in transplantation. Even though many might agree with this perspective, it is not clear that societal policies or educational efforts to devalue organs for rights holders apart from their donation are appropriate, in part because of the complex beliefs, sentiments, and rituals surrounding the body in various communities.

Third, we could attempt to reduce perceived risks, costs, and burdens of *acts* of donation. These risks, costs, and burdens—coupled with the organs' value to potential recipients—all combine to support the judgment that cadaveric organ donation is heroic or sacrificial, perhaps even too heroic or too sacrificial. Furthermore, because of these risks, costs, and burdens, some individuals or families may not discharge their obligation to donate—if they accept that moral framework. After all, some level of risks, costs, and burdens can defeat an obligation of beneficence.

Various opinion polls suggest that individuals while alive do not undertake donative acts of completing documents of gift for various reasons, some of which include the burden of contemplating their own deaths and the sense of risk, for instance, in having life-sustaining procedures terminated prematurely or death declared prematurely (see Childress 1997). In view of such opinion polls, several analysts in the 1980s thought that the major bottleneck in organ procurement was professional unwillingness to ask families following a relative's death, rather than familial unwillingness to donate. The problem, many supposed, was a shortage of *askers*, not a shortage of *donors* (as decision makers). Families' failures to give resulted from professionals' failure to ask. Hence, Arthur Caplan (1984) proposed "required request" directed at the decedent's next of kin. And many of us thought it would work. However, required request has failed to increase the supply of organs substantially even though it has perhaps prevented a decline in donations. In one study, Laura Siminoff and her colleagues discovered that now most families are asked. In her study, more than 70 percent of the families of organ-donor-eligible patients were asked, but only 46.5 percent agreed to donate organs (Siminoff, et al. 1995). We do not know exactly *how* they were approached. And, in general, we do not know much about why familial decision makers fail to donate in part because too much attention has focused on getting individuals to sign donor cards.

Even among families donating, "complaints about the lack of information on brain death, the cost of donation, the effect of donation on funeral arrangements, and health care providers' insensitivity were relatively common" (Siminoff et al. 1995, p. 16). We need efforts to reduce all these negative effects. For instance, misunderstandings about so called "brain death" are numerous and deep-seated, and they help to create and sustain distrust and mistrust because they increase agents' sense that a decision to donate is highly risky—it may lead physicians and other health care professionals to declare a "donor" dead before he or she is "really" dead.

Fourth, we could try to increase the perceived benefits of *acts* of donation. Those who donate report both positive and negative outcomes, in terms of meaning and significance of the act of donation (see, e.g., Siminoff et al. 1995, p.16). In the Texas case discussed earlier, the mother also noted: "I just can't believe people don't donate more. This was the best thing we could have ever done. Whoever the people are that got the organs, we're just grateful to them to keep part of him alive in this way. We're grateful they are living."

One barrier to proposals to increase the benefits of acts of donation to donors is that the dominant interpretation of the present system of organ procurement in the U.S. stresses its altruism and its voluntarism. Acts of transfer of organs are deemed to be altruistic, that is, purely other-directed, as well as voluntary. For example, in his excellent book, *The Most Useful Gift*, Jeffrey Prottas (1994, p. 50) writes: "the voluntary decision to donate must be based on altruistic motives; otherwise, it is not permitted." That is an overstatement, however. Indeed, for cadaveric donors, there is no inquiry into motives, as long as it is clear that financial com-

KENNEDY INSTITUTE OF ETHICS JOURNAL • MARCH 2001

pensation is not involved. Donors may have all sorts of mixed motives for donating—ranging from altruism, which is certainly important, to a sense of obligation, to a desire to find redemptive meaning in a tragic set of circumstances, to a hope that their loved one can live on in others, to a desire for praise, honor, fame, and so forth.

Once we recognize that motives are often, and perhaps usually, mixed and that the procurement system does not require pure altruism as the donor's sole motivation, then we can begin to consider not only how the society could remove disincentives to donation, but also how it might provide incentives–i.e., additional motivating reasons–without replacing a moral sense of altruism or moral obligation. Honoring the act of donation and the donor/source of the organs has certainly been one way, for example, through letters from the Surgeon General or president or through public ceremonies to honor donor families.

One question that arises is whether, within moral constraints, we could find more meaningful and powerful incentives, perhaps even financial ones. I will not here examine arguments for a market in organs, which I have opposed elsewhere as ethically unacceptable as well as politically infeasible, at least in the short-run, because it is currently illegal. Although some proposals to provide financial incentives for organ donation stop short of a market in organs, they are mistakenly characterized as "paid donation." Such proposals (1) fail to distinguish the logic of donation and the logic of sales, and/or (2) attempt to transfer the moral aura surrounding organ donation to sales.

No doubt, some proposals to provide financial incentives for organ donation are really ways to purchase organs. However, short of actually buying and selling organs, can financial incentives be used legitimately "as tools to improve the decision for donation"? Can they be used without blurring the line between donations and sales?

Providing some financial (and other incentives) has been labeled "rewarded gifting." According to William F. May (1991, p. 181), if the reward is given only when the gift of the organ has been provided, then it is hard to see how the transfer differs from a sale—"the transaction differs very little from an outright sale" (with all the attendant problems). But a "very little" difference may still mark a significant boundary between donations and sales, particularly if the "reward" represents an expression of communal solidarity with and gratitude to the donor/source.

My starting point is Thomas Peter's (1991) proposal of a pilot program to test the effects of providing a death benefit of $1,000 for recover-

CHILDRESS • REDUCING BARRIERS TO ORGAN DONATION

able donations. In his proposal, the benefit is provided not for acts of donation but for organs actually recovered. Hence, this proposal does indeed appear to be equivalent to a purchase/sale. However, some possible modifications might be more compatible with socio-moral practices of donation. We could provide the death benefit as a tangible societal expression of gratitude for *acts* of donation, not only for recoverable organs. Thus, as a regular practice, the society could cover the organ source's funeral expenses up to a certain level (say, $1,000) in order to express, quite concretely and tangibly, its gratitude for the act of donation, whether by the organ source while alive or by the family at the time of death, and to share in the disposition of the final remains, following the removal of donated organs. Such a practice of conveying gratitude would express communal solidarity with the deceased and the bereaved who donate or do not block donation.

I do not argue for this approach, even as a pilot experiment. I only want to suggest that, in principle, it could be developed in a way that would avoid sales/purchases along with some of the associated ethical problems. However, we should be quite cautious about tampering with policies and practices regarding organ donation, since it is probably more fragile than we often suspect. The wrong kinds of policies, and even the wrong kinds of experiments, could increase the failure to donate.

OTHER POSSIBLE DIRECTIONS IN POLICIES AND PRACTICES

My arguments about ways the society could make the act of cadaveric organ donation more reasonable for individuals and/or families—whether that act is deemed morally ideal or morally obligatory—suggest some other directions we should consider in our social policies and practices of organ procurement.

First, in addition to reducing perceived risks, costs, and burdens, we need in more general ways to reduce mistrust and distrust. These more general ways involve expressions of community toward, and solidarity with, individuals and families, so that individuals and families come to trust the overall system. Throughout I have stressed *expressing* rather than *imposing* community.

As we note the importance of trust, we can also see some important connections between organ procurement and organ distribution. Recall the numerous cynical comments about how quickly Mickey Mantle received a liver transplant. It is important to assure the public that donated organs are used in fair as well as effective ways, without priority to pa-

KENNEDY INSTITUTE OF ETHICS JOURNAL • MARCH 2001

tients who are rich, powerful, or famous. Many of the problems of public accountability in organ distribution appear at the point of admission to waiting lists rather than selection from waiting lists. Furthermore, the long and vitriolic debates about the United Network for Organ Sharing's (UNOS's) policies regarding liver allocation have aroused suspicions that allocation policies put transplant centers ahead of potential transplant recipients.

In addition, as the federal Task Force on Organ Transplantation (1986) argued more than 15 years ago, there are good reasons to eliminate ability to pay as a criterion for access to most transplants. Inability to pay is now rarely a problem for kidney transplantation because of the End-Stage Renal Disease Program of Medicare (but the limited coverage for post-transplant immunosuppressive medications does create problems of access). Inability to pay remains a major roadblock for patients needing other expensive transplants. The Task Force argued that it is unfair and even exploitative for the society to ask people, rich and poor alike, to donate organs if poor people would not have an opportunity to get on waiting lists if they needed a transplant. Hence, it is important to include all potential donors in the community of potential recipients.

Second, public education needs to be redirected in at least two ways. First, it must deal with some of the fundamental causes of distrust and mistrust, attitudes that are difficult to change. Those attitudes are reflected in various opinion polls, and they are more common among minorities, who view themselves as on the margins of the larger society and have less reason to trust it (see the summary in Childress 1997). One important part of public education that is both cognitive and attitudinal in nature concerns "brain death," which, as previously noted, is widely misunderstood and which, as a result, generates mistrust.

Public education also needs to target individuals as members of families—or families including individuals. Too often public education has concentrated on the individual's signed donor card as the desired outcome. However, the donor card expresses an individualistic, legalistic, and rationalistic approach to organ donation that downplays communities (families), practices, and non-rational aspects of decision making.

By contrast, and in line with several recent educational campaigns, individuals also should be encouraged to indicate their wishes to their families and to consider how they would make decisions about deceased family members. Donor cards can play a useful role in this process, especially if they are viewed as ways to stimulate familial conversation rather than as ways to effectively donate organs. These comments begin to suggest why society should avoid some proposed changes in law or social practices as misguided.

For example, one widely discussed proposal is mandated choice. In my judgment, such a policy would be excessively individualistic, rationalistic, and legalistic. It would require individuals to state their preferences regarding organ donations in conjunction with some other state-mandated task, such as renewing a driver's license or filing income tax forms. According to the American Medical Association (AMA) Council on Ethical and Judicial Affairs (1994, p. 809), "Requiring a decision regarding donation would overcome a major obstacle to organ donation—the reluctance of individuals to contemplate their own deaths and the disposition of their bodies after death—and individual autonomy would be protected and even enhanced."

The Council claims that such a policy would be both right and effective, that is, would both respect autonomy and increase the supply of transplantable organs. However, their explanation displays the proposal's deficiency: "Under mandated choice, individuals who feel this reluctance [to contemplate their own deaths and the disposition of their bodies after death] would have to confront it, thereby removing it as a barrier to donation" (AMA Council 1994, p. 809). In contrast to the Council's claim, mandating choice, at least without other major changes of the kind I am proposing, would probably decrease, rather than increase, the supply of organs. If forced to choose, many individuals would probably check "no," not because they oppose the donation of their organs after their deaths, but because they are afraid of being on record as donors of organs, with only the time of delivery to be determined. In saying "no," they would block their family's possible decision to donate.

In affirming that mandated choice is not only right but would also be effective, the Council appeals to "empirical evidence that mandated choice would be acceptable to the public and therefore effective in increasing the organ supply" (AMA Council 1994, p. 810). Putative empirical evidence is found in a survey in which 90 percent of the respondents indicated that they would support such a program of mandated choice. However, the Council's inference confuses public acceptance of a program with individuals' willingness to say "yes" if forced to make a choice. We do not have the evidence to support the claim that a legal mandate for individuals to make a decision about post-mortem organ donation will actually increase acts of donation. The factors that currently deter individuals and families from deciding to donate would also apply under mandated choice,

KENNEDY INSTITUTE OF ETHICS JOURNAL • MARCH 2001

and they would prevent mandated choice from increasing organ donation. However, if those factors were corrected, as I am arguing they should
be, then mandated choice would be unnecessary.

Proponents of mandated choice overemphasize a very individualistic,
rationalistic, and legalistic version of autonomy. They fail to see how people
might exercise their autonomy in various ways—for example, delegating
the decision to their family or not blocking their family's subsequent decision
may also be an exercise of autonomy and even altruistic in motivation.

According to the AMA Council (1994, p. 810), "The individual's interest in controlling the disposition of his or her own body and property
after death suggests that it is *ethically preferable* for the individual, rather
than the family, to decide to donate organs" (emphasis added). The AMA
Council (1994, p. 810) also indicates that this is what UAGA says: "The
Uniform Anatomical Gift Act's emphasis on individual autonomy and
individual decision making would be protected and enhanced by a system
of mandated choice, in which the donation decision would have to be
confronted before death and would have to be made by the individual
donor, not by a surrogate."

These statements represent basic misconceptions and fundamental confusions. The UAGA only identifies rights holders and the rights they hold.
It does not claim that it is ethically preferable for the individual to make
an express decision about donation. A system in which individuals have
the *right* to make their own decisions is, in my judgment, ethically preferable to any other system. However, such a system does not and need not
embody an ideal of human autonomy that implies that it is ethically preferable for individuals to determine, let alone be required to determine, in
an explicit way what will happen with their bodies after their deaths,
rather than, for instance, delegating this decision to others.

CONCLUSION

In conclusion, a fundamental question concerns how organ procurement can affirm individuals, rationality, and law without being excessively individualistic (e.g., in neglecting individuals in their communities),
excessively rationalistic (e.g., in neglecting various non-rational aspects
of individual and familial decisions and policies that influence those decisions), and excessively legalistic (e.g., in assuming that law can make all
the difference while neglecting social practices).

Drawing together various themes, I would characterize my approach
as communitarian in several respects, but firmly individualistic in others.

CHILDRESS • REDUCING BARRIERS TO ORGAN DONATION

A possible label would be liberal communitarian–it starts from and continues to affirm the UAGA's emphasis on individuals' rights to make their own decisions about donation. And it favors laws that would not allow the family to override the decedent's prior express wish to donate, just as current laws and social practices do not allow the family to override the decedent's prior express wish not to donate.

It is communitarian in that it recognizes the individual's and/or family's duty or obligation to rescue others through cadaveric organ donation under some circumstances, but that duty or obligation does not authorize claiming bodies and their parts against the decedent's or family's objections. It still appreciates the relevance for various purposes, including legislation, of a model of supererogation.

To hold that cadaveric organ donation is morally obligatory, at least in some circumstances, does not imply that we should evaluate failures to donate merely in terms of failures to discharge an obligation. We should still express community, rather than impose community through communal norms and sanctions for failures to donate. The society can make it easier and more reasonable for individuals and families to discharge an obligation (or live up to an ideal) of cadaveric organ donation in part by reducing actual and perceived risks, costs, and burdens of acts of donation.

My approach recognizes that individuals' (and families') willingness to donate generally presupposes their trust in the larger community, for example, in its criteria and procedures for determining death and for distributing donated organs. Also important is the society's expression of communal solidarity in individual and familial suffering, in part through the provision of health care. Indeed, it is morally and practically problematic to request organ donation from people who have difficulty obtaining basic health care, much less expensive procedures such as organ transplants. What is utterly indispensable is the expression of community in several ways, rather than the imposition of communal norms and sanctions in demanding the provision of organs.

It is important to educate the public not only or even primarily as individuals who are invited to sign donor cards as putatively effective means for the post-mortem transfer of organs, but as individuals who are members of communities, particularly small communities of families, who should communicate their preferences regarding donation to other members of the family, who should engage in moral discourse with other family members about organ donation, who should discern the views of other family members about organ donation, and who should themselves con-

KENNEDY INSTITUTE OF ETHICS JOURNAL • MARCH 2001

sider how to make decisions regarding other family members' organs in the event of death. Nevertheless, my approach remains "liberal" in that it recognizes and prioritizes individuals' legal and social rights to decide to donate or withhold their own organs after death, whether cadaveric organ donation is considered morally obligatory or ideal.

This paper has its origins in the André Hellegers Memorial Lecture at Georgetown University in 1995 and in the Alloway Lecture at the University of Toronto and the Canadian Bioethics Association in 1997. The author is indebted to these and other audiences for perceptive criticisms and helpful suggestions, but absolves them of any responsibility for the final product.

REFERENCES

AMA Council. American Medical Association Council on Ethical and Judicial Affairs. 1994. Strategies for Cadaveric Organ Procurement: Mandated Choice and Presumed Consent. *JAMA* 272: 809-12.

Beauchamp, Tom L., and Childress, James F. 1994. *Principles of Biomedical Ethics*, 4th ed. New York: Oxford University Press.

Caplan, Arthur L. 1984. Ethical and Policy Issues in the Procurement of Cadaver Organs for Transplantation. *New England Journal of Medicine* 314: 981-83.

Childress, James F. 1997. *Practical Reasoning in Bioethics*. Bloomington: Indiana University Press.

Dallas Morning News. 1995. A Hero in Death: Mantle Organ Donor Helped Save Six Lives. *The Atlanta Constitution* (7 August): 6C.

May, William F. 1991. *The Patient's Ordeal*. Bloomington: Indiana University Press.

National Conference of Commissioners on Uniform State Laws. 1987. *Uniform Anatomical Gift Act*. Chicago, IL: National Conference of Commissioners.

Peters, Thomas G. 1991. Life or Death: The Issue of Payment in Cadaveric Organ Donation. *JAMA* 265: 1302-5.

Prottas, Jeffrey M. 1994. *The Most Useful Gift: Altruism and the Public Policy of Organ Transplants*. A Twentieth-Century Fund Book. San Francisco: Jossey-Bass Publishers.

Siminoff, Laura; Arnold, Robert M.; Caplan, Arthur L.; et al. 1995. Public Policy Governing Organ and Tissue Procurement in the United States. *Annals of Internal Medicine* 123:10-17.

Task Force on Organ Transplantation. 1986. Organ Transplantation: Issues and Recommendations. Rockville, MD: Office of Organ Transplantation, Health Resources and Services Administration, U.S. DHHS, April.

[14]

Two Steps to Three Choices:
A New Approach to Mandated Choice

SUSAN E. HERZ

The Problem

Approximately 62,000 people in this country await organ transplants.[1] Ten years ago the waiting list numbered 16,000.[2] The line gets longer every day. Up to 30% of those waiting in line will die waiting.[3] We face a chronic shortage of organs. While demand for organs steadily increases, the number of cadaveric organ donors remains relatively constant: approximately 4,000 in 1988, and approximately 5,500 in 1997.[4] In response to this environment of scarcity, policymakers have considered initiatives in a number of domains.

Some design rationing schemes.[5] Others encourage interventions such as presumed consent, advance directives, required request, and/or market force. Each such policy directly aims to lessen the disparity between supply and demand, but each fails to withstand pragmatic and/or ethical scrutiny. Waving a banner of hope in life and death situations, still other policymakers justify procedural shortcuts to resolve the complex issues that surround organ supply. Commentators use organ scarcity to help rationalize cloning,[6] controversial genetic research,[7] and cross-species organ and tissue transplantation.[8]

The deaths, the suffering, the rationing, the questionable policy initiatives, and the rush to develop extraordinary medical remedies may share roots in an ill-conceived construct. All operate within a scarcity paradigm. The myth: for lack of available organs, some people die. For lack of available organs, some people live without vision or kidney function or other life-enhancing condition. The reality: we do not lack organs. By one conservative estimate, medically suitable cadaveric potential donors outnumber actual donors three to one.[9] Further, according to a 1993 Gallup poll, 85% of Americans support organ transplants based on donation, and 69% would likely donate their own organs.[10] We stand in a universe brimming with available organs, asking questions about coping with scarcity. Meanwhile, available organs do not enter the supply stream and yes, people who might otherwise live, do die.

This article presents and defends the view that a system of mandated choice involving two steps to three choices constitutes the ethically and pragmatically preferred route for retrieving cadaveric organs for transplantation. It holds this option to the litmus of bioethical principles and pragmatism, notes the proposed system's strengths and weaknesses, and calls for pilot programs.

Two Steps to Three Choices: An Untested Approach

The first step of this approach would involve a broad based, ongoing educational campaign systematically informing the general public about issues sur-

A New Approach to Mandated Choice

rounding organ shortage. Previous tiptoeing around Americans' reluctance to accept death may lie at the heart of some failed initiatives. Death: patients don't want to think about it; doctors don't want to talk about it; policymakers don't want to offend those they seek to serve. Many people are reluctant to contemplate their own deaths, the deaths of others, bodily mutilation, disposition of their own bodies after death, disposition of others' bodies after death. The need for cadaveric organs calls for stout-hearted and culturally appropriate information sharing, media coverage, visible public debates, and other forms of far-reaching education. For purposes of this discussion, we note simply that as a first step, a sustained public–private partnership dedicated to comprehensive public education should carry the day.

As the second step of the proposed protocol—with stakeholders well informed about relevant issues—states would require legally competent adults to routinely document one of three responses to the question of posthumous organ donation: "yes," "no," or "let others decide." In other words, competent adults would be required to record a decision (1) bequeathing organs for medical use, (2) not bequeathing organs for medical use, or (3) directing others to decide. Such "others" could be family members, named individuals, or physicians.

Confidential, revocable, binding choices would be expressed in writings that determine the disposition of organs upon death. The mandate to express choice would be satisfied by individuals filing signed writings with a central repository of such information—for example the Registry of Motor Vehicles. People could change their minds with unlimited frequency, and the most recent writing would prevail. No rights or benefits would flow from a particular choice made, although the act of filing a choice would be required to complete the business at hand, in this case obtaining or renewing a driver's license.

No person would be authorized to execute a written expression of choice on behalf of another adult, whether the would-be donor or nondonor is characterized as competent, once-competent, or never-competent. This clear rule would help bypass concerns about coercion, motivation, violations of bodily integrity, intrusions upon autonomy, and other indicia of possible impropriety.

Safeguarding of confidentiality, a key feature of this system, would help protect choice-makers from concerns about coercion by family members, employers, or others. Fines imposed on violators would reflect the premium placed on confidentiality of choice. Only under carefully delineated circumstances would organ procurement organizations, physicians, and others have access to this information.

Once refined, this approach would make active choice relatively easy. With each decision earning neither penalty nor bonus, the process of education followed by the required expression of choice would invite potential donors to carefully consider and then communicate personal wishes. Registration of clear wishes would contribute profoundly to the peace of mind of choosers, physicians, and family members. Gone would be concerns about inaccurately second guessing the wishes of a loved one or patient. In some instances, of course, registration of choice would contribute profoundly to the peace of mind of organ recipients.

Such an undertaking may already enjoy a measure of baseline support. Even prior to educational initiatives and even without the three-choice menu, some members of the general public may support implementation of a mandated choice program.[11] In addition, for a number of years certain physicians[12] and

341

Susan E. Herz

lawyers[13] have proposed mandated choice. The American Medical Association's Council on Ethical and Judicial Affairs reviewed presumed consent and mandated choice as vehicles for cadaveric organ procurement, and concluded mandated choice was the more ethical and viable alternative.[14]

Nonetheless, apparently only one state has tried it. The Texas legislature put a law on the books in 1991 and removed it in 1997. The law required that people make a "yes" or "no" choice at the time of driver's license renewal. Although the positive response rate increased from 3% in 1994 to 20% in 1996, a number of concerns convinced policymakers that the system should be dissolved.[15] The absence of a public education campaign resulted in many Texans confronting the question for the first time when in line at the license renewal office. Often, registry employees did not even ask the question, and their computers defaulted to a "no." When this problem was discovered and corrected, the positive response rate rose rapidly. Nonetheless, "I don't know" continued to default to "no." The disparity between actual assents and the Gallup poll promise concerned policymakers and the program was withdrawn.

The approach suggested here differs from the Texas model significantly. First, implementation of the system would follow a broad-based educational campaign. Second, those who are undecided would be permitted to do as they always have: allow family members to decide. The difference here is that such choice would be articulated, at least informing survivors that the deceased was not categorically opposed to organ donation. A carefully designed strategy to pilot a mandated choice system remains untested.

Ethical Principles Honored

Bioethicists have studied American values and extracted a number of relevant gold standards including autonomy, beneficence, and justice.[16] It is against these three standards that we review the proposed policy. Because education per se as intervention does not raise bioethical issues, we address here the ethical underpinnings only of the second step: three-prong mandated choice. A two-prong mandated choice paradigm has been discussed in the literature, so certain arguments can be anticipated.

Autonomy

Choice Preserved. Required expression of choice preserves choice. The proposed scheme does not reward one choice over another, and does not coerce the making of a particular choice; it simply requires that the choice be explicit. According to the above referenced 1993 Gallup poll, 93% of respondents would honor family members' wishes regarding organ donation if those wishes were known. Requiring a clearly articulated selection would assure that those 93% knew or could ascertain their relatives' wishes, and would prohibit the remaining 7% from intervening against the wishes of the deceased.

Power Promoted. Not only would this system of mandated choice preserve choice, it would also give patients more power because decisions would be made on a routine basis, often in advance of life-threatening conditions. Under

A New Approach to Mandated Choice

such circumstances, individuals can be expected to think clearly, without undue influence. This obligatory execution of an advance directive would avoid the hazards of guesswork and projection that now threaten the integrity of substituted judgment determinations, guesswork that also threatens peace of mind for those designated to make such determinations.

Counterarguments. Commentators have voiced two considerations about autonomy. They claim that although requiring choice permits a choice not to donate, it does not permit a choice not to choose, thus violating the very autonomy we seek to preserve and enhance. But the emotional appeal of this argument overlooks the fact that "not choosing" is choosing. An apparent decision to bypass the donation question operates as a choice to let family members decide. Indeed, during every moment of legally competent adulthood, every American is making the choice to posthumously (1) donate organs, or (2) not donate organs, or (3) let family and physicians determine whether to donate his or her organs. The proposed protocol would simply record the decision so that during a time of profound grief no one need guess which of the three choices was the one most likely made. At this point the third choice may rank as the most common. Yet when the decision to let others decide is effectively communicated by lack of documented preference—as is so often the case—family and physicians are left guessing whether the chooser's silence should be deemed an unrecorded decision to donate. Consequently "not choosing" under the current system yields the same results as execution of an ambiguously drafted document. The three-choice intervention would recognize that Americans already make choices about posthumous disposition of their organs ("I'll say nothing and Uncle Joe will decide"). It simply requires an act to memorialize the choosing process. The resulting documentation would alter the context for family and/or physician who are asked to decide about organ donation because they would know that the deceased faced the question, chose to say neither yes nor no, and deliberately chose to let survivors' judgment reign.

Some challenge autonomy on the ground that autonomy is not an interest held by dead persons. Some see a bogus benefit in upholding the decisional integrity of dead persons.[17] This view fails to appreciate that mandated choice defers to the wishes of a living person, albeit *after* he or she has died. The legal system requires the same with disposition of real and personal property and even custody of children of the deceased. We honor deceased persons' wishes about willing their favorite chairs. Should we honor less their wishes about their own bodies?

Beneficence

Beneficence, a second bioethical beacon, is defined as promoting good, and preventing or removing evil or harm. A mandated three-prong choice program would meet this standard through at least three avenues.

Recipient Benefits. Should this system result in an increased number of donated organs, the most obvious manifestation of beneficence would be the gift of life to those who would otherwise die and the gift of enhanced life to those who would otherwise enjoy fewer of life's riches by reason of blindness, insulin

Susan E. Herz

dependence, or other condition relieved or cured by organ transplantation. Less obvious: recipients know that donors and nondonors have categorized themselves knowingly and voluntarily.

Choice-Maker Benefits. Less apparent might be benefits to the choice-maker. Those who choose not to donate may ineffably benefit from the self-expression involved in asserting their interests, and from the peace of mind accompanying reasonable certainty that their wishes will be followed. Those choosing to donate may similarly benefit intangibly. On an experiential level, many know a particular paradox whether or not they have articulated it: that people learn by teaching, speak by listening, empower themselves by empowering others, and perhaps most profoundly, receive by giving. Along these lines, Marcel Mauss, the French sociologist, wrote: "The theme of gift, of freedom and obligation in the gift, or generosity and self-interest in giving reappear in our society like the resurrection of a dominant motif long for-gotten."[18] Even if the act of giving did not include a simultaneous paradox-ical act of receiving, the act of giving may nonetheless create a rewarding experience.

Community Benefits. One can appreciate the benefit to community with or without subscribing to the communitarian view that the common good ranks above individual rights. The act of making a choice serves individual and community with equal force. When the individual chooses to donate organs, many benefit. At the outset, interlocking beneficiaries include the donor, the recipient, and family and physicians of both. The choice not to donate one's organs serves the group in like measure. Physicians and newly bereaved people are spared not only uncomfortable conversations, but also the guesswork of identifying the wishes of the deceased. Regardless of choice, once peoples' wishes are clear, society may profit from an unobstructed snapshot of values in this area.

Counterarguments. In response to the assertion that mandated expression of choice honors beneficence, some opponents presently argue that any good created by a system of mandated choice would be nullified by the harm of entering into a debtor-creditor relationship where the debt can never be repaid. Reluctance to enter into such relationship with the donor's family has been called the "tyranny of the gift," rooted in the offering of a "gift . . . beyond duty and claim."[19] However, mandated choice does not dictate creation or noncre-ation of a donation; it merely requires that individuals memorialize their wishes about posthumous disposition of transplantable organs. Even if the system did result in a greater number of gifts offered, would-be recipients would be under no compulsion to accept.[20]

Justice

Fair Process. At its bone, the notion of justice involves equity and fair play. Requiring expression of one of three choices would operate even-handedly. Each choice-maker would have the power to give or withhold organs, and each prospective recipient would have the power to accept or reject the offer.

A New Approach to Mandated Choice

Appearance of Fairness. Appearance of fairness may be as important as fairness itself. Public opinion research undertaken by the New England Organ Bank (NEOB) supports this adage in the organ procurement arena. According to NEOB's survey of 800 demographically representative respondents in Maine and Massachusetts, the most highly rated factor influencing willingness to donate is assurance of the fairness of the national organ distribution system.[21] The proposed three-choice intervention would beam a spotlight on the issue of organ demand, on the obligation of every competent adult to make a choice, and on the role of policymakers in making decisions about how to allocate resources. Light-of-day discussions about such issues would contribute to actual and apparent fairness and would appeal to the public's sense of fair play.

Counterarguments. One might argue that true justice requires both fair process and fair results as beacons and that attention to appearance of fairness may sacrifice attention to actual fairness. This mischaracterization of the argument misses the point that under a three-choice system, fair process and fair result do serve as twin beacons. This discussion simply acknowledges that fair process carries particular weight.

Opponents of the justice rationale might further argue that being forced to make a publicly recorded choice violates standards of fairness because the right of decisional privacy is sacrosanct. One ought to be able to make intimate decisions about disposition of bodily parts, opponents might argue, without government intervention. Even the legal system recognizes this right to private decisionmaking and jealously guards it from unfair encroachment. Yet even the legal system does not deem absolute this right to decisional privacy. Legitimate government interests may outweigh it. Assuring adequate supply of cadaveric organs may constitute such an interest. Further, under the proposed scheme confidentiality is vigorously protected, its breach subject to financial penalty. And even if a central repository's "knowledge" of an individual's decision were held to violate privacy interests, this information would rank as a minor cost compared to the priceless benefits accruing to individuals and society. The initial education outreach should carefully identify and address concerns associated with fairness.

Conclusions

Strengths

The strengths of this education-based, three-option system are clear. The system is ethically sound, consistent with key principles and values. It is pragmatic. It is acceptable. In one survey some 90% of respondents said they would support a program of mandated choice, while only 60% supported presumed consent.[22] Implementation could be administratively cost effective and streamlined. The three-choice model respects freedom of choice, allowing for all stripe of humanity, from those who would carry the banner for organ donation to those wanting to assure that bodies are buried intact.

A system of mandated choice would avoid pitfalls of alternative solutions. Unlike alternatives on the table, the intervention proposed here meets key bioethical standards; reflects the actual wishes of the donor; addresses cultural

Susan E. Herz

avoidance of death; neither presumes nor perpetuates scarcity of transplant organs; may help inspire trust in medicine; constitutes a fair, noncoercive, pragmatic, efficient response to a serious problem; and may even work. Given a chance, this protocol might expand the pool of potential donors and recipients, reducing the gap between the 62,000 waiting and the 5,500 donating.

Weaknesses

H.L. Mencken is credited with saying that "for every complex problem, there's an answer that is elegant, simple, and wrong." I hope his words do not apply, but the risk remains. A significant factor may have been overlooked or unexplored. We have scant empirical data. As Murray and Youngner put it: "Aside from opinion polls with their obvious limitations ... (we) have based organ recovery policy too often on little more than enthusiastic hunches."[23] Moreover, the opinion polls suggest that although most Americans think organ donation is a good idea, many would stop short of offering their own organs. Whether usable organ supply will increase remains an open question.

Implications

A pilot program to test a prototype of two steps to three choices must begin with a willingness to plan meticulously and a commitment to meet transplantation needs. The bottom line: You want something? Give the facts, then ask. Sharing the information and asking the question may take courage. Receiving the answer may give heart.

Notes

1. United Network for Organ Sharing. *Registrations and Patients on the UNOS National Patient Waiting List Last Updated March 17, 1999.* Richmond, Va.: United Network for Organ Sharing, 1998.
2. United Network for Organ Sharing, Division of Transplantation, Department of Health and Human Services. *1997 Annual Report of the United States Scientific Registry for Transplant Recipients and the Organ Procurement and Transplantation Network—Transplant Data: 1988–1996.* Richmond, Va.: United Network for Organ Sharing and Rockville, Md.: Department of Health and Human Services, 1997.
3. Council on Ethical and Judicial Affairs, American Medical Association. Strategies for cadaveric organ procurement: mandated choice and presumed consent. *JAMA* 1994;272:809–12.
4. See note 2, UNOS, DHHS 1997.
5. Annas GJ. The prostitute, the playboy, and the poet: rationing schemes for organ transplantation. *American Journal of Public Health* 1985;75(2):187–9. Munson R. *Intervention and Reflection: Basic Issues in Medical Ethics.* Belmont, Calif.: Wadsworth Publishing Co., 1996.
6. Robertson JA. Human cloning and the challenge of regulation. *New England Journal of Medicine* 1998;339(2):119–22.
7. Bach FH. Genetic engineering as an approach to xenotransplantation. *World Journal of Surgery* 1997;21(9):913–6.
8. Lambrights D, Sachs DH, Cooper DK. Discordant organ xenotransplantation in primates: world experience and current status. *Transplantation* 1998;66(5):547–61.
9. Gortmaker SL, Beasley CL, Brigham LE, Franz HG, Garrison RN, Lucas BA, et al. Organ donor potential and performance: size and nature of the organ donor shortfall. *Critical Care Medicine* 1996;24(3):432–9.
10. Gallup Organization. *Highlights of Public Attitudes toward Organ Donation.* Princeton, N.J.: Gallup, 1993.

A New Approach to Mandated Choice

11. Spital A. Mandated choice: a plan to increase public commitment to organ donation. *JAMA* 1995;273:504–6.
12. Spital A. The shortage of organs for transplantation: where do we go from here? *New England Journal of Medicine* 1991;325:1243–6.
13. Katz BJ. Increasing the supply of human organs for transplantation: a proposal for a system of mandated choice. *Beverly Hills Bar Journal* 1984;18:152–67.
14. See note 3, Council on Ethical and Judicial Affairs 1994.
15. Berry PH. Ethics in transplantation. *Texas Medicine* 1997.
16. Beauchamp TL, Childress JF. *Principles of Biomedical Ethics*, 4th ed. New York: Oxford University Press, 1994.
17. Glasson J, Orentlicher D, Waithe ME, Block JD, Murray TH, Youngner SJ. Mandated choice for organ donation [letters and response]. *JAMA* 1995;273:1176–8.
18. Quoted in Fox RC, Swazey J. *Spare Parts: Organ Replacement in American Society.* New York: Oxford University Press, 1992, at p. 32.
19. See note 18, Fox, Swazey 1992:39–40.
20. Lane H, Grodin M. Ethical issues in cochlear implant surgery: an exploration into disease, disability and the best interests of the child. *Kennedy Institute of Ethics Journal* 1997;7(3):231–51.
21. Strock B. Mandated choice and presumed consent: the silver bullets to solve the donor shortage? *UNOS Update* 1996;12(4):14–5.
22. See note 12, Spital 1991.
23. Murray TH, Youngner SJ. Organ salvage policies: a need for better data and more insightful ethics. *JAMA* 1994;272:814–5.

[15]

ETHICAL ISSUES IN LIMB TRANSPLANTS

DONNA DICKENSON AND GUY WIDDERSHOVEN

ABSTRACT

On one view, limb transplants cross technological frontiers but not ethical ones; the only issues to be resolved concern professional competence, under the assumption of patient autonomy. Given that the benefits of limb transplant do not outweigh the risks, however, the autonomy and rationality of the patient are not necessarily self-evident. In addition to questions of resource allocation and informed consent, limb, and particularly hand, allograft also raises important issues of personal identity and bodily integrity. We present two linked schemas for exploring ethical issues in limb transplants. The first, relying on conventional concepts in biomedical ethics, asks whether the procedure is research or therapy, whether the costs outweigh the benefits, and whether it should be up to the patient to decide. The second introduces more speculative and theoretically challenging questions, including bodily integrity, the argument from unnaturalness, and the function of the hand in expressing personal identity and intimacy. We conclude that limb transplants are not ruled out a priori, unlike some procedures that are prima facie wrong to perform, such as amputation of healthy limbs to relieve body dysmorphic disorders. However, their legitimacy is not proven by appeals to the interests of scientific research, cost-benefit, or patient autonomy.

INTRODUCTION

In April 1999, *The Lancet* published an Early Report on the six months' results of the first human hand allograft, performed in Lyon in September 1998.[1] The same clinical team performed a

---

[1] J.M. Dubernard, E. Owen, G. Herzberg, M. Lanzetta, X. Martin, H. Kapila *et al.* Human Hand Allograft: Report on the First 6 Months. *The Lancet* 1999; 353: 1315–1320.

ETHICAL ISSUES IN LIMB TRANSPLANTS   111

double human hand allograft in January 2000. In the interim, a US team at Louisville performed a similar procedure. Yet permission to perform further human hand allografts has again been refused by the St Mary's Hospital Trust Clinical Ethics Committee, on which one of the authors sits (DD). Following face-to-face evaluation of hand function in the transplant recipient six months after the operation, the committee reiterated its concerns that the level of function attained did not outweigh the risk. Doubts about 'the ethics of putting a patient through toxic immunosuppressive therapy for a non-vital operation' were also raised in a commentary on the *Lancet* report.[2] The recipient of the first hand transplant has recently announced that he is actually seeking to have it amputated, saying 'I've become mentally detached from it.'[3] This article explores the ethical arguments both for and against limb transplant, and particularly human hand allograft, with emphasis on the issues concerning identity which can be seen in the recipient's reaction.

On one view, hand transplants cross technological frontiers but not ethical ones. They raise no ethical questions that have not been answered long since, in favour of transplantation. There can be no objections except from unregenerate opponents of progress in science – according to one of the very few articles in medical ethics to have appeared on the issue of limb transplants. The article concludes in favour of cadaveric hand transplantation, provided professional and procedural standards of competence have been met (including field strength of the clinical team, scientific background of the innovation, and open public evaluation).[4]

Nonetheless, it is broadly agreed that doctors are not obliged to do everything which is technologically possible. We can stave off the moment of death over and over again in terminally ill patients, but there is a widespread dread of pointless 'high-tech' intervention. Modern medicine tends to generalise the application of technologically innovative procedures beyond their original target group, as epitomised by the widespread

---

[2] G. Foucher. Commentary: Prospects for Hand Transplantation. *The Lancet* 1999; 353: 1286–1287.

[3] C.Hallam, quoted in: 'Man with New Hand Doesn't Want It,' *International Herald Tribune*, 21–22 October 2000, p. 5.

[4] M. Siegler. Ethical Issues in Innovative Surgery: Should We Attempt a Cadaveric Hand Transplantation in a Human Subject? *Transplantation Proceedings* 1998; 30: 2779–2782, at 2782.

112   DICKENSON AND WIDDERSHOVEN

overuse of cardio-pulmonary resuscitation.[5,6] Specifically in transplant surgery, 'in every instance, the extension ... to organs beyond the original kidney, such as the heart, liver, lungs and pancreas, has raised questions and controversies in the mind of physicians and the general public.'[7] Are limb transplants a step too far down a slippery slope?[8]

Surprisingly little attention has been paid to possible ethical problems in limb transplants. Perhaps this is partly a function of what one study has identified as an 'ethics gap' between the medical and surgical literatures in their coverage of biomedical ethics.[9] Some concepts from conventional biomedical ethics may help us elucidate these particular surgical dilemmas: the boundaries of research, burdens and benefits, and patient autonomy.[10] But we will also introduce another set of more speculative and philosophically challenging concepts, which go beyond the scope of conventional biomedical ethics, in order to do justice to some of the unexpected questions that arise in limb transplantation. This second set of issues includes bodily integrity, unnaturalness, and personal identity.

RESEARCH BOUNDARIES, BURDENS AND BENEFITS, AND PATIENT AUTONOMY

Unlike life-saving transplants, the benefits of limb transplants do not self-evidently surpass the burdens. The risks of lifelong immunosuppressive medication, as well as the possible development of melanomas and other cancers, mean that a limb transplant may actually shorten life. It has been said of medicine that 'the art's most delicate aspect is not to shorten

---

[5] M. Hilberman, J. Kutner, D. Parsons, D.J. Murphy. Marginally Effective Medical Care: Ethical Analysis of Issues in Cardiopulmonary Resuscitation (CPR). *Journal of Medical Ethics* 1997; 23: 361–367.

[6] P.N.E. Bruce-Jones. Resuscitation Decisions in the Elderly: A Discussion of Current Thinking. *Journal of Medical Ethics* 1997; 22: 286–291.

[7] E. Friedman. Editorial: The Desperate Case: CARE (Costs, Applicability, Research, Ethics). *JAMA* 1989; 261: 1483–1490.

[8] B. Williams. 1985. Which Slopes are Slippery? In: Lockwood M (ed.) *Moral Dilemmas in Modern Medicine*. Oxford. Oxford University Press: 126–137.

[9] F. Paola, S.S. Barten. An 'Ethics Gap' in Writing About Bioethics: A Quantitative Comparison of the Medical and the Surgical Literature. *Journal of Medical Ethics* 1995; 21: 84–88.

[10] D. Dickenson, N. Hakim. Ethical Issues in Limb Transplants. *Postgraduate Medical Journal* 1999; 75: 513–515.

ETHICAL ISSUES IN LIMB TRANSPLANTS 113

life further, and not to diminish it.'[11] Other innovative transplant procedures, such as multi-organ transplants, may be criticised as having such unacceptably high mortality rates that they are properly characterised as more research than therapy, and possibly non-therapeutic research at that. Both the case of four-year-old Laura Davies and the two American paediatric cases described by Friedman[12] bear out this ethical qualm, with extensive lymphoma at autopsy in the latter cases.

One might want to argue, however, that medical science only advances by performing procedures at the limit of current knowledge. In that case, limb transplants would be more like research than therapy, and one could expect the risk-benefit ratio to be different. However, the Lyon and Louisville recipients clearly understood the procedure to be therapy, not research. Nor was this supposed research properly designed and evidentially sound. Simply because a procedure is new and unproven does not make it 'experimental' or 'research.' In any case, the standard for subjects' informed consent to participation in medical research is actually higher than for their agreement to therapeutic procedures.[13]

If limb transplants are not to be judged by research standards, the cost-benefit equation which they entail must be considered under the rubric of therapeutic interventions. The most obvious benefit of most other organ transplants, saving life, does not apply to limb transplants. The nearest similarity is to restoration of function, for example, through corneal transplants. However, artificial limbs currently provide a better level of function than the limb transplants so far performed, which does not hold for corneal transplants.

But who should decide on the acceptability of the cost-benefit equation? Here we would normally need to consider both resource allocation – e.g. the expense to the UK National Health Service of lifelong immunosuppressive medication – and benefits to the individual patient. In the case of the Lyon patient, who was paying privately for his own treatment, there was no public resource allocation question (except perhaps insofar as the UK surgeon's time was being diverted away from NHS patients). So the issue resolved itself into a matter of patient autonomy, the

[11] C. Elliott. Doing Harm, Living Organ Donors, Clinical Research, and The Tenth Man. *Journal of Medical Ethics* 1995; 21: 91–96.

[12] *Op. cit.*, note 7.

[13] J. Montgomery. 1997. *Health Care Law*. Oxford. Oxford University Press: 344.

114 DICKENSON AND WIDDERSHOVEN

third question on our list. The obvious patient autonomy argument in the case of an adult patient is that it is up to the patient to weigh the risks and benefits. If he chooses to accept the risks of an actually decreased life span, his autonomy deserves respect. But why?

Many people would phrase their answer in terms of 'whose body is it?', a liberal argument founded loosely on John Locke's assertion in *An Essay concerning Human Understanding* that 'Every man hath a property in his own person.' But Locke follows that sentence with another which ought to give us pause: 'The labour of his body, and the work of his hands, we may say, are properly his.' Locke says we own our labour, not our bodies. And we own our labour because it is the product of our moral agency, which is much closer to what Locke means by 'person' than is the physical body.[14,15]

In Locke's terminology, we own that with which we have mixed our labour. It is not literally mixing our bodies with natural resources which gives us a claim to property; that would be an incoherent metaphor. As Robert Nozick has famously pointed out in his fantastical example of pouring his tin of tomato juice into the sea and then claiming he owns the oceans of the world,[16] mixing one substance which I own with another which I do not possess does not make the second one mine. Similarly, it is not the physical contact between my body and the hoe or the land which entitles me to claim the harvest. If there is anything special about my work, it is not that it is the labour of my body, but that it represents my agency, a part of my self, my person.

Anglo-American common law views tissue taken from the body not as the property of the person from whose body it comes, but as *res nullius*, no one's property. What the law was traditionally concerned with was making sure that the tissue was not taken without consent, not with what happened to it afterwards; after all, it was presumed to be diseased. Of course we need not literally own our bodies to have rights over their inviolability; indeed, this is closer to the conventional position in law. Common law is more concerned with protecting the physical person from assault or other trespass, through the cornerstone of consent, than with establishing property rights in the body. But this is primarily a negative right, to be free of trespass to the

[14] J. Waldron. 1988. *The Right to Private Property*. Oxford. Clarendon Press.
[15] D. Dickenson. 1997. *Property, Women and Politics: Subjects or Objects?* Cambridge. Polity Press.
[16] R. Nozick. 1974. *Anarchy, State and Utopia*. New York. Basic Books.

person – not a positive right to demand any and all forms of procedure which I may think desirable.[17] So it is simply not good enough to say that I own my body and can request that whatever I like should be done to it.

Is the argument from autonomy more to do with the right to harm oneself if one chooses? We accept that argument in other procedures involving self-harm, such as donation of a kidney by a living donor. But where do we draw the line about self-harm? Donation of a kidney by a living donor entails a clear benefit to the recipient. What about the recent furore about amputation of healthy limbs to 'cure' victims of rare body dysmorphic disorders?[18] These patients have an obsessive belief that their body is incomplete with four limbs, but will be complete after amputation. Here there is no benefit to another person, but the surgeon who performed these procedures felt that he was justified by the threats of suicide or self-harm which these patients had made. (In one case, the patient had already asked a friend to shoot off one of her limbs.) Should we say that amputating healthy limbs is *prima facie* wrong – or at least, not part of the goals of medicine? After all, it carries unpleasant connotations of emotional blackmail, and of colluding with the patient's delusions.

That there should be a class of procedures which are *prima facie* wrong, even if patients request them, seems plausible. It is the underpinning notion behind mental health legislation, after all, that people's motives and desires are not always to be taken at face value. This is not just a matter of the law's distinction between the competent adult's *refusal* of treatment, which may occur on any grounds, or no grounds,[19] and the absence of a right to *request* whatever procedure one wants, although that is part of it. In more philosophical terms, the problem of other minds may mean that the clinician cannot ever fully understand the patient's motives for consenting to, refusing, or requesting a procedure; but that does not mean that the clinician has to conclude that the patient's desires must always be respected.[20]

Let us assume, then, that there is a class of procedures which it would be *prima facie* wrong for the clinician to propose (whether

[17] R. *v.* Secretary of State for Social Services, W. Midlands AHA & Birmingham AHA (Teaching), *ex parte* Hincks [1980] 1BMLR 93; R. *v.* Cambridge HA, *ex parte* B [1995] 2 All ER 129 (CA); [1995] 1 FLR 1055 (QBD).

[18] G. Seenan. Healthy Limbs Cut Off at Patients' Request. *Guardian.* 1 February 2000: p. 9.

[19] Re T [1992] 4 All ER 649.

[20] Re J [1991] 3 All ER 930.

116   DICKENSON AND WIDDERSHOVEN

or not the patient agreed) and wrong for the patient to request. If there is a class of procedures which are *prima facie* wrong to perform, what is in that class? Amputation of healthy limbs, in the absence of other justification than that so far encountered, is such a procedure, we suggest. The burden of proof is on the clinician who proposes it, or the patient who requests it, to show why it is not wrong, if further argumentation can be produced. But what about gender reassignment? Somehow that now seems more acceptable, but why? How do we know that the content of the class is not simply down to newness, strangeness, or the 'yuck' factor?

For our purposes, we only need to establish that the patient autonomy argument does not trump all. It may be wrong to take advantage of another's willingness to harm himself: motives are complex creatures.[21] Following extensive media coverage of a total artificial heart transplantation in 1982, some volunteers were even willing to 'donate' their hearts in the interests of advancing science, though they had no cardiac pathology.[22] In the hand transplant case, the risk is not necessarily certain death, and the benefit of the procedure is to the person undertaking the risk; but there may still be a distinction between respecting the patient's 'right' to harm himself and being the agent of possible harm. In interviewing the Lyon recipient, the St Mary's ethics committee was struck by evidence of possible thought disorder: he denied that his own arm, which had been reattached but failed to 'take', was really his, whilst he strongly believed that he would eventually find his 'own' arm again when an allograft was performed. With the hand showing signs of rejection two years later because of his failure to take immunosuppressive medication consistently, he now says, 'As it began to be rejected, I realised that it wasn't my hand after all.'[23] Perhaps he failed to take his immunosupressive medication precisely because he was

[21] We have excluded discussion of the profit motive in donors, for reasons of space limitation. For further discussion of paid organ donation and 'rewarded gifting' (in the context of other organs than limbs), see, *inter alia*: R.R. Bollinger. Ethics of Transplantation. D.J. Rothman, E. Rose, T. Awaya, *et al.* The Bellagio Task Force Report on Transplantation, Bodily Integrity and the International Traffic in Organs. *Transplantation Proceedings* 1997; 29: 2739–2745; C.A.E. Nickerson, J.D. Jasper, D.A. Asch. Comfort Level, Financial Incentives and Consent for Organ Donation. *Transplantation Proceedings* 1998; 30: 155–159; A.S. Dear. Guest Editorial: Paid Organ Donation–the Grey Basket Concept. *Journal of Medical Ethics* 1998; 24: 265–368.

[22] M. Shaw (ed.) 1984. *After Barney Clark: Reflections on the Utah Artificial Heart Program.* Austin. University of Texas Press.

[23] See note 3.

ETHICAL ISSUES IN LIMB TRANSPLANTS   117

under the delusion that the transplanted arm was his own long-lost limb.

How much room is there for critical examination of the patient's motives? The answer to this question depends on how one conceives of autonomy and the interaction between doctor and patient. Emanuel and Emanuel[24] define four models of the doctor-patient relationship:

1. The paternalistic model, in which the doctor knows best;
2. The informative model, in which the doctor merely conveys information and the patient decides;
3. The interpretative model, in which the doctor acts as a counsellor or adviser, helping the patient to clarify values;
4. The deliberative model, in which the doctor acts as a friend or teacher, eliciting the patient to critically examine his or her values in a process of communication and deliberation.

In the Lyon case, the surgeons seem to have followed the informative, legalistic model. The patient was asked to sign a detailed consent form and a legal contract, detailing risks in surgery and anaesthesia together with post-surgical risks of possible drug-related complications, malignancies, infections and long-term psychological complications.[25] The surgical team certainly gave the recipient enough information by the usual professional standards, and indeed more than enough to satisfy the rather minimal requirements of English law.[26] Yet one may doubt the scientific basis of the information given, and therefore the validity of the informed consent. As hand allograft is an 'experimental' procedure, there is an insufficient body of evidence on the basis of which patients can be informed. The team in Louisville chose to give the patient a reduced dose of immunosuppressive medication, reasoning that 'Because a hand transplant is not a life-saving procedure, the drug treatment will be less aggressive than that of other organ transplants.'[27] It is not clear whether the US recipient consented to receive a 'riskier' treatment regime, and if he did, on what evidential basis.

The interpretative and deliberative models imply that the surgeons should actually focus on the patient's reasons for wanting a hand allograft, given the risks involved. In the Lyon

---

[24] E.J. Emanuel, L.I. Emanuel. Four Models of the Physician-Patient Relationship. *JAMA* 1992; 267: 2221–2226.

[25] *Op.cit.*, note 1, 1316.

[26] Sidaway *v.* Bethlem RHG [1985] 1 All ER 643.

[27] Dr Jon Jones, quoted in *The Guardian*, 26 January 1999.

118   DICKENSON AND WIDDERSHOVEN

case, this raises some interesting questions. For nearly ten years, following the reamputation of his right forearm after an initial replantation failed, the recipient had refused an aesthetic or functional prosthesis. Was there an element of inability to accept the loss of his hand, and the failure of its replantation? The deliberative model draws our attention to such questions: patient autonomy is not a catch-all answer in this view, but rather the beginning of a questioning process. 'The conception of patient autonomy is moral self-development; the patient is empowered not simply to follow unexamined preferences or values, but to consider, through dialogue, alternative health-related values, their worthiness, and their implications for treatment.'[28] Of course, there is a considerable risk of slipping over into the paternalistic model here: of overbearing doctors overriding the patient's own values, rather than helping to draw them out. In limb transplants, however, where the motives may be complicated and the benefits might actually be outweighed by the harms, that seems much less of a risk than the converse: failing to examine the patient's decision jointly.

Let us review the issues raised thus far, and evaluate their impact on the ethical status of limb transplants. In this section we have raised three possible ethical objections to human hand allograft in particular:

1) *Is this therapy or research?* The 'defence' claimed that limb transplants are research, not therapy, and that they should be allowed because research pushes the boundaries of scientific knowledge forward. The fact that limb transplant is not (yet) a treatment of proven efficacy, however, does not make it research. So this objection still stands.

2) *Do the costs outweigh the benefits?* Even if limb transplants are not *prima facie* wrong to perform, they could be proven wrong with more extensive argumentation, most obviously cost-benefit analysis. In therapeutic treatment, the benefits to the patients should outweigh the possible risks and harms (which would not necessarily be true in research). However, limb transplant is not a life-saving therapy. This is the calculus on the benefit side; on the harm side we have lifelong immunosuppressive medication, which also carries heavy resource implications. In the view of our clinical ethics committee, the degree of function regained did not counterbalance the costs.

[28] See reference 24, 2222.

3) *Should the patient be the one to decide on the risk-benefit equation?*
   We might want to argue that it is the patient who should
   decide what risks are acceptable. If this is so, it is not so
   because patients straightforwardly own their bodies. The law
   has traditionally been concerned with protecting patients
   from unauthorised trespass to the person, but has been
   unwilling to say that doctors must go along with whatever
   trespass patients do authorise. There are some procedures
   which we want to view as outside the goals of medicine,
   whether the doctor or the patient proposes them. So we
   come back again to the question of whether limb transplants
   are among those procedures.

On balance, so far, drawing on all three of the 'standard'
arguments from bioethics, we have yet to show positive
reasons why limb transplants should be performed. Can
more unconventional arguments take us beyond this im-
passe?

BODILY INTEGRITY AND PERSONAL IDENTITY

Our first set of considerations was fairly standard bioethical fare,
although the application to limb transplants is new. The second
set is more speculative, but possibly more powerful. So far, we
have two 'no' results against limb transplants, and one 'not
proven'. The more speculative arguments, in our view, actually
favour limb transplants more than the standard ones; but they
also require the clinician to take into account some new and
unusual factors.

First, bodily integrity: an obvious issue in physiological terms is
that invasion of bodily integrity precipitates the immune system's
natural reaction, and the consequent need for lifelong
immunosuppressive therapy. But the issue is not only biological;
it is also symbolic, as is clear from the Lyon team's decision to
attempt to restore the normal appearance of the dead donor
through a prosthesis – in order, as they put it, to restore the
dignity of the donor. That the surgical team felt such a need itself
suggests that they felt all was not right. But what exactly is the
ethical importance of bodily integrity, and how does it bear on
the rightness or wrongness of limb transplants?

The symbolic importance of bodily integrity may explain the
emphasis put upon obtaining consent of family members for
organ transplants, contrary to the general principle in English
law that no one, not even a relative, can give or withhold consent

120   DICKENSON AND WIDDERSHOVEN

on behalf of an adult patient.[29] In the absence of consent from the patient, bodily integrity is normally sacrosanct. However, the Human Tissue Act 1961 requires doctors to consult relatives about organ donation if there was no previous consent from the deceased person. French law in relation to organ donation is based on the 'opt-out' principle; but in the UK, where the 'opt-in' system applies, consent must have been obtained from donors before their death. The position is complex in law, but essentially a spouse or relative has the power of veto.[30] In countries with the 'opt-out' system, it is also customary to request the relatives' permission, although this too carries no legal weight.[31] Since 1987, US doctors have been required by law to request relatives' permission for 'harvesting' organs of deceased patients who had not given a consent before death. Similarly in the Netherlands, a law has recently been enacted which gives patients the option of consenting or refusing donation of their own accord, or of leaving the decision to surviving relatives.

In passing, it is also important to note that the current donor card system in the UK may not cover limb transplants. The card reads:

I request that after my death
A.   any part of my body be used for the treatment of others, (tick box) or
B.   my kidneys (tick box), corneas (tick box), heart (tick box), lungs (tick box), liver (tick box), pancreas (tick box) be used for transplantation.

The donor could be excused for thinking that the list under B covers all parts of the body which can be donated. If so, then ticking A would not imply consent to donating limbs.

We have seen that the law gives an unusual level of power to relatives of organ donors, and that this may be linked to feelings about bodily integrity of the deceased. But there is another possibility, which raises an argument from unnaturalness. Is there a lingering sense among the Western general public that transplantation is somehow unnatural and wrong? This is a view which certainly persists in other cultures such as Japan.[32]

---

[29] Re T [1992] 4 All ER 627.

[30] For further detail, see: J. Montgomery. 1997. *Health Care Law.* Oxford. Oxford University Press: 427–430.

[31] B.W. Haag, F.P. Stuart. 1989. The Organ Donor: Brain Death, Selection Criteria, Supply and Demand. In: M.W. Flye (ed.) *Principles of Organ Transplantation.* Philadelphia. WB Saunders Co: 185.

[32] J.R. McConnell. The Ambiguity About Death in Japan: An Ethical Implication for Organ Procurement. *Journal of Medical Ethics* 1999; 25: 322–324.

All medical intervention is unnatural in that it constitutes interference with the natural order, although it is perfectly natural in the sense that we are ourselves part of that order.[33] (It may be that the argument from unnaturalness fulfils our need to maintain boundaries against which our choices have value[34]; but this says nothing about where the boundaries should be set.) One argument in favour of xenotransplants has been that all transplants are unnatural, and may affect our sense of bodily integrity, but that our human identity is not wrapped up in any of our organs. 'If the essence of humanity is seen as a capacity to transcend their level of organic existence, then a person's sense of identity should not, in theory, be threatened by a transfer of organs across species boundaries,' the Nuffield Council Working Party on Xenografts argued.[35]

If this is true of non-human organs, then *a fortiori* it should be true of any human transplant, whether of kidney, limb, or brain tissue. Yet there are two grounds for doubting whether it is true of human transplants. The first is the empirical evidence from transplant recipients, many of whom do report feeling disturbed at the sense of 'otherness' of part of a dead person's body in their own.[36] In principle, at least, this could be controlled through psychiatric testing and counselling of recipients. The more challenging question is philosophical: whether some organs, such as the hand, represent personal identity in a way that other organs do not. This leads into a third set of considerations, concerning personal identity.

Opponents of brain tissue transplants often fear that the procedure alters the recipient's identity in a profoundly problematic way – so that the person who gave consent to receiving the tissue is no longer the same person after the transplant.[37,38] Similarly, we need to consider the wider function of the hand in

---

[33] J. Hughes. Xenografting: Ethical Issues. *Journal of Medical Ethics* 1998; 24: 18–24.

[34] R. Norman. Interfering With Nature. *Journal of Applied Philosophy* 1996; 13: 1–11.

[35] Nuffield Council on Bioethics. *Animal-to-Human Transplants: The Ethics of Xenotransplantation.* 1996; London. Nuffield Council: 104.

[36] J. Craven, G.M. Rodin. 1992. *Psychiatric Aspects of Organ Transplantation.* New York. Oxford University Press: 169–171.

[37] G. Northoff. Do Brain Tissue Transplants Alter Personal Identity? Inadequacies of Some 'Standard Arguments'. *Journal of Medical Ethics* 1996; 22: 174–80.

[38] L. Burd, J.M. Gregory, J. Kerbeshian. The Brain-Mind Quiddity: Ethical Issues in the Use of Human Brain Tissue for Therapeutic and Scientific Purposes. *Journal of Medical Ethics* 1998; 24: 118–22.

122   DICKENSON AND WIDDERSHOVEN

relation to identity, as an instrument of physical intimacy, of contact with others, of consummate skill in artists and musicians, of agency itself – as witness the use of 'hand' to represent agency in such phrases as 'the hand of Fate', 'by his own hand', 'the hand of God'. The hand plays an unrivalled part in both shaping and standing for the story of both the recipient and the donor, in representing agency, and our language reflects this role.

It might be argued that hand allografts entail the transposition of an organ with personal qualities from one person to another. This goes beyond the issue of the hand's visibility, though that too is an issue. 'It may not be easy to live with a transplanted hand, which, unlike other common transplants, remains constantly in full view'[39] – a constant threat to the recipient's sense of his or her own psychological wholeness, arguably outweighing the physical wholeness for which the transplant was sought in the first place. An artificial hand or limb might arguably have the same effect, but on the other hand, there may be a crucial psychological difference. The recipient is not expected to believe that the artificial limb is his or her own, or another person's. There are no personal qualities to be transposed from one to another.

Personal identity, like bodily integrity, has a symbolic character: a person is not only a physical unity, but also a symbolic unity, presented towards others. The French philosopher Ricoeur calls this second notion of identity *ipse*, distinguishing it from the spatio-temporal *idem*.[40] Personal identity as *ipse* is created through interpersonal relations, built upon social practices and shared stories.[41] This kind of identity is not spiritual: it is embodied. Eminently expressive parts of the body, like the face and hand, represent this identity and the relationships with others which are implied in it. If such body parts are inserted into a completely different context, personal identity is at stake, and so are the interpersonal relationships connected with it.

Likewise, it may be conceivable that the intimacy which the hand can express is transformed as a result of transplantation, necessarily having an emotional impact on those who are intimately related to both donor and recipient. It is indeed unsettling to think that the hand with which one has once been intimate may now stroke another body. Even more than the issue

[39] *Op. cit.*, note 2, 1286.
[40] P. Ricoeur. 1991. Narrative Identity. In: D. Wood (ed.) *On Paul Ricoeur: Narrative and Interpretation.* London. Routledge: 188–199.
[41] G.A.M. Widdershoven. 1993. The Story of Life: Hermeneutic Perspectives on the Relationship Between Narrative and Life History. In: R. Josselson, A. Lieblich (eds.) *The Narrative Study of Lives.* Vol. 1. Newbury Park. Sage: 1–20.

of bodily integrity, the issue of personal identity seems to require extensive communication with close relatives in the case of limb transplantation. But is this enough? Perhaps what we really want to say is that the strangeness of hand transplants has nothing to do with their 'experimental' status, or with the 'yuck' factor, but with all that the hand represents. The hand occupies a privileged position, as the expression of both agency and intimacy – of our self and our relation to others.

Yet what is so morally special about intimacy? After all, someone like John Harris might argue, having someone to be intimate with is just a form of privilege, like having children. (Harris does not think we should give preference in allocating scarce resources of organs to those who have dependent children.[42]) One of us has argued elsewhere[43] that this is to view children merely as a consumer good, as a possession; the similar point here is that a view like Harris's is impoverished, and an inaccurate representation of how we come to be agents in the first place. It is through social contact, including the contacts of intimacy, that we become moral agents, on accounts which range from Aristotle's to Hegel's, and on into modern narrative, communitarian, feminist and hermeneutic perspectives. This gives intimacy a claim of precedence on our moral judgement. To the extent that the hand symbolises intimacy, it also gives the hand a special status.

The issues raised in this second section have been less standard and more speculative; or perhaps it is more accurate to say that they have less to do with principlist bioethics and more to do with a narrative or hermeneutic style of ethics, which focuses on the construction and symbolic representation of identity. What conclusions do they suggest?

1. *Symbolic importance of the donor's bodily integrity:* It is difficult to see that limb donation offends against the symbolic importance of bodily integrity any more than does soft tissue donation; the only difference is that it is more visible. However, it is by no means clear that the donor card system includes limbs, and there might be a valid challenge to any presumed consent from relatives. In law, at least, limb transplants might in fact be wrong to perform, without clear and unambiguous consent from the donor.

---

[42] J. Harris. 1985. *The Value of Life.* London. Routledge: 105.
[43] D. Dickenson. 1991. *Moral Luck in Medical Ethics and Practical Politics.* Aldershot. Gower.

124   DICKENSON AND WIDDERSHOVEN

2. *The argument from unnaturalness:* This, too, appears to fail. All transplants are unnatural; and what is unnatural is neither good nor bad, merely unnatural. So there is no objection to limb transplants on grounds of unnaturalness. The effect of this, however, is merely to confirm our initial hypothesis that limb transplants are not *prima facie* wrong to perform, rather than to provide a positive justification for them.

3. *Personal identity and intimacy:* Although these are the most abstract and perhaps speculative grounds for doubting the rightness of hand transplants, they are rooted in a view of human agency which has long historical roots and active current offshoots. The hand, as an expression of both agency and intimacy, occupies a different place in our moral sensibility than internal organs. Again, this is not a reason for absolutely prohibiting hand transplants, if those intimate with both donor and recipient consent, but it is a reason for thinking that the decision is not down to the individual donor or recipient alone.

CONCLUSION

Is it right to perform limb transplants, and in particular hand allografts? Several of our six criteria merely ratify our initial hypothesis that it is at least not wrong to do so. Two – bodily integrity and intimacy – cast rather more doubt on our hypothesis that limb transplant is not forbidden. Overall, we do not rule out hand allograft *a priori*: transplantation may be consistent with respect for the bodily integrity of both donor and recipient, and the recipient may be able to integrate the new limb into his or her personal identity in a satisfactory way. This will, however, require a great deal of effort from all involved, including family members of both donor and recipient. Our discussion shows that limb transplants are not ethically straightforward: rather, they pose deep ethical dilemmas about autonomy and identity, which certainly cannot be solved by concentrating only on professional standards of competence.[44]

Donna Dickenson
University of Birmingham, England

Guy Widdershoven
University of Maastricht, Netherlands

[44] *Op. cit.*, note 3.

[16]

On the Ethics of Facial Transplantation Research

Osborne P. Wiggins, University of Louisville
John H. Barker, University of Louisville
Serge Martinez, University of Louisville
Marieke Vossen, University of Louisville; University of Utrecht, The Netherlands
Claudio Maldonado, University of Louisville
Federico V. Grossi, University of Louisville
Cedric G. Francois, University of Louisville
Michael Cunningham, University of Louisville
Gustavo Perez-Abadia, University of Louisville
Moshe Kon, University of Utrecht, The Netherlands
Joseph C. Banis, University of Louisville

Transplantation continues to push the frontiers of medicine into domains that summon forth troublesome ethical questions. Looming on the frontier today is human facial transplantation. We develop criteria that, we maintain, must be satisfied in order to ethically undertake this as-yet-untried transplant procedure. We draw on the criteria advanced by Dr. Francis Moore in the late 1980s for introducing innovative procedures in transplant surgery. In addition to these we also insist that human face transplantation must meet all the ethical requirements usually applied to health care research. We summarize the achievements of transplant surgery to date, focusing in particular on the safety and efficacy of immunosuppressive medications. We also emphasize the importance of risk/benefit assessments that take into account the physical, aesthetic, psychological, and social dimensions of facial disfiguration, reconstruction, and transplantation. Finally, we maintain that the time has come to move facial transplantation research into the clinical phase.

Keywords

composite tissue
allotransplantation (CTA)
bioethics
reconstructive surgical
procedures
face transplant
immunosuppression
risk assessment
informed consent
identity

Open Peer Commentaries

Carson Strong, p 13
Francois Petit,
Antoine Paraskevas,
and Laurent Lantieri, p 14
Peter E M Butler,
Alex Clarke, and Richard E
Ashcroft, p 16
Arthur Caplan, p 18
Tod Chambers, p 20
Nichola Rumsey, p 22
George J Agich
and Maria Siemionow, p 25
E Haavi Morreim, p 27
Françoise Baylis, p 30
John A Robertson, p 32
Karen J Maschke
and Eric Trump, p 33
Rachel A. Ankeny
and Ian Kerridge, p 35
Sara Goering, p 37
Steven H Miles, p 39

Author's Response

Joseph C Banis, John H
Barker, Michael Cunningham,
Cedric G. Francois, Allen Furr,
Federico Grossi, Moshe Kon,
Claudio Maldonado, Serge
Martinez, Gustavo
Perez-Abadia, Marieke Vossen,
and Osborne P Wiggins, p W23
Howard Trachtman, p W38

Introduction: Advances in Transplant Surgery and Ethical Criteria

The field of transplantation surgery has always pushed the boundaries of medicine forward. In doing so it has repeatedly raised unprecedented ethical questions. Today, as teams around the world consider performing a human facial transplantation, the frontiers of medical ethics are again being tested. Not long ago the pressing ethical issues in transplantation concerned the scarcity of donated organs and the deaths of potential recipients that resulted from this lamentable scarcity (Veatch 2000). With the relatively recent advent of human hand transplantation, however, ethical reflection has shifted to the need to weigh the risks the patient assumes for the sake of receiving a donated organ that, unlike a heart or liver, is not necessary for his or her survival.

The aim of this essay is to address these ethical issues when they arise for human facial transplantation research. When considering facial transplantation research, the ethical concerns must be based on the scientific, surgical, psychological, and social dimensions of the procedure and its aftermath. Therefore, this article devotes considerable space to discussing these dimensions in so far as they have implications for ethics. The ethical questions that arise here are complex and, as we have indicated, unprecedented. Issues of the psychological hopes, anxieties, and stability of transplant recipients have always caused ethical concerns, but with facial transplantation the psychological and social dimensions loom much larger: what is at stake is a person's self-image, social acceptability, and sense of normalcy as he or she subjectively experiences them. To formulate these broad concerns in the language of medical research ethics, many of the "risks" and "benefits" of the surgery seem unpredictable.

The American Journal of Bioethics

As one of the teams preparing to perform human facial transplantation, a key part of our program at the University of Louisville consists of soliciting and incorporating professional discussion into our protocol. The purpose of this essay is to present our reflections on human facial transplantation research to the biomedical ethics community in order to solicit their responses. We view this essay as a component of the "open display and public and professional discussion" required for proceeding in an ethical manner toward the performance of an innovative surgical procedure. As the reader will see below, this is one of the four ethical criteria that Dr. Francis Moore stipulated for undertaking such procedures (Moore 1988, 1989). Our team adopted these criteria and is adhering to them as part our program's ethical guidelines. Throughout this essay we shall refer to the steps our team at the University of Louisville has taken to meet both Moore's criteria and the ethical standards applicable to all health care research.

In part I of this article, we sketch the surgical procedures that are presently utilized in treating facial disfigurements.

In part II, we presuppose the guidelines and regulations formulated by *The Nuremberg Code*, the *Declaration of Helsinki*, *The Belmont Report*, and various official documents that form the basis for the ethical evaluation of all health care research performed today, and we examine facial transplantation from this point of view. We accordingly address the permissibility of facial transplantation research in terms of risk/benefit assessment, informed consent, and privacy and confidentiality.

In part III, we address the criteria enunciated by Francis Moore for judging the acceptability of innovative surgery (Moore 1988, 1989; Siegler 1998). Since we believe that Moore's criteria prompt us to focus on issues not routinely included in the ethics of research, we also deem it important to examine facial transplantation in the light of these requirements.

In part IV, we raise the question, Is it time to perform a facial transplant? Based on parts II and III we summarize eight criteria that, we think, must be satisfied in order to answer this question in the affirmative. We then consider that we have satisfied these criteria at the University of Louisville and that therefore it is justifiable to move forward with performing an experimental facial transplant.

I. Present-Day Procedures for Treating Facial Disfigurements

Facial disfigurement can result from trauma, extirpation of tumors, major burns, severe infections, or congenital birth defects. Patients with such disfigurations number in the thousands (Lee and Mathes 1999). The most advanced treatments available today consist of reconstructing these defects by surgically reattaching the original tissues (Buncke 1996; Thomas et al. 1998), transferring autologous tissues from another part of the body (Angrigiani and Grilli 1997; Pribaz and Fine 2001), and/or using prosthetic materials to replace the missing tissues (Beumer, Roumanas, and Nishimura 1995). By far the best outcomes are achieved with the first alternative, when the original tissues can be salvaged and used to reconstruct the defect. Unfortunately, in most cases the original tissue cannot be salvaged, either because the trauma or disease causing the loss destroyed it beyond use or because the original tissues never existed in the first place (as in congenital birth defects).

When, as in most cases, the original tissues are not available, autologous tissue and/or prosthetic materials are used to reconstruct large tissue defects of the face. In these situations, complications caused by prosthetic materials (e.g., infection or rejection) are common, donor site morbidity (at the location from which the autologous tissues are taken) is almost always present, and multiple "revision" operations and prolonged rehabilitation are usually required. Moreover, functional and aesthetic recovery is usually poor, and the resulting deformity almost always leads to major psychosocial morbidity. The latter in turn often prompts these patients to retire to a secluded environment, becoming social recluses (Lefebvre and Barclay 1982; MacGregor 1990).

A possible solution to the above scenario is to reconstruct these severe facial deformities with identical tissues transplanted from brain-dead human donors (Composite Tissue Allotransplantation), as is done in solid organ transplantation. Composite Tissue Allotransplantation (CTA) in the form of human hand transplantation has recently received a great deal of attention in scientific circles and in the lay media. In the more than twenty hand transplants performed to date, the fact that the tissues used (human hands from brain-dead donors) were identical in both form and function to those originally lost has resulted in excellent early (five years) functional and aesthetic outcomes.

If facial transplantation were available for clinical application in the above-cited example, one could envision a single operation to replace the burned facial tissues with healthy donor tissues identical to the tissues destroyed in the accident. Following surgery, there would be a few revision operations giving the patient a normal appearance and nearly normal function, allowing him or her to return to a normal life in a relatively short time.

In spite of these advantages that facial transplantation has over current reconstructive methods, the main disadvantage is that patients receiving facial tissues from a donor would, like solid organ recipients, have to take potentially toxic immunosuppressive drugs for life in order to prevent rejection. The risks posed by these drugs raises the central question concerning facial transplantation: Do the benefits of facial transplantation justify the risks posed by the immunosuppressive drugs?

II. Official Ethical Codes for Research on Human Subjects

Here we shall address three of the main requirements of the ethics of research using human subjects: (1) risk/benefit assessments, (2) informed consent, and (3) privacy and confidentiality.

Risk/benefit assessments

Ethical codes governing medical and surgical research require careful risk/benefit analyses.

The *Declaration of Helsinki* states:

> Every biomedical research project involving human subjects should be preceded by careful assessment of predictable risks in comparison with foreseeable benefits to the subject or to others. Concern for the interests of the subject must always prevail over the interest of science and society. (Jonsen, Veatch, and Walters 1998)

The Belmont Report clarifies the extent of risks and benefits that need to be considered:

> Many kinds of possible harms and benefits need to be taken into account. There are, for example, risks of psychological, physical, legal, social and economic harm and the corresponding benefits. (Jonsen, Veatch, and Walters 1998)

The extent of risks and benefits may go beyond the individual subject, according to *The Belmont Report:* "Risks and benefits of research may affect the individual subjects, the families of the individual subjects, and society at large (or special groups of subjects in society)" (Jonsen, Veatch, and Walters 1998).

Risk/benefit assessments must be carried out by three different parties. The individual subjects themselves must make such comparisons. The investigative team must make them. And the Institutional Review Board (IRB) reviewing the research

proposal must perform them. Regarding the IRB's duties, the U.S. Department of Health, Education and Welfare's Institutional Guide, *On the Protection of Human Subjects,* states:

> The committee should carefully weigh the known or foreseeable risks to be encountered by subjects, the probable benefits that may accrue to them, and the probable benefits to humanity that may result from the subject's participation in the project or activity. If it seems probable that participation will confer substantial benefits on the subjects, the committee may be justified in permitting them to accept commensurate or lesser risks. (Jonsen, Veatch, and Walters 1998)

Risk/benefit assessment in facial transplantation

In the light of these codes we must seek to develop a clear understanding of the risks to which a patient treated with a facial transplant would be exposed in comparison with the possible benefits. The main risks are those related to the surgical transplant procedure and the lifelong immunosuppression medications that patients would have to take in order to prevent the transplanted tissue from being rejected. The expected benefits primarily would be improvements in quality of life in the form of restored function and aesthetic appearance and the concomitant improvement in the recipient's body image and sense of self. These benefits would probably also increase the recipient's ease and ability in social interactions with other people. While using transplanted tissues to reconstruct facial deformities would significantly improve a patient's quality of life, in most cases these procedures would not be life-saving in the strict sense of the word. This situation stands in contrast to life-saving treatments, like heart and liver transplants, in which the risk/benefit ratio is more readily conceptualized.

Below we discuss the risks and the benefits of facial transplantation and apply them to the "risk and benefit" lessons learned in solid organ transplants and the recent hand transplants.

General Risks of Organ Transplantation Compared to Face Transplantation

Risks Related to Surgery. While facial transplantation is a complex procedure, it does not pose more risks than conventional reconstructive procedures in which the patient's own tissue is used to repair the defects. In a 1998 multicenter study, Dupont et al. (1998) estimated this mortality to be no higher than 0.0567%, which was a figure far higher than that reported in most studies. In addition, compared to

Organ and Tissue Transplantation

The American Journal of Bioethics

conventional reconstructive procedures, facial transplant procedures would utilize tissues taken from a donor rather than from the patient's own body and would thus obviate the complications associated with donor site morbidity. Also, conventional reconstructive methods can require over 100 revision surgeries over many years whereas, if successful, facial transplantation would require only a few surgeries. Since each surgical procedure carries with it inherent risks, it could be argued that conventional reconstructive methods are associated with more risks than facial transplants.

Risks related to immunosuppression

The immunosuppression-related risks in facial transplantation are also expected to be the same as those experienced by the solid organ and hand transplant recipients, who receive the same drug regimens. The most common complications associated with the use of immunosuppressants include increased incidence of: (1) infections, (2) malignancies, and (3) end-organ toxicity. In rare instances malignancies associated with immunosuppressive therapy can result in death. The incidences of these complications, in the particular case of tacrolimus and mycophenolate mofetil/prednisone combination therapy (the drug regimen that would most likely be used in facial transplants), are as follows:

Infections: The incidence of opportunistic infections (bacterial, fungal, and viral, including CMV) reported in kidney transplant recipients using tacrolimus and mycophenolate mofetil (MMF) range from 8.4% to 31% (Daoud et al. 1998; Stratta 1997). When this complication occurs, the initial treatment usually consists of the appropriate antibiotic, antifungal, or antiviral agent. In rare cases it is necessary to lower the level of immunosuppression, or even to halt immunosuppressive drugs altogether.

Malignancies: In transplant recipients, there exists a 1.2% incidence of posttransplant lymphoproliferative disease (PTLD) and an 11.1% incidence of nonmelanoma skin carcinoma (reported over a three-year period of follow-up) (Mathew 1998). When malignancies occur in heart, lung, or liver transplant patients, immunosuppression must be continued because of the life-saving nature of the transplanted organ.

However, in facial transplantation, as in kidney transplantation, immunosuppression could be halted so that the patient's immune responsiveness against the tumor might be strengthened. Here, the recipient's life would not be put at risk by discontinuation of immunosuppression even though the consequence would be loss of the transplanted tissue.

End-organ toxicity: In solid organ recipients, tacrolimus has been reported to be associated with end-organ toxicity and presents itself in the form of post-transplant diabetes mellitus in 7 to 11.9% of recipients. Of these, approximately two-thirds are able to discontinue insulin within twelve months after transplant (Johnson et al. 2000; Miller 1999). Tacrolimus is also nephrotoxic, as evidenced by increased blood creatinine levels in approximately 20% of the recipients using this drug. Since organ toxicity is relatively drug-specific, substitution with different drugs often offers a solution in these cases. Combining tacrolimus with MMF makes it possible to reduce the tacrolimus doses and thus diminishes nephrotoxicity while maintaining adequate immunosuppression (de Mattos, Olyaei, and Bennett 2000).

In the case of end-organ toxicity, it could be argued that recipients of transplanted facial tissues have an advantage over solid organ recipients. This is due to the fact that facial tissue recipients could be potentially less susceptible to immunosuppression-related end-organ toxicity than solid organ recipients. This stems from the fact that by the time solid organ recipients receive their donor organ, they have often already experienced multiple organ problems from their underlying chronic disease. Once they receive their transplanted organ, the immunosuppressive drugs they must take often further damage their already debilitated organs. In the case of facial tissue recipients, serious underlying chronic disease would exclude the patient from transplantation, and consequently their organs should be healthy (Cendales and Hardy 2000). Therefore, it is reasonable to expect less end-organ toxicity with the immunosuppressive drugs in facial tissue recipients when compared with solid organ recipients.

Psychological Risks. The psychological risks that facial transplant recipients will confront will be similar to those experienced by solid organ transplant recipients, for example, a desperation that creates unrealistic hopes, fears that his or her body will reject the transplant, guilt feelings about the death of the donor, difficulty conforming to the treatment

On the Ethics of Facial Transplantation Research

regimen and its side-effects, and a sense of personal responsibility for the success of the procedure (Zdichavsky et al. 1999).

Moreover, the recipient of a new face must deal with a new appearance, but to some extent this resembles the risk of receiving a new hand, which also reshapes one's sense of one's appearance. What is unique to facial transplantation, however, is that facial appearance is intimately and profoundly associated with one's sense of personal and social identity. Therefore, the recipient of a face must adapt to his or her own responses to this new "identity" as well as to other people's responses to it. It is expected that such adaptations will not occur once and for all; rather, they will repeatedly occur and undergo modifications over time. Moreover, it will be impossible for the recipient of a transplanted face to escape a bright public spotlight, and such publicity will be invasive and long-term. Such risks might be mitigated by careful patient selection, ongoing monitoring, and psychiatric intervention, as indicated.

Social Risks. As in cases of solid organ and hand transplantation, the family of the recipient of a face will be responsible for care-giving and social and psychological support. The recipient and his or her family will also be subjected inevitably to intrusive publicity and media coverage. In addition to these risks to the family of the recipient, there are other risks that we might imagine affecting the larger society. For example, a successful facial transplant might be interpreted as conveying the message that a good quality of life cannot be achieved by people with disfiguring conditions. There also exists the possibility that the public may develop unrealistic expectations for the outcomes of such surgery, perhaps to the point of creating an inappropriate demand for its use in less worthy cases, such as cosmetic enhancement for the aging rich or for criminal identity concealment. The facial transplant research team cannot prevent these or other misconceptions. What the team can do is provide accurate information in order, it is hoped, to shape public opinions in a responsible manner.

General Benefits of Organ Transplantation Compared to Face Transplantation

Benefits associated with facial transplantation can be separated into three categories: functional benefits, aesthetic/psychological benefits, and social benefits. The relative value of these three types of benefits is important when assessing the risk/benefit

equation for a transplant candidate and developing a triage strategy. For example, a hand transplant provides predominantly functional and, to a lesser degree, aesthetic benefits. The combination of these two benefits contributes to the psychological benefit derived from this procedure. A transplanted hand takes the place of the lost/missing hand in the spatial resolution of the patient. This has important psychological implications and is a great benefit of this procedure. This was clear in the repeated statements by Louisville's first hand transplant recipient, in which he asserted that his transplanted hand gave him a sense of being "whole" and "complete" (Klapheke 1999).

Functional Benefits. Functional recovery of the facial tissues offers several important benefits. Depending on the extent of the original deformity, the anticipated benefits include restoration of blinking for eye protection, improved oral continence, and restoration of facial expression and sensory function.

Aesthetic and Psychological Benefits. The human face is unquestionably the most important aesthetic anatomical feature of the human body. Much of how other people react to us depends upon our aesthetic appearance. Moreover, the appearance of our face is the predominant anatomical feature by which we identify and differentiate ourselves from others. In a large number of cases facial disfigurement leads to depression, social isolation, and even the risk of suicide (Robinson, Rumsey, and Partridge 1996; Ye 1998). By replacing the disfigured face with a "normal" appearing/functioning face, facial transplantation would provide important psychological benefits.

Social Benefits. Closely related to functional, aesthetic, and psychological benefits is the enhanced social capacity of the subject. Although a period of adaptation will be required for both the subject and others involved, the subject's willingness and ease in engaging in social interactions should improve. Restoring the abilities to make facial expressions, enjoy an aesthetically acceptable appearance, and interact comfortably with others lends significant weight to the benefit side of the risk/benefit equation.

Informed consent

Ever since *The Nuremberg Code* (Jonsen, Veatch, and Walters 1998), informed consent has been fundamental to any research performed with human subjects. *The Belmont Report* grounds this requirement in the basic ethical principle of respect for persons

The American Journal of Bioethics

(Jonsen, Veatch, and Walters 1998). The *Report* states:

> Respect for persons requires that subjects, to the degree that they are capable, be given the opportunity to choose what shall or shall not happen to them. This opportunity is provided when adequate standards for informed consent are satisfied (Jonsen, Veatch, and Walters 1998).

On the Protection of Human Subjects: U.S. Department of Health, Education and Welfare's Institutional Guide specifies the main items to be covered by informed consent:

> The basic elements of informed consent are:
> A fair explanation of the procedures to be followed, including an identification of those which are experimental;
> A description of the attendant discomforts and risks;
> A description of the benefits to be expected;
> A disclosure of appropriate alternative procedures that would be advantageous for the subject;
> An offer to answer any inquiries concerning the procedures;
> An instruction that the subject is free to withdraw his consent and to discontinue participation in the project or activity at any time. (Jonsen, Veatch, and Walters 1998)

All prospective candidates being considered for facial transplantation in our program will be presented with an informed consent in both oral and written form. Investigators who will be involved in performing the transplant will discuss with the prospective subject all elements of the informed consent and will address any concerns or questions that the subject may have. Prospective subjects will in no way be coerced or manipulated regarding any part of the informed consent process.

To assure that the prospective candidate receives an objective perspective during and after the informed consent process, he or she will be encouraged to select a subject advocate who will assist him or her in understanding and deliberating about the various components of the procedure.

Here we shall not summarize the many items included in this informed consent process. However, we would like to note that item 6 in the *On the Protection of Human Subjects: U.S. Department of Health, Education and Welfare's Institutional Guide* cited above cannot be followed strictly in facial transplantation: the subject must conform to the research-treatment regimen as long as he or she has the transplanted facial tissue.

Privacy and confidentiality

The *Declaration of Helsinki* states:

> The right of the research subject to safeguard his or her integrity must always be respected. Every precaution should be taken to respect the privacy of the subject and to minimize the impact of the study on the subject's physical and mental integrity and on the personality of the subject. (Jonsen, Veatch, and Walters 1998)

In the case of transplantation research, there are two groups of persons whose privacy and confidentiality should be respected. The first is the donor and his or her family, and the second is the recipient and his or her family.

Facial Tissue Donor

The privacy and confidentiality of the donor and his or her family ought to be respected to the extent permitted by law. All reasonable efforts should be made to protect the donor's anonymity. Identifying information ought not to be publicly revealed. The donor's family must be informed, however, that the research team cannot prevent someone (e.g., a member or friend of the donor's family) who knows about the case from publicizing information on his or her own.

Facial Tissue Recipient

In the case of an innovative therapeutic procedure like facial transplantation, there are two reasons for concern about the confidentiality and privacy of the recipient and his or her family:

1. The full scientific reporting and discussion of this procedure and its results may be restricted too greatly by efforts to maintain the privacy of the subject. For example, in the publication of the outcomes of the operation it may be highly desirable, from a scientific point of view, to provide unaltered photographs of the face of the recipient. Also, in conference presentations it might be very helpful, again from a scientific point of view, to hear the recipient him- or herself speak about his or her experience and to respond to questions. Hence the mandate to respect privacy and confidentiality may conflict with scientific requirements.

2. The prospect of a facial transplant has already attracted significant media attention, and as the likelihood—and then the reality—of such a phenomenon develops, the interest of the media in it will inevitably become greater. It is difficult to

imagine, then, how the media can be kept from discovering the identity and much other information about the recipient and his or her family. Indeed, for the recipient, "privacy" may not be possible.

In a recent article entitled "High-Profile Research and the Media: The Case of the AbioCor Artificial Heart," E.H. Morreim carefully examined the issue of disclosure of information to the public (Morreim 2004). She pointed out that, from a scientific point of view, the ideal way to provide information to the public is through publications in refereed professional journals. Peer-reviewed publications are better able to provide accurate scientific information than are press releases that occur as the research project progresses. Nonetheless, she noted that high-profile research cannot enjoy such luxury in a society that prides itself on its "freedom of the press." She sought, then, to sort out the competing obligations to disclose information to the public, to maintain the research subject's privacy and confidentiality, and to publish the procedures and results of medical/surgical research in professional journals.

Morreim (2004) pointed out that in our society we must recognize "the right of free press" and the public's "desire to know" about heath care innovations. Freedom of the press, she asserted, "does not mean that anyone is required, in the first place, to provide a reporter with whatever information he wants" (Morreim 2004). Similarly with the public's "desire to know" some kind of information: it does not entail that anyone has the duty to produce the information (Morreim 2004).

Nevertheless, in keeping with our established policy of "open display and professional and public discussion and evaluation," we believe we are obligated to release to the press basic clinical and surgical information about facial transplants. This obligation, however, must be balanced against the research subject's right to privacy and confidentiality. Morreim (2004) seems to have concluded that "materially significant trends in the progress of the trial" should be disclosed to the public, and "Patients should not be permitted to veto the disclosure of such information" (Morreim 2004). Affirming the patient's right to privacy, however, she added,

> Patients should be able to control some kinds of information. Clearly, purely personal details such as marital status, education, occupation, and the like should be governed by the patient (Morreim 2004).

And, she continued,

> Additionally, patients and families should have the opportunity to review press releases in advance to correct errors, delete unsuitable personal information, and influence the tone of the report. (Morreim 2004)

These suggestions will guide our approach to press releases and to protecting the subject's privacy and confidentiality. Accordingly, we shall inform the subject and his or her family that we shall need to publish in professional journals some identifying information about the subject. We shall seek, however, to restrict such information to solely what is necessary for scientific purposes. In addition, we shall inform the subject at the outset that we shall provide press releases. As press releases are prepared, the general nature of the information that will be released will be disclosed to the subject and the subject's family, and they will be given the opportunity to review the information and offer suggestions. We shall also inform the subject that extensive media attention is likely to be forthcoming and that we cannot guarantee that their identities and other personal information will not be discovered and published by the media. As the press releases are prepared, we shall provide subjects and their families the opportunity to review them in advance and offer suggestions. Subjects and their families will remain at liberty to control personal information in so far as this can be done in the light of the intense media spotlight.

III. Francis Moore's Criteria for Innovative Surgical Procedures

In our facial transplantation program at the University of Louisville, in addition to the above ethical requirements, we have also adopted and are following criteria recommended by Dr. Francis Moore (1988, 1989). In 1988 article, Moore offered four criteria for determining whether it is ethically acceptable to employ an innovative surgical technique. His criteria were: (1) the scientific background of the innovation, (2) the skill and experience of the team ("field strength"), (3) the ethical climate of the institution, and (4) open display and public and professional discussion and evaluation (Moore 1988).

The scientific background of the innovation

This criterion requires that the scientific preparation for proceeding to carry out an innovative surgical procedure must have been carefully and fully developed. The scientific preparation for facial

The American Journal of Bioethics

transplantation is derived primarily from solid organ and hand transplantation research. In addition, unique to hand and facial transplantation, the risk vs. benefit equation in these non-life-saving procedures is being studied (Cunningham et al. 2004).

The vast majority of solid organ transplantation research that bears relevance to facial transplantation has focused on identifying and developing new immunosuppressive drugs and drug combinations that effectively suppress rejection while also causing minimal side effects. The relevant literature is full of basic science and clinical research describing the development and evaluation of these drugs (Gorantla et al. 2000). In 1997, experiments conducted in our laboratory in a large animal model (Ren et al. 2000) demonstrated that one of these new drug combinations (tacrolimus/MMF/prednisone) successfully prevented rejection of transplanted skin, muscle, bone, and other tissues making up the hand while causing minimal systemic toxicity (Jones et al. 1999; Shirbacheh et al. 1998). Based on these experiments, teams in Lyon (France), Louisville (USA), and Guangzhou (China) performed in 1998 and 1999 the first four human hand transplants using this same drug regimen (Dubernard et al. 1999; Francois et al. 2000; Jones et al. 2000).

From an immunological standpoint, since the face contains mostly the same tissues as the hand, it is reasonable to assume that the same immunosuppressive drug regimen found to be effective in the animal research that preceded human hand transplants and in the human hand transplants that followed should also be effective in facial transplantation.

In addition to this animal research, the scientific preparation for facial transplantation must include empirical studies that address the critical ethical questions that such procedures pose. We are therefore in the process of carrying out several studies that aim to answer the central question, "Do the benefits of facial transplantation justify the risks posed by the immunosuppressive drugs required to prevent rejection?" While the risks of immunosuppression are generally accepted for "life-saving" organ transplantation procedures, these same risks are questioned when it comes to "non-life-saving" or "quality-of-life improving" procedures like facial transplantation. To address this issue we designed a questionnaire-based study (Cunningham et al. 2004) to assess the amount of risk individuals are willing to accept to receive the benefits of facial transplantation. Our initial findings from over 250 individuals in four populations questioned (healthy normal subjects, upper extremity amputees, organ transplant recipients, and individuals with facial disfigurements) indicate that they would accept significantly more risk to receive a facial transplant than a single hand, double hand, larynx, foot, or even a kidney transplant (Banis et al. 2002). The last point is intriguing since kidney transplantation is a universally accepted treatment for which the risk vs. benefit ratio goes largely unquestioned.

Siegler (1998) has claimed that central to the ethical concerns with respect to these procedures is the question of whether "the equipoise consideration has been satisfied." He defined equipoise as "a situation of uncertainty in which the clinical investigator regards the potential outcome of an experiment or clinical trial as truly balanced between its potential for benefiting the patient or for causing unintended harms" (Siegler 1998). The key term here is "uncertainty." At stake is an uncertainty that remains at the point at which we have gained as much knowledge as we can through scientific studies; and therefore, additional knowledge can be attained only by actually performing the experimental procedure and following the outcome. We believe that facial transplantation has reached a position of equipoise because we are destined to remain uncertain about whether the benefits will outweigh the harms (or vice versa) until we perform the procedure and observe the actual results.

The Skill and Experience of the Team ("Field Strength")

Moore (1998, 1999) emphasized that the skill and experience of the team undertaking the innovative procedure is crucial. Obviously, such a procedure can be truly "tested" for its safety and efficacy only if the skills and experience of the team performing the procedure are unlikely to be the cause of failure. Moreover, the "field strength" of the team must be assured in order to protect the subjects from harm. *The Nuremberg Code* enunciates this ethical concern for beneficence:

> 8. The experiment should be conducted only by scientifically qualified persons. The highest degree of skill and care should be required through all stages of the experiment of those who conduct or engage in the experiment. (Jonsen, Veatch, and Walters 1998)

The team at the University of Louisville is composed of experts who have extensive experience in the scientific, clinical, surgical, and psychological areas pertinent to facial transplantation. This includes specialists in reconstructive surgery, head and neck surgery, transplant surgery, immunology, psychology, psychiatry, ethics, Institutional Review Board participation, and organ procurement. The reconstructive and head and neck surgeons on our team are familiar with and regularly employ the latest techniques described above to remove, transfer, and reconfigure autologous tissues to reconstruct facial deformities. Indeed, members of the team have pioneered many of the techniques used today for reconstructing complex facial deformities (Banis and Acland 1984). In addition, the team has acquired relevant skills and experience through having established a program for and performed successful human hand transplants. It is such "field strength," we think, that is necessary in order to take the next step of performing a human facial transplantation.

Ethical climate of the institution

What is at stake here is ultimately the motivation for undertaking the innovative procedure. Moore was concerned that the innovation not be performed mainly for the purposes of institutional or professional self-aggrandizement. He thought that it should rather be carried out primarily for its potential contributions to those people who are in need of the procedure. As he expressed it:

> When the epiphenomena of medical care, such as capital gain, investor profit, institutional representation, surgeon ego, municipal pride, and chauvinism, become the true objective of the procedure, then the ethical climate of the institution is no longer acceptable for therapeutic innovation (Moore 1988; Siegler 1998).

Adherence to this ethical requirement is essential but difficult to verify. How can we determine what a person's or an institution's motivations are? Usually people and institutions engage in sizable projects with a variety of motives for doing so.

We suggest that the ethical issues here pertain to possible conflicts of interest. If desires for enhanced reputation, financial reward, professional vanity, and so on motivate those involved to compromise the scientific, medical, surgical, or ethical aspects of the procedure, "then the ethical climate of the institution is no longer acceptable for therapeutic innovation." An institution may seek an enhanced reputation and even financial profit from being "the first" to advance therapeutic techniques. Indeed, numerous health care institutions highly prize their public reputations for being "first" with innovative procedures, and this usually does not lead

people to suspect unethical conduct. The desire to be first becomes unethical only when it motivates the institution to undertake the innovation in a manner that fails to follow strict scientific, medical, surgical, and ethical demands. The key question then becomes this: Have the institutions and professionals involved adhered as much as can reasonably be expected to scientific, medical, surgical, and ethical requirements in performing this new procedure? If these requirements have been met, then it matters little what other motivations may be operative. And this would seem to be the case especially in view of the fact that such motivations can usually not be detected or proven.

Open display and public and professional discussion and evaluation

Moore (1998) recognized that it is crucial that innovative surgical procedures be openly displayed before the broad community of professionals in the field as well as before the general public. In order to ensure that the issues surrounding facial transplantation would be submitted to public and professional discussion, evaluation, and criticism, we at the University of Louisville have organized and participated in several conferences addressing these manifold issues. Moreover, we have published the proceedings from these conferences in trade journals to make them accessible to as wide a professional audience as possible. Feedback we have received from public and professional discussion has allowed us to rethink and revise various components of our program. In fact, although our institutional review board proposal has been virtually complete for over three years, we have postponed submitting it for approval and have rather repeatedly fine-tuned it based on criticisms we have received from professional and public discussions.

Below we list the main examples of efforts we have made to meet Moore's recommendation of open display and public and professional discussion and evaluation.

In November 1997, we hosted the first International Symposium on Composite Tissue Allotransplantation in Louisville, Kentucky. The workshop brought together international experts in immunology, transplant, plastic, and hand surgery, research, and ethics to evaluate the scientific, ethical, and clinical barriers standing in the way of performing the first human hand transplants. After two days of discussion the consensus was reached that sufficient animal research had been done and that it was time

The American Journal of Bioethics

to move on to the clinical phase of this research (Barker et al. 1998).

In May 2000, we convened the 2nd International Symposium on Composite Tissue Allotransplantation in Louisville, Kentucky to share the early results of the first human hand transplants and invited teams who had performed other types of composite tissue allotransplantation procedures (namely, larynx, bone, tendon, and nerve). Three hand transplant teams reported encouraging early immunological and functional findings. They reported that the immunosuppressive drug regimen [tacrolimus/MMF/Prednisone] they were using effectively prevented hand rejection, allowed for good recovery of hand function, and caused minimal toxic side-effects in their first patients (Barker, Breidenbach, and Hewitt 2000).

We have also published discussions of the present and future state of composite tissue allotransplantation in professional trade journals (Barker, Vossen, and Banis 2004; Barker et al. 2002; Gorantla et al. 2001)

On November 19, 2003, our team participated in a public discussion at the Dana Center of the London Science Museum. At this gathering four professionals from various fields related to facial transplantation explained their work and their respective positions on the question of whether the time had come to perform human facial transplants. This two-hour event specifically focused on the public's participation and their opinions (Morris and Monaco 2004). Following this meeting the proceedings were posted on the Dana Center's website, and the public was invited to post its views. Finally, in addition to these public forums for discussion, we have also openly made our program available to the public in several sources of print, radio, and television media.

IV. Is It Time to Perform a Facial Transplant?

In light of the above discussion we would like to put forward a set of criteria for determining whether the point has been reached, in the preparation and development of this innovative surgical procedure, at which it is justified to perform an experimental facial transplant. The criteria we propose are these:

1. Moore's criterion of "scientific background of the innovation." The preparatory scientific groundwork has been laid through laboratory and clinical investigations of the pertinent medications, technology, procedures, and ethical issues. This

preparatory work has significantly reduced the risks of the proposed procedure.

2. Moore's criterion of "skill and experience of the team ('field strength')." The surgeons and clinicians involved in the research project possess the knowledge, experience, skills, and technical abilities needed for it.

3. Moore's criterion of "open display and public and professional discussion and evaluation." Items (1) and (2) above have been publicized so that professional and lay persons who have so wished have had sufficient opportunity to discuss and criticize the performance of the procedure. Moreover, these responses and criticisms have been seriously considered by the research team and have, when appropriate, influenced the revision of the research proposal.

4. Moore's critique of the "ethical climate of the institution." The innovation is not being performed for purposes of institutional prestige or professional recognition. It is rather the criteria enumerated here that are the truly governing ones.

5. The remaining uncertainties regarding facial transplantation and its consequences can be resolved either by proceeding to actually performing the procedure on human subjects or by postponing it and waiting for further developments. Undoubtedly, postponing the procedure would allow for the development of medical innovations. An analogy can be imagined in the manned mission to the moon. This venture would have been aided by the development of the microcomputer, digital camera, and other innovations produced during the past three decades. Such innovations, however, were not essential for a successful moon mission. We submit that, in an analogous way, future medical developments will provide only minimal knowledge compared to that which will be gained from performing the procedure. An example of this is in the knowledge gained from performing human hand transplants. Despite the arguments made against them as too precipitous and uncertain, over twenty hand transplants have been performed. As a result, the field has gained a wealth of knowledge based on direct evidence that would not have been possible if we had not dared to perform the procedure in the face of the uncertainties.

6. There exist informed subjects who, deeming the procedure beneficial, want to undergo it and who will not be able to undergo it if it is postponed in order to wait for further developments.

7. There exist indefinitely many other potential subjects who could in the future benefit from this procedure if it proves to be successful.

8. The procedure has been subjected to the established regulatory scrutiny and reviews, including approval by the relevant IRB.

If these eight criteria are satisfied, we submit that it would be justified to actually perform the experimental procedure on qualified, voluntary, and informed human subjects. Furthermore, we maintain that at the University of Louisville these criteria have been satisfied for the procedure of human facial transplantation. There arrives a point in time when the procedure should simply be done. We submit that that time is now. ∎

Received 9 March 2004; accepted 1 April 2004; revision received 4 April 2004; posted for commentary 5 April 2004.

Competing Interests Statement
The authors declare that they have no competing financial interests.

References

Angrigiani, C., and D. Grilli. 1997. Total face reconstruction with one free flap. *Plastic & Reconstructive Surgery* 99(6): 1566–1575.

Banis, J. C., Jr., and R. D. Acland. 1984. Managing the outer limits of reconstruction with microsurgical free tissue transfer. *Archives of Surgery* 119(6): 673–679.

Banis, J. C., P. C. R. Brouha, R. Majzoub, et al. 2002. *How much risk are individuals willing to accept to receive composite tissue allotransplantation reconstructive procedures?* Presentation at the Annual Meeting of the Association of Plastic Surgery, Seattle, WA.

Barker, J., M. Vossen, and J. C. Banis. 2004. Face transplantation. *International Journal of Surgery* 2:8–12.

Barker, J. H., W. C. Breidenbach, and C. W. Hewitt. 2000. Second International Symposium on Composite Tissue Allotransplantation. Introduction. *Microsurgery* 20(8): 359.

Barker, J. H., C. G. Francois, J. M. Frank, and C. Maldonado. 2002. Composite tissue allotransplantation. *Transplantation* 73(5): 832–835.

Barker, J. H., J. W. Jones, and W. C. Breidenbach. 1998. Composite tissue transplantation; A clinical reality? Transplantation Proceedings (Invited Editor), 30(6): 2686–2787.

Beumer, J., III, E. Roumanas, and R. Nishimura. 1995. Advances in osseointegrated implants for dental and facial rehabilitation following major head and neck surgery. *Seminars in Surgical Oncology* 11(3): 200–207.

Buncke, H. J. 1996. Microsurgical replantation of the avulsed scalp: Report of 20 cases. *Plastic & Reconstructive Surgery* 97(6): 1107–1108.

Cendales, L., and M. A. Hardy. 2000. Immunologic considerations in composite tissue transplantation: Overview. *Microsurgery* 20(8): 412–419.

Cunningham, M., R. Majzoub, P. C. R. Brouha, et al. 2004. Risk acceptance in composite tissue allotransplantation reconstructive procedures—Instrument design and validation. *European Journal of Trauma* 30(1): 12–16.

Daoud, A. J., T. J. Schroeder, M. Shah, et al. 1998. A comparison of the safety and efficacy of mycophenolate mofetil, prednisone and cyclosporine and mycophenolate mofetil, and prednisone and tacrolimus. *Transplantation Proceedings* 30(8): 4079–4081.

de Mattos, A. M., A. J. Olyaei, and W. M. Bennett. 2000. Nephrotoxicity of immunosuppressive drugs: Long-term consequences and challenges for the future. *American Journal of Kidney Disease* 35(2): 333–346.

Dubernard, J. M., E. Owen, G. Herzberg, et al. 1999. Human hand allograft: Report on first 6 months. *Lancet* 353(9161): 1315–1320.

Dupont, H., P. Mezzarobba, A. C. Degremont, et al. 1998. Early perioperative mortality in a multidisciplinary hospital. *Annales Francaise d'Anesthesie et de Reanimation* 17(7): 755–763.

Francois, C. G., W. C. Breidenbach, C. Maldonado, et al. 2000. Hand transplantation: Comparisons and observations of the first four clinical cases. *Microsurgery* 20(8): 360–371.

Gorantla, V. S., J. H. Barker, J. W. Jones, Jr., et al. 2000. Immunosuppressive agents in transplantation: Mechanisms of action and current anti-rejection strategies. *Microsurgery* 20(8): 420–429.

Gorantla, V. S., C. Maldonado, F. Johannes, and J. H. Barker. 2001. Composite Tissue Allotransplantation (CTA): Current status and future insights. *European Journal of Trauma* 27(6): 267–274.

Johnson, C., N. Ahsan, T. Gonwa, et al. 2000. Randomized trial of tacrolimus (Prograf) in combination with azathioprine or mycophenolate mofetil versus cyclosporine (Neoral) with mycophenolate mofetil after cadaveric kidney transplantation. *Transplantation* 69(5): 834–841.

Jones, J. W., S. A. Gruber, J. H. Barker, and W. C. Breidenbach. 2000. Successful hand transplantation. One-year follow-up. Louisville Hand Transplant Team. *The New England Journal of Medicine* 343(7): 468–473.

Jones, J. W., Jr., E. T. Ustuner, M. Zdichavsky, et al. 1999. Long-term survival of an extremity composite

The American Journal of Bioethics

tissue allograft with FK506-mycophenolate mofetil therapy. *Surgery* 126(2): 384–388.

Jonsen, A. R., R. M. Veatch, and L. Walters. 1998. *Source book in bioethics: A documentary history.* Washington, DC: Georgetown University Press.

Klapheke, M. M. 1999. Transplantation of the human hand: Psychiatric considerations. *Bulletin of the Menninger Clinic* 63(2): 159–173.

Lee, W. P., and D. W. Mathes. 1999. Hand transplantation: Pertinent data and future outlook. *The Journal of Hand Surgery* 24(5): 906–913.

Lefebvre, A., and S. Barclay. 1982. Psychosocial impact of craniofacial deformities before and after reconstructive surgery. *Canadian Journal of Psychiatry* 27(7): 579–584.

MacGregor, F. C. 1990. Facial disfigurement: Problems and management of social interaction and implications for mental health. *Aesthetic Plastic Surgery* 14(4): 249–257.

Mathew, T. H. 1998. A blinded, long-term, randomized multicenter study of mycophenolate mofetil in cadaveric renal transplantation: Results at three years. Tricontinental Mycophenolate Mofetil Renal Transplantation Study Group. *Transplantation* 65(11): 1450–1454.

Miller, J. 1999. Tacrolimus and mycophenolate mofetil in renal transplant recipients: One year results of a multicenter, randomized dose ranging trial. FK506/MMF Dose-Ranging Kidney Transplant Study Group. *Transplantation Proceedings* 31(1–2): 276–277.

Moore, F. D. 1988. Three ethical revolutions: Ancient assumptions remodeled under pressure of transplantation. *Transplantation Proceedings* 20(1 Suppl 1): 1061–1067.

Moore, F. D. 1989. The desperate case: CARE (costs, applicability, research, ethics). *JAMA* 261(10): 1483–1484.

Morreim, F. 2004. High-profile research and the media: The case of the AbioCor artificial heart. *Hastings Center Report* January/February:11–24.

Morris, P. J., and A. P. Monaco. 2004. Facial transplantation: Is the time right? *Transplantation* 77(3): 329.

Pribaz, J. J., and N. A. Fine. 2001. Prefabricated and prelaminated flaps for head and neck reconstruction. *Clinical Plastic Surgery* 28(2): 261–272, vii.

Ren, X., M. V. Shirbacheh, E. T. Ustuner, et al. 2000. Osteomyocutaneous flap as a preclinical composite tissue allograft: Swine model. *Microsurgery* 20(3): 143–149.

Robinson, E., N. Rumsey, and J. Partridge. 1996. An evaluation of the impact of social interaction skills training for facially disfigured people. *British Journal of Plastic Surgery* 49(5): 281–289.

Shirbacheh, M., J. Jones, W. C. Breidenbach, and J. H. Barker. 1998. *The feasibility of human hand transplantation.* Presentation at the Seventh International Federation of the Society for Surgery of Hand Congress, Vancouver, BC.

Siegler, M. 1998. Ethical issues in innovative surgery: Should we attempt a cadaveric hand transplantation in a human subject? *Transplantation Proceedings* 30(6): 2779–2782.

Stratta, R. J. 1997. Simultaneous use of tacrolimus and mycophenolate mofetil in combined pancreas-kidney transplant recipients: A multi-center report. The FK/MMF Multi-Center Study Group. *Transplantation Proceedings* 29(1–2): 654–655.

Thomas, A., V. Obed, A. Murarka, and G. Malhotra. 1998. Total face and scalp replantation. *Plastic & Reconstructive Surgery* 102(6): 2085–2087.

Veatch, R. M. 2000. *Transplantation ethics.* Washington, DC: Georgetown University Press.

Ye, E. M. 1998. Psychological morbidity in patients with facial and neck burns. *Burns* 24(7): 646–648.

Zdichavsky, M., J. W. Jones, E. T. Ustuner, et al. 1999. Scoring of skin rejection in a swine composite tissue allograft model. *Journal of Surgical Research* 85(1): 1–8.

Part V
Living Donor Transplantation

[17]

Autonomy's Limits: Living Donation and Health-Related Harm

RYAN SAUDER and LISA S. PARKER

In late December 1998, Renada Daniel-Patterson's father offered to donate a kidney to his daughter and ignited a controversy in the bioethics community. Renada had been born with only one kidney, which began to fail early in her childhood. At age 6, Renada had to receive dialysis three times a week. She was unable to attend school or venture very far from home. This pattern continued until Renada was 13, when Mr. Patterson called from prison to offer her his kidney. Renada was surprised to hear from her father, who was serving 12 years at California State Prison for burglary and drug convictions. Mr. Patterson was determined to be a compatible donor, and the family proceeded with the transplant operation. As a result of this surgery, Renada was able to live the life of a healthy girl for 2 years. Because the medication to prevent rejection of the transplanted organ made her feel ill and bloated and caused her to develop a hump on her back, Renada gradually began to skip doses. As a result, her donated kidney began to fail. It was under these circumstances that David Patterson offered to donate his second kidney to his daughter in 1998.

This situation presents several complicated ethical issues that deserve more thorough consideration than this forum can afford. However, the central question raised by the possibility of a person donating both of his kidneys concerns the nature and possible limits of autonomous decisionmaking: how much can one person be permitted to sacrifice in order to assist another? After identifying and briefly discussing other significant issues raised by this case, we will focus on this primary question.

Personal values and beliefs, including beliefs about altruism and responsibility, are obviously involved in people's decisionmaking about donating an organ (and also in seeking or accepting a donated organ). As in all decisions that involve balancing risks and benefits, empirical information is also relevant. For decisions about organ donation and transplantation, this empirical information includes data about the health-related risks of donation; the prospective recipient's prognosis and quality of life with, and without, transplantation; the availability and relative burdens of alternatives to transplantation, including the likelihood that a cadaveric organ will become available in a timely manner; the immediacy of the prospective recipient's need; and the likelihood of transplantation's success, which may vary with the timing of the operation, the quality and source of the transplanted organ, and the recipient's overall health and adherence to posttransplantation medical care. Thus, data as seemingly purely scientific as the likelihood that the recipient has developed or will develop antibodies that increase the likelihood of organ rejection are pertinent to the decisionmaking of prospective living organ donors and organ recipients.

Ryan Sauder and Lisa S. Parker

So too are data as obviously socially mediated as organ-donor rates among different racial groups. Prediction of both the likelihood and the importance of a recipient's adhering to posttransplantation medical regimes is notoriously difficult; moreover, social factors frequently play a role in recipients' adherence.[1]

According to the Health Care Financing Administration report, in 1998 more than 230,000 Americans were being treated for End Stage Renal Disease (ESRD)[2]; 1.8% of these dialysis patients were below 19 years of age, and 32.3% of the patients were Black.[3] This statistic demonstrates that African Americans, who compose only 12% of the American population, disproportionately suffer from ESRD.[4] This is due in part to greater incidence of hypertension and diabetes in the African-American population. Furthermore, because African-Americans (and members of other underserved populations) are more likely to experience a lack of access to healthcare, frequently cases of diabetes and hypertension are discovered later and treated less aggressively than in persons with better access to care. This fact certainly contributes to the greater proportion of Blacks suffering from ESRD.

The length of time that dialysis patients survive varies by age, sex, and race. The average for a White male between 40 and 44 years old is 6.9 years. The remaining years of life for a Black male of the same age is 10 years. A White female in the same age bracket will survive, on average, for 7.1 years; the average for a 40–44-year-old Black female is 9.8 years.[5] Aside from numbing of the skin and needle insertion, hemodialysis itself is not painful; however, dependence on hemodialysis affects patients' quality of life, as it generally requires frequent travel to a dialysis center and rather stringent dietary restrictions.

Kidney transplantation—with an organ from either a cadaveric or a living donor—provides an alternative to dialysis. In 1998, 9,343 persons donated kidneys for transplant: 5,327 cadaveric donors and 4,016 living donors.[6] These kidneys were used in 11,990 transplant operations.[7] Living kidney donation is a relatively safe procedure with an estimated mortality rate of 0.03% and a low rate of complications.[8] There is a better chance of organs' being compatible when the donor and recipient are of the same race.[9] Because some research demonstrates that antigenic similarity between donor and recipient improves success rates in transplantation, antigen-matching is one criterion used to allocate organs.[10] The HLA antigens used to determine compatibility occur in different proportions among various ethnic groups.[11] Although a disproportionate number of those awaiting transplantation are African-American, in 1998 only about 10% of cadaveric donors and 9.5% of living donors were Black.[12] To the degree that organs are allocated based on antigen-matching, then, Blacks have a reduced possibility of obtaining good matches and may therefore wait longer for a kidney (or receive an organ that is less antigenically compatible).[13]

As of August 1999, there were nearly 43,000 patients waiting for kidney transplantation.[14] The longest living adult kidney recipient to date was 34 years and 11 months posttransplantation. Similarly, the longest living pediatric recipient was 34 years and 7 months.[15] The option of transplantation permits recipients to maintain a normal diet and schedule and eliminates the need for dialysis. Recipients must, however, maintain a strict regimen of medications to prevent their bodies from rejecting the transplanted organ(s).

These data, when applied to Renada's case in particular, raise some difficult ethical issues. Her history of noncompliance in taking posttransplantation medications might suggest to some that Renada does not deserve to be the

Autonomy's Limits: Living Donation and Health-Related Harm

recipient of a second kidney—a second chance—especially because so many others are awaiting a "first chance," and because the option of dialysis means that refusal to provide her with a second transplanted organ is not an immediate "death sentence." In the absence of more specific details regarding the reasons behind and circumstances surrounding her noncompliance, however, this would be at best a tenuous and premature argument. The argument is undermined further when one considers that Renada's receipt of a second donor kidney would not in any way diminish the pool of donor kidneys available to other ESRD patients because the donated kidney was offered by her father, who presumably would not make it available for use by any other patient. (Of course, Renada's father, who would need dialysis to continue living, might join the list of those in need of kidney transplantation.)

It is noteworthy that Renada's body had already begun to reject one of her father's kidneys. Further testing would be required to determine whether her father is an eligible donor or whether she is likely to have developed antibodies to his tissues. Given the increased risks and obvious burden that would be placed on her father with the loss of his second kidney, it might be reasonable at least to demand that there be a greater-than-minimal chance of a successful operation and well-functioning kidney for Renada.

Some additional ethical concerns stem from Mr. Patterson's being a prisoner. If there were any evidence that he was being pressured to donate by those who have power over him in his institutional setting or who may influence the conditions for his release, there would be strong reason to question the voluntariness of his decision. However, most concern about his status as a prisoner has focused not on his vulnerability to pressure, but on society's vulnerability to increased costs because of his decision to donate.[16] Because the government generally pays for prisoners' healthcare, it has been argued that it is unfair for Mr. Patterson to elect to place an increased financial burden on taxpayers. Dialysis treatments are quite expensive (up to $50,000 per patient per year),[17] particularly if patients require off-site transportation to obtain the treatments. In fact, the majority of dialysis patients, not merely those who reside in state institutions, receive some governmental reimbursement for dialysis in accordance with the ESRD benefit of the Medicare program, and many receive further aid from state medical assistance programs. However, in this case, either Renada or her father will be on dialysis, so there would not necessarily be a net increase in expenditures (from some source) on dialysis. Concern about a prisoner further burdening taxpayers suggests an attitude toward those convicted of crimes that part of their punishment should include not being allowed to impose social costs to the same degree as nonprisoners. Only explicit articulation of this position, social debate and resulting social consensus about it, and its subsequent consistent implementation could justify basing public policy on this (now merely implicit) belief.

Some might argue that Mr. Patterson should not be permitted to donate his kidney and begin dialysis treatments because he might then receive special privileges in prison because of his health status. A frequent procedure viewed as onerous by most patients could be perceived as a reprieve of sorts for a person accustomed to monotonous incarceration. Such a claim, however, gives little credence to Mr. Patterson's ability to make an informed decision. Because his release date is in 2003, it would be remarkably myopic for him to choose to exchange a healthy kidney and relatively unimpeded lifestyle for a shortened

Organ and Tissue Transplantation

Ryan Sauder and Lisa S. Parker

lifetime on dialysis merely to acquire more frequent diversions in his current life situation. To regard Mr. Patterson's offer as self-centered is to presume a remarkable lack of foresight. Of greater concern might be the possibility that Mr. Patterson would hold unrealistic expectations that his donation might result in additional benefits for him; for example, a favorable parole board review or reconciliation with his estranged family. Such, often unrealistic, expectations are of concern with all living organ donation;[18] however, it is difficult to determine whether a prospective donor actually harbors such hopes, whether they are realistic or not, and whether they impede, or are actually factors in, autonomous decisionmaking.

The relevance of medico-scientific and social factors that constitute the context of the donation-transplantation decision cannot be disputed. Questions of costs to society arising from individual decisions have some relevance to ethical analysis of the permissibility of a person donating both of his kidneys and becoming dialysis-dependent. It would be unfair, however, to place disproportionate weight on these costs because they are so temporally proximate and certain in a case like this, when others' personal decisions place perhaps more distant burdens on society but are not subjected to similar scrutiny. Society, for example, condones (and frequently encourages) persons to pursue high-stress professional occupations or risky pastimes, despite knowledge of the emotional and financial burdens that such stressful employment or risky pursuits place on others (e.g., family members or members of an insurance pool). Similarly, although the health risks and financial costs associated with smoking are well documented, and smoking is currently subject to some social censure, the sale and use of tobacco products are not prohibited.

The central question presented by this case is one that would arise if prospective donor and recipient were both vastly wealthy and if there were no more than the usual level of medical uncertainty regarding the likelihood of the transplantation's being successful and benefiting the recipient. That question remains: how much can one person be permitted to sacrifice to benefit another? Three main issues are useful in addressing this question: the concept and requirements of autonomous choice, the relationship between self-endangerment and autonomy, and the interplay between a patient's sacrificial decision and the medical tenet "do no harm."

First, how can we understand the concept of autonomous choice? Traditionally, bioethics has conceived of autonomy as an individual's capacity for and right to self-governance in decisionmaking regarding her person and her actions. In other words, an individual should be able to decide and act in a manner that resonates with her values and belief system. Respect for autonomy has become a cornerstone value of contemporary bioethics that, along with recognition that individuals are often best situated to protect their own welfare interests, grounds the doctrine of informed consent.

Obtaining informed consent to medical interventions has typically required five components: (1) the decisionmaker's competence; (2) disclosure to the decisionmaker of any information particularly relevant to the decision, especially risks and benefits of the intervention; (3) the decisionmaker's understanding of the risks and benefits that are disclosed; (4) the voluntariness of the decision; and (5) communication of the final decision. Evidence of meeting these five requirements is generally deemed necessary to ensure autonomous choice in contexts requiring informed consent. In some contexts, however,

Autonomy's Limits: Living Donation and Health-Related Harm

although decisionmakers assert that their decisions are autonomous and accurately reflect deeply held values and preferences, their decisions appear not to meet standard informed-consent requirements.

Living organ donation, especially by those emotionally related to the recipient, is one such occasion. Frequently, a prospective donor, particularly a parent or sibling of the prospective recipient, will experience the decision to donate as automatic.[19] They frequently report feeling that they had no choice but to donate, and proceed to offer their organs willingly and without hesitation, sometimes even before hearing of the risks involved in such a donation.[20] Disclosure of risks frequently has no effect on the decision to donate.[21] These decisions hardly seem to meet the traditional requirements of informed consent. Failing to take risks of an intervention into account when deciding whether to consent to it, and feeling compelled to consent, are typically hallmarks of a failure of the informed-consent process. Yet we are reluctant to suggest that these prospective donors are not making autonomous decisions to donate and, consequently, that their decisions (and organs) should not be accepted.[22]

According to the traditional doctrine of informed consent outlined above, the decision to offer oneself as a living donor prior to full disclosure and consideration of risks is a red flag of invalid informed consent. Certainly, disclosure should be made and the potential donor should be prompted to consider carefully the risks. But to fail to accept a prospective donor's decision because it was made too immediately or on the basis of emotion, not rational and prudential consideration of foreseeable risks and benefits, would violate the spirit of informed consent in mistaken service of the supposed letter of the doctrine's requirements. To discount or declare invalid such a decision is to largely ignore the context in which the offer was made, the relevance of the relationships of the parties involved, and the importance of those relationships for the values of the decisionmaker. After all, informed consent seeks to ensure that patients make decisions that reflect their values. A parent, for example, may offer to donate a kidney to their child without hesitation or forethought. Although such a decision does not reflect the informed consent process traditionally considered necessary for autonomous decisionmaking in medical contexts, it may resonate with a clear history of self-sacrifice that marks many parent-child relationships. Additionally, by contributing to the well-being of their children, parents may be acting to fulfill their own chosen life plans. Although such a decision to donate does not meet each checklist requirement of informed consent, it does not appear irresponsible or uninformed when viewed in light of the value system previously adopted by the decisionmaker, a value system that informs the relationship between prospective donor and recipient. Indeed, such a decision may most truly fulfill the autonomy-oriented goal of informed consent for healthcare decisionmaking: to allow persons to act in medical contexts in ways that respect their autonomy by reflecting their deeply held values.

Intuitively, these decisions make sense, but this altered concept of acceptable contextual consent warrants further exploration. One specific concern is whether this understanding of autonomy and this apparent modification of informed consent to emphasize its spirit by reinterpreting the letter of its requirements would allow individuals to be too self-sacrificing. For the sake of a conception of autonomy that is more closely tied to individuals' deeply held values than to

Ryan Sauder and Lisa S. Parker

norms of rational deliberation, would this interpretation of the requirements of informed consent allow individuals to sacrifice too radically their own welfare? Or, does allowing individuals to eschew norms of prudence and rational deliberation, in their pursuit or preservation of deeply held values and interests, actually serve a deeper sense of autonomy and a higher sense of well-being?

If bioethics' commitment to promoting autonomous decisionmaking is not undertaken merely to ensure that decisions accord with values about which there is broadly held social consensus, if it instead seeks to ensure that individuals' decisions reflect their own values, then bioethics' doctrine of informed consent must be able to accommodate decisions that are altruistic and even self-sacrificing beyond the point that most people find acceptable. When the decisionmaker makes a convincing appeal to a deeply held, though perhaps idiosyncratic, value system, the decision should receive the prima facie respect of the bioethical and medical communities. Nevertheless, there are limits to autonomy, and there may be limits to what society or bioethical, legal, and medical communities may allow a person to consent to, even in pursuit of the most deeply held values.

Traditionally, the scope of a person's autonomy is limited by the rights or socially protected interests of others. In the case of Mr. Patterson's decision to donate his second kidney, however, the question is whether his own health-related interests should be protected from his autonomous decision to sacrifice them for the sake of both his values and his daughter's potential benefit. If we can assume that Mr. Patterson understands the burdens and risks that his donation would entail, should he be permitted to accept them? In answering this question, we must strive to avoid a medico-centric perspective that gives primary weight to health-related risks and benefits. We must give appropriate weight to the psychological and social benefits that Mr. Patterson may reasonably anticipate from donation of his second kidney. If his hopes were utterly unrealistic—if, for example, he mistakenly believed that his prison sentence would be commuted or that full reconciliation with his family would result from his donation—then we would have reason to question Mr. Patterson further and to question his understanding, appreciation, and weighing of the risks and benefits that he himself considers material to his decision.

Moreover, because his donation would place some potentially severe restrictions on his current and future lifestyle (e.g., dialysis, the possibility of a shortened life span), it would be important for Mr. Patterson to understand these realities, including the particular health-related risks that prison life, including suboptimal healthcare, may pose. He must also understand that other options are available for Renada (including continued dialysis and the possibility of a cadaveric kidney donation) and the chances that transplantation with his donated kidney will improve her quality of life. He should also be prompted to consider that his donation may impose some psychological and social burdens on Renada; for example, a sense of obligation or guilt, or a social bond to her father that she might not desire. He might not want to place her in the position of accepting a "gift of life" that so severely compromises his health. If, however, Mr. Patterson considered all of these factors and still wished to donate his second kidney, is there any reason not to permit him to do so?

If there were superior or comparable options available to Renada, as with dialysis there indeed seemed to be, then there is reason not to ask or to allow Mr. Patterson to sacrifice his health-related interests. If, however, there were no

Autonomy's Limits: Living Donation and Health-Related Harm

option, or no option that afforded Renada a similar quality of life in the reasonably foreseeable future, then the primary ethical barrier to permitting Mr. Patterson's donation might be concern about the medical profession's complicity in a procedure that so severely compromised one person's health-related interests for the benefit of another's.

Medicine is supposed to be governed by the norm: "first, do no harm." Of course, medical procedures often involve doing some harm for the greater benefit of the patient. Incisions are made to remove the tumor; side effects of chemotherapy are imposed and endured with the hope of cure or prevention of recurrence. These harms are imposed, however, for the direct health-related benefit of the person harmed. And, quite importantly, only the minimum harm that can reasonably achieve the desired benefit is imposed. The question Mr. Patterson's decision raises is whether medical practitioners can ethically be complicit in imposing harms on one person for the health-related benefit of another person (e.g., Renada) when the person harmed (e.g., Mr. Patterson) seeks and may reasonably receive social and psychological benefits and accepts the health-related harm. Our answer is a tentative "yes."

One additional constraint must be observed: the harm imposed must be the minimum harm that can be imposed to achieve the desired benefit. In other words, if Renada could be expected to receive a kidney from a cadaveric donor and in the meantime remain on dialysis, without considerable disruption of the quality of her life or risk to her eventual prognosis, then it might be appropriate to refuse to impose the health-related harm on Mr. Patterson that he is nevertheless willing to accept. To proceed to impose that health-related harm on Mr. Patterson when the benefit to Renada may be achieved by other means would be unjustified, even if Mr. Patterson were to insist that he wanted to achieve the psychological benefit of being such an heroic donor or of compensating for past wrongs. The situation would be somewhat analogous to a case in which a surgical patient asked for a more invasive procedure than was necessary to remove his tumor because he wanted not only to achieve health-related benefit but additional psychological benefit that might accrue to him during a prolonged recovery period. Our analysis of Mr. Patterson's offer to donate his second kidney takes seriously potential psychological and social benefits and weighs them along with health-related risks and potential benefits but does not consider them to themselves justify a medical practitioner's imposing health-related harm. This analysis of the prescription to "do no harm" departs from the traditional analysis by weighing risks and benefits across two people, but only in cases where the person to be harmed for the sake of another considers incurring that harm for the sake of the other to be in accordance with his values and where the harm imposed is the minimum commensurate with achieving the benefit to the other.

Someone might argue that with the acceptance of Mr. Patterson's second kidney for Renada, an additional patient awaiting kidney transplantation might benefit from the cadaveric kidney that Renada would not use. It would seem that so long as Mr. Patterson's incurring the health-related harm of being without kidneys is acceptable to him, there would always be some additional health-related benefit (albeit to some third person) of Renada's receiving his kidney that would justify his donation, even if Renada could pursue an alternative that did not impose such harms on Mr. Patterson. However, this is not the case. So far as we can tell, Mr. Patterson wants to donate his second

Ryan Sauder and Lisa S. Parker

kidney for the health-related benefit of Renada and for the social and psychological benefits he anticipates in virtue of potentially benefiting her. His is not
a desire to donate (to someone) out of general altruism and for the social and
psychological benefits that it might bring. In the determination of the acceptability of imposing the health-related harms that he accepts, it is the potential
benefits that Mr. Patterson actually anticipates (for himself and Renada) that
may justify imposing harm on him, if he chooses to accept that harm under
conditions of informed consent.

The considerations that may justify allowing Mr. Patterson to donate his
second kidney and that may justify the complicity of society, medicine, and
particular medical practitioners in his thereby being harmed do not justify
accepting his donation for the benefit of those outside the scope of his concern
(e.g., third parties on the waiting list) or taking that potential benefit into
account in balancing harms and benefits. They also would not justify imposing
an obligation to be self-sacrificing for the benefit of others in general or of
particular emotionally related others. If, however, such sacrifice reflects a
person's deeply held values and is consented to under conditions of informed
consent, the decision to make such sacrifice should be respected and provides
grounds for medical practitioners to violate the apparent prescription to do no
harm.

Conclusion

If there had been no comparable or superior treatment alternative available to
Renada, it might have been permissible to permit her father to incur the serious
health-related harm and future risks to his health that he expressed willingness
to accept. For his decision to donate his second kidney to be accepted, his
decision would have to fulfill the demands of informed consent. As with many
living donation decisions, that informed consent may be best evaluated in light
of the donor's relationship with the recipient and the value system that informs
the donor's decision, as well as traditional requirements designed to ensure
understanding of the risks and benefits—health-related, psychological, and
social—involved. Also, to act on a donation decision that imposes such severe
health-related harms and future risks, it must be the case that doing so
nevertheless imposes the most minimal harm commensurate with achieving
the health-related benefit for the recipient, and this health-related benefit that
may reasonably be anticipated must be a benefit that the prospective donor
actually seeks to achieve by his donation.

The permissibility of a prospective donor's acting in such an apparently
self-sacrificing manner lies in (1) the coincidence of his interests with the
benefit to accrue to the recipient, (2) his belief in this coincidence based on his
own values, (3) his informed consent to the myriad risks that he would incur
by donating, and (4) his donation imposing the minimum health-related harm—
when summed across donor and recipient—that may still achieve the health-
related benefit to the recipient that he desires. In the case of Renada and her
father, the fourth condition did not obtain; the availability of dialysis and the
prospect of receiving a cadaveric organ meant that the option of receiving Mr.
Patterson's second kidney was not the option that imposed the minimum
health-related harm (even assuming that he was an eligible donor and that the
chances of success were equivalent to those with a cadaveric organ). In this

Autonomy's Limits: Living Donation and Health-Related Harm

case, the reason for refusing Mr. Patterson's offer to donate would not reside with concerns about the autonomy of his decision nor with a blanket refusal to accept such self-sacrifice. Again, such self-sacrifice may be permitted if it is autonomously chosen and consented to with adequate understanding and if it imposes the minimum possible harm commensurate with the desired possible benefit.

Notes

1. Washington AW. Cross-cultural issues in transplant compliance. *Transplantation Proceedings* 199;31:S27–8; Sharp LA. A medical anthropologist's view on posttransplant compliance: the underground economy of medical survival. *Transplantation Proceedings* 1999;31:S31–3; Kasiske BL, Neylan III JF, Riggio RR, Danovitch GM, Kahana L, Alexander SR, White MG. The effect of race on access and outcome in transplantation. *New England Journal of Medicine* 1991;324:302–7.
2. National Kidney Foundation. End stage renal disease in the United States (25 Aug 1999). Available at: http://www.kidney.org/general/news/esrd.cfm
3. See note 2, NKF 1999.
4. National Kidney Foundation. Ten facts about African-Americans and kidney disease (25 Aug 1999). Available at: http://www.kidney.org/general/news/african-american.cfm
5. See note 2, NKF 1999.
6. United Network for Organ Sharing (UNOS). UNOS critical data: donor statistics (25 Aug 1999). Available at: http://www.unos.org/Newsroom/critdata_donors.htm
7. United Network for Organ Sharing (UNOS). UNOS critical data: main page, frequently requested data (25 Aug 1999). Available at: http://www.unos.org/Newsroom/critdata_main.htm
8. Najarian JS, Chavers BM, McHugh LE, Matas AJ. 20 years or more of follow-up of living kidney donors. *Lancet* 1992;340:807–10; Duraj F, Tydén G, Blom B. Living-donor nephrectomy: how safe is it? *Transplantation Proceedings* 1995;27:803–4.
9. Shelton DL. Ethical questions in father-daughter transplant. *American Medical News* 1999;42:31.
10. Gaston RS, Ayres I, Dooley LG, Diethelm AG. Racial equity in renal transplantation: the disparate impact of HLA-based allocation. *JAMA* 1993;270:1352–6.
11. See note 10, Gaston et al. 1993:1353.
12. See note 6, UNOS 1999.
13. Arnason WB. Directed donation: the relevance of race. *Hastings Center Report* 1991;21:13–9.
14. See note 6, UNOS 1999.
15. United Network for Organ Sharing (UNOS). UNOS critical data: milestones (25 Aug 1999). Available at: http://www.unos.org/Newsroom/critdata_milestones.htm
16. Nieves E. Girl awaits father's 2d (sic) kidney, and decision by medical ethicists. *New York Times* 5 Dec 1998;148:A1.
17. Josefson D. Prisoner wants to donate his second kidney. *British Medical Journal* 2 Jan 1999;318:7.
18. Simmons RG, Marine SK, Simmons RL. *Gift of Life: The Effect of Organ Transplantation on Individual, Family, and Societal Dynamics.* New Brunswick, N.J.: Transaction Books, 1987:161–4.
19. See note 18, Simmons, Marine, Simmons 1987:240–1.
20. See note 18, Simmons, Marine, Simmons 1987:246–7.
21. See note 18, Simmons, Marine, Simmons 1987:240–1.
22. Our analysis here draws on the argument presented in: Majeske RA, Parker LS, Frader J. An ethical framework for consideration of decisions regarding live organ donation. In: Spielman B, ed. *Organ and Tissue Donation: Ethical, Legal, and Policy Issues.* Carbondale: Southern Illinois Press, 1996:89–101.

[18]

Moral Agency and the Family: The Case of Living Related Organ Transplantation

ROBERT A. CROUCH and CARL ELLIOTT

Introduction

Living related organ transplantation is morally problematic for two reasons. First, it requires surgeons to perform nontherapeutic, even dangerous procedures on healthy donors—and in the case of children, without their consent. Second, the transplant donor and recipient are often intimately related to each other, as parent and child, or as siblings. These relationships challenge our conventional models of medical decisionmaking. Is there anything morally problematic about a parent allowing the interests of one child to be risked for the sake of another? What exactly are the interests of the prospective child donor whose sibling will die without an organ? Is the choice of a parent to take risks for the sake of her child truly free, or is the specter of coercion necessarily raised?

When it comes to moral decisions about the family, the tools of moral philosophy and the law have not always served us well, particularly when the question involves exposing one family member to risks for the sake of another. This raises an obvious question: since we all have families of one sort or another, why do we find it so difficult to think clearly about them? We would like to suggest that one reason we have such difficulty thinking clearly about living related organ transplantation and the family is that we have unthinkingly imported a certain picture of moral agency into our deliberations, and this has led us ineluctably to think about these problems in the wrong way.

"Philosophy is the battle against the bewitchment of our intelligence by means of language," wrote Wittgenstein in a famous passage of his *Philosophical Investigations*.[1] Language bewitches our intelligence by suggesting to us certain ways of thinking about philosophical matters. The manner in which we ask and answer questions, use metaphors, and offer descriptions all subtly influence the way in which we think about the world. Because we do not have a clear overview of our language, we can easily be led into philosophical confusion. As Wittgenstein puts it, "A philosophical problem has the form: 'I don't know my way about'."[2]

The authors gratefully acknowledge the support of the *Fonds pour la Formation de Chercheurs et l'Aide à la Recherche* (Québec, Canada). Selected portions of this manuscript were presented (by RAC) at the 8th Annual Canadian Bioethics Society Conference in Montreal (1996), and at the Annual Meeting of the Society for Health and Human Values, American Association of Bioethics, and the Society for Bioethics Consultation in Baltimore (1997), where it was granted the SHHV Student Interest Group paper award. Thanks to all those who offered comments on those two occasions.

Robert A. Crouch and Carl Elliott

One way that language can bewitch our intelligence, suggests Wittgenstein, is through the grammatical pictures suggested through language. "A *picture* held us captive. And we could not get outside it, for it lay in our language and language seemed to repeat it to us inexorably."[3] Something similar seems to happen very often in current bioethical thinking about children and the family. We want to argue that in thinking about the role of children and family members in organ transplantation, bioethics has been influenced by a certain grammatical picture of human agency. The picture is not of children and their parents located in a context of intimacy, but of sovereign, independent human agents free of the moral and emotional connections that typically bind family members to each other. It is a picture of human agency not unlike what Iris Murdoch (perhaps somewhat unfairly) calls the "Kantian man-God," an agent who is "free, independent, lonely, powerful, rational, responsible, brave, the hero of so many novels and books of moral philosophy."[4] We will argue that this picture, or something like it, represents a way of thinking about human agency that underlies many of the confusions that have arisen around living-related organ transplantation.

Coercion and Parent-to-Child Partial Liver Transplantation

In 1988 a surgical team at São Paulo Medical College Hospital and Clinics in Brazil performed the world's first living partial liver transplant, from a mother to her four-year-old child. Since that time surgical teams at a number of other universities have performed similar procedures, including a group at the University of Chicago, who in 1990 performed a mother-to-daughter partial liver transplantation for a child with biliary atresia. Because the liver ordinarily regenerates within four to six weeks after partial hepatectomy, surgeons involved in these early procedures believed that the procedure would involve no serious long-term risks to the donor. However, because of the novelty of these early procedures, the risks to the donor and the potential benefits to the recipient were at least partly unknown. Thus the ethical problem: should a transplant team offer a parent, under circumstances of uncertainty, the opportunity to donate part of her liver to her desperately ill child?

While partial liver transplantations are now more common, at the time of the early procedures many commentators objected on ethical grounds. Many of these ethical objections, rather surprisingly, appealed to notions of autonomy. Objectors argued that parents should not be offered the procedure because they will find it extremely difficult to refuse. The procedure was new and innovative, the risks uncertain, and parents, faced with the potential death of a child, may not be able to make a free choice to donate. "Does anyone really think parents can say 'No' when the option is certain death for their own son or daughter?" asked Arthur Caplan.[5] Commenting on the Chicago transplantation to the *New York Times*, George Annas said: "The parents basically can't say no."[6]

To be clear about just what these objectors are saying is important. They are not saying that parents can be pressured into donating by other family members or by the healthcare team. They are saying that parents might somehow pressure *themselves*. By virtue of their emotional ties to their child and their sense of moral obligation, parents will feel "forced" to donate. Here the more conventional image of coercion as a threat by another agent is turned inward; the threat comes not from another person but from the agent. More specifically,

Moral Agency and the Family

the threat comes from conscience and love for the child. This image of conscience as a coercive force is made explicit by Siegler and Lantos who, even while arguing that the transplantation is ethically acceptable, warn against the "internal coercion" created by guilt.[7]

Where does this argument get its persuasive force? What makes the argument so appealing to many thoughtful people? Even if the argument is misguided (as we believe it is), it does not strike most people—or at least most Westerners—as completely unreasonable. There is a sense in which a person often feels bound to act in accordance with conscience or emotional commitments, even if refusing is easy and without penalty. But without penalty for refusing, why would we say that conscience or love "forces" or "coerces" a parent to donate?

One reason may be the tension between the public and private faces of morality. Some parents may not want to donate, in fact, may not even feel morally obligated to donate, but would be ashamed to have this attitude revealed to anyone else, especially to family. The opinions of others can be powerful motivating forces; some might even call them coercive. And if public revelation of a decision can move a person to donate, through guilt or shame, then it is only a short, but misguided, step toward thinking of guilt or shame as coercive in themselves.

But perhaps a more important reason underlying the appeal of this argument is a picture of agency that identifies freedom with independence. Our language reflects this picture of agency back to us when we speak of the *bonds* of love or of being emotionally *tied* to another person. If these metaphors ring true to us, they do so because they evoke images that capture something of the actual experience of strong emotional commitments. It is true, for example, that families can be stifling, marriage confining, children limiting, divorce liberating. The attachments and commitments of the family can limit a person's independence, and if independence is identified with freedom—as it is in the American mythology of rugged frontiersmen and lonely cowboys—then these commitments will also be seen as limits on a person's freedom. The moral commitments associated with intimacy, such as loyalty and devotion, are seen as "coercive" because they motivate a person to actions that a completely independent person would not take. Thus parents who risk their own lives to donate organs to a child are not acting freely, because they are bound by moral and emotional ties to the child.

To resist this suggestion is important. Most parents make sacrifices of one sort or another for their children and do so not only freely but unhesitatingly. If we take seriously the argument that choices made for reasons of love and moral obligation are not free, we must admit that all parents who make financial sacrifices to send their children to college are somehow not making these sacrifices freely. What is more, to do so would mean that the less moral and emotional motivation a person has for donating an organ, the freer is his or her choice to donate. Thus if a child needs an organ, only strangers, not the child's parents, would be truly free to volunteer as donors.

The picture of agency underlying this concept of coercion is one that identifies the moral agent as completely free when he or she is self-interested and lacks any moral or emotional connections to other people. Morality and love are limits on freedom because they move a person to act for the sake of other people, rather than for self. Yet we have another name for agents who are

Robert A. Crouch and Carl Elliott

self-interested and lack deep emotional attachments: we call them sociopaths. If we are ever to get straight about the nature of voluntariness, we must recognize that moral and emotional commitments are not exceptional, are not constraints on freedom, but are rather a part of ordinary human life. More specifically, they are a part of ordinary *family* life that we must take seriously if we want to understand how family members can make free choices about organ donation.

The Best Interests Standard and Kidney Transplantation between Minor Siblings

In the preceding section we have tried to show how a certain picture of human agency can distort one's thinking about parent-to-child partial liver transplantation. Now we turn to the still more vexing question whether it is ethically justifiable to use a minor as a kidney donor for a sibling. These procedures are ethically problematic because the minor donor is often incompetent to consent to the procedure, and more importantly, because the procedure is not for the child's own benefit, but for the benefit of the sibling. We will suggest that an inappropriate picture of human agency has played into how the courts have considered this issue, particularly how they have constructed the minor donor's best interests.

Because the procedure is nontherapeutic for the donor, it is not surprising that sibling-to-sibling kidney transplantations have often wound up in the courts. What is more surprising is the reasoning and willingness of U.S. courts to authorize these transplants. In many cases, both the parents of the prospective donor and the courts have reasoned that it is in a minor donor's "best interests" to serve as a kidney donor for a sibling. Given the obvious risks of donation, one might well ask: How have the courts justified their decisions?

In a word, curiously. An early case is instructive. In *Masden v. Harrison*[8] the proposed donation took place not between young children but between 19-year-old twins. However, because the age of majority in Massachusetts was 21, the donor, Leonard, could not render a legal consent. Thus although Leonard had expressed his willingness to act as a donor for his brother (Leon), and had been found by the court to be sufficiently mature to understand the consequences of his decision to donate, neither his consent nor the consent of his parents was legally sufficient to authorize the transplantation. As a result, the justice in the declaratory judgment crafted a solution to the problem by highlighting the negative psychological impact that the death of the sick brother would have on the healthy prospective donor brother:

> I am satisfied from the testimony of the psychiatrist that grave emotional impact may be visited upon Leonard if the defendants refuse to perform this operation and Leon should die, as apparently he will . . . . Such emotional disturbance could well affect the health and physical well-being of Leonard for the remainder of his life. I therefore find that this operation is necessary for the continued good health and future well-being of Leonard and that in performing the operation the defendants are conferring a benefit upon Leonard as well as Leon.[9]

This construction of the problem had important consequences for later U.S. legal decisions. Two points are important. First, although the decision is written

Moral Agency and the Family

as if the donor were a minor incapable of consent, in fact he was 19 years old and probably quite capable of acting as a responsible moral agent. Second, perhaps as a result of the fact that the law did not recognize Leonard as a responsible moral agent able to consent knowingly to risks, the decision is framed in terms of Leonard's *own* interests. That is, the court suggests that donation would be not only in the interests of Leon, but also in the interests of Leonard, the donor. Satisfied that the operation would benefit both brothers, healthy and ill, the courts authorized the operation, and it was successfully carried out.

What the *Masden* court effectively did was to justify an adult's decision to donate a kidney to his brother using a decisionmaking framework more appropriate for a much younger child. Thus when later American courts followed the *Masden* court's lead, they produced rather eccentric results.[10] Consider briefly the following three examples.

First, in *Strunk v. Strunk*,[11] a Kentucky court authorized an intersibling kidney donation from Jerry Strunk, a 27-year-old institutionalized mentally incompetent person with a mental age of a six-year-old, to his dying 28-year-old brother Tommy. In reaching their conclusion, the court relied heavily upon the testimony of a court-appointed psychiatrist as well as an *amicus curiae* brief submitted by the Department of Mental Health of Kentucky. Because Tommy was Jerry's primary link to the rest of the family, and because Tommy was the only one who could understand Jerry's "defective" speech, it was felt that Tommy's continued survival was essential to Jerry's overall well-being. As the concurring justices wrote,

> it would not only be beneficial to Tommy but also beneficial to Jerry because Jerry [is] greatly dependent upon Tommy, emotionally and psychologically, and . . . his well-being would be jeopardized more severely by the loss of his brother than by the removal of a kidney.[12]

Second, consider *Hart v. Brown*,[13] a Connecticut case where a kidney donation from a seven-year-old girl to her twin sister was authorized partly on the ground that it would be in the donor child's "best interests" to donate. As part of their fact finding, the court heard from a psychiatrist who examined the prospective donor, Margaret, and testified that she had a "strong identification" with her ill sister, Kathleen. The psychiatrist testified further that the donor would be better off in a family that was happy than in a family that was distressed due to the loss of Kathleen and, more directly, that it would be a "very great loss" to the donor if her ill sister were to die.[14]

And finally, consider the Texas case *Little v. Little*,[15] in which the courts authorized kidney donation from a 14-year-old girl with Down syndrome to her brother on the ground that it was in her best interests to do so. In reaching its decision the Texas court argued in the first instance that the dangers of the donation to Anne were "minimal," and that although Anne might be frightened by the foreign surroundings of the hospital, nonetheless evidence suggested that Anne would not suffer psychological harm as a result of her participation. Moreover, the court argued, given (1) the existence of a close relationship between Anne and Stephen, (2) a genuine concern by each child for the welfare of the other, and (3) an awareness by Anne that Stephen was ill and that she was in a position to "ameliorate Stephen's burden," a decision to permit Anne's kidney donation would prevent negative psychological effects (e.g., guilt or

Robert A. Crouch and Carl Elliott

sadness) from occurring in the future if Stephen were to die because Anne was not permitted to help him.

What is going on in these three cases? What seems apparent is that when faced with a sick family member in need of a kidney, the courts interpreted their guiding decisionmaking principle—the best interests of the donor—as broadly as necessary in order to help the patient and her family. Equipped with the best interests standard, but confronted by a donor who would not benefit *physically* from donation, the courts used a much wider construct, one that considered potential "psychological" benefits. With these "psychological" benefits in mind, the courts argued that to donate a kidney would be in a child's "best interests."

Yet consider just what the courts are saying. They are saying that it is in the child's best interests to: (1) be exposed to the unfamiliar and frightening environment of a hospital; (2) be exposed to the risks attending the use of general anaesthetics; (3) be exposed to the potentially serious peri- and post-operative risks associated with the surgical removal of a healthy kidney; (4) be exposed to the potentially serious long-term risks associated with extended hyperperfusion of the remaining kidney, including unknown risks; (5) potentially experience the psychological trauma following a failed transplantation attempt; and finally, (6) potentially experience the "psychological benefits" following a successful transplantation attempt. As one jurist has written, the appeal to psychological benefits as a justification for authorizing donation is "pretty thin soup on which to base a decision."[16]

Why, then, have the courts used it so often? We want to suggest two reasons. First, the courts may have had in mind a picture of moral agency that identifies the agent's *interests* with *self-interests*, narrowly construed. What is clear is that the courts felt the need to justify the use of an incompetent kidney donor by showing that donating would somehow be in the donor's self-interest. And if the picture of moral agency is one of agents, sovereign, independent, and emotionally unconnected to other human beings, there will be little room for a concept of human interests that includes the interests of others. Thus the problem faced by the courts, which (apparently) wanted to approve the transplantation. Armed with this picture of the independent, rationally self-interested agent, but faced with what they implicitly realized to be beings whose interests were intimately bound up with the interests of their families, the courts quite understandably tried to construct arguments whereby a child would benefit "psychologically" by being used as an organ donor for a sibling. In effect, they said that the child could donate because to do so would be in the child's self-interest.

Now, one problem with this narrow construction—of interests *as* self-interests—is that it fails to recognize that an agent's interests (even self-interests) can include the interests of others. Joel Feinberg, for example, makes a helpful distinction between self-regarding interests and other-regarding interests.[17] Self-regarding interests are those interests that relate exclusively to the well-being of the agent himself or herself. Thus, self-regarding interests might include interest in remaining healthy or in becoming a successful writer. Other-regarding interests involve the desires that an agent has for the well-being of another person. Here, the agent may act to bring about the increased well-being of another person, and may in fact serve this other person's own interests at least partly as an end in itself. Thus an agent who acts in the service of other-

Moral Agency and the Family

regarding interests may do so partly for instrumental reasons (some of her *own* interests are served through the action) and partly because the end that is promoted (the well-being of *another* person) is important to the *other* person. So, for example, a father might choose to forgo a better and more expensive medical treatment for himself and settle for the treatment that his insurance covers in order to use the money to buy a house in a neighborhood that has better schooling for his children.[18] This parent, therefore, acts to promote the educational well-being of his children *for the sake of his children*; but at the same time a personal interest is being served, namely, the parental interest in seeing that his children get a good education and do well in life.

This picture of human agency seems fairly well established in the Western tradition. To be sure, the picture drawn above would need to be filled out more in order to pass for an adequate rendition of a human agent; for example, we would have to talk about the pull that morality can exert on an agent regardless of the interests it serves, or about the intrinsic importance of the agent's autonomy—"I will act *as I want to* even if it serves no other person's interests, and even if it runs counter to my own interests," as we can imagine one saying.[19] But the point is that a human agent can legitimately be thought of as one who acts to promote, or is at least mindful during deliberation of, self-regarding and other-regarding interests. Therefore, it is at least arguable that a prospective adult sibling donor might decide to donate a kidney because it will promote the well-being of the sibling, but also because the donor will, among other things, benefit from being able to continue the relationship with the sibling, or benefit "psychologically" from feelings of increased happiness and self-esteem as a result of having done something of profound importance for a loved one.[20]

But this reasoning points to the second problem in the U.S. courts' decisions. A concept of the interests an agent has in other people sounds quite reasonable *if* one is, in fact, talking about an agent—that is, about a competent adult. But is invoking agency—understood properly—reasonable in the case of a small child or a mentally incompetent adult? In many cases it is far from clear that the donor is mature and sufficiently mentally developed to have an important other-regarding interest in a sibling.

Contrast, for example, the reasoning of the *Masden* court with the court cases that followed. In the Masden case, we can reasonably assume that in making his decision to donate, the healthy brother Leonard gave consideration to what Feinberg has called other-regarding interests. We can also assume that, as a 19-year-old, Leonard was sufficiently mature to have developed interests of his own. Here to treat Leonard as an adult made sense because he *was* an adult, albeit not a *legal* adult. And although he was not a legal adult, he could reasonably be expected to experience psychological benefits from his donation experience, not only because he was emotionally mature enough for psychological benefits to be a realistic possibility, but because the act of donation could be thought of as serving Leonard's self-regarding and other-regarding interests; namely, his self-regarding interests in continuing his relationship with his brother and being spared the emotional trauma of losing him, as well as his other-regarding interest in (potentially) saving his brother's life.

Yet does this sort of construction make sense in the cases that followed? Arguably it does not, and we want to suggest that the reason has something to do with the courts' understanding of psychological best interests. Exactly what

Robert A. Crouch and Carl Elliott

the courts mean when they refer to psychological best interests is often unclear, but the meaning seems to involve at least the following points. First, the donation can have instrumental value to the donor: in donating, the donor may save the life of a sibling and will therefore have a sibling to grow up with and to share a life with, each of which brings with it certain identifiable social and emotional benefits to the donor. Second, *ceteris paribus*, growing up in a household unaffected by the tragic loss of a sibling or child is possibly more conducive to psychological stability and general mental health than growing up in a family that has been struck by loss. Third, even if the donation is ultimately unsuccessful, the donor may receive some comfort from the recognition that everything possible was done to help the sibling, and that the role played in the medical treatment was crucial, even if unsuccessful.

The important point here is that one of the necessary preconditions of receiving what the courts call psychological benefits is that the donor have sufficient cognitive development to recognize the *social* aspect of donation; that is, the donor must be aware not merely that his or her kidney has been removed, but rather that he or she has helped the sibling *by donating* in a way that few (perhaps no) others could ever do.[21] The distinction we are attempting to illustrate is similar to that captured by the shift in language use from "kidney extraction," or "nephrectomy"—a purely biological description—to "kidney donation"—a description of an act that takes place in a social context and carries specific meanings within that context.[22] Thus if the donor is not mentally developed to a sufficient degree, he will not only fail to understand why he is in the hospital and why he has been physically harmed, he will also fail to understand the important role that he has played in the care of his sibling. Thus he may well *not* receive any psychological benefits as a result of his donation.[23] Children and mentally incompetent persons are, in other words, human agents of a different sort from adults, and we must be careful about the interests that we take children or mentally incompetent persons to have.

Yet many courts appear to have had no such reservations. Was the *Hart* court correct, for instance, in ruling that it was in the best interests of a seven-year-old girl to donate a kidney to her twin sister? That a seven-year-old would have the depth of understanding to appreciate the significance of being used as a donor is not clear at all. However, a seven-year-old will grow older and more mature with time. As she gets older, her other-regarding interest in the life and health of her twin would develop, and her appreciation of the significance of the transplantation would grow richer and more complex.[24]

The same cannot be said of the Strunk and Little cases. The Kentucky court in *Strunk* reasoned that Jerry Strunk, a mentally incompetent adult with the mental age of a six-year-old, would be more severely jeopardized by the loss of his brother than by the loss of his kidney; the *Little* court authorized the transplantation of a kidney from a 14-year-old with Down syndrome, citing such benefits as "heightened self-esteem, enhanced status in the family, *renewed meaning in life*, and other positive feelings."[25] Yet because their mental conditions were static, in neither of these cases could the donor be expected to develop a more mature understanding of the transplantation over time. Nor could the donor be expected to develop a deeper other-regarding interest in the sibling as they grew older. If the positive "psychological" benefits of donating a kidney seem speculative for a seven-year-old who will eventually fully understand what was done to her, then they seem even more dubious for an incom-

Moral Agency and the Family

petent donor whose mental abilities will never increase and whose relationship with a sibling cannot be expected to grow more mature with time.[26]

Briefly put, the problem is that *as* minors and *as* mentally incompetent persons, the prospective donors would probably *not* be able to experience the psychological benefits because of their insufficiently developed mental, emotional, and moral capacities—in short, because they are human agents in a very different sense from adults.[27] Thus even if the courts are correct in their general identification of psychological benefits, and even if such benefits would materialize in an *adult* and outweigh the burdens associated with donation, we have reason to worry that the child or mentally incompetent person would not experience this benefit because of immaturity. Children and mentally incompetent persons simply do not fit the picture of human agency implicitly assumed in these cases.

Situating the Problem

The overarching point that we have attempted to make is simple: our thinking about living related organ transplantation has been affected by an implicitly assumed picture of human agency. This picture of the agent as essentially rational, independent, disengaged from others, and self-interested has, we believe, led many into error regarding either the *permissibility* of intrafamilial organ donations or the *ground* on which such donations can be authorized. We do not believe that the parent who is offered the chance to donate part of her liver to a dying child is coerced by her love for her child, or by the exhortations of her conscience; nor do we believe that the donation of a kidney by a minor child can be justified by an appeal to the donor's best interests, even when such interests include both self-regarding and other-regarding interests.

If we are to clear away the fog that has prevented us from seeing the issue clearly, we must strive to understand how our thinking about agency has influenced our thinking about living related organ transplantation. As Wittgenstein says, "A main source of our failure to understand is that we do not *command a clear view* of the use of our words."[28] We believe that the first step we must take to command a clear view is to situate the problems we have discussed squarely within the family. Once the problem is properly situated, the inadequacy of the picture of human agency that has dominated discussions of living-related organ transplantation will be put into sharper relief.

The picture of the human agent as independent and self-interested that has fueled so many errors in this context is an inadequate picture of the human agent *within the family*. To think of family members in this way is to miss what is of importance in family life and to human agency. In families, the important factor is that family members cherish each other simply for each other's sake, and that being devoted to "the family" and its members is a source of deep meaning and value in our lives and the lives of those around us. To be a member of a family is to recognize the importance of strongly "shared significances."[29] To share something in the strong sense, according to Charles Taylor, means that "the good we share in part effectively turns on our sharing; *the sharing in itself is valued*."[30] Nancy Sherman has expressed a similar idea more recently. Attempting to articulate what is important about community participation, Sherman has written:

Robert A. Crouch and Carl Elliott

> One can be in a community and strongly identify with its ends with-
> out there being a *sense* of community. In such a case, what seems to be
> lacking is the pleasure of mutual interaction. A common end may be
> prized, facilitated by cooperation and collective endeavour, but the
> goods of mutuality and responsiveness, *that sense of the shared journey*,
> may simply be lacking. And yet it is this sense that seems to come
> closest to the value of community per se.[31]

There are, we would claim, interests within families that can rightly be called
"strongly valued goods," that come (to an extent, at least) from the fact that we
are engaged in a shared journey. These interests include both the interests in
the family *qua* family, or family in the abstract (think of the sense in which we
have all, at one point or another in our lives, invoked the idea of "the family"
as a reason to do, or not to do something) and the interests in the family *qua*
particular individuals, or each member's love, commitment and concern for
each other member.[32] The main point here is that the concept of strongly valued
goods within the family brings to expression the idea of collectivism in the
family; as family members we share significances in our lives with other family
members in a deeper way than we do with non-family-members in our lives.
Indeed, as Sherman has pointed out, "We value creating a shared world, and
the mutuality that is defined by our interactions. The pleasure of mutuality and
the expansion of self that comes with it is a part of human flourishing."[33] The
importance of this mutuality runs deeper than an expansion of self, however; it
may even be described using the stronger language of "union," which, according to Sherman, involves:

> a sense of tracking something with another, of creating a sense of unity
> through an attunement to each other's moves. The operative virtue
> here is not respect, nor beneficence, nor even cooperation, though each
> may enter non-essentially. . . . what seems to be at stake is some mea-
> sure of transcendence; it is a relaxing of one's own sense of boundaries
> and control. *It is acknowledging a sense of union or merger.*[34]

Recognizing these meaningful characteristics of the family should convince
us that the picture of the independent and self-interested agent is inappropriate
in the context of the family. Rather, a more adequate picture of the human
agent within the family would involve, we believe, a recognition that the
interests of family members are often inextricably intertwined. We want to
replace the discrete and separable interests of family members with a more
realistic view, one that recognizes the conflict, confluence, and confusion of
interests characteristic of life within the family. These interests have their origins in the intimate context of the family and lay claim to our allegiance and to
our efforts. As Schoeman has revealingly said: "We *share our selves* with those
with whom we are intimate and are aware that they do the same with us.
Traditional moral boundaries, which give rigid shape to the self, are transparent to this kind of sharing."[35]

This richer understanding of human agency has implications for the two
cases we discussed above. We do things, and should be expected to do things,
for the family and for particular family members that we simply would not do
for non-family members. For the most part, such burdens come with the very
fact that we are bound to one another within a particular family. Thus if we

Moral Agency and the Family

view the agent's interests as being bound up with the interests of the family and its members, it should not strike one as ethically problematic that a mother might *naturally* want to donate part of her liver to her dying child. Neither love nor conscience constrains the mother's autonomy; rather, they give voice to her autonomy and say something about the kind of agent she is and the kind of family of which she is a member.

Why the use of the best interests standard may be inappropriate for thinking about kidney transplantations between minor siblings should now also be more apparent. The best interests standard is a formal and abstract framework; families are intimate and particular associations. The best interests standard is impartial; families are often partial and favoritist. Most crucially, the best interests standard is applied to an individual shorn of his or her associations; families are, or can be, intimate collectivities.[36] The interests of more than one person are at stake. To attempt to cram a formal relation into an intimate context does violence to the morally significant aspects of the family relationship. Indeed, the traditional reliance on the best interests standard when considering the use of minors as organ donors illustrates the extent to which this reasoning has disregarded the union of family members and their interests, thus missed some of the important moral consequences that flow from the family context. What is morally important and problematic about organ transplantation is precisely that it may *not* be in the best interests of the donor.

Should living-related kidney transplantations never be done? No, but justification must rest on other grounds that take account of the fact that such transplantations are done not to advance the interests of the child donor as an individual, but for the sake of another family member, and for the sake of the family as a whole. Justification must reckon honestly with the risks to the donor, the likelihood that the procedure will succeed, the possible benefits to the recipient, and the potential alternatives. It must take account of the fact that parents have obligations not only to the child who is to donate the kidney, but to the sick child who is to receive it, whose life and welfare may be in mortal danger. And most crucially, any justification for sibling kidney transplantation must cast a critical eye on the question whether parents can legitimately expect their children to bear some burdens for the sake of family interests, even interests that the children might not yet explicitly endorse.

Notes

1. Wittgenstein L. *Philosophical Investigations,* 3rd ed. Anscombe GEM, trans. Anscombe GEM, Rhees R, von Wright GH, eds. Oxford, UK: Basil Blackwell, 1967.
2. See note 1, Wittgenstein 1967:49.
3. See note 1, Wittgenstein 1967:48.
4. Murdoch I. *The Sovereignty of Good.* London: Routledge and Kegan Paul, 1970:80.
5. Arthur Caplan's comments are taken from *Knight-Ridder Newspapers* 1989;Dec. 14.
6. George Annas' comments are taken from *The New York Times* 1989;Nov. 27.
7. Siegler M, Lantos JD. Commentary: Ethical justification for living liver donation. *Cambridge Quarterly of Healthcare Ethics* 1992;1(4):320–25, at p. 323.
8. No.68651 Eq., Massachusetts, 12 June 1957.
9. Quoted in Curran WJ. A problem of consent: kidney transplantation in minors. *New York University Law Review* 1959;34:891–98 at 893; emphasis added. *Masden,* like *Huskey v. Harrison* and *Foster v. Harrison* after it, is an unreported judgment. Therefore, we are bound to the excerpts from the slip opinions that have been quoted in Curran's paper.

Robert A. Crouch and Carl Elliott

10. A clarification here is important. In both *Strunk v. Strunk* (see note 11) and *Hart v. Brown* (see note 13), unlike in *Little v. Little* (see note 15) where the best interests standard was explicitly adopted by the court, the justices in these two earlier cases held that the court's authority to authorize the minor donations rested with the common law substituted judgment doctrine. Although this is undoubtedly true as a strict matter of law, it is similarly beyond doubt that the justices would not have authorized the donations had they not found that the donation would be in the minor donor's best interests. Thus while the substituted judgment doctrine is prominent in the *language* of the courts, the point here is that the best interests standard dominates the *thinking* of the courts in all of these cases. Because of this, we will not discuss the substituted judgment doctrine here. For an excellent account of the substituted judgment doctrine in these and many other cases see Harmon L. Falling off the vine: legal fictions and the doctrine of substituted judgment. *Yale Law Journal* 1990;100(1):1–71.

11. *Strunk v. Strunk*, 445 S.W.2d 145 (Kentucky, 1969).

12. See note 11, *Strunk* 1969:149.

13. *Hart v. Brown*, 289 A.2d 386 (Connecticut, 1972).

14. See note 13, *Hart* 1972:389.

15. *Little v. Little*, 576 S.W.2d 493 (Texas, 1979).

16. In re Guardianship of Pescinski, 226 N.W.2d 180, 1975:182.

17. Feinberg J. *Harm to Others. Volume I: The Moral Limits of the Criminal Law*. New York: Oxford University Press, 1984:70–79. Feinberg identifies a further class of actions that are not self-interested, such as those done from principle or charity. Such acts are not done in the service of, and may be contrary to, the agent's own interests. They are mentioned here for the sake of completeness.

18. Nelson JL. Taking families seriously. *Hastings Center Report* 1992;22(4):6–12 at 9.

19. The agent may, of course, have an interest in doing anything at all, regardless of the ill consequences to himself or others, so long as it is freely chosen by him or herself.

20. The existence of such "psychological benefits" is widely noted in the empirical literature. See, for example Simmons RG, Marine Klein SD, Simmons RL. *Gift of Life: The Effect of Organ Transplantation on Individual, Family, and Societal Dynamics*. New York: John Wiley & Sons, Inc., 1974.

21. It is useful to note that the degree to which the mentally incompetent person is impaired should alter the way we think about such a prospective donor. Although many of the issues that arise in the context of organ (or tissue) donation by legally incompetent persons are similar whether the prospective donor is incompetent by virtue of tender age or by virtue of mental deficiency, the reader should not thereby conclude that there are no meaningful differences in the problems that are raised by these two classes of incompetent persons; nor should one infer that the conclusions that hold true for one group of incompetent persons hold true for the other group as well.

22. The rhetoric of "organ donation as gift" is useful to highlight in this context. On this see Fox RC, Swazey JP. *The Courage to Fail: A Social View of Organ Transplants and Dialysis*, 2nd ed. Chicago: University of Chicago Press, 1978; Fox RC, Swazey JP. *Spare Parts: Organ Replacement in American Society*. Oxford, UK: Oxford University Press, 1992; Murray TH. Gifts of the body and the needs of strangers. *Hastings Center Report* 1987;17(2):30–38; and Mauss M. *The Gift: Forms and Functions of Exchange in Archaic Societies*. Cunnison I, trans. Glencoe, Ill.: Free Press, 1954.

23. He may, of course, get some pleasure from being told that he helped his sibling. The degree to which this can be characterized as psychological benefit among mentally incompetent persons is surely both highly variable and highly speculative.

24. This, of course, raises the question: How young is too young to grow to appreciate the significance of donating a kidney? While it is perhaps true that a seven-year-old would remember her donation experience and appreciate the significance of that experience more with time, it seems that this sort of growing appreciation of an act performed in childhood would be forever lost on, say, a one-year-old who donated bone marrow to a sibling. In a recent case, *Curran v. Bosze* (566 N.E.2d 1319, Illinois, 1990), *a court appointed psychiatrist, asked whether a 3 1/2-year-old would benefit psychologically from donating bone marrow to a half-sibling, testified that in his opinion "the likely psychological benefits would be probably relatively small"* (Curran 1990:1336).

25. See note 15, *Little* 1979:499; emphasis added.

26. Precisely these reasons were given in an earlier case (*Camitta v. Fager*, No.73-171 Eq., Massachusetts, 5 September 1973) when the mental state of the prospective minor donor—a combi-

Moral Agency and the Family

nation of mild retardation and schizophrenia—were believed to preclude the possibility of psychological benefit accruing to the donor. As noted in Baron CH, Botsford M, Cole GF. Live organ and tissue transplants from minor donors in Massachusetts. *Boston University Law Review* 1975; 55:159–193, at p. 167, note 41.

27. An interesting treatment of Aristotle's and Plato's views about children and their different type of "agency" is found in Nussbaum MC. *The Fragility of Goodness: Luck and Ethics in Greek Tragedy and Philosophy.* Cambridge: Cambridge University Press, 1986:264–89.
28. See note 1, Wittgenstein 1967:49.
29. Taylor C. Hegel's ambiguous legacy for modern liberalism. *Cardozo Law Review* 1989;10:857–70 at 861.
30. See note 29, Taylor 1989:861; emphasis added.
31. Sherman N. The virtues of common pursuit. *Philosophical and Phenomenological Research* 1993;53(2):277–299 at 282; second emphasis added.
32. Patricia Smith has made the distinction between (1) family in the abstract and (2) family as a household of particular individuals, and argued that different family obligations are associated with the different senses of the family. See Smith P. Family responsibility and the nature of obligation. In: Myers DT, Kipnis K, Murphy CF, Jr., eds. *Family Matters: Rethinking the Philosophy of the Family.* Ithaca: Cornell University Press, 1993:41–58.
33. See note 31, Sherman 1993:278.
34. See note 31, Sherman. 1993:282; emphasis added.
35. Schoeman F. Rights of children, rights of parents, and the moral basis of the family. *Ethics* 1980;91(4):6–19 at 8.
36. Nelson HL, Nelson JL. *The Patient in the Family: An Ethics of Medicine and Families.* New York: Routledge, 1995:63–72. This excellent book is indispensable to any discussion of the role of the family in medical decisionmaking.

[19]

ORGAN DONATIONS BY INCOMPETENTS AND THE SUBSTITUTED JUDGMENT DOCTRINE

JOHN A. ROBERTSON*

INTRODUCTION

This Article deals with a problem that often arises in the development and application of biomedical knowledge—the need to inflict suffering on incompetent persons to benefit others. The practice takes many forms. Incompetents are used as subjects in medical experimentation and as a source of tissue and organ transplants; they are covertly killed or allowed to die, as occurs in the pediatric nursery with defective newborns; their reproductive ability is curtailed through compulsory sterilization; and their behavior is modified by intrusive procedures.[1] Because these activities appear inconsistent with the autonomy and dignity usually accorded individuals, ascertaining their justifiable limits is an important enterprise with controversial legal and ethical implications. To elucidate the issues, this Article will discuss the use of incompetents in intrafamilial organ—especially kidney—transplants and will focus particularly on the validity of the substituted judgment doctrine in resolving these dilemmas.

The high priority which our society accords persons and our recognition of their inherent dignity and value are the sources of the dilemmas posed by biomedical innovation,[2] for nearly all bioethical issues arise from a clash between respect for persons (and subsidiary values such as fairness and equality) and some other interest.[3] Ethical difficulties with organ transplants, brain death, sterilization, abortion, experimentation, cloning, genetic screening, psychosurgery, behavior modification and euthanasia all derive from respect for persons.

The threat to this value takes many forms. Sometimes the threat is inequality, as when scarce medical resources are allocated on the basis of

* Assistant Professor, University of Wisconsin Law School.
This research was supported by the Program in Medical Ethics of the Department of History of Medicine, University of Wisconsin Medical School, and benefitted from the encouragement and devil's advocacy of Norman Fost. I am also indebted to Marshall Breger for valuable comments on an earlier draft, and to David LeGrand for able research assistance.
1. Lovaas, Schaffer, & Simmons, *Building Social Behavior in Autistic Children by Use of Electroshock Treatment*, 1 J. EXPERIMENTAL RESEARCH IN PERSONALITY 99-109 (1965); S. RACHMAN & J. TEASDALE, AVERSION AND BEHAVIOR DISORDERS (1964); A. BONDURA, PRINCIPLES OF BEHAVIOR MODIFICATION (1969).
2. The notion that a person is an autonomous being with inherent dignity and value and whose life and actions are—to the greatest extent compatible with the rights of others—to be controlled by his own choices, has been a dominant theme in the philosophy and politics of Western civilization since the Enlightenment. *See, e.g.*, Kant, *Fundamental Principles of the Metaphysics of Morals* in PROBLEMS OF MORAL PHILOSOPHY 2336 (2d ed. P. Taylor 1972); C. FRIED, AN ANATOMY OF VALUES: PROBLEMS OF PERSONAL AND SOCIAL CHOICE 34-39, 138 (1970). *See also* R. NOZICK, ANARCHY, STATE, AND UTOPIA (1974); C. FRIED, MEDICAL EXPERIMENTATION: PERSONAL INTEGRITY AND SOCIAL POLICY 67-78, 94-104 (1974).
3. For example, a physician's interest in career advancement or the welfare of future patients. *See, e.g.*, B. BARBER, J. LALLY, J. MAKARUSHKA & D. SULLIVAN, RESEARCH ON HUMAN SUBJECTS (1973); J. KATZ, EXPERIMENTATION WITH HUMAN BEINGS 435-514 (1972).

ORGAN DONATIONS   49

social worth,[4] or incompetents rather than consenting adults are used in experimentation.[5] Or the threat may be manipulation that seems inconsistent with human dignity, as in behavior modification or cloning.[6] The spectres of both inequality and manipulation are implicated when one person's interests are sacrificed for the benefit of others: when people are sterilized against their will, subjected to research without their consent, or pronounced dead by criteria of brain death.[7] From our present vantage point—that is, with present values and notions of humanhood[8]—solutions to the problems posed by biomedical innovation necessarily must be consistent with respect for persons.

Traditionally, the device that adjusts our knowledge to our ethics has been the concept of consent. The free, knowing and intelligent consent of a competent person to participation in the development or use of biomedical knowledge appears prima facie to satisfy the requirement of respect for persons, since respect for persons means respecting a person's autonomy. The problem of euthanasia may be seen in this light. In general, we feel revulsion at involuntary euthanasia,[9] and most doubts about voluntary euthanasia involve ascertaining the validity of the subject's consent, such as whether a living will executed at a prior date is sufficient evidence of present consent.[10] Similarly, the ethical and legal issues in genetic screening and counselling revolve around questions of disclosure and full consent

---

4. Katz, *Process Design for Selection of Hemodialysis and Organ Transplant Recipients*, 22 BUFF. L. REV. 373 (1973); Dukeminier & Sanders, *Medical Advances and Legal Lag: Hemodialysis and Kidney Transplantation*, 15 U.C.L.A. L. REV. 357 (1968).

5. Goldman, *Was Dr. Klugman Justified in Giving the Children Hepatitis?*, MEDICAL WORLD NEWS 20-31 (1971).

6. L. TRIBE, CHANNELLING TECHNOLOGY THROUGH LAW 155-86, 304-64 (1973).

7. Determining death on the basis of a flat electroencephalogram or similar indicia that brain activity has ceased, however decided, involves a social policy judgment that the interest in maintaining life at any cost is secondary to the other interests implicated in pronouncing a person dead, including use of the body as a source of organ transplants. *See* Capron & Kass, *A Statutory Definition of the Standards for Determining Human Death: An Appraisal and a Proposal*, 121 U. PA. L. REV. 87 (1972).

8. Biomedical and other technology may alter present conceptions of self, humanhood and other values to such an extent that in the relatively near future the concerns expressed here will seem quite odd. *See* Tribe, *Ways Not to Think About Plastic Trees: New Foundations for Environmental Law*, 83 YALE L.J. 1315, 1323-26 (1974).

9. *See* Kamisar, *Some Non-Religious Views Against Proposed "Mercy-Killing" Legislation*, 42 MINN. L. REV. 969 (1958); *Study Finds Most Favor Fast Death*, N.Y. Times, Oct. 31, 1973, at 6, col. 1. Most proponents of euthanasia stop short of recommending involuntary euthanasia, with the exception of defective newborns and the long-term comatose patient. *See* Robertson, *Involuntary Euthanasia of Defective Newborns: A Legal Analysis*, 27 STAN. L. REV. 213 (1975); McCormick, *To Save or Let Die—The Dilemma of Modern Medicine*, 229 JAMA 172 (1974); Gustafson, *Mongolism, Parental Desires, and the Right to Life*, 16 PERSPECTIVES IN BIOL. AND MED. 529 (1973); Duff & Campbell, *Moral and Ethical Dilemmas in the Special Care Nursery*, 289 N. ENG. J. MED. 890 (1973); Paper by R. Burt, *Authorizing Death for Anomalous Newborns*, National Symposium on Genetics and Law, Boston, Mass. May 22, 1975, published in A. Milunsky & G. J. Annas, ed., GENETICS AND THE LAW 435 (1975). Jonson, Phibbs, Tooley & Garland, *Critical Issues in Newborn Intensive Care: A Conference Report and Policy Proposal*, 55 J. PED. 756-68 (1975).

10. Kutner, *Due Process of Euthanasia: The Living Will, A Proposal*, 44 IND. L.J. 539 (1969); Kutner, *The Living Will, Coping with the Historical Event of Death*, 27 BAYLOR L. REV. 39 (1975); D. MAGUIRE, DEATH BY CHOICE (1974). Technically the criminal law does not permit active euthanasia to which the deceased has consented, no matter how clear and unquestioned his consent. *See* W. LAFAVE & A. SCOTT, CRIMINAL LAW 408 (1972).

to procedures that may reveal genetic data that stigmatize or restrict a person's later choices.[11] In general, the major thrust of public policy toward research with human subjects has concerned the development of institutional mechanisms for assuring that competent adults participating in research have given their informed consent.[12]

More difficult issues arise when the mental or social condition of the patient or subject precludes legally effective consent to a personal intrusion. In such situations, respect for persons usually entails prohibiting the intrusive activity.[13] Sterilization of the retarded poses ethical difficulties because a highly intrusive procedure is performed for which consent is not possible. Similarly, the use of children and the institutionalized mentally impaired in experimentation cannot be rationalized in terms of consent precisely because they are incapable of consent. The question of withholding treatment from defective newborns is likewise troublesome, as is the use of children and the retarded in bone marrow and kidney transplants.

Of course, some medical procedures can be justified even when the person involved is incapable of consent—primarily when the procedure will benefit the incompetent.[14] If the procedure advances the incompetent's interests by providing a benefit, respect for persons is maintained.

In the absence of benefit, however, one may still argue, on a utilitarian basis, that an absolute prohibition on the use of incompetents is unjustified. Individual cases, the argument goes,[15] must be decided by balancing the

---

11. COMMITTEE FOR THE STUDY OF INBORN ERRORS OF METABOLISM, NATIONAL RESEARCH COUNCIL, NATIONAL ACADEMY OF SCIENCES, GENETIC SCREENING: PROGRAMS, PRINCIPLES AND RESEARCH (1975). For example, such screening may reveal that a person has an extra Y chromosome, that he is a carrier of sickle cell trait or numerous other genetic traits which may, for example, affect marital and reproductive decisions or lead to insurance or employment problems.

12. Curran, *Governmental Regulation of the Use of Human Subjects in Medical Research: The Approach of Two Federal Agencies,* 98 DAEDALUS 542 (1969).

Truly "informed" consent often appears to be a mythical goal seldom achieved in practice. Leonard, Chase & Childs, *Genetic Counseling: A Consumer's View,* 287 N. ENG. J. MED. 433 (1972); Epstein & Lasagne, *Obtaining Informed Consent: Form or Substance,* 123 ARCH. INT. MED. 682 (1969). This is because variables such as the authority of the physician, the time, place and manner of informing, the amount of information provided, and the education of the subject seem to affect the subject's understanding of what is being communicated to him. Unless review procedures take account of these other influences, the consent process is likely to be more a formal than a substantive safeguard of the interests of research subjects. *See* Fost, *A Surrogate System for Informed Consent,* 233 JAMA 800 (1975).

13. Exceptions are made in the cases of prisoners who would ordinarily have the mental capacity to consent but who, because of their confinement, might be more susceptible to coercive influences. *See* Bailey v. Mandel, Civil Action No. K-74-110 (D.C. Md. 1974).

14. Strunk v. Strunk, 445 S.W.2d 145 (Ky. 1969); Baron, Botsford & Cole, *Live Organ and Tissue Transplants From Minor Donors in Massachusetts,* 55 B.U.L. REV. 159 (1975).

Decisions as to whether a procedure constitutes a benefit may be made by a court. *See, e.g.,* Strunk v. Strunk, *supra;* Hart v. Brown, 29 Conn. Supp. 368, 289 A.2d 386 (Super Ct. 1972), or by a legally designated surrogate, *see, e.g.,* Bonner v. Moran, 126 F.2d 121 (D.C. Cir. 1941). *See generally* Curran & Beecher, *Experimentation in Children,* 210 JAMA 77 (1969).

15. Though the two do not necessarily yield similar results, the same result may often be reached on biomedical issues whether one's approach is that of "rule" or "act" utilitarianism. A rule permitting organ transplants from incompetents could be justified on grounds of utility, even though every specific result justified on utilitarian grounds would not yield a rule similarly justified. *See generally* D. LYONS, FORMS AND LIMITS OF UTILITARIANISM (1965).

benefits to be derived by others from the intervention with the costs to the incompetent. Failure to conduct productive experimentation on fetuses, children, or the retarded may deny future patients, some of whom are in the same class, beneficial medical knowledge which may prolong their lives or reduce their suffering. Where the risks to the incompetent are minimal or, if substantial, less than the harm that would occur to the class deprived of the benefits, the research would, under this view, occur.[16] Such utilitarian arguments may be made with regard to nontreatment of severely damaged newborns, and sterilization of sexually active persons of low I.Q. In all these instances the ethically questionable act seems necessary to save the lives or reduce the suffering of others, or protect society at large.

The problem, of course, is that utilitarianism conflicts with the strictest respect for persons. Utilitarian principles may justify intrusions into persons entailing pain, harm, or suffering—or, simply, their use as a means to others' utility, thus prima facie violating their character as autonomous, dignified beings.[17] Accepting a utilitarian standard to justify intrusions directed against incompetents will facilitate extending a balancing approach to marginally compelling situations, perhaps even where the person subject to the intrusion is capable of withholding consent.

Given, however, that enormous benefits may flow from such nonconsensual intrusions, one may argue that maintaining respect for persons is an exercise in moral form over moral substance. Direct and tangible suffering, even death, may result from strict refusal to allow intrusions which will not benefit the incompetent. Moreover, the costs to the incompetent will often appear slight, insubstantial, or merely statistical, and considerably less than the benefits realized by the beneficiaries of departures from the rule of respect.[18] Perhaps abstract moral principles should jealously be guarded. But the price of maintaining respect in many situations, measured by the suffering not alleviated, will often seem exorbitant.

An absolutist approach to respect for persons is thus likely to be met with little sympathy; moreover, the short run gains of utilitarian compromise may be extremely attractive. Yet a strictly utilitarian approach also has its costs. Aside from the problems of comparing interpersonal utilities,[19] weighing and comparing utilities in particular situations is slippery business and subject to bias and abuse. Even if utilitarian decision-making is structured by procedural due process, including judicial review, the dangers of a utilitarian approach, even to utilitarians, may seem great.

---

16. HEW experimentation policy is basically utilitarian. Institutional review committees must determine whether "[t]he risks to the subject are so outweighed by the sum of the benefit to the subject and the importance of the knowledge to be gained as to warrant a decision to allow the subject to accept these risks; . . ." 45 C.F.R. § 46.2(b)(1) (1974).

17. *See* notes 11-16 and accompanying text *supra*.

18. For example, the risk to life from unilateral nephrectomy has been estimated to be 1 in 4,000 or about the ordinary risk in driving, *see* note 42 *infra*, while the recipient's life will often be saved as a result of a transplant.

19. J. RAWLS, A THEORY OF JUSTICE 22-27, 90-91 (1971).

The long-run social effects of such a precedent will be unpredictable, perhaps including the destruction of traditional moral values upon which the cohesiveness of society depends.[20]

Can a middle position that retains the flexibility of utilitarianism without damaging the ethic of respect for persons be fashioned for these situations? If so, such a position would forestall further utilitarian incursions. At the very least, it would reduce the pressure to dilute the formal ethic, and preserve its power as a beaconlight guiding technological developments.

The legal-ethical dilemma that arises when the organ of an incompetent person is sought for transplantation to a close relative is a useful setting to explore this question. Unlike other situations in which incompetents suffer harm primarily to benefit others, in the case of transplants the life of an identifiable person hangs in the balance. Conducting medical research on incompetents may ultimately provide knowledge that will save life or reduce suffering, but one cannot predict in advance whether any particular research will have this effect, much less that the life of a particular person will depend on its occurrence.

The transplant case also differs from other situations because the risk imposed on the donor is often minimal. If abortion is viewed as imposing harm on the fetus to "benefit" the mother, the harm imposed is hardly minimal. Likewise passive enthanasia involves imposing death on the defective newborn primarily to protect family and society from the psychic and financial burdens of raising such a child. In both cases a benefit short of saving life is sought at the expense of the incompetent's death. The transplant situation, by contrast, starkly presents a compelling case—a limited risk and pain is to be imposed on a person incapable of consent in order to save another's life. If respect for persons does not permit this intervention, then *a fortiori* less compelling cases will not be permitted. If the transplant can be squared with libertarian principles, then a similar analysis can be fruitfully applied to the other situations.

I. *Lausier v. Pescinski* AND THE BENEFITS RULE

The grant or receipt of an organ is structured by a set of social norms regulating gift-giving and family obligations, and by a biological, psychological and sociological screening process which Professors Fox and Swayze call "gatekeeping."[21] Gatekeeping involves the selection, on medical, psychiatric and social grounds, of those patients who will receive, and the persons who will give, organs.[22] Although the initial screening may take

---

20. The good of one individual is seldom strong enough to withstand the combined utility of many. Thus scarce resources, including personal rights and even life, may be allocated on the basis of social worth criteria. *See* Alexander, *Medical Science Under Dictatorship*, 241 N. ENG. J. MED. 39 (1949); Rawls, *supra* note 19, at 22-27.

21. FOX & SWAYZE, THE COURAGE TO FAIL 6-7 (1974).

22. *Id.* at 6-10, 32-39.

place within the family circle,[23] the final decision usually rests with the transplant surgeon. He is faced with a conflict between protecting donors from nontherapeutic harm and saving the life of a diseased person.[24]

Sometimes the screening process conducted by the family and physician will lead to a decision that a person legally and perhaps physically incapable of consent is the best donor. Such a decision may result from simple medical factors, intra-familial conflict, or unconcern for the incompetent. In the case of an incompetent, however, the physician does not make the final gatekeeping decision. Intrusions into the body of an incompetent to benefit another cannot be authorized by the incompetent's guardian[25] without judicial approval.

Judicial approval for intra-family transplants from incompetent donors has been obtained in most cases.[26] The first appellate case on the question, the 1969 Kentucky Court of Appeals decision of *Strunk v. Strunk*,[27] was a notable impetus. The court permitted a kidney transplant from a 27-year-old incompetent to his 28-year-old brother, finding that the incompetent, who had close relations with the recipient, would benefit from his continuing to live. Subsequent decisions have relied heavily on the benefit rule of *Strunk*.

In *Lausier v. Pescinski*,[28] the most recent appellate decision in this area, however, the court declined to assume power to authorize transplants from incompetents. The case is the only reported decision denying a transplant in an immediate life and death situation,[29] and thus is an almost ideal context in which to consider the ethical questions raised by requests for transplants from incompetents. The case also juxtaposes the two com-

---

23. *Id.* at 6.

24. *Id.* at 9, 36.

25. Generally the guardian of an incompetent must protect the best interests of the incompetent and do nothing to injure him. *See, e.g.,* WIS. STAT.. ANN. § 880.08 (1971).

26. The trend began with three Massachusetts cases, Foster v. Harrison. Equity No. 68674 (Mass. Sup. Jud. Ct. Nov. 20, 1957); Huskey v. Harrison, Equity No. 68666 (Mass. Sup. Jud. Ct. Aug. 30, 1957); Masden v. Harrison, Equity No. 68651 (Mass. Sup. Jud. Ct. June 12, 1957), *summarized and discussed in* Curran, *A Problem of Consent: Kidney Transplants in Minors,* 34 N.Y.U.L. REV. 891 (1959). *See also* Santiago-Delphin, Simmons, Simmons, Tierney, Bernstein, *et al., Medico-Legal Management of the Juvenile Kidney Donor,* 6 TRANSPLANTATION PROCEEDINGS 441 (1974) [hereinafter cited as SANTIAGO-DELPHIN]. Since 1957, Massachusetts courts have authorized on numerous occasions transplants involving legally incompetent donors. *See, e.g.,* Nathan v. Flanagan, Civil No. J74-109 (Mass. Sup. Jud. Ct. 1974) (bone marrow); Nicosia v. Peter Bent Brigham Hosp., Equity No. 73-8 (Mass. Feb. 26. 1973) (kidney). Trial courts in other states have followed Massachusetts' example. *See, e.g.,* Hart v. Brown, 29 Conn. Supp. 368, 289 A.2d 386 (Super. Ct. 1972); Howard v. Fulton-DeKalb Memorial Hosp. Auth., Civil No. B-90430 (Ga. Super. Ct. Nov. 29, 1973); *In re* Sharpe, Equity No. 44476 (Md. Cir. Ct. Dec. 28, 1973) (bone marrow); Children's Memorial Hosp. v. Lewis, No. 73CH6936 (Ill. Cir. Ct. Nov. 21, 1973).

Because lower courts decide most of these cases, the cases tend to be unreported. Thus it is not claimed that the two reported cases denying transplants, *In re* Richardson, 284 So. 2d 185 (La. App.), *cert. denied,* 284 So. 2d 338 (La. 1973). and Lausier v. Pescinski, 67 Wis. 2d 4, 226 N.W.2d 180 (1975), are the only cases in which courts have denied transplants. *See, e.g., In re* Gilmore, (Wis. Cty. Ct., Dodge County, Juneau, Wis. May 3, 1974) (kidney).

27. 445 S.W.2d 145 (Ky. 1969).

28. 67 Wis. 2d 4, 226 N.W.2d 180 (1975).

29. A kidney transplant from an incompetent was also denied in *In re* Richardson, 284 So. 2d 185 (La. App. 1973), but it is highly unlikely that the transplant would have prolonged the donee's life, since the donee died shortly thereafter from other causes.

peting legal justifications for judicially authorized transplants—the requirement of benefit to the incompetent and the "substituted judgment" doctrine.

The facts of the case were straightforward enough. Mrs. Elaine Jeske, the mother of six children, contracted glomerulonephritis[30] in early 1970. In March of 1971 she underwent a total nephrectomy[31] and at that time was placed on a list for cadaver organs.[32] A suitable cadaver did not become available and, faced with discouraging prospects for procuring one, Mrs. Jeske's doctors turned to family members as possible donors. All others in the family being either unsuitable or unwilling[33] to donate, exclusive attention focused on Mrs. Jeske's brother, Richard Pescinski. Richard, described as a "catatonic schizophrenic"[34] with the mental age of twelve, no lucid intervals[35] and no hope of recovery, had been institutionalized for 20 of his 38 years. On January 4, 1974, another sister, Janice Lausier, was appointed general guardian for Richard,[36] and she then petitioned the county court to approve a transplant.

The county court denied the guardian authority to consent, concluding that "neither [it] nor the guardian has absolute authority to substitute its judgment for that of the ward."[37] The Wisconsin Supreme Court affirmed, holding that both it and the county court lacked the power to authorize a

---

30. Chronic glomerulonephritis is characterized by the progressive destruction of the glomerular portion of the nephron, which removes waste material from the blood. Record on Appeal to Wisconsin Supreme Court, *In re Pescinski*, No. 28617, 177 [hereinafter cited as Record].

31. *Id.* at 182-83.

32. *Id.* at 182. Because of the problems attending long-term dialysis, some of which had already developed, it was felt "highly desirable and conceivably rather urgent that she receive a kidney transplant." *Id.* at 185.

33. The availability of donors other than Richard from within the Pescinski family was an issue contested throughout the proceedings. *See, e.g., id.* at 193-94 (hearing to authorize tests to determine Richard's suitability as a donor); *id.* at 245-47 (hearing on petition to authorize the transplant). Both of Mrs. Jeske's parents were considered too old and unwell to undergo a nephrectomy, and her sister Janice was eliminated as a diabetic. *Id.* at 188, 193-94, 205. Her brother Ralph, a dairy farmer and the father of ten, was advised by his own physician "not to get involved—his first responsibility was to his own family." *Id.* at 278. None of Mrs. Jeske's children were considered because her surgeon "as a matter of principle" refused to take organs from those below the age of consent. *Id.* at 205, 271. After the conclusion of the *Pescinski* litigation, her eldest son, then 20, agreed to a transplant but was found incompatible. Author's Telephone Interview with Eugene Kershek (Mrs. Jeske's counsel), July 7, 1975.

34. Record, *supra* note 30, at 140.

35. *Id.* at 225. This diagnosis came from the director of the institution in which Richard was living. Two other witnesses at the trial, an administrative assistant at the home and a social worker, testified to the contrary, ascribing Richard with some "lucid moments." *Id.* at 285-86, 300-01. For example, the social worker testified that Richard has "been more or less lost in the shuffle. I think that Richard probably will never be able to return to the community, but I think he can reach a more higher level than he is functioning on now." In response to a question concerning what kind of things Richard can do she answered:

> It depends on his mood at the time. He attends lots of social functions. He needs some encouragement, but he does attend. He goes to the monthly dance. He plays checkers and bingo, things like this, and lately he has been participating in group discussions. It takes a lot of extra attention to get Richard to speak out on his own. He responds to direct questions, but rarely initiates conversation on his own, but he will with encouragement.

Id.

36. *Id.* at 7.

37. *Id.* at 124.

non-consensual transplant. This rule, enunciated in cold language at the end of an 1100 word opinion,[38] appeared to be a sentence of death for Mrs. Jeske.[39]

The court's opinion relied upon the requirements of consent and benefit articulated in *Strunk:*

> An incompetent particularly should have his own interests protected. Certainly no advantage should be taken of him. In the absence of real consent on his part, and in a situation where no benefit to him has been established, we fail to find any authority for the county court or this court, to approve this operation.[40]

This cursory analysis failed to address either of the two key issues before the court: (1) the power of the guardian, the county court or the supreme court to authorize a transplant, and (2) the meaning of an incompetent's best interests or benefit when his sibling's life is at stake.

The court supported its conclusion as to its own lack of power by properly noting a lack of specific statutory authority and by citing Wisconsin cases prohibiting the making of gifts from an incompetent's estate.[41] But neither the absence of a statute not the limited case law preclude a special rule for procuring body organs where the donor's risk is not great[42] and a life is at stake, if the court has the broad powers of a court of equity. In indicating that there would be a different result if the incompetent were benefited, the court impliedly admitted that, at least in some circumstances, it has the equitable power to permit a transplant. Thus, the court did not say that it wholly lacked power to order the transplant, but only that it chose not to exercise it in the instant case. Its rationalization of the result as outside the power of Wisconsin courts simply does not succeed.[43]

The decision is correct, then, only if the court was right in requiring a showing of benefit to the incompetent donor. The clear merit of the benefits rule is that it maintains respect for persons. Though there may be no right

---

38. Only 430 words of the opinion dealt with the court's reasons for denying the transplant.

39. The court filed its opinion on March 4, 1975. As of January 14, 1976, she was still alive but had severely deteriorated and was non-ambulatory. Author's Telephone Interview with Eugene Kershek, Jan. 14, 1976.

40. 67 Wis. 2d at 8, 9, 226 N.W.2d at 182.

41. Kay v. Erickson, 209 Wis. 147, 244 N.W. 625 (1932); Estate of Evans, 28 Wis. 2d 97, 125 N.W.2d 832 (1965).

42. A doctor testifying at the *Pescinski* hearing gave figures of one death in 4,000 kidney transplants in the United States and Canada in the last decade. He found the risk roughly comparable to the risk of driving in Wisconsin, where 1,000 automobile deaths from a population of 4,000,000 occur each year. Record, *supra* note 30, at 260-61.

43. The lone dissenter, Justice Roland Day, rejected the majority's consent-benefit analysis. He asserted the consent requirement to be inapplicable when the subject is an incompetent with "no lucid intervals." 67 Wis. 2d at 10, 226 N.W.2d at 182. Brushing aside benefit as "pretty thin soup" on which to base a decision as to whether or not the donee is to be permitted to live," he turned to the substituted judgment doctrine's standard of what the donor would do if competent. *Id.* at 10-11, 12, 226 N.W.2d at 182-83. He concluded that "in all probability" Richard would consent, because "for him it would be a short period of discomfort which would not affect his ability either to enjoy life or his longevity." *Id.* at 12, 226 N.W.2d at 183.

to improve the lot of a competent person against his will,[44] where the person is incompetent respect for persons requires that we act for his benefit or best interests.

The benefit rule, however, may be questioned on several grounds, and many compelling cases fall outside even an expansive definition of benefit. Because the incompetent does not benefit, the intrusions entailed in the sterilization of the severely retarded, experimentation with children and the institutionalized, or in situations such as *Pescinski,* must always be denied, although competent persons in those situations might have chosen otherwise.

Moreover, the benefits test can be and has been so vaguely and loosely applied as to permit arbitrary manipulation for utilitarian ends. The test contains no criteria or standards for determining what constitutes a benefit, or the amount of benefit that must be shown in a particular case. Courts have readily determined that such intangible psychological factors as the traumatic impact of the recipient's death on the donor, or the denial to him of the psychic pleasures he receives from interaction with the recipient are benefits that justify transplants.[45] Even in cases where testimony on the psychic effects appears substantial, as in *Strunk,* skepticism about relying on such evidence of benefits seems warranted.[46] At times this testimony appears contrived, as when the donor is too young to have developed the deep ties with the sibling that the testimony suggests.[47]

The ultimate rationale for the benefits test must also be questioned. The claim is that, when a non-consensual physical intrusion that benefits others confers net benefits on the incompetent, the intrusion is consistent with respect for persons. Yet the presence of benefit does not justify nonconsensual intrusions on competent persons. Rather, the determinative factor appears to be consent or choice—persons may choose or consent to actions which bring them little or negative benefit. Respect for persons requires that incompetents be similarly treated. We should treat incompetents as they would choose to be treated in a given situation. Where the

---

44. *See* notes 84-85 and accompanying text *infra.*

45. Baron, *et al., supra* note 14, at 171; *see* Hart v. Brown, 29 Conn. Supp. 368, 289 A.2d 386 (Super. Ct. 1972); Strunk v. Strunk, 445 S.W.2d 145 (Ky. 1969).

46. Steinfield, J., dissenting in *Strunk,* stated: "It is common knowledge beyond dispute that the loss of a close relative or a friend to a six-year-old child is not of major import. Opinions concerning psychological trauma are at best most nebulous." 445 S.W.2d 145, 150 (Ky. 1969). *See also* Lausier v. Pescinski, 67 Wis. 2d 1, 10-11 (1975) (Day, J., dissenting); Note, *Equity-Transplants-Power of Court to Authorize Removal of Kidney from Mental Incompetent for Transplantation into Brother,* 16 WAYNE L. REV. 1460, 1465-67 (1970); Note, *Transplantation-Incompetent Donors: Was the First Step or the Last Taken in Strunk v. Strunk?,* 58 CALIF. L. REV. 754, 759-63 (1970).

When tested in an adversary proceeding, psychiatrists have admitted that testimony about future psychological detriment or benefit to children under twelve is highly speculative, Baron, Botsford & Cole, *supra* note 14, at 171, and some courts are beginning to discount the importance of benefit. *See* Camitta v. Schillinger, Equity No. 74-18 (Mass. Sup. Jud. Ct. Jan. 31, 1974), *cited in* Nathan v. Farinelli, Equity No. 74-87 at 6-7 (Mass. Sup. Jud. Ct. July 3, 1974).

47. Baron, Botsford & Cole, *supra* note 14, at 171.

wishes or preferences of the incompetent are known, we are obligated to act in accordance with them.[48] Where his wishes or intentions have not been articulated and cannot be known, the existence of net benefits serves as a convenient surrogate for determining what he would have chosen, because it is reasonable to assume that an incompetent would want that which benefits him. The benefit rule should thus be subservient to the obligation to do what the incompetent person wants: if there is a conflict between the self-interest and inferred desire of an incompetent, the incompetent's putative choice should prevail.

Indeed, a test focusing on the inferred wishes of the incompetent, *i.e.*, the substituted judgment doctrine, is widely accepted to permit gifts to be made from incompetents' estates.[49] Like bodily intrusions, such gifts do impose a risk on the incompetent—the risk of future financial ruin—yet the courts recognize and apply a principled alternative to the benefit test.

The remainder of this Article will examine in detail the doctrine of substituted judgment and its application to transplants from incompetents.[50] After an account of the doctrine in the probate area, a justification for applying it to transplants will be advanced.

II. Substituted Judgment and Organ Transplants From Incompetents

A. *Substituted Judgment—The Precedents*

Under the substituted judgment doctrine—at least since the 1816 case of *Ex parte Whitebread*[51]—courts have authorized gifts from the incompetent's estate to persons to whom the incompetent owes no duty of support.[52] The substituted judgment doctrine requires the court to "don the

---

48. If a competent person knowingly and voluntarily signs a paper saying it is his intention to give a $10,000 gift to X every year even if it harms his estate, or he does not want medical treatment if unconscious, respect for persons requires, if the person becomes incompetent, that we honor that intention, even if his "objective benefit" from the action is negative. *See* note 96 and accompanying text *infra*.

49. *See* notes 51-83 and accompanying text *infra*.

50. Despite the apparent relevance of the substituted judgment doctrine, the incompetent transplant cases seldom have been based on it. *Strunk*, which contains the most detailed exposition of the doctrine, seems to fall back upon a benefits rule, basing its approval of the transplant on the benefit that the incompetent donor was likely to derive and not on the fact that he would have consented to the transplant if competent. 445 S.W.2d at 148. A few other cases mention the doctrine, but are decided on other grounds. *See, e.g.*, Hart v. Brown, 29 Conn. Supp. 368, 289 A.2d 386 (Super Ct. 1972).

51. *Ex parte* Whitebread, a Lunatic, 2 Mer. Rep. 99 (1816).

52. *See* In re Guardianship of Brice, 233 Iowa 183, 8 N.W.2d 576 (1943); *In re* Buckley's Estate, 330 Mich. 102, 47 N.W.2d 33 (1951). The formulations of the doctrine vary. *See, e.g.*, Marsh v. Scott, 2 N.J.S. 240, 63 A.2d 275 (1949) (if "he could consent"); *In re* Johnson, 111 N.J. Eq. 268, 162 A. 96 (N.J. Chan. 1932) (if "he had the capacity to act"); Citizens' State Bank v. Shanklin, 174 Mo. App. 639, 161 S.W. 341 (1913) (if "he had been of right mind").

Sometimes the rule is more specifically articulated to refer to what the incompetent would have done if suddenly cured. Kemp v. Arnold, 234 Mo. App. 154, 113 S.W.2d 143 (1938). Other formulations do the reverse and look to the choice he would make if "he had remained in possession of his faculties." *In re* Heeney, a Lunatic, 2 Barb. Ch. Rep. 326 (1847).

mental mantle of the incompetent"[53] and to "substitute itself as nearly as may be for the incompetent, and to act upon the same motives and considerations as would have moved her."[54] Motives of charity and altruism,[55] self-interest,[56] and even the desire to minimize estate taxes[57] have all been imputed to an incompetent on this basis. To determine whether the incompetent, if sane, would have made a gift, the courts look to several factors that would move one in the incompetent's situation—the needs of the donee, the relationship to the incompetent, the degree of intimacy both before and during incompetency, the ward's past expressions or manifestations of concern or gift-giving, the present and future requirements of the incompetent himself, the extent of others' dependency upon him, and the size and condition of the estate—"giving to these and any other pertinent matters such weight as the incompetent, if sane, probably would have given."[58]

The decisions have had little difficulty squaring the concept with a duty to act in the best interests of the incompetent. The justifications asserted include benefit to the incompetent,[59] his likely ratification of the imputed choice upon recovery,[60] or the satisfaction of intentions and patterns of conduct commenced before the period of incompetency.[61] A notion of respect for persons has been implicit in the doctrine: it is in the incompetent's best interests to be treated as nearly as possible as the person he would be if his incompetence had never occurred. As an early commentator on the doctrine put it:

> Acting for the general welfare and advantage of a person does not mean merely supplying his or her physical wants or investing his or her money wisely. It is as much to the general advantage and welfare of a mother, for example, that the health of her children be preserved and that they be cared for in sickness, as it is that she herself be provided with a proper means of support.[62]

1. *The Standards.* Although the substituted judgment doctrine is recognized in most American and British jurisdictions either in judicial[63] or

---

53. *In re* Carson, 39 Misc. 2d 544, 241 N.Y.S.2d 288, 289 (Ulster County Ct. 1962).
54. City Bank v. McGowan, 323 U.S. 594, 599 (1944).
55. *In re* Flagler, an Incompetent Person, 248 N.Y. 415, 162 N.E. 471 (1928); *see* Note, *Insane Persons: Allowance From Surplus Income of Incompetent for Third Persons to Whom No Legal Duty is Owing,* 14 CORNELL L.Q. 89 (1928).
56. *Ex parte* Whitebread, 2 Mer. Rep. 99 (1816).
57. *In re* Dupont, 41 Del. Ch. 300, 194 A.2d 309 (1963).
58. *In re* Brice, 233 Iowa 183, 187, 8 N.W.2d 576, 579 (1943); *In re* Fleming's Estate, 173 Misc. 851, 19 N.Y.S.2d 234 (Kings County Ct. 1940).
59. *Ex parte* Whitebread, 2 Mer. Rep. 99 (1816); *In re* Evans, L.R. 21 Ch. D. 297 (C.A. 1882); *In re* Darling, L.R. 39 Ch. D. 208 (C.A. 1888).
60. *See, e.g.,* The Earl of Carysfort, Cr. & Ph. 76, 41 E.R. 418, L.C. (1840); *In re* Thomas, a Lunatic, 2 Ph. 169 (1846).
61. *See* notes 67-70 and accompanying text *infra.*
62. Carrington, *The Application of Lunatics' Estates for the Benefit of Dependent Relations,* 2 VA. L. REV. 204, 204-05 (1914).
63. The doctrine was first recognized in the United States in *In re* Willoughby, a Lunatic, 11 Paige 257 (N.Y. 1844), which affirmed the Chancellor's power to support from a lunatic's surplus income one not next-of-kin to whom the lunatic had no legal obligation of support if

Organ and Tissue Transplantation

ORGAN DONATIONS

statutory[64] form, there is wide variation in the facts and circumstances upon which courts find that an incompetent, if competent, would make a gift. The varying results reveal internal tensions which limit the scope of the substituted judgment doctrine in the estate area and its applicability to other situations. The main tension stems from attempting to discern what in fact the incompetent would have done, if competent. The courts invariably focus on the desires and preferences which the incompetent would have had if he never had become incompetent, or if he had, if he recovered and essentially retained his pre-incompetency preference schedule. But there is an alternative approach. The courts could ask what a person in the incompetent's situation would do if he had legal capacity; that is, the courts could act to maximize the present subjective interests of the incompetent.[65] If this interpretation were chosen, crucial differences could develop in the application of the substituted judgment doctrine to transplants.[66]

The major issue to which the courts have addressed themselves is what facts and circumstances constitute sufficient evidence of what an incompetent would do if competent. The courts have had to choose between a subjective and an objective standard, the first requiring an actual indication of donative intent to the recipient, the second focusing on what the incompetent would be wise, prudent or reasonable to do. Where an estate is ample to meet the needs and legal obligations of the incompetent, the result reached has thus depended on the weight courts have given to past evidence of gifts, or intention to give, to the applicant; the reasonable person standard; and a factor combining aspects of both subjective and objective standards—the closeness of the applicant to the incompetent. The trend has been toward the objective standard.

a. *Past Evidence of Gift or Intention to Give.* In substituting their judgment for the incompetent, courts will only rarely refuse to recognize evidence that the incompetent while competent made gifts to the applicant,

the Chancellor was satisfied "beyond all reasonable doubt, that the lunatic himself would have so provided if he had been of sound mind." *Id.* at 259-60. *See also In re* Heeney, 2 Barb. Ch. 326 (1847). Several other jurisdictions followed New York in recognizing substituted judgment as an equity power. *See* Hambleton's Appeal, 102 Pa. 50 (1883); *In re* DeNissen's Guardianship, 197 Wash. 265, 275, 84 P.2d 1024, 1028 (1938); Sheneman v. Manring, 152 Kan. 780, 783-84, 107 P.2d 741, 744 (1940). But the doctrine has not been recognized in states in which the probate and other courts charged with the care and management of incompetents had only limited statutory powers and no general equitable jurisdiction. *See In re* Guardianship of Estate of Neal, 406 S.W.2d 496 (Tex. Civ. App. 1966); Kelly v. Scott, 215 Md. 530, 137 A.2d 704 (1958); Lewis v. Moody, 149 Tenn. 687, 261 S.W. 673 (1924).

64. The statutes fall into two classes. One form permits the guardian or the court to make gifts to family, immediate relative, or specified relatives if the estate is ample enough, without further inquiry as to how the incompetent would have acted. *See, e.g.,* N.J.S.A. 3A:20-4. These statutes depart from the underlying basis of common law substituted judgment. They require no showing of legal obligation to the recipient, prior contact, or, most significantly, circumstances suggesting that the incompetent would have made the gift if competent.

The other class of statutes is more directly in keeping with the purposes of substituted judgment. They allow gifts to designated relatives only if the circumstances show that the incompetent if competent would have made the gift. *See, e.g.,* CAL. PROBATE CODE § 1558 (West 1954).

65. *See* notes 90-95 and accompanying text *infra.*

66. *See* notes 103-23 and accompanying text *infra.*

or expressed an intention to do so. If the incompetent has previously expressed an intention to help a person and has in fact done so in the past, the courts assume that he would make the gift, if competent, or, alternatively, assume that, if he recovered, he would not blame a surrogate for continuing a pattern he had established while competent.[67] Therefore, every effort is made to fulfill a previously expressed intention or continue a practice of support or gifts for a needy person.[68] By the same token, in many cases of collateral or non-blood relationship, a lack of previously expressed donative intention is determinative,[69] however compelling the applicant's need.[70]

b. *Relationship.* If evidence of past gifts or intention to give is absent, the closeness of the applicant's relationship to the incompetent may provide sufficient assurance that the incompetent would have made the gift if competent. This inference is usually confined to the immediate family—the spouse and minor children. It is sometimes extended to parents and adult children and occasionally applied to grandchildren and siblings living with the incompetent. Beyond this immediate circle, courts have been reluctant to exercise their power of substituted judgment.

This limitation to close relatives may appear harsh and unduly restrictive. Cousins, nieces and nephews, in-laws and other collateral relatives have suffered because courts usually refuse to believe that a lunatic, with the capacity to act, will choose to assist needy relatives simply because they are related.[71] In some circumstances less conservative courts do conclude from the closeness of a relationship that the incompetent, if competent, would make a gift, even if the incompetent had expressed no view on the subject.[72]

---

67. The early case of Hambleton's Appeal, 102 Pa. 50 (1883), made clear the importance of previously expressed intent. There, an elderly man had persuaded his nephew to give up a lucrative business and to move with his family to care for him. The Pennsylvania Supreme Court, giving controlling weight to the intentions of the lunatic while still sane, sanctioned the arrangement's continuance after the uncle became incompetent:
[T]he duty of the court [was] to maintain and carry forward [his] affairs . . . as they were when his mind failed him. . . . We look only to the lunatic's disposition of things when sane . . . and with it the court had no right to interfere except for good cause shown.
Id. at 53, 55.
68. Thus the court in *Ex parte* Haycock, 5 Russ. 154 (1828), refused to permit the committee of a lunatic's estate to sell furniture which would benefit his estate, but which he had bequeathed to a particular individual while sane.
69. *See* Kemp v. Arnold, 234 Mo. App. 154, 113 S.W.2d 143 (1938); *In re* Brice's Guardianship, 233 Iowa 183, 8 N.W.2d 576 (1943).
70. *See, e.g., In re* Trusteeship of Kenan, 261 N.C. 1, 134 S.E.2d 85 (1964) (approval for charitable gifts denied despite tax advantages and however "wise and prudent" they might seem, absent facts showing gift program prior to incompetency); Monds v. Dugger, 176 Tenn. 550, 144 S.W.2d 761 (1940); *In re* Evans, 21 Ch.D. 297 (1882) (relief denied to impoverished 81-year-old clergyman, the father of eight children, one of whom was dependent upon him, and one of eight next-of-kin first cousins, where there was no showing that incompetent had made any payment to him while competent).
71. *See In re* Johnson, 111 N.J. Eq. 268, 162 A. 96 (1932); Monds v. Dugger, 176 Tenn. 550, 144 S.W.2d 761 (1940); *In re* Schley, 201 Misc. 522, 107 N.Y.S.2d 884 (Queens County Ct. 1951); *In re* Kernochan, 84 Misc. 565, 146 N.Y.S. 1026 (1914).
72. *See In re* Bond, 198 Misc. 256, 98 N.Y.S.2d 81 (Steuben County Ct. 1950) (gift to

c. *A Reasonable Person Standard.* Where evidence of past donative intention or action or close blood relation is absent, and absent a contrary intent, a court may still authorize a gift on the ground that it would have been bestowed by a reasonable or prudent person in the incompetent's circumstances.[73] If the court's function is to treat the incompetent's property as he himself would want it treated, and no evidence of his intentions exist, then should it not be assumed that he would act as a similarly situated, reasonable person? Indeed, requiring actual evidence of subjective intent, such as expression of intention or practice when sane, would make the doctrine inapplicable in many situations—such as that of the congenital incompetent, or where insanity or senility onsets gradually—in which it is difficult to determine any pattern of sane intentions.[74] Undue reliance on subjective manifestations of intention overlooks the changes time creates in the needs of friends and relatives, in the affluence of the incompetent, or in other circumstances which could not be foreseen when the incompetent was sane.[75]

Advocates of a subjective standard would argue that the incompetent, if competent, might not prefer to act as a reasonable person in his circumstances would. But the force of this argument is lessened by the limitations which may be placed on the use of an objective standard: it should be used only in the absence of sufficient evidence of the incompetent's intent and preferences, and never to contradict them, however unwise or imprudent they might seem.[76]

Although courts have been reluctant to infer the incompetent's intent under a reasonable person standard,[77] a trend can be discerned toward a more objective standard which adequately protects the incompetent from undue risk.[78] The most explicit exposition of an objective standard has

---

sister who had cared for incompetent); *In re* Calasantra, 154 Misc. 493, 278 N.Y.S. 263 (County Ct. 1935) (gift to sister with whom incompetent had lived before his illness); Kemp v. Arnold, 234 Mo. App. 154, 113 S.W.2d 143 (1938); De Wald v. Morris, 397 S.W.2d 738 (Kan. Ct. App. 1965).

73. The earliest pronouncement on substituted judgment, *Ex parte* Whitebread, 2 Mer. Rep. 99 (1816), supports this approach, suggesting that until the lunatic recovers the court acts properly if it applies the incompetent's property "in such manner as the Court thinks it would have been wise and prudent in the Lunatic himself to apply it, in case he had been capable." *Id.* at 102.

For a forceful argument for an objective test, *see* Hale & Thompson, *The Surplus Income of a Lunatic,* 8 HARV. L. REV. 472, 473-74 (1895).

74. *In re* Guardianship of Christianson, 56 Cal. Rptr. 505, 520 (1967).

75. *Id.*

76. *See* Paper by Capron, *Experimentation and Human Genetics: Problems of Consent* 9-10. National Symposium on Genetics and Law, Boston, Mass. May 22, 1975, published in A. Milunsky & G. J. Annas, ed., GENETICS AND THE LAW (1976).

77. *Cf. In re* Trusteeship of Kenan, 261 N.C. 1, 134 S.E.2d 85 (1964); Monds v. Dugger, 176 Tenn. 559, 144 S.W.2d 761 (1940); *In re* Evans, 21 Ch.D. 297 (1882).

78. *In re* Flagler, 248 N.Y. 415, 162 N.E. 471 (1928), is an important case in this regard. There the court permitted a gift of $12,000 and a $1,000 annuity to a second cousin in ill health from an $11,000,000 estate. Rather than insisting on positive evidence of the incompetent's charitable inclinations, Judge Lehman was persuaded by the lack of evidence that she would not be moved by the moral and charitable considerations of her cousin's plight. *Id.* at 419 and 472. To limit the risk of violating the incompetent's actual intentions, the court limited the gift to the bare minimum needed. *Id.* at 420 and 472.

occurred in situations where a gift is sought to reduce estate taxes and preserve a larger distribution upon death. Early cases on the issue either denied the gift because of lack of evidence of subjective intent[79] or permitted it because there was evidence that the incompetent had intended to make such distributions and save taxes.[80] New York and California courts, however, have since firmly established an objective or reasonable person test for making these gifts. They have reasoned that despite the incompetent's failure to evidence his wishes to make gifts to obtain tax advantages, a reasonable person in his situation would certainly try to enlarge his estate by minimizing taxes.[81] The courts, however, have been careful to honor any subjective intent manifested in plans for testamentary distribution, even to the point of denying the gift.[82]

2. *Applicability to Organ Donations.* For over 150 years the substituted judgment doctrine has regulated the judicial response to claims of needy relatives upon incompetents, and has permitted depletion of incompetent estates with no direct benefit to them solely to help others. The rationale for this practice—that respect for persons requires courts to follow the putative wishes of the incompetent were he otherwise, even if such a course provides no direct benefit to the incompetent—is prima facie relevant in determining whether tissue and organs may be taken from incompetents to benefit close relatives in need. If property can be invaded because of minimal risk to the incompetent's interests, then presumably the body could also be invaded if the risks are commensurate.[83]

B. *Substituted Judgment–A Philosophical Rationale*

Although intrusions that yield a net benefit to the incompetent do not generally violate respect for persons, a transplant from an incompetent will not necessarily show disrespect for his person even if such benefit is absent. Non-beneficial transplants from those legally incapable of consent are consistent with and even required by respect for persons if it is clear that the incompetent, if competent, would have consented to the transplant.

The argument has several steps. The doctrine of respect for persons

---

79. Bullock Estate, 10 Pa. Dist. and Co. R. 2d 682, 44 Del. Co. Rep. 171 (1956); *In re* Trusteeship of Kenan, 261 N.C. 1, 134 S.E.2d 85 (1964).

80. *In re* Dupont, 41 Del. Ch. 300, 194 A.2d 309 (1963).

81. *See In re* Carson, 39 Misc. 2d 544, 241 N.Y.S.2d 288 (Ulster County Ct. 1962); *In re* Christianson, 56 Cal. Reptr. 505 (1967). *See also* Strange v. Powers, 358 Mass. 126, 260 N.E.2d 704 (1970); *In re* Morris, 111 N.H. 287, 281 A.2d 156 (1971); *In re* Trott, 118 N.J. Super. 436, 288 A.2d 303 (1972).

82. *See In re* Carson, 39 Misc. 2d 544, 546-47, 241 N.Y.S.2d 288, 290-91 (Ulster County Ct. 1962); *In re* Christianson, 56 Cal. Reptr. 505, 524, 248 Cal. App. 2d 398, 427 (1967). *See also In re* Turner, 61 Misc. 2d 151, 157, 305 N.Y.S.2d 387, 391 (Westchester County Ct. 1969).

83. The fact that the substituted judgment doctrine arose as a justification for disposing of the property of wealthy lunatics does not render the doctrine inapplicable to the transplant situation. The risks to the incompetent from a transplant may be slight, depending on the precise nature of the physical intrusion. *See* note 18 *supra*.

holds that people are free to make choices according to their own conception of their interests. This freedom generally prevails even if we disagree with the person's choice of ends or means—provided there is no unjustifiable infringement on the rights of others.[84] Thus our society respects a person's decision to refuse medical care in certain circumstances,[85] to use mind-altering drugs,[86] and possibly to commit suicide.[87]

If a person because of age or mental disability cannot select or communicate his preferences, respect for persons requires that the integrity of the person still be maintained. As stated by Rawls, maintaining the integrity of the person means that we act toward him "as we have reason to believe [he] would choose for [himself] if [he] were [capable] of reason and deciding rationally."[88] It does not provide a license to impute to him preferences he never had or to ignore previous preferences.

> Paternalistic decisions are to be guided by the individual's own settled preferences and interests insofar as they are not irrational, or failing a knowledge of these, by the theory of primary goods.[89]

If preferences are unknown, we must act with respect to the preferences a reasonable, competent person in the incompetent's situation would have.

There are several reasons for treating incompetents in this way. One is that if the person recovered or became competent, and was informed of our actions, he would be most likely to ratify a decision that attempted to ascertain and do that which from the circumstances it appeared that he would have wanted done.[90] For such an attempt would continue to regard him, even during his incapacity, as an individual with free choice and moral dignity, and not as someone whose preferences no longer mattered. Even if we were mistaken in ascertaining his preferences, the person could still agree that he had been fairly treated, if we had a good reason for thinking he would have made the choices imputed to him.

In addition, if a person were to decide in advance how he would want

---

84. The classic statement of this position is by Mill:
   . . . the principle requires liberty of tastes and pursuits, of framing the plan of our life to suit our own character, of doing as we like, subject to such consequences as may follow; without impediment from our fellow creatures, so long as what we do does not harm them, even though they should think our conduct foolish, perverse, or wrong. . . . The only freedom which deserves the name is that of pursuing our own good in our own way, so long as we do not attempt to deprive others of theirs, or impede their efforts to obtain it. Each is the proper guardian of his own health, whether bodily, *or* mental and spiritual. Mankind are greater gainers by suffering each other to live as seems good to themselves than by compelling each to live as seems good to the rest.
J. S. MILL, ON LIBERTY 16-17 (Atlantic Monthly Press ed. 1921).
   85. *See* cases cited in Cantor, *A Patient's Decision to Refuse Life—Saving Medical Treatment*, 26 RUTGERS L. REV. 228 (1973).
   86. *Cf.* Ravin v. State, 43 U.S.L.W. 2502 (Alas. June 10, 1975).
   87. *See* Cantor, *supra* note 85, at 254-58.
   88. J. RAWLS, *supra* note 19, at 209.
   89. *Id.* at 249.
   90. *Id.*

to be treated if he lost his rational faculties, he would be likely to choose a scheme that, to the extent possible, approximated what he would do if rational.[91] His moral worth is recognized since he is treated as the person he was, that is, as a person with the final ends and beliefs he previously expressed.[92] Moreover, since incompetents are treated as persons in other important respects,[93] consistency requires that, when questions arise concerning their treatment in particular situations, they also be treated as persons with wants and preferences. By failing to treat them as we treat competent persons, in similar situations, ascertaining and respecting their lawful choices, we might undercut respect for the incompetent persons in other situations, and eventually diminish respect for all persons.

In most situations respect for the person of incompetents will result in actions which benefit or are in the best interest of the incompetent. A competent person will ordinarily satisfy his wants and preferences. To the extent that the benefits rule advances the incompetent's previously expressed preferences, or procures him more of the primary goods[94] if his preferences are unknown, there is a firm basis for ascribing to him choices which yield a net benefit.

If the incompetent's apparent best interests conflict with the choice he would make if competent, respect for persons requires that his imputed choice have priority. Thus, the fact that a Jehovah's Witness is unconscious does not justify transfusing blood to save his life, if he has previously made it clear that under no circumstances would he want a transfusion and he would not be required to accept a transfusion if conscious.[95] Nor should an unconscious person be maintained on an artificial life-support system contrary to previously expressed preference if he would have been permitted to refuse treatment when conscious. By a parity of reasoning, the absence of benefit to the incompetent should not prevent an

---

91. Dworkin, *Paternalism*, in MORALITY AND THE LAW 119-22 (Wasserstrom ed. 1971).

92. In Rawlsian terms, one would focus on what a person would choose in the "original position"—the hypothetical pre-societal situation in which individuals confront the world and their realities from behind a veil of ignorance, knowing only the general laws of psychology, economics and the like, but nothing about their own characteristics, preferences or interests. *See* J. RAWLS, *supra* note 19, at 249-50.

A person in the original position will want to insure himself against the possibility that his powers will be undeveloped or that they will not be able rationally to advance his interests. *Id.* at 249. For this purpose he will adopt principles "to protect [himself] against the weakness and infirmities of [his] reason and will in society." *Id.* Since one would want to guarantee the integrity of his person and his final ends and beliefs, he would authorize others to act on his behalf and to do what he would do for himself if he were rational, when he became incapable of looking after his own good. *Id.* at 249-50. Paternalistic decisions are then to be guided by the individual's own settled preferences and interests so long as they are not irrational, or, lacking knowledge of these, by the theory of primary goods: we act for him as we would act for ourselves from the standpoint of the original position. *Id.* at 249.

93. *E.g.*, they are protected by the criminal law.

94. Primary goods are "things that every rational man is presumed to want. These goods normally have a use whatever a person's rational plan of life." J. RAWLS, *supra* note 19, at 62. Examples are rights and liberties, powers and opportunities, income and wealth (social primary goods), and health and vigor, intelligence and imagination (natural primary goods).

95. *In re* Brooks, 32 Ill. 2d 361, 205 N.E.2d 435 (1965). *Contra*, JFK Memorial Hospital v. Heston, 58 N.J. 576, 279 A.2d 670 (1971).

intervention when a choice in favor of the intervention can be imputed to the incompetent. In short, if respect for persons dictates honoring the wishes of competents even when their objective interests are impaired, a like rule should apply to incompetents.

One objection to this approach might be that it is absurd to treat an incompetent as he would choose to be treated if he were competent, when he is not competent, perhaps never has been, and may never be. The actual situation of the incompetent diverges from how he is treated or regarded under the substituted judgment doctrine. But it is precisely such a divergence that respect for persons requires and which generally confers benefits on the incompetent. Eliminating this divergence would mean that we treat the incompetent in all respects as a non-thinking, non-choosing, irrational being—in short, as a non-person.

A more substantial problem is specifying precisely what it means to "choose as the incompetent would, if competent." It could mean what the person would have chosen if he had never become incompetent—if he had remained in possession of his faculties. But what if the incompetency is congenital, or the person is a child? Alternatively, it could mean the choice made by the incompetent if his incompetency were suddenly lifted for a moment, only to have the clouds of unreason later descend. Or it could mean the person's choice if he were permanently to recover competency. This latter interpretation would be appropriate in the situation of children who will develop the faculty of reason or persons temporarily psychotic; but not in that of the retarded, the senile, or the chronically insane. Proper application of the substituted judgment test depends on specifying the precise characteristics of the situation into which competency is projected when the court substitutes its judgment for that of the incompetent.

If respect for persons means that we accede to a person's choice of ends and means, respect for incompetent persons requires that they be similarly treated. It must be determined what choices a competent person with the characteristics, tastes, preferences, history and prospects of the incompetent would make to maximize his interests or wants—both those he presently has and those he is likely to have in the future. These characteristics might include present incompetency, a period of previous incompetency, and the possibility of future incompetency. His interests or wants will thus vary with the length of the incompetency; his preferences as an incompetent; the identity and preferences established before becoming incompetent; and the likelihood of regaining competency. A competent person with the characteristics of this incompetent cannot very well maximize satisfaction of his preferences if he ignores factors such as present incompetency and future institutionalization which will determine present and future preferences as an incompetent. To assign the incompetent characteristics as if he had never become incompetent would be to misdescribe him. The divergence between the wants thus assigned him and his actual wants is, in fact, of greater significance than the divergence between his actually being incompetent and the treatment of him as competent for the purposes of the substituted judgment doctrine. The latter divergence merely enables us to respect and honor the wants of the incompetent by treating him like a competent person who would try to maximize his wants. The former distorts what his wants are and thus risks abusing his person by never recognizing or satisfying his wants. It acts not to advance his interests, but to advance the interests of a person who superficially resembles the incompetent.

The extent to which the preferences to be maximized depend on recognition of present, past and future incompetency will of course vary with particular situations. A 30-year-old man experiencing a transient psychosis has reasonable prospects of resuming his former social role upon recovery and thus of maintaining his prior preferences. To maximize his wants during his incompetency we must take into account the fact that previous preferences will soon be reasserted. The fact of incompetency alters some of his present wants, but it does not allow us to ignore altogether his past preferences.

Suppose, however, that the prognosis for recovery of the 30-year-old man is nil. He faces an indefinite future of incompetency and institutionalization, in which he will be unable to advance his own interests as an incompetent. The fact of future incompetency has significantly altered his situation and thus his present interests. If he had been an avid mountain-climber while competent and would be likely to continue this sport upon recovery, it would be pertinent to whether a kidney transplant, which would limit such activity, should occur. But the fact that a kidney transplant would interfere with his climbing would not be relevant if he had no chance of climbing again. Choosing for him on the basis of a set of preferences which would exist only if he were competent would thus be inappropriate. Respect for persons only demands that we make the best and most reasonable choice for a person given his wants and preferences in the circumstances he is presently and likely to be in, and not the circumstances in which we, if omnipotent, would like to place him.

A third situation is that of a child or a person with a long history of incompetency who will attain competency in the future. This case resembles the first, in that the incompetent's preferences must take account of future competency, but differs from the first two situations in that no preferences have been established during a prior period of competency. The interests to be maximized include the incompetent's existing tastes and preferences and the tastes and preferences the person is likely to have in the future when competent. Since the latter are unknowable, it would be in his interest to preserve maximum flexibility.

The fourth situation is that of one who has only a brief history of competency or none at all and no expectation of competency in the future. Severely mentally retarded persons and persons who become incurably insane or incur brain damage at an early age, *inter alia,* fall into this category. To respect the dignity and integrity of such a person the task of substituted judgment will be to ascertain his actual interests and preferences, which will be circumscribed by his present and future incompetency.

In each of these situations the wants or interests of a person in the incompetent's situation will include his present wants in the state of incompetency. But how do we ascertain the wants of an incompetent? Should they be granted any validity at all? If the incompetent lacks the capacity to communicate his preferences in the ways that people ordinarily do, it may be more difficult or perhaps impossible to know them. If he somehow communicates preferences, his very incompetency means that his preferences are not necessarily to be honored. But it would be erroneous to conclude that none of the expressed wants of incompetents should be satisfied. Incompetency encompasses several types of mental impairment, including the inability to have certain wants, the possession of bizarre wants, or the inability to choose among or satisfy conflicting preferences. Thus some expressed wants, if they appear irrational and indicative of his incompetency (such as a desire to fly) need not be honored. Expressed wants not in this category, however, should be satisfied.[96] Clearly, they define, in part, his interests, of which respect for persons must take account.

Respect for persons, as argued above, requires that previously expressed preferences, or preferences we think the incompetent has or would have, should also be honored. What if a past preference conflicts with a present preference? The present preference should be honored if so doing will have a favorable or trivial impact on the attainment of other wants, present or future, attributed to the incompetent. Present preferences should not be respected if they will foreclose achieving other expressed wants or wants the incompetent would be presumed to have if competent.[97] Overriding a present want in order to satisfy an imputed want is justified especially if it permits the satisfaction of other present wants.[98] Substituted

---

96. Thus respect for persons requires that to the extent feasible we permit an incompetent to watch television 16 hours a day, engorge himself on ice cream, or to satisfy preferences which are not irrational, up to the point of injury to others. Respect for persons does not require that an incompetent be permitted to mutilate himself. For a rationale of this position, *see* J. RAWLS, *supra* note 19, and Shapiro, *Legislating the Control of Behavior Control: Autonomy and the Coercive Use of Organic Therapies,* 47 So. CAL. L. REV. 237, 276-96 (1974).

97. Thus an incompetent need not be allowed to injure himself by banging his head against a wall.

98. Although treating an incompetent as a person capable of altruism on the basis of evidence that he would so choose if competent seems questionable because he cannot, while incompetent, realize any of the satisfactions of altruism, so treating him might still lead to a greater willingness of society to satisfy his actual present wants.

judgment thus combines subjective and objective elements. The subjective elements are the present tastes and preferences of the incompetent and those which he might have if competent, if he has a reasonable chance of becoming so. The objective aspect is the determination of what a reasonable person with the characteristics and present and future wants of the incompetent would choose to maximize his interests.

C. *The Doctrine Applied to Transplants*

The gift of organs and tissues to other persons is not a rare occurrence. While cadavers are the chief source of transplanted body parts, living donors frequently provide skin, bone marrow and kidneys to close relatives, and blood to strangers.[99] Indeed, cultural norms of obligation and gift-giving create strong pressures for intra-family body gifts, particularly from spouse to spouse, parent to child, or even sibling to sibling.[100] Should a practice so widely practiced and approved among ordinary persons be foreclosed merely because the donor is legally incompetent to make gifts? The substituted judgment doctrine would permit transplants from incompetents in situations where the incompetent, if competent, would donate an organ.

III. Considerations in the Application of the Substituted Judgment Doctrine.

A. *Welfare of the Donor*

It is useful to think of the decision to donate organs in terms of its effect on the donor's welfare. As Kenneth Arrow points out,[101] one's welfare may depend on his enhancing some other person's welfare. Kidney donors, for example, report heightened self-esteem, renewed meaning in life, and other positive feelings including transcendental or peak experiences from their gift of life to another.[102] Their decision to donate brings

---

99. See *The 11th Report of the Human Renal Transplant Registry*, 226 JAMA 1197 (1973); *see also* Titmuss, The Gift Relationship (1971).

100. 52.6% of the kidneys transplanted in the United States from 1951 through 1973 (7,000) were from living donors, 17.7% of them siblings. *The 11th Report of the Human Renal Transplant Registry*, 226 JAMA 1197, 1198 (1973). Fellner and Marshall found an instantaneous willingness of close family members to donate. *Kidney Donors—The Myth of Informed Consent*, 126 Amer. J. Psychiatry 1245 (1970). Fellner and Schwartz found that only 46% of their respondents thought there was less than an even chance that they would donate one of their kidneys to a stranger in need, with only 24% definitely ruling this out. *Altruism in Disrepute*, 284 N. Eng. J. Med. 582, 583 (1971).

101. *Gifts and Exchanges*, 1 Philos. and Public Affairs 343, 348 (1972).

102. Fellner, *Organ Donation—For Whose Sake?*, 79 Annals of Internal Medicine 589, 591 (1973); Eisendrath, Guttmann & Murray, *Psychological Considerations in the Selection of Kidney Transplant Donors*, 129 Surg. Gynecol. and Obstet. 243 (1969); Sadler, Davison, Carrol & Kountz, *The Living, Genetically Unrelated Kidney Donor*, 3 Seminar Psychiatry 86 (1971); Fox, *A Sociological Perspective on Organ Transplantation and Hemodialysis*, 169 Ann. N.Y. Acad. Sci. 406 (1970).

praise from the recipient, family, friends and even the public.[103] Often it enhances their status in the family, as occurs with adolescent donors[104] and those who offer to donate as a way of being reaccepted after a previous rejection by the family.[105] Indeed, there may be competition among family members to give.[106] Gift giving norms also involve obligations to repay, the satisfaction of which the donor will enjoy in various forms possibly over many years.[107] Thus, whatever the complicated motivations of the donor, his altruism seldom has a zero or negative return.[108] If a competent organ donor will often experience an increase in personal welfare from donating his organ, could not the utility of an incompetent person in this situation also be enhanced sufficiently that a reasonable person with his present and future preferences might choose to undergo the pain and risks of a transplant?

The graft of an incompetent's organ to save or prolong the life of a close relative is problematic precisely because of the costs imposed on the donor. If the risk were trivial, a question of principle would still exist, but the changes and consequences of abuse would be lowered. To make a substituted judgment concerning an organ transplant, it is essential to be clear about the effect of the transplant on the donor,[109] since a competent person similarly situated is likely to consider the consequences to himself. To an incompetent, who may be less able to understand the transplant procedures or to adapt to the unfamiliar surroundings of a hospital, the risks of an organ transplant may be even greater.[110]

---

103. *Id.; Brother Donates Marrow to Sister,* Boston Sunday Globe, June 1, 1975, at 8, col. 3.

104. Bernstein & Simmons, *The Adolescent Kidney Donor: The Right to Give,* 131 AM. J. PSYCHIAT. 1338, 1340 (1974); SANTIAGO-DELPHIN, *supra* note 26, at 443-44.

105. Simmons, Fulton, & Fulton, *The Prospective Organ Transplant Donor: Problems and Prospects of Medical Innovation,* 3 OMEGA 319, 327 (1972). *See also* Eisendrath *et al., supra* note 102.

106. Fellner & Marshall, *supra* note 100, at 82.

107. FOX & SWAYZE, *supra* note 21, at 5, 15-20.

108. However, the donor may experience depression if the transplant fails, and, after the transplant, may miss the attention he had hitherto received. *See* sources cited in note 102 *supra.*

109. *See* for accounts of experiences with kidney transplants Bennett & Harrison, *Experience with Living Familial Renal Donors,* 139 SURG., GYNECOL., AND OBSTET. 894, 896 (1974); Santiago, Simmons, *et al., Life Insurance Perspectives for the Living Kidney Donor,* 14 TRANSPLANTATION 131, 132-33 (1972); Penn, Halgremsen, Ogden & Starzel, *Use of Living Donors in Kidney Transplantation in Man,* 100 ARCH. SURG. 226, 230 (1970); Liljequist, *General Health and Renal Function in Kidney Transplantation Donors 8-30 Months After Nephrectomy,* in C. FRANKSSON, KIDNEY TRANSPLANTATION 88 (1968); Straffron, Kiser, Stewart, Hewitt, Gifford & Nakamoto, *Four Years' Clinical Experience with 138 Kidney Transplants,* 99 J. UROLOGY 479 (1968). An organ donor must normally be hospitalized which itself presents certain risks. *See* Schimmel, *The Hazards of Hospitalization,* 60 ANNALS OF INTERNAL MEDICINE 100, 101 (1964). In addition, the transplant procedures may engender fear and depression in the donor. Eisendrath *et al., supra* note 102, at 245. The evidence to date suggests that nephrectomy has not reduced the longevity of donors. To minimize the risks to the donor, he should be guaranteed both short and long-term medical care, conditions which the court in authorizing the transplant could make. *Cf.* Baron *et al., supra* note 14, at 189-92; *see also* J. Savage, *Organ Transplantation With an Incompetent Donor, Kentucky Resolves the Dilemma of Strunk v. Strunk,* 58 KY. L.J. 129, 146 (1970).

110. *See generally* G. THORNE, UNDERSTANDING THE MENTALLY RETARDED (1965).

A competent person would be likely to take into account the benefits to him flowing from the donation of an organ, and so must a court in substituting its judgment for that of an incompetent. Of course, the benefit factor need not be dispositive, as it would not ordinarily in the case of a competent. While a transplant will not confer a direct physical benefit on the donor, it might, if successful, preserve the life of a person with whom the donor has close relations, upon whom he is dependent, or from whom he will receive more love, care, attention, or intimacy. Thus a person may very well conclude, even as a purely rational utility-maximizer, that such benefits outweigh the costs of a transplant, whether he will be competent or incompetent in the future. The ratio of benefits to costs may be all the greater in favor of the transplant if the recipient is the one person who cares for the incompetent.[111] The psychological welfare of an incompetent may depend on knowing that other members of his family are in good health; he may therefore benefit from donating an organ even if he does not receive more love and care as a result of the donation. Finally, the social role and responsibilities, present and future, of the incompetent should be taken into account in substituting judgment, just as it would be a factor in the decisionmaking of a competent person, since the question of whether a donation would increase a person's utility would depend on the person's present and likely future social and occupational role.[112] Use of an institutionalized incompetent might inspire his attendants to devote special care and attention to him, out of a sense of obligation or otherwise. Or, as a condition or natural result of the organ donation, it might be decided to assure the incompetent the best of medical care, which could facilitate later maximization of preferences even as an incompetent. Possibly the social obligation to repay gifts may lead the family of the recipient to repay the donor with increased love and attention.

Of course, such factors would have to be determined on a case-by-case basis. Depending upon the nature of the incompetency and the likelihood of recovery, results under the substituted judgment standard will vary. The incompetent may not be able now, nor in the near future to comprehend the meaning of charity or the social norms surrounding gift-giving, and thus may lack the capacity to taste the immediate psychological fruits of altruism. Similarly, the demands of role or relation may have little meaning. Nonetheless, even under such circumstances there may be benefit to the incompetent from a donation.

---

111. The prevailing case law generally finds benefit if a close or dependent relationship exists between the incompetent and the recipient. *See* notes 71-72 and accompanying text *supra*.

112. If the incompetent is likely to recover and undertake strenuous employment, as, for example, a professional football player, the net benefit to him of a transplant to a close family member is likely to be less great than if the incompetent, upon expected recovery, would take a job as a bookkeeper.

Of course, the impact of donation on the incompetent's social role is relevant only if there is a possibility of recovery to perform that role.

B. *Material Compensation*

What would an incompetent person, if competent, decide to do if as a condition of the transplant a money payment were made to him? Offers of money in exchange for organs have not yet been considered by the cases.[113] According to economic theory, there should be a point at which money is worth more to an incompetent than retention of the desired organ.[114] However, the amount the incompetent would be paid as damages in a legal proceeding to recover for loss of a kidney might not be sufficient *ex ante* to induce him to give up his kidney.[115] The latter standard of course would be the one relevant to substituted judgment. An analysis of the value to the incompetent of the kidney would focus on three elements: (a) the loss of productive time; (b) pain and suffering; and (c) the impairment of body wholeness.

In taking account of loss of productive time, not merely wage earnings should be considered: household production must be accounted for as well.[116] The likelihood of recovery by the incompetent will also affect the calculation of loss of productive time. If we assume that the incompetent will not have future earnings, the value to him of the organ can be calculated by the probability of reduction of his capacity to use time, and the opportunity or service cost of that. We thus arrive at a figure roughly equal to the value of the kidney to the incompetent. A rational maximizer in the incompetent's position would thus be better off if he traded the kidney for any amount greater than that figure.[117]

While pain and suffering vary with individuals and are notoriously hard to measure, courts and juries have had considerable experience with compensating pain and suffering, and some rough guidelines exist.[118] Since suffering of an incompetent may be aggravated by his failure to understand the intrusive procedures involved in a transplant, compensation should cover this pain as well.

An element of pain and suffering particularly associated with the donation of an organ is the discomfort, which may be later felt more acutely if the incompetent recovers, that he is no longer whole and is more vulnerable. He might also consider that his incompetency was exploited. Of course this need not be the case: suffering may be alleviated by the incompetent's pride to have been the source of another's life.

113. The guardian ad litem in *Pescinski* implied that a monetary benefit to his client would suffice to justify the transplant. *See* note 28 and accompanying text *supra*.

114. One is reminded of Professor Friedman's statement, "Benefit is not identical with money, but there is, also, a firm correlation." Friedman, *The Renounceable Will: The Problem of the Incompetent Spouse*, 1958 Wis. L. Rev. 400, 409.

115. Komesar, *Toward a General Theory of Personal Injury Loss*, 3 J. Legal Studies 457, 468-77, 480-85 (1974).

116. *Id.*

117. The existence of a cash payment might make the incompetent—if he recovered competency—feel that he was regarded as ungenerous because he would save a relative's life only for money and not out of altruism. There is obviously no such danger where the incompetent's state is permanent.

118. Komesar, *supra* note 115, at 477-80.

COLUMBIA LAW REVIEW [Vol. 76:48

In calculating the amount of payment which would induce a competent in the situation of the incompetent to agree to an organ donation, offset should be made to the extent that it would otherwise be in the incompetent's interests to have the transplant occur. Some monetary compensation may be critical where other benefits to the incompetent are minimal or not clearly greater than the loss incurred by the donor.

In general, payment can alleviate doubts about the application of the substituted judgment doctrine in a particular case, by adding an incentive that in combination with such factors as family ties may eliminate doubt as to what the incompetent would do if competent.[119] However, some incompetents who will never become competent may not be able fully to realize, because of the nature of their incompetency, the benefits—symbolic or material—which flow from money payment. Such a reality could not be ignored in making a substituted judgment. Yet if some of the tastes and preferences of an incompetent are unsatisfied due to scarcity of resources —and there is no reason why an incompetent would not feel the effects of scarcity—a transfer of resources to him could enhance his welfare.[120] Only if he is so insentient or so well provided that the marginal benefit of additional resources is zero would payment have no effect on the choice which a rational person in his position would make. It is difficult to imagine that an incompetent institutionalized for years in county and state institutions, whose income is social security payments could not be benefitted by a money transfer.

The mere fact of payment does not, as in eminent domain proceedings, justify taking the organ. Rather, the inquiry under the substituted judgment theory is whether the existence of some payment would so enhance or increase the incompetent's welfare that a reasonable person, trying to protect the incompetent's interests, would choose to undergo the pain and risks to obtain that benefit. Payment will not automatically lead to a donation on substituted judgment grounds, but it may tip the scales in favor of allowing a donation where the incompetency is of such a nature that otherwise the transplant would not be permitted.

No doubt many will find highly objectionable that a wealth transfer can justify under the substituted judgment doctrine an organ donation which would not otherwise be permitted.[121] But wealth transfers to incompetents do not entail a market system for supplying organs and tissue.[122] Because of the limited ability of incompetents to express their preferences and the

---

119. Payment by the recipient may also provide a disincentive to seek the organ of an incompetent and thus act to reduce the use of incompetents as organ sources. *See* note 123 *infra*.

120. Wants of the incompetent that could be satisfied by money include not only those for which the incompetent has expressed a desire—e.g., a color television or warmer clothes—but also those which he objectively needs—e.g., psychiatric, medical or educational services.

121. *See, e.g.,* TITMUSS, *supra note* 99 (a forceful argument against a market system for the supply of blood).

122. *See* Note, *The Sale of Human Body Parts,* 72 MICH. L. REV. 1182 (1974).

difficulties in inferring them, we can, while prohibiting such transactions between competents, allow payment for the organs of incompetent persons to ensure the correct exercise of substituted judgment. In a sense, one is always compensated—in self-satisfaction—for his altruism. Where the form of repayment is likely to be of no value to the giver, then use of a more meaningful form should not be objectionable.[123]

C. *Summary*

Because the actions of most people can be analyzed in terms of exchange, which is based on assessment of cost and benefit, the elements of exchange become important in applying substituted judgment. For this reason the doctrine often reaches the same result as the benefit rule. However, because substituted judgment retains its clear focus on what a competent person in the position of the incompetent—a unique position— would do, it greatly expands a benefit approach to include subjective increases in utility that have not been recognized or even discussed under the benefits rule.

Courts have sometimes hesitated to consider psychological benefits to the incompetent in applying the benefits rule, largely for fear of abuse.[124] The substituted judgment doctrine allows consideration of such benefits while mitigating the danger of abuse, since the best interest inquiry is focused on the interests of the incompetent as they presently exist from his own particular vantage point. Substituted judgment provides a structured solution which forestalls resort to potentially expansive utilitarian balancing.

IV. FURTHER POLICY IMPLICATIONS OF A SUBSTITUTED JUDGMENT APPROACH

Objections to substituted judgment that still must be explored are that the doctrine treats incompetents unequally and will facilitate utilitarian uses of incompetents in other situations.

---

123. Still, arguments against such transactions may be made on the basis of their effect on human dignity: an incompetent's poverty should not be allowed to coerce him to undergo a transplant operation, *see id.* at 1217-18; TITMUSS, *supra* note 99, at 245-46, nor should the donee's poverty prevent him from obtaining one. The force of the latter argument is mitigated if the money payment to an incompetent donor is made from the public treasury. 42 U.S.C. §§ 426(e), (f), and (g) (Supp. IV 1974), which provide coverage for expenses related to renal transplant and dialysis could be read to include compensation to an incompetent kidney donor. Of course, payment by the government would eliminate the disincentive to use an incompetent donor which would exist if the cost of compensation were borne by the recipient alone. But this disincentive would be significant only for someone with money. Poor people should not be denied transplants simply because they do not have the funds to compensate an incompetent donor. In addition, payment to incompetents will not reduce the gifts otherwise being made by competent persons if competents are prohibited from engaging in market transactions, and if alternative organ sources must first be exhausted before an incompetent's organ can be used. In theory, the substituted judgment doctrine would permit incompetents to be used as a source of blood, skin or kidneys for strangers if a large enough payment or some other benefit were forthcoming. Indeed, an incompetent likely to remain so might have no other source of income and thus be greatly disadvantaged if unable to engage in such transactions. But money payments should be determinative only after a rigorous inquiry in which the incompetent is represented, and the inquiry must reveal that the incompetent will in fact realize a net benefit.

124. *See* note 46 and accompanying text *supra.*

A. Equality: Incompetents as Organ Banks?

Since tissues or organs are not taken from competent persons without their explicit consent even if another's life is at stake,[125] removing organs from incompetents without their explicit consent is prima facie to treat them unequally.[126] But is there unequal treatment in any meaningful sense? Ordinarily a person is capable of formulating and communicating his own choices. Where the person is incapable of having or communicating certain preferences, at least two alternatives are presented. We may conclude that respect for persons requires that we always presume that he says no to any intrusive procedure. But if, in fact, he would have chosen the procedure, he has been treated unequally in a real sense, because, unlike competents, he has been prevented from realizing his choices. Another alternative is to treat the incompetent as nearly as possible as if he were competent—capable of formulating and communicating a choice. Thus equal treatment requires resort to substituted judgment which, in some circumstances, will lead us to an imputation of consent to an intrusive medical procedure. The doctrine does not treat incompetents differently from competents in the matter of respecting their choices or, what is the same, respecting their persons. Thus, the effect of substituted judgment is not to infer a choice to donate because a reasonable person, comparing costs and benefits, might so choose, or because a person has a moral obligation to donate an organ to a sibling.[127] Since organs are not taken from competents on that basis, neither should they be taken from incompetents. Rather, the difference arises in the method of ascertaining what those choices are, though in both cases the best method available is used. If A could speak but could not write, and B could write but could not speak, would they be treated equally by heeding only their spoken words? Surely ascertaining the choices of incompetents on the basis of previous actions, stated intentions and the like is not to treat them unequally, when no other method of ascertaining their choices exists. Indeed precisely such a method is used when a competent,

---

125. If a private individual took another's organ without consent, he would be subject to civil and criminal sanctions. Cf. Annas & Glantz, Psychosurgery: The Law's Response, 54 B.U. L. Rev. 249, 253-54 (1974). If the state by statute sanctioned such a procedure, there would be serious questions about the statute's constitutionality, as authorizing a taking without compensation or an impingement upon rights of substantive due process. Note, Compulsory Removal of Cadaver Organs, 69 Colum. L. Rev. 693 (1969).

126. Under the doctrine of implied consent, intrusions on the bodies of temporarily unconscious persons are permissible when the intrusion is for the person's benefit. See W. Prosser, Handbook of the Law of Torts 101-03 (1971). A substituted judgment analysis would reach the same benefit. Some intrusions to benefit others are allowed, to serve the public interest in effective law enforcement, for example by testing the blood of a suspect. See Cupp v. Murphy, 412 U.S. 291 (1973); Schmerber v. California, 384 U.S. 757 (1966), or to ensure public health through compulsory immunization, see Holcomb v. Armstrong, 39 Wash. 2d 860, 239 P.2d 545 (1952); Jacobsen v. Massachusetts, 197 U.S. 11 (1905). However, the justifications for such intrusions are non-discriminatory, since they apply to competents and incompetents alike.

127. The limited circumstances in which one may justifiably impute to an incompetent the choice of benefitting another because of moral obligation are demonstrated by Richard McCormick, Proxy Consent in the Experimentation Situation, 18 Perspectives in Biology and Medicine 2 (1974).

because of temporary unconsciousness or unavailability, is unable to communicate his preferences.[128] Obviously, an absolute equality could be achieved by simply ignoring consent,[129] actual or imputed, and ordering organ donations on the basis of other factors. Both competents and incompetents would then be equal in their degradation, since respect for personal choices is the sine qua non of respect for persons.

Nor will incompetents as a result of application of the substituted judgment doctrine be used as organ sources more frequently than competents. If the evidence clearly indicates that the incompetent would not be a donor if he were capable of making the choice for himself, then he cannot be so used any more than a competent who refuses to consent can be used.

The substituted judgment doctrine does, of course, require a fairly sophisticated analysis and inquiry and may lead to practical problems of implementation. Therefore, in order to avoid damaging the interests of the incompetent, limitations on the use of the substituted judgment doctrine in organ transplant cases should be established. A per se rule against transplants which have no reasonable chance of saving or prolonging the recipient's life is warranted, because transplanting the organ of an incompetent is unlikely to enhance his welfare in such a situation.[130] Moreover, even a competent donor would be unlikely to consent to a transplant if it did not have a reasonable chance of saving someone's life.

In addition, courts should not apply the substituted judgment doctrine unless alternative sources of an organ have been investigated and found wanting. Such a limitation, though somewhat inconsistent with the general approach of the substituted judgment doctrine, is necessary to guard against abuse of incompetents. The substituted judgment doctrine must be kept in perspective as a means of attaining the larger value of respect for persons. Abuse of the substituted judgment doctrine, likely unless transplants from incompetents are authorized only after exhaustion of alternative sources and only for intrusions that will benefit relatives or intimates of the incompetent,[131] would undoubtedly undermine the respect that should be accorded to all persons.

128. The law regarding non-consensual representation of the interests of one party by another, found in legal doctrines of virtual representation, standing and class actions, is based on the idea that the representative will act in the matter as the person represented would act if before the court. Padway v. Pacific Mutual Life Insurance Company, 42 F. Supp. 569 (E.D. Wis. 1942); Lightle v. Kirby, 194 Ark. 535, 108 S.W.2d 896 (1937). *See also* Capron, *supra* note 76, at 15-18. These doctrines, like the doctrine of implied consent, note 126 *supra,* also may be usefully understood in terms of substituted judgment, because they authorize actions without actual consent in situations where it is likely that the affected person, if able to communicate his preferences, would agree with the course chosen.

129. Legislation to this effect would be constitutional only if the interests advanced by the transplant were found to be "compelling state interests," which justified the violation of fundamental rights entailed. *See* Note, *Compulsory Removal of Body Organs,* 69 Colum. L. Rev. 693 (1969).

130. If the incompetent's organ will not reasonably save the recipient's life, it is unlikely that he will be rewarded for a gift which seems superfluous, though there are situations in which this perhaps may not apply.

131. Such a rule might be superfluous for transplants of kidneys, skin, bone marrow, and

B. *The Problem of the Slippery Slope*

A final policy concern is that any deviation from a requirement of actual consent could open the door to social worth or utilitarian assessments in non-transplant situations of incompetents and competents alike, leading to further and massive incursions on the autonomy and dignity of individuals. This "slippery slope" or "entering wedge" argument pervades medical ethical debates. Does the substituted judgment indeed propel us down a "slippery slope"? Despite social tendencies to deny to the institutionalized and mentally disabled adequate treatment, civil rights and dignity, recent recognition of the rights of incompetent persons, particularly their right to respectful care and treatment, has been a major step toward a more humane and dignified treatment of the mentally handicapped.[132] Much of this progress has resulted from an emphasis on the similarities as human beings between incompetent and competent persons. One might argue that if the law recognizes a class of situations in which actual consent required of competent persons is waived for incompetents, leading to highly intrusive and dangerous surgery for the benefit of others, then support would be given to common notions that incompetents, are second class citizens. Yet if such an impact is possible at all, it could occur only by a misunderstanding or misinterpretation of substituted judgment. For the substituted judgment doctrine is explicitly non-utilitarian, and makes no claim that the rights of incompetents may be overridden to advance the interests of others, where the rights of competents may not be similarly overridden. Rather than detract from respect for the persons of incompetents, the substituted judgment doctrine, properly understood, actually fosters such respect. For it seeks to treat incompetents as competents are treated—as creatures of choice, with the autonomy and dignity of choice, and whose choices as best as we can ascertain them are to be respected. It thus stands as a further elaboration of the personhood of incompetents.

Nor is the substituted judgment doctrine advanced here likely to produce results which disrespect the persons of incompetents if applied to other biomedical issues—such as experimentation, sterilization and contraception, or euthanasia. Rather than support a prohibition on all non-therapeutic experimentation or sterilization, as many would now recom-

---

so forth, since without blood relation the incompetent probably would not be a good match for the donee. However, if a national tissue typing data bank system were operating, an incompetent could conceivably be found an acceptable match to a stranger.

132. O'Connor v. Donaldson, 422 U.S. 363 (1975); Jackson v. Indiana, 406 U.S. 715 (1972); New York St. Ass'n for Retarded Children, Inc. v. Rockefeller, 357 F. Supp. 752 (E.D.N.Y. 1973); Mills v. Board of Education 348 F. Supp. 866 (D.D.C. 1972); Herr, *Civil Rights, Uncivil Asylums, and the Retarded*, 43 U. CINN. L. REV. 679 (1974); Schoenfeld, *Human Rights for the Mentally Retarded: Their Recognition by the Providers of Service*, 4 HUMAN RIGHTS 31 (1974); American Assoc. of Mental Deficiency, *Rights of Mentally Retarded Persons*, 11 MENTAL RETARDATION 56, 57 (October 1973); Herr, *Retarded Children and the Law: Enforcing the Constitutional Rights of the Mentally Retarded*, 23 SYR. L. REV. 995 (1973).

mend, rigorous application of the doctrine would permit non-therapeutic experimentation[133] and sterilization[134] of incompetents in particular circumstances. In each case, however, the decision would be made in accordance with the interests of the incompetent, as a reasonable person with the incompetent's characteristics, preferences and prospects would see them. On the other hand, the doctrine is unlikely to support decisions in favor of passive euthanasia of defective newborns[135] or the chronically vegetative.[136] Thus applying substituted judgment to organ transplants need not open the door to abuse of incompetents in other areas of biomedical concern.

CONCLUSION

The substituted judgment doctrine gives a principled solution to the problem of imposing non-consensual harm on incompetents to benefit others. Since a court making a substituted judgment always seeks to do for the incompetent what he would do if capable of formulating and communicating his own choices, it never deviates from the demands of respect for persons. Consistent with that respect, however, it recognizes that a person's welfare, rightly understood, may depend on helping others.

This substituted judgment improves upon both utilitarianism and the benefit rule that has dominated the cases. Where utilitarianism slights the interests of the incompetent for the sake of a greater individual or social good, substituted judgment begins and ends in loyalty to the incompetent, but without the narrow focus of the benefit rule on direct, tangible returns. Balancing and judgment, as always, remain, but their scope is limited and always subject to the litmus of asking whether we, had we the wants, characteristics and prospects of the incompetent, would choose to give our tissue or organs to the person in need. The current dilemma concerning

133. An incompetent may have more of his present or likely future preferences satisfied through participation in non-therapeutic research, *e.g.*, if it led to better medical care, more attention and privileges, or money payments. Of course, these gains would have to be net of the risks. The point is that on a case-by-case analysis the substituted judgment approach does not *ipso facto* foreclose non-therapeutic experimentation. What the incompetent would choose, however, is not the sole factor determining public policy concerning research with incompetent subjects.

134. An incompetent may also gain from loss of reproductive capacity in certain cases— e.g., where reproduction will not satisfy the person's tastes and preferences, and may, in fact, impede satisfaction of other tastes and preferences. Again, a case-by-case approach would not *ipso facto* foreclose compulsory sterilization or contraception and may provide ethically sound grounds for the cases where interference with reproductive capacity seems justified.

135. Except for the situation in which the newborn is in incessant pain or will survive only a few days, it will be hard to conclude that from its perspective no life is better than the life it now has. *See* Robertson, *supra* note 9.

136. Substituted judgment will yield a decision to terminate life support systems of a chronically vegetative person only where the person is in incessant unstoppable pain. A prior executed statement of intent, which appears to have been made voluntarily after reflection and with knowledge, might also lead to nontreatment, though even there one may question whether the patient's present interests require execution of prior wishes. In most other situations, however, while it may be in the interests of others to terminate care, it will not be in the patient's interests, at least not under the substituted judgment doctrine. For discussion in a recent case, *see* In re Karen Quinlan, An Alleged Incompetent, Sup. Ct. N.J., Morris Co., No. C-201-75, 30-31 (Nov. 10, 1975).

organ transplants from incompetent donors requires ethical and legal clarity if harm is not to be inflicted unjustifiably either on incompetent persons or on relatives in dire need. The confusion in the cases rests on a confusion as to the demands of respect for persons. Substituted judgment can dispel that confusion and structure, if not simplify, the inquiry before the court. The doctrine can also clarify the debate on other bioethical dilemmas, pointing the way to resolutions that maintain respect for persons.

Part VI
Specific Classes of Donors

[20]

TAKING THE CAMEL BY THE NOSE: THE ANENCEPHALIC AS A SOURCE FOR PEDIATRIC ORGAN TRANSPLANTS

*Jay A. Friedman**

A newborn infant with a seriously defective heart lies in the intensive care unit of a California hospital, its life dependent on the slim possibility that a suitable donor heart can be found for transplantation. In another room lies a second infant born with a congenital malformation called anencephaly.[1] It has a healthy heart, but most of its brain is lacking. It will inevitably die within hours or days, but current determination-of-death statutes prohibit organ removal from such an infant until its minimal brain matter completely ceases to function. While the anencephalic infant deteriorates toward certain death, physicians stand by helplessly as the first baby dies of heart failure.[2]

Recent advances in organ transplant technology have opened a Pandora's box of ethical issues with which physicians, ethicists and lawyers must grapple. One particularly agonizing issue is the complicated debate over whether physicians should be permitted to remove organs from anencephalic babies at birth for purposes of transplantation.[3] The issue has struck deep chords not only within the medical and legal communities but in society in general. One account in the popular press succinctly sums up the issue:

> The dilemma is this: Does it matter if the child dies 24 or 48 hours before he might otherwise, particularly if that act will

* B.A., Brooklyn College of the City University of New York, 1983; J.D., Columbia University School of Law 1988. I wish to thank Harold Edgar and Mark Geistfeld for their helpful comments on earlier drafts of this Article. I must also express my gratitude to the firm of Dewey Ballantine, with whom I am associated. The firm's encouragement and generous provision of support services made this Article possible. All rights reserved.

1. For a precise description of anencephaly see infra notes 19–29 and accompanying text.

2. See Peabody, Emery & Ashwal, Experience with Anencephalic Infants as Prospective Organ Donors, 321 New Eng. J. Med. 344 (1989) (describing protocol in which physicians waited unsuccessfully for anencephalic infants to satisfy current criteria of brain death).

3. See generally Arras & Shinnar, Anencephalic Newborns as Organ Donors: A Critique, 259 J. A.M.A. 2284 (1988); Caplan, Should Foetuses or Infants Be Utilized as Organ Donors?, 1 Bioethics 119 (1987); Capron, Anencephalic Donors: Separate the Dead from the Dying, Hastings Center Rep., Feb. 1987, at 5; Harrison, Commentary, The Anencephalic Newborn as Organ Donor, Hastings Center Rep., Mar.–Apr. 1986, at 21; International Consensus Conference on Anencephalic Donors, Transplantation Proc., Aug. 1988, Supp. 5, at 1–82; Landwirth, Should Anencephalic Infants Be Used as Organ Donors?, 82 Pediatrics 257 (1988); Medearis & Holmes, On the Use of Anencephalic Infants as Organ Donors, 321 New Eng. J. Med. 391 (1989); Note, Death Unto Life: Anencephalic Infants as Organ Donors, 74 Va. L. Rev. 1527 (1988).

give life to four or five other kids? . . . We run up against the starkest possible test of Kantian versus utilitarian ethics. The utilitarian ethic, summed up by the slogan "the greatest good for the greatest number," would surely permit, indeed dictate, that the dying child be used as an organ donor. The Kantian ethic prohibits using—and certainly killing—one person for the sake of another.[4]

That the issue should engender intense debate is not surprising, for it raises fundamental legal and moral questions that must be resolved. By setting familiar themes of life and death in an unfamiliar context, the debate has shaken the solidity of long-held beliefs about life's beginning and end. By considering the propriety of removing organs from an independently breathing infant in order to benefit others, the debate raises the possibility that not all offspring of human parents qualify as "persons" accorded individual rights. Perhaps the most important question brought into focus by the controversy is this: when faced with the Hobson's choice between the certain death of two individuals as opposed to the death of one, under what circumstances should the law require that both die?

This Article argues for modification of existing law to permit parents to donate organs of anencephalic infants before brain death has occurred in order to insure the availability of usable organs. Parts I through III outline the medical and legal issues raised by the use of anencephalics as organ donors and summarize the previously unsuccessful attempts to resolve the issues in favor of using anencephalics as donors. Part I describes the current crisis in obtaining organs for pediatric transplants, defines anencephaly and explains why infants born with that condition are a suitable source of organs. Part II discusses the difficulties current legal rules pose for organ donation by anencephalics. Part III then analyzes two approaches to solving the dilemma. It argues that the first solution, a protocol designed to allow transplantation while comporting with the applicable brain death statute, has instead injured the very interests the statute was created to protect. Part III concludes with an introduction of the second solution: statutory changes, such as those recently proposed in the California and New Jersey legislatures, that focus on amending either the relevant determination-of-death or organ-donation statutes to permit anencephalics to serve as donors.

The remainder of the Article is devoted to arguments supporting these proposals for statutory change. Part IV surveys legal develop-

---

4. Krauthammer, Five Babies vs. One Principle: Which Is Worth More?, Wash. Post, Dec. 11, 1987, at A27, col. 1. Other accounts in the popular press include Rothenberg & Shewmon, Anencephalic Infants: Means to an End or Ends in Themselves? No Life Should be Traded for Another, L.A. Times, Dec. 10, 1987, § 2, at 11, col. 1; Walters, Anencephalic Infants: Means to an End or Ends in Themselves? Transplant of Their Organs can Save Lives, L.A. Times, Dec. 10, 1987, § 2, at 11, col. 3.

ments in analogous factual settings and concludes that the utilization of anencephalics as donors would not be inconsistent with developing legal doctrine. Part V introduces a theory of personhood which provides a coherent framework for understanding the proposed statutes and defends the theory against criticisms that it lacks empirical support and is therefore overly subjective. It also examines the motivations underlying existing determination-of-death statutes (which conflict with personhood theory) and argues that the considerations supporting such statutes have no relevance to anencephaly. Part VI demonstrates that such proposed statutes suffer from no constitutional infirmities. Part VII completes the defense of the California and New Jersey statutes by showing why slippery-slope concerns raised by opponents of these proposals do not warrant abandoning a position that is otherwise meritorious.

I. ORGAN TRANSPLANTATION AND THE ANENCEPHALIC NEONATE

The bright promise held out by organ transplant technology to those threatened with organ failure has been dimmed somewhat by the extent to which the demand for such vital commodities has consistently outstripped supply.[5] For the very youngest patients this crisis is particularly acute, giving rise to a controversial proposal for the utilization of a source as yet largely untapped: the anencephalic neonate.

A. *The Problem: High Demand, Low Supply*

The unhappy imbalance between the need for transplantable organs and the supply of such organs is attributable to a number of causes. If the donor organs are taken from cadavers, consent must first be obtained from the potential donor while alive or from the next-of-kin after death, a practice that has reduced the number of organs available for transplantation.[6] Even when organs can be obtained, whether from cadavers or consenting live donors, they must be matched to the recipient to reduce the risk of graft rejection by the recipient's immune system.[7] Another major difficulty is that both cadaver organs and those

---

5. See generally Iglehart, Transplantation: The Problem of Limited Resources, 309 New Eng. J. Med. 123 (1983); Schwartz, Bioethical and Legal Considerations in Increasing the Supply of Transplantable Organs: From UAGA to "Baby Fae," 10 Am. J.L. & Med. 397 (1985); Note, Patient Selection for Artificial and Transplanted Organs, 82 Harv. L. Rev. 1322 (1969); Note, Scarce Medical Resources, 69 Colum. L. Rev. 620 (1969).

6. See, e.g., J. Harris, The Value of Life 119 (1985); An Appalling Panorama, 281 Brit. Med. J. 1028, 1028 (1980) (following British television program in 1980 that suggested that not all organ donors were in fact dead at the time of donation, thousands of potential donors tore up their consent cards).

7. This concern has been alleviated to a large extent by the introduction of the drug cyclosporine, which was approved by the U.S. Food and Drug Administration in November 1983. Use of cyclosporine has been found to increase one-year survival rates for liver recipients from 30% to 65–70%. Iglehart, supra note 5, at 125. For kidney

removed from a living donor are viable for only a limited time, ranging from several hours for a liver or heart to about one and one-half days for a kidney.[8] The shortage of organs available for infants is even more severe than the shortfall that exists for children and adults.[9] Approximately 1 in 5,000 infants is born with end stage renal disease.[10] That translates into 400 to 500 children in the United States each year who need new kidneys. The same number need new hearts, and another 500 require replacement livers.[11] All of the foregoing difficulties are compounded by the small size of newborns, which requires that only organs from other infants can be used for transplantation.[12] However, very few suitable infant donors are available.[13] The result is disheartening indeed—an estimated forty to seventy percent of the children under age two on transplant waiting lists die before donors can be found.[14]

In response to the need for improving the system of organ transplantation, Congress enacted the National Organ Transplant Act of 1984, which provided for the establishment of a national Organ Procurement and Transplantation Network and grants to organ pro-

transplants, some transplant surgeons have reported survival rates of 80–90% after use of cyclosporine became widespread. Human Organ Transplantation: Societal, Medical-Legal, Regulatory, and Reimbursement Issues 19 (D. Cowan, J. Kantorowitz, J. Moskowitz & P. Rheinstein eds. 1987). See generally U.S. Dep't of Health and Human Servs., Pub. Health Serv., Health Resources and Services Administration Office of Organ Transplantation Report to the Secretary and the Congress on Immunosuppressive Therapies (1985), reprinted in id. at 402–05.

8. See Schwartz, supra note 5, at 399; Note, The Sale of Human Body Parts, 72 Mich. L. Rev. 1182, 1220–21 (1974).

9. See Annas, The Paradoxes of Organ Transplantation, 78 Am. J. Pub. Health 621, 621–22 (1988). For a discussion of the unique problems associated with transplantation in children, see Guttman, Organ Transplantation in Children, 11 Pediatric Annals 910 (1982); Lum, Wassner & Martin, Current Thinking in Transplantation in Infants and Children, 32 Pediatric Clinics N. Am. 1203 (1985).

10. Broyer, Incidence and Etiology of ESRD in Children, in End Stage Renal Disease in Children 9, 14 (R. Fine & A. Gruskin eds. 1984) [hereinafter End Stage Renal Disease].

11. See The Anencephalic as a Source for Pediatric Organ Transplants: A Question of Medical Ethics: Hearings on Cal. S. 2018 Before the Cal. Legislative Senate Subcomm. on the Rights of the Disabled 9 (1986) [hereinafter Subcommittee Hearings].

12. See, e.g., English, Is Cardiac Transplantation Suitable for Children?, 4 Pediatric Cardiology 57 (1983).

13. See Capron, supra note 3, at 5 (cadaver organs come primarily from the victims of automobile accidents, very few of whom are newborns); Caplan, supra note 3, at 120 (describing difficulties associated with using infants who have suffered sudden infant death syndrome (SIDS) as donors); id. at 127 (noting that mechanical substitutes for the heart, liver and pancreas will not be developed in the near future).

14. Subcommittee Hearings, supra note 11, at 7; Blakeselee, New Attention Focused on Infant Organ Donors, N.Y. Times, Dec. 14, 1987, at A18, col. 1; see also Bailey, Donor Organs from Human Anencephalics: A Salutary Resource for Infant Heart Transplantation, Transplantation Proc., Aug. 1988, Supp. 5, at 35 (most infants accepted for cardiac transplantation at Loma Linda University Medical Center die waiting for an acceptable donor to be found).

curement agencies.[15] The Network's responsibilities are largely concentrated on improving the dissemination of relevant information to facilitate organ transplants.[16] However, these largely procedural reforms have not translated into substantive gains.[17]

B. *Anencephalic Infants as a Source of Donors*

The crisis in pediatric organ transplantation has given birth to a controversial proposal for the utilization of a source of organs as yet untapped: the two to three thousand anencephalic babies born in the United States each year.[18] Anencephaly is the most serious of a group of defects involving arrested development of the neural tube, in which the tube of tissue that forms the spinal cord and from which the brain develops fails to close.[19] It is a lethal congenital malformation in which the cerebrum (often called the forebrain or "higher brain") and the cerebellum are absent, while the midbrain and the pons (which comprise the brainstem or "lower brain") are usually present.[20] The ap-

---

15. National Organ Transplant Act, Pub. L. No. 98-507, 98 Stat. 2339 (1984) (codified as amended at 42 U.S.C.A. §§ 273–274 (Supp. 1989)).

16. See 42 U.S.C.A. § 274(a)–(b) (Supp. 1989). The Act also prohibited the sale of organs, id. § 274(e), a practice that provides a telling commentary on the desperate nature of the situation.

17. See Blakeslee, Law Thwarts Effort to Donate Infants' Organs, N.Y. Times, Sept. 9, 1986, at C1, col. 1.

18. Anencephaly occurs in the United States at a rate that ranges from .50 to 1.00 per 1,000 births. Rosner, Risemberg, Bennett, Cassell, Farnsworth, Landoldt, Loeb, Numann, Ona, Sechzer & Sordillo, The Anencephalic Fetus and Newborn as Organ Donors, 1988 N.Y. St. J. Med. 360, 360. Some studies estimate that the number of anencephalics born each year in the United States is between 1,000 and 1,800, Subcommittee Hearings, supra note 11, at 6, while the Centers for Disease Control puts the number as high as between 2000 and 3000. Capron, supra note 3, at 5.

19. Anencephaly arises during the process of neurulation, a well-defined period between the seventeenth and thirtieth day after ovulation. Lemire, Neural Tube Defects, 259 J. A.M.A. 558, 558 (1988). Other such defects include microcephaly (an abnormally small head), encephalocele (in which some of the meninges and brain tissue are outside of the skull) and holoprosencephaly (in which the brain does not properly divide into hemispheres).

20. Nakano, Anencephaly: A Review, 15 Developmental Med. & Child Neurology 383, 384 (1973). The brain has three general anatomic divisions that perform different tasks. The cerebrum is usually referred to as the "higher brain" because it controls consciousness, thought, language, memory and feeling. The cerebellum is the structure responsible for the regulation and coordination of complex voluntary muscular movement. The brainstem, which is composed of the midbrain, the pons and the medulla oblongata, is also known as the "lower brain" because it controls the spontaneous, vegetative functions such as respiration, blood pressure, temperature, swallowing, yawning and neuroendocrine control. See President's Comm'n for the Study of Ethical Problems in Medicine and Biomedical and Behavioral Research, Defining Death: A Report on the Medical, Legal and Ethical Issues in the Determination of Death 15 (1981) [hereinafter Defining Death]; Smith, Legal Recognition of Neocortical Death, 71 Cornell L. Rev. 850, 857 (1986). Scientists acknowledge, though, that the physical location of neurological functions may not be as compartmentalized as this. See infra notes 222–23 and accompanying text.

pearance of an anencephalic is unique: the vault of the skull (in which the cerebrum is located) is absent, the brain appears as a mass of exposed tissue,[21] and the infant's face has but "a short forehead that just slopes off and goes down to the neck."[22] Because of these remarkable features, the diagnosis of anencephaly[23] is unmistakable.[24]

Since it possesses no cerebrum, an anencephalic can never experience consciousness.[25] Even its rudimentary brainstem is insufficient to maintain spontaneous biological activity for very long; 40% of all anencephalics are stillborn, while of the remainder 65% die within the first day of life, an additional 30% die by the end of the first week and only 1.5% survive as long as one month.[26] For the same reasons, the prospects of a cure for anencephaly are nonexistent. Instead, efforts at combatting the condition are focused on identifying its etiology[27] and preventing its occurrence.[28] In short, it is a defect which is "incompatible with life."[29]

The diagnosis of anencephaly is often made prenatally,[30] giving parents ample time to consider how best to cope with the situation.

---

21. Nakano, supra note 20, at 384.

22. Ricks, Scientists Hunt for Cause of "Brain-Missing Babies," U.P.I. (Regional News), Dec. 22, 1987 (quoting Dr. William Goldie).

23. In liveborn anencephalic infants the condition is diagnosed by the depressed skull and protruding eyes. Nakano, supra note 20, at 384.

24. See Arras & Shinnar, supra note 3, at 2284; Parachini, Science, Ethics Clash over Infant Organ Donations Bill, L.A. Times, Dec. 2, 1986, § 5, at 1, col. 2, 5, col. 4 (quoting Dr. Michael Harrison, transplant surgeon, Univ. of Cal. at San Francisco).

25. See supra note 20 and accompanying text.

26. Baird & Sadovnick, Survival in Infants with Anencephaly, 23 Clinical Pediatrics 268, 270 (1984); Subcommittee Hearings, supra note 11, at 64 (testimony of Leslie Rothenberg, Adjunct Assistant Professor of Medicine and Director, Program in Medical Ethics, UCLA Medical Center). A recent intensive study of anencephaly reports one case of survival for as long as fourteen months but cautions that cases of unusually long survival may have been erroneously diagnosed as anencephaly. Medical Task Force on Anencephaly, The Infant with Anencephaly, 322 New Eng. J. Med. 669, 671 (1990).

27. No firm conclusions have been reached as to the cause of anencephaly, but many epidemiological clues have been pursued. Among the environmental factors that some scientists believe are related to the occurrence of anencephaly are the ingestion of nitrite-cured meat, blighted potatoes, salicylites, hard water, antineoplastic and anticonvulsant drugs, as well as anesthetics and infectious agents. Lemire, supra note 19, at 559. Others speculate that nutrient deficiencies may lie at the root of the problem. Stevenson, Kelly, Aylsworth & Phelan, Vascular Basis for Neural Tube Defects: A Hypothesis, 80 Pediatrics 102, 102 (1987).

28. There is some evidence that vitamin supplementation during pregnancy can reduce the risk of giving birth to an anencephalic baby. See Smithells, Sheppard, Schorah, Seller, Nevin, Harris, Read & Fielding, Apparent Prevention of Neural Tube Defects by Periconceptional Vitamin Supplementation, 56 Archives of Disease in Childhood 911 (1981).

29. Ricks, supra note 22.

30. Pregnancies involving neural tube defects, such as anencephaly, exhibit higher levels of alpha-fetoprotein (AFP) in the amniotic fluid. See Randle, Alpha-Fetoprotein Levels in Amniotic Fluid in Normal Pregnancy and in Pregnancy Complicated by Anencephaly, 80 J. Obstetrics & Gynaecolology Brit. Commonwealth 1054, 1054 (1973).

Several parents have rejected the option to undergo a therapeutic abortion, choosing instead to carry the fetus to term despite the additional hardships that such a course usually entails.[31] They generally do so in the hope of wresting some positive meaning from this tragedy by donating their child's organs to other imperiled newborns[32] whose lives can be saved by such donations.[33] Because the anencephalic's organs (other than the brain) develop normally, it is a suitable transplant donor.[34] To the surprise of those parents, such efforts have met an obstacle created in part by the realities of medicine and in part by the laws of society.[35] The complication arises from the way in which an

---

By the 13th to 15th week of pregnancy, AFP reaches peak levels, allowing diagnosis and confirmation by either ultrasound or amniocentesis. Lemire, supra note 19, at 559.

31. See, e.g., Blakeslee, supra note 14, at A18, col. 1; Fost, Organs from Anencephalic Infants: An Idea Whose Time Has Not Yet Come, Hastings Center Rep., Oct.–Nov. 1988, at 5 (pressure to permit organ donation comes in large part from parents of anencephalic infants).

Some evidence suggests that the increase in prenatal detection of anencephaly will mean a sharp drop in the availability of these donors as more women will choose to terminate such pregnancies. For example, in California about 50% of all pregnancies are screened during the second trimester, and approximately 95% of the detected anencephalics have been electively aborted. See Shewmon, Anencephaly: Selected Medical Aspects, Hastings Center Rep., Oct.–Nov. 1988, at 11, 12; see also Medearis & Holmes, supra note 3, at 392 (similar findings in study of Boston hospital).

However, these statistics are far from conclusive. First, as the authors of these studies concede, data from California and Boston are atypical of the nation as a whole. See Shewmon, supra, at 12; Medearis & Holmes, supra note 3, at 391. Mandatory offering of AFP screening has been in effect in California since 1986, and the urbanized, highly educated population served by Brigham and Women's Hospital is probably more apt to request prenatal screening than a similar sample from elsewhere in the country. Second, the large number of elective abortions is not surprising given the current legal climate, which makes organ procurement from anencephalics exceedingly difficult. One might well expect more willingness on the part of expectant mothers to complete their pregnancies if such legal strictures were removed. Finally, the question of whether to permit the use of anencephalics as donors is one that can and should be considered independently of the quantitative benefits to be expected therefrom, for saving even a few lives is an achievement of major significance.

32. See, e.g., Blakeslee, supra note 14, at A18, col. 1.

33. See id.; Rovner, Infants Without Brains, Washington Post, Jan. 26, 1988, Health Section, at 16, col. 1. Up to five children can be saved from the organs donated by one. See Rosner, Risemberg, Bennett, Cassell, Farnsworth, Landoldt, Loeb, Numann, Ona, Sechzer & Sordillo, supra note 18, at 361.

34. See Flake, Harrison, Sauer, Adzick, LaBerge, Krummel & Thaler, Auxiliary Transplantation of the Fetal Liver II: Functional Evaluation Of an Intraabdominal Model, 22J. Pediatric Surgery 559, 562 (1987); Peabody, Emery & Ashwal, supra note 2, at 349; cf. Botkin, Anencephalic Infants as Organ Donors, 82 Pediatrics 250, 251 (1988) (finding somewhat higher rate of malformation in organs from anencephalics, "but not to a degree that would preclude their use in transplantation."). But cf. Baird & Sadovnick, Congenital Malformations Associated with Anencephaly in Liveborn and Stillborn Infants, 32 Teratology 355 (1985) (finding a higher than normal incidence of abnormalities in anencephalic infants in organs other than the brain).

35. During the late 1960s a few medical centers in the United States and France did attempt to utilize organs obtained from anencephalics for transplantation to other in-

anencephalic dies. Because of the lack of higher brain function, the baby's respiratory system intermittently lapses. These incidents repeat with increasing frequency until respiration ceases entirely, by which time the baby's oxygen-starved organs are so severely damaged that they are no longer suitable for transplantation.[36]

II. LEGAL OBSTACLES TO UTILIZING ANENCEPHALICS AS DONORS

The only course of action open to transplant surgeons is to remove the necessary organs from the anencephalic sometime during the infant's brief life span, preferably as close to birth as possible. Because the impending birth of an anencephalic is usually known weeks in advance,[37] it is often feasible for the medical team involved to locate an appropriate recipient and arrange for the transplant to be performed at the optimal time.[38] However, removal of the donor's vital organs would immediately result in termination of the infant's heartbeat and respiration, thereby exposing the physician who performed the procedure to homicide charges. From the standpoint of criminal law, therefore, two inquiries are relevant. First, had the donor's life commenced? Then, if the answer is affirmative, was the donor considered legally dead before the removal of its organs? Under current statutes, the answer to both questions is straightforward.

A. *Life's Beginning: The Live Birth Rule*

The law of homicide requires that the victim be a living human being. At common law, the killing of a fetus was not homicide unless the fetus had been "born alive."[39] Being born alive required that the fetus be totally expelled from the mother and demonstrate "a clear sign of independent vitality," such as respiration, although respiration was

---

fants. The results of one such series of experiments at an American medical center were sufficiently encouraging to induce the researchers involved in the surgery to continue. However, the transplants stopped when the legal concerns discussed herein were raised regarding the eligibility of anencephalics for organ donation. See Martin & Noseworthy, Surgical Aspects of Transplantation: Technique and Complications, *in* End Stage Renal Disease, supra note 10, at 458, 463; see also Martin, Gonzalez, West, Swartz & Sutorius, Homotransplantation of Both Kidneys from an Anencephalic Monster to a 17-Pound Boy with Eagle-Barrett Syndrome, 66 Surgery 603 (1969).

36. See Peabody, Emery & Ashwal, supra note 2, at 349; Rovner, supra note 33, Health Section, at 16, col. 1.

37. See supra note 30 and accompanying text.

38. See Discussion of Bailey, Donor Organs from Human Anencephalics: A Salutary Resource for Infant Heart Transplantation, Transplantation Proc., Aug. 1988, Supp. 5 at 39, 39–40; Blakeslee, supra note 14, at A18, col. 1 (after an anencephalic donor was identified, doctors performed a premature cesarean section on a second infant suffering congenital heart disease in order to procure the donor heart at the optimal time).

39. Shedd v. State, 178 Ga. 653, 654, 173 S.E. 847, 847 (1934); Adrams v. Foshee, 3 Iowa 273, 279 (1856); Jackson v. Commonwealth, 265 Ky. 295, 296, 96 S.W.2d 1014, 1014 (1936).

not strictly required.[40] In the United States, the "born alive" requirement[41] has come to mean that once the fetus is "fully brought forth" from the body of its mother[42] it is considered a human being.[43] This conclusion is supported by *Roe v. Wade*,[44] which implies (in dictum) that live birth is both a necessary and sufficient condition for the existence of human life to which homicide laws might attach.[45] Since the portions of the anencephalic's brain that control breathing are intact,[46] these infants are capable of spontaneous respiration. Thus, upon birth they qualify as "human beings" under the relevant homicide statutes.

B. *The Meaning of Death*

1. *Legal Standards of Death.* — Because the precise location of the line dividing life and death significantly affects legal outcomes in diverse areas,[47] the law has always fixed definitive criteria of death. Historically, the absence of heartbeat and breathing were accepted by the medical profession and the common law as the definitive criteria of death.[48] No close scrutiny or penetrating inquiry was needed to vali-

---

40. Atkinson, Life, Birth, and Live-Birth, 20 L.Q. Rev. 134, 135 (1904).

41. This requirement is generally followed in the modern cases. See, e.g., People v. Greer, 79 Ill. 2d 103, 116, 402 N.E.2d 203, 209 (1980); Hollis v. Commonwealth, 652 S.W.2d 61, 62 (Ky. 1983); State v. Gyles, 313 So. 2d 799, 800–01 (La. 1975).

Some of the modern codes define a person for purposes of the law of homicide as meaning a human being who has been born and was alive at the time of the homicidal act. See, e.g., Ala. Code § 13A-6-1 (1982); Alaska Stat. § 11.41.140 (1989); Colo. Rev. Stat. § 18-3-101 (1986); Del. Code Ann. tit. 11, § 222(18) (1987); Hawaii Rev. Stat. § 707-700 (1988); Mont. Code Ann. § 45-2-101(27) (1989) (defining "human being"); Neb. Rev. Stat. § 28-302 (1989); N.Y. Penal Law § 125.05 (McKinney 1987); Tex. Penal Code Ann. § 1.07(17) (Vernon 1974) (defining "individual"). This is also the definition in Model Penal Code § 210.0(1) (1980).

42. Jackson v. Commonwealth, 265 Ky. 295, 296, 96 S.W.2d 1014, 1014 (1936). Some cases add that the child must have established an "independent circulation." See State v. Winthrop, 43 Iowa 519, 523 (1876); cf. Wallace v. State, 10 Tex. App. 255, 271 (1881) (finding that respiration conclusively establishes requirement of independent circulation).

43. See, e.g., Hodgson v. Anderson, 378 F. Supp. 1008, 1017 (D. Minn. 1974) (a fetus who is "born alive and is capable of living independently of its mother . . . becomes a person—protected by the usual constitutional rights"), appeal dismissed on other grounds sub nom. Spannaus v. Hodgson, 420 U.S. 903 (1975), aff'd in part and rev'd in part on other grounds sub nom. Hodgson v. Lawson, 542 F.2d 1350 (8th Cir. 1976); Maine Medical Center v. Houle, No. 74-145, slip op. at 4 (Mc. Super. Ct. Feb. 14, 1974) (brain-damaged child born with severe physical malformations was nonetheless "at the moment of live birth . . . a human being entitled to the fullest protection of the law").

44. 410 U.S. 113 (1973).

45. Id. at 161 ("In areas other than criminal abortion, the law has been reluctant to endorse any theory that life, as we recognize it, begins before live birth . . ..").

46. See supra note 34 and accompanying text.

47. See infra notes 51–53 and accompanying text.

48. See Defining Death, supra note 20, at 5; see also Smith v. Smith, 229 Ark. 579, 586, 317 S.W.2d 275, 279 (1958); In re Estate of Schmidt, 261 Cal. App. 2d 262, 273, 67 Cal. Rptr. 847, 854 (1968).

date the cardiopulmonary standard in the minds of the medical and legal communities. Whether the standard was appropriate because heart and lung function deserved special significance in interpreting the phenomenon of death, or whether it was merely a convenient signpost indicating that death (whatever "death" may mean) had already occurred was a moot question. Until the medical profession became capable of artificially maintaining respiratory and cardiac functions, there was no need to consider such issues; at the time a person's heart or lungs ceased functioning the complete deterioration of all other organs followed immediately. For practical purposes, the entire individual died all at once.[49]

The advent of the artificial respirator, along with sophisticated techniques for sustaining comatose patients, transformed the "simple" process of dying.[50] Medical science became capable of supporting the biological functions of such patients for long periods of time, even in the complete absence of brain function.

These new technologies created uncertainties which forced society to reexamine established notions of death. For instance, should a life insurance company be able to deny death benefits to the spouse of a comatose patient who will never regain any brain function?[51] May the decision of when to terminate the life-support systems of such patients turn on considerations of maximizing tax advantages?[52] Suppose a criminal shoots someone in the head and causes the victim to fall into an irreversible coma, sustained only by artificial ventilation. Should the

---

49. See K. Gervais, Redefining Death 2 (1986).

For situations in which the precise moment of death did matter, the common law clung to the cardiopulmonary standard with a tenacity that sometimes produced absurd results. A cogent example is Gray v. Sawyer, 247 S.W.2d 496 (Ky. 1952), in which a husband and wife were killed by a locomotive and the issue of survivorship became important to determine inheritance. A newly discovered witness testified that the wife, decapitated, was bleeding "from near her neck and blood was gushing from her body in spurts." The court accepted the testimony of doctors who "expressed the opinion that Mrs. Gugel had survived her husband for a fleeting moment" because "a body is not dead so long as there is a heart beat and that may be evidenced by the gushing of blood in spurts." Id. at 497.

50. Respiration is normally accomplished by neural impulses from the brain that stimulate the muscles in the diaphragm to expand, causing the lungs to fill with air. Therefore, in the complete absence of brain function, unaided respiration cannot take place. The artificial respirator (or ventilator) is a mechanical device that performs the function of the thoracic muscles and also controls the rate and depth of breathing. Defining Death, supra note 20, at 15–16. Associated advances in medical technology that prolonged the process of dying include intravenous hydration, nasogastric feeding and bladder catheterization. Id. at 21.

51. See Thornton & Staff, Death and the Life Insurance Policy: What Hath Modern Medicine Wrought?, 36 Okla. L. Rev. 285, 290–91 (1983).

52. See Jorrie & Standley, The Tax Advantages of Lingering Death, 48 Tex. B. J. 1070, 1072–73 (1985) (recommending that tax attorneys obtain a durable power of attorney to delay or withhold death directives from attending physicians in order to achieve favorable tax treatment by delaying the moment of death).

defendant be acquitted on grounds that the removal of the victim from the respirator by the physician is a superseding cause of death because under a cardiopulmonary standard the victim was alive after the shooting?[53]

Additional strong incentives existed to update criteria of death. The rise in transplant surgery was one such factor, since the viability of organs drops rapidly after respiration and circulation stop.[54] The prime candidates for organ donation are otherwise healthy persons who have suffered fatal head injuries but are biologically sustained on artificial respirators. Even the organs of these potential donors will deteriorate over time. Therefore, commentators began to argue in favor of expanding the definition of death in order to facilitate organ transplants.[55] Many commentators also felt that the utilization of scarce and costly medical resources for patients who would never regain any brain function needlessly prolonged the psychological and financial strain on grieving families and prevented some patients with reversible conditions from gaining access to such facilities.[56]

Accompanying these pressures to update the legal definition of death were medical advances that made it possible to accurately determine the irreversible loss of all brain functions. One of the earliest and most well-known efforts in this process, a 1968 report issued by the Harvard Medical School (later referred to as the "Harvard Criteria"), provided a three-part test for determining when brain death has occurred.[57]

In response to these fundamental social and medical changes,

---

53. See, e.g., People v. Eulo, 63 N.Y.2d 341, 355, 472 N.E.2d 286, 294, 482 N.Y.S.2d 436, 444 (1984) (judicial construction of statutory term, "death," to embrace a determination that a person has suffered irreversible cessation of the functioning of the entire brain, despite absence of statute specifically recognizing "brain death").

54. See supra note 8 and accompanying text.

55. See Defining Death, supra note 20, at 23.

56. Id. at 24.

57. These criteria are:

1) *Unreceptivity and unresponsivity.* The patient shows a total unawareness to externally applied stimuli and inner need, and complete unresponsiveness, even when intensely painful stimuli are being applied.

2) *No movements or breathing.* All spontaneous muscular movement, spontaneous respiration, and response to stimuli such as pain, touch, sound or light are absent.

3) *No reflexes.* Among the indications of absent reflexes are: fixed, dilated pupils; lack of eye movement even when the head is turned or ice water is placed in the ear; lack of response to noxious stimuli; and generally, unelicitable tendon reflexes.

Ad Hoc Comm. of the Harvard Medical School to Examine the Definition of Brain Death, A Definition of Irreversible Coma. 205 J. A.M.A. 337, 337–38 (1968).

In addition, a flat electroencephalogram (EEG) was recommended as a confirmatory test, and all tests were to be repeated at least 24 hours later without showing change. See id. Less stringent criteria have since been proposed for determining whole brain

thirty-five states and the District of Columbia have enacted statutory definitions of death that include a provision for brain death.[58] Nineteen of those jurisdictions[59] have patterned their statutes after the Uniform Determination of Death Act (UDDA),[60] a model statute drafted in 1980 that adopts an alternative test under which an individual who meets either the cardiopulmonary or brain death standard of death is considered dead.[61] Significantly, every such statute yet adopted requires that "whole brain death" occur in order to satisfy the "brain death" prong of the test.[62] In addition, a Presidential Commis-

---

death. *See, e.g.,* Cranford, Minnesota Medical Association Criteria: Brain Death: Concept and Criteria, 61 Minn. Med. 600 (1978).

58. Ala. Code § 22-31-1(b) (1975); Alaska Stat. § 09.65.120 (1983); Ark. Stat. Ann. §§ 82-537 to -538 (1976 & Supp. 1985); Cal. Health & Safety Code §§ 7180–7183 (West 1970 & Supp. 1986); Colo. Rev. Stat. § 12-36-136 (1977 & Supp. 1985); Conn. Gen. Stat. Ann. § 19a-278(b) (West 1985 Special Pamphlet); D.C. Code Ann. § 6-2401 (1982); Fla. Stat. Ann. § 382.009 (West 1986 & Supp. 1990); Ga. Code Ann. § 88-1716 (1979 & Supp. 1984); Hawaii Rev. Stat. § 327C-1 (1976 & Supp. 1984); Idaho Code § 54-1819 (1981); Ill. Ann. Stat. ch. 110 1/2, ¶ 302 (Smith-Hurd 1978); Iowa Code Ann. § 702.8 (West 1976); Kan. Stat. Ann. § 77-205 (1984); La. Rev. Stat. Ann. § 9:111 (West 1965 & Supp. 1986); Me. Rev. Stat. Ann. tit. 22, §§ 2811–2813 (1964 & Supp. 1985); Md. Health-Gen. Code Ann. §§ 5-201 to -202 (1982 & Supp. 1985); Mich. Comp. Laws Ann. § 333.1021 (West 1980); Miss. Code Ann. § 41-36-3 (1981); Mo. Ann. Stat. § 194.005 (Vernon 1983); Mont. Code Ann. § 50-22-101 (1983); Nev. Rev. Stat. § 451.007 (1979); N.M. Stat. Ann. § 12-2-4 (1978); N.C. Gen. Stat. § 90-323 (1985); Ohio Rev. Code Ann. § 2108.30 (Baldwin 1987); Okla. Stat. Ann. tit. 63, § 1-301(g) (West 1975); Or. Rev. Stat. § 146.001 (1984); Pa. Stat. Ann. tit. 35, §§ 10201–10203 (Purdon Supp. 1984); R.I. Gen. Laws § 23-4-16 (1985); Tenn. Code Ann. § 68-3-501 (1982); Tex. Rev. Civ. Stat. Ann. art. 4447t (Vernon 1976 & Supp. 1986); Vt. Stat. Ann. tit. 18, § 5218 (1968 & Supp. 1985); Va. Code Ann. § 541.1-2972 (1988); W. Va. Code §§ 16-10-1 to -3 (1985); Wis. Stat. § 146.71 (Supp. 1985); Wyo. Stat. § 35-19-101 (Supp. 1985).

59. Statutes of this type exist in California, Colorado, the District of Columbia, Georgia, Idaho, Kansas, Maine, Maryland, Mississippi, Montana, New Mexico, Ohio, Oregon, Pennsylvania, Rhode Island, Tennessee, Vermont, Virginia and Wisconsin. *See supra* note 58.

60. 12 U.L.A. 322–23 (Supp. 1990).

61. The UDDA provides:

§ 1. [Determination of Death]. An individual who has sustained either (1) irreversible cessation of circulatory and respiratory functions, or (2) irreversible cessation of all functions of the entire brain, including the brain stem, is dead. A determination of death must be made in accordance with accepted medical standards.

§ 2. [Uniformity of Construction and Application]. This Act shall be applied and construed to effectuate its general purpose to make uniform the law with respect to the subject of this Act among states enacting it.

62. The term "whole brain death" refers to the total and irreversible dysfunction of all components in the intracranial cavity, including both cerebral hemispheres, brain stem and cerebellum. Korein, The Problem of Brain Death: Development and History, 315 Annals N.Y. Acad. Sci. 19, 20 (1978). The concept implies the loss of integrated functioning among the various systems of the body, a task accomplished by the brain during life. It does not, however, imply the destruction of every neuron in the brain or the cessation of metabolic activity on the cellular level. Defining Death, *supra* note 20, at 33.

sion[63] appointed to study, among other topics, the "ethical and legal implications of . . . the matter of defining death, including the advisability of developing a uniform definition of death"[64] issued a report endorsing the adoption of the UDDA.[65] No state has yet adopted a "higher brain function" or "neocortical" standard, which would define death in terms of the irreversible cessation of cognitive, nonspontaneous brain activity that precludes the possibility of any form of consciousness.[66]

The cardiopulmonary, whole brain and neocortical models differ sharply in diagnostic practice. Under the older, more restrictive, cardiopulmonary statutes, a person who has lost all brain function but whose breathing is being maintained by mechanical support systems is not considered "dead." Persons who are brain dead but continue to breathe with the aid of a mechanical respirator *are* considered dead in jurisdictions that have adopted whole brain definitions of death. Finally, the neocortical standard is most expansive in that it classifies even individuals who can breathe on their own as dead if they lack all higher brain functions.

The higher brain concept also represents a philosophical view of death fundamentally different from that embodied in either the whole brain or cardiopulmonary formulations. The former equates personhood with consciousness and the cognitive functions, arguing that since these abilities are what set humanity apart from other species, their loss can be equated with death.[67] In contrast, proponents of the

---

63. Legislation creating the President's Commission for the Study of Ethical Problems in Biomedical and Behavioral Research was enacted in Pub. L. 95-622, 92 Stat. 3412, 3438 (1978) (codified at 42 U.S.C. § 300v (1982)).

64. Id. at 3439 (codified at 42 U.S.C. § 300v-1(a)(1)(B)).

65. Defining Death, supra note 20, at 2. For a general discussion defending the Commission's choice of the whole brain standard, see id. at 31–43.

66. "Neocortical death" refers to the destruction of the two cerebral hemispheres, which together comprise the cerebrum. Korein, supra note 62, at 21. Consciousness, thought, memory and feeling are located in the cerebrum, while the brainstem and cerebellum, which continue to function after neocortical death, control spontaneous functions such as respiration, swallowing, yawning and sleep-wake cycles. See supra note 20. The terms "irreversible noncognitive state," "persistent vegetative state," "appalic syndrome" and "cerebral death" are used interchangeably with "neocortical death." Korein, supra note 62, at 21. The term does not encompass the state known as "locked-in syndrome," in which all four extremities and the lower cranial nerves are paralyzed yet the patient still retains consciousness. F. Plum & J. Posner, The Diagnosis of Stupor and Coma 6 (3d ed. 1980).

Several commentators have suggested that a neocortical standard should be adopted. See Buchanan, The Limits of Proxy Decisionmaking for Incompetents, 29 UCLA L. Rev. 386, 403–06 (1981); Kluge, The Euthanasia of Radically Defective Neonates: Some Statutory Considerations, 6 Dalhousie L.J. 229, 249–54 (1980); Smith, supra note 20, at 852.

67. If neocortical functions—the capacity to think, feel, communicate, or experience our environment—are the key to human life, then the loss of neocortical functions should be the key to human death. If the irreversible loss of an or-

whole brain view maintain that it represents merely an updated set of criteria to diagnose death, but that the underlying phenomenon being diagnosed is identical whether traditional cardiopulmonary criteria or whole brain criteria are used.[68] According to these proponents, breathing and circulation were never held to constitute "life" in and of themselves; they were merely conclusive evidence of integrated functioning among the interdependent bodily systems. Immediately upon cessation of respiration and heartbeat, the brain would die, and death would occur when the various systems of the body ceased to function as an integrated whole. The introduction of mechanical life-support systems succeeded in camouflaging this reality by artificially maintaining each subsystem individually—the respirator, heart pump, drugs and other medical resources each performing one function of the lower brain.[69] Criteria of whole brain death permit physicians to recognize this fact and declare patients in such a condition to be dead.

2. *Applying the Legal Standards to Anencephalics.* — At birth, the anencephalic neonate can breathe without the aid of any mechanical means. Unlike cardiac function, which is involuntary and can continue independently of the brain, respiratory activity can occur only when the lungs receive the appropriate neural impulses from the brain.[70] Since anencephalics at birth are capable of spontaneous respiration, they clearly have not reached the point of total cessation of brain function. Therefore, they do not satisfy the requirements set forth in either the whole brain death statutes or (a fortiori) the statutes which refer solely to cardiopulmonary and respiratory activity as the determinant of death. Therefore, under current criminal statutes, the procurement of vital organs from an independently breathing anencephalic newborn would be considered the proximate cause of the baby's death, and the physician who procured such organs would be open to homicide charges.[71] The fact that an anencephalic infant certainly would have

---

ganism's essentially significant attributes characterizes death, and if in humans the significant attributes are the capacity for consciousness and higher cortical functions rather than for autonomic bodily integration, then people who have lost these distinguishing features of human life should be treated as dead.

Smith, supra note 20, at 860.

68. See Korein, supra note 62, at 27. The President's Commission similarly declared: "Thus, brain-based criteria do not introduce a new 'kind of death,' but rather reinforce the concept of death as a single phenomenon—the collapse of psycho-physical integrity. The statute merely allows new ways to recognize that this phenomenon has occurred." Defining Death, supra note 20, at 58. But see K. Gervais, supra note 49, at 16–44 (arguing that whole brain death criteria represent a fundamental departure from traditional cardiac-centered standards).

69. See Defining Death, supra note 20, at 32–33.

70. Id. at 16.

71. Analogous suits have arisen against doctors for removing organs for transplantation from patients declared dead on the basis of brain-oriented criteria in jurisdictions where no law recognizing a brain death standard had been enacted. See, e.g., Ain, DA Warns on Organ Removal, N.Y. Daily News, May 9, 1984, at 23. In jurisdictions that

died anyway within a matter of hours or days does not constitute a defense for the physician who intervenes by removing the child's organs, for it is well settled that the merest shortening of human life is punishable as homicide.[72] Furthermore, the common law has for centuries held that one may not give up one's own life or authorize another to take it.[73] Therefore, the proxy consent obtained from the parents of the donor cannot serve as a valid defense to the charge of homicide any more than the direct consent would have had the child been capable of giving it. Anencephalics cannot serve as organ donors until they have reached the stage of whole brain death, at which point their organs are damaged beyond repair and are no longer suitable for transplantation.

III. THE SEARCH FOR SOLUTIONS

There exist two possible approaches to solve the difficulties in obtaining organs from anencephalics. One solution is to amend existing statutes in a manner that would enable anencephalics to be used as donors. The second method is to attempt to obtain organs from these infants without violating the law. This technique requires physicians to maintain artificial ventilation of the neonate while "hoping" that the infant's brain will fail (due to any number of possible causes) within a short time after birth. One hospital has developed such a pioneering effort, but, as is sometimes the case, the cure proved worse than the disease.

A. The Loma Linda Protocol

1. *A Brief Description.* — On December 18, 1987, Loma Linda University Medical Center released the first protocol in the United States developed to deal with the use of anencephalics as organ donors.[74] It

---

have adopted the whole brain definition of death, the intentional termination of the life of a person who has not yet reached the point of total cessation of brain function (e.g., a vegetative patient) is punishable as homicide. Thus, in a recent Florida case a young father who shot and killed his irreversibly unconscious three year old daughter received a mandatory sentence of twenty-five years to life. See Griffith v. State, No. 73,998 (Fla. Sup. Ct. Mar. 29, 1990) (Westlaw Fla. Library). With regard specifically to anencephalics, a Pitt County, North Carolina grand jury returned an indictment against two hospital employees accused of causing the death of an anencephalic baby by mechanical compression of the infant's chest. See Mother Wants Former Hospital Employees Prosecuted, A.P. (Domestic News), Apr. 30, 1985. There is little reason to doubt that the removal of organs for transplant purposes from an anencephalic would similarly qualify for criminal sanctions under current law.

72. Commonwealth v. Bowen, 13 Mass. 356 (1816) (willfully accelerating death, by however short a space of time, involves the full guilt of murder); accord Regina v. Murton, 176 Eng. Rep. 221, 222 (1862).

73. See O. Temkin, W. Frankena & S. Kadish, Respect for Life in Medicine, Philosophy, and the Law 76 (1977) (citing John Locke, The Second Treatise of Government, in Two Treatises of Government § 6, at 288–89, § 135, at 375–76 (P. Laslett ed. 1960)).

74. See Sahagun & Steinbrook, Hospital Issues Policy on Brain-Dead Babies' Use as Organ Donors, L.A. Times, Dec. 19, 1987, Part I, at 33, col. 1. The protocol was discon-

set forth guidelines under which such infants could be utilized as donors in a manner consistent with applicable brain death statutes. Under the protocol, babies born with anencephaly would be sustained with a respirator for a maximum of seven days.[75] During that period, doctors would remove the respirator every twelve hours in order to determine whether brain death had occurred.[76] To avoid any conflicts of interest, such a determination would be made by two Loma Linda physicians unaffiliated with the transplantation team, and, if necessary, an outside consultant would confirm the findings.[77] This artificial ventilation preserved the baby's organs in a condition suitable for transplantation, so that if brain death did occur during the prescribed period the organs could be immediately used. Finally, in order to ensure proper respect for the newborn, the protocol specified that babies who were not yet brain dead at the end of seven days would have their life support discontinued and be allowed to die.

2. *A Critical Evaluation.* — The Loma Linda protocol represents a valiant effort to please everyone: to accede to the wishes of grieving parents seeking to salvage some meaning from their child's brief life, to provide desperately needed organs for critically ill newborns, and to comply with relevant brain death statutes. As is common with such efforts, the protocol ultimately failed to please anyone.

Dissatisfaction of the medical community resulted from uncertainty as to whether anencephalic babies are capable of experiencing pain.[78] If they do feel pain, artificially prolonging the lives of these infants by hooking them up to respirators would inflict additional pain upon unconsenting subjects solely for the benefit of others. Since organ removal for transplantation can be accomplished painlessly under

---

tinued for further study after trials with 12 infants resulted in no transplants. See Peabody, Emery & Ashwal, supra note 2, at 350.

75. Anencephalic Organ Donation Comm. of Loma Linda Univ. Medical Center, Considerations of Anencephalic Infants as Organ Donors: A Working Document 3 (1987) [hereinafter Protocol].

76. Id. at 4.

77. Sahagun & Steinbrook, supra note 74, Part I, at 33, col. 1.

78. The grimaces and crying of these children have convinced some physicians that they can feel pain, even though they are missing the portions of the brain that apparently respond to pain stimuli. See Rovner, supra note 33; see also Discussion of Outstanding Issues, Transplantation Proc., Aug. 1988, Supp. 5, at 69, 71 [hereinafter Outstanding Issues]. Indeed, even in the case of brain dead patients who have lost all brain function, there remain doubts about whether they cannot experience pain. As one commentator noted, "[t]he UAGA and brain death statutes, even if enough to guarantee the diagnostic certainty of brain death in the case of organ donation, do not assure that a biomort is brain dead to the extent that it experiences no pain when maintained over a prolonged period of time." Martyn, Using the Brain Dead for Medical Research, 1986 Utah L. Rev. 1, 15.

Other physicians, however, categorically state that anencephalics cannot feel pain. See Paris & Fletcher, Infant Doe Regulations and the Absolute Requirement to Use Nourishment and Fluids for the Dying Infant, 11 L. Med. & Health Care 210, 211 (1983) ("Since they have no brain, they have no perception of pain, no hunger, no suffering.").

anesthesia, the effort to comply with statutory brain death requirements via the Loma Linda protocol performed an indefensible cruelty upon its subjects that otherwise could have been avoided.

Conscious of these criticisms, physicians at Loma Linda proposed to administer a painkiller, Demerol, if the newborns exhibited any signs of distress.[79] That decision, however, could lead to even greater complications in properly diagnosing brain death. One of the crucial prerequisites to adopting the whole brain definition of death in many states was that the clinical indicators used be completely reliable.[80] Moreover, one of the primary reasons for rejecting a neocortical standard of death in favor of whole brain death was the relative lack of certainty involved in the diagnosis of neocortical death.[81] However, there are four complicating conditions in whose presence brain death cannot be diagnosed with certainty.[82] The first such condition is ingestion of certain sedative drugs.[83] The irony of the Loma Linda protocol is therefore apparent. Anencephalics cannot be utilized as organ donors at birth because the states have rejected a neocortical standard of death in favor of a whole brain death standard. That choice was predicated upon the greater reliability of diagnosis involved in whole brain death. Yet, by attempting to comply with the brain death statute, physicians are forced to administer drugs whose effect is to render the diagnosis of death much less reliable than corresponding tests for determining neocortical death in patients who are not receiving drugs.

In order to alleviate these concerns, physicians at Loma Linda proposed to administer another drug, Narcan, to counter the effects of the Demerol.[84] However, even if such measures proved successful in neutralizing the effects of the sedatives, there is another element involved in the protocol that would vitiate the required certainty of brain death.

---

79. Protocol, supra note 75, at 3; see Sahagun & Steinbrook, supra note 74, Part I, at 33, col. 1.

80. See Defining Death, supra note 20, at 25.

81. See Bernat, Culver & Gert, On the Definition and Criterion of Death, 94 Annals Internal Med. 389, 391 (1981); Defining Death, supra note 20, at 40; Korein, supra note 62, at 27; Walton, Epistemology of Brain Death Determination, 2 Metamedicine 259, 270 (1981).

82. Defining Death, supra note 20, at 165–66. Criteria for reliable recognition of brain death are not available in the presence of drug intoxication, hypothermia or shock, nor do reliable criteria exist for diagnosing brain death in infants and young children.

83. The physicians who drafted Guidelines for the President's Commission warned: Drug intoxication is the most serious problem in the determination of death, especially when multiple drugs are used. Cessation of brain functions caused by *the sedative* and anesthetic drugs . . . may be completely reversible even though they produce clinical cessation of brain functions and electrocerebral silence. In cases where there is any likelihood of sedative presence, toxicology screening for all likely drugs is required. If exogenous intoxification is found, death may not be declared until the intoxicant is metabolized or intracranial circulation is tested and found to have ceased.
Defining Death, supra note 20, at 165 (emphasis added).

84. See Sahagun & Steinbrook, supra note 74, Part I, at 33, col. 1.

The criteria for diagnosing brain death have proven less than completely reliable with regard to one sector of society—very young children, particularly newborns.[85] According to one bioethicist, "there are cases of kids popping awake after brain wave instruments indicated they were dead."[86] Thus, while the diagnosis of lack of higher brain function in an anencephalic is 100 percent accurate,[87] the corresponding determination of absence of basal brain function is actually less positive in all newborns than in the general population. Moreover, a task force studying the problem concluded that traditional brain death criteria are inapplicable to infants below the age of seven days.[88] Since the Loma Linda protocol was limited by its own terms to trials not exceeding one week,[89] the attempt to establish brain death in that period seems futile.

A second drawback of the brain-death criteria embodied in the protocol is that they actually fall short of meeting all the requirements specified in standard tests of brain death, even as applied to newborns. Normally, in addition to apnea, a patient must exhibit a lack of reflexes and responses to external stimuli in order to be declared brain dead.[90] However, anencephalics do possess reflexes.[91] Arguably then, the protocol does not even satisfy its own objective of complying with current brain-death statutes. Moreover, the use of less stringent criteria may eventually lead to the relaxation of standards applied to other newborns, for whom extra vigilance is needed to insure that the loss of brain function is irreversible.

In addition to these practical reservations expressed by critics, the protocol also suffers from an ethical defect. The procedures employed by Loma Linda are founded upon the assumption that while it is morally impermissible to remove organs from one human being for the benefit of another, it is nevertheless justifiable to modify the normal

---

85. The medical consultants to the President's Commission described the third condition in which a determination of brain death would be unreliable:

> The brains of infants and young children have increased resistance to damage and may recover substantial functions even after exhibiting unresponsiveness on neurological examination for longer periods than do adults. Physicians should be particularly cautious in applying neurologic criteria to determine death in children younger than five years.

Defining Death, supra note 20, at 166.

86. Blakeslee, supra note 17, at C9, col. 3.

87. See supra note 24 and infra notes 227–28 and accompanying text.

88. Task Force on Brain Death in Children, Guidelines for the Determination of Brain Death in Children, 80 Pediatrics 298, 298 (1987).

89. See supra text accompanying note 75.

90. See supra note 57.

91. Physicians at Loma Linda are not alone in their decision that it is appropriate to modify these criteria in the case of anencephaly. The International Consensus Development Conference on Anencephalic Donors, which met in Ontario, Canada in January 1987, also concluded that the ability to initiate a reflex such as blinking or swallowing is not a vital function of the brain stem and may therefore be dispensed with in this situation. Outstanding Issues, supra note 78, at 73.

course of treatment by prolonging a patient's life solely to benefit others. Yet, in a parallel context, a Congressional commission reached the opposite conclusion.

Following the 1973 Supreme Court decision legalizing abortion, the press reported that live, aborted fetuses were being used for medical research in ways that many people found shocking.[92] In response, Congress created the National Commission for the Protection of Human Subjects of Biomedical and Behavioral Research[93] to study the issue of how to deal with such abortuses in the most appropriate manner. In its report,[94] the Commission distinguished between viable and nonviable fetuses.[95] A viable fetus is to be treated as an infant and not exposed to anything more than minimal experimental risks.[96] More leeway was granted in the use of nonviable fetuses. However, the Commission concluded that no steps should be taken that would terminate the heartbeat or respiration of a nonviable fetus[97] or in any way "alter the duration of life of the nonviable fetus *ex utero*."[98]

The conceptual relationship between the anencephalic newborn and a nonviable fetus *ex utero* is a close one. Both are capable of inde-

---

92. Cases of such research are surveyed in Mahoney, The Nature and Extent of Research Involving Living Human Fetuses, *in* National Comm'n for the Protection of Human Subjects of Biomedical and Behavioral Research, Appendix: Research on the Fetus 1-1 (1975) [hereinafter Appendix]; see also Note, Fetal Experimentation: Moral, Legal, and Medical Implications, 26 Stan. L. Rev. 1191, 1191 (1974) (live, aborted babies have had their chest wall cut open in order to observe their heartbeat).

93. See National Research Act of 1974, Pub. L. No. 93-348, 88 Stat. 342 (codified at U.S.C. § 289l-1 (1982)).

94. National Comm'n for the Protection of Human Subjects of Biomedical and Behavioral Research, Report and Recommendations: Research on the Fetus (1975) [hereinafter Research on the Fetus].

95. The results of the Commission's study were subsequently codified as federal regulations with which all research financially supported by the Department of Health and Human Services must comply. See HHS, Additional Protections Pertaining to Research, Development and Related Activities Involving Fetuses, Pregnant Women, and Human In Vitro Fertilization, 45 C.F.R. §§ 46.201–46.211 (1989). For a summary of the regulations, see Friedman, The Federal Fetal Experimentation Regulations: An Establishment Clause Analysis, 61 Minn. L. Rev. 961, 970–76 (1977).

The federal regulations define a viable fetus as one that is "able, after either spontaneous or induced delivery, to survive (given the benefit of available medical therapy) to the point of independently maintaining heartbeat and respiration." 45 C.F.R. § 46.203(d) (1989). This section also specifies that "[t]he Secretary may from time to time, taking into account medical advances, publish in the Federal Register guidelines to assist in determining whether a fetus is viable for purposes of this subpart." Id. A nonviable fetus is defined as "a fetus *ex utero* which, although living, is not viable." Id. § 46.203(e).

96. Id. § 46.209(a).

97. Id. § 46.209(b)(2).

98. See Research on the Fetus, supra note 94, at 68. This result is codified at 45 C.F.R. § 46.209 (1989), which imposes three conditions that must be met before a nonviable fetus can be used as a subject of research. The first such condition is that vital functions of the fetus will not be artificially maintained. Id. § 46.209(b).

pendently sustaining respiration, albeit for a limited time. Consequently, both qualify under the current statutory framework as living persons. The necessity for protocols such as the one developed at Loma Linda results from the recognition that research on any living subject should comply with such restrictions. The protocol is therefore flawed in its refusal to relate this prohibition to the broader principle of respect for human dignity from which it stems. A complete acceptance of this principle would demand prohibiting interference with the anencephalic's natural lifespan for purposes nonbeneficial to the subject, a restriction that physicians at Loma Linda are unwilling to impose upon themselves.

B. *Proposals For Statutory Change*

One point emerges clearly from the preceding analysis: efforts to utilize anencephalics as organ donors within the framework of existing statutes are fraught with medical, legal and ethical difficulties. The solution is to recognize this fact and amend the law in the most appropriate fashion, an approach that has been attempted in California and New Jersey.

1. *A Brief Description.* — On February 19, 1986, California State Senators Marks, Nielsen and Rosenthal introduced a bill[99] to amend sections 7180–7183 of the California Health and Safety Code, the sections representing California's adoption of the UDDA.[100] The proposed amended sections read as follows:

> 7180. (a) An individual who has sustained either (1) irreversible cessation of circulatory and respiratory functions, or (2) irreversible cessation of all functions of the entire brain, including the brain stem is dead. Additionally, an individual born with the condition of anencephaly is dead. A determination of death must be made in accordance with accepted medical standards.
>
> 7180.5. "Anencephaly," as used in this chapter, means markedly defective development of the brain, together with absence of the bones of the cranial vault and the cerebral and cerebellar hemispheres, and with only a rudimentary brain stem and some traces of basal ganglis present.[101]

---

99. Cal. S. 2018 (1986).

100. Unif. Determination of Death Act, 12 U.L.A. 322–23 (Supp. 1990). The proposed statute is identical to the UDDA except that it adds the provision on anencephaly.

101. The bill also amended sections 7181 and 7182 of the statute to require that the diagnosis of anencephaly be independently determined by another physician not a part of the transplant team. Cal. S. 2018, §§ 3–4 (1988). In addition, section 7183 of the Health and Safety Code was amended to stipulate that the preceding sections 7180–7182 would not become operative unless the United States Department of Health and Human Services made a written finding that the proposed state law was in conformity with federal law and the rules and regulations adopted pursuant to federal law. Id. § 5.

A similar bill permitting organ retrieval from anencephalics was also introduced in the New Jersey State Assembly. In contrast to the California bill, which focuses on modifying the definition of death, the New Jersey version seeks to achieve the same result by amending that state's adoption of the Uniform Anatomical Gift Act (UAGA).[102] Section 2(a) of the UAGA specifies that any gift of organs takes effect upon the death of the donor.[103] The proposed statute would eliminate this requirement in the case of anencephalics.[104]

The introduction of the bill in the California State Legislature created a storm of controversy, questions and uncertainty.[105] Due to the confusion and consternation surrounding the bill, Senator Milton Marks, its primary sponsor, eliminated the proposed substantive changes in the determination-of-death law. In its stead, the legislature passed an amended version of the bill that merely required a state panel to examine the legal, medical and ethical issues pertaining to the original proposal.[106]

2. *The Critics' Views.* — The statutory approach to the problem carries considerable appeal as a way of bypassing the medical obstacles to transplantation by redefining the ground rules. Nevertheless, this method raises problems of its own. Two separate criticisms of the original California proposal effectively underscore the difficulties associated with legislatively altering the status of anencephalics.

Alexander Capron's objection focuses on the distinction between a dying person and one who is dead:

> Adding anencephalics to the category of dead persons would be a radical change, both in the social and medical understanding of what it means to be dead and in the social prac-

---

102. N.J. Stat. Ann. § 26:6-57 to -65 (West 1987 & Supp. 1989). For the 1987 amendments to the UAGA, not adopted in New Jersey, see 8A U.L.A. 2-53 (Supp. 1990).

103. N.J. Stat. Ann. § 26:6-58(a) (West 1987); see also UAGA § 1(1), 8A U.L.A. 7 (Supp. 1990) (containing current uniform provision).

104. The bill, in pertinent part, provides:

A parent of an anencephalic infant, either prior to or upon the birth of that infant, may submit to the attending physician or surgeon a written request for the donation of the body of that infant, or a part thereof, to any of the donees for any of the purposes stated in section 3 of the "Uniform Anatomical Gift Act" . . . to which the attending physician or surgeon shall consent in writing if the requested donation is medically suitable of purpose and safety, and if one of the parents does not object to the donation, regardless of whether the infant has sustained an irreversible cessation of circulatory and respiratory functions or an irreversible cessation of all functions of the brain stem.

State of N.J. Assembly Bill No. 3367 (1986).

105. The commotion was in part due to the confusion by some people of anencephaly with hydrocephaly, a condition commonly known as "water on the brain," that can cause brain damage or death. See Blakeslee, supra note 17, at C9, col. 4. Others were simply unsure about the exact nature of anencephaly and how it differed from other neurologic defects. See Subcommittee Hearings, supra note 11, at 9.

106. See Subcommittee Hearings, supra note 11, at 27–28.

tices surrounding death. Anencephalic infants may be dying, but they are still alive and breathing. Calling them "dead" will not change physiologic reality or otherwise cause them to resemble those (cold and nonrespiring) bodies that are considered appropriate for post-mortem examinations and burial.[107]

Gilbert Meilaender's critique implicitly builds upon Capron's concerns by pointing out that if a dying person is accorded rights then the use of anencephalics as donors violates those rights:

> To intervene in this baby's living and dying in ways we normally reject (because we think it an indignity to a dying subject) would be to do here what we normally think it wrong to do—and to do so for reasons entirely unrelated to the case of Baby Z. What we *accomplish* thereby would be good; what we *do* would not.[108]

IV. LEGAL ANALOGIES SUPPORTING STATUTORY CHANGE

The Article now examines several areas of law as a means of questioning the normative assumptions about the treatment of rights-bearing entities that lie at the heart of the above critiques. The first section of this part focuses on the right to bodily integrity that underlies the objections to any form of nonvoluntary organ procurement. The following sections provide support for the idea that this right is not absolute, particularly in situations where biological life exists only marginally. Part V then follows with an overarching theory of personhood that places these exceptions to the bodily integrity rule in perspective and provides the proposed statutes with a coherent philosophical and legal basis.

A. *The "Bad Samaritan" Principle*

Since organ procurement from anencephalics forces the donor to rescue the recipient, an appreciation of the ramifications involved in organ procurement must start with the common-law rule that one has no duty to come to the aid of another person in distress, even when the rescuer would risk no harm thereby.[109] Narrow exceptions to the rule

---

107. Capron, supra note 3, at 6.

108. Meilaender, Commentary: The Anencephalic Newborn as Organ Donor, Hastings Center Rep., Mar.–Apr. 1986, at 23.

109. See, e.g., Bradberry v. Pinellas County, 789 F.2d 1513, 1518 (11th Cir. 1986) (defendant county had no duty to rescue decedent who swam too far off shore because county did not create defendant's peril); Handiboe v. McCarthy, 114 Ga. App. 541, 151 S.E.2d 905 (Ct. App. 1966) (no duty to rescue child licensee drowning in swimming pool); Osterlind v. Hill, 263 Mass. 73, 160 N.E. 301 (1928) (proprietor of canoe rental service had no duty to rescue intoxicated patron whose canoe tipped over); Yania v. Bigan, 397 Pa. 316, 155 A.2d 343 (1959) (no duty to rescue business invitee who, at defendant's insistence, jumped into a water-filled trench and drowned). See generally Restatement (Second) of Torts § 314 (1965); Prosser and Keeton on Torts § 56 (W. Keeton 5th ed. 1984).

exist; for example, if the rescuer stands in a special relationship to the victim or has voluntarily begun to render assistance, he must complete the rescue with reasonable care.[110] Nevertheless, the general no-duty rule has drawn strong criticism from those within the Anglo-American legal tradition[111] and has been rejected by other legal systems outside of that tradition.[112] The rule's endurance testifies to the high value our society places on the concept of individual autonomy.

When the rescue requires forcible intrusion on the body of another, as in the organ-donation situation, the interest of the subject in being free from coercion is much stronger. Consequently, even when competing interests dictate that an intrusion be required, only minor intrusions are permissible.[113] The parameters of what might be considered a "minor" intrusion have been developed within the context of the fourth amendment's prohibition against unreasonable searches and seizures.[114] In *Schmerber v. California*,[115] the Supreme Court articulated a balancing test weighing the individual's interest in "human dignity" against the interest of society in requiring the intrusion, noting that "[t]he integrity of an individual's person is a cherished value of our society."[116] The *Schmerber* Court concluded its analysis with the caveat that its holding "that the Constitution does not forbid the States minor

---

110. See W. LaFave & A. Scott, Criminal Law ¶ 3.3(a)(1), at 203 (2d ed. 1986) (criminal law imposes duty on parents to rescue child). Other such relationships include common carriers and passengers, innkeepers and guests, and the responsibility of a ship to save a crew member who has fallen overboard. Id. ¶ 3.3(a)(1), at 203–04; Prosser and Keeton on Torts supra note 109, § 56, at 376–82.

111. See, e.g., Ames, Law and Morals, 22 Harv. L. Rev. 97, 113 (1908) (legal obligation should correspond to moral duty); D'Amato, The "Bad Samaritan" Paradigm, 70 Nw. U.L. Rev. 798, 804 (1975) (suggesting criminal sanctions for failing to rescue).

112. For example, the German criminal code provides:

Anybody who does not render aid in an accident or common danger or in an emergency situation, although aid is needed and under the circumstances can be expected of him, especially if he would not subject himself thereby to any considerable danger, or if he would not thereby violate other important duties, shall be punished by imprisonment not to exceed one year or a fine.

StGB § 330(c), translated in Feldbrugge, Good and Bad Samaritans: A Comparative Survey of Criminal Law Provisions Concerning Failure to Rescue, 14 Am. J. Comp. L. 630, 655–56 (1966). Professor Feldbrugge goes on to cite criminal statutes from twenty-three countries imposing a duty to rescue and punishing its breach. Id. at 655–57.

113. For example, the state interest in preserving the public health legitimates compulsory vaccinations. See Jacobson v. Massachusetts, 197 U.S. 11, 28–29 (1905).

114. U.S. Const., amend. IV. The fourth amendment is the source of significant restrictions stemming from the right to bodily integrity even when no intrusion per se is involved. Thus, the Fifth Circuit noted in the context of strip searches: "In a civilized society, one's anatomy is draped with constitutional protections." United States v. Afanador, 567 F.2d 1325, 1331 (5th Cir. 1978).

115. 384 U.S. 757 (1966).

116. Id. at 772. The Court applied this balancing test in deciding that a state may forcibly require a person suspected of drunken driving to submit to a blood test without violating the suspect's fourth amendment right not to be subject to unreasonable searches and seizures. Id. at 771–72.

intrusions into an individual's body under stringently limited conditions in no way indicates that it permits more substantial intrusions, or intrusions under other conditions."[117] That warning bore fruit in *Winston v. Lee*,[118] in which the Court held that the balancing test generally does not permit compelled surgical intrusions into an individuals's body for evidence.[119]

One exception in which the state does subject individuals to the threat of serious physical injury or death is mandatory military service.[120] In that instance, though, the interests of one person are not being subjugated to the needs or wishes of another individual. Rather, society in general is the beneficiary of a compulsory draft. This crucial distinction leaves no foothold for extending the exception to instances in which one person is called upon to come unwillingly to the aid of another by donating part of his body.

Cases involving rescues that would require the donation of a body part are understandably rare.[121] Indeed, only once has a court faced the question of whether a major intrusion on the body of one individual can be compelled to benefit another. In *McFall v. Shimp*,[122] thirty-nine year old Robert McFall suffered from aplastic anemia, a disease of the bone marrow that required McFall to receive a bone marrow transplant.[123] The only compatible donor was found to be the plaintiff's

---

117. Id. at 772.

118. 470 U.S. 753 (1985).

119. The surgery in *Winston* required the use of a general anesthetic, which the Court found overly intrusive because it involved "a virtually total divestment of respondent's ordinary control over surgical probing beneath his skin." Id. at 765; see also United States v. Crowder, 543 F.2d 312, 316 (D.C. Cir. 1976) (en banc) (allowing minor surgery to remove a bullet lying superficially beneath the skin of defendant's arm while denying permission to remove a second bullet lodged in the thigh because the latter procedure involved a greater risk of damage to the suspect's leg), cert. denied, 429 U.S. 1062 (1977).

Bodily invasions *are* permissible when they are in the defendant's own best interest. For example, in People v. Bracamonte, 15 Cal. 3d 394, 404, 540 P.2d 624, 631, 124 Cal. Rptr. 528, 535 (1975), the defendant swallowed balloons that the police suspected contained narcotics. The court pointed out that if the prosecution could have shown that the balloons would likely break open in the suspect's stomach, thereby endangering his health, then stomach pumping would have been justified, and any evidence obtained thereby would have been admissible. See generally Note, Nonconsensual Surgery: The Unkindest Cut of All, 53 Notre Dame L. Rev. 291 (1977); Comment, Search and Seizure: Compelled Surgical Intrusions?, 27 Baylor L. Rev. 305 (1975).

120. Selective Draft Law Cases, 245 U.S. 366, 378 (1918).

121. One reason for the scarcity of such cases is that they require an identifiable defendant, that is, a single individual or limited group of persons who alone are in a position to render aid. Otherwise, the hypothetical invoked by Dean Prosser to justify the law's unwillingness to create a duty to rescue comes into play: "A man is starving to death in the middle of a city and no one feeds him. Whom can he sue?" Discussion of the Restatement of the Law, Second, Torts, 37 A.L.I. Proc. 171 (1960).

122. 10 Pa. D. & C.3d 90 (C.P. Allegheny County 1978).

123. Case Comment, Coerced Donation of Body Tissues: Can We Live with *McFall v. Shimp?*, 40 Ohio St. L.J. 409, 410 (1979).

first cousin, David Shimp, who refused to donate his bone marrow.[124] In desperation, McFall sought a preliminary injunction requiring Shimp to undergo the transplant. Despite the tragic circumstances,[125] the court's decision was unequivocal. Judge Flaherty denied plaintiff's request, stating that "[o]ur society, contrary to many others, has as its first principle, the respect for the individual, and that society and government exist to protect the individual from being invaded and hurt by another."[126]

These restrictions on interference with another's bodily integrity (of which *Shimp* is an extreme example) emphasize the very limited scope of necessity as a justification in this context.[127] Would the result be otherwise if the victim of the intrusion faced imminent death in any event? Put somewhat differently, does the firm principle that dying persons are accorded full rights weaken when the element of necessity is added?[128]

Here, too, the precedents are few. The best known is *Regina v. Dudley and Stephens*,[129] in which four crewmen stranded at sea in a lifeboat faced certain death by starvation. Three were married; the fourth, a boy who was in the most weakened condition and therefore likely to die first, was not.[130] Based on these considerations, the three men killed the boy and survived by eating his flesh until rescued. The survivors were convicted of murder.[131]

---

124. Id. at 410–11.

125. Robert McFall died on August 10, 1978, two weeks after the case was filed. See id. at 414.

126. *McFall*, 10 Pa. D. & C.3d, at 91. The opinion continued:

This request is not to be compared with an action at law for damages, but rather is an action in equity before a chancellor, which, in the ultimate, if granted, would require the forceable submission to the medical procedure. For a society which respects the rights of *one* individual, to sink its teeth into the jugular vein or neck of one of its members and suck from it sustenance for *another* member, is revolting to our hard-wrought concepts of jurisprudence. Forceable extraction of living body tissue causes revulsion to the judicial mind. Such would raise the spectre of the swastika and the Inquisition, reminiscent of the horrors this portends.

Id. at 92.

127. Contrast the tort of invading another's property, for which a privilege of necessity does exist. See, e.g., People v. Roberts, 47 Cal. 2d 374, 377, 303 P.2d 721, 723 (1956); Ploof v. Putnam, 81 Vt. 471, 474, 71 A. 188, 189 (1908).

128. Note that when the dying "person" is actually a nonperson in the eyes of the law, as in the case of fetuses, a much stronger case can be made for the defense of necessity. Thus, in pre-*Roe* jurisprudence under statutes that proscribed the "unlawful" termination of a pregnancy without attention to exceptions, the courts nonetheless recognized the need for such a defense when a therapeutic abortion was medically indicated. See Commonwealth v. Wheeler, 315 Mass. 394, 395, 53 N.E.2d 4, 5 (1944); The King v. Bourne, [1939] 1 K.B. 687, 694.

129. 14 Q.B. 273 (1884).

130. Id. at 274–75.

131. Id. at 288; see also United States v. Holmes, 26 F. Cas. 360 (C.C.E.D. Pa. 1842) (No. 15,383) (crewman convicted of manslaughter for throwing fourteen male

These precedents support what critics of organ procurement from anencephalics implicitly assume: that dying persons have full rights and that those rights encompass the decision not to come to the assistance of others. Therefore, the extremity of the need for such organs is not a relevant factor, for no balancing process is involved. While this may be correct as a general rule, there are significant exceptions to the rule that may indicate that the anencephalic's right to bodily integrity may not be absolute.

B. *Forced Cesareans*

A growing number of cases have ordered pregnant women to submit to various forms of medical intervention, including cesarean sections, in order to preserve the well-being of their fetuses.[132] Although

---

passengers overboard in order to save leaking lifeboat); Fuller, The Case of the Speluncean Explorers, 62 Harv. L. Rev. 616 (1949) (discussing hypothetical case of explorers who, in order to survive, choose one of their party by lot to be killed and eaten).

A contrary German example is illustrated by the Judgment March 5, 1949, *Obersten Gerichtshof für die Britische Zone Entscheidungen Des Obersten Gerichtshof für die Britische Zone in Strafsachen* [OGHSE] 321. In that case, the defendant physician was being tried for serving on a committee that selected mentally ill persons for euthanasia. In defense, he asserted that he had knowingly participated in condemning innocent persons to death solely in order to save other patients by falsely representing them as being cured, and striking their names from the lists of those condemned. Id. at 322. The lower court had decided that the accused may be entitled to a "personal immunity," based not any specific provision of law but rather on an "extrastatutory necessity." However, the appellate court subsequently reversed this decision, finding that the legal concept of "necessity" from which the lower court derived its notion of "personal immunity" cannot be applied where the compared values are both human life. Id. at 334.

The Model Penal Code does provide that necessity is a justification applicable to all offenses including homicide. Model Penal Code § 3.02 & comments (1962). The situations offered as illustrations involve the deflection of an existing threat (for example, a flood) from many potential victims to one. Judith Thomson perceptively distinguishes between the Model Penal Code principle and the legal doctrines prohibiting the rescue of several individuals dying from organ failure by removing organs from another without her consent. In the former scenario, the actor did not create the threat that menaces the one, and therefore the "wrong" suffered by the one is not of his doing. The surgeon who would kill one person as a means of procuring organs to save five cannot take refuge in the same claim, for organ failure threatens the five, while the potential threat to the one is the organ-retrieval operation. Thomson, The Trolley Problem, 94 Yale L.J. 1395, 1406–08 (1985).

132. See, e.g., In re A.C., 533 A.2d 611, 617 (D.C. 1987) (validating a court-ordered cesarean section of a sedated, terminally ill woman whose consent was unclear), rev'd on reh'g en banc, No. 87-609 (D.C. Apr. 26, 1990) (Westlaw, Dist. Col. library); In re Madyun Fetus, 114 Daily Wash. Law Rep. 2233 (D.C. Super. Ct. 1986) (court-ordered cesarean section), aff'd, No. 86-1149 (D.C. July 2, 1986); Jefferson v. Griffin Spalding County Hosp. Auth., 247 Ga. 86, 274 S.E.2d 457 (1981) (same); Raleigh Fitkin-Paul Morgan Memorial Hosp. v. Anderson, 42 N.J. 421, 424, 201 A.2d 537, 538 (holding, prior to *Roe v. Wade*, that a pregnant woman could be forced to undergo a blood transfusion in order to protect her fetus), cert. denied, 377 U.S. 985 (1964); Gallagher, Prenatal Invasions & Interventions: What's Wrong with Fetal Rights, 10 Harv. Women's L.J. 9, 11 (1987) (citing eleven cases involving coerced cesarean sections); Rhoden, The Judge

it is true that the parent-child relationship is one of the special relationships in which the law imposes a duty to rescue,[133] these cases cannot be interpreted as falling within that exception. Nor can they be explained by viewing pregnancy as a voluntary rescue that, once undertaken, must be completed successfully. The magnitude of the intrusion on the mother's body and the significance of the risk involved render these interpretations untenable, for nowhere else does the law require a rescuer to complete such an arduous and dangerous rescue.[134] The only adequate explanation for these decisions is the recognition that the preservation of potential human life at times justifies major intrusions on the sanctity of individual rights.[135] The teaching of these cases bears particular significance to the anencephalic issue, for if parents are required to aid fetuses who are not persons as a matter of constitutional law, certainly the states could permit rescues where the beneficiaries are full persons in the eyes of the law.

A closely related phenomenon is the proliferation of living-will statutes and the insertion of "pregnancy clauses" in the majority of such statutes.[136] Pregnancy clauses prevent a pregnant woman from exercising her right to decline medical treatment when terminally ill, in order to preserve the life of her fetus. The effect of such statutes thus replicates the results reached in the mandatory cesarean cases.

The most recent judicial pronouncement in this area reverses this trend. *In re A.C.*[137] involved a pregnant woman hospitalized with cancer who had, at the time the case arose, "at best, two days left of se-

---

in the Delivery Room: The Emergence of Court-Ordered Cesareans, 74 Calif. L. Rev. 1951, 1951 nn.3–4 (1986) (citing other unpublished cases involving court-ordered surgery); Comment, In re A.C.: Foreshadowing the Unfortunate Expansion of Court-Ordered Cesarean Sections, 74 Iowa L. Rev. 287, 300 (1989).

133. See supra note 110.

134. See Nelson, Buggy & Weil, Forced Medical Treatment of Pregnant Women: "Compelling Each to Live as Seems Good to the Rest," 37 Hastings L.J. 703, 753–55 (1986); Rhoden, supra note 132, at 1977–81.

135. See, e.g., Jefferson v. Griffin Spalding County Hosp. Auth., 247 Ga. at 89, 274 S.E.2d at 460 ("[W]e weighed the right of the mother to practice her religion and to refuse surgery on herself, against her unborn child's right to live. We found in favor of her child's right to live.").

136. Living-will statutes are laws that enable competent adults to select a course of medical treatment that will be followed should they become terminally ill. See, e.g., Ark. Stat. Ann. §§ 20-17-201 to -218 (1987); Cal. Health & Safety Code §§ 7185–7195 (West 1970). "Pregnancy clauses" are legislatively enacted exceptions to such statutes which provide that an individual's election to terminate medical treatment shall be given no effect if the individual is pregnant and terminating treatment would harm the fetus. See, e.g., Conn. Gen. Stat. Ann. § 19a-574 (West Supp. 1990); Del. Code Ann. tit. 16, § 2503(d) (1983). Most living will statutes also contain pregnancy clauses. See Note, Pregnancy Clauses in Living Will Statutes, 87 Colum. L. Rev. 1280, 1281 n.2, 1282 n.10, 1283 n.11 (1987) (citing living-will statutes with and without pregnancy clauses).

137. 533 A.2d 611 (D.C. 1987), rev'd on reh'g en banc, No. 87-609 (D.C. Apr. 26, 1990) (Westlaw, Dist. Col. Library).

dated life."[138] The hospital administration sought and was granted a court order allowing the performance of a cesarean section without A.C.'s consent.[139] The procedure was performed, but both mother and child died shortly thereafter.[140]

The appellate court's initial opinion[141] recognized the significance of a person's interest in bodily integrity[142] and the consequent weakening of the state's interest in preserving the child's health when the two interests collided. However, in the final analysis, the court felt that considerations of bodily integrity were not dispositive:

> The Caesarean section would not significantly affect A.C.'s condition because she had, at best, two days left of sedated life; the complications arising from the surgery would not significantly alter that prognosis. The child, on the other hand, had a chance of surviving delivery, despite the possibility that it would be born handicapped. Accordingly, we concluded that the trial judge did not err in subordinating A.C.'s right against bodily intrusion to the interests of the unborn child and the state, and hence we denied the motion for stay.[143]

Upon en banc rehearing, the appellate court reversed its earlier decision and held that the trial court should have attempted to ascertain the mother's wishes by the procedure known as substituted judgment.[144] Those wishes cannot normally be overridden by the results of a balancing test, as the original appellate opinion suggested. The court conceded, however, that situations might arise in which the use of a balancing test, rather than a substituted judgment procedure, would be appropriate.[145]

The stringent limitations on infringing another's bodily integrity enunciated in *In re A.C.* represent only one judicial viewpoint on this

---

138. Id. at 617

139. Id. at 612.

140. Id.

141. The Court of Appeals opinion describing these events was written after the fact in order to "assist others and to test [the] court's decision with analysis of precedent." Id. at 611. A few months later, the court vacated the opinion of the motions division, ordering an en banc rehearing of the case. In re A.C., 539 A.2d 203 (D.C. 1988). Upon rehearing the full case on the merits, the original decision was reversed. *A.C.*, No. 87-609 (D.C. Apr. 26, 1990) (Westlaw Dist. Col. Library).

142. *A.C.*, 533 A.2d at 615–16.

143. Id. at 617.

144. *A.C.*, No. 87-609 (D.C. Apr. 26, 1990).

145. Again, in virtually all cases the decision of the patient, albeit discerned through the mechanism of substituted judgment, will control. We do not quite foreclose the possibility that a conflicting state interest may be so compelling that the patient's wishes must yield, but we anticipate that such cases will be extremely rare and truly exceptional.

Id. But see id. (Belson, J., concurring in part and dissenting in part) (arguing that a balancing test *is* the appropriate approach).

question.[146] Moreover, the unique situation presented by anencephaly is perhaps the best example of the "truly exceptional"[147] instances in which bodily integrity may be compromised. The core difference between the original motions division opinion in *In re A.C.* and the subsequent en banc reversal lies in defining the scope of rights possessed by the terminally ill. Although the cesarean section was clearly detrimental to A.C.'s health, the motions division assigned little weight to that factor because her physicians predicted that she would in any event soon succumb to cancer.[148] The en banc opinion rejected such analysis, asserting that "it matters not what the quality of a patient's life may be; the right of bodily integrity is not extinguished simply because someone is ill, or even at death's door."[149]

Even if appropriate for terminally ill patients generally, however, the reasons supporting the protective standard applied in the en banc opinion do not apply to anencephalics. One legitimate reason for rejecting the initial opinion is that it disregarded the existence of interests peculiar to terminally ill patients. In A.C.'s case, the court-ordered surgery foreclosed any choices she might have made concerning the circumstances of her death—for example, whether to die alone in a hospital operating room or at home with family and friends.[150] In contrast to A.C., however, anencephalic infants have no such interests.[151]

---

146. This view seems to conflict with several other judicial rulings on the subject. See supra note 132.

147. *A.C.*, No. 87-609, (D.C. Apr. 26, 1990).

148. See *A.C.*, 533 A.2d at 617. Similarly, the court distinguished Colautti v. Franklin, 439 U.S. 379 (1979), and Thornburgh v. American College of Obstetricians and Gynecologists, 476 U.S. 747 (1986), which stand for the proposition that the mother's well-being carries primacy over the health of her fetus in situations where the two interests might conflict. A.C.'s case, said the court, was different in that her good health was not being sacrificed to save her child's life. *A.C.*, 533 A.2d at 615 n.4. The court, without more explanation, seemed to accept the idea that a terminally ill patient has a substantially diminished interest in bodily integrity.

See also Mahowald, Silver & Ratcheson, The Ethical Options in Transplanting Fetal Tissue, Hastings Center Rep., Feb. 1987, at 9. The authors advocate the permissibility of transplanting organs and tissues from nonviable abortuses under certain conditions. In order to satisfy the requirements of informed consent, they adopt Richard McCormick's following suggestion:

with respect to the participation of children in low-risk experimentation, membership in a community may justify the procedure. The situation [of organ transplantation from nonviable abortuses] may be considered "low risk" on the basis of the donor's inability to survive, regardless of whether the transplantation takes place.

Id. at 14 (footnote omitted); see also Note, Medical Breakthroughs in Human Fetal Tissue Transplantation: Time to Reevaluate Legislative Restrictions on Fetal Research, 13 Vt. L. Rev. 373, 383 (1988) (adopting view of Mahowald, Silver and Ratcheson that "[t]he burden to the nonviable fetus [in being a tissue donor] is irrelevant because death is imminent").

149. *A.C.*, No. 87-609 (D.C., Apr. 26, 1990).

150. See Comment, supra note 132, at 298.

151. See infra notes 176–86 and accompanying text.

They never gain consciousness and thus can never form preferences concerning the circumstances of their death. Similarly, in reasoning that one who is terminally ill can suffer little harm in being compelled to undergo surgery, the original opinion failed to acknowledge that while one's interests *after* death may merit no protection, it is nevertheless appropriate to protect an individual's *existing* interests in how she will be treated after she becomes incompetent or dies.[152] Since anencephalics are incapable of ever possessing interests, even according to the en banc opinion, a decision to utilize their organs for transplantation should not be inappropriate.

C. *The Nonviable Fetus* ex Utero

A persuasive metaphor for anencephaly lies in the controversy surrounding permissible modes of experimentation upon the nonviable fetus *ex utero*. Such fetuses have undergone live birth but, like the anencephalic infant, will survive for a very brief time only.[153] In

___

152. The enforceability of a living will is an example of one way in which our legal system protects such interests. See supra note 136; infra note 186 and accompanying text.

153. The Peel Commission Report, issued in 1972, defined a "pre-viable" fetus as follows: "one which, although it may show some but not all signs of life, has not yet reached the stage at which it is able, and is incapable of being made able, to function as a self-sustaining whole independently of any connection with the mother." See The Use of Fetuses and Fetal Material for Research ¶ 6 (1972) [hereinafter The Peel Report], reprinted in Appendix, supra note 92, at 19-1, 19-2. Presumably, heartbeat and respiration are prominent examples of "signs of life" that, although present, are not sufficient to confer viability on a fetus which cannot "function as a self-sustaining whole" independent of the mother. This definition clearly seems to contemplate the case of a very immature fetus *ex utero*, which cannot be sustained under present technology. Such a fetus, although it may be able to breath without assistance, is nonviable because it cannot become a stable organism and hence faces imminent death. Under this definition, anencephalics are also nonviable despite their ability to breathe on their own and to maintain a heartbeat. Since their respiratory function will soon begin to deteriorate due to the lack of a developed brain, see supra note 36 and accompanying text, they too face imminent death and are therefore nonviable.

Federal guidelines limiting research grants, contain a slight modification of the Peel Commission definition: " 'Viable' as it pertains to the fetus means being able, after either spontaneous or induced delivery, to survive (given the benefit of available medical therapy) to the point of independently maintaining heart beat and respiration." HHS, Additional Protections Pertaining to Research, Development and Related Activities Involving Fetuses, Pregnant Women, and Human In Vitro Fertilization, 45 C.F.R. § 46.203(d) (1989). This definition seems to rely solely on the ability to breathe and maintain a heartbeat without mechanical assistance to determine "survival." If this interpretation is correct, then anencephalics, who are able to do so, would be considered viable. However, further reading of the regulations indicates that this reading of section 46.203(d) is incorrect. Section 46.209(b) provides: "No nonviable fetus may be involved as a subject in an activity covered by the subpart unless: . . . (2) [e]xperimental activities which of themselves would terminate the heart beat or respiration of the fetus will not be employed." The regulations thus assume that there will be some nonviable fetuses capable of respiration. Therefore, some criteria other than respiration and heart beat must be necessary for viability. The regulations are silent on what those criteria

England, the Peel Commission, appointed to study the ethical and legal implications of fetal research, reached a conclusion that treated non-viable fetuses in substantially the same manner as dead fetuses.[154] The Commission's recommendations permit experimentation that would terminate vital functions of the nonviable fetus provided that essentially the same restrictions applicable to dead fetuses[155] are observed.[156] In the United States as well, federal regulations as initially promulgated stated that:

> No nonviable fetus may be involved . . . in an activity . . . unless: (1) Vital functions of the fetus will not be artificially maintained *except where the purpose of the activity is to develop new methods for enabling fetuses to survive to the point of viability.*[157]

This last clause permitted experimentation not benefiting the subject upon which it is performed, a significant departure from the treatment accorded live fetuses upon whom such nontherapeutic experimentation that might harm the fetus is forbidden.[158] These regulations have been amended to conform with the predominating live birth standard and

---

might be. The best interpretation would seem to be that the Peel Commission definition, which emphasizes the capability to function as a self-sustaining organism, should be read into the regulations. An organism that begins dying from the moment of expulsion would be considered nonviable under such a definition, and thus anencephalics would be included among the nonviable.

154. The Peel Report, supra note 153, ¶¶ 32–35, reprinted in Appendix, supra note 92, at 19-8 to 19-9.

155. These provisions proscribe any such research when parental objection exists. They also forbid any experimentation in the operating theater or place of delivery and any monetary payment for fetuses or fetal material. See The Peel Report, supra note 153, Recommended Code of Practice, ¶ 3(ii)–(iv), reprinted in Appendix, supra note 92, at 19-13.

156. These are:

[(i) The conditions concerning research on dead fetuses set forth supra note 155.]

(ii) Only fetuses weighing less than 300 grammes are used.

(iii) The responsibility for deciding that the fetus is in a category which may be used for this type of research rests with the medical attendants at its birth and never with the intending research worker.

(iv) Such research is only carried out in departments directly related to a hospital and with the direct sanction of its ethical committee.

(v) Before permitting such research that ethical committee satisfies itself: (a) on the validity of the research; (b) that the required information cannot be obtained in any other way; and (c) that the investigators have the necessary facility and skill.

The Peel Report, Recommended Code of Practice, ¶ 4, reprinted in Appendix, supra note 92, at 19-13.

157. 40 Fed. Reg. 33,528 (1975) (emphasis added), amended by 43 Fed. Reg. 1759 (1978).

158. 45 C.F.R. § 46.209(a) (1989). For this reason the regulations governing non-viable fetuses drew strong criticism. See Horan, Fetal Experimentation and Federal Regulation, 22 Vill. L. Rev. 325, 338–40 (1976–1977); Research on the Fetus, supra note 94, at 77, 79–80 (dissenting statement of Commissioner Louisell).

are no longer consonant with the Peel Commission's position.[159] However, it was a growing appreciation of the highly developed neurological structure possessed by nonviable fetuses and the accompanying capacity to experience pain that spurred the modification of the regulations.[160] The anencephalic is distinct from nonviable fetuses in its lack of such neurological structures. Therefore, the original morally significant decision to decline to recognize the significance of borderline biological life in both the Peel Report and the original HEW regulations retains its full import when applied to anencephalics. This conclusion is buttressed by the fact that organ procurement from anencephalics who do not meet whole brain death criteria is currently permissible in Germany and Japan.[161]

D. *"Monsters" and the Law of Homicide*

This notion of not giving full credence to biological life is not a recent development. Historically, many societies refused to accord newborns with full status as persons. Though such attitudes fostered practices that are not worthy of emulation, they reinforce the conclusion that universal rights to bodily integrity are not ingrained in our culture as absolutes. The historical prejudices expressed themselves in the widespread practice of infanticide—in some societies sanctioned by the state, in others formally prohibited but tacitly accepted. The ancient Greeks feared that defective persons would transmit undesirable traits onto the next generation and therefore actively promoted killing such children at birth. Grecian law thus allowed infants to be exposed to the elements until the time they would be admitted to the family through a special ceremony, the *amphidromia*.[162] By the Middle Ages,

---

159. See 45 C.F.R. § 46.209(b)(1)–(2) (1989).

160. See Appendix, supra note 92, at 2-4, 2-7, 14-18; National Commission for the Protection of Human Subjects of Biomedical and Behavioral Research: Research on the Fetus, 22 Vill. L. Rev. 300, 321–22 (1976–1977) (statement of Commissioners Lebacqz & Jonsen).

161. See Holgreve, Beller, Buckholz, Hansmann & Kohler, Kidney Transplantation from Anencephalic Donors, 316 New Eng. J. Med. 1069, 1069 (1987) (courts in Federal Republic of Germany accept concept that anencephalic fetus at term "has never been alive despite the presence of a heartbeat"); Ohshima, Ono, Kinukawa, Matsuura, Tsuzuki & Itoh, 132 J. Urology 546 (1984).

162. Feen, Abortion and Exposure in Ancient Greece: Assessing the Status of the Fetus and "Newborn" from Classical Sources, in Abortion and the Status of the Fetus 283, 285 (W. Bondeson, H. Englehardt, S. Spicker & D. Winship eds. 1983).

According to bioethicist H.T. Engelhardt, Aristotle also endorsed selective infanticide: "Let there be a law that no deformed child shall live . . . ." H. Englehardt, The Foundations of Bioethics 228 (1986) (quoting 7 Aristotle, Politics, 1335b, reprinted in The Basic Works of Aristotle 1302 (R. McKeon ed. 1941)). In Rome, there seems to have been a duty to kill deformed infants. Cicero remarks in passing that "[a] dreadfully deformed child ought to be killed quickly, as the Twelve Tables ordain." Id. (quoting Cicero, de Legibus III, 8, 19).

Other societies have also sought to ensure purity of the gene pool by selectively killing defective infants. The Nuer tribe has traditionally defined such neonates as "hip-

infanticide had acquired the stamp of official condemnation in England,[163] yet few cases of infanticide were tried in the king's courts. Instead, these instances were dealt with by ecclesiastical authorities who regarded infanticide as a venial sin that could be handled under the traditional requirements of penance: one year on bread and water and two more years without wine or meat for intentionally smothering an infant.[164]

Grossly deformed infants were even then subject to a double standard. The common law recognized a class of nonhuman beings, "monsters" who were the products of human conception but were not considered human beings.[165] Human beings were "reasonable creatures in being," a term denoting the capacity (presently or prospectively) to reason.[166] This principle was carried forward in the first nationwide German penal code, the so-called Carolina, which was in force in a substantial part of Europe from its enactment in 1532 until 1871. In contrast to Roman law, which punished the killing of slaves only as the destruction of property, the Carolina Code drew no distinctions between human beings as far as homicide was concerned, with the exception of abortion and monster killing.[167] Such creatures were presumed to lack souls, and were therefore not considered persons to whom the statutes governing the protection of human life applied.[168]

Writing during the reign of Henry III, Bracton states that a monster is not a human being; Blackstone substantially repeats that view, though neither wrote in the context of homicide.[169] Similarly, an early

popotamuses" who were born to human parents through some mistake. The appropriate treatment for hippopotamuses was, of course, to return them to their natural habitat by tossing them in the river, which is exactly what tribal adults did with these infants. T. Beauchamp & J. Childress, Principles of Biomedical Ethics 121 (1979).

163. Punishment for child murder in medieval Europe, when meted out at all, was usually directed at (often unwed) mothers on the lower end of the socioeconomic scale and took cruel forms. A notable example was the practice of "sacking," in which the infanticidal mother was put in a sack and submerged in water for six hours, while a choir standing by sang Psalm 130, "Out of the depths I cry to Thee." R. Weir, Selective Nontreatment of Handicapped Newborns: Moral Dilemmas in Neonatal Medicine 11 (1984).

164. Id. at 12–13.

165. See Dickens, The Infant as Donor: Legal Issues, Transplantation Proc., Aug. 1988, Supp. 5, at 50.

166. Id.

167. Eser, "Sanctity" and "Quality" of Life in an Historical-Comparative View, *in* S. Wallace & A. Eser, Suicide and Euthanasia: The Rights of Personhood 103, 104–05 (1981).

168. Id. at 107.

169. See 2 W. Blackstone, Commentaries *246; H. Bracton, *De Legibus et Consuetudinibus Angliae* 203–04 (G. Woodbine ed., S. Thorne Trans. 1968); 4 H. Bracton, *De Legibus et Consuetudinibus Angliae* 361–62 (G. Woodbine ed., S. Thorne trans. 1977).

Two rationales have been put forth in explanation of the historic denial of personhood to newborns, particularly defective ones. The first substantially undercuts the authority of these long-standing doctrines. It is the belief in "hybridity," the notion that

New York case discussed in dictum the question of previable infants in deciding whether one may inherit through a stillborn child. It concluded that one could not inherit through such a child, stating that "children born dead, or in such an early state of pregnancy as to be incapable of living, although they be not actually dead at the time of their birth, are considered as if they had never been born or conceived."[170] Among modern writers, Professor Glanville Williams recognizes the propriety of infanticide when confined to a small group of highly impaired neonates.[171]

Without resorting to theories of ensoulment, these sources lend weight to the notion that an anencephalic may be viewed as a biologically functioning entity that is something less than a person.[172] The next part of this Article attempts to develop a reasoned framework by which those beings who command the full protection of the prohibition against homicide—persons—can be distinguished from those who do not.

---

these anomalous infants must have been the product of an animal paternity. G. Williams, The Sanctity of Life and the Criminal Law 21 (1957). By definition, then, they could be denied status as human beings since they lacked full human parentage. The second is exemplified by English physician Charles Mercier's thoughts:

> In comparison with other cases of murder, a minimum of harm is done by it. . . . The victim's mind is not sufficiently developed to enable it to suffer from the contemplation of approaching suffering or death. It is incapable of feeling fear or terror. Nor is its consciousness sufficiently developed to enable it to suffer pain in appreciable degree. Its loss leaves no gap in any family circle, deprives no children of their breadwinner or their mother, no human being of a friend, helper or companion. The crime diffuses no sense of insecurity. No one feels a whit less safe because the crime has been committed.

Id. at 18 (quoting C. Mercier, Crime and Insanity 212–13 (1911)).

170. Marsellis v. Thalhimer, 2 Paige Ch. 35, 41 (N.Y. Ch. 1830).

171. It seems probable that the medical practice [of passively allowing these newborns to die without actively causing their deaths] is unduly cautious, and that a creature that is clearly a monster in the old-fashioned sense could lawfully be put to a merciful death. This appears to be a reasonable deduction from the rule stated by the [sic] Bracton and the other institutional writers that a monster is not a man. . . . The only possible objection, apart from the extreme view that even a monster is the abode of an immortal spirit, is the difficulty of drawing the line; but all moral and legal rules require a line to be drawn somewhere.

G. Williams, supra note 169, at 22. In a previous paragraph, Professor Williams notes that "[f]ortunately, the question whether a monster is human has small practical importance for the most extreme cases, because the acephalous, ectocardiac, etc., monster will usually die quickly after birth." Id. at 21–22. When considering the use of anencephalics for transplantation purposes, however, the question of whether the infant is human or not is of paramount importance despite the fact that death will soon follow.

172. Dr. Leonard Bailey, a transplant surgeon at Loma Linda, echoed this idea when he termed the anencephalic infant a "nonperson human derivative." Goldsmith, Anencephalic Organ Donor Program Suspended; Loma Linda Report Expected to Detail Findings, 260 J. A.M.A. 1671 (1988).

V. Towards a Theory of Personhood

The preceding materials indicate a tension inherent in our received legal and moral tradition. The law of rescue reflects a deep commitment to Kant's Mere Means Principle: "Act in such a way that you always treat humanity, whether in your own person or in the person of any other, never simply as a means, but always at the same time as an end."[173] Thus, the reluctance to intrude on an individual's freedom of action (and bodily integrity) in order to further the interests of another lies at the root of the resistance to proposals for organ procurement from anencephalics.[174]

Despite the entrenched position of Kantian thought, there are signs of erosion at the edges of life and death which imply a willingness to subdue rights-based claims in the face of important practical considerations.[175] Yet, if we analyze the purposes served by ascribing rights, it should become clear that there exist entities to which we would find it natural not to ascribe rights. Since the Kantian ethic applies only to rights holders, no violence is done to the Mere Means Principle by utilizing such entities to procure crucial benefits for others. This understanding will facilitate an appreciation of why the California statute does not abridge firmly established moral and legal norms.

A. *Elements of a Theory*

To have a right is to possess a (moral or legal) claim *to* something or *against* someone. The ascription of rights to a particular individual is a means of protecting that individual's interests. This concept can be better appreciated by considering why it is that mere things do not have rights.[176] For example, statutes exist prohibiting the destruction of

---

173. I. Kant, Groundwork of the Metaphysics of Morals 96 (H. Paton trans. 1964); see generally I. Kant, The Metaphysical Elements of Justice (1965). Ronald Dworkin accurately sums up this reluctance to subjugate the individual for the greater good by pointing out that rights trump utilities. R. Dworkin, Taking Rights Seriously xi (1977).

The alternative viewpoint, utilitarianism, evaluates actions solely by reference to their consequences. See, e.g., Hare, Ethical Theory and Utilitarianism, *in* Utilitarianism and Beyond 23, 25 (A. Sen & B. Williams eds. 1982). According to a utilitarian view, an act that is intuitively wrong but that results in the greater good is not merely permissible, but imperative. A utilitarian might therefore favor involuntary organ retrieval from terminally ill patients. See, e.g, Harris, The Survival Lottery, *in* Killing and Letting Die 149 (B. Steinbock ed. 1980) (defending view that it is morally permissible to kill one person in order to obtain transplantable organs that would save several others); J. Harris, supra note 6, at 21 ("[I]n cases where [sic] we have to choose between lives where we cannot save all at risk, we should choose to save as many lives as we can.").

174. See, e.g., supra note 108 and accompanying text. Even though an anencephalic's death is inevitable, the Kantian view would not condone direct human intervention that would instead become the direct cause of death. See J. Finnis, Fundamentals of Ethics 112–20 (1983).

175. See supra text accompanying notes 132–72.

176. See generally Feinberg, The Rights of Animals and Unborn Generations, *in* Philosophy & Environmental Crisis 43 (W. Blackstone ed. 1974).

flowers and antiquities.[177] We even pay persons to devote their principal energies to the task of ensuring that such things flourish.[178] Yet we rightly do not think of such laws as protecting the rights of plants or ancient ruins. Since such objects lack desires or wishes, they cannot possess interests, and without interests they cannot be said to have a "good" of their own that warrants protection. Rather, it is our own sensibilities and wishes that are the objects of these laws.

Philosophers and ethicists have relied on this premise to draw a distinction between human beings and persons. The former term denotes an uncontroversial genetic observation: the offspring of human parents is a member of the species *Homo sapiens* in the same way that a labrador's offspring are members of the canine species. Persons can be viewed as a subset of humanity:[179] those humans who possess certain attributes attain the status of persons. Thus, while all offspring of humans are also human, they are not necessarily persons. Only persons, rather than all humans, have rights, and it is only persons whose autonomy must be respected. By outlining the theory of personhood below, it will become apparent that anencephalics constitute a class of humans that are not persons.

Those writing on the topic of personhood have attempted to answer the question "what properties must a being possess in order for it to have a right to life?" Typically, the response is given in the form of a list of characteristics which represent a rough sketch of the necessary, and perhaps sufficient, conditions for being a person. Rationality[180] and self-consciousness[181] are the common denominators among the

177. See, e.g., 16 U.S.C. § 726(c) (1988) (flowers); id. § 433 (antiques).

178. See, e.g., id. §§ 554, 554a (National Forest Service rangers).

179. It is not even necessarily true that the subset of persons is entirely contained within the set of humans. Writers on this subject have persuasively argued that higher species of apes, robots and sentient extraterrestrials all should be treated as people despite their biological inhumanity. See, e.g., H. Engelhardt, supra note 162, at 107; Feinberg, The Problem of Personhood, in Contemporary Issues in Bioethics 109, 110–11 (T. Beauchamp & L. Walters eds. 2d ed. 1982); Puccetti, The Life of a Person, in Abortion and the Status of the Fetus, supra note 162, at 169, 174–75.

180. Among the 15 criteria Joseph Fletcher lists that form a composite picture of man are minimal intelligence ("any individual . . . who falls below the I.Q. 40-mark . . . is questionably a person; below the 20-mark, not a person") and neocortical function ("In a way, this is the cardinal indicator, the one all others are hinged upon"). Fletcher, Indicators of Humanhood: A Tentative Profile of Man, Hastings Center Rep., Nov. 1972, at 1, 3; see also Feinberg, supra note 179, at 109, 114 (finding ability to reason to be central to the concept of personhood); Warren, Do Potential People Have Moral Rights?, 7 Can. J. Phil. 275, 283 (1977) (same).

181. See Feinberg, supra note 179, at 109, 114 (requirements of "consciousness" and "self-awareness"); Fletcher, supra note 180, at 1 (criteria of personhood include "self-awareness"); Tooley, In Defense of Abortion and Infanticide, in Contemporary Issues in Bioethics, supra note 179, at 215, 221–22 (requirement of a capacity for a sense of self); Warren, On the Moral and Legal Status of Abortion, in Contemporary Issues in Bioethics, supra note 179, at 250, 256 (requirements of "consciousness" and "self-awareness").

various inventories. Those who posit a nonbiological basis of personhood there is uniformly agree that without these traits personhood is impossible.[182] There is also a third trait which is closely linked to these two, namely, a sense of futurity and the capacity for desires about one's future.[183] The significance of this triad lies in the connection between the rights individuals may possess and the corresponding desires they entertain. The moral prohibition against violating an individual's rights exists only if by doing so one frustrates that individual's desires for some valued thing. As Michael Tooley explains: "If you do not care whether I take your car, then I generally do not violate your right by doing so."[184]

That moral strictures against violating an entity's rights do not extend to nonpersons is similarly demonstrated by our moral position vis-á-vis higher animals. Beasts experience pain and pleasure, yet we normally have no duty to refrain from killing them, provided we do so humanely and in the furtherance of legitimate human interests.[185] It is only persons—beings capable of cognition—who possess a full panoply of rights.

Two classes of entities pose a difficulty for this argument, in that we apparently ascribe rights to such entities though they are incapable of formulating interests. The first counterexample is dead people. Promises made to individuals who subsequently die are enforced by the law after their death, as are testamentary dispositions, even though enforcement (or the lack of it) cannot be said to benefit (or harm) the dead person.[186] This practice, however, flows from the interest we all have while yet alive that our wishes after death be respected. The interests survive the person, but their origins lie in the sentient mind of the person who once held them.

The second context in which rights are imputed to nonsentient entities involves fetuses.[187] Indeed, it is precisely this anomaly which has led advocates of abortion to reject such rights and conclude that abor-

---

182. Some authors have added another general characteristic: the capacity to be a moral agent. H. Tristram Engelhardt quotes Kant's comment that "[a] person is [a] subject whose actions are capable of being imputed [that is, one who can act responsibly]. Accordingly, moral personality is nothing but the freedom of a rational being under moral laws." Engelhardt, Medicine and the Concept of Person, in Contemporary Issues in Bioethics, supra note 179, at 94, 95.

183. Fletcher, supra note 180, at 2; Tooley, supra note 181.

184. Tooley, A Defense of Abortion and Infanticide, in The Problem of Abortion 51, 60 (J. Feinberg ed. 1973).

185. See Feinberg, supra note 176, at 56.

186. For example, a decedent's wishes expressed in his will regarding the disposition of his remains prevail over the wishes of the surviving spouse and children. See, e.g., In re Eichner's estate, 173 Misc. 644, 18 N.Y.S.2d 573 (1940); Feller v. Universal Funeral Chapel, Inc., 124 N.Y.S.2d 546 (Sup. Ct. 1953).

187. Children, even very young ones, are properly considered to have rights, which often must be exercised through representation by a proxy. Young people have desires much as mature people do, though they may be incapable of verbalizing them or appre-

tion is morally permissible. The syllogism used is straightforward: (1) only persons have a right to life, (2) an entity that lacks rationality, self-consciousness and desires about its future is not a person, (3) a fetus lacks all of these criteria, hence (4) a fetus is not a person and therefore has no right to life.[188]

A crucial difficulty with this argument is the fact that fetuses have the potential for achieving personhood in the course of normal development. Opponents of abortion justify their position by citing the potential these beings have of becoming interest holders and the reality that these emerging interests require protection now if they are to be realized at all.[189] Those justifying abortion respond that it is a logical error to deduce actual rights from mere potential qualification for those rights.[190] Australian philosopher Stanley Benn summarizes this position: "A potential president of the United States is not on that account Commander-in-Chief."[191]

The debate surrounding nonstandard rights holders also has consequence in determining the proper treatment of entities in two categories contiguous to fetuses and the dead: neonates and those who are comatose. The attribution of personhood to individuals in the latter category can be interpreted as a vindication of their prior interests in being cared for should they ever reach such a state.[192] Neonates, on the other hand, have rights only because of their potential for sentience. Those who reject the significance of potentiality are forced to admit that strictures against harming infants flow instead from the interests which parents as rational entities have in these beings, much like the interests infringed when one appropriates another's animal without

---

ciating how those interests can best be furthered. Consequently, the law appoints parents or guardians to safeguard those rights.

188. See, e.g., H. Engelhardt, supra note 162, at 217–20; Warren, supra note 181, at 250, 255–56.

189. See Feinberg, supra note 176, at 43, 62–64. A more extreme view is that the potential capacity for rational thought is itself sufficient to classify fetuses as persons. This outlook is developed in Noonan, Deciding Who is Human, 13 Nat. L.F. 134, 135–36 (1968).

190. See Feinberg, supra note 179, at 109, 113; H. Engelhardt, supra note 162, at 110–12. Various thought experiments are invoked to illustrate this point. Michael Tooley, for example, hypothesizes the discovery of a chemical that, when administered to newborn kittens, would lead them to develop the capacity for self-awareness and rational thought. He argues that current mores that regard the destruction of surplus newborn kittens as not morally wrong (or only marginally so) would not be affected by the manufacture of this new chemical. Assuming there is no morally relevant distinction between artificial and natural potentiality for becoming persons, then naturally potential persons have no more right to life than such kittens have. See Tooley, Abortion and Infanticide, 2 Phil. & Pub. Aff. 37, 60–62 (1972).

191. Benn, Abortion, Infanticide, and Respect for Persons, in The Problem of Abortion, supra note 184, at 92, 102.

192. See Correspondence, 2 Phil. & Pub. Aff. 419, 421 (1973) (reply of M. Tooley). For criticism of this justification, see Robertson, Involuntary Euthanasia of Defective Newborns: A Legal Analysis, 27 Stan. L. Rev. 213, 249–50 (1975).

permission.[193]

The proposals to harvest vital organs from anencephalics are premised on an analysis identical to that used to justify abortion. The moral stricture against harvesting organs applies only to persons. These infants can no more satisfy even minimal criteria of personhood than can fetuses.[194] Moreover, even though many of us would agree that the potential for development inherent in fetuses and infants merits protection, that argument disappears in the case of anencephalics, for such entities will never qualify as persons in the sense put forth by proponents of personhood theory. In view of the enormous benefits to be derived from proposed transplantation protocols, there is every reason to take advantage of such crucial sources of organs. Of course, as is the case with normal neonates, the treatment accorded these infants generates intense parental emotion. Therefore, it certainly would be immoral to remove organs from anencephalics without parental consent.[195] But once such consent is forthcoming, we must realize that no person's rights are violated by procurement.[196]

---

193. See, e.g., H. Englehardt, supra note 162, at 108, 112–13 (arguing that infants are not strictly persons, but are treated by society as such in order to promote other valid interests). Compare Sumner, Abortion, *in* Health Care Ethics 162, 171 (D. VanDeVeer & T. Regan eds. 1987) ("If . . . the result [of interpreting personhood in terms of self-consciousness and rationality is] that the killing of such a victim [i.e., an infant or a young child] is really a property offense, then we are entitled to conclude that [we] ha[ve] somehow gone seriously wrong.") with Warren, supra note 181, at 250, 259 (The conclusion that infanticide is wrong for reasons analogous to those that make it wrong to destroy great works of art "will no doubt, strike many people as heartless and immoral; but remember that the very existence of people who feel this way . . . is reason enough to conclude that [infants] should be preserved.").

194. The debate among philosophers on this and related topics is often couched in terms of "personhood." Calling anencephalics "nonpersons" carries with it unpleasant connotations of disrespect for these entities. Such terminology, however, is merely a shorthand way of recognizing that while the infant's biological existence may briefly continue, human life as we value it does not exist. Whether one speaks in terms of a definition of personhood which modifies the live-donor rule, or in terms of a definition of death which modifies the whole-brain-death standard, the result is the same: biological life without the associated legal protections that attach to "persons." The California and New Jersey bills, see supra notes 101–04 and accompanying text, are thus conceptually identical even though the New Jersey version makes no reference to amending the relevant determination-of-death statutes.

195. Unlike the New Jersey statute, the California version makes no mention of parental consent as a prerequisite for organ removal; its sole concern is with amending the definition of death. Existing legal doctrines would nevertheless permit organ removal only after obtaining parental consent. See infra notes 299–302 and accompanying text.

196. The situation is sharply different when the interests of two persons compete in an arena that can satisfactorily accommodate only one set of interests. Prevailing ethical norms proscribe any attempt to weigh the relative worth of one individual against another. For example, during the 1960s and early 1970s hemodialysis emerged as a successful treatment for patients with end-stage renal disease. However, the necessary equipment was extremely expensive, and there simply were not enough hemodialysis machines to fill the demand. See Rettig, The Policy Debate on Patient Care Financing

B. *Criticism of the Theory*

Critics of personhood theory, however, point out that among the lists of attributes offered as indicia of personhood no single viewpoint finds support in any set of evidentiary or factual findings.[197] Therefore, they assert, any choice among the competing theories must necessarily be an arbitrary one.

One can usefully approach this problem by differentiating claims of arbitrariness that relate to the margins of personhood theory, from those that strike at its core. The various theories of personhood, despite their bewildering diversity of viewpoints, all cluster about a common center of essential attributes relating to the capacity for thought and self-awareness.[198] When considered as a group, then, there are sound reasons for choosing from among this set of definitions of humanity, rather than adopting a view that would deny personhood to all those under ten years of age or all non-Aryans. Certainly, at the margin the charge of arbitrariness has some effect, since different philosophies may dispute the personhood of hard cases such as neonates.[199] But it is precisely such arguments to which an observation of Justice Holmes

---

for Victims of End-Stage Renal Disease, 40 Law & Contemp. Probs., Autumn 1976, at 196, 201–04. During this period some machines were allocated on the basis of criteria that purported to measure the social worth of the individuals competing for the treatment. The Seattle Artificial Kidney Center, for example, selected patients on the basis of " '. . . age and sex of patient; marital status and number of dependents; income; net worth; emotional stability, with particular regard to the patient's capacity to accept the treatment; educational background; nature of occupation; past performance and future potential; and names of people who could serve as references.' " Alexander, They Decide Who Lives, Who Dies, Life, Nov. 9, 1962, at 102, 106. These policies led one pair of commentators to remark that the standards excluded "creative nonconformists, who rub the bourgeoisie the wrong way but who historically have contributed so much to the making of America. The Pacific Northwest is no place for a Henry David Thoreau with bad kidneys." Sanders & Dukeminier, Medical Advance and Legal Lag: Hemodialysis and Kidney Transplantation, 15 UCLA L. Rev. 357, 378 (1968). Eventually, widespread discomfort with such selection procedures led to the passage of the Social Security Amendments of 1972 under which most patients were reimbursed through Medicare for dialysis treatments. See Social Security Amendments of 1972, Pub. L. No. 92-603, § 299I, 86 Stat. 1329, 1463–64 (1972) (codified as amended at 42 U.S.C. § 426-1 (1982)). The sharply increased funding indirectly led to a greater supply of equipment, thereby alleviating the problem to a large extent. See Mehlman, Rationing Expensive Lifesaving Medical Treatments, 1985 Wis. L. Rev. 239, 259.

197. See, e.g., Rhoden, The New Neonatal Dilemma: Live Births from Late Abortions, 72 Geo. L.J. 1451, 1467 (1984); Robertson, supra note 192, at 248; cf. McMillan, Ancient Admonitions and the Sanctity of Personhood, in Euthanasia and the Newborn 253, 259 (R. McMillan, H. Engelhardt & S. Spicker eds. 1987) ("[A] major objection is that personhood, like beauty, is seen to reside largely in the eye of the beholder."); Puccetti, supra note 179, at 169, 175 ("[I]t might turn out that the concept of a person is only a free-floating honorific that we all happily apply to ourselves, . . . rather as those who are *chic* are all and only those who can get themselves considered *chic* by others who consider themselves *chic*.").

198. See supra notes 180–83 and accompanying text.

199. See supra note 191 and accompanying text.

provides an apt reply: "[W]here to draw the line . . . is the question in pretty much everything worth arguing in the law."[200] Moreover, as a minimum, it should be acceptable to all sides to exclude entities who fail to meet the common criteria. Anencephalics, who lack the capacity or potential for even the most minimal level of cogitation and social interaction, clearly are such entities.[201] Perhaps they are not the only such entities.[202] But, once having agreed to postulate a nonbiological basis of personhood, anencephalics certainly fall on one side of every line that conceivably can be drawn.

This approach, however, begs the question to some extent, for it implicitly assumes that *some* nonbiological criteria of personhood are justifiable.[203] This assumption, which lies at the core of personhood theory, creates problems on two fronts. First, like many philosophical axioms, it is difficult to defend.[204] Second, it raises the apparent internal inconsistency that exists between personhood theory and the prevailing legal structure. This clash results from the operation of the twin doctrines of live birth and whole brain death, which seem to reject the moral position that some forms of physical existence are not equivalent with personhood.

---

200. Irwin v. Gavit, 268 U.S. 161, 168 (1925).

201. Professor Robertson, a critic of those who would deny treatment to handicapped newborns on the grounds that they are not persons, nevertheless recognizes this fact. In concluding his critique of such theories, he concedes that in the most extreme cases there may be some justification for relying on them: "Finally, the only group of defective newborns who would clearly qualify as nonpersons is anencephalics, who altogether lack a brain, or those so severely brain-damaged that it is immediately clear that a sense of self or personality can never develop." Robertson, supra note 192, at 251.

202. This may pose a difficulty—one that I shall later address. See infra notes 287–97 and accompanying text.

203. See R. Macklin, Mortal Choices: Bioethics in Today's World 219–20 (1987).

204. Mary Anne Warren concludes her analysis of the morality of abortion by pointing out that: "If the opponents of abortion were to deny the appropriateness of these five criteria [of personhood], I do not know what further arguments would convince them. We would probably have to admit that our conceptual schemes were indeed irreconcilably different, and that our dispute could not be settled objectively." Warren, supra note 181, at 256. If the belief that all human offspring are persons was solely religious in nature one could perhaps answer, as Herbert Wechsler and Jerome Michael did with regard to religious objections to voluntary euthanasia, that "[t]hose who hold the faith may follow its precepts without requiring those who do not hold it to act as if they did." Wechsler & Michael, A Rationale of the Law of Homicide: I, 37 Colum. L. Rev. 701, 740 (1937). However, the sanctity of human life is undoubtedly grounded in the secular concept of dignity and respect for all human beings as well. Hence, it is entirely appropriate that we consider such viewpoints. See In re Eichner, 102 Misc. 2d 184, 189, 423 N.Y.S.2d 580, 584 (Sup. Ct. 1979) ("Parenthetically, the Court notes that insofar as evidence concerning religious subjects has been considered, it has been the Court's consistent purpose solely to examine the evidence for the light it sheds on the secular concerns of the Court." (citing In re Quinlan, 70 N.J. 10, 355 A.2d 647 (1976))), aff'd sub nom. Eichner v. Dillon, 73 A.D.2d 431 (1980), modified sub nom. In re Storar, 52 N.Y.2d 363, 420 N.E.2d 64, 438 N.Y.S.2d 266 (1981); Caplan, supra note 3, at 121–22.

The next subpart of this Article tackles these two difficulties. It begins with some observations about the legitimacy of a decision to select a nonbiological position despite the lack of empirical support. The Article then examines the considerations adduced in support of the whole brain standard, which reveals that the reluctance to accept neocortical death is largely practical, rather than doctrinal. These practical objections are less apt when applied to anencephaly, and therefore a different rule should control in this special situation.

C. *Medical Reality*

The objection that nonbiological formulations of personhood are not susceptible to empirical proof[205] can be understood to mean that legislative adoption of such a theory would be unwise or illegitimate. Yet, closer scrutiny reveals the weakness of this claim. First, current medical practices demonstrate a crucial inconsistency from which traditional biological theories of personhood suffer. Several writers have noted that there is absolutely no morally significant change in the fetus between the moments immediately preceding and following birth.[206] This underlies society's reluctance to sanction very late abortions in most situations.[207] Indeed, the choice of birth as a point of demarcation for personhood is largely interpretable in terms of the ease with which the standard could be administered.[208] Commentators have noted the incongruity of permitting late abortions for certain genetic defects while requiring treatment for premature infants born with the same defects at the same gestational age.[209]

Anencephaly is the only condition upon which there is wide agreement that even very late third trimester abortions are morally permissible.[210] Why do the considerations which uniquely permit late abortion

---

205. See supra note 197 and accompanying text.

206. See, e.g., R. Weir, supra note 163, at 146–47 (view of ethicist Paul Ramsey that birth " 'is a comparatively unimportant point in the development of the life God calls into being' "). The only physical differences are that a fetus does not breathe air and is physically attached to the mother. Yet, as one commentator has noted, a newborn still attached to the umbilical cord retains these characteristics and is nonetheless considered a full-fledged person. See Note, Technological Advances and *Roe v. Wade*: The Need to Rethink Abortion Law, 29 UCLA L. Rev. 1194, 1206 n.80 (1982).

207. Rhoden, Trimesters and Technology: Revamping *Roe v. Wade*, 95 Yale L.J. 639, 669 (1986); cf. Chervenak, Farley, Walters, Hobbins & Mahoney, When is Termination of Pregnancy During the Third Trimester Morally Justifiable?, 310 New Eng. J. Med. 501, 502 (1984) ("it can be argued that our moral obligations to the third-trimester, possibly-viable fetus are stronger than our obligations, for example, to a preimplantation embryo").

208. See Capron, The Law Relating to Experimentation with the Fetus, *in* Appendix, supra note 92, at 13-26.

209. See, e.g., Rhoden, supra note 197, at 1489; Comment, Premature Infants: A Legal Approach to Decision-Making in Neonatal Intensive Care, 19 U.S.F.L. Rev. 261, 280 (1985).

210. Chervenak, Farley, Walters, Hobbins & Mahoney, supra note 207, at 502; see

for anencephaly suddenly cease to apply at the time of birth? The contrast between the refusal to perform very late abortions on other fetuses and the practice regarding anencephalics indicates that physicians and society regard these neonates as nonpersons.[211] The reluctance to interfere with these infants immediately following birth is explainable only as a wish to conform with legal prohibitions.[212] Ideally, the causal relationship should be reversed; that is, the law in this area should reflect social consensus and medical reality.

Moreover, the position that all products of human conception are persons is equally unprovable. Thus, the controversy surrounding anencephaly represents a classic case of ethical pluralism, similar to the debate which raged about abortion prior to *Roe v. Wade*. In that area, decision making by majoritarian democratic processes was considered an appropriate means of resolving the problem.[213] Prochoice and prolife advocates attempted to persuade each other of the soundness of their respective positions, though at the bottom of the debate lay the reality that "the difficult question of when life begins" is one upon which "those trained in the respective disciplines of medicine, philosophy, and theology are unable to arrive at any consensus."[214] The resulting "abortion map" was a patchwork quilt of states that proscribed or permitted abortion in varying degrees.[215] A similar approach should be valid in deciding about anencephaly. The various state legislatures should not be prevented from choosing, by majority fiat, a theory of personhood that seems most correct to its members.

---

also Rovner, supra note 33, Health Section, at 16, col. 1 (physicians will abort anencephalic fetuses up to the moment of birth).

211. This argument has been advanced by two West German physicians, W. Holzgreve and F.K. Boller, who have performed kidney transplants utilizing anencephalic neonates as donors. Letter from W. Holzgreve and F.K. Boller to the Editor, 317 New Eng. J. Med. 961 (1987).

212. One neurosurgeon, Dr. Ivan, admits:

Ethically, I see no difficulties in taking a resuscitated anencephalic child to the operating room with beating heart, even though . . . the child may be able to breathe on its own. My problem is with the law because the law says there should be total irreversible absence of all brain functions.

Girvin, Brain Death Criteria—Current Approach to the Non-Anencephalic, Transplantation Proc., Aug. 1988, Supp. 5 at 26, 31.

213. See, e.g., Baron, Legislative Regulation of Fetal Experimentation: On Negotiating Compromise in Situations of Ethical Pluralism, *in* 3 Genetics and the Law 431, 438–39 (A. Milunsky & G. Annas eds. 1985) (decrying *Roe* decision for its effect of foreclosing legislative compromise as a means of resolving the abortion controversy); Schneider, State-Interest Analysis in Fourteenth Amendment "Privacy" Law: An Essay on the Constitutionalization of Social Issues, 51 Law & Contemp. Probs. 79, 110–18 (1988) (arguing that political, rather than judicial, solutions to issues such as abortion "give people some sense of control over their environments and their lives").

214. Roe v. Wade, 410 U.S. 113, 159 (1973).

215. See, e.g., George, The Evolving Law of Abortion, 23 Case W. Res. L. Rev. 708, 740–42 (1972) (collecting and discussing restrictive and permissive state statutes on abortion issues).

D.   *Rejection of the Neocortical Standard—Implications for Anencephaly*

The second line of argument against personhood theory claims that such theories are inconsistent with the widespread rejection of a neocortical standard of death. A study of the development of the whole brain death standard will enable us to better judge how the incongruity between law and medicine arose and whether it should be corrected. When considering what definition of death should replace the common-law cardiopulmonary standard, the President's Commission enumerated several basic requirements that any potential standard had to fulfill. According to the Commission, the new definition should limit the change in the law to the minimum needed to achieve the goal of defining appropriate behavior towards respirator-assisted comatose persons.[216] It should reflect "scientific knowledge and clinical reality."[217] Most importantly, the proposed standard had to "accurately reflect the social meaning of death and not constitute a mere legal fiction."[218]

Applying these general criteria to the specific problem under study, the Commission concluded that it was most appropriate to broaden the definition of death to include whole brain death, but not to encompass neocortical death. One important reason for rejecting the neocortical view was the prerequisite that any standard adopted reflect "scientific knowledge and clinical reality."[219] The criteria for whole brain death are highly reliable.[220] Although reports do surface of brain-dead patients "returning to life," experts agree that such instances, which occur most frequently when organ donation is contemplated, can be attributed to a lack of proficiency or care in correctly applying the criteria.[221]

The corresponding situation with regard to neocortical death is far less clear. Neuroscientists agree that functions such as cognition and consciousness result from complex interconnections between the

---

216. Defining Death, supra note 20, at 7.

217. Id.

218. Id. at 31.

219. Id. at 7.

220. See supra note 57 and accompanying text.

221. Thus, in one case an eighteen-year-old patient who had suffered severe injuries in a motor vehicle accident was declared brain dead after 12 hours of treatment at an outlying hospital. Permission was obtained from his parents to remove his kidneys for transplantation, whereupon he was transferred to a university hospital for the purpose of organ procurement. There, he was reevaluated and received more intensive treatment. Eventually he was released with only a slight impairment of higher cognitive functions. Capron, Determination of Death *in* Medicolegal Aspects of Critical Care 115 (K. Benesch, N. Abramson, A. Grenvik & A. Meisel eds. 1986); see also Girvin, supra note 212, at 28–29; Ivan, Brain Death in the Infant and What Constitutes Life, Transplantation Proc., Aug. 1988, Supp. 5, at 17, 25 (citing headline in British newspaper which stated "patient pronounced dead prior to removal of kidneys for transplantation starts breathing on the operating table").

brainstem and the cerebral cortex.[222] Therefore, because it is impossible to be certain that with the shutdown of specific areas of the brain a complete loss of cognitive functions occurs, "the 'higher brain' may well exist only as a metaphorical concept, not in reality."[223] The difficulty of formulating reliable diagnostic criteria is thus a principal obstacle that has prevented the adoption of neocortical death as a standard.[224]

A closely related problem is the difficulty of distinguishing between a patient who is neocortically dead and one who exists in the state known as "locked-in syndrome." Those in the latter category have undergone paralysis of all four lower extremities and the lower cranial nerves, yet retain consciousness,[225] and therefore can not be grouped with neocortically dead patients who have lost all consciousness. Because those suffering from "locked-in syndrome" cannot communicate with others, their condition mimics that of a neocortically dead patient.[226]

None of these considerations are relevant to anencephaly. In contrast to the uncertainty surrounding the diagnosis of higher brain death, the diagnosis of anencephaly is completely accurate.[227] It is a

---

222. Defining Death, supra note 20, at 15.

223. Id. at 40.

224. Id.; see also Bernat, Culver & Gert, supra note 81, at 391; Korein, supra note 62, at 27; Walton, supra note 81, at 270; Youngner & Bartlett, Human Death and High Technology: The Failure of the Whole-Brain Formulations, 99 Annals Internal Med. 252, 258 (1983). The current situation may be changing, however, with the advent of positron emission tomography (PET) scanning. By viewing on a video screen the flow of tracers labeled with positron-emitting isotopes in the patient's bloodstream, scientists are now capable of studying the chemistry of selected subregions of the brain and thereby evaluating higher brain functions. See Smith, supra note 20, at 879–80.

225. See generally F. Plum & J. Posner, supra note 66, at 6.

226. This problem was crucial in Brophy v. New Eng. Sinai Hosp., Inc., No. 85-E0009-G1, slip. op. at 6–12 (Mass. P. & Fam. Ct. Dep't. Oct. 21, 1985), set aside and remanded, 398 Mass. 417, 497 N.E.2d 626 (1986), in which the trial court denied a request to terminate the administration of nutrition and hydration to an irreversibly unconscious patient due in part to uncertainty as to whether Brophy was completely unconscious. Medical science is just beginning to devise methods, such as PET screening, which can reliably differentiate between locked-in syndrome and neocortical death. See Smith, supra note 20, at 879–83.

227. See Bailey, supra note 14, at 35, 37; Caplan, Ethical Issues in the Use of Anencephalic Infants as a Source of Organs and Tissues for Transplantation, Transplantation Proc., Aug. 1988, Supp. 5 at 42, 48; supra notes 23–24 and accompanying text. Some critics who oppose the utilization of anencephalics cite examples of misdiagnosis of anencephaly. E.g., Capron, supra note 3, at 6; Medearis & Holmes, supra note 3, at 392 ("too many errors have been made for the diagnosis to be considered reliable as a legal definition of death."). Anecdotal evidence of misdiagnosis of anencephaly nevertheless should not be taken as a significant obstacle in the way of transplantation, particularly in the context of mistaken referrals to regional or national transplantation centers. Similar mistakes are committed in the diagnosis of whole brain death, notwithstanding the widespread agreement that whole brain death can be diagnosed with complete certainty. See supra note 221. Given the lower level of sophistication and

condition so unique that it cannot be confused with any less severe deformity.[228] The possibility of "recovering" any higher brain functions, a concern regarding the potential adoption of neocortical death for all those in vegetative conditions, is nonexistent for anencephalics who lack the entire higher cortical structure.[229] Nor is there even a remote possibility of artificial substitutes being devised which could improve the anencephalic's condition. Thus, while the law should not be defined by the state of scientific progress at any single point in time,[230] the possibility of developing any cure for anencephaly is sufficiently remote that it can be ruled out for purposes of formulating a legal approach to the problem. Moreover, proposed solutions such as the one in California treat anencephaly as *sui generis*, a single exception to the prevailing whole brain death criteria.[231] The addition of but a single case to the category of those who are legally dead does no violence to the "minimum change" envisioned by the President's Commission.[232]

---

expertise at local levels, such errors are not extraordinary. Since organ transplants are performed at sophisticated facilities, society can be confident that the relevant criteria will be applied with skill and care at the final stage preceding transplantation, whether the donor is an anencephalic or a person who has undergone whole brain death.

In addition, fears of misdiagnosis may be allayed by the utilization of more strict criteria for identifying anencephaly. A recent study of anencephaly notes that while errors in diagnosis have been described in the literature, use of the following four criteria guarantees virtual certainty of diagnosis:

    (1) A large portion of the skull is absent;

    (2) The scalp, which extends to the margin of the bone, is absent over the skull defect;

    (3) Hemorrhagic, fibrotic tissue is exposed because of defects in the skull and scalp;

    (4) Recognizable cerebral hemispheres are absent.

With such criteria, two months was the longest survival for an anencephalic infant that could be confirmed by the authors of the study. Medical Task Force on Anencephaly, supra note 26, at 670–71.

228. See Arras & Shinnar, supra note 3, at 2284.

229. Dr. Michael Harrison, who is a leading proponent of the use of anencephalics as organ donors, stresses this point: ·

> The whole-brain definition of death was drafted to protect the comatose patient whose injured brain might recover function. However, failure of the brain to develop is clearly different from injury to a functioning brain, and it was simply not considered when the brain-death definition was formulated. The extreme caution and safeguards needed in pronouncing brain death after brain injury should not apply to anencephaly, in which the physical structure necessary for recovery is absent.

Harrison, Organ Procurement for Children: The Anencephalic Fetus as Donor, The Lancet, Dec. 13, 1986, at 1385; see also Botkin, supra note 34, at 252.

230. See generally Rhoden, supra note 207, at 691–96.

231. See supra notes 99–101 and accompanying text.

232. See Ethics and Social Impact Comm., Transplant Policy Center, Ann Arbor, Mich., Anencephalic Infants as Sources of Transplantable Organs, Hastings Center Rep., Oct.–Nov. 1988, at 29 (arguing that "anencephalics have an absolutely unique status, and must, in the interest of human decency and beneficence, be treated uniquely").

Another compelling reason for the choice of a whole brain standard was the insistence by the members of the President's Commission that any definition, no matter how cogent the arguments for its adoption, also intuitively make sense to lay people.[233] On a matter so fundamental the Commission felt that any legislation that was at odds with deeply ingrained emotional attitudes toward death would be met with unease and mistrust. Such unease might actually reduce, rather than increase, the number of organ donations. Because a change in the law would remove the certainty once associated with the declaration of death, next-of-kin might become overcautious in accepting the idea that their loved one has died and suspicious of any requests for organ donation.[234]

Anxiety over a possible irrational backlash generated by "gut feeling" should not be dismissed lightly, since societal attitude is a crucial factor in the success of any effort to increase the supply of transplantable organs. A 1985 Gallup poll revealed that among people who were aware of organ transplants 85% were very or somewhat likely to donate the organs of their deceased loved ones,[235] yet the number willing to donate their own organs has been put at 45%,[236] this last figure down from 70% in the late 1960s.[237] Even more startling is the reported figure for those who have actually signed their organ donor cards, which ranges from 1.5% to 19% according to some studies,[238] and as high as approximately 25% according to others.[239]

This disparity between hypothetical good intentions and actual willingness to donate stems from a visceral discomfort with the entire business of organ transplantation. In the Gallup poll mentioned above, two reasons were most frequently given as "very important" for the reluctance by most to sign donor cards: "They might do something to me before I am really dead" (23%) and "I'm afraid the doctors might hasten my death if they needed my organs" (21%).[240] Reactions such as these led a transplant surgeon to admit feeling that "I am the vulture hiding at the foot of the bed."[241] Should people perceive organ pro-

---

233. Defining Death, supra note 20, at 7.

234. See Capron, supra note 3, at 8–9; Medearis & Holmes, supra note 3, at 392.

235. Childress, Artificial and Transplanted Organs, 1 Biolaw § 13, at 304 (1986).

236. Id. A more conservative report puts the figure at 24%. Freedman, The Anencephalic Organ Donor: Affect, Analysis, and Ethics, Transplantation Proc. Aug. 1988, Supp. 5 at 57, 59.

237. Childress, supra note 235, at 304.

238. Kaufman, Huchton, Megan, McBride, Beardsley & Kahan, Kidney Donation: Needs and Possibilities, 5 Neurosurgery 237, 240 (1979); Stuart, Veith & Cranford, Brain Death Laws and Patterns of Consent to Remove Organs for Transplantation from Cadavers in the United States and 28 Other Countries, 31 Transplantation 238, 239 (1981).

239. Freedman, supra note 236, at 59.

240. Childress, supra note 235, at 308.

241. Freedman, supra note 236, at 59. Dr. Freedman continues by elaborating on the specific images conjured in people's minds by the process of transplantation:

curement from anencephalics as a willingness on the part of the medical profession to adhere to a less rigid standard for determining death, the number of overall donations may well decrease as a result of the fears cited in the Gallup poll. There is some merit, then, in concerns that the utilization of anencephalics and those who have suffered neocortical death as a source of organs may win one battle but lose the war.

Nevertheless, the Commission's conclusions, influenced considerably by these apprehensions, may have been unnecessarily cautious. Admittedly, individuals without neocortical functions seem very much alive. These patients breathe spontaneously, they may have sleep-wake cycles, and they may yawn, react to light, blink, swallow and maintain a heartbeat. Such patients can survive for years with basic medical and nursing care, often without a respirator.[242] However, the corresponding situation involving whole brain dead persons is not much different.

Patients who have suffered whole brain death whose bodies are being maintained with the support of ventilators and other life-support equipment present a disquieting paradox to those responsible for their

---

It is remarkable how many levers of horror heart transplantation manages to pull. It is a concatenation of the two most venerable figures of horror, together with several disparate themes of the literature. The venerable figures are, of course, the vampire and Frankenstein's monster. The theme of Dracula may be recast as the preservation of one through the living substance of the other. The themes of Frankenstein are many, and include the overweening pride of medicine, science and progress, unnatural life, and grave-robbing. Other horror themes that may be associated with transplantation include the premature burial and the unquiet grave, the mad scientist, and cannibalism.

Id. at 59–60.

Even health professionals are not immune from such uneasy feelings. Some have reported sensing a "presence" or "spirit" in the room during organ retrieval. See Youngner, Allen, Bartlett, Cascorbi, Hau, Jackson, Mahowald & Martin, Psychosocial and Ethical Implications of Organ Retrieval, 313 New Eng. J. Med. 321, 322 (1985).

Associations of this type probably account for the third and fourth most common reasons for unwillingness to sign donor cards: a dislike of "thinking about dying," followed by a dislike of "the idea of somebody cutting me up after I die." See Childress, supra note 235, at 308.

242. Neocortically dead patients require artificial feeding (given intravenously or through nasogastric tubes) and antibiotics for pulmonary infections. Their bodies are "exercised" by physical therapists. One individual survived for more than 37 years in a condition of irreversible coma. See The Guinness Book of World Records 24 (D. McFarlan ed. 1989).

Bioethicist Alexander Capron, a critic of the neocortical death concept, summarizes the situation:

It would be highly controversial—and, indeed, would be rejected by most people—to call people who are in a coma but who still breathe on their own "dead," especially when the purpose is to allow removal of their vital organs, which *would* then cause their death as that term is now used. This was the nightmarish scenario that took place in the Jefferson Institute in Robin Cook's novel, *Coma*.

Capron, supra note 3, at 8.

care and to those who were close to them during life.[243] While legally and medically they are dead, these cadavers remind us more of living patients than of those patients who have suffered cardiac arrest and are being prepared for burial. Their chests move up and down rhythmically. Their hearts continue to pump oxygenated blood, thereby causing their skin to retain the warmth and healthy color that common experience tells us is a characteristic of living people.[244] They produce urine which must be collected and disposed of.[245] They exhibit reflexes which are sufficiently complex to mislead lay people into believing that the supposedly deceased person lying in front of them is actually alive.[246] They are even capable of reproduction, certainly a *sine qua non* of life in a physiologic sense.[247] While this state of physiologic life cannot continue indefinitely (as is the case with those in irreversible comas who retain brainstem function), cardiopulmonary functions have been reported to survive for as long as sixty-eight days after complete loss of brain functions.[248]

These peculiarities produce a considerable degree of psychological ambivalence among next-of-kin and medical personnel associated with

243. See generally Martyn, supra note 78, at 8–10 (discussing need of relatives facing "the life-in-death paradox" to grasp the fact of death while witnessing sustained signs of life); Youngner, Allen, Bartlett, Cascorbi, Hau, Jackson, Mahowald & Martin, supra note 241, at 321 (describing "the life processes of. . . dead patients").

244. Younger, Allen, Bartlett, Cascorbi, Hau, Jackson, Mahowald & Martin, supra note 241, at 321. It is true that these processes could not continue without the intervention of mechanical means of respiration and parenteral nutrition. However, many critically ill patients in intensive care units require these and other forms of artificial life support. Therefore, at the intuitive level it is difficult to distinguish brain-dead cadavers from living patients.

245. See Youngner, Drawing the Line in Brain Death, Hastings Center Rep., Aug. 1987, at 43, 44 (letter to the editor).

246. For example, bending the neck of a brain-dead patient will sometimes cause the patient to raise his arms. Ivan, supra note 221, at 17; see also Letter to the Editor from J. Eric Jordan & Eric Dyess, 35 Neurology 1082 (1985) (five to six minutes after cardiac activity and respiration had ceased "the patient crossed both arms over his chest and began to sit up"). In addition, when an organ is being retrieved from a brain-dead cadaver the donor often shows "dramatic increases in . . . blood pressures as well as in heart rate after incision." Wetzel, Setzer, Stiff & Rogers, Hemodynamic Responses in Brain Dead Organ Donor Patients, 64 Anesthesia & Analgesia 125, 126 (1985).

247. Pregnant women who have suffered brain death have been maintained on artificial life-support systems until parturition. See Dillon, Lee, Tronolone, Buckwald & Foote, Life Support and Maternal Brain Death During Pregnancy, 248 J. A.M.A. 1089, 1090 (1982); Shrader, On Dying More than One Death, Hastings Center Rep., Feb. 1986, at 12, 12 (thirty-one-week old fetus delivered by cesarean section nine weeks after his mother had been determined to be brain dead). Similarly, there is no reason why a male in the same condition could not serve as a sperm donor. H. Engelhardt, supra note 162, at 209.

248. Parisi, Kim, Collins & Hilfinger, Brain Death with Prolonged Somatic Survival, 306 New Eng. J. Med. 14, 17 (1982). It is theoretically possible for organs in a brain-dead body to function until old age wears out the heart. Grenvik, Brain Death and Permanently Lost Consciousness, in Shoemaker, Thompson & Holbrook, Textbook of Critical Care 968, 969 (1984).

the organ retrieval process. Nevertheless, the opportunity to benefit from an expanded pool of organ donors was seen as a positive result of the adoption of the whole-brain-death standard by those involved in drafting the UDDA.[249] It is entirely possible that the statutory recognition of whole brain death by the various states was itself a powerful socializing force that paved the way for public acceptance of organ donation from such cadavers. Nor have the emotional conflicts generated by using whole brain dead cadavers as organ donors adversely affected organ donation.[250] If the conceptual difference between whole brain death and neocortical death was well understood and firmly rooted in the public mind, the President's Commission might be correct in fearing that the leap from one standard to the next would engender widespread distrust. Yet, recent evidence indicates that even among health professionals the whole brain standard itself is regarded as a "new" type of death.[251] From a legislative standpoint, therefore, it seems that any initial public misgivings would diminish over time as the public became better informed about the specifics of anencephaly and as the benefits obtained became publicized.[252]

In addition, the number of anencephalic children whose status would be changed by current proposals, while large enough to make a meaningful difference to potential recipients, is too small to generate the type of widespread, grass-roots reaction feared by critics. Furthermore, unlike the case of adult cadavers for which the impetus for organ donation most often comes from outside the family, the parents of anencephalics often initiate the proposal to donate their child's organs and are ardently in favor of changing current law.[253] Since those directly affected by proposed changes are not psychologically at risk, any concerns must be confined to the public at large. When so stated, it behooves us to ask whether the concrete interests of those children who could enjoy life saving benefits as a result of these proposals do not take precedence over general societal misgivings.[254]

---

249. See Defining Death, supra note 20, at 23.

250. See Girvin, supra note 212, at 29.

251. See, e.g., Youngner, Landefeld, Coulton, Juknialis & Leary, "Brain Death" and Organ Retrieval: A Cross-Sectional Survey of Knowledge and Concepts Among Health Professionals, 261 J. A.M.A. 2205 (1989); see also Strachan v. John F. Kennedy Memorial Hosp., 109 N.J. 523, 527, 538 A.2d 346, 348 (1988) (after informing parents that son was brain dead, hospital refused to remove respirator without a court order or parental permission).

252. Although the apprehension with which the bill on anencephaly was greeted in California might dissuade legislators from supporting these proposals, such caution is unwarranted. A significant part of the turmoil surrounding the introduction of Senator Marks' bill in California resulted from a lack of understanding about anencephaly and about the bill's effect on other seriously ill newborns, see supra note 105, rather than from any fundamental philosophical arguments.

253. See supra notes 31–33 and accompanying text.

254. Another related cost-benefit argument made by some is that the utilization of anencephalics is an unjust use of limited resources for the benefit of a few babies. Such

VI. Constitutional Considerations

The notion of changing the status of these infants by amending the statutory definition of death necessarily implicates the constitutional guarantees of due process and equal protection.[255] Admittedly, the proposed California statute makes no mention of fourteenth amendment personhood. Nevertheless, in order to counter the claim that an anencephalic's substantive due process right to life is violated by such a statute, one can answer only that dead people (as anencephalics would be under the statutes) are not persons within the meaning of the fourteenth amendment.[256] Thus, the power to fix criteria of death implicitly carries with it the power to decide who is a person for constitutional purposes. A state legislature, however, possesses no revisory authority with which it could assert an interpretation of the constitution different from one already rendered by the federal courts.[257] Therefore, advo-

---

efforts at developing spectacular, high-technology medical care, it is maintained, could produce more beneficial results if directed towards widespread, preventative therapies. See Subcommittee Hearings, supra note 11, at 48 (testimony of Sister Maureen Webb, Consultant for Respect Life and Bioethics [sic], Diocese of Oakland). This argument contains some truth to it; in part, it reflects a preoccupation with saving identifiable lives rather than statistical lives. The attitude may be an irrational one, yet it persists. See generally, C. Fried, An Anatomy of Values: Problems of Personal and Social Choice 207–36 (1970) (discussing different reactions people have to endangered identifiable lives versus statistical lives); Fried, The Value of Life, 82 Harv. L. Rev. 1415, 1419–22 (1969). However, there is surely no guarantee that funds conserved by foregoing neonatal organ transplants will be diverted to these kinds of preventative health measures. It therefore seems ill-advised to trade away immediate benefits for a future, hypothetical good which may not even be achieved.

255. U.S. Const. amend. XIV.

256. Cf. Simon v. United States, 438 F. Supp. 759, 761 (S.D. Fla. 1977) (stillborn children are not "persons" within the meaning of the fourteenth amendment).

257. For example, in rejecting an effort by a state legislature to ban abortion by defining the point at which life begins, a district court stated:

Nor does the Rhode Island legislature have the power to determine what is a "person" within the meaning of the Fourteenth Amendment. Such a question is purely a question of law for the courts, independent of any power in the state legislature to create evidentiary presumptions. . . .

"Clearly the Federal courts must reserve ultimate authority to say what the meaning of the Fourteenth Amendment is. Surely the States could not, by legislative or judicial fiat, overturn the Dartmouth College case, 4 Wheat. 518, 4 L.Ed. 629 (1819), by finding that a charter was not a 'contract'; or overturn Goldberg v. Kelly, 397 U.S. 254, 90 S.Ct. 1011, 25 L.Ed.2d 287 (1970), by finding that the right to welfare benefits was not 'property'; or overturn Pierce v. Society of Sisters, 268 U.S. 510, 45 S.Ct. 571, 69 L.Ed. 1070 (1925), by finding that the right of parents to send their children to private school was not a 'liberty'; or overturn Brown v. Board of Education, 347 U.S. 483, 74 S.Ct. 686, 98 L.Ed. 873 (1954), by finding that black children were not 'persons' . . . ."

Doe v. Israel, 358 F. Supp. 1193, 1201 (D.R.I.) (quoting Professor Thomas Emerson), aff'd, 482 F.2d 156 (1st Cir. 1973), cert. denied, 416 U.S. 993 (1974).

There is some question whether the Supreme Court's decision in *Katzenbach v. Morgan*, 384 U.S. 641 (1966), recognized some degree of revisory authority in Congress under section 5 of the fourteenth amendment. That decision upheld the constitutional-

cating statutory change embodies a prediction that the federal courts would, if confronted with the issue, find that such a statute did not violate the constitution.

What analysis would the Supreme Court utilize to give content to the meaning of "person" in the fourteenth amendment? Curiously, there is almost no discussion of this fundamental question in the literature.[258] In common usage, anencephalics might be deemed persons, but that alone bears little weight.[259] In *Roe v. Wade*,[260] the Supreme Court briefly considered the issue of personhood as it relates to fetuses.[261] The conclusion there—that a fetus is not a person for fourteenth amendment purposes—was reached largely on the strength of the finding that abortion statutes existing at the time of the amendment's adoption were liberal, indicating that the framers of the amendment did not intend the term "person" to include the unborn.[262] This interpretive method would probably lead to a similar conclusion about anencephalics. As previously noted,[263] the common law did not view seriously defective infants as full-fledged persons entitled to the protec-

---

ity of federal legislation barring enforcement of New York's English literacy requirement as a valid exercise of Congress' power under section five of the fourteenth amendment to enforce the provisions of that amendment. The *Katzenbach* Court thus seemed to defer to Congress' judgment that such literacy requirements violated the fourteenth amendment. See id. at 650–54. Yet, seven years earlier in *Lassiter v. Northhampton County Bd. of Elections*, 360 U.S. 45 (1959), the Court held that literacy tests did not violate the fourteenth and fifteenth amendments absent some showing of discriminatory application. Id. at 50–54. For discussions of Congress' power to interpret constitutional provisions, see Cohen, Congressional Power to Interpret Due Process and Equal Protection, 27 Stan. L. Rev. 603, 620 (1975); Cox, The Supreme Court, 1965 Term—Foreword: Constitutional Adjudication and the Promotion of Human Rights, 80 Harv. L. Rev. 91, 103–07 (1966); Estreicher, Congressional Power and Constitutional Rights: Reflections on Proposed "Human Life" Legislation, 68 Va. L. Rev. 333, 414 (1982). However, even such authority would only empower Congress to *expand*, but not to contract, the limits of fourteenth amendment personhood. See *Katzenbach*, 384 U.S. at 651, n.10.

258. "Human beings are of course the intended beneficiaries of our constitutional scheme. The Constitution was consecrated to the blessings of liberty for ourselves and our posterity—yet it contains no discussion of the right to be a *human* being; no definition of a person . . . ." L. Tribe, American Constitutional Law § 15-3, at 1308 (2d ed. 1988).

259. The notoriously shifting meaning of words in the constitutional dictionary, which does not consider child pornography, New York v. Ferber, 458 U.S. 747, 764 (1982), or obscenity, Roth v. United States, 354 U.S. 476, 485 (1957), or "fighting words," Chaplinsky v. New Hampshire, 315 U.S. 568, 572 (1942), as "speech" for first amendment purposes, indicates that the interpretive process looks to result rather than etymology for guidance.

260. 410 U.S. 113 (1973).

261. Id. at 156–59.

262. Id. at 158. The Court also surveyed the usage of the word as it appears in other constitutional clauses, such as the listing of qualifications for various elective federal offices and provisions regarding extradition and found that it had no prenatal application. Id. at 157. Those clauses are equally inapplicable to anencephalic infants whose entire existence will span only a few brief days.

263. See supra notes 165–66 and accompanying text.

tion of the law against homicide. Even in jurisdictions in which that position no longer prevailed by 1868 (the year of the fourteenth amendment's adoption), the competing interests that shaped the common law at that time were not the same as those that inform the debate over the status of anencephalics. The choice of "birth" (i.e., emergence from the mother with some biological function) as the point for determining "personhood" was made in the context of interests such as a person's hypothetical interest in being free to kill a newborn or behave negligently toward it.[264] Had organ transplantation technology been available during the mid-nineteenth century, the balancing of a different set of interests might have led to a different statutory regime regarding entities such as anencephalic newborns and thus to a different definition of personhood.

One source the Court might look to for a definition of the term person is state law, a technique it has employed in seeking to define other fourteenth amendment terms such as "property."[265] With regard to procedural due process, the result of such an approach is that "a state may . . . avoid all due process safeguards . . . merely by labeling them as not constituting 'property.' "[266] Thus, the state's definition of personhood might itself foreclose any further constitutional challenges to the statute.[267]

Even if state law does not define the boundaries of constitutional personhood, it seems plausible to view that concept as incorporating an irreducible minimum above which states should be free to rationally

---

264. The choice of birth as a dividing line is understandable in light of the ease of administration and uniformity that it provided. The capacity for making more complex evaluations involving the nature and severity of various birth defects did not exist then, but is appropriate for use in determining personhood when modern technology is available.

265. See, e.g., Board of Regents v. Roth, 408 U.S. 564, 577 (1972).

266. Bishop v. Wood, 426 U.S. 341, 354 n.4 (1976) (Brennan, J., dissenting). It is important to realize why this interpretive technique exemplified in *Roth* does not conflict with the assertion of the court in *Doe v. Israel*, 358 F. Supp. 1193, 1201 (D.R.I.), aff'd, 482 F.2d 156 (1st Cir. 1973), cert. denied, 416 U.S. 993 (1974), that a state legislature has no authority to define fourteenth amendment terms. In *Doe*, the court was speaking to the question of which institution has the ultimate authority to determine the meaning of the fourteenth amendment when the interpretations of the court and the legislature conflict. In *Roth* (and in this Part of the Article), the issue was what sources the Court would look to as aids in a de novo inquiry regarding the meaning of constitutional terms. *Roth*, 408 U.S. at 576–78.

267. It is open to question whether the Court would use a similar approach in deciding all interpretive questions that might arise under the fourteenth amendment, particularly those pertaining to substantive due process rights to life and liberty. In *Smith v. Organization of Foster Families for Equality and Reform*, 431 U.S. 816 (1977), the Court held that, "unlike the property interests [discussed in] *Roth*, the liberty interest in family privacy has its source, and its contours are ordinarily to be sought, not in state law, but in intrinsic human rights, as they have been understood in 'this Nation's history and tradition.' " Id. at 845 (citing Moore v. East Cleveland, 431 U.S. 494, 503 (1977)).

legislate.[268] Whether a particular statute infringes upon that minimum boundary is a question that should be decided by reference to existing techniques for identifying legislation that draws impermissible distinctions. Thus, if the criteria used fell into established suspect classifications, one would expect the court to apply strict scrutiny.[269] Conversely, when the relevant legislative criteria are purely medical in nature, as is the case with anencephaly, the more relaxed rational basis test would govern.[270] Nor can the decision to reclassify only anencephalics, while leaving unchanged the status of other newborns who will die in infancy, be challenged on equal protection grounds. Such a scheme suffers from no constitutional infirmity, for it is well accepted that legislative reform may proceed "one step at a time, addressing itself to the phase of the problem which seems most acute to the legislative mind."[271] Therefore, the Court should permit the states to expand the definition of death to include anencephalic infants.

VII. THE SLIPPERY SLOPE ARGUMENT

The prior discussion demonstrates that the import attached to physiologic existence alone is unwarranted. Yet, the intuition may remain that there is some fundamental moral significance about live birth and whole brain death. The explanation behind such intuitions, I submit, lies not in these standards themselves but in the fear that once we have taken this first step, the rest of the camel is sure to follow,[272] with disastrous consequences. Joseph Fletcher, after proposing his fifteen

---

268. That states should enjoy considerable latitude in defining death is intuitively persuasive when one considers that the statutory adoption of whole brain death did not generate controversy as to its constitutionality. For example, one deliberative body, in issuing a report endorsing the whole brain criteria, termed it a standard "constitutional on its face." See The N.Y. State Task Force on Life and the Law, The Determination of Death 13 (1986).

269. Thus, the ability of states to circumvent strict scrutiny by defining a disfavored class of people as "dead" is surely cabined by the requirement that the criteria used not be racial or ethnic in nature. See, e.g., Brown v. Board of Educ., 347 U.S. 483 (1954) (racially segregated schools violate the fourteenth amendment's equal protection clause); Strauder v. West Virginia, 100 U.S. 303 (1879) (striking down murder conviction by a jury limited by state law to white males).

270. Under that standard, the Court has been willing to uphold any classification based "upon a state of facts that reasonably can be conceived to constitute a distinction, or difference in state policy." Allied Stores v. Bowers, 358 U.S. 522, 530 (1959). Even viewing anencephalics as physically handicapped should not trigger strict scrutiny by the courts, since the Supreme Court has held that those handicapped by mental retardation do not constitute a quasi-suspect class. City of Cleburne v. Cleburne Living Center, 473 U.S. 432, 442-46 (1985).

271. Williamson v. Lee Optical, 348 U.S. 483, 489 (1955); see also McDonald v. Board of Election Comm'rs, 394 U.S. 802, 809 (1969) (citing *Williamson*).

272. "[T]his is the first case [permitting a government agency to dictate the makeup of a newspaper's pages]. This is the first such case, but I fear it may not be the last. The camel's nose is in the tent." Pittsburgh Press Co. v. Pittsburgh Comm'n on Human Relations, 413 U.S. 376, 402 (1973) (Stewart, J., dissenting).

criteria of humanhood, closed with a dire warning: "Divorced from the laboratory and the hospital, talk about what it means to be human could easily become inhumane."[273] To redefine the status of anencephalics by declaring them nonpersons might push society down a slippery slope towards similar treatment for other seriously deformed infants.[274] This fear of the slippery slope must be addressed if we are to allow the utilization of anencephalics as organ donors.

A. *Involuntary Euthanasia*

Though often lumped together under the "slippery slope" rubric, this argument actually takes two distinct forms to which different considerations apply. The first involves the assertion that any step in this direction will eventually lead to the elimination of people who merely are regarded by society as undesirable.[275] Those sharing this apprehension concede that such a result would be a perversion, rather than an outgrowth, of the proposed policy change towards anencephalics. The distinction between removing organs from an infant on the brink of death and the extermination of those whom society might deem a burden is clear. Yet, future generations might be unwilling to draw such a distinction.

The issue of whether the transition from voluntary and nonvoluntary[276] forms of euthanasia to involuntary euthanasia is likely

---

273. Fletcher, supra note 180, at 4; see also Bok, Ethical Problems of Abortion, 2 Hastings Center Studies 33, 41 (1974) ("Slavery, witchhunts and wars have all been justified by their perpetrators on the grounds that they held their victims to be less than fully human.").

274. See, e.g., Ferrell, Brain-Defective Baby; Source of New Heart Ignites Ethics Debate, L.A. Times, Nov. 11, 1987, part 1, at 1, col. 3; Rothenberg & Shewmon, supra note 4.

275. The horrors of Nazi Germany serve as a constant reminder of man's inhumanity. For example, by authority of an informal letter signed by Hitler, 275,000 persons were killed as "useless eaters." See Silving, Euthanasia: A Study in Comparative Criminal Law, 103 U. Pa. L. Rev., 350, 356 n.23 (1954). Yale Kamisar argues vigorously for the proposition that "*it* [i.e., such practices] *can happen here unless we darn well make sure that it does not.*" Kamisar, Some Non-Religious Views Against Proposed "Mercy-Killing" Legislation, 42 Minn. L. Rev. 969, 1038 (1958).

The temptation to take advantage of such theories is especially pronounced in situations where some persons stand to benefit from their application. In Iran, for example, prisoners condemned to death have been declared nonhumans. The government then forcibly removes their eyes for transplantation to injured soldiers. See Krauthammer, supra note 4, at A27, col. 1. Financial gain also provides a strong motivation to disregard human life. Thus, Dr. W. Sackett, a Florida legislator who is also a physician, suggested that the state could save five billion dollars over the next fifty years if all Down's Syndrome patients were allowed to succumb to the pneumonia they frequently contract. See G. Larue, Euthanasia and Religion 5 (1985).

276. The term nonvoluntary euthanasia is used to describe situations in which the patient is incompetent to communicate his desire regarding what course of treatment to pursue. Involuntary euthanasia refers to the killing of competent persons against their will. But cf. Note, Voluntary Active Euthanasia for the Terminally Ill and the Constitu-

has been extensively debated.[277] Those arguments need not be reviewed here, but several salient points should be mentioned. As with every appeal to slippery slope anxieties, "the cost of accepting [such arguments] is the continued prohibition of some conduct that is actually acceptable."[278] The extent to which this concern militates against accepting the slippery slope position is a function of the magnitude of the interests thereby denied. As a consequence of the continued illegality of euthanasia, we accept that some individuals suffering intolerable and unmitigable pain will be refused an appropriate form of relief.[279] When we forego obtaining vital organs from anencephalics, however, much weightier interests are sacrificed. A viable liver can enable the potential recipient to experience a life that can be productive

---

tional Right to Privacy, 69 Cornell L. Rev. 363, 365–66 (1984) (describing both practices as involuntary euthanasia).

277. See Wechsler & Michael, supra note 204, at 739 n.148; Kamisar, supra note 275, at 1030–41. Kamisar points out that such a transition did occur in recent times in the Third Reich, whose policies on euthanasia sprang from an "acceptance of the attitude . . . that there is such a thing as life not worthy to be lived." Id. at 1032 (quoting Alexander, Medical Science Under Dictatorship, 241 New Eng. J. Med. 39, 44 (1949)). Kamisar then seeks to refute the argument that such practices, while possible in a dictatorship, cannot occur in a democratic society such as ours. He cites the experience of Japanese-Americans who were held in prison camps for many months without proffer of charges. That shameful chapter in American history was also the result of a slippery slope. Initially, a curfew requirement was imposed on those of Japanese ancestry, a measure that was upheld in Hirabayashi v. United States, 320 U.S. 81 (1943). That decision was then cited as authority for the confinement of those citizens in prison camps in Korematsu v. United States, 323 U.S. 214, 217–19 (1944); see also In re Eichner, 102 Misc. 2d 184, 199–200, 423 N.Y.S.2d 580, 591 (Sup. Ct. 1979) (fear that a decision permitting cessation of treatment based on the right to privacy would "invite unrestrained applications" of the doctrine), modified, 73 A.D.2d 431, 426 N.Y.S.2d 517 (1980), modified sub nom., In re Storar, 52 N.Y.2d 363, 420 N.E.2d 64, 438 N.Y.S.2d 266 (1981).

Glanville Williams is more sanguine about our ability to prevent such horrors. He notes that soldiers kill with legal impunity during wartime, yet that has in no way expanded the scope of acceptable killing. G. Williams, supra note 169, at 316. He maintains that American democratic processes provide protection against the dangers of the slippery slope. See also Gelfand, Euthanasia and the Terminally Ill Patient, 63 Neb. L. Rev. 741, 764–65 (1984) (the gap between voluntary and involuntary euthanasia should be portrayed as a chasm rather than a slope); Note, Equality for the Elderly Incompetent: A Proposal for Dignified Death, 39 Stan. L. Rev. 689, 727–28 (1987) (guidelines governing right to refuse treatment may be narrowly drawn).

278. President's Comm'n for the Study of Ethical Problems in Medicine and Biomedical and Behavioral Research, Deciding to Forego Life-Sustaining Treatment 29–30 (1983); see also Schauer, Slippery Slopes, 99 Harv. L. Rev. 361, 368–69 (1985) (slippery slope arguments necessarily concede that the instant case is being dealt with in an acceptable fashion).

279. Professor Kamisar acknowledges the validity of this interest at the beginning of his article, assuring all that in the case of an incurable pain-racked cancer victim, "I would hate to have to argue that the hand of death should be stayed." Kamisar, supra note 275, at 975. He then proceeds to argue at length for precisely that viewpoint, concluding that while it may be an "evil" for these patients to continue to suffer, it can be justified on the ground of the social interests to be protected. Id. at 1042.

for many years to come. Candidates for euthanasia, in contrast, by definition suffer from an incurable illness. Their suffering is finite. Therefore, the benefit to be derived from using anencephalics in transplants is of a greater degree and should not be rejected solely because of eventualities that may never materialize.

One might also consider what it is that renders slippery slope appeals compelling in a particular setting. Professor Schauer has identified the factors which contribute to their efficacy.[280] Important among these factors is the counterintuitive nature of the principles at risk of being violated at some future time.[281] For example, arguments of this type are especially popular in the area of free speech, because the rights being protected are difficult for jury and judge alike to appreciate. Often, the parties whose freedom we are asked to defend, such as the Nazis or the Hare Krishnas, espouse unpopular philosophies.[282] Similarly, in criminal procedure cases, it is often clear that the defendant is in fact guilty of the crime charged.[283] Thus, any curtailment of constitutional rights in these areas is likely to be expanded in the future given the nature of the litigants involved.

Such considerations would not come into play if anencephalics were made available as organ donors. There is nothing counterintuitive about the principles at stake here. Any attempt to expand the category of nonpersons would certainly be met with strong resistance rather than passive acquiescence.

Finally, this form of the slippery slope argument arises with regard to another dilemma in bioethics—that of withholding treatment from the seriously ill. Nevertheless, such practices have existed for some time, both informally[284] and formally,[285] and no one has charged that,

---

280. See Schauer, supra note 278, at 368–78.

281. Id. at 376–77.

282. See, e.g., National Socialist Party of Am. v. Village of Skokie, 432 U.S. 43 (1977) (per curiam); Collin v. Smith, 578 F.2d 1197 (7th Cir.), stay denied, 436 U.S. 953, cert. denied, 439 U.S. 916 (1978); International Soc'y for Krishna Consciousness, Inc. v. Barber, 506 F. Supp. 147 (N.D.N.Y. 1980), rev'd, 650 F.2d 430 (2d Cir. 1981); Edwards v. Maryland State Fair and Agricultural Soc'y, 476 F. Supp. 153 (D. Md. 1979) aff'd in part and rev'd in part, 628 F.2d 282 (4th Cir. 1980).

283. Compare Davies, A Hard Look at What We Know (and Still Need to Learn) About the "Costs" of the Exclusionary Rule: The NIJ Study and Other Studies of "Lost" Arrests, 1983 Am. B. Found. Res. J. 611, 680 (estimating rate of lost convictions due to illegal search or seizure at between 2.8% and 7.1% for those arrested on felony drug charges) with United States v. Leon, 468 U.S. 897, 908 n.6 (1983) (noting that the small percentages reported in such studies "mask a large absolute number of felons who are released because the cases against them were based in part on illegal searches or seizures").

284. The prevalence of selective nontreatment of newborns was first publicized in 1973 by two doctors at Yale-New Haven Hospital. See Duff & Campbell, Moral and Ethical Dilemmas in the Special-Care Nursery, 289 New Eng. J. Med. 890 (1973).

285. See, e.g., 42 U.S.C. § 5106g(10) (Supp. 1989) (withholding of treatment from infant not child abuse if patient is irreversibly comatose or if treatment would merely prolong dying).

974   COLUMBIA LAW REVIEW   [Vol. 90:917

for example, treatment is disproportionately withheld from minority children. Let us borrow a page from first amendment jurisprudence and weigh the "gravity of the 'evil,' discounted by its improbability."[286] When balanced by the expected benefits to be gained from utilizing anencephalics as donors, the scales tip decisively in favor of taking the risk.

B. *Line-Drawing Revisited*

There is, though, a second form of the slippery argument advanced by some—one more difficult to refute. I am referring here to the "where-do-you-draw-the-line?" variation. If sapient life is necessary for personhood, why limit the list of potential organ donors to anencephalics? Other defects also cause early mortality and prevent the possibility of conscious life from developing.[287] Since there is no natural boundary separating anencephaly from these other severe anomalies, perhaps it would be advisable to forego the admittedly legitimate use of anencephalics in order to prevent the scope of potential donor sources from being widened. It is feared that such an undesirable expansion might include other seriously defective newborns[288] and nonviable aborted fetuses.[289]

A claim such as this masquerades as a slippery slope argument, in that it supposedly points to an unappealing consequence of the theory of personhood, and by doing so purports to prove the theory false. Yet, the consequence is really no more or less appealing than the first step under consideration—the proposed utilization of organs from

---

286. Dennis v. United States, 341 U.S. 494, 510 (1951) (quoting lower court opinion by Hand, J., 183 F.2d 201, 212 (2d Cir. 1950)).

287. Infants born with renal agenesis or infantile polycystic kidneys can survive for only a few weeks after birth. Chervenak, Farley, Walters, Hobbins & Mahoney, supra note 207, at 502. Other such conditions include Potter's syndrome and trisomy 13. Arras & Shinnar, supra note 3, at 2285. Hydranencephaly, in which the brain has been destroyed by a major vascular event or disease during pregnancy, permits survival for only a few months, though some such children survive for several years without ever gaining consciousness. R. Weir, supra note 163, at 41–42.

288. Infants afflicted with conditions such as hydranencephaly or microcephaly actually may be more suitable as donors than anencephalics. Because such newborns tend to survive for a somewhat longer period than do anencephalics, their organs are more developed. This extra development eliminates some difficulties that occur with the use of organs obtained from the very youngest neonates, such as the tendency of vessels to clot. See Capron, supra note 3, at 7.

289. See Subcommittee Hearings, supra note 11, at 49 (testimony of Sister Maureen Webb, Consultant for Respect Life and Bioethics [sic], Diocese of Oakland). This feeling that abortuses may also be at risk needs some qualification. The arguments regarding anencephaly can in no principled way be extended to encompass the case of a viable abortus that has the potential with proper care to thrive. Therefore, while the first type of slippery slope argument, see supra notes 275–86, may be applicable to such fetuses, the line-drawing variation being considered here is not applicable. Our analysis therefore will be confined to nonviable abortuses and other neonates with severe birth defects.

anencephalics. After all, such other donors are no more capable of attaining the criteria of personhood than are anencephalics. If my arguments in support of this first step are convincing, then the supposedly embarrassing implications it entails are no longer embarrassing.[290] An appeal to the implications involved is really a facade, then, for those who dislike the implications of the initial step.

Nevertheless, there are some valid practical reasons for refraining from expanding determination of death statutes to be contiguous with the personhood criteria.[291] Thus, even this weak sort of argument may persuade some that any expansion of the sphere of acceptable organ donors would be disastrous, and hence any initial action in this direction ill-advised. All slippery slope arguments rest on some asserted empirical evidence indicating that a future slide is likely.[292] In this case, such fears are primarily fueled by the intuition that where no natural stopping point exists along a continuum the possibility of future encroachment is greater than in cases where a well-defined boundary can be identified. However, this belief is incorrect.

The flaw in such reasoning can be demonstrated by examining the bases underlying the slippery slope argument. Part of its strength lies in the linguistic imprecision which necessarily accompanies all legal formulae devised by society. The imprecision may arise either intentionally,[293] unavoidably,[294] or negligently. In any case, the advocate

---

290. Apropos is a remark made by the philosopher H.P. Grice. When confronted at a conference with the objection that a theory of his had a seemingly unacceptable implication, he replied: "See here, that's not an *objection* to my theory—*that's* my theory." Rachels, Killing and Starving to Death, *in* Moral Issues 163 (J. Narveson ed. 1983).

291. See supra notes 216–54 and accompanying text (describing problems of uncertainty of diagnosis and fear of public backlash as major reasons for rejecting wholesale incorporation of neocortical standard of death).

292. See Schauer, supra note 278, at 381–83.

293. The formulator of a rule may choose to articulate standards in language less rigid than otherwise necessary in order to preserve flexibility. Contrast, for example, the highly precise rules of the Bankruptcy Code with much of first amendment jurisprudence, which employs standards such as "clear and present danger," Brandenburg v. Ohio, 395 U.S. 444, 447 (1969) or "public figure," Curtis Publishing Co. v. Butts, 388 U.S. 130 (1967). The resulting sacrifice in precision is deemed to be compensated for by the greater adaptability inherent in the more general phrasing. This technique is frequently used in judicial opinions, which often cannot deal specifically with all the permutations that may arise in future situations. See Schauer, supra note 278, at 370–73.

294. Linguists refer to this phenomenon as "open texture," the concept that new situations previously unimagined may arise that would cause seemingly precise language (at the time of writing) to become vague (in the face of unforeseen developments). See Waismann, Verifiability, *in* Essays on Logic and Language 117 (A. Flew ed. 1st ser. 1951); Margalit, Open Texture, *in* Meaning and Use 141 (A. Margalit ed. 1979). Compare the People ex rel. Fyfe v. Barnett, 319 Ill. 403, 150 N.E. 290 (1926) with Commonwealth v. Maxwell, 271 Pa. 378, 114 A. 825 (1921). Both Illinois and Pennsylvania had statutes providing that prospective jurors shall be selected from lists of eligible voters. At the time of the enactment of these statutes, only males were eligible

making the slippery slope argument claims that any move from the current state of affairs to the instant case will eventually lead to the danger case because of the inherent looseness in the rule created to address the instant case.

A subtle consideration is that a line artificially drawn at some point in a spectrum can often be less fuzzy than boundaries which correspond to some sort of natural division. The firmness of the line is actually a function of the degree of precision in the language used, rather than the setting in which this particular line happens to be laid down.[295] Moreover, some concepts lend themselves to exact definition while others do not. The proposal to permit organ removal from anencephalics offers a prime example of a concept capable of precise formulation in just one word. Anencephaly is a condition that can be clinically confused with no other; nor does the visual appearance of anencephalics resemble that of other neonates.[296] In addition, the biological lifespan of anencephalics is shorter than that of infants afflicted with other serious diseases.[297] There can therefore be no doubt in the future about where this particular cutoff is situated. This in itself is a

---

to vote in both states. Subsequently, the nineteenth amendment to the federal constitution gave women the right to vote, giving rise to the question whether they were eligible to serve as jurors under the respective statutes of the two states. *Fyfe* held they were not, while *Maxwell* reached the opposite conclusion. See also Moore, The Semantics of Judging, 54 S. Cal. L. Rev. 151, 200–02 (1981) (discussing problem of open texture).

295. A cogent example is the reduction in the size of juries from twelve to six in Williams v. Florida, 399 U.S. 78 (1970) (criminal cases) and Colgrove v. Battin, 413 U.S. 149 (1973) (civil cases). In both, the argument was made that if jury size could be diminished to six, why not to five or four—or one? See *Williams*, 399 U.S. at 126, *Colgrove*, 413 U.S. at 180–82. This argument failed simply because the Supreme Court declared that five was not a sufficient number of jurors, while six was. See Ballew v. Georgia, 435 U.S. 223, 239 (1978). The line between five and six, once drawn, is more firm than the distinction between a "sufficiently large jury" and an "insufficiently large jury." Of course, this relates only to the ability of future decision makers to determine the precise *location* of the line. It does not explain *why* the line was drawn there, thus leaving the possibility open that it would be moved in the future to some other point on the continuum by lawmakers unwilling or unable to understand the reason why it was put there at first. Yet, that problem did not seem to trouble the Court in the jury cases. See Schauer, supra note 278, at 379–80.

296. See supra notes 21–24 and accompanying text.

297. Practically speaking, infants suffering from other serious disabilities have not been seriously considered as donors because doing so would involve the sacrifice of a greater period of biological life. Botkin, supra note 34, at 253. The difference, of course, is in degree rather than in kind, precisely as in the jury cases. See supra note 295. The Court confessed that there existed no clear line between a jury of six and one of five. *Ballew*, 435 U.S. at 239 (1978). Both suffer from the same defects of impaired group deliberation and inaccurate fact finding when compared with a jury of twelve, with the defect becoming progressively worse as jury size diminishes. Id. at 232–39. The Court, however, was satisfied with a rule that says "till here, but no further" in order to accommodate the interest of the various states in having less expensive and more expeditious trials. See id. at 243–44.

powerful safeguard against future deterioration of the established position.

CONCLUSION

"There is only one argument for doing something; the rest are arguments for doing nothing."[298]

One concern shared by participants on both sides of the controversy is that these infants be treated with respect and dignity as befits all human offspring. It bears emphasizing that proposals to legitimate organ procurement from anencephalics do not displace parental choice regarding what conduct is most appropriate. Parents who feel, as some writers have suggested,[299] that the donation of life-giving organs is the highest form of dignity accorded the anencephalic infant, would be able to fulfill such wishes if statutory change was adopted. Alternatively, parents who disapprove of the idea of organ procurement would retain the power of decision even under a statutory scheme that declared a child born with anencephaly to be dead. As next of kin, it is they who have the right to donate organs of the deceased child for transplantation purposes.[300] Another possible analogy supporting parental choice is the notion that individuals possess property rights in excised body parts.[301] Therefore, recognizing that children born with anencephaly are not alive would not invite disrespectful treatment on the part of physicians who might wish to utilize these subjects for transplantation or experimentation purposes.[302] The decision would rest in the hands

---

298. J. Harris, supra note 6, at 116 (quoting F. Cornford, The Microcosmographia Academica (1908)).

299. See Caplan, supra note 3, at 128.

300. UAGA § 2(b), 8A U.L.A. 15, 34 (1983). The UAGA has been adopted by all 50 states and the District of Columbia. See id., at 15–16 (table of jurisdictions where act has been adopted); see also Georgia Lions Eye Bank, Inc. v. Lavant, 255 Ga. 60, 335 S.E.2d 127 (1985) (holding that relatives have a quasi-property interest in the bodies of their next of kin), cert. denied, 475 U.S. 1084 (1986).

301. See, e.g., Moore v. Regents of the Univ. of Cal., 202 Cal. App. 3d 1230, 249 Cal. Rptr. 494 (Ct. App.), review granted, 47 Cal. 3d 6, 763 P.2d 479, 252 Cal. Rptr. 816 (1988) (patient possesses property interest in his excised spleen and is consequently entitled to share in profits from commercially valuable cell line developed using his spleen tissue); Robertson, Embryos, Families, & Procreative Liberty: The Legal Structure of the New Reproduction, 59 S. Cal. L. Rev. 939, 974 (1986) (parents have property interests in unused gametes they have produced). See generally Note, She's Got Betty Davis['s] Eyes: Removal of Cadaver Organs Under the Takings and Due Process Clauses, 90 Colum. L. Rev. 528, 542–60 (1990) (surveying property rights in the body).

302. Since the parents have the power to direct the disposal of their child's remains, any unauthorized removal or use of body parts by others would give rise to both civil and criminal liability. See, e.g., Palmquist v. Standard Accident Ins. Co., 3 F. Supp. 358, 359–60 (S.D. Cal. 1933) (surviving spouse obtained damages against coroner who, without authority, retained deceased's body); Diebler v. American Radiator & Standard Sanitary Corp., 196 Misc. 618, 619, 92 N.Y.S.2d 356, 357 (Sup. Ct. 1949) (same); Trammel v. City of New York, 193 Misc. 756, 82 N.Y.S.2d 762 (Sup. Ct. 1948) (same), aff'd, 276 A.D. 781, 93 N.Y.S.2d 299 (App. Div. 1949). In addition, grave robbing statutes

978   *COLUMBIA LAW REVIEW*   [Vol. 90:917

of those whose love for the infant will guide them in selecting a plan that will give meaning to the child's brief existence. Whether that plan involves transplantation or instead simply permits events to run their natural course in the solitude of a hospital room, we can be sure that their choice will be the appropriate one.

Breaking new ground in the law is not an easy thing to do. The praises of stability are well sung. Nevertheless, preservation of the status quo was never the objective of our legal system. Oliver Wendell Holmes once remarked: "It is revolting to have no better reason for a rule of law than that so it was laid down in the time of Henry IV. It is still more revolting if the grounds upon which it was laid down have vanished long since, and the rule simply persists from blind imitation of the past."[303] Law is a mirror of society—as the world changes, so does its reflection captured in the mirror.

Anencephalic newborns pose both a challenge and an opportunity for society. This Article has shown that current attempts to meet this challenge within the framework of existing law create new problems which result in a blend of poor medicine and ill fitting law. Far preferable is for society to recognize that the existing rejection of the concept of neocortical death is predicated upon rationales which have no relevance to anencephaly. This treatment is not a form of disrespect. It is rather an affirmation that from tragic circumstances great good can be brought forth.

---

have been used as the basis for potential criminal liability in prosecutions against physicians who have performed unauthorized experiments on fetal remains. See Capron, supra note 208, at 13-7 to 13-8.

Another related ethical concern, in the fetal transplant context, is that women may become pregnant with the intention of having an abortion to aid an ailing relative. See, e.g., Lewin, Medical Use of Fetal Tissue Spurs New Abortion Debate, N.Y. Times, Aug. 16, 1987, at A1, col. 4 (citing case of California woman who considered becoming artificially inseminated with her father's sperm, aborting the resultant fetus, and transplanting brain tissue from the abortus into her father's brain to combat the Alzheimer's disease from which he suffered). This fear is obviously nonexistent in the context of anencephaly, for a woman cannot intend to conceive a fetus afflicted with anencephaly.

303. Holmes, The Path of the Law, 10 Harv. L. Rev. 457, 469 (1897).

[21]

ANENCEPHALICS AS ORGAN SOURCES

SHARON E. SYTSMA

ABSTRACT. In recent years, the need for infant organs for transplantation has increased. There is a growing recognition of the potential use of anencephalics as sources of organs. Prevalent arguments defending the use of live anencephalics for organ sources are identified and criticized. I argue that attempts to deny the applicability of the "dead-donor rule" are either question-begging or based on false premises and that attempts to skirt the Kantian dictum against treating others as a means only are not successful. I contend that the apparent utilitarian justification for live anencephalics as organ sources is unsatisfactory for two reasons: first, because it ignores the undermining effect the policy would have on parental values and sentiments central to social welfare; and second, because attempts to respond adequately to the slippery slope argument against live anencephalic use are unconvincing.

Key words: anencephalics, ethics, live donor transplantation, medical ethics, organ transplantation

1. INTRODUCTION

Presently our laws require that organs be taken only from brain-dead human beings. In recent years, the demand for infant organs for transplantation has increased, and there is a growing recognition of the potential use of live anencephalics as sources of organs.[1] Given both the intense need and a changing mentality, a continued effort to change our current organ transplant requirements is underway. The American Medical Association has announced its approval of live anencephalic organ use.[2] Some have argued that the use of live anencephalic organs is not only morally permissible, but morally required.[3] Under this persuasion, John McDonald,[4] president of both the American Society of Transplant Surgeons and the United Network for Organ Sharing, is working towards and expects a change in the law which would permit the use of live anencephalics as organ sources. Walters[5] reports that in a survey of informed physicians and ethicists, 57% of physicians and 72% of ethicists find no moral objections to the practice, though many were opposed because of social concerns.

Since the policy calling for live anencephalic organ transplants marks such a significant aberration from traditional policies, the burden of justification for its moral permissibility lies with its proponents. Proponents of

20   SHARON E. SYTSMA

live anencephalic organ transplantation must pursue one of the following options: 1) they must put forth arguments showing that taking organs from anencephalics does not violate the current "dead donor" rule (inapplicability approach); 2) they must put forth arguments for making an exception for the anencephalic, which would apply to the anencephalic but not to other similar cases (exclusionary approach); or 3) they must show that the "dead donor" rule should be changed (revisionist approach).

In this paper, I review and critically evaluate the prevalent arguments in defense of the use of anencephalics for organ sources, and I further the attempt to construct a resistance to this policy. I argue that the inapplicability approach is based on premises which are either obviously false or hopelessly question-begging, and also that attempts to skirt the Kantian dictum against treating others as a "means only" are unconvincing. However, I do not base my resistance to live anencephalic organ use on Kant's principle because of its ineluctable indeterminacy: honesty demands the admission that it is not always clear when we are treating another as a means only. Instead, I argue against the exclusionary and the revisionist approaches on the grounds that a policy for using live anencephalic as organ sources threatens natural emotive attachments central to the existential meaning of parenthood – emotions which are serviceable to society, and thus deserving of protection. I also defend the slippery slope argument against this policy by challenging the claim of its opponents that anencephalics constitute a class by themselves.

2. THE INAPPLICABILITY ARGUMENT

The inapplicability argument refers to a determination that using anencephalics as organ sources does not invalidate the "dead donor" rule. One argument within the inapplicability approach calls the anencephalic brain dead.[6] According to the Uniform Determination of Death Act (UDDA), a human being is not dead unless both the higher and the lower brain have ceased functioning. Since all anencephalics suitable for organ transplantation have at least a functioning brain stem, it is erroneous to classify them as brain dead, at least without further argument. Another argument calls the anencephalic "brain absent," thereby making the determination of brain death irrelevant.[7] Again, this attempt ignores the presence of the brain stem; that the anencephalic has a partial brain and is biologically alive is an incontestable fact.

Other attempts within the inapplicability approach deny that the anencephalic is a human being, or a person, or a being with a right to life.[8] If the terms "human being" or "person" are used in the "moral sense," such arguments beg the question. Even if arguments are provided for why anencephalics are not persons, the fallacy is still committed. For instance, Serafini,[9] after arguing that anencephalics are not persons because they have no mental life, goes on to assert that "because anencephalics are not persons, there are no reasons – based on questions of personhood – why anencephalics cannot be killed, and, it is hoped, be used as sources of organs." The inference depends on the very questionable missing premise that only persons have a moral status.

If "human being" means membership in our species, then the anencephalic is one, and further argument must be given to show that it can be treated differently than other human beings. If "person" means having person-like capacities, the anencephalic is excluded; nevertheless, many human beings who are not "persons" in this sense are accorded a right to life – for example, other infants and the severely demented. Again, further argument is required to defend the moral permissibility of taking the lives of only anencephalics for the sake of others. To begin by denying that the anencephalic has a right to life also hopelessly begs the question: it is to assume just what is supposed to be proven.

3. EXCLUSIONARY AND REVISIONIST ARGUMENTS

Most exclusionary and revisionist approaches towards the use of anencephalics as organ sources rely on a utilitarian appeal: the anencephalic is undoubtedly going to die, and very soon. It has no interests. Another child's life, or perhaps even several other children's lives, assuming more than one of the anencephalic's organs are healthy, might be saved if a transplant is performed. Infants who need organ transplants require *infant* organs. It is better to save one life than to allow two or more to perish. Therefore, we should either make an exception for the anencephalic, or revise our "dead donor" rule, so that we may retrieve organs from anencephalics, and possibly from others who cannot be said to have interests and who will never have interests again. Our focus is shifted away from our caring tendance of the dying infant toward the dramatic prospect of altering the course of nature and saving another infant's life. As Walters'[10] survey of physicians and ethicists indicates, this argument has for many an irresistible appeal.

Objections to this apparent utilitarian appeal can be framed in either deontological or utilitarian terms. Realizing how well the Kantian dictum against treating others as a means only is grounded in ethical tradition,

22   SHARON E. SYTSMA

supporters of live anencephalic organ use have devised a variety of attempts
to reconcile their policy with the deontological emphasis on intrinsic worth.
I will examine these attempts and then further examine the issue from a
utilitarian perspective.

Kant's[11] third formulation of the Categorical Imperative prohibits treating
humanity, whether in our own person or in that of others, merely as a means
to an end. All rational beings, he claims, have intrinsic and not merely
extrinsic worth, which is a function of autonomy. Understandably, many
would think that in removing the organs of the anencephalic we are treating
it as a mere means to another's good.[12]

Supporters of anencephalic organ use argue that the Kantian dictum
doesn not apply to anencephalics, or indeed, to any human being that is not
capable of autonomy. "Regardless of the interpretation of Kant's categorical imperative," Walters and Ashwal[13] claim, "it appears that he did not
have non-self-aware humans in mind in his philosophizing. Therefore, to
apply Kant's standard to anencephalic infants is beyond – not necessarily
contrary to – his writings." Some argue that the Kantian dictum does not
apply to anencephalics because only beings who have "ends" in the sense
of "goals" are beings who must be treated as "ends," that is, beings worthy
of respect. Beings who are thought of as "ends in themselves" are interpreted as beings who are presently capable of constructing aims – ends –
for themselves. Thus Graber[14] concludes that it is impossible to treat the
deceased "as ends" because "they no longer have any values, goals, or
wishes for us to honor or promote," and the same would hold for anencephalics. Graber[15] claims: "We are not using a person as a means in an
objectionable way by decisions to harvest organs, as long as the decisions
and associated procedures accord with the dignity, delicacy, reverence,
and respect appropriate to the human status of the dead or dying individual."

The error of conflating "having ends" with "being an end" underlies
Jecker's[16] inference that using anencephalics as organ donors upon parental
request is permissible. Relying on Engelhardt's[17] notion of infants as
"persons-in-a-social-sense," Jecker[18] proposes that for beings who are not
persons in themselves, but only persons in relation to others, we treat them
"as ends" by constructing ends for them: "The idea is that such treatment
does not involve treating anencephalic infants as a mere means, because
the infant's ends are inextricably linked to the parents' ends and the
treatment advances important ends parents hold." We respect such infants
as ends by respecting the ends of their parents. I believe that these conclusions are based on an illegitimate interpretation of Kant's view.

Despite his claims that intrinsic worth is due to freedom and rationality,
Kant[19] himself refers to children as "persons," as "citizens of the world,"

ANENCEPHALICS AS ORGAN SOURCES   23

and as beings with rights, deserving of respect. He claims that neither infanticide nor the abandonment of children is morally permissible, that all children have an innate right to be cared for by their parents, and that children should not be looked upon nor treated as property. These comments indicate that Kant did think of infants and children as having intrinsic worth, a view in keeping with the general prohibition against infanticide.[20] Therefore, when Kant speaks of "man and any rational being" existing "as an end in himself, *not merely as a means*," he is attributing "absolute worth" not only to "rational men" but to members of "mankind," that is, the human species. He did not equate "having ends" with "being an end," as both Graber and Jecker do. For Kant, being "an end" means "having intrinsic worth," not "having goals and desires." Apart from Jecker's questionable interpretation of Kant's dictum, the suggestion that we respect an infant's ends by respecting its parents' ends is a problematic and dangerous proposal, one which even Engelhardt[21] does not consistently uphold. Engelhardt[22] argues that we should respect parental autonomy *unless* doing so encourages a lack of respect for the care of children, or if doing so will lead to unnecessary suffering on the part of the child. Such a claim is inconsistent with the view that infants have moral status only in and through their parents.

What is not clear is whether Kant thought of the intrinsic worth of children as a result of their potentiality for autonomy or as a result of their coming into the world (without their consent) due to the actions of beings who are autonomous. Kant might have thought of the intrinsic worth of children as due to their being members of our species, "one of us." To suggest that infants have moral status because they belong to our species does not make one automatically guilty of "speciesism." One could hold this view and also hold that members of other species have special obligations to members of their own species, and also recognize that we do have some obligations to members of other species. Kant's[23] view of offspring as beings who are born "endowed with freedom" unfortunately does nothing to help us resolve the question of why he attributed a moral status to infants and children.

Thomasma[24] argues that the treatment of anencephalics as an organ source is justified precisely because these infants lack any qualities of "personhood," and any potentiality for autonomy. He does not support the use of other beings who are "nonpersons" for organ sources. Persons in a persistent vegetative state or who are permanently comatose are "former persons," who have a value history, and had the opportunity to make a decision to offer their organs. Also, there is an (albeit extremely remote) possibility that a person in a permanent vegetative state might come out

24   SHARON E. SYTSMA

of his or her coma. Normal infants, most defective infants, and even fetuses are potential persons and therefore, according to Thomasma,[25] appropriate subjects of deontological concern.

Thomasma[26] does allow that beings who lack either former or potential personhood are deserving of respect, since they are human beings (they have "ontic value"), but he claims that the respect for their lives "takes the form of utilitarian concern, of benefiting others through transplant of tissue organs." The moral imperative to respect life for these non-persons is transformed away from respecting their lives into respecting the means within them which can be used to preserve the lives of others. This view allows Thomasma[27] to draw an analogy between childbearing and organ donation: "The moral choice of a mother who bears a child is to give life support. The same choice follows naturally when that child cannot sustain its own life. Then the choice of the mother, subject to objections of the father, might be to donate the organs of that being in order to continue to choose life support."

Thomasma[28] concludes that the anencephalic has no right to life, and the parents may make the decision to donate its organs. The argument is not convincing because there still remains the possibility that our obligation to children is *not* to be understood as a function of their potentiality for personhood, but is due to the fact that through our actions we have brought them into existence. I will pursue this line of thought further later in the discussion.

Another attempt to avoid the accusation of treating anencephalics as a means only is to simply deny that this is what we are doing. For example, Walters and Ashwal,[29] defending respirator use to obtain anencephalic organs, write: "No, this does not treat such infants as means only, but admittedly utilizes them as means primarily." The claim is that we can impose respirator use, surgically remove vital organs, all the while maintaining a respect for the intrinsic worth of the anencephalic. Our respect for the infant as an end can sufficiently be demonstrated by the fact that the usual rituals in the treatment of cadavers are observed.

This view unfortunately highlights the limits of Kant's third formulation of the Categorical Imperative as a normative guide. Sometimes it is just not clear whether we are treating a person as a means only. Is the claim that we are not using the anencephalic as a means only legitimate, or is it the epitome of sophistry and self-deception? Can we fulfill whatever obligation we have towards the anencephalic by "respectfully" removing its organs, and afterwards providing ritualistic burial? We would not make this claim if the "organ source" were an autonomous living being kidnapped by an underground organ market syndicate. Nor do I think we would make this claim if the organ source were a deceased person whose religious views prohibited the decision to be an organ donor, or even a deceased person who for whatever reason expressed a reluctance to volunteer as a donor. I do not think that even when a person personally chooses to donate his or her organs that we have a sufficient guarantee that we are truly respecting the person as an end, for it may be that the donor doesn't have sufficient self-respect, and the offering of organs is done out of a misguided self-sacrificial attitude. The clearest cases in which it is conceivable that we can respect persons as ends while taking their organs are those in which persons have made autonomous decisions to sacrifice their organs as a gift to others.

4. PARENTAL RESPONSIBILITIES AND CONCERNS

Currently, we allow next of kin to donate organs of their deceased relatives. The presumption is that the relatives *care* about the deceased, and will make a decision in keeping with his or her wishes. The decision to donate organs is left to the relatives who have the responsibility of the disposition of the body. Thus, respect for the deceased is maintained. If relatives made a decision contrary to the known previous wishes of the deceased, or if individuals without proper authority chose to have the organs donated, respect for the deceased would be violated. Supposing that allowing relatives to donate organs of their deceased is in keeping with respect for persons, would the offering of the live anencephalic's organs by its parents also be? Many will think not. What relevant difference can be pointed to in order to explain this perception?

While it is obvious that the responsibility of the next of kin of the deceased is to provide for the disposition of the body, the responsibility of the next of kin (the parents) of the living, but dying, infant is *caring*. What "caring" entails depends on the situation of the child. Normally, it implies protection and nurturing. If nurturing the child involves means which would not be beneficial, but would only prolong the dying process and increase suffering, then foregoing those means would be permissible. If the child's disease involved excruciating and uncontrollable pain, caring might even involve using means which foreseeably will shorten its life. It does not seem that caring *for the child* could ever allow killing it *in order to* save another. This may have been the insight that guides Meilaender[30] to propose that in order to refrain from treating the anencephalic infant as a means only we must refrain from doing anything which we would not ordinarily do in the care of a dying infant.

The deontological prohibition against using the anencephalic as an organ source coheres with the notion that parents have special obligations to their children. Thus, Thomasma's[31] claim that childbearing and organ donation are analogous is thrown into question. The "moral choice" of the parent is not simply to provide "life-support"; and despite the fact that some parents have been willing, the choice to donate one's own infant's organs to save another life cannot be said to "naturally" follow, given the fact that special obligations to one's own children are universally recognized. The denial that we are treating anencephalic infants as means only strains credulity because of this sense of special obligation.

The predominant, even if not universal, view that parents should not be morally required to donate their anencephalics' organs is revealing. Consider the parents who are protective of their anencephalic, refusing respirator use for organ retrieval purposes which would artificially prolong the life of the infant, or indeed any treatment which is not designed specifically with their infant in mind. I believe their steadfast protection of the child, even knowing the child will die soon, inspires not only sympathy, but admiration. A policy allowing anencephalic organ transplantation would undermine this perception.

Having highlighted the special obligation between parents and children, we can return to the utilitarian analysis. Utilitarianism has often been criticized for leading to conclusions which violate our sense of special obligations. The utilitarian defense is that the importance of these special obligations must be factored into the utilitarian calculation. A policy allowing parents to donate the organs of their live anencephalic may undermine this sense of special obligation because it would trivialize the parents' emotional attachment and natural protective inclination, the weakening of which could ultimately be detrimental to the society. Social utility is served by natural familial sentiments. Many of us experience a natural emotive response which condemns any proposal to treat one human being as a means to save another no matter how bleak the prognosis. However, emotional responses do not by themselves constitute moral grounds. Nevertheless, they are relevant; and they may prevent us from prematurely giving our assent to otherwise logical sounding arguments or even motivate us to counter such arguments.[32]

The symbolic appeal concerning the value of existential parental emotive attitudes can be broadened. Some proponents of the dead donor rule argue that adhering to that rule is symbolic of our respect for the dying and of our resistance to the tendency to think of others as sources of body parts.[33] Though not ultimately convinced by either side of the issue, Arnold and Youngner[34] recognize the importance of these symbolic appeals: "Symbols keep us attuned to what we consider important. As such they shape our self-conception and how we organize our communities."

Parents are not the only ones who experience an emotive repulsion against a proposal for live anencephalic organ use, or whose emotive responses need protecting. If medical professionals are convinced that anencephalic organs ought to be transplanted, they too must overcome their emotive tendencies which would otherwise prevent them from killing their patients. Van Cleve,[35] in interviews studying the experience of nurses who had the opportunity to care for anencephalics being treated as potential organ sources, found that while 56% responded positively and without reservation to the opportunity to care for anencephalics, many respondent's enthusiasm wavered as they participated in such programs. Sixty-five percent reported concern for the dignity of the infant and 68% expressed concern about the possibility of pain in the infant. Among those actually caring for the anencephalics, feelings of "stressors" were cited more often than feelings of satisfaction, and many reported that they experienced no feelings of satisfaction at all. These are not emotional reactions we should desire to be numbed or disregarded in our nurses. The safeguarding of these emotions is an important strategy for averting a slippery slope effect.

5. THE SLIPPERY SLOPE EFFECT

Most opponents of the policy for live anencephalic organ use are worried about a slippery slope effect. Capron[36] has argued against the revisionist approach by showing that redefining death to allow for anencephalic organ use might lead to harvesting organs from others for whom life is no benefit, including the comatose, permanently vegetative, senile, and other infants with similar neurological defects. Churchill and Pinkus[37] warn against redefining death for utilitarian reasons because of the same concern. They argue that the definition of death formulated by the President's Commission in the early eighties was motivated in the spirit of philosophical and social inquiry, but not by the interests of society or the medical community in saving lives.

Proponents have countered that a slippery slope effect is not likely because anencephalics are in a class by themselves, so using them for organs will not lead to using others for organs. Harrison,[38] director of a fetal transplant program, states with confidence: "This category can be narrowly defined, and cannot be expanded to include individuals with less severe anomalies or injuries." The Ethics and Social Impact Committee in Ann Arbor, Michigan claims that anencephalics are "absolutely unique"

28   SHARON E. SYTSMA

and that there is no possibility of confusion between anencephaly and other genetic anomalies.[39]

Thomasma's[40] response to an envisioned slippery slope effect is to point out that the anencephalic is in a class by itself *(sui generis)*. The anencephalic is neither a potential nor a former person. The anencephalic is in a class separate from the class of persons in a vegetative state, and from other infants. However, there still remains the possibility that the slippery slope effect could extend to infants with other neurological defects who are facing immanent death. Shewmon,[41] for example, points to instances where infants with other conditions have been diagnosed as anencephalics. Capron[42] argues that other neurological defects such as hydranencephaly and microcephaly are "*conceptually* indistinguishable" from anencephaly: they all are lethal neurological conditions. Shewmon[43] admits that diagnosis in most cases is dependable, but nevertheless claims that "the commonly encountered contention that 'anencephaly' is so well defined and so distinct from all other congenital brain malformations that misdiagnoses cannot occur and that organ-harvesting policies limited to 'anencephalics' cannot possibly extend to other conditions, is simply false." Infants with severe cases of microcephaly with encephalocele, for instance, can have a greater life expectancy than less severe cases of mero-anencephaly. Infants with amniotic band syndrome are not considered anencephalics by some, but are by others.

Truog and Fletcher[44] suggest a revision of the definition of death which they think adequately separates the anencephalic from other classes of defective infants, and also from the permanently vegetative. They assert that the arguments supporting the Uniform Determination of Death Act (according to which the brain-dead are considered dead) are applicable also to anencephalics, so anencephalics should be considered dead. The President's Commission, they argue, ignores the evidence of continued brain function in the central nervous system even after "brain-death" has occurred. The justification of restricting the demand of brain-death to the upper and lower brain could only be that upon the death of the upper and lower brain, death is surely imminent. Since the anencephalic is also surely imminently dead, they conclude that the anencephalic should be considered dead. Accordingly, Truog and Fletcher[45] put forth the following alternative definition of death: People are dead "if they have a distinct and precisely definable condition characterized by the absence of integrated brain function, such that somatic death is uniformly imminent." Moreover, Truog and Fletcher[46] claim that "from a theoretical view" their analysis "invalidates any concerns about a 'slippery-slope' extension of [their] proposal to other handicapped adults or infants."

While this definition of death would exclude the permanently vegetative and almost all other infant defects and diseases, it is not clear that other
severe neurological conditions are not "characterized by the absence of
integrated brain function." So Shewmon's and Capron's point still holds.
Further, the claim that anencephalics are imminently dead ignores the albeit
rare instances where anencephalics live for weeks, or even months.[47] Most
importantly, however, the distinctions between anencephalics and other
similar cases are so sophisticated and subtle, that they might elude even
those in the medical profession. Truog and Fletcher[48] admit this, and
recognize that while there are *theoretical* considerations supporting the
sui generis status of anencephalics, *pragmatic* concerns must be "seriously
considered" before we change our definition of death. In short, the "slippery
slope" still threatens.

If the justification for anencephalic organ transplants is that these infants
are not self-conscious and will die soon, what difference does it make that
the infant will die in a day or in a week, a month, or two years? The denial
that a slippery slope effect could take place for other such infants is
unconvincing because the justification applies logically to other conditions as well.[49] The impetus to call for live anencephalic use based on the
urgent need for infant organs and a concern for greater likelihood of
success, surely would suggest the use of similar conditions which further
guaranteed success. Hydraencephalics have more viable organs.

Furthermore, just because there is some way to distinguish between the
anencephalic and other groups does not guarantee that the distinction
between appropriate and inappropriate organ sources will be maintained
accordingly. Some scholars are not disturbed by the prospect of a slippery
slope effect. Graber[50] acknowledges and embraces the applicability of the
justification for those who are permanently comatose or in a vegetative
state, or indeed, for "any of the categories of patients who, although not
yet dead, are imminently dying." Nevertheless, I must agree with those,
like Arthur Caplan,[51] who believe that such a policy would have a deleterious effect on organ transplant programs, because people could become
afraid to donate their organs for fear that the medical profession will not
treat them in their dying hours in view of their own best interest, but rather
as a viable organ source. The policy could also have damaging consequences for the well-being of society, much more so than even a proposal
for active voluntary euthanasia, because of its frank utilitarian appeal that
accommodates and encourages judgements that some lives can be sacrificed for others.

30   SHARON E. SYTSMA

6. CONCLUSION

I have argued that proponents of anencephalic organ transplantation have not successfully come to grips with the Kantian prohibition against treating others as a means only. Such a policy is likely to evoke a sense of outrage and abhorrence in many attending to the issue, not the least, those health care providers who are called upon to assist the transplant operations. Catholic moralists are at odds as to whether even inducing abortion for anencephalic fetuses to protect the mother from risks is morally permissible – so far are they from accepting a utilitarian justification of live anencephalic organ use.[52] I have also suggested that a utilitarian analysis does not clearly indicate support of such a policy. If anencephalic organ transplantation is sanctioned by the legal system, parents of prenatally diagnosed anencephalics will very likely begin to think that they had an obligation to bring the fetuses to term, and to donate their infants' organs. What should be thought of as a supererogatory act becomes morally required. This effect could weaken parental protective emotive attitudes. Our concern for altruism should not encourage us to abandon our existential meaning and integrity as parents and caretakers. The legal sanctioning of anencephalic organ transplantation tarnishes and thereby jeopardizes the ideal of parenthood. Qualities we admire as virtuous and as having a social utility should not be compromised at the level of policy. Indeed, the term "altruism" is strained when applied to the offering of one's own infant for the good of another. Altruistic acts involve sacrifices on one's own part, not on that of another.

If such a proposal were sanctioned, parents of infants that require organs for survival will feel an obligation to have the transplant surgery take place if an organ were available. The view that a human being with a defective organ has a right to another human being's organ, whatever their condition, is a perversion of morality, turning an "imperfect duty" into a "perfect one."

REFERENCES

1. Diaz JH. The anencephalic organ donor: A challenge to existing moral and statutory laws. *Critical Care Medicine* 1993;21(11):1781.
2. American Medical Association Council on Ethical and Judicial Affairs. The use of anencephalic neonates as organ donors. *J Am Med Assoc* 1995; 273(20): 1614–1618.
3. Zaner RM. Anencephalics as organ donors. *J Med Phil* 1989;14(1):72.
4. McDonald J. Too many organs going to waste. *Shreveport Times*, 1988 Apr 3:8(col 2).
5. Walters JW. Anencephalic infants as organ sources. *Bioethics* 1991;5(4):326–341.
6. Holzgreve W, Beller FK, Buchholz B, et al. Kidney transplantation from anencephalic donors. *New Engl Med* 1987;316:1069.

7. Harrison M. The anencephalic as organ donor. *Hasting Center Report* 1986;16:21. Also: Bailey LL. Donor organs from human anencephalics: A salutary resource for infant heart transplantation. *Transplant Proceedings* 1988;20:35–38.
8. Cefalo RC, Engelhardt HT. The use of anencephalic tissue for transplantation. *Med Phil* 1989;14(1):89. Also: Zaner R. (1989):69 and Serafini A. Is coma morally equivalent to anencephalia? *Ethics and Behavior* 1993;3(2):187–198.
9. Serafini: 196.
10. Walters.
11. Kant I. *Fundamental Principles of the Metaphysics of Morals*. Abbott T, trans. Indianapolis: Bobbs-Merrill Co., Inc., 1949:46.
12. Churchill LR, Pinkus RLB. The use of anencephalic organs: historical and ethical dimensions. *The Milbank Quarterly* 1990;68(2):147–169.
13. Walters JW, Ashwal S. Organ prolongation in anencephalic infants: ethical & medical issues. *Hastings Center Report* 1988;5:21.
14. Graber G. Should abnormal fetuses be brought to term for the sole purpose of providing infant transplant organs? *Biomedical Ethics Reviews* 1989.
15. Graber: 18.
16. Jecker N. Anencephalic infants and special relationships. *Theoretical Medicine* 1990;11:333–342.
17. Engelhardt HT. Ethical issues in aiding the death of young children. In: Marvin K, ed., *Beneficent Euthanasia*. New York: Prometheus Books, 1975.
18. Jecker: 339–340.
19. Kant I. *The Metaphysics of Morals*, trans. Mary Gregor. New York: Cambridge University Press, 1991:98–100.
20. Post S. History, infanticide, and imperiled newborns. *Hastings Center Report* 1988;18(4):14–33.
21. Englehardt, 1975.
22. Ibid.
23. Kant: 98.
24. Thomasma DC. Anencephalics as organ donors. *Biomedical Ethical Reviews* 1989;25–54.
25. Ibid: 43.
26. Ibid. Also, Ethics and Social Impact Committee, Transplant Policy Center in Ann Arbor, Michigan. Anencephalic infants as sources of transplantable organs. *Hastings Center Report* 1988;18(5):28–30.
27. Thomasma: 48
28. Ibid.
29. Walters and Ashwal: 21.
30. Meilaender G. The anencephalic newborn as organ donor: commentary. *Hastings Center Report* 1986;16:23.
31. Thomasma: 48.
32. Callahan S. The role of emotion in ethical decision-making. *Hastings Center Report* 1988;18:9–14. Also, Bennett J. The conscience of Huckleberry Finn. *Philosophy* 1974;49(April).
33. May W. Attitudes toward the newly dead. *Hastings Center Studies* 1973;1(1):3–13. Also, Fox R. "An ignoble form of cannibalism": reflections on the Pittsburgh protocol of procuring organs from non-heart-beating-cadavers. *Kennedy Inst Ethics J* 1993;3:231–239. And Weisbard AJ. A polemic on principles: reflections on the Pittsburgh Protocol. *Kennedy Inst Ethics J* 1993;3:217–230.
34. Arnold RM, Youngner SJ. The dead donor rule: should we stretch it, bend it, or abandon it? *Kennedy Inst Ethics J* 1993;3(2):263–278.
35. Van Cleve L. Nurses' experience caring for anencephalic infants who are potential organ donors. *J Pedi Nurs* 1993;8(2):79–84.

32   SHARON E. SYTSMA

36. Capron, AC. Anencephalic donors: separate the dead from the dying. *Hastings Center Report* 1987;17:5–9.
37. Churchill L, Pinkus R. The use of anencephalic organs: historical and ethical dimensions. *Milbank Quart* 1990;68(2):147–169.
38. Harrison: 21.
39. Ethics and Social Impact Committee: 29. Also see Zaner: 70.
40. Thomasma: 42–43.
41. Shewmon A. Anencephaly: selected medical aspects. *Hastings Center Report* 1988;18:12. Also by Shewmon, The use of anencephalics as organ sources. *J Am Med Assoc* 1989;261(12);1773–1781.
42. Capron: 8.
43. Shewmon: 12.
44. Truog RD, Fletcher J. Brain death and the anencephalic newborn. *Bioethics,* 1990;4(3):199–215.
45. Ibid: 214.
46. Ibid: 214.
47. Shewmon: 1988.
48. Truog and Fletcher: 214.
49. Fost N. Organs from anencephalic infants: an idea whose time has not yet come. *Hastings Center Report* 1988;5:5–11.
50. Graber: 22.
51. Caplan A. *Moral Matters: Ethical Issues in Medicine and the Life Sciences.* New York: John Wiley & Sons, Inc., 1995:77.
52. Walsh JL, McQueen MM. The morality of induced delivery of the anencephalic fetus prior to viability. *Kennedy Ins Ethics J* 1993;3(4):357–369.

[22]

FETAL TISSUE TRANSPLANTS*

JOHN A. ROBERTSON**

Fetal tissue divides readily and contains the precursor cells for many important somatic functions. Tissue transplant from aborted fetuses may thus restore function in persons suffering from degenerative neurological diseases, from diabetes and from a variety of blood and immune system disorders. Although still highly experimental, the clinical potential of fetal tissue warrants further investigation.

Yet many people have voiced strong ethical objections to fetal tissue transplants.[1] Right to life groups fear that it will legitimate and encourage abortion.[2] Others foresee women becoming pregnant and aborting to produce fetal tissue, possibly creating a market for abortion. The most extreme opponents urge legal prohibitions on tissue transplants from induced abortions and a ban on federal funding of fetal tissue re-

---

* Copyright 1988 John A. Robertson.

** Baker & Botts Professor, University of Texas at Austin, School of Law. This article is based on a paper presented at The Health Law Teachers Conference of the American Society of Law and Medicine, University of Pennsylvania, June 3, 1988. Portions of this article appear in *Rights, Symbolism and Public Policy in Fetal Tissue Transplants*, HASTINGS CENTER REP. (1988) (*forthcoming*).

The author gratefully acknowledges the comments of Richard Markovits, Douglas Laycock, Mike Sharlot, Nicholas Terry, George Annas, Arthur Caplan, Albert R. Jonson, Pat Cain, Jean Love, Alan Fine, Mary Mahowald and Stuart Youngner on an earlier draft of this paper.

1. While research with live fetuses *ex utero* and fetuses about to be aborted has previously been the subject of controversy, research on dead aborted fetuses has long occurred without much conflict. The novelty of fetal brain tissue transplants has reopened an ethical, legal and policy debate about disposition of aborted fetuses.

2. Lewin, *Medical Use of Fetal Tissue Spurs New Abortion Debate*, N.Y. Times, August 16, 1987, at 1, col. 5.

search. More moderate opponents call for strict regulation of the circumstances in which fetal tissue is obtained, including a ban on the sale of fetal tissue and intrafamilial or designated tissue donations.[3]

The emerging controversy over fetal tissue transplants illustrates once again the power of medical innovation to challenge ethical norms and social practices. The challenge must be met if medical progress in this important area is to occur. To guide the development of public policy, this article examines key ethical, legal and policy issues presented by fetal tissue transplants.

I. BENEFITS, TISSUE SOURCE AND CONTROVERSY

Scientists have engaged in research with fetal tissue for many years, but only recently has the possibility of transplanting fetal tissue to cure or alleviate symptoms in sick patients seemed feasible on a large scale.[4] Before addressing ethical and legal issues, a brief description of the potential benefits and sources of fetal tissue transplants and the ethical controversy they have engendered is in order.

A. *Potential Applications*

While physicians have performed relatively few transplants to humans thus far, considerable animal research involving human fetal tissue suggests that it may be an effective therapy for at least two severe chronic diseases—Parkinson's disease and diabetes. Research also indicates human fetal tissue has potential application to a wide variety of other disorders.

Parkinson's disease is a chronic, progressive degenerative disease that affects more than 1.5 million Americans. The disease causes the brain to lose the capacity to produce essential neurotransmitters. As a result, the patient suffers from tremors, rigidity, paralysis and eventually dies. Extensive work with animal models suggests that inserting fetal cells in the affected part of the brain will produce the missing neurotransmitters in quantities sufficient to alleviate symptoms and prevent further deterioration.[5] Patients suffering from other central nervous system disorders,

---

3. For a discussion of these issues, see *infra* notes 140-57 and accompanying text.

4. *See* Lewin, *supra* note 2.

5. Rohter, *Fetal Tissue Aids Two Parkinson Cases*, N.Y. Times, Jan. 7, 1988, at B13, col. 1; Fine, *The Ethics of Fetal Tissue Transplants*, HASTINGS CENTER REP., June-July 1988, at 5. Fine describes the disease as occurring

when neurons degenerate in the region of the midbrain called the substantia nigra. Nor-

such as Alzheimer's disease, amytropic lateral sclerosis, and Huntington's chorea, may also benefit from fetal transplants.[6]

Fetal transplants also offer a promising therapy for the million Americans who suffer from juvenile diabetes. While the disease is manageable to varying degrees with exogenous insulin, the lives of these people are often shortened by accelerated atherosclerosis, renal disorders and other serious problems. Extensive animal studies suggest that transplantation of fetal pancreatic islet cells into the diabetic patient could produce a normal supply of insulin and prevent further symptoms. Successful fetal islet transplants could benefit an estimated 700,000-900,000 of these patients, at great savings to the community.[7]

While patients with Parkinson's disease and diabetes are the most likely beneficiaries of fetal tissue transplants, other patients may also benefit. Fetal liver, the source of the hematopoietic cells which produce the blood and immune system, may provide an effective remedy for radiation sickness, aplastic anemia and other hemoglobinopathies. Future applications to sickle cell anemia and thalassemia, to diseases of the immune system, such as AIDS and rheumoarthritis, and to diseases of aging are also possible.[8]

Research with fetal tissue may also yield essential information about the oncogenesis of early development cancers; the regulation, growth, development and regeneration of tissue as an alternative to transplant therapy; the effect of environmental factors on the fetus; the genesis of diseases of development, such as respiratory distress syndrome and hemoglobinopathies; and the pathogenesis of the HIV virus implicated in AIDS. Fetal tissue may also serve as a source of biologic substances for research and therapy.[9]

---

mally, fibers from these cells secrete the chemical dopamine in forebrain regions important for regulating movement. In the absence of normal dopamine secretion, the patient suffers from a variety of impairments including rigidity, difficulty initiating movements and tremors.

Id.

6. *See supra* note 2.

7. Statement of Kevin Lafferty, Ph.D., National Disease Research Interchange Meeting on Fetal Transplants (April 11, 1988).

8. Statement of Dr. Robert Gale, National Disease Research Interchange Meeting on Fetal Transplants (April 11, 1988).

9. Statement of Dr. William Raub, National Disease Research Interchange Meeting on Fetal Transplants (April 11, 1988).

B. Source and Supply of Fetal Tissue

The one and a half million abortions performed annually in the United States appear adequate to supply fetal tissue for research and therapy for the foreseeable future. Nearly eighty percent of induced abortions are performed between the sixth and eleventh weeks of gestation, at which time neural and other tissue is sufficiently developed to be retrieved and transplanted.[10] Abortions performed at fourteen to sixteen weeks provide fetal pancreases used in diabetes research, but it may be possible to use pancreases retrieved earlier.

Past research with fetal tissue has used fetal tissue obtained through informal contacts between researchers and physicians doing abortions, usually in the same institution. Recently, intermediary organizations that retrieve fetal tissue from abortion facilities and distribute it to researchers have arisen.[11] One may expect more such bodies to develop, with most fetal tissue retrieved by specialized tissue or organ procurement agencies. In some cases, for-profit firms that specialize in processing the tissue for transplant may enter the field.[12]

Answers to several questions related to the needed supply of fetal tissue must await further research. For example, the number of fetuses needed to produce a successful neural or pancreatic graft is unknown.[13] Progress in replicating and growing fetal cell lines in culture may reduce the number of aborted fetuses needed for therapeutic purposes. The ability to freeze fetal cells will enhance the ability to tissue-type and study for infection, and allow retrieved tissue to be transported long distances as solid organs and other tissue now are. Major questions about histocompatibility remain unsolved. In the long run, drugs that directly supply the missing biological factors or substances will probably replace fetal tissue transplants.[14]

---

10. Fine, *supra* note 5, at 6-7.

11. The National Disease Research Interchange of Philadelphia, Pennsylvania is one such intermediary.

12. Hana Biologies, Inc., a publicly traded company, is now acquiring fetal tissue to study the possible development of fetal islet cells for transplant to diabetic patients.

13. Statement of Drs. Kevin Lafferty and Lars Olson, at NIH Panel on Fetal Tissue Transplantation Research (Sept. 21, 1988).

14. Statement of Dr. William Moscona, NIH Panel on Fetal Tissue Transplantation Research (Sept. 21, 1988).

C. The Ethical Controversy

Ethical duties of beneficence require curing disease and alleviating suffering wherever possible. If fetal tissue transplants will help patients suffering from Parkinson's disease, diabetes and other disorders, a prima facie obligation to pursue those remedies exists, defeasible only if fetal tissue could not be ethically obtained.[15]

Fetal tissue for transplant is obtained from intentional destruction of fetuses—a legal practice that many persons view as immoral.[16] In their view, research or therapy with aborted fetuses legitimizes or even encourages abortion, opening the door to women conceiving and aborting solely to get tissue for transplant. The good to patients, in their view, is outweighed by the harm to fetuses and the denigration of women that thereby occurs.

The fetal tissue transplant controversy thus has an architecture similar to many bioethical debates, with a novel twist because of the contested status of the fetus and abortion. Respect for the needs of sick patients appears to conflict with respect for prenatal human life and larger societal moral concerns. Closer analysis is necessary to show whether this apparent conflict is real and how it may or should be resolved.

The following discussion assumes that the experimental or clinical use of tissue from aborted fetuses is medically justified to cure, alleviate symptoms of, or greatly improve the quality of life of patients suffering from a variety of life-threatening or seriously debilitating diseases.[17] It first analyzes ethical objections based on fetal and maternal welfare and then discusses legal and regulatory issues.

II. ISSUES OF FETAL STATUS AND WELFARE

The main ethical objection to fetal tissue transplants is the need to rely

---

15. Lewin, *supra* note 2. These issues arise even though tissue is obtained from a fetus that is clearly dead. Further ethical problems would arise if tissue had to be procured from an aborted fetus that was still alive. *See infra* notes 175-82 and accompanying text.

16. Wide opposition to *Roe v. Wade*, 410 U.S. 113 (1973) continues to exist. *See* ABORTION AND THE CONSTITUTION (D. Horan, E. Grant & P. Cunningham ed. 1988).

17. The assumption of great benefit subtly changes the nature of the current debate, since there is no guarantee at the present time that the great potential of fetal tissue transplants in curing disease or alleviating symptoms will be achieved. The case for incurring the symbolic costs of creating and destroying fetuses to obtain tissue for transplants weakens considerably as the certainty or magnitude of benefit falls. (For a definition of "symbolic costs" see *infra* note 51). The success factor should thus be factored into the ethical and legal analysis that follows.

448   WASHINGTON UNIVERSITY LAW QUARTERLY   [Vol. 66:443

on induced abortions to obtain fetal tissue.[18] Like cadaveric organ procurement, fetal transplants depend upon a death to enable good to another to occur. But cadaveric organs are obtained only after the tragic death of the organ source, with strict protections ensuring that the source's interests are not compromised for the purpose of procuring organs.[19]

By contrast, the death of the fetus that provides tissue for transplant is deliberate. The donor—the woman providing the tissue—chooses to kill the fetus for reasons usually unrelated to tissue procurement. Although the abortion producing the tissue is legal and occurs for reasons unrelated to tissue procurement, many people who view abortion as immoral argue that procuring fetal tissue disrespects and exploits the aborted fetus. They fear that fetal tissue transplants will legitimize and further entrench abortion, and even lead to pregnancy and abortion to produce tissue for transplant.[20] Accordingly, they would drastically limit or even prohibit all fetal tissue transplants, or at least remove the government from funding research or therapy with fetal tissue.

Because ethical objections based on concern for the fetus are at the heart of the fetal tissue transplant debate, an extended analysis of the ethical legitimacy of fetal tissue transplants from induced abortions follows. A key distinction in this analysis is between tissue obtained from fetuses aborted for family planning reasons and fetuses aborted to obtain tissue for transplant.

A.   Use of Fetuses Aborted For Family Planning Purposes

Over a million and a half abortions occur in the United States every year, and over ninety-five percent of them occur in the first trimester.[21] Whether pregnancy occurs from contraceptive failure or sheer negligence, most of these abortions are done to avoid an unwanted preg-

---

18. Tissue from spontaneously aborted (miscarried) fetuses is not an adequate substitute because of the probability that fetal pathology triggered the miscarriage, and the indeterminate delay between fetal death and expulsion from the uterus. In addition, enormous logistical problems in recovering and processing such tissue can arise. *See* Fine, *supra* note 5, at 6.

19. Cadaveric organ sources must be brain dead, as determined by physicians who have no role in the transplant itself. The death of the organ source usually results from events such as trauma, accident, suicide or homicide that are illegal or socially undesirable. The person consenting to use of the cadaveric organs does not usually cause the death of the organ source.

20. Lewin, *supra* note 2.

21. Henshaw, Binkin, Blaine & Smith, *A Portrait of American Women Who Obtain Abortions,* 17 FAMILY PLANNING PERSPECTIVES 90, 91 (1985).

nancy—broadly speaking, for family planning purposes.[22] The aborted fetuses, often macerated or a mass of tissue, are then incinerated or otherwise discarded.[23] Fetal tissue transplants would, presumably with the mother's consent, salvage some of that tissue to benefit patients suffering from serious disease.

Two ethical arguments have been made against use of tissue from abortions induced to end an unwanted pregnancy.[24] Both rest on the premise that abortion is morally abhorrent, a premise not universally held in our pluralistic society. If the premise is rejected, the use of fetal tissue from family planning abortions poses no major ethical problem.[25] Even assuming the immorality of abortion, however, it does not follow that tissue transplants from such abortions are also immoral. These ethical objections are insufficient to justify a ban on tissue transplants from fetuses aborted to end an unwanted pregnancy.[26]

1. Complicity in Abortion

A major ethical objection to use of tissue from family planning abortions is the idea of complicity in the abortion that provides the fetal tissue. The premise here is that knowingly profiting from an evil done to others makes one a moral accomplice in the commission of that evil.[27] If

---

22. The term "family planning abortions" might seem unnecessarily euphemistic to some persons. The intent is to denote those abortions that will occur regardless of research with fetal tissue or fetal tissue transplants. In most cases they are sought because of the woman's desire to avoid taking on family or childrearing responsibilities, and thus are designated, for want of a better term, abortions done for "family planning" purposes.

23. Some jurisdictions have enacted fetal disposal laws that aim to protect public health or demonstrate respect for aborted fetuses. *See infra* note 134.

24. A third "ethical" objection is that research is further "exploitation" of the fetus that has already been "exploited" by the abortion. But this objection misunderstands the practice at issue. Fetal tissue for transplant is obtained from dead fetuses. Once dead, the fetus no longer can be "exploited" or harmed. Statement of Dr. John Wilkie, National Right to Life Committee, NIH Panel on Fetal Tissue Transplant Research (Sept. 22, 1988).

25. Other ethical issues such as the content, the process and the timing of obtaining informed consent and the risk of commercialization would also arise, but these pose no major barrier to conducting such research.

26. However, recipients, physicians, and other participants in the transplant process who object to use of fetal tissue from aborted fetuses should be entitled to know the source of fetal tissue that is being transplanted, so that they may refuse to participate.

27. People's practice in this regard is inconsistent and not easily subject to clear lines. It is said that behind every great fortune lies a crime, yet we seldom seek to parse out those connections. As Henry Fairlie has noted, "[W]ith whatever corruptions and brutality an American fortune has been amassed, it is laundered within one generation. The money sticks, but not the filth." Fairlie, *Shamala: A Washington Success Story*, THE NEW REPUBLIC, Aug. 22, 1988 at 21, 22. Thus, by not

induced abortions are evil, transplanting fetal remains makes one morally complicitous in the evil that makes the transplant possible.

Yet even proponents of the complicity argument are not quite so extreme, recognizing that not all situations of later benefit make one an accomplice in the evil act from which benefits are derived. For example, James Burtchaell, a leading articulator of the complicity objection, claims that complicity occurs not merely from partaking of benefit, but only when one enters into a "supportive alliance" with the underlying evil that makes the benefit possible.[28] In discussing different relationships to an underlying evil, he distinguishes "a neutral or even an opponent and an ally from the way in which one does or does not hold oneself apart from the enterprise and its purposes."[29] Later he states that "it is the sort of association which implies and engenders approbation that creates moral complicity. This situation is detectable when the associate's ability to condemn the activity atrophies."[30]

In light of Burtchaell's analysis of complicity, it is unclear why he finds the researcher using fetal tissue from an elective abortion necessarily to be an accomplice to the abortionist and the woman choosing abortion. The researcher and transplant patient ordinarily will be removed from the abortion process: they will not have requested the abortion, and will have no knowledge of who performed it or where it occurred. A third party intermediary will procure the tissue for the researcher.[31] The abortion will have occurred for reasons unrelated to tissue procurement. The researcher and transplant patient might even be morally opposed to abortion, and surely will suffer no moral disintegration because they

---

inquiring closely into the origin of the money used in most transactions, the market system "dirties" everyone's hands. The grocer who sells food to the physician who performs abortions enables the physician to continue his work and the grocer is paid with the proceeds from previous abortions. See G. HIGGINS, KENNEDY FOR THE DEFENSE 34-35 (1980) for a graphic presentation of this dilemma for a criminal defense attorney.

28. Burtchaell, *Case Study: University Policy on Experimental Use of Aborted Fetal Tissue,* IRB: A REVIEW OF HUMAN SUBJECTS RESEARCH, July-Aug. 1988, at 7. He acknowledges that complicity is a contingent relationship which depends on judgment over which reasonable persons might disagree. *Id.* at 8. While Burtchaell poses the question as one of complicity, one might argue that the problem is really one of "dirty hands" or association with the previous evil, which raises a different set of concerns. The extent to which one's hands are "dirtied" is even more clearly a matter of judgment.

29. *Id.* at 9.

30. *Id.*

31. *See supra* notes 11, 12, and *infra* notes 102-06 and accompanying text.

choose to salvage some good from an abortion that will occur regardless of their research or therapeutic goals.

The donation of organs and cadavers from homicide victims provides a useful analogy. Families of murder victims (or coroners if no family is known) are often asked to donate organs and bodies for research, therapy and education. If they consent, organ procurement agencies will coordinate the retrieval and distribution of organs. No one would seriously argue that the surgeon who transplants the victim's kidneys, heart, liver, or corneas into a needy recipient is thereby an accomplice in the homicide that made the organs available for transplant, even if he knows their source. Nor is the recipient of the transplanted organs or the medical student who uses the cadaver of a murder victim to study anatomy an accomplice in the homicide.

If organs from murder and accident victims may be used without complicity in the murder or accident that makes the organs available, then fetal remains could also be used without complicity in the abortion.[32] The physician and patient benefiting from the homicide or abortion do not, by salvaging some good from an independently caused death, become moral accomplices in the death that makes organs available.

Burtchaell's approach to the problem of complicity assumes that researchers necessarily applaud the underlying act of abortion, thereby allying themselves with it. One may benefit from another's evil act, however, without applauding or approving of that evil. X may disapprove of Y's murder of Z, even though X gains an inheritance or a promotion as a result. Indeed, one might even question Burtchaell's assumption that X has complicity in Y's prior act even if he subsequently applauds it. Applauding Y's murder of Z might show a design to bring about the murder it the first place, or be viewed as insensitive or callous. But it alone would not make one morally responsible for—an accomplice in—the murder that has already occurred. In any event, the willingness to derive benefit from another's wrongful death does not create complicity in that death because it is a contingent event over which the persons who benefit had no control.[33]

---

32. For example, suppose X murdered Y, a woman who was three months pregnant at the time. Surely if her husband, Z, could consent to donation of Y's organs for transplant to A, he should be free to consent to donation of the dead fetus' organs to B as well, even though the fetus has been intentionally killed. Intentional, legal killing by abortion should not change B's ability to obtain fetal organs for transplant.

33. The question of encouraging future abortions, which are performed to obtain tissue for

452   WASHINGTON UNIVERSITY LAW QUARTERLY   [Vol. 66:443

The complicity argument against use of aborted fetuses often draws an analogy to the reluctance to use the results of unethical medical research carried out by the Nazis. Burtchaell and others have argued that it would make us retroactive accomplices in the Nazi horrors to use the products of their unethical and lethal research.[34] As our discussion of organ donation from homicide victims shows, however, the idea of retroactive complicity from accepting benefits produced from an earlier evil act claims more than most people are prepared to accept.[35] A clear separation between the perpetrator and beneficiary of the immoral act breaks the chain of moral complicity for that act.

Thus, one could rely on Nazi-generated data without approving the horrendous acts of Nazi doctors that made such knowledge possible. Nor would it necessarily dishonor those unfortunate victims. Indeed, it could reasonably be viewed as retrospectively honoring them by saving others. The Jewish doctors who made systematic studies of starvation in the Warsaw ghetto in order to reap some good from the evil being done to their brethren were not accomplices in that evil.[36] Nor should one

---

transplant, is more accurately described as a problem of complicity. This subject is treated *infra* notes 37-39 and accompanying text.

34. Burtchaell distinguishes between use of tissue specimens left over from a lethal experiment, and use of a drug that was developed on the basis of that research, without explaining why complicity would occur in the one case but not in the other. *See* Burtchaell, *supra* note 28 at 10. Note that the claimed complicity is not in torturing the subjects by experimentation, but in benefitting from the unethical experiment done by others.

Others have objected to citing Nazi data, as demonstrated by a recent controversy over whether the Environmental Protection Agency (EPA), in considering regulation of certain gasses, should rely on data from lethal experiments that the Nazis performed on concentration camp victims. The EPA refused to rely on the data, in order to demonstrate its horror and disapproval of the Nazi practices. Shabecoff, *Head of E.P.A. Bars Nazi Data in Study on Gas*, N.Y. Times, March 23, 1988, at 1, col. 5. While other data may have been available that made reliance on the Nazi studies unnecessary, one commentator noted that to use unethically obtained data even to save lives "would put us at risk of retrospectively participating in their torture and death." Howard Spiro, *Let Nazi Medical Data Remind Us of Evil*, Letter to the Editor, N.Y. Times, April 19, 1988, at 30, col. 5. A similar issue has arisen over whether Nazi hypothermia studies may be used in devising ways to save people swept into icy seas. *Minnesota Scientist Plans to Publish Nazi Experiment on Freezing*, N.Y. Times, May 12, 1988, at 28, col. 3. At issue here are questions of "dirty hands" and retroactive approval rather than complicity in the strict sense. *See supra* note 28.

35. *See supra* notes 31-32 and accompanying text.

36. L. TUSHNET, THE USES OF ADVERSITY: STUDIES OF STARVATION IN THE WARSAW GHETTO (1966). Indeed, on a recent visit to a former concentration camp in Austria, the Pope commented that the Holocaust is "a great gift" to us, because it forces us to confront and reflect on the evil in man. Are we in complicity with the evil done by the Nazis if we make use of this "gift" that grows out of the evil destruction of millions of persons? *John Paul Cites Suffering of Jews*, N.Y. Times, June 26, 1988, at 6, col. 1.

consider accomplices the doctors and patients who now benefit from their studies.

Thus, persons opposed to abortion could reasonably find that use of fetal tissue from abortions occurring for reasons unrelated to tissue procurement does not make one an accomplice in the abortion that makes the tissue available. If the complicity claim is doubtful when the underlying immorality of the act is clear, as with Nazi-produced data or transplants from murder victims, it is considerably weakened when the act making the benefit possible is legal and its immorality is vigorously debated, as is the case with abortion. The risk of retroactive complicity in an abortion performed for reasons unrelated to tissue procurement does not ethically justify denying fetal tissue to researchers or needy transplant recipients.

2. *Legitimize, Entrench and Encourage Abortion*

A second objection is that salvaging tissue for transplant from aborted fetuses will make abortion less morally offensive and more easily tolerated both for individual pregnant women and for society. Those who object believe the result will be to so dilute the perceived immorality and undesirability of abortion as to transform it into a morally positive act. This will encourage abortions that would not otherwise occur, and dilute support for reversing the legal acceptability of abortion, in effect creating complicity in future abortions.[37]

But the feared impact on abortion attitudes is highly speculative, particularly at a time when few fetal transplants have yet occurred. There is good reason to think that fetal tissue transplants will have little effect on abortion attitudes and practices. For example, the possibility of donating tissue for transplant may have little effect on individual abortion decisions. The main motivation for most abortions is the desire to avoid the burdens of an unwanted pregnancy. The fact that fetal remains may be donated for transplant may be of little significance in the total array of factors that lead a woman to abort a pregnancy.

Even if women feel better for having donated fetal tissue, the possibility of donation alone would lead few women to abort who would not otherwise have done so. Tissue donation may even have little impact on

---

37. While fetal tissue donations might, on the margin, produce more abortions than would otherwise occur, the concern is not with women who conceive for the purpose of obtaining tissue for transplant. *See infra* notes 47-60.

those women who are highly ambivalent or undecided about abortion, particularly if the decision to abort must first be made before notice of the opportunity to donate is offered.[38] Of course, some women might find the chance to donate fetal tissue the deciding factor, but it seems unlikely that this possibility will greatly increase the number of abortions that will occur. Speculation of such effects alone does not justify losing the substantial benefits that fetal tissue transplants can bring.

Nor does the mere fact that fetal tissue is donated for research and transplant mean that a public otherwise ready to outlaw abortion would refrain from doing so. The continuing legal acceptance of abortion flows from the wide disagreement that exists over early fetal status. If a majority agreed that embryos and fetuses should be respected as persons despite the burdens placed on pregnant women, such possible secondary benefits of induced abortion as fetal tissue transplants would most likely not prevent a change in the legality of abortion. At the very least, there is enough doubt about the point to prevent such speculations from stopping the great good that fetal tissue may provide.[39]

Indeed, one could make the same argument against organ transplants from homicide, suicide and accident victims. One could argue that the willingness to use their organs might encourage or legitimate those practices, or at least make it harder to enact lower speed limits, or seatbelt, gun control and drunk driving laws to prevent them. After all, the need to prevent fatal accidents, murder and suicide becomes less pressing if

---

38. It is difficult to tell whether a general knowledge that fetal tissue transplants occur will influence the decision of women contemplating abortion even when they are not specifically asked to donate until after they have decided about the abortion. In a somewhat analogous context, the right to donate organs for transplant is not thought to lead families to remove life support systems prematurely. The issue of whether informed consent to abortion constitutes an inducement is discussed *infra* note 82.

39. Although people strongly opposed to abortion might disagree with this analysis, one could reasonably find the effect of fetal transplant on individual and social practices of abortion to be marginal, especially if techniques to separate abortion and retrieval of fetal tissue are firmly in place. Any resulting encouragement of abortion is likely to be too slight to justify foregoing the more likely benefits from fetal tissue research and therapy.

To pursue the point somewhat further, suppose that fetal tissue transplants increased the number of abortions by X over the next 5 years, but fetal transplants saved $X + Y$ lives over that same period. At low values of X and high values of Y fetal transplants would not be unethical, since X measures unknown or statistical increases in abortion, not unlike the statistical lives lost in selecting a particular automobile or road design, or building tunnels and suspension bridges. Nor does the fact that the increased deaths from abortion will occur intentionally change the outcome. Laws permitting the possession of handguns also produce intentionally caused deaths (usually illegally). Such statistical risks of intentional or unintentional death become an acceptable cost of achieving the social policies in question.

some good to others might come from use of victim organs for transplant. However, the connection is too tenuous and speculative to ban organ transplants on that basis. It is also tenuous and should be rejected as a basis for prohibiting fetal tissue transplants.

In sum, fetal tissue transplants, though dependent on abortions induced to prevent unwanted pregnancy, can be sufficiently divorced from such abortions as to be separately evaluated. Given that abortion is legal and occurring on a large scale, the willingness to use resulting tissue for transplant neither creates complicity in past abortions nor appears to encourage substantially more abortions than would otherwise have occurred. Such ethical concerns are not sufficient, given the possible good to others, to justify banning use of fetal tissue for research or therapy.

B. Aborting to Obtain Tissue for Transplant

A more widely shared ethical objection to procuring tissue from induced abortions is the incentive that it will give women to become pregnant and abort solely to obtain tissue for transplant. Most commentators assume that conception and abortion for tissue procurement is so clearly unethical that the prospect hardly merits discussion. To discourage such a practice, they would ban all tissue transplants from related persons.[40] Indeed, some persons would even ban any use of fetuses aborted for family planning reasons simply to minimize the risk that conception and abortion for transplant purposes will occur.

1. The Need: Unlikely at Present Time

The need to abort solely for transplant purposes could arise in two situations that do not presently exist. One situation would arise if histocompatibility between the fetus and recipient were necessary for effective fetal transplants. In that case, tissue from abortions done currently for family planning reasons would be less desirable or even useless for transplant purposes.[41] Female relatives, spouses or even unrelated compatible persons engaged for that purpose might then seek to get pregnant

---

40. Mahowald, Silver & Ratcheson, *The Ethical Options in Transplanting Fetal Tissue*, HASTINGS CENTER REP., Feb. 1987, at 9. *See also* Fine, *supra* note 5. An exception is Mary Warren, in a brief comment that appeared before the current debate arose. Warren, Maquire & Levine, *Can the Fetus Be an Organ Farm?*, HASTINGS CENTER REP. 23-25 (1978).

41. However, random matching of tissue and immunosuppression of poorer matches would still occur, as it does with solid organ transplantation, so that family planning abortions might still be an important source of tissue for transplant.

in order to obtain properly matched fetal tissue for transplant.[42]

The second situation would arise if the supply of tissue from family planning abortions proved inadequate to meet the demand for fetal tissue. For example, the supply of fetal tissue would be reduced if the incidence of surgical abortions were lowered due to medical alternatives such as RU 486 or more effective contraceptive practices.[43] On the other hand, demand for fetal tissue would greatly increase if fetal tissue transplants proved successful for a large class of patients, such as those suffering from Parkinson's disease or diabetes.[44] Pressure on supply might also occur if tissue from several aborted fetuses were needed to produce one viable transplant.

At this stage of research, however, it appears likely that the million plus abortions that occur annually in the United States to end unwanted pregnancies are more than adequate to supply fetal tissue for most current research and transplant purposes.[45] Histocompatibility between tissue source and recipient does not appear necessary for effective fetal tissue transplants. Indeed, fetal tissue may be immunologically privileged or easily rendered so, thus reducing the chance of rejection and the need for genetic matching. Progress in propagating cell lines from aborted fetuses will reduce even more the number of fetuses that are needed. As research progresses, fetal transplants may be eventually replaced by the chemical that the transplant serves to produce.[46]

At present, the question of aborting to obtain tissue for transplant is a red herring, because there is little advantage to be gained from such abortions and no one is recommending them. Yet the fear that women will conceive and abort to produce tissue for transplant has figured so largely in the current controversy that the ethics of the practice deserve careful attention—in the unlikely event the need for such abortions arises. Anal-

---

42. In most instances the conception would probably occur via artificial insemination, with appropriately matched or chosen sperm. However, *in vitro* fertilization and egg donation for matching purposes might also occur.

43. RU 486 is an experimental hormonal drug which terminates early pregnancies without the use of a surgical procedure. Cousinat, Le Strat, Ulmann, Baulieu & Schaison, *Termination of Early Pregnancy by the Progesterone Antagonist RU 486 (Mifepristone)*, 315 NEW ENG. J. MED. 1565 (1986). Kolata, *France and China allow Sale of a Drug for Early Abortion*, N.Y. Times, Sept. 24, 1988, at 1, col. 1.

44. Fine has shown that current abortions could supply patients suffering from Parkinson's disease, but would be inadequate if fetal tissue transplants successfully treated additional diseases such as diabetes. Fine, *supra* note 5, at 6.

45. *Id.*

46. *See supra* note 14.

ysis will show that such a practice is ethically more complex and defensible than most commentators have assumed.

2. A Hypothetical Situation

What if the hypothetical possibility became real and diabetes or other diseases could be effectively treated only with tissue from a fetus that was genetically related to the recipient? Or the supply of fetal tissue from elective abortions did not meet the needs of persons with Parkinson's disease? Consider first the situation where a woman eight weeks pregnant with her husband's child learns that tissue from her fetus could cure severe neurologic disease in herself or a close relative, such as her husband, son or daughter, father or mother, or brother or sister. May she ethically abort the pregnancy to obtain tissue for transplant to the relative or herself? Further, if she is not yet pregnant, may she conceive a fetus that she will then abort to obtain tissue for transplant to herself or to her relative?[47]

To focus analysis of this situation on fetal welfare, assume in each case that no other viable tissue source exists, and that the advanced state of the neurologic disease has become a major tragedy for the victim and family. The woman has voluntarily raised the possibility of abortion to obtain tissue without any direct pressure or inducements from the family or others. Her husband agrees to an abortion for transplant purposes if she is willing, but exerts no pressure on her to abort or to conceive for transplant purposes.

The main concern in this situation is the harm done to the fetus.[48] We discuss first the ethics of aborting for this purpose when the woman is already pregnant, and then we discuss the situation of conceiving in order to abort for transplant purposes.

a. The Woman is Already Pregnant

If the woman is already pregnant, the question is whether an abortion

---

47. If conception and abortion for intrafamilial donation is acceptable, the question of impregnating an unrelated woman for this purpose, presumably by noncoital means such as artificial insemination, may then be addressed. Patients without female relatives available to produce fetal tissue may have to recruit unrelated persons for this purpose. No doubt all patients needs would not be met unless the donor were paid, which raise the troubling issue of commercialization. *See infra* notes 155-56 and accompanying text.

48. Concerns about maternal health and welfare would also arise, but these would seem comparable to or less than similar concerns regarding bone marrow and kidney donations, which are permitted—indeed, are applauded. *See infra* notes 72-77 and accompanying text.

may ethically be done to obtain tissue for transplant, when in the absence of the need for tissue, the pregnancy would be carried to term. In short, may a first trimester fetus be sacrificed to procure tissue for transplant?

Assuming a clear and substantial benefit to the recipient, ethical assessment of this situation depends on the value placed on early fetuses and the reasons deemed acceptable for abortion. Although some people think that fetuses (and even fertilized eggs and preimplantation embryos) have the full value of persons, many people find the fetus' inherent status to depend on the stage of gestational development.[49] An ethically sound distinction may be made between fetuses that have developed to such a level of neurologic and cognitive capacity that they are sentient and thus have interests in themselves, and those which are so neurologically immature that they cannot experience harm. While aborting fetuses at that earlier stage prevents them from achieving their potential, it does not harm or wrong them, since they are insufficiently developed to experience harm.[50]

Although aborting the fetus at that early stage presumably does not harm the fetus, it may impose "symbolic costs" in terms of the general reduced respect for human life that a willingness to abort early fetuses connotes.[51] Still, the abortion may be ethically acceptable if the good

---

49. The following analysis assumes that early abortions are ethically acceptable. A more complete analysis of this position is found in Robertson, *Gestational Burdens and Fetal Status: A Defense of Roe v. Wade*, 13 AM. J. L. & MED. 189 (1988). It should also be noted that rejection of this premise in favor of treating the fetus as a moral subject with rights from the time of conception would not necessarily lead to the conclusion that abortion is impermissible, as Judith Jarvis Thomson has shown in Thomson, *A Defense of Abortion*, 1 PHIL. & PUB. AFF. 47 (1971). In those instances, e.g., rape, contraceptive failure, etc., a woman would not violate the fetus's right in terminating the pregnancy in order to produce tissue for transplant. Her motivation in avoiding gestation would not affect her right to do so because she has no independent obligation to continue the pregnancy. Under this approach, however, a woman would not have a right to abort if she had conceived for that purpose.

50. All fetuses may have the potential to develop into persons, but only some fetuses—the later ones—have advanced to the point of sentience and thus have interests in themselves. Potentiality alone does not give interests or rights in the not yet existent entity who could be brought into being. Bigelow & Pargetter, *Morality, Potential Persons and Abortion*, 25 AM. PHIL. Q. 173, 178 (1988); Singer & Dawson, *IVF Technology and the Argument from Potential*, 17 PHIL. & PUB. AFF. 87, 95-96 (1988). The point at which the fetus develops interests may be drawn at viability because roughly at this stage the fetus attains sufficient physiologic development to be sentient and thus have interests in its own right. *See* Robertson, *supra* note 49.

51. The symbolic costs consist of that impact on the lives of actual persons, including the moral tone or atmosphere of society, that results from the attitude toward potential persons symbolized by the willingness to prevent their emergence into being after conception has occurred. The existence and magnitude of those costs is, of course, a matter of debate and controversy.

sought by abortion sufficiently outweighs the symbolic devaluation of life that occurs when fetuses that cannot be harmed in their own right are aborted. Many persons find that the burdens of unwanted pregnancy outweigh the symbolic devaluation of fetal life. Others would require a more compelling reason, such as protecting the mother's life or health, avoiding the birth of a handicapped child, or avoiding the burdens of a pregnancy due to rape or incest.

Compared to these reasons for abortion, terminating a pregnancy to obtain tissue to save one's own life or the life of a close relative seems equally, if not more, compelling. Indeed, aborting to obtain tissue would seem as compelling as even the most stringent reasons for permitting abortion, e.g., saving the mother's life or health, avoiding a handicapped birth, or avoiding pregnancy due to rape or incest. And certainly if abortion in the case of an unwanted pregnancy is deemed permissible, abortion to obtain tissue to save another person's life is.

If tissue from the fetus is transplanted into the mother to save her own life, the situation is very close to one in which abortion is justified to save the mother's life or health.[52] If the mother may abort to save her own life, however, should she be disqualified from aborting to save the life of another? To say "yes" would elevate narcissism over altruism. In short, aborting an early fetus to get tissue to save oneself or one's close relative seems as ethically sound a reason for aborting as other reasons that are generally accepted. In fact, many persons would find this motive more compelling than the desire to end an unwanted pregnancy.

Of course, aborting a wanted pregnancy to prevent severe neurologic disease in oneself or a close relative would hardly be done joyfully, and would place the mother in an excruciating dilemma, not unlike the situation in William Styron's *Sophie's Choice*.[53] In this case, a fetus that could be carried to term would have to be sacrificed to save a parent, spouse,

---

52. The difference here is that the fetus itself is not threatening the mother's health, but is the means by which the mother's life will be saved. Yet in each case the death of the fetus protects the mother. If an innocent fetus can be sacrificed in one case, could it be sacrificed in another? If the fetus had the moral status of a person, this distinction would be crucial if the mother were not otherwise permitted to terminate the pregnancy. *Supra* note 49. Indeed, the fetus could not in that case be sacrificed even to save many lives. Thomson, *The Trolley Problem*, 94 YALE L.J. 1395 (1985).

53. Styron presents the dilemma of the Nazis forcing a mother to select one of her children to be murdered, or lose them both. If the early fetus does not itself have rights, the Sophie's Choice analogy is inapt, since the choice in the fetal context is between a potential child and an actual child or adult. However, the choice is still painful because the potential child would have become actual but for the need to produce tissue for the person in need. (I am indebted to Judith Areen for this

sibling or child who already exists. Such a tragic choice would engender loss or grief in the mother, whatever the decision reached by her. Yet one cannot say that the choice to abort is ethically impermissible, if early abortion of unwanted pregnancies, or abortion for more compelling reasons, is acceptable. In all such cases the fetus is being sacrificed or used as a means to advance other goals. There is no sound basis for distinguishing use of fetal tissue for transplant, if sacrifice of the fetus to pursue those other goals is permitted.

Public attitudes toward a woman aborting an otherwise-wanted pregnancy to benefit a family member most likely would reflect attitudes toward abortion generally.[54] Those who are against abortion in all circumstances will object to abortions done to treat severe neurologic disease in the mother or a family member. Similarly, persons who accept family planning abortions should have no objection to abortion to procure tissue for transplant, because the fetal status is no more compelling and the interest of the woman in controlling her body and reproductive capacity is similar.

Since neither group forms a majority, however, persons who object to family planning abortions but who accept abortions that are necessary to protect the mother's health, in cases of rape or incest, or to prevent a handicapped birth, will determine whether a majority of people approve of abortions for transplant. It is conceivable that many persons in this swing group would find abortion acceptable if performed to obtain tissue for transplant into a family member. The benefit of alleviating severe neurologic disease is arguably as great as the benefits in the cases they accept as justifiable abortion.[55] Indeed, they are likely to view abortion for transplant purposes as more compelling than abortions done for family planning purposes. If this group accepts abortion to procure tissue for transplant to a family member, a clear majority in favor of the practice would exist.[56]

---

analogy). For this reason the abortion may be more difficult than abortion of a pregnancy undertaken to obtain tissue for transplant.

54. Public attitudes alone do not determine the ethical acceptability of a practice. They do, however, show that the ethical analysis presented may be in keeping with the considered judgment of many persons.

55. If they accept abortion to prevent serious harm to the mother, then they should approve an abortion to procure tissue for transplant to the pregnant woman. *But see supra* note 49. If the fetus may be sacrificed to save the mother, then abortion to procure comparable benefits to others should also be permitted.

56. *America's Abortion Dilemma*, NEWSWEEK, Jan. 14, 1985, at 22.

b. Conceiving and Aborting for Transplant Purposes

What then about the situation where the woman is not yet pregnant, but seeks to conceive in order to abort and obtain tissue for transplant? If histocompatibility between tissue source and recipient is needed, most pregnancies would have to be deliberately planned for that purpose. If a woman already pregnant may abort to obtain tissue for transplant, is there an ethical objection to conceiving for that purpose and then aborting?

In terms of fetal welfare, no greater harm occurs to the fetus conceived in order to be aborted, as long as the abortion occurs at a stage at which the fetus is insufficiently developed to experience harm, such as during the first trimester.[57] Of course, such deliberate creation may have greater symbolic or moral significance, because it denotes a willingness to use fetuses as a means to serve other ends. However, aborting when already pregnant to procure tissue for transplant (or to save the mother's life, prevent a handicapped birth, or avoid unwanted pregnancy) also denotes a willingness to use the fetus as a means to other ends. Deliberate creation of fetuses to be aborted may enhance the perception that human life is being systematically devalued, but reasonable persons could find that the additional symbolic devaluation is negligible, or in any case, insufficient to outweigh the substantial gain to recipients that deliberate creation provides. As long as abortion of an existing pregnancy for transplant purposes is ethically accepted, conceiving in order to abort and procure tissue for transplant should also be ethically acceptable when necessary to alleviate great suffering in others.[58]

---

57. The situation is thus distinguishable from one in which the entity created did develop interests before being sacrificed for the good of others. *See also supra* note 53.

58. Some insight into the symbolic concerns that arise when fetuses are created and then aborted for transplant purposes may be gained by considering analogous situations with embryo research, embryo farming and fetal reduction.

The ethics of embryo research generally accept research with excess embryos produced in the attempt to achieve pregnancy through *in vitro* fertilization (IVF) for legitimate scientific purposes. *See* Robertson, *Embryo Research*, 24 U.W. ONTARIO L. REV. 15, 35-36 (1986). Yet several national ethics bodies have recommended and two Australian states have enacted legislation against conceiving embryos solely for research purposes, even though similar British and Canadian bodies have approved it. *Id.* at 35-36.

Because embryo research is permitted if the embryos were by-products of IVF attempts at pregnancy, such research poses no greater harm to embryos when they are created solely for research purposes. The opposition to creating embryos for research purposes is a symbolic, moral concern that should be balanced against the need to obtain embryos in this way to conduct research. Given that important research on egg freezing and the microinjection of sperm cannot be conducted otherwise, there is a strong argument for permitting research on embryos created for that purpose. The

462   WASHINGTON UNIVERSITY LAW QUARTERLY   [Vol. 66:443

Many people will resist this conclusion, even if they accept abortion to procure tissue when the woman is already pregnant. Whether rationally or not, they assign moral or symbolic significance to the fact of deliberate creation for abortion, and are less ready to sanction such a practice. Others who accept abortion for tissue procurement when the woman is already pregnant will find insufficient differences in deliberate creation to outweigh the resulting good. Public acceptability of such a practice thus

---

situation is distinguishable, however, because unlike fetuses conceived and aborted to obtain tissue, the preimplantation embryos in question have not developed even the rudiments of a neurologic system or differentiated other organs.

A variation on this issue would arise if embryos produced by IVF could be grown in culture outside of the body long enough to produce the tissue necessary for transplant. Since embryos cannot develop *in vitro* for more than six to eight days, they are not now a source of tissue for transplant. Suppose, however, that it became possible to culture embryos long enough for tissue farming purposes. Because implantation in a woman does not occur, there is no pregnancy to be aborted. However, an early embryo would be created and destroyed in order to obtain tissue for transplant. If obtained very early in development, the embryo would not have developed to the point at which it itself had interests or rights, and thus would not be harmed by the practice. Yet symbolic concerns with deliberately creating and destroying human life would still arise. The policy issue would be whether the benefits from this tissue source outweighed the symbolic costs of creating and destroying embryos to obtain tissue for transplant. *See* Robertson, *Embryos, Families and Procreative Liberty: The Legal Structure of the New Reproduction*, 59 S. CAL. L. REV. 939, 985-86 (1986).

The growing practice of selective reduction of multiple fetuses resulting from the use of fertility drugs or the transfer of several IVF-produced embryos also presents an issue of deliberately creating fetuses that will be destroyed to serve other goals. Selective reduction or abortion of quintuplets or quadruplets to twins can be justified by the benefits to the mother and to the surviving fetuses. Selective reduction increases the chance of a full term delivery and healthy survival, rather than premature birth and a high risk of death or serious handicap in all. Berkowitz, *Selective Reduction of Multifetal Pregnancies in the First Trimester*, 318 NEW ENG. J. MED. 1043 (1988).

The problem, however, is that the need for the selective reduction usually arises from the mother's decision to take fertility drugs to achieve pregnancy, knowing that multifetal pregnancy and hence need for selective reduction might arise. The mother's wish to reduce the number of fetuses seems less ethically justified when the need results from her deliberate actions, rather than arises naturally. Again, the ethical concern is symbolic—the deliberate devaluation of fetal life that occurs in the willingness to risk creating fetuses that will then be aborted. Of course, the good of achieving pregnancy might be taken to outweigh the symbolic harm, particularly if the abortion is early in the first trimester. *See* Holder & Henifin, *Case Studies: Selective Termination of Pregnancy*, HASTINGS CENTER REP., Feb.-March 1988, at 21 (1988).

Other instances of creating embryos or fetuses with the intention or high risk that they would be destroyed arise with reports of "pregnancy doping" by eastern european female athletes and abortion or embryo selection for sex determination purposes. In the first instance women are reported to have become pregnant in order to raise hormone levels to enhance athletic performance, and then abort. In the second, women abort to avoid the birth of a child of a gender that is undesired because of its association with X linked genetic disease (usually male) or for social reasons (usually female). The ethics of these practices depends upon the stage of development at which abortion occurs, the importance of the benefits derived, the risks to the women and the symbolic costs associated with intentional destruction of prenatal life.

depends on how the swing group views the fact of deliberate creation for the purpose of abortion, assuming it would accept abortion to procure tissue when the pregnancy is not planned for that purpose.

In sum, deliberate creation of fetuses to be aborted for tissue procurement is more ethically complex and defensible than the widespread dismissal it has received would suggest.[59] Such a practice is, of course, not in itself desirable, but, in a specific situation of strong personal or familial need, may be justified. Further ethical analysis of the situation should await actual development of the need. In the meantime, the fear that fetal tissue transplants will encourage women to abort to obtain tissue for transplant should be more carefully scrutinized as the main concern driving policy. If the specific need arises, aborting to obtain tissue for a family member may be more defensible than many previously thought.

III. ISSUES OF MATERNAL AUTONOMY AND WELFARE

While the controversy over fetal tissue transplants has centered on fetal status, issues of maternal autonomy and welfare also deserve consideration. Respecting the woman's decision to abort and to dispose of fetal remains, however, may conflict with the need to protect women from undue pressure and inducements to abort, to donate fetal tissue, or to change the timing and method of abortion. Are limitations on the woman's choice about abortion and disposition of fetal remains ethically justified, or do they constitute unnecessary paternalism? The following discussion considers these issues in the context of the mother's role in disposing of fetal tissue, the process of obtaining consent, and changes in the timing and method of abortion.

A. Maternal Disposition of Fetal Remains

Maternal autonomy over the decision to abort and to donate fetal tissue is a central ethical concern once fetal tissue transplants are deemed acceptable. Yet some ethicists would deny the woman authority to donate fetal remains because she has chosen abortion, or because they fear that dispositional authority will induce women to become pregnant and abort in order to produce fetal tissue. This discussion considers each argument separately.

---

59. Most commentators who recommend a ban on such abortions have not thoroughly analyzed the issue, perhaps because the need for such abortions has not yet arisen. Mahowald et al, *Transplantation of Neural Tissue from Fetuses*, 235 SCIENCE 1308-09 (1987) (letter to editor).

1. The Mother's Right to Dispose of Fetal Tissue

Federal research regulations and the Uniform Anatomical Gift Act, effective in every state, give the mother the right to make or withhold donations of fetal remains for research or therapy.[60] Some ethicists, however, would deny women this right on the ground that the decision to abort disqualifies her from playing any role in disposition of fetal remains.[61] This argument is mistaken on two grounds and would lead either to procuring fetal tissue without parental consent or to a total ban on fetal transplants.[62]

The major premise of this argument is that the person disposing of cadaveric remains acts as a guardian or proxy for the deceased. Because the mother has chosen to kill the fetus by abortion, she is no longer qualified to act as the proxy or guardian of the fetus that she has abandoned.[63]

One mistake here is the assumption that the person who disposes of cadaveric remains acts as a guardian or proxy for the deceased. Deceased persons or fetuses no longer have interests to be protected, as persons with guardians or proxy decision-makers have. Rather, control of human remains is assigned to next-of-kin because of their own interests in making anatomical gifts and in assuring that the remains are treated

---

60. UNIF. ANATOMICAL GIFT ACT § 3, 8A U.L.A. 8-9 (West Supp. 1987). The UAGA makes the mother's consent determinative "unless the father objects." *See also* 45 C.F.R. § 46.209(d) (1987). These provisions require that the father also consent to use of fetal tissue unless he is unavailable to consent.

61. Mahowald, *Placing Wedges Along a Slippery Slope: Use of Fetal Neural Tissue for Transplantation*, 36 CLINICAL RESEARCH 220 (1988); Burtchaell, *supra* note 28, at 8. Presumably they would disqualify the father who agreed to the abortion from consenting as well. Only where the father opposed the abortion would he have a right to donate fetal tissue for transplant.

This argument might have some force in the case of a parent who kills a child or a spouse who murders a spouse. Although determining burial or organ donation rights is usually not an incentive to murder, perhaps the murderer should lose the right to determine organ donation and burial in those cases, just as they lose the right to collect inheritance or life insurance. Riggs v. Palmer, 115 N.Y. 506, 513, 22 N.E. 188, 190 (1889). A woman who aborts is not committing murder, however. She is doing a legal act, indeed, a legal act enshrined as a basic constitutional right.

62. The latter is the goal of some persons taking this position. Burtchaell, for example, uses the claimed inappropriateness of the mother as disposer of fetal remains to argue that they should not be used at all, because it would be "undignified" to use human remains without the consent of next-of-kin. Burtchaell, *supra* note 28, at 8. This position is thus another way to challenge the ethical acceptability of fetal tissue transplants.

63. In an analogous situation, a woman who aborts does not automatically lose custody of an infant born alive as the result of an abortion procedure that attempted to kill the fetus. She is entitled to both substantive and procedural due process before her parental prerogatives may be terminated. *See* Keith v. Daley, 764 F.2d 1265, 1271 (7th Cir. 1986); Wynn v. Carey, 599 F.2d 193, 195 (7th Cir. 1979).

respectfully by burial or cremation. It is not a right which they earn because they have protected the kin's interest when alive. Nor is the right assigned to them because they are best situated to implement the deceased's prior wishes concerning disposition of his cadaver.[64] Indeed, the latter concern is particularly inappropriate in the case of an aborted fetus, which could have had no specific wishes concerning disposition of its remains.

A second mistake is the assumption that a woman has no interest in what happens to the fetus that she chooses to abort. As a product of her body and potential heir that she has for her own reasons chosen not to bring to term, she may care deeply about whether fetal remains are contributed to research or therapy to help others. Given that interest, there is good reason—and no compelling contrary reason—to respect her wishes, as current law presently does.[65] Indeed, in cases of conflict between the mother and the father over disposition, one could argue that the mother's wishes should control because the fetus was removed from her body.[66]

Thus, granting the woman who aborts the right to dispose of fetal remains does not undermine or conflict with any of the purposes served in giving next-of-kin dispositional control of human remains. There is not good reason to override existing law and traditional practice in this area.

Alternative policies would pose even greater problems, requiring either that fetal remains be used without parental consent or not at all. Neither

64. Some persons argue that the next-of-kin is to decide how the deceased would want to be treated if able to tell us, or how they would have wanted to be treated if previously asked about it. Caplan, *Should Fetuses or Infants be Utilized as Organ Donors*, 1 BIOETHICS 135 (1987). There is little evidence that this idea underlies the family's traditional right to decide on burial.

65. *See supra* note 60. The law treats the aborted fetus as the woman's property for the purpose of disposition and anatomical gifts, just as other excised tissue is treated as property in this sense. Although the fetus is genetically different than other removed body parts, its source in the woman's body makes her claim to dispose of it a strong one. (Would not a kidney that had been transplanted to a patient be that patient's if later removed?) Perhaps a more accurate description is that the aborted fetus is the woman's "quasi-property," because her dispositional authority is not unlimited. She may have no right to sell it or display it publicly. Even if she could not demand payment for donation to research, she could still determine whether donation for research will occur. *Cf.* Moore v. Regents of the Univ. of Cal., No. BO 21195, slip. op. (Cal. App. July 21, 1988).

66. Both the Uniform Anatomical Gift Act and federal research regulations permit the father to veto her decision to donate. *See supra* note 60. It is unclear why he should have this authority, however, because donation for research will create no later obligations in him, as might occur if the woman donated a frozen embryo to another couple without his consent and a child were born. If conflicts of this sort arise, the right of the father to veto the mother's donation should be reconsidered.

alternative is acceptable. Public policy in the United States has vigorously rejected routine salvage of body parts without family consent as a way to increase the supply of organs for transplants.[67] Even presumed consent, which presumes the family's consent in the absence of actual objection, has been largely rejected.[68] Depriving the mother (and father who agrees to the abortion) of the power to veto fetal tissue transplants would single out fetal tissue for transplant use without family consent. Such a radical change in tissue procurement practice is not necessary to satisfy the need for fetal tissue and would serve only to punish women who abort.[69]

A proposed alternative to a policy of fetal tissue procurement without maternal consent is to ban fetal tissue transplants altogether in order to prevent the mother from donating fetal tissue. However, this solution burns the house to roast the pig, in effect making tissue transplants from aborted fetuses ethically unacceptable. As we have seen, however, a ban on all fetal transplants, whether to discourage abortions or to symbolize opposition to abortion, is not justified.[70]

In sum, the ethical case for denying dispositional control of fetal remains to the woman who aborts is not persuasive. The woman cannot require that fetal remains be used for transplant because no donor has the right to require that intended donees accept the anatomical gift,[71] but she should retain the existing legal right to veto use of fetal remains for transplant or other purposes. Her consent to donation of fetal tissue should be routinely sought by those who retrieve fetal tissue.

---

67. Robertson, *Supply and Distribution of Hearts for Transplantation: Legal, Ethical and Policy Issues*, 75 CIRCULATION 77, 79 (1987).

68. Only twelve states allow presumed consent for cornea donations. DEPARTMENT OF HEALTH AND HUMAN SERVICES, ORGAN TRANSPLANTATION: ISSUES AND RECOMMENDATIONS, REPORT OF THE TASK FORCE ON ORGAN TRANSPLANTATION, April, 1986, p. 30.

69. Such a result would not, however, violate any fundamental right to control disposition of bodily parts. *See infra* note 125. Nor would it violate any moral right of the woman per se according to ethicist Albert R. Jonsen, Jonsen, *Transplantation of Fetal Tissue: An Ethicist's Viewpoint*, 36 CLINICAL RESEARCH 215, 219 (1988).

70. *See supra* notes 20-46 and accompanying text. Indeed, there would also be serious constitutional problems as well. *See infra* notes 92-101 and accompanying text.

71. The Uniform Anatomical Gift Act permits the designated donee to reject the anatomical gift. Indeed, persons who sign organ donor cards often have their gifts refused before they reach the donee, because organ procurement agencies generally require more authorization to donate than a signed organ donor card.

2. *Will Maternal Consent Encourage Abortion?*

A second reason for denying women dispositional control of fetal remains is the fear that it will lead them to become pregnant and abort in order to obtain fetal tissue for transplant. As we have seen, there is little reason now to think that women will abort to obtain tissue for transplant. The possibility of donation will be a minor factor in the decision to abort, and no need now exists to seek fetal tissue from sources other than abortions performed to end unwanted pregnancy.

If the need to abort to produce fetal tissue did arise, however, the mother's dispositional control over fetal remains would be essential. Unless she could donate fetal remains for transplant and designate the recipient, it would be difficult to draw upon this source of fetal tissue.

Three arguments against a woman's voluntary use of her reproductive capacity in this way can be made. The first argument, based on respect for the welfare of the fetuses that are conceived only to be aborted, has been discussed above, and found wanting in situations where a close family member would be saved from death or serious loss of health.[72]

A second argument, briefly treated here, is the need to protect women from the physical burdens of a pregnancy and abortion they would not otherwise undergo. Banning conception and abortion to procure fetal tissue on paternalistic grounds cannot be reconciled with a woman's autonomy. The physical and psychological burdens of an abortion are not so substantial that women should for their own good be barred from freely assuming them. If women are already pregnant, aborting will probably be less physically hazardous and intrusive than going to term, even though grief and psychological complexities doubtlessly may occur.[73]

If women conceive in order to abort, the physical and psychological risks incurred by them may be reasonably viewed as equivalent to or less than the risks associated with kidney or bone marrow donation, both of which ordinarily entail greater physical intrusion.[74] The benefits to the

---

72. *See supra* notes 47-59 and accompanying text.

73. Depending on the circumstances and previous experiences and psychological make-up of the woman, the abortion might be experienced with at least the grief that accompanies a miscarriage, which can be substantial. The feeling of loss here will by compounded by the notion that this was a pregnancy that might have gone to term. On the other hand, the satisfaction at doing good for a close relative could overcome or negate these feelings.

74. Although the physical intrusion may be less in abortions, the woman loses a fetus and potential child, and not just renewable tissue or a functionally superfluous kidney. The psychologi-

recipient are comparable in each case, and the sacrifice made by the donor should be equally permitted—and applauded. In terms of maternal welfare, there is no reason to treat pregnancy to procure tissue for transplant differently than kidney and marrow donations.[75]

A third argument is that women would thereby be viewed as "vessels" or "machines" to produce fetal tissue, thus denigrating their inherent worth as persons. The problem with this argument is that the same charge can be made against any living donor, whether of kidney, bone marrow, blood, sperm or egg. Insofar as persons donate body parts, they may be viewed as mere tissue or organ producers, with their full reality as persons obliterated by their tissue-producing role. Indeed, women who bear children are always in danger of being viewed as child-breeders. Such views oversimplify the complex emotional reality of organ and tissue donation and of human reproduction. While perceptions of pregnancy and procreative capacity may eventually be affected, the danger that fetal tissue donors would be so narrowly viewed would not justify barring women from freely assuming that role to provide sick patients needed tissue for transplant.[76]

Such donations, however, are ethically acceptable only because the risks are freely chosen. To assure that consent is protected, special attention should be given to consent procedures that will protect the woman from being coerced or unduly pressured by prospective donors and their families, just as occurs with living related kidney and marrow donors. Special consent procedures, including waiting periods, consent advisors and monitors, and other devices to guarantee free, informed consent are

---

cal impact will accordingly be greater, since loss of a fetus cannot be equated with loss of a kidney or bone marrow.

75. This is true even if the donor is unrelated to the recipient and is recruited solely for that purpose, because unrelated bone marrow and even kidney donations do occur. Paying the donor to conceive and abort does not change the balance of risks, even though it may induce certain women to volunteer for this procedure. A ban on such donations would deny recipients a great benefit, a factor that should be considered in deciding whether to interfere on paternalistic grounds with the autonomous choice of the woman. In any event, the donor's decisional process should be closely monitored to assure that it is free and informed.

76. This argument assumes that no money will be paid for her donation. *See infra* notes 91-102 and accompanying text. Even so, the practice of using one's reproductive capacity to produce tissue for transplant may alter or at least complicate perceptions of female reproductive function. Indeed, it would be surprising if some such effect did not occur. That does not mean, however, that women would be so depersonalized that they should be deprived of these choices over their bodies, and needy recipients deprived of transplants.

clearly justified, even though a total ban on such donations is not.[77]

B. The Process of Obtaining Consent

If the woman retains the right to determine whether fetal tissue is used for research or therapy, tissue procurement procedures should respect that right. The main ethical concern then is to assure that her choice about tissue donation and the abortion is free and informed.

To that end, current federal regulations require, and many commentators recommend, that consent to tissue donation be clearly separated from consent to the abortion. A clear separation of the two decisions will assure that tissue donation is not a prerequisite to performance of the abortion.[78] Also, it will prevent the prospect of donating fetal remains from influencing the decision to abort.[79]

At present, the recommended procedure is to have the request to donate fetal tissue made only after the woman has consented to the abortion. The alternative of waiting until the abortion has been performed may not be practical.[80] In addition, the person requesting consent to tissue donation and performing the abortion should not be the person using the donated tissue in research or therapy. This constraint is widely followed in cadaveric organ procurement.

While these procedures are, on the whole, sound, two problems should be noted. Withholding information about fetal tissue donation until after consent to abort is obtained may deprive women of information that is material to their decision to abort, thus preventing their decision from being fully informed. However, only a small group of women would be materially affected by this constraint. Information about tissue donation will not be material to women who choose to abort without that knowledge, since their decision is not affected by the possibility of donation. In

---

77. *See* Robertson, *Taking Consent Seriously: IRB Intervention in the Consent Process*, IRB A REVIEW OF HUMAN SUBJECTS RESEARCH, May 1982, at 1.

78. Cases might rarely arise in which a physician would not do the abortion unless it were specifically for transplant purposes. This, however, will not be the case with tissue retrieved from family planning abortions.

79. A clear separation of the abortion and donation decisions would prevent the prospect of donating fetal remains from influencing the decision to abort except to the extent that publicity about fetal transplants will make women generally aware of the prospect of donation.

80. The woman's capacity to consent after the abortion may be diminished due to anesthesia or the emotional effects of the abortion itself, and the time that viable fetal tissue may be retrieved is short.

470   WASHINGTON UNIVERSITY LAW QUARTERLY   [Vol. 66:443

any event, they will be informed of donation options after they decide to abort.

The group most affected by this policy are women who decide against abortion after discussing the matter with a physician or abortion facility, but who would have chosen to abort if they had been informed that they might donate fetal tissue for transplant. This group would probably not be large. Further, women who are so ambivalent about abortion that tissue donation would reverse a decision against abortion could be required to raise the issue themselves.[81] Given the small size of the group and the benefits of clearly separating the abortion and donation decision in family planning abortions, the policy is defensible.[82]

A second potential problem is that separating the person requesting the tissue donation from the person performing the tissue transplant might not effectively guard the woman from pressure to donate. This practice would not prevent the person who obtains consent for the abortion from also requesting the tissue donation, albeit at a later point in time. If the same person requests both, particularly if it is the physician performing the abortion, and the abortion facility has a financial interest in maximizing tissue procurement, the risk of undue pressure or manipulation of the woman to donate might occur. Since abortion facilities will not be able to sell fetal tissue,[83] this danger may be minimal. To reduce

---

81. At that point, the person obtaining consent could inform them of that possibility or even refuse to discuss it until after the decision to abort is made. But if such knowledge is generally in the air, the ambivalent woman may take it into account or condition her acceptance of the abortion on use of the remains in research or therapy.

Informing women of the chance to donate if they are ambivalent is not, however, an "inducement ... offered to terminate [the] pregnancy. . ." that is prohibited by the federal regulations. 45 C.F.R. § 46.206(b) (1987). Even if the information is given before consent to the abortion, it is not an inducement unless offered specifically for the purpose of "inducing" the woman to terminate the pregnancy and donate the tissue. It would simply be informing the woman of her option to donate fetal tissue.

82. If women undecided or ambivalent about abortion do raise the question, the physician should inform them of fetal tissue donation options. Providing such information should not be considered an illegal inducement to abortion, even if it has the effect of leading women to choose abortion when absent the information they would not have done so, because no valuable consideration to abort is offered. *See* National Institutes of Health, Report of the Panel on Fetal Tissue Transplantation Research, (forthcoming). When the woman does not inquire and thus is not informed of donation options, however, it is unclear whether legal doctrines of informed consent have been violated. Only women who would have aborted if so informed, but who choose not to because ignorant of that possibility, could make such a claim.

83. *See infra* notes 103-04 and accompanying text. Although abortion facilities cannot sell fetal tissue, they can recoup the expenses of procuring the tissue. Loose accounting of reimbursable costs could make it financially advantageous to them to retrieve as much tissue as possible. A payment of

such influences, perhaps the person who obtains consent to the abortion should not also request the tissue donation.

C. Changes in Timing and Method of Abortion

Federal regulations (and most commentators) state that "no procedural changes which may cause greater than minimal risk to the fetus or pregnant woman will be introduced into the procedure for terminating the pregnancy solely in the interest" of the research activity.[84] Although this policy is partially intended to protect fetuses from later or more painful abortions,[85] a main concern is to protect women from postponing pregnancy or undergoing more onerous abortion procedures than they otherwise would, solely to obtain tissue for transplant. Once again, a potential conflict arises between maternal autonomy and paternalism.

Some changes in abortion procedures to enhance tissue procurement pose little additional risk to the woman and should be permitted. For example, reductions in the amount of suction, use of a larger bore needle, and ultrasound-guided placement of the suction instrument in evacuation abortions might facilitate the retrieval of tissue and organs from first trimester aborted fetuses by increasing the chance that tissue will be removed whole and unmacerated.[86]

More problematic would be changes in abortion methods that increase the risks and burdens of the abortion. Such methods include substitution of prostaglandin induction or hysterotomy[87] for less risky methods, or postponement of an early first trimester abortion to later in the first trimester, or to the second trimester. Apart from her desire to facilitate

---

$25-$50 per fetal pancreas retrieved may be financially attractive to abortion facilities and lead them to seek donations and cut corners in the consent process. Strict rules about what counts as reimbursable procurement costs may be necessary to prevent profiteering in this way.

84. 45 C.F.R. § 46.206(a)(3)-(4) (1987).

85. This would be a concern later in the second trimester when the nervous system is so developed that the aborted fetus experiences pain. Also, delaying abortion might be viewed as using the fetus as a means that symbolically devalues human life. *See supra* note 51. If abortion at the later time is otherwise ethically acceptable, the issue is similar to the problem of creating embryos or fetuses solely for research or tissue procurement purposes. *See supra* notes 57-59 and accompanying text.

86. Statement of Dr. George Allen, *supra* note 5. The use of ultrasound might involve some increased cost, which all persons undergoing abortion would then pay. However, this change could be independently justified as in the patients' interest to protect against perforations and should be routinely done even though it is not now the practice.

87. A hysterotomy is a surgical incision into a uterus to remove a fetus, or abortion by Caesarean section.

472   WASHINGTON UNIVERSITY LAW QUARTERLY   [Vol. 66:443

tissue donation, these changes would appear to be against the woman's interest.

Can such paternalistic interference with the mother's choice be justified? While a libertarian might disagree, asking the woman to take on these extra burdens can be ethically justified only if they were necessary to obtain viable tissue. If sufficient tissue can be obtained without such changes, then it would not be ethically sound to ask a patient to assume extra burdens, even the burdens of slightly delaying the abortion.[88] Sufficient fetal tissue for research and therapy may now be obtained without changes in individual abortion procedures, therefore, the federal rules against such changes remain sound.

A different policy should be considered if changes in timing or method of abortion become necessary to procure viable tissue for transplant. If the need were clearly shown, there is no objection in principle to asking a woman to assume some additional burdens for the sake of tissue procurement. If the woman is already pregnant and determined to have an abortion, the additional risks of postponing the abortion a few weeks, or even changing to a prostaglandin abortion, would seem well within the range of risks that persons may voluntarily choose to benefit others.[89] Indeed, the risks would seem no different than those that a woman who conceives for transplant purposes assumes, or the risks that a kidney or marrow donor takes on. Special IRB review[90] and other consent procedures to protect the woman's autonomy, however, would be in order.

IV. COMMERCIALIZATION OF FETAL TISSUE

In addition to ethical concerns about fetal and maternal welfare, opponents of fetal tissue transplants have raised the specter that fetal tissue procurement will lead to a commercial market in abortions and in fetal tissue. Paying money to women to abort, or to donate once they abort, is generally perceived as damaging to human dignity. Commercial buying

---

88. This is a basic principle of medical ethics, evident in research rules, which do not permit a subject to accept freely all risks, but only those risks that have a reasonable chance of procuring useful knowledge. *See* 45 C.F.R. § 46.111(a)(2) (1987). Further, the risks to the subject must be so outweighed by the sum of the benefit to the subject and the importance of the knowledge to be gained, as to warrant a decision to allow the subject to accept those risks.

89. Abortion by hysterotomy raises a more difficult issue, because it is major surgery no longer used to terminate pregnancy. It would be a rare case, however, in which a hysterotomy would be necessary to obtain viable tissue for transplant.

90. IRB refers to Institutional Review Boards, established by Congress to oversee federally-funded scientific research. *See* 46 C.F.R. § 101-409 (1987).

and selling of fetal tissue raises similar concerns. Such market transactions risk exploiting women and their reproductive capacity, and denigrating the human dignity of aborted fetuses by treating them as market commodities.[91]

Most commentators and advisory bodies that have considered fetal tissue transplants recommend that market transactions in abortions and fetal tissue be prohibited.[92] The National Organ Transplant Act of 1984, which bans the payment of "valuable consideration" for the donation or distribution of solid organs, was amended in 1988 to ban sales of fetal organs and "any subparts thereof."[93] In addition, several states prohibit the sale of fetal tissue and organs.[94]

At present such policies are easily supported, for they would appear to

---

91. For opposition to markets in body products generally, see R. TITMUSS, THE GIFT RELATIONSHIP: FROM HUMAN BLOOD TO SOCIAL POLICY (1972); Radin, *Market Inalienability*, 100 HARV. L. REV. 1849 (1987); Murray, *Gifts of the Body and the Needs of Strangers*, HASTINGS CENTER REP., April 1987, at 30-35 (1987).

92. *See supra* note 61.

93. The National Organ Transplant Act, Pub. L. No. 98-507, 1984 U.S. CODE CONG. & ADMIN. NEWS (98 Stat) 2339 (codified at 42 U.S.C. § 274e (Supp. II 1984)). This law originally did not list the brain as an organ covered by the Act, though the liver and pancreas were listed. Arguably, pancreatic islet cells and fetal liver tissue were covered, even if fetal brain cells were not, on the theory that such cells and tissue were a subpart of the covered organ, and that Congress could not have intended only to ban the sale of the full organ and not subparts such as tissue and cells. Congress amended the Act in 1988 by changing the definition of "human organ" to mean "the human (including fetal) kidney, liver, heart, lung, pancreas, bone marrow, cornea, eye, bone and skin or any subpart thereof and any other human organ (or any subpart thereof, including that derived from a fetus) specified by the Secretary of Health and Human Services by regulation." CONG. REC. H10214, Oct. 13, 1988. Fetal cells and tissue of the named organs as subparts are now more clearly covered. Presumably the brain, as an organ, could be added to the list by the Secretary. Fetal neural tissue of interest to Parkinson's disease patients would then be covered as a subpart of the brain. However, payment for fetal brain tissue would not be banned until the Secretary issued the necessary regulation.

Assuming that fetal tissue is covered as a "subpart" of the named organs, a major issue that arises under the act will be whether firms that obtain, process and distribute fetal tissue for transplant may be able to "sell" the processed tissue to doctors and patients and receive profit in addition to their processing costs. If the act does not permit profit as part of the "reasonable payments" for processing tissue, it could have a negative effect on future developments in this field. For further discussion of this point, see *infra* notes 101-106, 156 and accompanying text.

94. ARK. STAT. ANN. § 82-439 (Supp. 1985); FLA. STAT. ANN. § 873.05 (West Supp. 1987); ILL. ANN. STAT. ch. 38, § 81.54(7) (Smith-Hurd 1983); LA. CIV. CODE ANN. art. 9:122 (Supp. 1987); ME. REV. STAT. ANN. tit. 22, § 1593 (1964); MASS. GEN. LAWS ANN. ch. 112, § 1593 (1964); MICH. COMP. LAWS ANN. § 333.2690 (West 1980); MINN. STAT. ANN. § 145.422 (West Supp. 1986); MO. REV. STAT. § 188.036 (1988); NEV. REV. STAT. § 451.015 (1985); N.D. CENT. CODE § 14-02.2-02 (1981); OHIO REV. CODE ANN. § 2919.14 (Anderson 1985); OKLA. STAT. tit. 63, § 1-735 (1987); PA. CONS. STAT. § 3216 (Purdon 1983); R.I. GEN. LAWS § 11-54-1(f) (Supp. 1987); TENN. CODE ANN. § 39-4-208 (Supp. 1987); TEX. PENAL CODE ANN. §§ 42.10, 48.02 (Vernon 1974

have little impact on the supply of fetal tissue for research and therapy. Given the general willingness of Americans to donate blood, organs and other tissue, there is little reason to think that women who abort unwanted pregnancies would not donate fetal tissue altruistically.[95] Indeed, many women who abort are likely to donate fetal remains in the hope that some additional good might result from the abortion.[96] Paying them to donate—buying their aborted fetuses—is thus unnecessary.

Nor at present is there any need to hire women to conceive and abort to provide tissue for transplant. As noted previously, the million plus annual abortions for family planning reasons is more than adequate to supply fetal tissue needs for the near future. Even if histocompatibility between the fetal tissue and recipient became essential, relatives rather than paid recruits would be the prime candidates for pregnancies and abortions to produce fetal tissue.[97]

But what if altruistic donations did not produce a sufficient supply of fetal tissue for transplant, or the need for histocompatible tissue required hiring women to be impregnated to produce a sufficient supply of fetal tissue? Would such payments be unethical? Should current legal policy still be maintained? Answering those questions would require balancing the risks of exploitation and the symbolic costs of perceived commodification (i.e. making fetuses subject to market transfer) against the need to increase tissue supply to benefit needy patients and the rights of women to determine use of their reproductive function.

No doubt many people would object to hiring women to conceive and abort, and insist on maintaining current laws. However, if pregnancy and abortion to produce fetal tissue is ethically defensible, then money payments in some circumstances may also be defensible, given obligations of beneficence and respect for persons, the lack of alternative tissue sources, and social practices in which some tissue donors are paid.[98]

---

and Supp. 1988); WYO. STAT. § 35-6-115 (1986). *See also* Note, *Regulating the Sale of Human Organs*, 71 VA. L. REV. 1015 (1985).

95. Physicians testified at the NIH Panel on Fetal Tissue Transplant Research that over 90% of women who were asked to donate fetal tissue agreed, a rate that compares favorably with the 70% rate of cadaveric organ donation from families of brain dead persons. *See* Task Force Report, *supra* 68, at 28.

96. It does not follow, however, that the donation is the determinative factor in deciding to abort, even if women who donate feel better about their decision to abort.

97. However, some unrelated women would be recruited for this purpose, since many patients might not have a relative available who is willing to conceive and abort to provide them with fetal tissue. One can imagine the creation of agency or brokerage services to provide this service for a fee.

98. For example, sperm donors are generally paid, and the emerging custom with egg donation

Legal policy might then be reconsidered to permit payments when essential to save the life or protect the health of transplant recipients who have no other alternatives.[99] Resolution of this difficult issue, however, should await the actual occurrence of the need to pay to obtain fetal tissue for transplant.

Current bans on buying and selling fetal tissue do not—and should not—prohibit reasonable payments to recover the costs of retrieving fetal tissue. Although paying organ donors is illegal under federal law, the law and ethics of organ procurement allow for payment of costs incurred in the acquisition of organs.[100] Organ donor families, for example, are not asked to pay for the costs of maintaining brain dead cadavers or for surgically removing the organs that they donate. The same principle should apply to fetal tissue donations.[101] Two related issues concern paying the donor's abortion expenses and paying other tissue retrieval costs.

A. *Paying Abortion Expenses*

Paying the cost of the abortion should be ethically and legally acceptable only in those instances in which the abortion is performed solely to obtain tissue for transplant. In that case, paying for the abortion is not a fee to donate tissue, but rather is payment of the costs of acquiring the donated tissue, comparable to paying the cost of the nephrectomy that makes a kidney donation possible. Other out-of-pocket costs incurred by the donor could also be reimbursed without violating federal law or ethical constraints.

In contrast, when the abortion is performed for reasons unrelated to

---

is to pay women up to $1200 to undergo ovarian stimulation and surgical removal of eggs under general anesthesia. Robertson, *Technology and Motherhood: Legal and Ethical Issues in Human Egg Donation,* 39 CASE W. RES. (1988) *(forthcoming).*

   99. In fact, the laws prohibiting hiring women to conceive and abort might unconstitutionally violate a patient's right to effective medical care. *See infra* notes 155-56 and accompanying text.

   100. 42 U.S.C. § 274e (Supp. II 1984). However, state organ sale laws are not always consistent in allowing recovery of the reasonable expenses of organ procurement. *See supra* note 94, at 1031-32. Also, state laws against sale of aborted fetuses might not distinguish payments for the expenses of the abortion from sale of the aborted fetus.

   Note also that while most states ban baby selling, they do permit the payment of medical expenses associated with the birth of the baby that is then adopted. *See, e.g.,* N.J. STAT. ANN. § 9:3-54 (West Supp. 1988).

   101. Paying expenses may not violate state and federal laws against selling organs and tissue, but it is unclear whether they would constitute an "inducement" within the federal research regulations. *See supra* note 81.

tissue procurement, paying abortion expenses amounts to paying the women to donate the tissue. This payment would constitute a sale of fetal tissue and should not be tolerated as long as fetal tissue sales are prohibited.[102] In any event, the willingness of most women to donate without a fee should make payment of abortion expenses unnecessary.

B.   Retrieval Costs and Tissue Retrieval and Processing Agencies

Because physicians who will use fetal tissue clinically ordinarily will not perform the abortion that provides the tissue, a system of specialized agencies that acquire fetal tissue from abortion clinics and distribute it for research or clinical use is likely to develop. These agencies may remove the relevant tissue from the aborted fetus and process it in certain ways to prepare it for therapeutic use, including propagating a line of cells from smaller tissue samples. Such agencies may be nonprofit or for-profit.

What role will money payments play in the operation of retrieval and processing agencies? Under existing law the agencies will be unable to pay women to donate fetal tissue. However, they should be free to pay the costs of personnel directly involved in retrieval, whether employees of the procurement agency or of the facility performing the abortion. For example, a tissue retrieval agency may reimburse the abortion clinic for using its space and staff to obtain consent for tissue donations and to retrieve tissue from aborted fetuses.[103] However, the abortion facility could not charge the agency a fee beyond reasonable expenses incurred in retrieving fetal tissue at their facility.[104]

In distributing fetal tissue to researchers and physicians, retrieval agencies should, of course, be able to recoup the expenses of procuring the tissue, including overhead and other operating expenses of the agency itself. Such payment is consistent with organ transplant recipients (or their payors) paying for the costs of organ procurement, including overhead and other operating costs of the organ procurement agency involved.

---

102. This is an example of how workable lines can be drawn that can minimize commercialization without preventing tissue procurement. *See infra* notes 104-06.

103. Statement of Fred Voss, Vice-President, Hana Biologies, Inc., NIH Panel on Fetal Tissue Transplantation Research (Sept. 21, 1988).

104. It will be important to develop clear lines here so that abortion facilities do not sell fetal tissue and thus offer inducements to persuade undecided women to donate or even to abort. Some dilemmas may arise in implementing such rules. Liberal reimbursement rules for the facility's retrieval costs, for example, could enable them to offer abortions to poorer women at reduced rates.

If the firm processing tissue is a for-profit enterprise, some profit margin should also be recognized in the amount it charges the recipient of the tissue. While some persons might argue that recognizing any profit amounts to a sale of fetal tissue that risks treating fetal tissue as a market commodity, a clear distinction can be drawn between buying and selling fetal tissue, and reimbursing for-profit tissue processing agencies for their costs of providing tissue, including the cost of inducing capital investment in the firm.[105] Persons who organize resources and invest capital to provide viable fetal tissue for transplant are performing a useful social activity. Fears about treating donors and fetuses as commodities might justify policies against selling fetal tissue, but they should not prevent giving for-profit firms the incentives necessary to organize and provide the services in question.[106]

V. LEGAL BARRIERS TO FETAL TISSUE TRANSPLANTS

Our examination of the ethical issues shows that transplants of tissue from aborted fetuses may ethically occur in many circumstances. Nevertheless, some legal barriers to research and therapeutic use of tissue from aborted fetuses exist. The analysis first addresses state bans on research and therapeutic use of aborted fetuses, and then considers the constitutionality of such restrictions.

A. State Bans on Research With Aborted Fetuses

The Uniform Anatomical Gift Act specifically permits use of tissue from aborted fetuses for research, education and transplantation.[107] Yet eight states have enacted statutes that prohibit research with aborted fetuses, and proposals for similar laws in other states can be expected.[108]

---

105. While lines here might get blurry, this would seem no more objectionable than paying Federal Express to ship tissue, which payment would include some "profit" or return on capital to Federal Express. Furthermore, it would seem no more objectionable than the "selling" of organ transplants, medical services, drugs and hospital space in which for-profit entities throughout the health care system engage.

106. The concerns really center on symbolic perceptions from allowing for-profit firms to operate in this area. But the physicians who transplant the tissue, the overnight agency that ships it, the hospital in which the transplant occurs, etc. all are making a profit. There is no good reason why the firm processing the tissue should not profit as well, especially if no other entity would provide the service. The wisdom and constitutionality of laws banning all "commercialization" of fetal tissue may thus be questioned. *See infra* note 155.

107. National Conference of Commissioner on Uniform State Laws, UNIFORM ANATOMICAL GIFT ACT (UAGA), 8A U.L.A. 34 (1987).

108. ARIZ. REV. STAT. ANN. § 36-2302 (1986); ARK. STAT. ANN. § 82-438 (Supp. 1985); ILL.

State laws that make it a crime to acquire or use tissue from aborted fetuses for research or therapy could have a major impact on further development of and access to fetal tissue transplant therapies. The scope of existing laws and their constitutionality thus deserve attention.

The eight states that now ban research with aborted fetuses enacted those laws as part of an effort after *Roe v. Wade* to restrict abortion and limit fetal experimentation.[109] Because legislative history is sparse and these provisions were usually part of a comprehensive regulation of abortion and fetal experimentation, it is difficult to ascertain the precise purpose of each state law. One surmises that a main purpose was to remove an incentive for abortion, even though there was little evidence of women aborting solely for research purposes.[110] No doubt a second purpose was to make a symbolic statement about the perceived immorality of abortion, by preventing any legitimating benefit from use of aborted fetuses. Legislators may also have been concerned with protecting fetuses that had been or were going to be aborted from the harm of experimentation.[111]

The extent to which these statutes prohibit use of fetal tissue from induced abortions depends, of course, on their precise wording.[112] None of them draw a distinction between research on fetuses aborted to get

---

ANN. STAT. ch. 38, para. 81-54(7) (Smith-Hurd 1983); IND. CODE ANN. § 35-1-58.5-6 (West 1986); LA. REV. STAT. ANN. § 1299.35.13 (West 1986); N.M. STAT. ANN. §§ 24-9A-3, 24-9A-4, 24-9A-5 (1986); OHIO REV. CODE ANN. § 2919.14 (Anderson 1985); OKLA. STAT. tit. 63, § 1-735 (Supp. 1981).

Missouri has enacted a law that prohibits physicians from performing, and persons from utilizing, fetal tissue or organs for "medical transplantation," if they know that the woman procured the abortion to obtain tissue or organs for transplant to herself or another. H.B. No. 1479, 84th Gen. Ass., 2d Reg. Sess. (1988) (to be codified at MO. REV. STAT. § 188.036). Because this statute does not apply to "medical transplantation" of fetal tissue or organs from abortions that occur for reasons other than tissue procurement, it will not prevent research or therapeutic transplants with fetal tissue from family planning abortions. The constitutional validity of such a ban is considered *infra* notes 140-56.

109. Baron, *Legislative Regulation of Fetal Experimentation, printed in* GENETICS AND THE LAW III, 431-35, (Milunsky & Annas ed. 1985).

110. *Id.* Terry, *"Alas! Poor Yorick," I Knew Him Ex Utero: The Regulation of Embryo and Fetal Experimentation and Disposal in England and the United States,* 39 VAND. L. REV. 420 (1986).

111. *See* Baron, *supra* note 109; Fletcher and Ryan, *Federal Regulations for Fetal Research: A Case for Reform,* 15 LAW, MEDICINE AND HEALTH CARE, 126-28 (Fall 1987). While fetuses that were to be aborted or that had emerged alive from the abortion could be harmed by experimentation, it is difficult to see how fetuses that were dead due to an induced abortion could be harmed by experimentation. For example, proper respect for the dead does not preclude research, education and transplantation use of cadavers.

112. In some cases these statutes may prevent research with spontaneously aborted fetuses as well.

tissue for experimentation and those aborted for family planning purposes.[113] In addition, six of the eight states only prohibit "experimentation" with aborted fetuses.[114] Thus, tissue from aborted fetuses could be used for therapeutic, but not experimental, purposes in those states.[115]

Moreover, all research uses of fetal tissue from induced abortions are not necessarily banned. Oklahoma, Ohio, Louisiana, Indiana, and Illinois make criminal the act of "experimenting upon the remains of a child or an unborn child resulting from an abortion."[116] But experimental use of fetal tissue is not necessarily research "upon" that tissue. For example, a research project that transplants fetal brain tissue into persons with Parkinson's disease is an experiment upon the recipient of the transplant, and not upon "the remains of a child or unborn child." Because criminal statutes are to be strictly construed, such a reading is cogent and tenable in those five states.

Statutes in Arizona, New Mexico and Arkansas are more broadly worded, and would exclude experimental transplants that clearly have the recipient as the experimental subject. The Arizona law states that "no person shall knowingly use any human fetus or embryo, living or dead, or any parts, organs, or fluids of such fetus resulting from an induced abortion for any medical experimentation or scientific or medical investigation."[117] Similarly, the New Mexico law prohibits clinical research activity "involving" a fetus.[118] These laws would prohibit experimental transplants (but not nonexperimental therapy) in the respective states, but it would not prohibit the procurement of fetal tissue in those states for experimental or other use in other states.[119]

The Arkansas law is the most broadly worded. It states that no person "shall possess either a fetus born dead as a result of a legal abortion, or any organ, member, or tissue of fetal material resulting from a legal abortion."[120] Under this wording, no fetal tissue or organs could be "pos-

---

113. An exception is the recently enacted Missouri statute. *See supra* note 108.

114. Arkansas is the exception because of its ban on "possession" of the organ, tissue or material of an aborted fetus. ARK. STAT. ANN. § 82-438 (Supp. 1985).

115. However, under the laws as now written, the research could be done in a state where it is legal, and therapy based on that research could be provided in states which now ban experimentation.

116. *See, e.g.,* OHIO REV. CODE ANN. § 2919.14 (Anderson 1985).

117. ARIZ. REV. STAT. ANN. § 36-2302 (1986).

118. N.M. STAT. ANN. §§ 24-9A-3, 24-9A-5 (1986).

119. However, Indiana would prohibit use of such tissue procured out of state as well. IND. CODE ANN. § 35-1-58.5-6 (West 1986).

120. ARK. STAT. ANN. § 82-438 (Supp. 1985).

sessed" in Arkansas for any reason, whether medical or educational, research or therapeutic, and whether or not procured in Arkansas. Presumably possession would include the possession of fetal tissue for the period of time from when it is obtained until after it is transplanted, thus placing the persons performing and receiving the tissue transplant in violation of the statute.[121]

B. Constitutionality of State Bans on Research with Aborted Fetuses

Existing state bans on research with aborted fetuses are vulnerable to attack under the United States Constitution on several grounds, including lack of a rational basis, vagueness, overbreadth and substantive due process interference with fundamental rights of pregnant women, and perhaps even of transplant recipients. In the only legal challenge to date, a federal district court struck down the Louisiana law on the grounds that it served no rational purpose, interfered with the right to have an abortion, and was vague.[122] The Fifth Circuit Court of Appeals affirmed the district court on the ground of vagueness only, finding that the definition of "experimentation" was too imprecise to give adequate notice about which medical uses of aborted fetuses were permitted and which were not.[123] The court thus left open the question of whether a better drafted statute would withstand substantive attack.[124]

In assessing the substantive arguments against bans on use of fetal tissue, it is useful to distinguish between bans on use of tissue procured from abortions performed for family planning reasons and abortions performed solely to obtain fetal tissue. Since existing laws do not make this distinction, they are vulnerable to arguments under either rubric.

1. Bans on Use of Fetal Tissue From Family Planning Abortions

Laws banning research or other use of fetal tissue from abortions performed to avoid pregnancy would strike at the heart of fetal tissue research, and make further progress in this field exceedingly difficult. By

---

121. The recipient would "possess" the fetal tissue as well because it would be in his body at all times, and as a result of a choice on his part, assuming he knew the source.

122. *Margaret S. v. Edwards*, 597 F. Supp. 636 (1984), *aff'd*, 794 F.2d 994 (5th Cir. 1986).

123. *Margaret S. v. Edwards*, 794 F.2d 994 (5th Cir. 1986). A concurring judge was willing to find the Louisiana statute invalid on grounds other than vagueness. *Id.* at 999-1004 (Williams, J., specially concurring). *See also* Note, *State Prohibition of Fetal Experimentation and the Fundamental Right of Privacy*, 88 COLUM. L. REV. 1073 (1988).

124. In theory, a statute void for vagueness can always be redrafted to overcome the vagueness problem.

banning all experimental use of fetuses from induced abortion, eight states have such laws at the present time, and more may be in the offing. Even if problems of vagueness are overcome, such laws could be attacked as lacking a rational basis, interfering with the woman's right to abort and infringing the recipient's right to receive health care.[125]

a. Is There a Rational Basis?

Banning experimental or therapeutic fetal tissue from abortions occurring for family planning reasons might not even satisfy the minimal rational basis test for legislation under either a due process or equal protection rubric.

Opponents of such laws would argue that they violate basic due process because no rational purpose is served in banning research (or therapeutic) uses of aborted fetuses.[126] The abortions have been performed to end unwanted pregnancy, and not to procure tissue for transplant. A ban on research will not protect the fetus, which is dead and no longer has interests to be protected. Nor is a ban necessary to show respect for human life, since research or therapeutic use of human cadavers has long been consistent with proper respect.

Such laws may also be effectively challenged as lacking a rational basis on equal protection grounds.[127] Several current statutes permit therapeutic but not experimental use of aborted fetuses. In addition, none of

---

125. *See Infra* note 126. Such laws are not subject to attack on the basis of a fundamental right to dispose of tissue independent of the abortion decision. As Commonwealth v. Edelin, 371 Mass. 497, 359 N.E.2d 4 (1976), makes clear, the right to abort does not necessarily give the woman the right to control disposition of the aborted fetus. If the aborted fetus is alive she may have a legal duty to treat it, despite her wishes to the contrary. Nor is there a fundamental right in the next-of-kin to control disposition of cadaveric or fetal remains. Tillman v. Detroit Receiving Hospital, 138 Mich. App. 683, 360 N.W.2d 275 (1984); State v. Powell, 11 Fla. 557, 497 So. 2d 1188 (1986), *cert. denied*, 107 S. Ct. 2202 (1987). Thus, laws prohibiting or mandating anatomical gifts would not violate a fundamental right to dispose of cadaveric remains from oneself or others.

126. If the interest protected is not fundamental, due process requires that the legislation be rationally related to a valid state purpose. Williamson v. Lee Optical Co., 348 U.S. 483, 491 (1955). *See* Roe v. Wade, 410 U.S. 113, 173 (1973) (Rehnquist, J., dissenting). However, in *Roe v. Wade* the Supreme Court majority held that a woman's interest in making the decision to abort is protected as a fundamental right. *Id.* at 152-53. Therefore, a state statute interfering with this right would be subject to strict judicial scrutiny. Strict scrutiny requires that the state interest be compelling and the state's means be narrowly drawn to protect only the compelling state interest. *Id.* at 155.

127. Even if the interest protected were not fundamental, and thus not judged under a strict "compelling interest" test, the legislation must still be "rationally related to a legitimate government interest." City of Cleburne v. Cleburne Living Center, 473 U.S. 432 (1985). If the purpose of the law was to demonstrate the human worth of the fetus, it would be irrational to ban research on aborted fetuses while permitting therapeutic uses of aborted fetuses.

the eight states forbid the experimental use of other human remains, such as victims of accident or violent crime. Thus, one could argue that these distinctions are irrational, because no valid purpose is served by singling out aborted fetuses for an experimental ban while permitting therapeutic uses of aborted fetuses and permitting both experimental and therapeutic uses of other human remains.[128]

Proponents, on the other hand, would argue that such laws are rationally related to discouraging abortion, because it will prevent women undecided about abortion from deciding to abort on the basis of tissue donation. Also, such laws serve the purpose of announcing the state's strong respect for prenatal life, even if that life has been taken, by reminding us that prenatal life is not to be exploited for the good of others.[129] Further, restricting experimental but not therapeutic use of aborted fetuses is justified as rational at a time when no therapeutic uses have been clearly established and the full costs of a broader ban are not clear. Nor, given the special need to protect fetuses subject to abortion, is it irrational to ban experiments on aborted fetuses but not other human cadavers. Finally, this ban might discourage doctors from persuading women to abort to obtain fetuses for research.

While the rational basis test is notoriously easy to meet, courts may well find (as did the district court and one judge at the appellate level in *Margaret S. v. Edwards*)[130] that such broad restrictions, particularly when therapeutic use of aborted fetuses and other human cadavers is permitted, serve no rational purpose. Resolution of the issue may well depend on whether judges considering such a challenge perceive such a broad ban as serving a state goal of protecting prenatal life in any meaningful way. Arguably, it does not.

b. *Interference with the Right to Abort*

If courts found such bans rational, the laws would still have to satisfy a stricter standard of scrutiny if they interfered with or significantly burdened the woman's decision to abort.[131] Because these laws do not pre-

---

128. *See* Margaret S. v. Edwards, 794 F.2d 994 (5th Cir. 1986) (argument that statute unconstitutional under rational basis test) (J. Williams, concurring); Margaret S. v. Edwards, 597 F. Supp. 636 (1985) (invalidated statute under rational basis test).

129. The state may take steps to protect prenatal life as long as it does not impinge on fundamental rights in doing so. Maher v. Roe, 432 U.S. 464 (1977).

130. *See supra* notes 122-23.

131. *See supra* note 126.

vent abortions sought solely for family planning purposes, but only restrict disposition of fetal remains, it may be hard to show an interference with reproductive decisionmaking.

One ground for finding such interference would be that a ban on research impinges on the woman's future reproductive decisionmaking, by preventing her from obtaining information directly relevant to her future decisions about pregnancy and childbearing.[132] Research on topics unrelated to reproduction, however, such as Parkinson's disease or diabetes, would not fall into that category.[133] A more narrowly drawn statute could meet that objection.

Another argument would be that such a statute necessarily impinges on the decision to abort because the very purpose of the law is to influence perceptions of fetal status so that women will not seek abortions in the future. Official elevation of fetal status in this way burdens or interferes with the autonomy of women contemplating family planning abortions, by announcing the state's support of prenatal life, thus leading women, who otherwise would abort, not to abort.[134] Indeed what other

---

132. A ban on research with aborted fetuses (whatever the reason for the abortion) might also interfere with a decision to abort, or with other reproductive decisions to the extent that it prevents the development of information that would affect abortion and other reproductive decisionmaking. *See* Note, *State Prohibition of Fetal Experimentation and the Fundamental Right of Privacy*, 88 COLUM. L. REV. 1073, 1078-85 (1988). For example, the district court in Margaret S. v. Treen, 597 F. Supp. 636 (E.D. La. 1984), *aff'd on other grounds sub nom.*, Margaret S. v. Edwards, 794 F.2d 994 (5th Cir. 1986), found that a prohibition on research on fetal tissue could deny a woman information that might influence her own future pregnancies. In addition, a prohibition on research might curtail the development of prenatal diagnostic techniques such as amniocentesis by making it impossible to examine fetal tissue that had been aborted. However, these considerations would apply only insofar as the statute banned research on those topics; they would not apply to interference with other kinds of research.

133. *See supra* note 132. However, one could argue that successful tissue transplants for those diseases would lead women to get pregnant and abort in the future solely to obtain tissue for transplant.

134. *See* Reproductive Health Serv. v. Webster, 851 F.2d 1071, 1076-77 (8th Cir. 1988). Also instructive here is the fate of fetal disposal laws. While constitutional challenges to fetal disposal laws have usually succeeded on vagueness grounds, some federal district courts have struck down for other reasons disposal laws that required aborted fetuses to be interred, buried or cremated. The courts held that the laws convey the message that a fetus is a human being deserving the respect and dignity of a formal burial, thus equating abortion with the taking of a human life. If such laws were shown to burden the woman's decision to abort, they would be invalid. Such a burden was found when the law required the woman to choose the means of disposal prior to the abortion. Leigh v. Olsen, 497 F. Supp. 1340 (D. N.D. 1980). In another case the burden was less clear because the woman would be informed of these options 24 hours after the abortion procedure. Margaret S. v. Edwards, 794 F.2d 994, 997-98 (5th Cir. 1986) (struck down on other grounds). *See also* Planned Parenthood Ass'n v. City of Cincinnati, 822 F.2d 1390, 1399 (6th Cir. 1987).

purpose can attend such a ban, but an attempt to show the worth of the fetus so that women will refrain from abortion?

The assumption underlying this objection, however, is that the state must remain neutral about protecting prenatal status, and can never "speak" on the issue for fear that its speech will persuade listeners to change their future behavior. As the abortion funding cases make clear, however, the state is not disqualified from speaking on abortion as long as no interference thereby occurs.[135]

Prohibiting the donation of fetal remains for research or therapy announces the government's view of the importance of respecting prenatal life, but it does not prevent abortions for women who are not aborting to produce fetal tissue for transplant. They may consider the government's message and act on it or not, as they choose. If the state is free to communicate its views about prenatal status, the ban on use of fetal remains will not unconstitutionally interfere with the decision to abort, even if some women then decide not to abort.[136]

c. The Right to Life or Health of the Recipient

Even if laws against tissue transplants with fetuses aborted for family planning reasons met a rational basis test and did not impermissibly interfere with a woman's right to abort, they still might interfere with the right of potential transplant recipients to receive medical treatment necessary for their life or health.

While the interest in receiving medical treatment has not, except in the context of abortion and contraception, received explicit constitutional protection, a cogent argument for such a right can be made.[137] Consider

---

135. Harris v. Mcrae, 448 U.S. 297 (1980); Beal v. Doe, 432 U.S. 438 (1977); Poelker v. Doe, 432 U.S. 519 (1977) (per curiam). For further development of this point, see Hirt, *Why the Government Is Not Required to Subsidize Abortion Counseling and Referral*, 101 HARV. L. REV. 1895 (1988).

136. Some cases have suggested that the state's right to communicate its views regarding prenatal life is limited, because the purpose is to influence the woman's abortion decision. Of course, that may be the purpose, but if the influence occurs merely from the presentation of information (here, the information that the state takes a negative view of abortion), unconstitutional interference does not occur. It is another matter, however, if the purpose of the law is to deprive women of dispositional rights because they have aborted. Although a woman has no independent fundamental right to control disposition of fetal or other tissue removed from her, depriving her of control over fetal remains is not valid if the purpose is to penalize the underlying choice of procuring tissue by abortion.

137. *Roe v. Wade* talks about the "right of the doctor and his patient to decide upon medical care." However, courts have not recognized this point explicitly in other cases, with the exception of Ballard v. Andrews, 498 F. Supp. 1038 (S.D. Texas 1980). The district court in *Margaret S. v. Treen*

a situation in which a willing physician and patient wish to treat a life-threatening illness with fetal tissue freely donated for that purpose—a treatment shown by extensive research abroad to be safe and effective for its intended purpose.[138] State law, however, prohibits transplants with tissue from aborted fetuses in order to make a symbolic statement about its view of the worth of fetuses. Would such a law, which we assume would meet a rational basis test, be valid?

The validity of such a law would turn on whether the fourteenth amendment right not to be deprived of "life or liberty without due process of law" protects the right to receive safe and effective medical treatments from willing physicians. A strong argument for subjecting such a statute to a scrutiny stricter than rational basis can be made on the basis of the plain meaning of the constitutional text.[139] The state, by this prohibition, would be directly depriving the patient of "life," for without the tissue transplant he would die. Moreover, the state prohibition would deprive him of "liberty" if the ban on treatment impaired the patient's physical mobility (as would be the case if severe Parkinson's disease or diabetes were not treated). In either case, under strict scrutiny, the purpose of deterring abortions or making a symbolic statement of fetal worth would not justify the state's interference with the patients's life or liberty.

While such an expansion of due process is novel, judicial recognition of a person's fundamental right to receive medical treatment necessary to restore life or physical movement should lie within accepted parameters of constitutional interpretation. Requiring the state to show more than disapproval of abortion to justify deprivation of a person's life or liberty

---

also recognized such a right in finding that a ban on research with aborted fetuses might violate the "right to health" of the woman by denying her information of medical benefit beyond reproductive decisionmaking by prohibiting procedures of immediate medical benefit to her, such as pathological examination of tissues. 597 F. Supp. 636, 673 (E.D. La. 1984) *aff'd on other grounds sub nom.,* Margaret v. Edwards, 794 F.2d 994 (5th Cir. 1986). *See also* Planned Parenthood v. Ashcroft, 462 U.S. 476, 486-87 (1983) (state may require pathological examination of fetal tissue from abortions done in abortion clinics to protect health and safety of woman).

138. A more exotic hypothetical will focus the point even more sharply. Suppose the patient's life depends upon taking a certain medicine derived only from the roots of a naturally occurring plant—ginseng—that flourishes in the upper Midwest. A religious minority has come to believe that removal of ginseng from the ground will cause the death of persons somewhere in the world, and persuades the state to ban sale and possession of ginseng. Would such a law, which would deprive other persons of the means necessary for them to live, be constitutional? In deciding that question, should not a test more rigorous than rational basis be applied?

139. *See supra* note 127.

486   WASHINGTON UNIVERSITY LAW QUARTERLY   [Vol. 66:443

(by preventing access to the only effective treatment possible) is not an arbitrary judicial decision even if the ban on fetal tissue transplants from aborted fetuses survives other attacks, it should not survive this one.

2. State Bans on Intrafamilial Transplants and Donor Designation of Recipients

Rather than a broad ban on all use of fetal tissue, such as those that currently exist in eight states, many commentators recommend a more discriminating approach. They would ban fetal tissue transplants only from abortions and pregnancies undertaken solely for that purpose, and not from all family planning abortions. To achieve this purpose, they recommend enacting a ban on fetal tissue donations to friends or family members, or alternatively, denying the woman who aborts the right to designate the recipient of a fetal tissue donation.[140] Since future developments might create a need for such abortions, the constitutionality of such bans deserves attention.

Bans on donor designation of recipient or intrafamilial donations create a "Chinese Wall" between the tissue source and recipient to prevent women from becoming organ farms, to prevent "abuse" or "degradation" of the reproductive process and to protect women from family pressures to conceive and abort to provide tissue.[141] Concerns for fetuses undoubtedly also enter into the movement for such laws.

While these purposes would easily satisfy a rational basis test, they would appear to interfere with a woman's reproductive rights and the recipient's right to effective health care.

a. Interference with the Right to Abort

A two-step evaluation is necessary to assess the impact on reproductive decisionmaking of laws that limit the donor's designation of recipients of fetal tissue. The first step is to consider their effect on women who are already pregnant and wish to abort in order to donate fetal tissue to a relative or friend in need. The second step considers the effect of such laws on decisions to become pregnant in order to produce fetal tissue for transplant.

A ban on donor designation of fetal tissue recipients would prevent a

---

140. *See, e.g.*, Danis, *Fetal Tissue Transplants: Restricting Recipient Designation*, 39 HASTINGS L.J. 1079 (1988). For a statute that is framed in terms of the woman's motivation, see MO. REV. STAT. § 188.036 (1988).

141. *See* Danis, *supra* note 140, at 1092.

pregnant woman from aborting in order to provide fetal tissue to a particular recipient. Does removal of a particular motivation for abortion interfere with or burden the fundamental right to terminate pregnancy?

The argument is strong that it does. *Roe v. Wade* [142] appears to create a right to terminate pregnancy regardless of the woman's motive for the abortion. While the Court emphasized a woman's interest in avoiding unwanted children as the underlying value or interest at stake in the abortion decision, it imposed no limits on her right to terminate based on her reasons for choosing to abort. [143] The clear implication is that a pregnant woman's motive in ending her pregnancy is irrelevant, and that state laws that conditioned abortion on particular motivations would be invalid. [144] Dislike of pregnancy and children, vanity, personal convenience or sheer malice may all motivate a woman in deciding to terminate pregnancy. A legal right to end pregnancy in order to obtain tissue for transplant thus follows.

If this reading of *Roe* is correct, then prohibiting a pregnant woman from aborting to provide fetal tissue by denying her the right to designate a donor, or to donate to a relative, is invalid absent a compelling state interest for this interference with the abortion decision. [145] Clearly, the goal of preventing abortions or protecting fetuses from degradation would not suffice as compelling state interests because the woman's right to devalue the fetus relative to other values is protected. Nor would preventing her from being coerced or pressured into aborting for a family member suffice either, because there are less restrictive ways of protecting her autonomy without banning all abortions to produce tissue. [146] A

---

142. 410 U.S. 113 (1973).

143. *Id.* at 155.; *see* Robertson, *supra* note 49.

144. An inquiry into motive for aborting a pregnancy would, in any case, be difficult to enforce because a woman could easily lie about her motives for the abortion, claiming that her purpose was to avoid the gestational burdens that pregnancy invariably involves. *But cf.* Mo. Rev. Stat. § 188.036 (1988).

145. The point is quite subtle, because the woman who may not designate the recipient is still free to abort. Also, the woman has no inherent right to dispose of fetal tissue or designate the recipient. Yet denying this right could interact with the abortion decision by limiting her autonomy over that choice. An analogy would be a law that required all profits from publication of sexually explicit, but nonobscene, films and books go to charity to help abused women. Although one could still publish such material, the incentive to do so is lost if profits cannot be made. Since motivation in publishing protected material is irrelevant to its legitimacy, such a ban would be unconstitutional. Similarly, a ban on designating the recipient of fetal tissue should also be unconstitutional, because it interferes with a motive for abortion, even though it does not prohibit the abortion per se, anymore than publication of the sexual material is prohibited per se.

146. Doctors have developed such techniques for recruiting family members for kidney trans-

ban on research use of aborted fetuses, enacted to prevent abortions done to obtain fetal tissue, would thus appear invalid.

b. Interference with the Right to Conceive

If the state could not ban abortion to produce fetal tissue when the woman is already pregnant (either directly or by banning intrafamilial or donor designation of fetal tissue recipients), could it nevertheless ban conception and pregnancy undertaken to procure tissue for transplant? To pursue that goal, it would have to fashion a law that banned only conceiving for that purpose, because, as argued in this Article, the woman's right to abort to produce tissue—once pregnant—is protected.[147] Would a precisely drafted law that penalized only conception to procure tissue for transplant, and not the abortion itself, be valid?

The validity of such a law would depend upon whether a woman has a right to initiate a pregnancy in order to produce fetal tissue for transplant by abortion. Judicial recognition of such a right would depend on several factors, including whether the parties are married, the woman's relationship to the intended recipient, and whether conception occurs coitally or noncoitally.

A strong argument for such a right (and against such a law) would arise in the case of a married couple that conceives to produce tissue for one of the partners, their offspring, or parents. The Supreme Court has been so protective of the sexual privacy of married couple that any restriction on marital conception would probably be subject to the strictest scrutiny.[148] Preventing fetuses from being treated as "mere means," or protecting women from the physical and symbolic effects of being a "tissue farm" would not seem substantial enough to justify the intrusion on the couple's sexual privacy.[149]

The Court is more likely to uphold a law directed against coital conception by unmarried persons for tissue procurement purposes. The key

---

plants. They interview the potential donor and if they find that he has been pressured or is reluctant to donate, the physicians then inform all parties that the donor is excluded on medical grounds.

147. A ban on donor designation of recipients or on intrafamilial donation would not achieve the purpose of banning only conceiving to procure tissue for transplant because it would also ban *abortions* to procure tissue for transplant. Drafting and implementing such a law would, therefore, be difficult. *But cf.* Mo. REV. STAT. § 188.036 (1988).

148. *See, e.g.*, Griswold v. Connecticut, 381 U.S. 479 (1965); Robertson, *Procreative Liberty and the Control of Conception, Pregnancy and Childbirth*, 69 VA. L. REV. 405 (1983).

149. No doubt the married couple's privacy would be protected even if conception occurred noncoitally.

is whether the Court would recognize a fundamental right of heterosexual sexual privacy. If it did, unmarried coitus would presumably be protected to the same extent as marital sex, whatever the motivation (and result) of the coitus. If unmarried coitus were not constitutionally protected, then the state could prohibit unmarried sexual intercourse performed with any motivation, including a desire to produce fetal tissue for transplant. Given the Court's restrictive view of sexual privacy in *Bowers v. Harwick*,[150] one cannot be confident that laws against conception by unmarried persons for transplant purposes would fall.

What then about noncoital conception to produce fetal tissue by a woman not married to the intended recipient or source of sperm? The right asserted here is not sexual autonomy per se, but the right to control one's body and reproductive capacity. The Court's decisions concerning birth control and abortion, however, have not been based on a general right to control one's body or reproductive capacity. Even though unmarried persons have a right to avoid conception and gestation, or to carry a pregnancy to term once they have conceived, it does not follow that single persons have a right to conceive in order to go to term, or conceive in order to abort.[151] If confronted with the question, the Court is more likely to reject rather than recognize such a right.

Yet even restrictions on unmarried conception might be vulnerable to attack if the woman is artificially inseminated to provide fetal tissue for a sibling, a parent, a child or herself. Protection of one's own health and family autonomy would then be added to the claim of a right to control one's body and reproductive capacity. Given the blurry contours of family autonomy, courts may well recognize the right to conceive when the intended recipient is the woman's child, parent or sibling, the woman herself, or the intended recipient has provided the sperm to produce the fetal tissue in question.[152] By contrast, a woman unrelated to the recipi-

---

150. Bowers v. Hardwick, 478 U.S. 186 (1986), upheld a state sodomy statute applied to homosexual activity on moral grounds alone, because homosexuals did not have a fundamental right of sexual privacy. Although *Bowers* dealt with homosexual rights, it hardly reassures persons who claim a right to heterosexual privacy outside of marriage. It may be that courts will also decline to apply strict scrutiny to fornication and sodomy laws applied to heterosexuals, thus allowing the enforcement of particular moral views to satisfy the rational basis test courts use for legislation that does not interfere with fundamental rights.

151. *See* Robertson, *supra* note 148, at 416-17.

152. While the Court has extended the notion of family privacy in the context of zoning restrictions, Moore v. City of East Cleveland, 431 U.S. 494 (1977), and decisions to marry or raise children, Zablocki v. Redhail, 434 U.S. 374 (1978), it is difficult to predict how it would treat the novel question presented here. In any event, in the absence of laws specifically banning such conception,

ent probably could be barred from conceiving to produce fetal tissue that is not genetically related to the recipient.[153]

In sum, laws that prohibit the woman who aborts from designating the recipient of fetal tissue are invalid because they would prevent women from aborting to obtain tissue for transplant. In addition, they might infringe on the right of married couples to conceive as they will, and the possible right of family members to contribute tissue or organs from their body to save the life of a family member. However, arrangements to produce fetal tissue that is not genetically related to the recipient could be banned without interfering with fundamental *reproductive* rights.

c. The Recipient's Right to Medical Treatment

Even if laws against designation of donees, aimed at preventing abortion and becoming pregnant to produce fetal tissue, did not interfere with reproductive rights, they would still have to be tested against the recipient's right to receive essential health care. As we have seen, one can make a cogent argument for such a right when conception and abortion are necessary to obtain the fetal tissue essential to save the life or health of a sick patient.[154] The courts should then require that the state have a more compelling purpose than demonstrating respect for fetuses or preventing women from becoming "organ farms" if such interference with the life and liberty of sick patients is to be justified. Absent more compelling justification, such laws would be invalid.

The patient's right to health care would even cast doubt on laws that banned payments to women to get pregnant and abort. If family planning abortions did not meet demand for fetal tissue transplants or if histocompatibility became important, it might be essential to pay women to undergo conception and abortion in order to provide the needed tissue.

---

the incest laws are not themselves a barrier to noncoital conception by a relative with the gametes of a family member in order to provide them or others with fetal tissue. Of course, artificial impregnation with the sperm of a family-related recipient or the relative of a recipient might raise powerful psychological feelings in the woman, the recipient or the sperm donor, and brush up against some of the policies behind incest and consanguineous marriage laws. The difference is that neither sexual intercourse, which incest laws ban, nor marriage and birth of offspring, which laws against consanguineous marriage aim to prevent, is occurring. *See generally* Coleman, *Incest: A Proper Definition Reveals the Need for a Different Legal Response*, 49 MO. L. REV. 251 (1984).

153. States could ban such practices because conceiving to produce fetal tissue that is not genetically related to the recipient presumably does nothing to further one's own health or family autonomy. States may thus be able to stop programs that rely on nonrelated women to produce fetal tissue for transplant without violating *reproductive* freedom.

154. *See supra* notes 137-39 and accompanying text.

Laws banning payment would then interfere with the life or liberty of recipients, and should be tested by a stricter scrutiny than if the effect on recipients were marginal. With such serious deprivations, symbolic concerns about commodification or denigration of human dignity might be found to be an insufficient justification for such laws.[155]

Even if payments to donors are not necessary to procure tissue, fees paid to for-profit agencies organized to retrieve and process fetal tissue from aborted fetuses may be. Statutes banning the sale of fetuses may be worded in ways that would prevent for-profit firms from charging the profit that is essential for them to operate in this field.[156] If they did have that effect, however, and nonprofit firms did not fill the gap, the courts should apply the same rigorous scrutiny in determining the constitutionality of the law they would apply to any restrictions that deprived recipients of the tissue transplants necessary for their health.

VI. FEDERAL RESEARCH FUNDING AND REGULATION OF FETAL TISSUE TRANSPLANTS

Federal regulations and federal funding policies for human subject research will play an important role in the development and diffusion of fetal tissue transplants. Federal research regulations will have a strong influence on fetal tissue procurement and research practices far beyond research that is directly funded by the federal government.[157] In addition, as a major player in biomedical research, federal funding may be essential for the research necessary to perfect tissue transplants.

---

155. These concerns might not amount to a compelling state interest because they are moralistic concerns over which reasonable people widely disagree. In general, symbolic or moralistic concerns do not trump fundamental rights. The same argument could be made against federal and state laws that prohibit sale of organs. *See supra* notes 93-94. The constitutionality of laws against organ sales has not yet been challenged, perhaps because the lack of organs for transplant is due to considerations other than the lack of financial incentives to motivate donors. *See* Robertson, *supra* note 67, at 80.

156. A statute that banned all "commercial use" of aborted fetuses, such as exists in Nevada, would arguably prevent for-profit firms from processing and distributing fetal tissue for profit. NEV. REV. STAT. § 451.015 (1985). The benefits to patients of for profit operations, however, may clearly outweigh the symbolic gains of not sanctioning any commercial operations with fetal tissue. After all, physicians are paid to perform abortions. *See supra* notes 93, 101-06 and accompanying text.

157. This is because institutions that receive federal funds generally must comply with federal research regulations even if the research itself is not federally funded. 45 C.F.R. § 46.201-211 (1987). Also, such regulations have great influence, and are likely to be followed even when not legally obligatory.

A. Current Federal Regulations for Fetal Research

In 1975, in the aftermath of *Roe v. Wade* and great controversy over
fetal research, Congress created the National Commission for Protection
of Human Subjects of Biomedical and Behavioral Science Research to
advise on policy for research with fetuses and other human subjects.[158]
Its recommendations for federally funded fetal research were promulgated in 1976 as regulations[159] that specify additional duties of institutional review boards "in connection with activities involving fetuses [and]
pregnant women."[160]

While these regulations focus on research with live fetuses that have
been or were intended to be aborted, one provision addresses the use of
dead fetuses in research. That provision states: "Activities involving the
dead fetus, macerated fetal material, or cells, tissue, or organs excised
from a dead fetus shall be conducted only in accordance with any applicable state or local laws regarding such activities."[161]

A striking feature of this regulation, which is still in effect, is that it
implicitly rejects the arguments against fetal tissue research canvassed in
this article. Research with dead aborted fetuses may be conducted as
long as state or local law permits it. With a few exceptions, state or local
law permits research with aborted fetuses when the mother consents. Indeed, most states currently permit even research with fetuses conceived
and aborted to obtain tissue for transplant.[162]

Other provisions of the regulations restrict the circumstances of fetal
tissue procurement. They require that:

(3) Individuals engaged in the activity will have no part in: (i) Any decisions as to the timing, method, and procedures used to terminate the pregnancy, and (ii) determining the viability of the fetus at the termination of
the pregnancy; and

(4) No procedural changes which may cause greater than minimal risk
to the fetus or the pregnant woman will be introduced into the procedure
for terminating the pregnancy solely in the interest of the activity.

(b) No inducements, monetary or otherwise, may be offered to terminate
pregnancy for the purposes of the activity. . . .[163]

---

158. National Research Act, Pub. L. No. 93-348, § 202(b), 88 Stat. 342 (1974).
159. 45 C.F.R. § 46.201-211 (1987).
160. National Commission for Protection of Human Subjects of Biomedical and Behavioral Research, Report and Recommendations: Research on the Fetus. 45 C.F.R. § 46.205 (1987).
161. 45 C.F.R. § 46.210 (1987).
162. *See supra* notes 108-20 and accompanying text.
163. 45 C.F.R. § 46.206(3),(4) (1987).

These restrictions are typical of the protections recommended by other commentators and advisory bodies for fetal procurement, and generally are sound.[164] However, some potential problems should be noted. A restrictive interpretation of "inducement" could prevent any discussion with a pregnant woman prior to a decision to abort of her right to donate fetal remains even though she might seek such information.[165] If changes in the timing or method of abortion become necessary to procure viable tissue, the regulations would prevent obtaining the tissue, even though the woman freely consented and the changes did not so increase the risk to the mother or to the fetus as to be ethically unacceptable.[166] Finally, there are limitations on who may request such changes, which could block access to fetal tissue.[167] If such provisions become barriers to obtaining fetal tissue, they should be reexamined to assure that they are ethically justified.

B. Federal Funding of Fetal Tissue Research and Therapy

While existing federal regulations permit transplants with tissue from aborted fetuses, the question of whether the federal government should

---

164. *See supra* notes 77-89 and accompanying text.

165. Providing her with the requested information may be prohibited because it might serve as the motivating factor in deciding to have an abortion. But this interpretation of "inducement" should be rejected. *See supra* note 81.

166. *See supra* notes 84-89 and accompanying text.

167. The question here is whether the person requesting permission for the abortion or consent to donation could request the woman to postpone the timing or change the method of abortion in order to procure viable tissue for transplant. The answer to this question depends upon the interpretation of the term "activity" as used in 45 C.F.R. § 46.206 (1987).

If the "activity" is the use of the donated tissue for research, then the person requesting permission for abortion and donation is not, strictly speaking, "engaged in the activity" and could make the request. This interpretation views the tissue recipient as the subject of research and not the fetus that is aborted or the pregnant woman.

On the other hand, if the "activity" is the abortion producing the fetal tissue, then even a person on the staff of the abortion facility who does not request consent to or perform the abortion may be unable to request such changes from the woman. So restrictive an interpretation would mean that no such requests could ever be made unless proposed by the woman undergoing the abortion. Such an interpretation should lead to a reevaluation of the policy behind the regulation. If concerns about risk are met, and there is no threat of undue influence or making access to abortion contingent on consent to postponement or a riskier method, then it is not clear what is gained by such a restrictive interpretation of the regulations—other than blocking access to fetal tissue.

It appears that the Office of Protection of Research Risks (OPRR), which is the main implementing agency of these regulations, takes the position that the woman and fetus that is going to be aborted are the subject of the activity. However, it is not clear that the OPRR would find that personnel at the abortion facility are barred from proposing such changes to a woman who has already agreed to undergo an abortion.

fund fetal tissue research nevertheless remains.[168] A special panel was recently convened by the National Institutes of Health (NIH) to advise the Assistant Secretary for Health on whether research programs involving fetal tissue transplants should be supported within or without NIH.[169] The panel recommended support for such research, with restrictions on tissue procurement comparable to the existing federal regulations.[170]

The question of federal funding of fetal tissue research merely repeats the issues discussed earlier in this article. Because funding decisions ordinarily to not interfere with or infringe constitutional rights, the government is not obligated to fund fetal tissue research (or therapy), no matter how desirable it appears.[171] As the NIH panel found, however, the arguments strongly favor funding of such research. Of overriding importance is the potential benefit to thousands of patients suffering from severe disease. Federal research funding may be necessary to develop new therapies, such as fetal tissue transplants, to treat those diseases. Federal funding will also allow the government to play a more active oversight role than if it leaves the field entirely to private funding, as occurred with *in vitro* fertilization research.[172]

The arguments against federal research funding come from right-to-life groups that would remove the federal government entirely from any financial support of abortion in the United States. They fear that federal financing of fetal tissue research will place an imprimatur of legitimacy on abortion, and encourage abortion in subtle or even direct ways.

The NIH panel found that the abortion producing fetal tissue for transplant research is sufficiently independent of research with that of fetal tissue that federal funding of abortion may occur without implicating the government in abortion. Fears that research with tissue from family planning abortions will legitimize abortion or retroactively impli-

---

168. The federal government has funded research with fetal tissue for many years. Last year, for example, $12,000,000 of such research was funded. It is only the prospect of fetal brain transplants that has led to the concern about funding of such research, perhaps because of the greatly increased demand for fetal tissue that is foreseen.

169. Kolata, *Federal Agency Bars Implanting of Fetal Tissue*, N.Y. Times, April 16, 1988 at 1, col.5.

170. Specter, *Fetal Tissue 'Acceptable' for Research*, Washington Post, Sept. 17, 1988, at 1, col. 3.

171. The United States Supreme Court made this clear in finding that governmental refusal to fund abortions for the indigent did not violate their constitutional rights. *See supra* note 135.

172. By funding no IVF research the federal government has left the field to private sector actors, who are free to research as they wish without any federal oversight.

cate the government and recipients in the abortion itself are too speculative to justify foregoing the potential benefits of fetal tissue transplant research.[173]

One can make the same arguments for funding research even when pregnancy and abortion have occurred for the purpose of producing tissue for transplant. Such a decision would, of course, be politically and ethically more controversial. If the need were established, however, the government could still fund the resulting research without also funding the abortion that makes the research possible, though arguments that the government is too closely implicated in such abortions will be strongly voiced.

If the politics of abortion lead to withdrawal of direct government funding of research with tissue from family planning abortions, the government should continue to fund other unrelated research at institutions that conduct research with aborted fetal tissue with nonfederal funds.[174] While the government is free to so restrict its research funds, the symbolic gains of refusing to fund other medical research in institutions doing nonfederally funded research with aborted fetuses are too few to justify the burden on researchers. Surely at that point the government's link to abortion is too attenuated to claim any complicity in or encouragement of abortion.

Finally, the symbolic costs that arise when one considers federal support of fetal tissue research would also arise if fetal tissue transplants became a proven therapy for Parkinson's disease, diabetes or other diseases. While the government is not constitutionally obligated to fund a given therapy, the arguments for federal funding of treatment are even stronger than for federal funding of research, because the benefits to patients are clearer. A policy of denying Medicare or Medicaid funding for therapeutic procedures using tissue from induced abortions would deprive needy patients of essential therapies in order to avoid speculative concerns about governmental complicity and encouragement of abortion. A more prudent approach would be to fund all therapies that meet the general funding standards for these programs. At the very least, the gov-

---

173. *See supra* notes 27-39. A person opposed to abortion might reasonably conclude that the pro-life cause is set back only marginally, if at all, by government funding of research with fetuses aborted for reasons unrelated to tissue procurement. In any event, the government will not be funding the abortion that produces the tissue for transplant.

174. *See* Grove City College v. Bell, 465 U.S. 555 (1984). This case would permit the government to withold such funds if it chose.

ernment's funding policies should distinguish between therapies dependent on tissue retrieved from family planning abortions and those dependent on tissue from abortions performed to provide tissue for transplant.

VII. TISSUE RETRIEVAL FROM LIVE FETUSES

The analysis of fetal tissue transplants has assumed that the fetus is dead when the tissue is taken. This assumption is realistic because ninety percent of abortions occur in the first trimester by suction curretage, which invariably fragments the fetus, killing it in the process.[175] In some cases, especially when the abortion occurs later in the pregnancy and different abortion methods are used, fetuses may emerge alive, though nonviable, from the abortion procedure. Could tissue be taken (with the mother's consent) from such fetuses if other sources of viable tissue were not available?

Fetuses that are alive and separate from the mother are legal persons, and have all the rights of newborn infants even though their prematurity is the result of a legal attempt through abortion to cause their death. If they are viable, legally they must be kept alive and reasonable efforts made to resuscitate them.[176] If they are nonviable but still alive (e.g., have spontaneous heart and lung action, or are not yet brain dead), there is no legal obligation to resuscitate or to attempt to sustain their life.[177]

However, retrieving tissue or organs for transplant from nonviable living fetuses before their death is legally restricted. Federal regulations narrowly limit the activities that may be carried out on nonviable fetuses *ex utero*. A nonviable *ex utero* fetus cannot be a subject in an activity unless: (1) "vital functions of the fetus will not be artificially maintained," (2) "experimental activities which of themselves would terminate the heartbeat of respiration of the fetus will not be employed," and (3) the purpose is "the development of important biomedical knowledge which cannot be obtained by other means."[178]

Under this regulation, nonviable fetuses could not be artificially maintained until organs and tissue were removed, unless the purpose of the

---

175. Fine, *supra* note 5, at 5-6.

176. Commonwealth v. Edelin, 371 Mass. 497, 359 N.E.2d 4 (1976).

177. There may be a legal obligation to attempt to sustain their life if the brief continuation of their lives is in their interest. Terminally ill and inevitably dying patients still might have interests in having their lives prolonged, even though they cannot be prolonged for very long.

178. 45 C.F.R. § 46.209 (1987).

research was to enable fetuses to survive to the point of viability.[179] In addition, organs and tissue could not be harvested if the harvest procedure itself "would terminate the heartbeat or respiration of the fetus," and the removal of organs and tissue for experimental transplants was itself considered part of the "experimental activity."[180]

State homicide laws would also restrict tissue retrieval from nonviable *ex utero* fetuses until they were pronounced dead under normal heart-lung or brain dead criteria. Removal of tissue or organs before death would technically constitute murder, if the removal were the immediate cause of death. The burdens and benefits of amending the law should be considered when the need to retrieve organs and tissue from nonviable, *ex utero* fetuses is shown.[181] In any event, even though commentators sometimes do not distinguish between ethical objections to procuring tissue from live, nonviable fetuses and the quite different objections to obtaining tissue from dead fetuses, policy should clearly separate the two. Ethical and legal objections to taking tissue from live, nonviable fetuses do not apply when the aborted fetus is dead.[182]

VIII. POLICY ISSUES IN DISTRIBUTING FETAL TRANSPLANTS

Resolution of the ethical issues that arise in fetal tissue procurement is essential for research to proceed with fetal tissue transplants. If supply side issues are solved and fetal transplants prove to be an effective therapy for Parkinson's disease, diabetes and disorders of the blood and immune system, difficult demand side issues will then arise. These issues include the costs of such therapies, whether they should be financed with both public and private funds, and whether special qualifications should be required of physicians who offer fetal tissue transplants. If scarcity of

---

179. Protocols for maintaining anencephalic newborns on respirators for seven days after birth in order to determine brain death for organ donation purposes thus would be prohibited, if the infant involved qualified as a fetus under the federal regulations. *See* Walters & Ashwal, *Organ Prolongation in Anencephalic Infants: Ethical and Medical Issues*, HASTINGS CENTER REP. Oct.-Nov. 1988 at 19.

180. See discussion of this point at *supra* notes 176-77.

181. Robertson, *Relaxing the Death Standard for Pediatric Organ Donations*, in ORGAN SUBSTITUTION TECHNOLOGY: ETHICAL, LEGAL AND PUBLIC POLICY ISSUES 69-77 (Mathieu ed. 1988).

182. However, problems may arise in determining brain death in a very premature infant. Uniform standards for determining brain death in such infants do not exist. Fine, *supra* note 5, at 6. The federal regulations define "dead fetus" as a "fetus *ex utero* which exhibits neither heartbeat, spontaneous respiratory activity, spontaneous movement of voluntary muscles, nor pulsation of the umbilical cord (if still attached)." 45 C.F.R. § 46.203(f) (1987).

viable tissue becomes a problem, important issues of allocation and distribution of fetal transplants will also arise.

Discussion of these issues is premature until more is known about the success of fetal tissue transplants for particular disorders. In any event, cost and scarcity issues are not unique to fetal tissue transplants. They would arise with any new treatment that could drastically improve the lot of millions of patients, and exist now with organ transplantation. The demand side, however, might affect the number of fetuses needed to serve patient needs, and thus cannot be ignored completely as long as abortion remains controversial.

IX. CONCLUSION

This survey of issues suggest that ethical and legal concerns should not bar research with fetal tissue transplants as a therapy for serious illness. Although many persons have ethical reservations about abortion, a wide range of opinion would likely support many research uses of fetal tissue, particularly when the abortions occur for reasons other than tissue procurement. In any event, constitutional status bars the government from banning all research and therapeutic uses of aborted fetuses, though it is not required to fund research or therapy with fetal tissue.

The use of fetal tissue inevitably implicates the strong feelings that abortion engenders. The disparate issues raised, however, can be treated separately, so that ethical concerns and the politics of abortion do not impede the progress of important research. For example, transplants with fetal tissue from family planning abortions do not necessarily entail approval of pregnancy and abortion undertaken to produce tissue for transplant. Nor will recognition of the mother's right to donate fetal tissue inherently cause fetuses to be bought and sold, or women to be paid to abort.

In the final analysis, fetal tissue transplants raise questions of symbolic costs as much as questions of rights. The symbolic costs involved in using fetal tissue to cure serious disease cut in many directions. Sorting out the symbolic and rights-based concerns about fetal tissue transplants will help to respect both important ethical values and progress in medical science.

[23]

Contemporary Transplantation Initiatives: Where's the Harm in Them?

David P.T. Price

Two contemporary strategies in cadaver organ transplantation, both with the potential to affect significantly expanding organ transplant waiting list sizes, have evolved: elective ventilation (EV) and use of nonheart-beating donors (NHBDs).[1] Both are undergoing a period of critical review. It is not clear how widely EV is practiced around the world. In Great Britain, the Royal Devon and Exeter Hospital was the first hospital to develop an EV protocol (the Exeter Protocol), in 1988, after which other British hospitals followed suit.[2] In the 1980s, new NHBD protocols of two distinct types were implemented worldwide, although both rely on death confirmed by traditional cardiopulmonary criteria. The first type involves the removal of organs immediately after death, the preeminent example being the University of Pittsburgh Medical Center Protocol (the Pittsburgh Protocol). The second involves the perfusion and cooling of kidneys immediately following death and subsequent organ removal.[3] Protocols of this type have sprung up in Holland, Great Britain (for example, at Leicester General Hospital), Italy, France, Spain, Japan, and the United States (for example, the Regional Organ Bank of Illinois).[4]

All these initiatives are designed to minimize warm ischemia time during which organs sustain damage due to the interruption of blood supply, thus affecting their viability for transplantation. EV protocols target patients in deep irreversible coma and believed to be dying imminently of intracranial hemorrhage. Such patients are transferred, with the consent of relatives, to intensive care units so that artificial ventilation can be initiated as soon as respiratory arrest occurs, thus preserving the organs until brain death can be established. The Pittsburgh NHBD Protocol seeks to control the time and place of death of patients (with a wide range of clinical conditions) who are expected to die shortly and who are dependent on life-sustaining treatment, for example, mechanical ventilation. After such a patient or his/her surrogate(s) has agreed to withdrawal of further life-sustaining measures and, on a separate occasion, the patient or the family have requested organ donation, lifesupport is withdrawn and the organs removed immediately following death.[5] NHBD perfusion protocols seek to avoid organ deterioration by cooling the organs while still inside the body, immediately following death, but prior to removal. These are essentially temporary measures initiated in most instances to allow sufficient time for authorization for organ donation to be obtained. Typically, an incision is made in the patient's groin, a catheter inserted into the femoral artery, and perfusion carried out. Unlike the alternative form of NHBD protocol (for instance, Pittsburgh) and EV protocols, in some instances neither the deceased nor the family has previously authorized the procedures to be carried out.[6] By contrast with EV, NHBD protocols have a relatively long history. NHBDs were in fact the main source of organ donation prior to the acceptance and use of heart-beating donors in the 1970s,[7] and their use is on the increase once more.

In October 1994, the Department of Health of England and Wales issued guidelines warning that EV for transplantation purposes is unlawful.[8] This moratorium followed closely on the heels of an independent King's Fund Institute Report, which advised that EV constitutes unlawful battery because it is not intended for the therapeutic benefit. It concluded that were EV to continue in Britain, its legality would have to be established by statute.[9] The English Law Commission recently recommended giving power to the secretary of state to introduce regulations governing this practice, should EV be deemed to be defensible.[10]

Volume 24:2, Summer 1996

A tension is, however, evident between legal and ethical perspectives on EV.[11] The King's Fund Institute Report endorsed EV from an ethical position, as has the British Medical Association (BMA), which commented that "[w]e recognise the risk of appearing to undervalue, and thus symbolically harm the status of dying patients, but believe that the important and tangible benefits to others may justify the action."[12] The legality of NHBDs is still to be tested, but certain similar legal and ethical issues arise under the Pittsburgh Protocol as with respect to EV. "Nonbeneficial" procedures are carried out, such as the (still living) patient being heparinized, prepped, and draped for the subsequent organ procurement.[13] Concerning this, Joanne Lynn remarks that "the current understanding that all interventions prior to a determination of death must be justified on the basis of the patient's welfare is challenged by the new protocol because it opens the possibility of implementing interventions to preserve organs during the time needed to confirm death, and possibly before death has occurred."[14] It is suggested, though, that a distinction exists between situations where patient consent was expressly obtained and those where only family authorization was relied on, just as the absence of explicit patient consent is the major stumbling block to EV, despite relatives' assent.

By contrast with the above protocols, although the sole purpose is again benefit to others, NHBD perfusion and cooling procedures are carried out on the newly, rather than the nearly, dead. Consequently, they raise issues slightly different from those raised by the other procedures. Albeit procedures on the dead are likely to be viewed as less objectionable than on the living, as Stuart Youngner states,

> [t]he moral questions raised by the postmortem infusion without family consent are more substantial than its advocates contend. For instance, if the controversy about practicing intubation on dead patients is any indication, there is little consensus about the moral acceptability of performing invasive procedures on dead patients to benefit others. Critics believe that these procedures are unethical because they are disrespectful of the dead, disregard families' wishes, and foster undesirable attitudes in health care professionals. The practice is also legally ambiguous.[15]

Thus, although relatives have certain powers in relation to the disposition of the body of a deceased, where such procedures are initiated without prior authorization, they are not without legal and ethical implications.

Such contemporary transplantation practices force consideration of our proper attitudes toward, and proper treatment of, the nearly dead and the newly dead. They are principally justified on the basis of utilitarian arguments, exemplified by the remarks of the BMA. But does treating these beings as potential organ donors genuinely harm them

by treating them (thereby transgressing Kant's proscription) merely as means to the ends of others?[16] Or, alternatively, is harm illusory to either dead or insentient living persons? It has been argued that deontological objections to the use of corpses for the benefit of others are misplaced because the dead body is no longer a person. John Harris goes further and argues that it is only to *persons*, that is, those individuals who have the capacity to value their existence (which would exclude the subjects of EV), that respect is owed. The BMA, however, recognized the possibility of at least "symbolic" harm in the context of EV, a point also expressed in the King's Fund Institute Report. Joel Feinberg, who endorses a utilitarian approach in the context of the (mis)treatment of the dead, reiterates this point: "symbolism is the whole point of the discussion, the sole focus of concern and misgiving."[17] But is *harm* being minimized here by describing it as "symbolic"? Is this simply an appeal to sentiment or a reflection of deeper seated principles? William May argues that the linking of symbols and sentiment underestimates the significance of symbols and their influence in organizing communities—it is not simply a matter of private and internal feelings.[18] As regards the dead, the Law Reform Commission of Canada (LRC) supports the argument that the dead *can* be harmed, but asserts that "[w]hat remains refractory is providing a coherent philosophical explanation of this intuition."[19] If the dead can be harmed, then *a fortiori* so can still living insentient individuals.

Cadavers are potentially useful for a myriad of purposes, graphically set out by Willard Gaylin over twenty years ago.[20] The newly dead may help advance medical science, treatment, and education through research and certain other procedures (for instance, intubation techniques) performed by medical students to advance their training. The newly dead are also occasionally kept on ventilatory support after brain death has been confirmed, to assist the psychological adjustment of relatives to the death.[21] Deceased (brain dead) pregnant women have had their "existence" prolonged in the hope of allowing doctors to bring a live born baby into the world.[22] The nearly dead insentient patient also has many potential uses for the benefit of others. Reports even document that pregnant women left in comas following an accident have "given birth" to premature babies, following measures taken deliberately to keep the patient alive to this end. Similar issues are raised in these contexts, so the debate here has broader ramifications.

I examine whether implementation of any of the above protocols implicates any "harm" in legal or ethical terms to such organ donors. I stress the crucial link between notions of dignity and the rights of autonomy of the individual, and I seek to resolve the ethical and legal dilemmas raised by these new initiatives. I do this primarily by extrapolating the autonomy of the once competent living person to the fullest extent. The LRC of Canada has commented that "[w]hat emerges from these competing considerations over medical benefits, potential mistreatment and respect for the dead is disagreement over the necessity for consent as a means of balancing the concerns."[23] A similar remark could have been made about the (insentient) nearly dead. Altruism is a right not a duty, capable of being exercised only by a person having the power of choice. The noncompetent living should not routinely be used to benefit others in a way that the competent could not be. Out of respect for the dead, we must appreciate that public policy vests certain decision-making rights in relatives, a factor that may force open a distinction between the different protocols and donor types and the interests of relatives.

The first part of this paper considers the legal aspects of EV and NHBD protocols. The second part considers the same practices from an ethical perspective. The third offers general comments and observations regarding these protocols. And the final section suggests the way forward for debate and for practical resolution of some of the difficulties here, and then considers the need for legislation.

Legal issues

The dying

In Great Britain, no national laws specifically address EV, nor has any legal authority considered the practice. However, in *Re F (Mental Patient: Sterilisation)*[24] and *Airedale NHS Trust v. Bland*,[25] the British House of Lords considered the legality of carrying out or discontinuing medical treatment on incompetent patients. The former case concerned the proposed sterilization of a mentally retarded adult woman; the latter, the withdrawal of nutrition and hydration through a nasogastric tube from a patient in a persistent vegetative state (PVS). The House of Lords unequivocally endorsed the applicability of the "best interests" test to such cases. In spite of this, neither case concerned procedures performed exclusively in the interests of others, thus begging the question whether the same test would be applicable in such a context.[26] The Law Commission, though, had no doubt that the best interests test *would* (but not necessarily *should*) be applicable to EV.[27] This is a safe prediction; English law is wedded to the best interests test in respect of decision making for incompetent adults. Consequently, no account may be taken of others' interests, and no power of proxy decision making exists, whether through a substituted judgment or another approach. Although relatives may have a right to be consulted about the treatment of incompetent relatives, in order for a doctor to reach a proper decision on the patient's best interests, they have no right to have their wishes respected.[28] Accordingly, the exclusive and heavy reliance on

relatives' consent under the Exeter Protocol was clearly misplaced in English law.

Even in U.S. jurisdictions, which permit reliance on substituted judgment with respect to nontherapeutic procedures performed on mentally incompetent persons, there would appear to be a need to establish that a potential benefit to the individual exists. It would not appear to authorize a court or relatives to permit nontherapeutic procedures prior to death, in accordance with the Pittsburgh Protocol or an EV protocol, where the views of the formerly competent person were not clearly stated.[29] Moreover, it would not be feasible to rely in this context on the provisions of section 1(2) of the British Human Tissue Act 1961 or the analogous provisions in the U.S. Uniform Anatomical Gift Act 1987 (UAGA),[30] both of which provide for organ removal authorization by surviving relatives, because such powers cannot take effect until the patient is dead.

In *Bland*, their Lordships made numerous statements about the legality of EV in Great Britain. Lord Browne-Wilkinson stated that "if there comes a stage where the responsible doctor comes to the reasonable conclusion ... that further continuance of an intrusive life support system is not in the best interests of the patient, he can no longer lawfully continue that life support system: to do so would constitute the crime of battery and the tort of trespass to the person."[31] These fairly sweeping views would certainly outlaw EV as this could confer no benefit on the patient; likewise, presumably, procedures performed prior to death in accordance with a Pittsburgh-type protocol. In essence, the British courts have moved to a position where there would be a perceived *harm* to such persons were such medical procedures to be carried out, and not just harm to relatives. The LRC of Canada stated that the "legal obligation to accord respect echoes the Hippocratic duty to care. To care is to treat the dying with dignity, to respect the integrity of the dead human form and to comfort the family, honouring and accommodating their needs and wishes as they confront the death of a relative."[32]

The nature of this duty was further elucidated in *Bland* by Lord Justice Butler Sloss, who said that Mr. Bland has the right to be respected. Consequently, he

> has the right to avoid unnecessary humiliation and degrading invasion of his body for no good purpose.... I cannot believe that a patient in the situation of Mr Bland should be subjected to therapeutically useless treatment contrary to good medical practice and medical ethics which would not be inflicted upon those able to choose. It is an affront to the right to be respected.[33]

The task here is to flesh out the substance of this duty of respect, and the notion of "dying with dignity."

Volume 24:2, Summer 1996

The dead

In common law, in England and Wales, there can be no property in a corpse. Directions by the deceased (whether in a will or otherwise) made while alive, as to the disposal of the body after death, create no legal duties on others to respect those wishes,[14] although the next of kin have a right to possession for burial purposes. However, many jurisdictions have legislation that prohibits the unnecessary mutilation of the cadaver specifically in the context of transplantation, for example, Italy, Argentina, Singapore, and the Philippines. Several of these laws make explicit not only the proscribed conduct but also its rationale. Belgian law, for instance, states that "[t]he removal of organs ... shall be carried out in such a way as to respect the remains of the deceased and spare the feelings of the family."[15] Although these provisions have no direct application to NHBD cooling protocols, because no organs are being removed at that point, they illustrate the type(s) of excesses and harm that should be guarded against even in the context of a legitimate activity involving the corpse, that is, potential indignity to the deceased and injury to the feelings of the deceased's family.

Moreover, many jurisdictions have laws stipulating "proper" treatment of the corpse generally. In British common law, it is an offense to offer "indignities or indecencies to the dead," to "indecently mutilat[e]" a corpse, to prevent burial, and to outrage "public decency."[16] Criminal offenses are proscribed for the mistreatment of the dead in the United States and in other jurisdictions.[17] Laws prohibiting the desecration of dead bodies or requiring decent burial attach importance to the dignity of the deceased person as a social value and, according to the LRC of Canada, to respect for the emotional and religious sentiments of the next of kin, and for the moral tranquillity of society at large, the protection of public health, and the minimization of public nuisances. NHBD cooling procedures are clearly no threat to public health nor do they bear any of the characteristics of a public nuisance.

The courts also clearly recognize notions of respect and dignity with regard to the dead human form. Where no good purpose is furthered by continued (cellular) existence after death, it should not be artificially extended. In the High Court in *Re A*,[18] Justice Johnson said that it would be contrary to the interests of A, a brain-stem dead child of nineteen months, and unfair to the nursing and medical staff at the hospital, for his body to be subjected to the "continuing indignity" to which it was subject, that is, continued ventilation, hydration, and nutrition. However, it is the validity of the purpose that is central. A recent Nuffield Council on Bioethics Report suggests that common law may legitimate the use of a corpse for certain "good" purposes beyond those specifically authorized by statute, although no law addresses this point.[19] If so, this would prevent any common law offenses from being applicable in circumstances where no excesses occur. The (legitimate) purpose would color perceptions as to what constitutes "mutilation," "indignity," or "indecency." In the United States, courts have held that making a small incision in the groin to determine the extent of an abscess was not a mutilation of the corpse, nor was an unauthorized embalming.[40] The King's Fund Institute Report also considered that, because society sanctions coroners performing autopsies as well as the embalming process, it is unlikely in Great Britain that the minimally invasive incision associated with NHBD cooling procedures would be viewed as unreasonable and unethical mutilation of the cadaver.[41]

Ethical issues

The nearly dead

Despite the recent guidelines issued to transplant centers about the unlawfulness of EV, the Code of Practice governing transplantation in the United Kingdom (drawn up by the Department of Health), while stating that any tests or treatment carried out on a patient before he/she dies must be for his/her benefit and not solely to preserve organs, adds that

> [v]ery occasionally it will be considered certain that death will inevitably occur shortly.... [I]n these cases doctors should seek the agreement of relatives for the initiation of artificial ventilation to preserve organ function before death has been diagnosed. If it is not possible to obtain the relatives' views before the situation arises, doctors should exercise their judgement in the light of the circumstances of the individual case whether or not to initiate artificial ventilation, so as to enable enquiries to be made about the views of the deceased and the relatives about the removal of organs after death has been diagnosed.[42]

This provision would sanction temporary ventilation with relatives' permission and even *without* relatives' consent in certain circumstances. Is this view ethically sustainable? Harris suggests that we would want others to respect not just ourselves but also our friends and relations who, although alive, are no longer "persons" (that is, no longer capable of social interaction); however, "[w]here its organs or tissues can be used to save the lives of other people who have not lost personhood but who may be in danger of losing their personhood through death or some other cause, then we have a motive for keeping alive the body of the former person so that the tissue and organs remain alive and usable."[43] The Exeter Protocol necessitates relatives' consent; thus, relatives themselves would not be harmed by such procedures (as is the case where relatives' consent has been obtained under the Pittsburgh Protocol).

But is the comatose patient harmed, and, if so, in what way? The King's Fund Institute Report stated that EV is not clinically deleterious to the deeply comatose individual and does not cause distress (although it leaves unanswered the question whether any procedures could be *clinically* deleterious to an unconscious insentient patient[44]). The King's Report continues: "Even if the moment of brain stem death can be shown to have been postponed for a short period in the electively ventilated patient, this does not automatically indicate that the patient's interests have been abused."[45]

By contrast, many view the deliberate prolonging of a patient's dying as unacceptable for any reason.[46] Paul Ramsey contends it is unethical to do so because God is being prevented from receiving His servant home, whom He has called.[47] However, it has been convincingly demonstrated that it is not possible to distinguish clearly between those who are dying and those who are not; consequently, prolonging dying is merely an oblique way of describing treatment that prolongs *life*.[48] The view that extending dying itself offends the dignity of the dying process therefore stands in stark contrast to traditional vitalist views that the primary purpose of medicine is to extend life.[49]

But, in any event, what is "dying with dignity"? It is surely not the extension of life per se that precludes dying with dignity, but rather the *manner* of that prolongation and the *reason* for it. This dignity is linked to potential benefit to the subject. The House of Lords in *Bland* considered medical treatment without any therapeutic purpose, that is, futile treatment, given simply to prolong a patient's life, to be inappropriate and to be withheld.[50] This dignity is also linked to the right of autonomy. In the Court of Appeal in *Bland*, Lord Justice Hoffmann said that

> the sanctity of life is only one of a cluster of ethical principles which we apply to decisions about how we should live. Another is respect for the individual human being and in particular for his right to choose how he should live his own life. We call this individual autonomy or the right of self-determination. And another principle, closely connected, is respect for the dignity of the individual human being: our belief that quite irrespective of what the person concerned may think about it, it is wrong for someone to be humiliated or treated without respect for his value as a person.[51]

While linked to autonomy, dignity is a broader concept with its own inherent core. Nonetheless, procedures which would otherwise compromise dignity are justifiable where specific consent has been given for them by that individual, just as is the case with certain procedures performed on the cadaver. The Superior Court of Quebec in *Nancy B v. Hôtel-Dieu de Québec*[52] held that constantly keeping the patient on the respirator without her consent constituted an intrusion and interference on her human dignity and personal privacy. Although Nancy B was competent and refused further treatment, in the context of nontherapeutic procedures it is the *absence* of consent that is central, whether or not the person has capacity. Utilitarian benefits to others cannot offset the loss of dignity to the individual.

The newly dead

In considering the ethical acceptability of *in situ* perfusion of organs, we must ask whether cutting into a corpse can constitute a harm to the (now dead) individual, and, if so, what *kind* of harm? It has been asserted *inter alia* by Youngner that it is impossible to inflict harm on a dead patient.[53] Our views here, though, will probably be significantly influenced by our attitudes to the "self" when a person has died.[54] The LRC of Canada commented that "[u]nder one view, persons are seen as inseparable from their bodies. Consequently, the dignity of the human body is inseparable from the dignity of the person. This nexus survives death, because the body symbolizes the person who once lived."[55] The manner of treatment after death has historically been regarded as at least partially reflective of the respect, or lack of it, accorded to the once living individual. In the nineteenth century, for instance, public dissection of the legally executed cadaver was viewed as an ingredient of the punishment itself.[56] In this context, loss of dignity is unrelated to actual or surrogate psychological suffering or awareness.[57] It reflects on the once living person.

Philosophers have long debated whether a dead person can be morally harmed. Views differ. Some, such as Ernest Partridge, contend that the dead have no interests and are consequently beyond harm or benefit.[58] By contrast, Bonnie Steinbock convincingly asserts that the

> common saying that the dead are beyond harming refers ... to the fact that the dead cannot be hurt, angered or distressed. But, their surviving interests can be defeated, and when this happens, the subject of posthumous harm is the antemortem person, for it is the antemortem person who cared about what would happen after he died.[59]

The difficulty is isolating which interests survive the interest-bearer's death. Desires, wants, and aims are crucial to the concept of interests, and the vast majority of us have legitimate wishes, desires, and wants concerning what happens to our corpse which can be thwarted by others or events.[60]

Moreover, some aspirations can *only* be fulfilled after our deaths, for example, the posthumous disposal of one's property by will. Raymond Belliotti argues that only if the

Volume 24:2, Summer 1996

object of our interests and desires *is* (not simply believed to be) realized, are those interests and desires fulfilled. Thus, despite Russell Scott's remark that the "very idea of applying the notion of personal autonomy to a corpse is absurd; at most, personal autonomy is only artificially extended beyond death,"[61] notions of autonomy *can* seemingly stretch beyond the point of death; but it is not the corpse's autonomy but that of the former living person represented by the corpse. The LRC of Canada suggested that respecting the wishes of a person about treatment of their body after death gives rise to a "fuller sense of autonomy."[62]

Questions also arise about the interests of others. The LRC of Canada stated that

> [m]inimally invasive experimentation or medical education techniques may not disfigure or mutilate the newly dead or otherwise violate their bodily integrity. However, even marginally invasive techniques such as intubation might be considered an indignity or mistreatment, if consent is not obtained from a family that considers such techniques offensive, outrageous or violative of religious beliefs.[63]

The difficulty here is balancing the harms and possible aspirations in the absence of such consent. The right to permit use of a deceased loved one's organs for transplantation is viewed by many as an important psychological and emotional issue at such a distressing time—it can even form part of the grieving process. Cutting into a corpse may be perceived as mutilation from a purely physical perspective; but it may also be viewed as the preservation of rights of autonomy from another—an issue on which I expand below. Without implementing NHBD cooling protocols, some of these other interests and values may not be effectuated. Moreover, even if relatives are wronged by these procedures, this would only amount to "offense" (in Feinberg's terminology), which is of a lesser order of importance than "harm" in the overall scale of wrongs and may therefore have to be "weighed in the balance."[64]

General comments

Advance directives are recognized in Great Britain and the United States as having legal effect after a patient has lost capacity.[65] Consequently, no ethical or legal obstacles should arise if patients have expressed their consent to EV in advance, although an advance directive does not *require* that EV be performed. As Allan Buchanan states,

> Instead of being seen simply as devices for protecting the patient or for exercising autonomy for its own sake, they might in addition become vehicles for new forms of altruism, new ways of exercising the virtue of charity. For example, instead of specifying that if

one comes to be in a persistent vegetative state all means of life support are to be withdrawn, a person with a strong sense of social obligation might instead request to be sustained in such a condition until his organs and other transplantable tissues are needed to save or enhance the lives of others.[66]

The BMA has remarked that "[p]atient autonomy could be preserved if patients were able to express their views on this practice in advance, either through some form of advance directive or re-worded donor card but public knowledge about this practice is not yet widespread."[67] Clearly, some already hospitalized patients will not be in a condition to consent prospectively to EV procedures. The Royal College of Nursing has advanced the contentious view that expressed consent to organ donation given by a competent patient implies consent to all procedures necessary to keep the organs viable for transplantation, including EV prior to brain death.[68] Certainly, implicit consent can be found to cooling procedures after death where consent to donate organs has been given by the deceased; but it is more difficult to accept the Royal College's view about EV protocols to take effect *before* death (similarly regarding analogous pre-death procedures under the Pittsburgh Protocol). Explicit consent must be the rule; implicit consent would only be supportable if the patient expressly accepted the specific protocol as a package, including such procedures. But even if the opposite view were conceded, difficult legal issues would arise where the individual did not, while alive, authorize organ donation after death. In such instances, absent proxy consent being legally recognized, such procedures cannot be legitimated.

The King's Fund Institute Report stated that, in the absence of expressed authorization, the issues raised by NHBD cooling protocols are very similar to those raised by the more general *presumed consent* debate. However, it also considered that, although organ removal and NHBD cooling procedures involve cutting into a corpse without consent, it is a "less significant" presumption in the latter context, that is, the individual and/or the family would not object to minimally invasive surgery.[69] It is noteworthy that the Regional Organ Bank of Illinois specifically relied on the presumed consent rationale to support its NHBD protocol. However, the notion of presumed consent to cooling procedures is especially problematic in jurisdictions, such as the United Kingdom and the United States, that have opting-in transplant regimes, which require explicit consent to organ donation.

But, although the deceased in these jurisdictions might not have been carrying donor cards nor orally expressed their affirmative views before death, the lack thereof is no certain indication of an objection to organ donation, let alone perfusion and cooling procedures. It appears that the majority of persons not carrying donor card nevertheless *do* wish to donate.[70] Such individuals may well wish to donate, be apathetic on the matter, or have deliberately left it to the family to decide.

Under Anglo-American law, the wishes of the deceased assume priority.[71] If these are unknown, then relatives have the right to decide whether the deceased's organs should be used for transplantation purposes. The deceased's true wishes in such instances may be unascertainable without contacting the relatives. However, if perfusion is not initiated in many instances *before* relatives are (that is, can be) contacted, the organs will cease to be viable. This minimal "holding operation" is akin to keeping a brain dead patient on a ventilator briefly while such approaches are made, authorizations sought, and the organ(s) removed. Public policy recognizes a legitimate purpose in this latter context, similarly the administration of drugs and fluids to maintain the condition of the organs.[72] Intubation is an invasive procedure, as are many other maintenance functions that are routinely performed on such cadavers, for which the permission of relatives will not invariably have been obtained. Arguably, dignity here is also *potentially* compromised, but the compromise is avoided by virtue of the overriding purposes and values served thereby.

Furthermore, in both the United Kingdom and the United States, permission of relatives is sought for organ removal even where the deceased has previously made a specific request to donate organs after death, although such permission is not required by law. It is unclear from the literature whether relatives' permission is sought in all cases where the NHBD cooling procedure is employed, even where specific donor consent exists. Where the latter exists, no legal or ethical objection can be made against the use of such procedures, regardless of the views or practices of the medical practitioners involved.

Conclusion

The High Court of New Zealand, in *Auckland Health Board v. Attorney-General*, has stated that the values of human dignity and personal privacy belonged to everyone, whether living or dying.[73] Absent consent or individual benefit, potential benefit to others is not sufficient per se to negate infringement of respect and dignity, certainly not as regards the still living. The real danger is that the incompetent may be "used" solely for the benefit of others, simply by virtue of their inability to object.[74] Symbolic harm here is real harm. Psychological suffering is not an invariable determinant of the existence of harm.

Steinbock advances a similar perspective for patients in PVS and the deceased. She maintains that the only interests PVS patients have are those that have survived their permanent loss of consciousness. Ante-vegetative persons can have surviving interests just as ante-mortem persons do. "However," she asserts,

it should not be assumed that keeping someone alive in a persistent vegetative state does not harm his (anti-vegetative) interests. Most people do not regard the prospect of living in a vegetative state with equanimity. The idea of existing as a permanently unconscious body fills many people with distress and horror.... We have as much reason to respect this sort of surviving interest as any other.[75]

These sentiments are echoed by Lord Justice Hoffmann in *Bland*. He said:

The fallacy in this argument is that it assumes that we have no interests except in those things of which we have conscious experience. But this does not accord with most people's intuitive feelings about their lives and deaths. At least a part of the reason why we honour the wishes of the dead about the distribution of their property is that we think it would wrong them not to do so, despite the fact that we believe that they will never know that their will has been ignored....[76]

Nevertheless, although the notion of dignity has discrete content, it is an elusive one, one that varies according to culture, time, the nature and purpose of the procedure, and whether the person is still alive. The Nuffield Council on Bioethics Report on Human Tissue observed that persons from different cultures may have varying opinions as to what would constitute degrading forms of medical treatment or degrading ways of treating dead bodies; however, it still considered that this variation does not entitle us to disregard bodily degradation or to regard it as something less than a serious form of injury.[77] The King's Fund Institute Report also highlighted the evolving notion of dignity, stating that

such procedures [for example, EV] prevent the 'good death' in a more fundamental sense, regardless of how the relatives feel. A peaceful and dignified departure ... whatever one's religious beliefs, is simply not possible if one's mortal remains are being moved from pillar to post.... But we should remind ourselves that acceptable modes of dying whilst attached to various forms of machinery would no doubt have seemed undignified to some. As the rationales for new practices are understood, new contexts for dying become acceptable. It may not be long before actively managing death to save other lives is as "good" and dignified a form of dying as any other.[78]

And, Madan observes that "those who still see some virtue in these ideas [dignity and freedom], will find it remarkable how across many cultures (and not only in Christian,

Volume 24:2, Summer 1996

Hindu and Jain cultural traditions) loss of autonomy, and loss of control over oneself in the context of death, are seen to result in undignified death, that is death which lacks nobility, distinction and illustriousness."[79] These remarks highlight the symbiotic, although fluid, relationship between autonomy and dignity in this context.

Harris argues that if having respect for the dead requires us to tolerate harm to the living, we should not abandon our notions of respect for the dead; instead, we should modify our concept of what such respect involves. He goes on to advocate automatic and routine organ removal regardless of the deceased's or relatives' wishes, thereby turning the discussion on its head. In effect, he is saying that the deceased would not wish to be perceived as having been uncharitable, and that to assume as much would be a mark of *dis*respect.[80]

Most of us would not go so far. James Orlowski, George Kanoti, and Maxwell Mehlman claim that corpses are entitled to less respect than the living, and that, in the case of intubating newly dead bodies, such respect is limited to avoiding disfigurement or ridicule.[81] Concepts of dignity and respect therefore still retain meaning and relevance for the dead, although they are more limited and may more easily give way to the needs of others. Ignoring the earlier formed desires and aspirations of the newly dead constitutes a violation of their (ante-mortem) right to respect and autonomy. John Hardwig argues that "each of us can imagine things that we would not want done to our bodies after we are dead, and as a matter of practice, we do continue to respect the autonomy of dead persons."[82] I submit that the deontological argument still has force as an extension of the respect for the former person's autonomy, but that, where such autonomy is not infringed and relatives do not object, no objection can be raised against using the cadaver for others' benefit. NHBD cooling protocols more obviously further autonomy interests than, for example, intubation procedures for medical training purposes.

Rights of autonomy in decision making are inevitably projected forward, and ignoring a person's wishes expressed earlier clearly casts doubt on whether (with the benefit of hindsight) that person truly had autonomy at that earlier point in time. As Feinberg states, "[e]vents after death do not retroactively produce effects at an earlier time, ... but their occurrence can lead us to revise our estimates of an earlier person's well-being, and correct the record before closing the book on his life."[83] What was possessed at a particular time can take into account later occurring events. If a person, while competent, completed an advance directive, we would probably say, if the wishes therein were ignored when that individual did lose capacity, that it was the autonomy of the "person" at the point when the statement was made that was infringed. We would retrospectively project the harm onto the earlier competent entity.[84] Thus, a similar process is at work when we assess the im-

pact on the once living person of frustrating such a person's wishes after death as when we respect decisions by competent persons that take effect when competence is lost.

However, to treat the dying as potential organ donors, without their authorization, is to treat incompetent but *living* individuals as already dead, just as physicians were motivated in some instances to treat anencephalic infants (who were not dead by traditional criteria) either as never having been born alive or as already being dead so to enable physicians to use them as organ donors. The Pittsburgh Protocol carries with it the same dangers as EV protocols and for the same reasons—relatives' rather than patient's consent is used to justify performing nontherapeutic procedures prior to death.

The line between the dying and the dead is thin, but it must remain demarcated. Superficial similarities between EV and NHBD protocols and between different NHBD protocols must not blind us to this. It is for the living to dictate the uses of their (still living) body where the procedures implicated have no potential benefit for them. Respect for incompetent patients requires that decision making be made in their best interests where no advance directive has been made. We cannot assume high levels of altruism—such supererogatory actions are laudable but not obligatory in our culture. The personal rights of relatives are reserved for intrusions on the individual only *after* death, when the wishes of the deceased are not explicit.

I submit, however, that practical changes to everyday processes could solve many of the dilemmas. Donor cards should be amended to include a provision that may be deleted by an unwilling individual; alternatively, a separate but related donor card authorizing EV should be created.[85] Either way, the potential subject of the procedure would need full information about the procedure and its risks, including the possibility of PVS. Greater public awareness of EV and NHBD practices is desirable.[86] Expressed rather than implied consent is a surer and fairer way forward, so that EV and Pittsburgh Protocol procedures are only carried out on patients who were competent immediately prior to their implementation and who have previously expressed their wishes. Indeed, if EV is to be accepted, legislation is vital; legal safeguards should include a requirement for a medical assessment of a futile prognosis and imminent death, confirmed independently by a noninvolved party. In respect to NHBD cooling protocols, legislation is less urgent, but it would be desirable to assuage concerns and to avoid civil actions brought by relatives for undue emotional harm and distress. Currently, bills are pending in the legislatures of three U.S. states, each of which addresses issues concerning NHBDs. A similar bill is under consideration in the Netherlands.[87]

The severe organ shortage demands that initiatives with the potential to impact significantly on transplantation rates must be evaluated fully, critically, and reasonably—objections should not be founded on flimsy ethical or technical legal grounds. Individual autonomy is not a value that can be easily overridden or evaded, in the interests of others or society. No tension arises between ethical and legal attitudes to NHBD cooling protocols. Where death has incontrovertibly occurred, they are both ethically and legally defensible. However, an undeniable tension exists between legal and ethical perceptions of EV and Pittsburgh-type protocols. I submit that the law's approach to EV, as it is has been practiced to date, is soundly based and may even be a surer guide to proper ethical assessment than more direct "ethical" appraisals. The harm may be symbolic in one sense, but autonomy and dignity are fundamental values for the living and for the dead.

References

1. As of June 7, 1995, 29,058 persons were on the kidney transplant waiting list in the United States, compared to 24,973 persons as of December 31, 1993. UNOS Correspondence, Data Request No. 061395-2, June 14, 1995. In the United Kingdom, the renal transplant waiting list has grown from 1,923 in 1980 to 5,000 as of June 30, 1995. United Kingdom Transplant Support and Services Authority, Transplant Updates.

2. See T. Feest et al., "Protocol for Increasing Organ Donation After Cerebrovascular Deaths in a District General Hospital," *Lancet*, 335 (1990): 1133–35. Adopting the protocol doubled the donation rate over nineteen months. See M. Salih et al., "Potential Availability of Cadaver Organs for Transplantation," *British Medical Journal*, 302 (1991): 1053–55. Worldwide estimates are that there are about forty potential candidates for EV per million. See A. Hibberd et al., "Potential for Cadaveric Organ Retrieval in New South Wales," *British Medical Journal*, 304 (1992): 1339–43.

3. Studies in the 1970s, by Starzl, Turcotte, Schweizer, Bankowski, Garcia-Rinaldi, Johnson, and others established the feasibility of preserving and using organs from NHBDs. See F.T. Rapaport, "Alternative Sources of Clinically Transplantable Vital Organs," *Transplantation Proceedings*, 25 (1993): 42–44.

4. In Maastricht, Holland, 20 percent more kidneys were procured by these means over a ten-year period. See G. Kootstra et al., "Twenty Percent More Kidneys Through a Non-Heart-Beating Program," *Transplantation Proceedings*, 23 (1991): 910–11. In the United Kingdom, Leicester reported a 38 percent increase in donor organs as a consequence of implementing this strategy. Nathan estimates that implementation of Pittsburgh-style protocols could result in a 20 to 25 percent increase in donor organs. See M.A. De Vita et al., "History of Organ Donation by Patients with Cardiac Death," *Kennedy Institute of Ethics Journal*, 3 (1993): at 125.

5. The patient must be apneic and unresponsive, for at least two minutes, to one of three electrocardiographic criteria. See S.J. Youngner et al., "Ethical, Psychosocial, and Public Policy Implications of Procuring Organs from Non-Heart-Beating Cadaver Donors," *JAMA*, 269 (1993): at 2771. The Pittsburgh Protocol is set out in the *Kennedy Institute of Ethics Journal*, 3 (1993): A1–A15. A similar protocol has been in place at the King's College Hospital, Dulwich, England, since 1988. See A.O. Phillips et al., "Renal Grafts from Non-Heart Beating Donors," *British Medical Journal*, 308 (1994): 575–76.

6. Potential donors are those who have come off bypass during cardiothoracic surgery, intraoperative neurosurgical

deaths, rapidly deteriorating intracerebral bleeds and subarachnoid hemorrhages, failed resuscitation in coronary care units, cardiac arrests on hospital wards, deaths in accident and emergency departments, or deaths from primary brain tumors in a hospice environment.

7. NHBDs initially became less popular because of concerns about the viability of organs from such donors. Even today, some of these organs fail to function and there is an increased incidence of acute tubular necrosis. NHBDs are still the main source of cadaver donors in countries such as Japan where the society is generally reluctant to accept fully the concept of brain death.

8. Acute Services Policy Unit, *Identification of Potential Donors of Organs for Transplantation* (Health Services Guidelines (84)1, 1994).

9. King's Fund Institute Report, *A Question of Give and Take: Improving the Supply of Donor Organs for Transplantation* (London: King's Fund Institute, Research Report 18, 1994): at 64.

10. Law Commission Report, *Mental Incapacity* (London: HMSO, Law Comm. No. 231, 1995): at para. 6.26. The commission also thought that EV was illegal in Great Britain.

11. Although some controversy arises over the issue, I do not intend to debate whether patients subjected to EV are truly dead, an issue which also recurs in debates about the application of the Pittsburgh Protocol, nor whether EV is unethical either because it constitutes an improper use of intensive care facilities (especially where such facilities are in short supply) or because of the risk that the practice itself will increase the risk of persons ending up in PVS.

12. British Medical Association, *Medical Ethics Today: Its Practice and Philosophy* (London: BMA, 1993): at 323. The British Transplantation Society, the ethical committee of the Royal College of Physicians, and the Royal College of Nursing have all expressed similar views.

13. M.A. De Vita et al., "Procuring Organs from a Non-Heart-Beating Cadaver: A Case Report," *Kennedy Institute of Ethics Journal*, 3 (1993): at 380.

14. J. Lynn, "Are the Patients Who Become Organ Donors under the Pittsburgh Protocol for 'Non-Heart-Beating Donors' Really Dead?," *Kennedy Institute of Ethics Journal*, 3 (1993): at 168.

15. Youngner et al., *supra* note 5, at 2770.

16. May has noted a "tinge of the inhuman in the humanitarianism of those who believe that the perception of social need easily overrides all other considerations." W. May, "Attitudes Towards the Newly Dead," *Hastings Center Studies*, 1, no. 2 (1973): at 5. While May is referring to the routine cutting up of corpses for organ removal, his remark has equal force in this analogous situation.

17. J. Feinberg, "The Mistreatment of the Dead," *Hastings Center Reports*, 15, no. 1 (1985): at 31. Sidney Callahan, by contrast, states that "[u]nlike Feinberg, I would be especially slow to label the moral sentiments or responses of others as squeamishness, or sentimentality, or irrationality," and he advocates an approach to ethical decision making involving a personal equilibrium in which emotion and reason are both activated and in accord. See S. Callahan, "The Role of Emotion in Ethical Decisionmaking," *Hastings Center Reports*, 18, no. 3 (1988): at 9, 14. It should be noted, though, that Feinberg also recognizes that harm can be caused (posthumously) to the now deceased by obstructing the fulfillment of certain interests.

18. W. May, "Religious Justifications for Donating Body Parts," *Hastings Center Reports*, 15, no. 1 (1985): at 38.

19. Law Reform Commission Report, *Procurement and*

Volume 24:2, Summer 1996

Transfer of Human Tissues and Organs (Ottawa: Law Reform Comm., Working Paper 66, 1992): at 45.

20. W. Gaylin, "Harvesting the Dead," *Harpers*, 249 (1974): 23–28.

21. See F. Miedema, "Medical Treatment after Brain Death: A Case Report and Ethical Analysis," *Journal of Clinical Ethics*, 2, no. 1 (1991): 50–52.

22. It is reported that four babies have been born as a result of such a practice. See J. Mason and A. McCall Smith, *Law and Medical Ethics* (London: Butterworths, 4th ed., 1994): at 289.

23. See Law Reform Commission, *supra* note 19, at 114.

24. *In Re F (Mental Patient: Sterilisation)*, [1990] 2 A.C. 1 (H.L.).

25. *Airedale NHS Trust v. Bland*, [1993] 1 All E.R. 821 (H.L.).

26. An alternative, "not against the interests" test, has been applied to nontherapeutic procedures performed on minors. See *S v. S*, [1970] 3 All E.R. 107 (H.L.). But with respect to adults, unlike children, no one is there to make the decision on their behalf or to be accountable for it. In fact, even in *Bland*, Lord Mustill had reservations about the best interests test as applied to PVS patients. See *Airedale NHS Trust*, All E.R. at 894 (stating that such individuals have "no best interests of any kind").

27. The Law Commission also generally approved the application of the best interests test in the context of medical procedures performed on the mentally incompetent. See Law Commission Report, *supra* note 10. It did consider that the test would *not* be appropriate for determining decisions relating either to elective ventilation or to the withdrawal of artificial nutrition or hydration. *Id.* at paras. 6.17–6.39, 6.24.

28. The High Court of Justice reached such a view in the case of a PVS patient in *Re G*, [1995] 3(1) *Med. L. Rev.* 80. In *Bland* and *Re F*, the House of Lords specifically rejected the substituted judgment approach that is prevalent in the United States.

29. See *Strunk v. Strunk*, 445 S.W.2d 145 (Ky. 1969) where the Kentucky Court of Appeals permitted an adult mentally incompetent twin to donate a kidney to his brother using a substituted judgment approach. The court found that, on balance, the procedure would do more (psychological) good than (physical) harm and would thus benefit the incompetent twin. Similarly, in cases like *Hart v. Brown*, 289 A.2d 386 (Conn. 1972), the Connecticut Superior Court permitted a twin to donate a kidney to his seven-year-old identical twin, utilizing a substituted judgment approach. That court found that benefit would accrue to the donating twin from the procedure. However, certain U.S. courts, for example, the Wisconsin Supreme Court, in *In re Guardianship of Richard Pescinski*, 226 N.W.2d 180 (Wis. 1975), have denied a power to authorize such a procedure on the basis of substituted judgment.

30. See U.A.G.A. §§ 1, 3 U.L.A. (1987). The Uniform Anatomical Gift Act has been enacted in all fifty U.S. states.

31. *Airedale NHS Trust v. Bland*, [1993] 1 All E.R. 821, 882–83. This was the majority opinion (Lords Lowry and Goff concurring).

32. Law Reform Commission Report, *supra* note 19, at 173.

33. *Bland*, [1993] 1 All E.R. at 848.

34. *Williams v. Williams* (1882) Ch.D. 659. Greater rights generally exist in the United States for a deceased to direct the manner and place of his burial. See A. Sadler and B. Sadler, "Transplantation and the Law: The Need for Organized Sensitivity," *Georgetown Law Journal*, 57 (1968–69): at 5.

35. Law of 13 June 1986, § 12. Austrian law states that organ removal may not result in "disfigurement of the cadaver that is incompatible with the dignity of the deceased." Bundesgesetzblatt für die Republik Österreich, June 1, 1982, § 62a(1).

36. S. White, "An End to D-I-Y Cremation?," *Medicine, Science and the Law*, 33 (1993): at 151.

37. For instance, in California it is an offense to mutilate a corpse. See Cal. Health & Safety Code, § 7052 (West Supp. 1988). In Pennsylvania, it is an offense to abuse a corpse. See 18 Pa. Con. Stat. Ann., § 5510 (Supp. 1990). Section 182(b) of the Canadian Criminal Code states that "[e]veryone who ... improperly or indecently interferes with or offers any indignity to a dead human body or human remains ... is guilty of an indictable offence." Canadian Criminal Code, 1892, 55 & 56 Vict., ch. 29 (Can.).

38. *In Re A*, [1992] 3 *Med. L. Rev.* 303.

39. Nuffield Council on Bioethics Report, *Human Tissue: Ethical and Legal Issues* (London: Nuffield Council, 1985): at 64.

40. D. Anaise et al., "An Approach to Organ Salvage from Non-Heartbeating Cadaver Donors under Existing Legal and Ethical Requirements for Transplantation," *Transplantation*, 49 (1990): at 293. See also *People v. Bullington*, 80 P.2d 1030 (Cal. Dist. Ct. App. 1938).

41. King's Fund Institute Report, *supra* note 9, at 66. Such procedures are not disfiguring and may not even result in any apparent change in the physical appearance of the corpse.

42. Department of Health, *Cadaveric Organs for Transplantation* (London: Dept. of Health, 1983): paras. 22, 26. Interestingly, this latter paragraph does not appear in the Australian Code, thus entirely reversing the effect of their guidelines on EV. See National Health and Medical Research Council, *An Australian Code of Practice for Transplantation of Cadaveric Organs and Tissues* (Canberra: The Council, 1989): § 6. Resuscitation is always permissible where breathing has stopped; but it is not clear whether the person is brain dead or whether brain death will inevitably occur. In these cases, the intervention is intended to be *therapeutic* for the patient.

43. J. Harris, *The Value of Life* (London: Routledge, 1985): at 242.

44. Michael De Vita et al. have made similar remarks in respect of the Pittsburgh Protocol, arguing that "[n]either procedure harmed that patient, but clearly neither provided benefit to or was indicated for that patient." De Vita et al., *supra* note 13, at 378.

45. King's Fund Institute Report, *supra* note 9, at 65.

46. For example, Park et al., letter, "Organ Donation," *British Medical Journal*, 306 (1993): 145, in response to reports of EV practices.

47. P. Ramsey, *The Patient as a Person* (New Haven: Yale University Press, 1970): at 210.

48. H. Kuhse and P. Singer, "Prolonging Dying is the Same as Prolonging Living—One More Response to Long," *Journal of Medical Ethics*, 17 (1991): 205–06.

49. Speaking extrajudicially, in 1976, Lord Hailsham, the former Lord Chancellor, said that "[t]he law at the moment is perfectly plain: if you have got a living body, you have to keep it alive, if you can." See *The Listener*, July 8, 1976, at 15.

50. *Airedale NHS Trust v. Bland*, [1993] 1 All E.R. 821. See, for example, Lord Goff, *id.* at 870.

51. *Id.* at 851.

52. *Nancy B v. Hôtel Dieu de Québec*, (1992) 86 D.L.R. (4th) 385 at 391.

53. Youngner, *supra* note 5, at 323.

54. May has commented that the complete identification of person with body "does not terminate abruptly with death." May, *supra* note 16, at 3. Kass graphically describes our instinctive responses to the cadaver. He suggests that our instinctive response (which he considers sound) is to treat the mortal remains of the deceased person with respect. L. Kass, "Thinking

about the Body," *Hastings Center Reports*, 15, no. 1 (1985): 20–30.

55. Law Reform Commission Report, *supra* note 19, at 40.

56. As in the public dissection of William Burke, who was convicted and executed for murdering individuals whose bodies he sold to Scottish anatomists.

57. Adam Smith remarked that "[t]he idea of that dreary and endless melancholy which the fancy naturally ascribes to their condition ... arises altogether from our lodging ... our own living souls in their **inanimated** bodies, and thence conceiving what would be our emotions in this case." See D.D. Raphael and A.L. Macfie, eds., *Adam Smith: Theory of Moral Sentiments* (Oxford: Oxford University Press, 1976): at 13. This does not accurately encapsulate the nature of the harm inflicted.

58. E. Partridge, "Posthumous Interests and Posthumous Respect," *Ethics*, 91 (1981): at 243–44. See also B.B. Levenbook, "Harming Someone After His Death," *Ethics*, 94 (1984): 407–19. Callahan argues that interests can survive a person's death but can only be carried on by *living* interest-bearers. See J. Callahan, "On Harming the Dead," *Ethics*, 97 (1987): 341–52.

59. B. Steinbock, *Life Before Birth: The Moral and Legal Status of Embryos and Fetuses* (New York: Oxford University Press, 1992): at 26. This view parallels that of George Pitcher, who stated that "if we allow our unfettered intuition to operate on certain examples, it becomes abundantly clear that we think the dead can indeed be wronged." See G. Pitcher, "The Misfortunes of the Dead," *American Philosophical Quarterly*, 21, no. 2 (1984): 183–88. However, he also argues that it is only *anti-mortem* not *post-mortem* persons who are capable of being harmed after the person has died.

60. See R. Belliotti, "Do Dead Human Beings Have Rights?," *The Personalist*, 60 (1979): 201–10. Feinberg also asserts that the dead are harmed whenever their interests are "set-back" in any way. See J. Feinberg, *Harm to Others* (Oxford: Oxford University Press, 1984): at 34.

61. R. Scott, *The Body as Property* (New York: Viking Press, 1981): at 260.

62. Law Reform Commission Report, *supra* note 19, at 45.

63. *Id.* at 114–15.

64. Feinberg, *supra* note 60, at 45.

65. See generally the British Medical Association, Code of Practice, *Advance Statements about Medical Treatment* (London: BMJ Publishing Group, 1995); *Airedale NHS Trust v. Bland*, [1993] 1 All E.R. 821; *Re T (Adult: Refusal of Treatment)*, [1992] 4 All E.R. 649; and *Re C (Adult: Refusal of Medical Treatment)*, [1994] 1 W.L.R. 290. In the United States, most states have living will statutes. See I. Kennedy and A. Grubb, *Medical Law: Text with Materials* (London: Butterworths, 2nd ed., 1994): at 1334–39; and Patient Self-Determination Act, 42 U.S.C. §§ 1395cc, 1396a (1994).

66. A. Buchanan, "Advance Directives and the Personal Identity Problem," *Philosophy and Public Affairs*, 17 (1988): at 278.

67. British Medical Association, *supra* note 12, at 28.

68. Royal College of Nursing, *Review of the Legal, Ethical and Nursing Issues of Harvesting of Organs* (London: RCN, Mar. 1993).

69. King's Fund Institute Report, *supra* note 9, at 66.

70. In England and the United States, relatively few persons complete and carry donor cards or other expressed authorization for organ donation. In the United Kingdom in 1992, approximately 27 percent of persons had donor cards, but only one in five persons actually carried one. See King's Fund Insti-

tute Report, *supra* note 9, at 66. This compares with a figure of 25 percent of persons found in 1987 to be carrying such cards/authorizations at any one time in the United States. See R.W. Evans and D.L. Manninen, "US Public Opinion Concerning the Procurement and Distribution of Donor Organs," *Transplantation Proceedings*, 20 (1988): 781–85.

71. In the United Kingdom and the United States, existing relatives are always contacted prior to organ removal, although this is not legislatively mandated. In presumed consent systems, the wishes of relatives typically have a central place, subordinate only to the wishes of the deceased.

72. Department of Health, *supra* note 42, paras. 24, 32, 34.

73. *Auckland Health Board v. Attorney-General*, [1993] 1 N.Z.L.R. 235, 245.

74. Norman Cantor has stated that "[i]t is useful for every citizen to know that, in the event he or she is incompetent during the dying process, human dignity will be respected." See N. Cantor, "Conroy, Best Interests, and the Handling of Dying Patients," *Rutgers Law Review*, 37 (1985): at 570.

75. Steinbock, *supra* note 59, at 30.

76. *Airedale NHS Trust v. Bland*, [1993] 1 All E.R. 821, 853.

77. Nuffield Council on Bioethics Report, *supra* note 39, at 6.7–6.9.

78. King's Fund Institute Report, *supra* note 9, at 65. Commentators like Ivan Illich have linked the lack of dignity in contemporary notions of death and dying to the "medicalization" of death and the invasion of life by technology. See I. Illich, *Medical Nemesis: The Exploration of Health* (London: Calder & Boyars, 1975).

79. T.N. Madan, "Dying with Dignity," *Social Science and Medicine*, 35 (1992): at 431.

80. See Harris, *supra* note 43, at 221–22.

81. J. Orlowski, G. Kanoti, and M. Mehlman, "The Ethical Dilemma of Permitting the Teaching and Perfecting of Resuscitation Techniques on Recently Expired Patients," *Journal of Clinical Ethics*, 1 (1990): at 203.

82. J. Hardwig, "Treating the Brain Dead for the Benefit of the Family," *Journal of Clinical Ethics*, 2 (1991): at 55.

83. Feinberg, *supra* note 60, at 93.

84. I largely ignore Derek Parfit's contentious assertions that the competent and incompetent individual are separate "persons." I argue, as does Buchanan, that in cases where the individual has suffered catastrophic neurological damage, no new, different person can exist even if the earlier "person" has ceased to exist. Buchanan, *supra* note 66, at 283.

85. The latter strategy is favored by Jean McHale. See J. McHale, "Elective Ventilation—Pragmatic Solution or Ethical Minefield?," *Professional Negligence*, 11, no. 1 (1995): at 25. In Great Britain, a new central computerized registry was set up in 1995; it might feasibly record individuals' wishes regarding EV.

86. The Leicester NHBD protocol was advertised in the local press (*Leicester Mercury*) without any adverse comment. See K. Varty et al., "Response to Organ Shortage: Kidney Retrieval Programme Using Non-Heart Beating Donors," *British Medical Journal*, 308 (1994): 575.

87. It would appear that, in the Netherlands, the implementation of such NHBD protocols without relatives' permission is unlawful because relatives' permission is required by law for any medical procedure carried out on a cadaver. See M. Booster et al., "In Situ Perfusion of Kidneys from Non-Heart Beating Donors: The Maastricht Protocol," *Transplantation Proceedings*, 25 (1993): 1503–04.

[24]

Should organs from patients in permanent vegetative state be used for transplantation?

R Hoffenberg, M Lock, N Tilney, C Casabona, A S Daar, R D Guttmann, I Kennedy, S Nundy, J Radcliffe-Richards, R A Sells, for the International Forum for Transplant Ethics

A shortage of donor organs limits most transplant programmes: some patients die of otherwise untreatable end-organ failure, others, in chronic renal failure, are obliged to continue with costly and distressing dialysis procedures. We discuss whether organs taken from patients in a permanent vegetative state (PVS) could be used for transplantation once a decision has been taken to withdraw treatment and allow the patient to die. In the USA, there are an estimated 10 000–25 000 adult patients and 4000–10 000 children in PVS;[1] figures for the UK are likely to be substantially less pro rata, perhaps 1000 in all. The UK figure applies to all those who have been vegetative for longer than 3 months, many of whom die within the first year, so no decision would be taken to withdraw treatment in their lifetimes and they would not be regarded as potential organ donors. As yet, few court decisions have given consent to withdraw treatment from such long-standing cases, but the numbers may increase as the process becomes more widely accepted. There would be obvious benefits if this potential source of organs were to be made available for transplantation, but some arguments have been adduced against this proposition.

First, there is continuing uncertainty and controversy about the definition and diagnosis of PVS, higher brain death, and the recognition of residual consciousness. Errors in diagnosis could result in faulty prognosis.[2,3] Therefore, no decisions should be taken to end the life of patients thought to be in PVS. However, Andrews and colleagues[2] affirm that an accurate diagnosis of PVS can be made if the patient is assessed over a period of time by an experienced team, and that the fear of misdiagnosis should not constitute an argument against ending the life of a patient. Second, the ruling of the UK's House of Lords in the case of Tony Bland[1] allowed all treatment including food and water to be withdrawn from patients who had been in PVS for longer than 1 year without evidence of recovering cerebral function, on the grounds that later restoration of function would be highly improbable. This ruling has been

---

Lancet 1997; **350**: 1320–21

1 Sherborne House, Sherborne, UK (Prof R Hoffenberg FRCP);
Department of Social Studies in Medicine, McIntyre Medical
Sciences Building, Montreal, Quebec, Canada (Prof M Lock PhD);
Brigham and Women's Hospital, Boston, MA, USA
(Prof N Tilney FACS); Catedra de Derecho y Genoma Humano,
Universidad de Deusto, Bilbao, Spain (Prof C Casabona LLD);
Department of Surgery, College of Medicine, Sultan Qaboos
University, Sultanate of Oman (Prof A S Daar MD); Royal Victoria
Hospital, Montreal (Prof R D Guttmann FRCPC); Faculty of Law,
King's College, London, UK (Prof I Kennedy LLD); Department of
Gastrointestinal Surgery, All India Institute of Medical Sciences,
New Delhi, India (Prof S Nundy FRCS); 21 Huddleston Road, London
(J Radcliffe-Richards BPhil); and The International Forum for
Transplant Ethics, Renal Transplant Unit, Royal Liverpool University
Hospital, Liverpool L7 8XP, UK (Prof R A Sells FRCS)

Correspondence to: Prof R A Sells

challenged by reports of exceptional individuals who first evinced such recovery after this time.[2] For example, Andrews[3] commented on a recently reported case of a man who first showed signs of recovery of function more than 5 years after the original injury, but emphasised that this case was "the exception which shouldn't make the rule".

These arguments apply to the general decision to withdraw treatment from patients in PVS; this decision has received legal sanction in the UK and is permitted without overt legal agreement in many other jurisdictions. We are aware of the difficulty involved in making a correct diagnosis of PVS, and, particularly, of distinguishing the locked-in syndrome. However, in this paper we discuss the possible use of organs taken from those patients in whom a decision has already been taken to withdraw treatment and allow them to die. The actual cause of their unresponsive condition is not in this sense relevant.

Once the decision has been taken to withdraw treatment and allow a patient in PVS to die, what are the arguments against the use of their organs for transplantation? First, the law distinguishes between passively allowing to die and actively accelerating death. The former may be permissible, the latter is not. Thus, it would be unlawful to cause the death of a patient by the act of organ removal. Patients with whole-brain or brain-stem death are deemed in law to be dead. When cardiopulmonary support is withdrawn, spontaneous function of the heart and lungs rapidly ceases, the circulation stops, and immediate organ retrieval is allowed. By contrast, patients in PVS are not regarded as dead; they have higher brain death, but retain brain-stem function and are not, therefore, recognised as dead by the US (whole brain) or UK (brain stem) criteria. In the case of PVS, life-support is the provision of nutrition and fluids. When this support is withdrawn, the heart and lungs continue to function until they fail 10–12 days later because of inanition, electrolyte imbalance, or dehydration. By this time, the organs are no longer in optimum condition and a poor outcome of transplantation is to be expected. To obtain viable transplantable organs, death would have to be accelerated, which is unlawful. If you wait for patients in PVS to die after withdrawal of treatment, the organs are unusable; if you accelerate death, you are acting illegally. So the argument goes that patients in PVS cannot be suitable organ providers. In addition, health-care workers with experience of seeking consent from relatives for the use of organs from patients with whole-brain or brain-stem death anticipate objections if requests are made about patients in PVS. Similarly, opposition among the general public to this practice might damage the overall programme for organ donation.

In the possible use of organs of patients in PVS one may ask three separate, but linked, questions. First, should patients in PVS be maintained by supportive treatment until they die "naturally", which could take many years; or

THE LANCET

might it be morally or legally permissible to accelerate their death? In the UK, the House of Lords accepted that Tony Bland was alive after 3 years in PVS, but argued that continued treatment was futile because there was no hope of recovery. Since he was regarded as non-sentient, non-cognitive, and wholly unaware of his predicament, he could not be said to have any interest in being kept alive, or, for that matter, in being allowed to die. An American Multi-Society Task Force review of PVS supported the view that "a persistent PVS can be judged to be permanent 12 months after a traumatic injury in adults and children; recovery after this time is exceedingly rare and almost always involves severe disability".[1] For non-traumatic causes, the 12-month period is reduced to 3 months. The choice of 12 months as a reasonable time to consider withdrawal of treatment is supported by the British Medical Association[6] and the American Neurological Association.[7] In favour of withdrawal are the lengthy distress of the patient's family and the medical staff who care for a patient whose condition will never improve, and the large amount of skill, effort, and money devoted to the care of such patients. The overall annual cost of keeping patients in PVS alive in the USA has been estimated at between one and seven billion dollars.[1] It is not a responsibility of doctors to preserve life at all costs, especially if treatment would be inordinately painful, damaging, or futile. In such circumstances, a doctor's duty of care to a patient may cease and be directed instead to the interests of the family, carers, or society. It is morally, and now in the UK legally, acceptable to accelerate the death of the patient by withdrawal of treatment.

Second, once the decision has been taken to end the life of a patient in PVS, how should it be done? Should life be allowed to drain away slowly after withdrawal of solid and liquid sustenance, or could a case be made for a more speedy termination of life? Since patients in PVS are presumed to be non-sentient, it is unlikely that they experience distressing thirst or hunger when food and fluids are withdrawn. Such distress would be a strong argument in favour of a more expeditious mode of death, for example, administration of a lethal drug. Indeed, if patients in PVS are thought to be sentient or capable of experiencing pain, discomfort, or distress either before or after a decision has been taken to withdraw food and fluids, a strong case could be made on humane grounds for routine administration of palliative analgesic or psychotropic therapy. A more speedy end to life may also reduce the misery imposed by a long drawn-out death on family, nursing staff, and others. At present, UK and US law accepts that in some circumstances patients in PVS may be permitted to die slowly through omission of therapy, but no active steps may be taken to accelerate the process.

Third, is it legally, morally, or practically possible to procure organs from patients in PVS for transplantation? The fact that these patients are legally deemed to be alive is a major obstacle to the use of their organs for any purpose. If one has to wait until death, as it is defined in law, then organs will be unsuitable for transplantation. An earlier act of retrieval would kill the patient and is illegal. As the law stands, there is no way out of this dilemma, and it is not possible to use the organs of patients in PVS for transplantation. From a moral point of view, the critical decision is whether or not to terminate life. Although we recognise that there are intuitive psychological distinctions between killing a person and allowing them to die, we believe that, though the means by which death is attained has legal implications, there is no clear moral distinction between allowing to die by omission of treatment and more actively ending life, for instance, by injection of a fatal substance. The outcome is the same.

In the judgment by the House of Lords, Lord Mustill expressed his own uneasy feeling that "however much the terminologies may differ the ethical status of the two courses of action is for all relevant purposes indistinguishable"—what the law refers to as a distinction without a difference. If the legal definition of death were to be changed to include comprehensive irreversible loss of higher brain function, it would be possible to take the life of a patient (or more accurately to stop the heart, since the patient would be defined as dead) by a "lethal" injection, and then to remove the organs needed for transplantation, subject to the usual criteria for consent. Another approach would be not to declare such individuals legally dead, but rather to exempt them from the normal legal prohibitions against "killing" in the way that was considered for anencephalic infants.[7] Arguments in favour of one of these steps would be humanitarian, to obviate the futile use of resources needed to keep alive an individual with no hope of recovery, and to make available organs suitable for transplantation. If such a step were legally permissible, it would be essential to separate the decision to let the patient die from the steps taken to procure organs. In other words, the medical team that decides, in consultation with the family, that no further benefit would come from continued treatment, must be separate and independent from those who request organ donation and from the team that secures the organs.

The recent debate about anencephalic neonates as potential organ donors[7] is relevant to our discussion of patients in PVS, since they are in many ways analogous. The Council on Ethical and Judicial Affairs of the American Medical Association stated in 1995 that it is ethically permissible for an anencephalic neonate to be an organ donor, although still legally alive by virtue of the current definition of death.[7] A survey of leading medical experts in anencephaly and in ethics showed that two-thirds of physicians regarded this decision as "intrinsically moral".[7] If changes in public thinking and the law were to make possible the use of organs from patients in PVS, it would be necessary, as in the case of abortion, to include a conscience clause allowing doctors and nurses the right to refuse to take part in the procedure. For religious, cultural, and other traditional reasons, it is likely that the proposal would be rejected, nevertheless, the arguments in favour are sufficiently compelling to justify serious debate.

References

1 Multi-Society Task Force on PVS. Medical aspects of the persistent vegetative state. *N Engl J Med* 1994; **330:** 1499–1508 (part 1) and 1572–79 (part 2).
2 Andrews K, Murphy L, Munday R, Littlewood C. Misdiagnosis of the vegetative state: retrospective study in a rehabilitation unit. *BMJ* 1996; **313:** 13–16.
3 Crawford R. Misdiagnosing the persistent vegetative state. *BMJ* 1996; **313:** 5–6.
4 House of Lords. Report of the Select Committee on Medical Ethics. Session 1993–94. London: HM Stationery Office, 1994.
5 Andrews K, cited by Dyer C. Hillsborough survivor emerges from permanent vegetative state. *BMJ* 1997; **314:** 996.
6 British Medical Association Discussion paper on treatment of patients in PVS. London: BMA, 1992.
7 American Neurological Committee on Ethical Affairs Report on PVS. *Ann Neurol* 1993; **33:** 386–90.

Part VII
Organ Allocation

[25]

Putting Patients First in Organ Allocation: An Ethical Analysis of the U.S. Debate

JAMES F. CHILDRESS

Introduction

Organ allocation policy involves a mixture of ethical, scientific, medical, legal, and political factors, among others. It is thus hard, and perhaps even impossible, to identify and fully separate ethical considerations from all these other factors. Yet I will focus primarily on the ethical considerations embedded in the current debate in the United States about organ allocation policy. I will argue that it is important to *put patients first*—in the language of the title of one of the major public hearings[1]—but even then significant ethical questions will remain about exactly *how* to put patients first.

I would not characterize the current organ-allocation system in the United States as fundamentally unfair or unjust, in part because there are debates about various criteria of fairness and justice and in part because the United Network for Organ Sharing (UNOS), the national Organ Procurement and Transplantation Network (OPTN) operating under a contract with the federal government's Department of Health and Human Services (DHHS), has made substantial progress over time. However, I do believe that organ allocation policy can be further improved—largely by putting patients across the nation first, apart from particular professional and institutional interests—and that the proposed DHHS regulations point in the right direction. Nevertheless, I cannot endorse the DHHS plan in toto largely because it does not adequately attend to the probability of successful outcomes among transplant candidates for particular organs. In my judgment, this criterion needs more attention, both on its own terms and in relation to medical urgency, than the DHHS regulations suppose.

Debates about the Community of Ownership of Donated Organs

I had the good fortune to serve as vice-chair of the federal Task Force on Organ Transplantation, which in April 1986 issued its report *Organ Transplantation: Issues and Recommendations*.[2] One of this task force's major responsibilities, as mandated by the National Organ Transplant Act, was to make "recommendations for assuring equitable access by patients to organ transplantation and for assuring the equitable allocation of donated organs among transplant centers

This paper originated in my testimony before the Joint Hearing of The House Commerce Committee Subcommittee on Health and Environment and The Senate Labor and Human Resources Committee "Putting Patients First: Resolving Allocation of Transplant Organs," June 18, 1998. It benefited from discussions with audiences at Yale University and the University of Pittsburgh, Spring, 1999.

James F. Childress

and among patients medically qualified for an organ transplant." It took me some time to discern that our debates about "equitable access" and "equitable allocation" were, in part, debates about who "owns" donated organs.

Apart from special cases of directed donation to named recipients, donated organs *belong to* the community, the public, and not to procurement and transplant teams. This fundamental conviction undergirded the Task Force's deliberations about and recommendations for equitable organ allocation: Donated organs should be viewed as scarce public resources for use for the welfare of the community. Organ procurement and transplant teams receive these donated organs as "trustees" and "stewards" on behalf of the whole community. Thus, they should not have unlimited dispositional authority over donated organs.

Over the years since the Task Force's report, the term "community" has been widely but variously used.[3] Unfortunately, it has often been excessively narrowed. In the current debate it frequently means the "transplant community,"[4] which is sometimes limited to transplant surgeons, professionals, and their institutions, though it sometimes includes organ donors, organ recipients, transplant candidates, and their families. But even the latter interpretation of "community" is still too narrow because it fails to include the larger community, which comprises not only all these parties but all of us as *potential donors* and *potential recipients* (and relatives of potential donors and potential recipients). Policies of organ allocation should be designed *for* the public as a whole.

This view of community ownership of and dispositional authority over donated organs provides strong support for wide and diverse public participation in setting the criteria for allocating donated organs. Calls for public participation stem in part from the nature of organ procurement in the United States—it depends on voluntary, public gifts; that is, gifts by individuals and their families to the community. Indeed, there are important moral connections between policies of organ procurement and policies of organ allocation. On the one hand, the success of policies of organ procurement may reduce scarcity and hence obviate some of the difficulties in organ allocation. On the other hand, distrust is a major reason for the public's reluctance to donate organs, and policies of procurement may be ineffective if the public perceives the policies of organ allocation as unfair and thus untrustworthy.[5] In short, public participation—for example, in the Organ Procurement and Transplantation Network (OPTN)—is very important and even indispensable to ensure actual and perceived fairness. "Organ allocation falls into the region of public decision-making," as Jeffrey Prottas insists, "not medical ethics and much less medical tradition."[6] Thus, policies of organ allocation should be designed, in part, *by* the public.

Two additional points about community ownership of donated organs and public participation in setting organ allocation criteria merit attention. First, while observing that prior to 1986 organs donated for transplantation had effectively belonged to the surgeons who removed them, Prottas contends that the fundamental philosophical shift to community ownership effected by the Task Force report both changed matters and left them the same. On the one hand, professional dominance remains, in part because of technical expertise and medical gatekeeping. On the other hand, professional dominance is now more circumscribed and publicly accountable. With organ allocation now in the public domain, in part because transplant professionals had sought governmental assistance for transplantation, there are now more participants, particularly public participants, and the terms of the debate have changed:

Putting Patients First in Organ Allocation

> Alternative allocation systems are now defended in public debate, and
> equity as well as efficiency must be considered and defined. Physi-
> cians dominate the debate, through knowledge as well as power, but
> they must justify their actions now as trustees of the public. The
> organs are no longer theirs.[7]

Second, some ambiguities about community ownership persist in debates in
the OPTN and elsewhere about policies of organ allocation: Do donated organs
belong to the national community or to regional, state, or local communities?
Whereas different answers to this question may or may not lead to different
policies, they certainly create different presumptions and pose different problems. Nevertheless, from either starting point, various arguments may support
using organs on one geographical level rather than another. If we start from
local (or state or regional) "ownership" of donated organs, then organs would
be allocated first in the local community, perhaps subject to some requirements
to "share" organs (e.g., a zero-antigen mismatch in kidney transplantation). If,
however, the relevant community for organ distribution is the national community, as I believe it is, then that community has the right and the responsibility to allocate the organs to patients anywhere in the country according to
acceptable standards and logistical constraints. Nevertheless, it may and often
should allow organs to be used at the local level, if, for instance, transporting
those organs would jeopardize their viability for transplantation. Such logistical problems remain especially important for heart and lung transplantation,
somewhat important for liver transplantation (where the situation has improved),
but only modestly important for kidney transplantation.

Although logistical problems thus remain variably important, there is nothing more than anecdotal evidence, to the best of my knowledge, to warrant the
additional common claim that local allocation provides a substantial incentive
for organ donation that would be lost under a national system. A truly national
approach should reduce the relevance of "accidents of geography" in organ
allocation and allow such geographical factors to enter only when and where
they are clearly relevant for transplantation outcomes.

In short, it is now time to return to the Task Force's conception of the national
community as the relevant community of dispositional authority in organ allocation and to take steps to minimize "accidents of geography"—accidents regarding where transplant candidates live or are listed—in organ allocation to the
greatest extent possible with the use of the best available technologies for each
type of organ. The moral point is not that the local community should "share"
some organs it obtains with the larger, national community—the language of
"sharing" suggests that the local community "owns" the donated organs. Rather,
donated organs belong to the national community, and the "trustees" and "stewards" of those organs should allocate them according to criteria that minimize
"accidents of geography" in putting patients first.

Principles of Just, Fair, and Equitable Allocation

Justice and Morally Relevant and Irrelevant Characteristics

To state the last point differently, it is, in my judgment, generally *unjust* to use
"accidents of geography" in organ allocation because they are not morally

James F. Childress

relevant to who should receive donated organs (unless, again, local or regional priority is required because transporting the organs would be impossible or would adversely affect their viability for transplantation). But what exactly is justice, and how should principles of justice function in organ allocation?

Justice, which may be defined as rendering to each person his or her due, includes both formal and material criteria. The *formal* criterion of justice involves similar treatment for similar cases or equal treatment for equals. Various *material* criteria of justice specify relevant similarities and dissimilarities among parties and thus determine how particular benefits and burdens will be distributed.[8] There is debate about the *moral relevance* and *moral weight* of different material criteria, such as need, merit, societal contribution, status, and ability to pay. Different theories of justice tend to stress different material criteria. However, some material criteria may be acceptable in some areas of life, such as employment, but not in others, such as the allocation of scarce life-saving organ transplants.

Even though principles of justice permit rationing under conditions of scarcity, they rule out allocation criteria that are based on morally irrelevant characteristics, such as race or gender. However, it is much easier to agree on what is unjust, such as distribution by gender or race, than on what is just. A fundamental question concerns which material criteria satisfy the requirements of justice and are justifiable for organ allocation. As I have argued, public participation is one way—but only one way and by no means sufficient—to reduce possible biases from particular professional or institutional interests in the public process of determining which material criteria are relevant to organ allocation. In short, public participation is one way to put patients first.

Just Material Criteria in Organ Allocation: Patient Need, Probability of Success, and Time on the Waiting List

There is general agreement that three material criteria are relevant, just, and justifiable in organ allocation—patient need, probability of a successful outcome, and time on the waiting list. These are recognized in UNOS policies, which attempt to balance them but which then allow local priority to produce "accidents of geography." They are also evident in the DHHS regulations, which, however, pay insufficient attention to the probability of a successful outcome, particularly in relation to the other two criteria.

The first two material criteria—patient need and probability of a successful outcome—appear at two major stages in organ allocation: (1) forming a waiting list by determining the pool of transplant candidates, and (2) allocating available organs to patients on the waiting list. The third material criterion—time on the waiting list—obviously applies only at the second stage of allocation. The difficult ethical and practical questions at each stage involve *specifying* the criteria—what exactly do they mean, how can we measure them, and so forth?— and *weighting* them in case they conflict—should one take priority over the others, should allocation policies attempt to balance them, and so forth? Even though there is little dispute about the general relevance of these three criteria, and much of that dispute focuses on waiting time rather than the other two criteria, vigorous and widespread debate occurs about how to specify and weight all three criteria.

Putting Patients First in Organ Allocation

Setting Criteria for Admission to Waiting Lists

There is general agreement that the waiting list of transplant candidates should be formed according to the medical criteria of need for and probability of benefiting from an organ transplant. However, consensus breaks down at the point of specification that requires determining whether to define these medical criteria broadly or narrowly, where to set the standards for need or for minimal efficacy, and which factors are relevant in determining both need and probable benefit. It also breaks down in determining which of these criteria should have priority in case of conflict.

Vigorous efforts have been undertaken, particularly through UNOS, to develop fair policies of allocating organ to patients *on* waiting lists, but it has been more difficult to ensure equitable access *to* waiting lists, perhaps in part because of transplant-center discretion. And yet, decisions about who will be admitted to the waiting list appear to constitute a primary source of unequal access to organ transplants. In the absence of minimum criteria for admission to the waiting lists for organ transplants, transplant teams have had the sole authority to decide whether and when to register a patient. According to a recent report, "a patient can be registered at any time before the transplant is urgently needed and can electively turn down available organs while accumulating waiting time that may misrepresent the patient's medical condition."[9]

It is thus essential to avoid the inappropriate, unnecessary, unfair, and premature listing of transplant candidates. DHHS rightly proposes a performance goal for the OPTN of defining "objective and measurable medical criteria to be used by all transplant centers in determining whether a patient is appropriate to be listed for a transplant."[10] These criteria should establish minimum medical need, as DHHS indicates, but they should also attend to probability of success, which DHHS doesn't adequately address or stress (even though it is mentioned more or less in passing).

Point Systems for Allocating Organs

It is obviously necessary to have point systems for allocating organs across the national community. Such systems appear to provide objective, public, and impartial ways to allocate organs by reducing institutional and professional discretion and possible bias. They thereby assure the public that all patients will be treated as equals according to the standards reflected in the point system.

With the exception of time on the waiting list, the material criteria explicitly used in different point systems for organ allocation are largely medical in that they involve medical techniques used by medical personnel and arguably influence the transplant's likely success or failure. They are not, however, value free.[11] Selecting different factors and then assigning to them various weights (points) reflect various values. The vigorous debate about how much weight each criterion should have is only partly technical and scientific (e.g., the impact of HLA matching in kidney transplantation); it is to a great extent ethical. Let me take one example: In kidney transplantation, such factors as quality of antigen match and logistical score focus on the chance of a successful outcome; both medical urgency and panel-reactive antibody in different ways focus on patient need; and time on the waiting list introduces a nonmedical factor, even though it may overlap with panel-reactive antibody because sen-

James F. Childress

sitized patients tend to wait longer for transplants. The points assigned to these various factors thus reflect value judgments about the relative importance of patient need, probability of success, and waiting time. Similar observations apply to other organ transplants.

Specifying and Balancing Patients' Needs and Probable Benefits

Both patient need for a transplant and the probability of a successful transplant are ethically relevant in selecting patients for the waiting list and in selecting patients to receive a particular organ. I would argue that both the urgency of medical need and the probability of successful outcome should be used to determine which candidate should receive a particular organ, after the pool of transplant candidates has been established by the same criteria. Obviously, a patient's risk of imminent death is a strong reason for allocating an organ to that patient. But a major reason for also considering the probability of a successful outcome is to avoid wasting the gift of life. Organs are donated for effective use, and providing an organ to a patient who has only a very limited chance of success increases the probability that he or she will then need another transplant for survival, further reducing the chances for others as well as for his or her own successful transplantation.

It is important to specify as completely as possible both criteria. The DHHS regulations quite rightly require further specification of medical need, according to status categories that adequately differentiate patient needs.[12] One important reason is that medical urgency is a manipulable category, which has reportedly been abused at times by physicians eager to protect their own patients by declaring them medically urgent to increase their chances for a transplant.[13] However, the DHHS regulations, in my judgment, do not adequately attend to the probability of success, which is also morally relevant.

To be sure, after concentrating on medical urgency as the primary criterion, the DHHS preamble and regulations often add a proviso to the effect that the application of the criterion of medical urgency is limited by medical judgment about not wasting an organ through a transplant that would be futile. For instance, the standard of equalizing waiting times within the medically urgent status emphasizes "that the sickest categories of patients should receive as much benefit as feasible under this standard, in accordance with sound medical judgment."[14] And among the "key constraints on organ allocation" that DHHS would require the OPTN to take into account is a limited version of the probability of a successful outcome: "There are patients with urgent need for whom transplantation is futile. Organs cannot be used without an assessment of the immune system and other physical conditions of patients."[15]

This DHHS proviso is important, but it is also necessary to try to build this ethical criterion of probability of success into the publicly formulated criteria of allocation rather than leaving it to medical discretion. This will be very difficult to accomplish—for instance, what counts as a success when we consider length of graft survival, length of patient survival, quality of life, rehabilitation?—and it may even be ultimately impossible. However, with both medical and public input in an open process conducted over time, we should be able to determine whether we can specify this criterion, along with status categories having to do with urgency of need. At the very least, through this process, it might be possible to set certain minimum thresholds of probable benefit.

Putting Patients First in Organ Allocation

One reason further specification is needed is that even judgments of "futility" are subject to considerable debate. For instance, as used in the medical literature, "medical futility" may mean (1) a procedure cannot be performed because of a patient's biological condition, (2) a procedure will not produce the intended physiological effect, (3) a procedure cannot be expected to produce the benefit that is sought, and (4) the anticipated benefits of a procedure will be outweighed by its burdens, harms, and costs. Given that the last is really a judgment of utility, rather than futility, only the first three should count, but even they are not objective and value free. For instance, some clinicians hold that a treatment is futile only if there is no chance it will be effective, whereas others label a treatment as futile if its chance of success is 13% or lower.[16] Clearly, a public process is needed to provide greater specification of "sound medical judgment" in this regard.

Such a public process will also need to consider how to *balance* these two morally relevant criteria of patient need and probable success. Tensions between medical urgency and probability of success may vary greatly depending on the organ in question. For instance, the category of medical urgency will probably not be as important when an artificial organ can be used as a backup (for example, dialysis for end-stage renal failure). In liver transplantation, to take another example, the dominant practice has been to give the sickest patient the highest priority (within the local area), but "medical utility" (and some would include cost-effectiveness) would often dictate placing the liver in a fitter patient to realize the greatest medical benefit (at the lowest cost). Another reason for some attention to those with a higher probability of benefit is that "as time goes on . . . the fitter patients become increasingly ill, their survivability on the waiting list declines, and their operative risk soars."[17] It is not possible to determine generally, apart from different types of organ transplants, what weights to assign to urgency of patient need and probability of success; what is needed is a public process to consider and determine their respective weights for organ-specific allocation policies.

The Moral Relevance of Time on the Waiting List
and of Seeking to Equalize Waiting Times

It is fair to allocate organs according to both medical need and probability of success, but when there are no substantial differences in degree of medical need and probable benefit among various transplant candidates, it is fair to use their time on the waiting list (or queuing or first-come, first-served) to break the tie. Indeed, if two or more patients are equally good candidates for a particular organ according to the medical criteria of need and probability of success, using their different times on the waiting list may be the fairest way to make the final selection. Such an approach presupposes that there is a firm (and morally acceptable) consensus on what constitutes substantial differences in medical need and probability of success, as well as on criteria for admission to the waiting list.

Some critics charge that time on the waiting list is morally irrelevant or even morally pernicious. For example, Olga Jonasson argues that "length of time on the waiting list is the least fair, most easily manipulated, and most mindless of all methods of organ allocation."[18] She is right if this criterion is used by itself without regard to the other important criteria of urgency of need and proba-

James F. Childress

bility of success or if it is viewed as the primary criterion. But the use of waiting time in patient selection, when medical need and probability of success are roughly equal, can be justified by various principles and values, such as fair equality of opportunity. Nevertheless, ethical and practical problems do arise in its application. For instance, when does the transplant candidate's waiting time start—when the patient seeks medical treatment for the condition that leads to end-stage organ failure or when the patient is registered with the OPTN, to take just two possibilities? The latter has been used, but, as critics note, it is easy to manipulate, for example, by putting patients on the list as early as possible and well before their condition really merits such placement. Hence, DHHS is rightly requiring that the OPTN set minimum standards across transplant centers for admission to the waiting list.

Also, the fairness of using time on the waiting list as a criterion depends in part on background conditions. For example, some people may not seek care early because they lack insurance; others may receive inadequate medical advice about how early to seek transplantation; and so forth. It will help, in line with the DHHS regulations, to establish not only firm standards for admission to the waiting list but also firm status categories and then to count only the time within a particular status: "The relevant 'tie-breaker' will no longer be total waiting time, perhaps years, but will become waiting time within a group of patients with equal medical urgency."[19] Such a development will facilitate the fair use of waiting time as a criterion of allocation.

If it is ethically acceptable, as I have argued, to use different times on the waiting list to break ties among transplant candidates, based on medical need and probability of success, is it also ethically important to try to reduce unequal waiting times among patients in particular status categories and across geographical boundaries? DHHS' performance goal is to make average waiting times as equal as possible among patients with similar degrees of need (here I would go beyond the DHHS regulations and include probability of success too, at least above a certain threshold). The goal is to equalize average waiting times within similar categories of transplant candidates. Inequalities, such as a fivefold difference in waiting times for liver transplants, should serve as triggers to inquire into ways to reduce the inequalities. It is a legitimate public goal to try to equalize, as much as possible, times on the waiting list, given that those times have some bearing on suffering, on urgency of need, and on probability of success, in addition to being independently significant. Increasing equality, through reducing arbitrary differences in time on the waiting list among otherwise similar transplant candidates, is required by formal justice.

Conclusions

Organ allocation poses a "tragic choice."[20] Short of adequately increasing the supply of transplantable organs, we cannot fully realize all our values at the same time. Hence, it is morally imperative to seek the best possible balance of the whole range of relevant values, which are reflected in the material criteria of patient needs, probability of success, and waiting time.

First, we need to defuse the moral rhetoric about various organ-allocation systems. Several organ-allocation systems appear to fall within the range of ethically acceptable or relatively just and fair systems, but all of them require

Putting Patients First in Organ Allocation

moral fine-tuning in the name of justice and fairness. And various participants in the debate appear to be acting in good faith, even when they seriously disagree.

Second, society should seek to further specify, to weight, and to balance patient need, probable success, and waiting time through a process that involves the fullest possible and most diverse public participation. Obviously, ethically acceptable allocation criteria cannot be formulated without the substantial input of transplant surgeons and other physicians, as well as other healthcare professionals and scientists. Nevertheless, donated organs belong to the whole community, and procurement and transplant teams receive those organs on behalf of the whole community, for which they serve as "trustees" and "stewards."

It is time to put patients first and to devise procedural and substantive criteria to protect current and future patients' rights and welfare. By putting patients first, we should be able to find common ground or reach an overlapping consensus. One way to do so is to ask, along the lines of the Golden Rule or the Rawlsian social contract, behind the veil of ignorance, which set of criteria we would find acceptable for allocating organs to ourselves or to our families, without knowing our own or our families' precise circumstances. This is a fair way to reflect on possible material criteria for just organ allocation.

Third, the morally relevant community of ownership of, or dispositional authority over, donated organs is the national community, subject to logistical constraints that must be met in order to provide viable organs for transplantation. Thus, the allocation system should focus on patients across the country and should minimize, as much as possible, "accidents of geography." This is the main point at which I would criticize the OPTN's current system—the procedural assignment of priority to the local community in allocation, even in combination with other substantive criteria (such as medical urgency in liver allocation), results in an unacceptable patchwork of allocation and produces various inequalities across the country. The alternative is not a single, national list that ignores the potential impact, for instance, of shipping organs great distances on the probable success of the transplant. What is required is a shift in orientation—to thinking about donated organs as belonging to the national community and then to specifying and balancing allocation criteria in part according to logistical realities.

The failure to take a national perspective has now resulted in further fragmentation, as states have adopted laws that require organs donated within their boundaries to be used for patients within their boundaries and to be shared with other states only if no patient within their states could benefit from the organ. Such a result should have been anticipated by various participants in this debate over the last few years. Medical and political boundaries may not coincide. (Obviously, it is also important to consider the limitations of national boundaries, but I cannot do so here.[21])

Fourth, several of DHHS' proposed regulations should move organ allocation in even more equitable directions. In particular, I have argued that it is essential to set minimum criteria for access to waiting lists for various organ transplants and also to set uniform status categories, such as medical urgency. With these changes, which the OPTN is already pursuing, at least to some extent, it may be possible to use differences in waiting time more fairly as a criterion of allocation, when medical urgency and probability of success are roughly equal among transplant candidates. Furthermore, with these changes, it should be possible to begin to reduce inequalities of waiting time, in part

James F. Childress

because patients will be admitted to the waiting list in a more consistent way and because their status will be clearer. It is ethically desirable to reduce inequalities of waiting time, both because equality is an important value and because longer waiting times often correlate with longer suffering, further deterioration, and lower chances of successful outcomes.

This point may not come through the recent Institute of Medicine (IOM) report, *Organ Procurement and Transplantation*, as clearly as it might.[22] This report criticizes certain uses of waiting time as an allocation criterion but, rather than rejecting waiting time altogether, calls for its "appropriate consideration." It properly notes that although "disparities in overall median waiting times for liver transplants have been cited as an indicator of the unfairness of the current system," those disparities do not provide "an appropriate measure of the fairness of the system." Thus, the report recommends discontinuing the use of waiting time as an allocation criterion for liver transplant candidates in certain statuses. Those in statuses 2B (who require continuous medical care and satisfy other conditions) and 3 (who require continuous medical care but do not satisfy the other conditions for 2B) are not as severely ill as those in statuses 1 (whose death from fulminant liver failure is expected in fewer than 7 days) or 2A (who are in intensive care for treatment of chronic liver failure and who are expected to die in fewer than 7 days). Those in statuses 2B and 3 present such a heterogeneous population in terms of range of severity of illness that waiting time is an inappropriate allocation criterion. The IOM report recommends that "an appropriate medical triage system ... be developed to ensure equitable allocation of organs to patients in these categories." I concur: waiting time should be a tie-breaker when urgency of medical need and probability of successful treatment are roughly equal.

My biggest problem with the proposed DHHS regulations, which the IOM report generally affirms, is not that they emphasize medical urgency—it is appropriate to emphasize this criterion particularly for liver transplants in contrast to kidney transplants—but that they do so without sufficient attention on the level of policy to probable benefit and to balancing probable benefit with medical urgency. Some process needs to be devised, in the OPTN or elsewhere, with both professional and public participation, to work out a fuller conception of "medical utility," which includes both urgency of need and probability of benefit.

Fifth, it is essential to stress, as the proposed DHHS regulations do, ongoing monitoring and evaluation and appropriate revision of any organ-allocation system for various reasons, including to determine whether a particular point system has discriminatory effects and needs modification, whatever modeling programs might have predicted originally. For instance, in 1995 UNOS determined that it needed to alter its point system for allocating cadaveric kidneys in order to eliminate points previously assigned to some levels of HLA match and to increase the role of time on the waiting list, in part to increase the access and to reduce the waiting time of African Americans seeking cadaveric kidney transplants.[23]

Sixth, the so-called green screen is a major source of unequal access to extrarenal organ transplantation in the United States. At this time, a patient's ability to pay, either directly or through third-party coverage, is an important de facto material criterion for access to extrarenal transplants. The strategies that DHHS has recommended for the Department and for the OPTN in trying to make access more equal may help in small ways, but, in the final analysis,

Putting Patients First in Organ Allocation

this issue must be addressed by the society as a whole, with the involvement of the federal and state governments.

Many of the arguments for providing funds to ensure equitable access to organ transplantation are similar to arguments for providing funds for other medical procedures. But one argument, used by the Task Force, specifically focuses on the *distinctiveness* or *uniqueness* of organ transplantation, particularly because of the social practices of procurement of organs for transplantation. This argument identifies an important moral connection between organ procurement, including organ donation, and organ distribution and allocation. In its efforts to increase the supply of organs, our society requests donations of organs from people of all socioeconomic classes—for example, through public appeals for organ donations or through state "required request" and "routine inquiry" statutes, which mandate that institutions inquire about an individual's or family's willingness to donate, or even request such a donation. However, it is unfair and even exploitative for the society to ask people, rich and poor alike, to donate organs if their own access to donated organs in cases of end-stage organ failure would be determined by their ability to pay rather than by their medical need, probability of success, and time on the waiting list.

This principled argument may be combined with an argument that focuses on the consequences of different policies. There are legitimate worries about the impact of unequal access to organ transplants (based on inability to pay) on the system of organ procurement, which includes gifts of organs from individuals and their families. There is substantial evidence that attitudes of distrust limit organ donation; this distrust appears to be directed at both organ procurement (e.g., the fear the potential donors will be declared dead prematurely) and organ distribution and allocation (e.g., the concern that potential transplant recipients from higher socioeconomic classes will receive priority).[24] Thus, it is not at all surprising that after Oregon decided to stop providing Medicaid funds for most organ transplants "a boycott of organ donations was organized by some low-income people."[25] And cynical comments about how quickly some famous people receive scarce organ transplants reflect public suspicion of organ allocation policies.

Finally, as the previous point suggests, there are important moral connections between organ procurement, including organ donation, on the one hand, and equitable access to organ transplantation and equitable organ allocation, on the other hand. It is obvious that increasing the supply of organs would reduce some problems of organ allocation, but, perhaps less obviously, public trust in the organ allocation system also appears to be important for the public donation of organs. As the Task Force on Organ Transplantation stressed,

> there is increasing public demand that the criteria for patient selection be public and fair. This demand stems in part from the nature of the organ procurement system, which depends on voluntary gifts to strangers. Indeed, because of the close connection between organ procurement and the politics of organ distribution, it is essential that the criteria for patient selection are fair and are perceived to be fair. Otherwise, distrust may perpetuate the scarcity of organs."[26]

Our fragile system of organ transplantation depends for its very existence on public trust and thus on the public's willingness to entrust their or their

James F. Childress

relatives' organs to the trustees and stewards who will allocate them on behalf of the national community to which the organs belong.

Notes

1. The Joint Hearing of The House Commerce Committee Subcommittee on Health and Environment and The Senate Labor and Human Resources Committee. *Putting Patients First: Resolving Allocation of Transplant Organs*. 18 Jun 1998.
2. National Task Force on Organ Transplantation. *Organ Transplantation: Issues and Recommendations*. Apr 1986.
3. Mongoven A. Federal hearings on liver transplant allocation and donation. *BioLaw* 1997;2:S373–89.
4. United Network for Organ Sharing. *The UNOS Statement of Principles and Objectives of Equitable Organ Allocation: UNOS Update*. 20 Aug 1994.
5. Childress JF. Some moral connections between organ procurement and organ distribution. *Journal of Contemporary Health Law and Policy* 1987;3:85–110.
6. Prottas JM. Nonresident aliens and access to organ transplant. *Transplantation Proceedings* 1989;21:3428.
7. Prottas JM. The most useful gift: altruism and the public policy of organ transplants. San Francisco, Calif.: Jossey-Bass Publishers, 1994:153.
8. Beauchamp TL, Childress JF. *Principles of Biomedical Ethics*, 4th ed. London/New York: Oxford University Press, 1994:chap. 6.
9. United Network of Organ Sharing, U.S. Department of Health and Human Services. *1994 Annual Report of the U.S. Scientific Registry for Transplant Recipients and the Organ Procurement and Transplantation Network, Transplant Data: 1988–1993*. Richmond, Va.: UNOS, and Bethesda, Md.: Division of Organ Transplantation, Bureau of Health Resources Development, Health Resources and Services Administration, U.S. Department of Health and Human Services, 1994:V-3.
10. Department of Health and Human Services. 42 CFR Part 121, Organ procurement and transplantation network: final rule. *Federal Register* 1998;63:16296.
11. Brock D. *Ethical Issues in Recipient Selection for Organ Transplantation*. Boulder, Colo.: Westview Press, 1988:86–99.
12. See note 10, Department of Health and Human Services 1998.
13. Monaco AP. Comments in roundtable discussion. *Transplantation Proceedings* 1989;21:3418.
14. See note 10, Department of Health and Human Services 1998:16314.
15. See note 10, Department of Health and Human Services 1998.
16. See note 8, Beauchamp, Childress 1994:289.
17. Jonasson O. Waiting in line. *Transplantation Proceedings* 1989;21:3391.
18. See note 17, Jonasson 1989:3392.
19. See note 10, Department of Health and Human Services 1998.
20. Calabresi G, Bobbitt P. *Tragic Choices*. New York: Norton, 1978.
21. Childress JF. *Practical Reasoning in Bioethics*. Bloomington: Indiana University Press, 1997:230-2.
22. Committee on Organ Procurement and Transplantation Policy, Division of Health Sciences Policy, Institute of Medicine. *Organ Procurement and Transplantation: Assessing Current Policies and the Potential Impact of the DHHS Final Rule*. Washington, D.C.: National Academy Press, 1999.
23. See note 9, UNOS, DHHS 1994:V-6-7, passim.
24. See note 5, Childress 1987. See note 21, Childress 1997.
25. Welch HG, Larson EB. Dealing with limited resources: the Oregon decision to curtail funding for organ transplantation. *New England Journal of Medicine* 1988;319:171-3.
26. See note 2, National Task Force on Organ Transplantation 1986:85.

[26]

The subtle politics of organ donation: a proposal

Stephanie Eaton   *University of Edinburgh, Edinburgh*

Abstract

Organs available for transplantation are scarce and valuable medical resources and decisions about who is to receive them should not be made more difficult by complicated calculations of desert. Consideration of likely clinical outcome must always take priority when allocating such a precious resource otherwise there is a danger of wasting that resource. However, desert may be a relevant concern in decision-making where the clinical risk is identical between two or more potential recipients of organs. Unlikely as this scenario is, such a decision procedure makes clear the interdependence of organ recipient and organ donor and hints at potential disadvantages for those who are willing to accept but unwilling to donate organs (free-riders). A combined opting-out and preference system weakens many of the objections to opting-out systems and may make the decision to donate organs on behalf of their deceased relatives easier for families.

(*Journal of Medical Ethics* 1998;24:166–170)

Keywords: Organ donation; free-riding; opting out

Inferring the wishes of donors

The system for potential organ donor recruitment in the UK operates such that persons indicate willingness to be an organ donor by the carrying of a donor card or the completion of a section of the driver's licence; it is also possible to express consent in what is known as a "living will". Such a system of opting-in through donor cards etc gives a firm indication of the deceased's views but is inadequate because of low public participation in the scheme. The Human Tissue Act 1961 requires that relatives be consulted about organ donation in the absence of any indication from the deceased. Where there is no evidence of consent, families may be called upon to make decisions at a difficult time without certain knowledge of the prior views of the deceased. Without such knowledge, families are often reluctant to give permission for organ donation; understandably hospitals do not wish to seem coercive at times of grief and as a result potential organs are lost.

As is well known, some countries have an arrangement of opting-out of potential donation of organs, a system which it is generally agreed gives rise to a greater availability of organs for transplantation. It is assumed in these countries that all citizens agree to become organ donors unless they have actively taken steps to indicate that in the relevant circumstances they would *not* wish to do so.[1] The policy of assuming consent gives rise to the criticism that those who are unable or too slow to take the necessary steps to opt-out and who are subsequently candidates for donation may have their organs used in violation of their strongly held wishes. This argument has successfully been used in a number of countries considering a system of opting-out and, as a result of the rejection of opting-out, the supply of much needed organs for transplantation has remained low.[2]

The availability of organs for transplantation from brain stem dead patients is reduced because of an understandable tendency to conservatism by families in those cases where the prior wishes of their deceased relative are not known. Yet it is known that a large majority of persons express a willingness to be postmortem donors[3] so in many cases this caution may be unfounded or may even be in breach of strongly held wishes to donate. Conservatism in these cases often results from a reluctance to guess what would have been the choice of the deceased: it is not the case that families believe that the deceased would have refused to donate organs, merely that they do not feel comfortable presuming consent. As the burden of decision-making usually falls upon the family without warning, a process of reasoning that helps to infer the wishes of the deceased could be a comfort to them.

A family's reluctance to guess the wishes of the deceased may lead it to refuse organ donation. By contrast, when a person's future is under consideration in a medical emergency, relatives do not hesitate to assert and act on his or her presumed desires with some confidence. No caution is exhibited in most cases where an unconscious patient is unable to consent to life-extending or enhancing medical intervention. In these cases the presumption is that, absent any indication to the contrary, the patient would consent to the treatment. Thus, we assume even without a positive statement to this effect, that a person would consent to undergo invasive surgery in order to prolong his or her life. Potential organ recipients are usually in a position to communicate their willingness to undergo transplantation.[4] However, if it were the case that the operation that was to be carried out without express consent was an organ transplantation, the patient's best interests would ensure the transplant went ahead.

As a default assumption, it is clear that doctors, transplant managers and families would expect a patient to permit a life-extending or life-improving transplant if it was in his or her clinical best interests. So, it is our assumption that most persons would, if their condition required it, be prepared to be recipients of organs. The analogous assumption, that most persons would if the circumstances arose, be prepared to donate organs, does not apparently hold: we are much more cautious about using organs in the absence of any positive evidence that the person had previously been willing to do so.

This asymmetry of inference results from the caution of families of potential donors and a failure to recognise the contingent interdependence of potential recipients and donors. It might be argued that there is no genuine interdependence between donors and recipients, for the donor is never dependent on the recipient and the recipient is totally reliant on the donor for the organ. However, there is a contingent interdependence between all persons prior to any particular person becoming identified as either a potential donor or a prospective recipient. An opting-out system recognises this interdependence. In the absence of a contrary declaration, an opting-out system assumes the consent of a person to donate and, at the same time, gives that person the right to be clinically and morally evaluated on equally favourable terms as any other potential recipients of an organ should he or she need an organ transplant. The recognition that access to potential benefits presupposes a preparedness to contribute gives us the justification for a general presumption of consent to organ donation, while the procedures for opting-out ensure the right to individual exception is protected.

Free-riding

Those persons who would be prepared to be organ recipients without the corresponding willingness to be organ donors are free-riders in the system, predisposed to benefit without ever consenting to contribute. The decision to opt-out from potential organ donation, if made by someone who would accept an organ transplant, is an overt expression of that individual's preparedness to be a free-rider. While the liberal state and society must allow this position to be held, the free-rider must accept the moral and practical consequences of the position. The practical consequences of opting-out would entail that the person who is a free-rider is liable to be discriminated against in the allocation of organs to recipients.

Resource allocation in medicine is an unavoidable aspect of management in hospitals. The problem is at its most difficult when resources are scarce; or their utilisation is expensive; or the consequences of lack are serious; or all three, as is the case with organ transplantation.[5] In such cases, where a limited resource must be allocated to someone, it seems reasonable that the free-rider should be penalised for his or her uncharitable views concerning his or her own potential contribution. Free-riding would seem to be possible in other areas of medicine, for example, in blood donation, although the relative availability of blood products makes the application of the concept unnecessary. Free-riding has also raised moral questions in other areas of life, for example non-union members who gain a union-procured pay increase. However, the scarcity of organs for transplantation and the lack of currently viable alternatives such as artificial organs or interspecies donation[6] make the application of free-riding criteria appropriate in this area.

Doctors are trained in making and balancing clinical judgments, and taking free-riding into account must only be contemplated after it has been established that the situation is clinically neutral ie where there is no medical or surgical advantage to be gained by transplanting into one potential recipient rather than another. Considering whether a patient is a free-rider adds a moral element to the clinical judgment of the doctor, the result of which may be the withholding of treatment from that individual. This would seem to be in contravention of standard medical ethics that seek to exclude moral judgments such as "desert" from clinical decisions and almost certainly doctors would be reluctant to take sole responsibility for such ethically grounded decisions. However, in cases where a resource is extremely limited, it is sometimes appropriate for moral criteria, such as free-riding, to be used to differentiate between patients.

It might be thought that there would be a dilemma when the probability of the success of a transplant into a person who had been predisposed to donate, the "generous recipient", is low while the likelihood of a successful outcome for the person who has opted-out of donation, the "selfish recipient",[7] is high. In all cases it is the clinical decision that must take priority on utilitarian grounds, as presenting less chance of the resource being wasted in an adverse clinical outcome such as organ rejection. In these cases, where the "selfish recipient" would benefit over the "generous recipient", the priority of the clinical judgment over the moral judgment might seem to undermine the point of using the concept of free-riding in the first place. Of course, the priority of the clinical over the moral may mean that in practice there is seldom or never a disadvantage as a consequence of free-riding. But the value of the concept of "free-riding" lies less in its application by doctors to specific cases than in the *political* possibilities it brings forward. Its usefulness lies in the fact that it promotes a discourse which leads to a greater acceptance of the presumption of consent and it may also make decisions easier for families of potential donors.

Essential interdependence

If it is agreed that most people would consent to benefiting from transplant technology and that free-riding is a morally precarious position to hold, it is possible to arouse people's awareness to the moral consequences of the stance which they are taking when they choose to opt-out. Where people still choose to opt-out knowing that this constitutes free-riding, they should be made aware that they may be disadvantaged in the future if they should ever become potential recipients of organs.[8] Such disadvantage counterbalances the unfairness of free-riding and since the decision as to who receives an organ will be clinically neutral, there can be no utilitarian argument against the application of the free-riding criterion. The organ to be transplanted goes, other things being equal, to the person who has not declined to donate organs him/herself. How many people would be content to be free-riders when the question of organ donation is put in these terms is not known. What is likely, however, is that once made explicit the concept of "free-riding" will stimulate discussion and bring the essential interdependence of potential organ recipients and donors to the forefront of public debates on organ donation.

The person who chooses to opt-out must consider his or her willingness to be a recipient of an organ, and must recognise the inevitable consequence that any willingness entails, that of free-riding. Publicity that promotes the idea that an opted-out person may be less likely to receive a transplant if he or she ever needs one, forces opters-out to reconsider their own moral standards. It is hoped that the unease that will be felt when opting-out is acknowledged as being a form

of free-riding will have the consequence that few people will choose to opt-out. As well, knowledge of the moral and practical consequences for someone who chooses to opt-out of organ donation while not wanting to exclude him/herself from the benefit of a future transplant can be used to neutralise the difficulties of consent that appear to hinder the straightforward acceptance of opting-out systems. Where a person has not made a declaration stating that he or she wishes to opt-out, and where it is believed that he or she would not have refused the benefits of transplant technology for him or herself, it can safely be assumed that he or she would have consented to be a donor, given the charitable - and not unreasonable - assumption that this person is not a free-rider. Given this assumption, and the obligations which result from being a member of a community of interdependent potential donors and recipients, a decision that infers the consent of that person to donate organs is possible.

As well as deterring potential opters-out, wider knowledge of the concept of free-riding resolves some of the difficulties that families face when making decisions on behalf of their deceased relatives. The use of free-riding makes clear the links between the instinct to be charitable ie to donate, and a broader picture which includes a default assumption of self preservation, ie to receive. Thus, families who accept that their prematurely dead would have wished to continue living, and who believe that their relative was not a free-rider, might be satisfied that their relative would have consented to organ donation as part of this broader web of rights, duties, obligations and fairness. Similarly, in cases where a person would have been unable to make decisions due to youth or incompetence, the default assumption is that he or she would take an opportunity to improve and extend his or her life through transplantation if this were necessary, that he or she was not a free-rider, and therefore would not have chosen to opt-out.

Conceivably, it is a violation of the principle of consent to assume without evidence an altruistic motive to donate organs. It is not a violation of the principle of consent to pre-suppose self-interest, nor is it a violation of medical ethics to combine the concept of self-interest with concepts of interdependence and obligation. A system which relies on publicising the disadvantages that may be incurred by free-riders in order to increase the supply of potential donors demonstrates that tacitly agreeing to organ donation is, in part, an act of self-interest. The system must also have a default assumption that its citizens are *not* free-riders. This assumption can be made on at least three grounds: the empirical evidence of support for organ donation; the expectation that most people would naturally wish to avoid the disadvantages that might accrue from opting-out, and the conviction that many citizens recognise the mutual interdependence of themselves and their fellow citizens to be particularly close in the case of organ donation and as a result they are happy to accept their duty to be potential donors. If we accept these assumptions then we should be able to support the introduction of an opting-out system.

The conjunction of tacit consent with a free-riding rationale must be used with caution. It is not difficult to see how this argument could be extended to the use of other body parts in research or treatment. It is important to stress that the free-riding distinction should only be used in situations that are clinically neutral and that its principal function is in the political arena, in making clear the interdependence of all persons as potential organ donors or organ recipients. Awareness of free-riding forces "selfish" opters-out to recognise the consequences of their choice; moral impropriety and the possibility of disadvantage, should the situation of their own need ever arise.

Prior volunteers only - Jarvis's modest proposal

A comparable proposal to increase the availability of organs by appealing to self-interest and penalising those who withhold consent to post-mortem donation was made recently by Jarvis.[9] He puts forward what he terms a "modest proposal" that advocates the rationing of organs by limiting transplantation to those who had previously consented to be donors themselves should the situation arise. Put negatively, those who do not opt-in to potential donation on the Jarvis scheme are disqualified from the possibility of a transplant or placed behind those who have opted-in.[10] As has been noted by Gillon,[11] this proposal blocks an individual's access to a particular treatment on the basis of assumed moral blameworthiness. This is a particularly harsh and final punishment for what may, in many cases, be inaction rather than a considered decision never to donate. Given the very low probability that an individual will become a candidate either for donation or receipt of organs, opting-in can hardly be seen as compelling or urgent, especially for young, healthy people. The Jarvis proposal creates the opposite problem to that of opting-out systems, ie how could one ever know that a person had really chosen to reject potential donation rather than been merely negligent? Although opting-in to potential donation

(with the consequence that one also opts-in to potential receipt) seems like a one-off insurance policy with no (or an insubstantial) premium, it is arguable whether the take-up of this type of insurance will be all that much higher than is the carrying of donor cards at the present time.

As Jarvis accepts, the proposal encounters other problems, such as obtaining the consent of children and the inadequately autonomous. He suggests excluding these groups from the scheme, thereby leaving unresolved a significant practical problem concerning the transplantation of organs into children who, because of their size, can often only utilise organs donated by other children. As Gillon notes, there are ways to overcome this problem: registration of consent by parents of young children, and allowing health workers and others to make decisions on behalf of mentally impaired people.[12] However, as Gillon's suggestion illustrates, accurately to register the entire population of potential organ donors (which would surely be impossible anyway) the Jarvis proposal would require a large bureaucratic structure to administer it. This would hardly seem cost-effective when viewed against the comparatively small number of persons who are candidates for organ donation each year. In addition, as organs are not uncommonly transported long distances for transplantation into suitable recipients, the exercise would have to cover all those countries that share data and collaborate in the matching of recipients with available organs. In this respect at least, the Jarvis proposal is far from "modest".

Instead of a complicated and expensive registration scheme, it is much more efficient to involve only those persons for whom organ donation is an issue, ie the families of brain stem dead patients. The Jarvis proposal is averse to the current practice of asking families for their consent. Presumably, on the Jarvis scheme doctors would have to forgo the removal of organs in those cases where the deceased had not opted-in, even when the families know that the deceased would have consented. It is known that there are wide variations in the response of the general public to low-probability risk.[13] If, as seems possible given current opting-in schemes, there is a low level of registration, the presumption that this failure to opt-in represents strongly held wishes not to donate may in fact have an effect contrary to that which Jarvis intends, ie a reduction in the number of available organs. With no scope for a decision to be taken by the family of the deceased this could effectively reduce the potential donor population rather than increase it.

However, the most unsatisfactory consequence of the Jarvis proposal would be the wastage of organs as a result of the ineligibility of a suitable recipient. The Jarvis proposal assumes that the matching of organs and donors is straightforward but, unfortunately, this is rarely the case. Not every organ that becomes available suits the needs of several potential recipients, and the Jarvis proposal, which has the consequence of excluding suitable potential recipients from the list of those eligible to receive an organ, runs the risk of wasting the very resource the availability of which he is trying to increase. This proposal may increase the numbers of those who have made clear their willingness to donate organs in the event of their death but it has the effect of reducing the demand for donor organs artificially, by excluding certain people from the pool of potential recipients, and possibly wasting organs as a result. Even in the less extreme version of Jarvis's proposal, where those who have not opted-in are placed at the end of the queue, time constraints in the matching and transportation of organs make this procedure unnecessarily risky.

The moral element in transplant decisions cannot be denied. Decisions about rationing and the quality of a person's life are increasingly a part of modern medical practice, for example in the refusal to operate on a cigarette smoker or the decision not to administer life-extending treatment to a profoundly ill neonate. Decisions that are justified on the basis of clinical outcome may disguise an underlying ethical determination of the most worthy patient as well as a utilitarian calculation as to the best use of resources. So, the potential for the moral as well as clinical ordering of potential transplant recipients, however difficult, must be acknowledged. Unfortunately, the Jarvis proposal fails to provide a method for safely discriminating on moral grounds and presents serious practical problems in its implementation.

Conclusion

A system of opting-out is the most efficient form of obtaining consent for the use of organs in transplantation. The obstacle of tacit consent is reduced by the belief that the majority of people would wish to benefit from the technology if they needed it and are not free-riders. As a result, a donor's prior wishes cannot be violated by the donation of his or her organs unless it is known that he or she would not have wished to receive (or donate) organs; or if he or she was known to be a free-rider with respect to transplantation and to understand the potentially detrimental consequences of this position.

In order to secure consent, families must be satisfied that their deceased relative would have taken the decision to donate. Families should be comforted by the knowledge that it is both empirically and morally likely that the deceased would have chosen to donate organs. Reaching this conclusion is made easier for the families within an opting-out system where the deceased has given no evidence of a reluctance to donate, and where it is agreed that the deceased was not a free-rider. Such a system provides a minimally administered means of enabling the relatives of brain stem dead patients to take decisions to donate on behalf of their deceased and be confident in those decisions.

Stephanie Eaton, BA, MSc, is a PhD student at the Centre for Law and Society, University of Edinburgh, Edinburgh.

References

1 In practice many countries with opting-out systems still seek to obtain the authorisation of relatives for the use of organs for transplantation. See Haag BW, Stuart FP. The organ donor: brain death, selection criteria, supply and demand. In: Flye MW, ed. *Principles of organ transplantation.* Philadelphia: W B Saunders Company, 1989: 185.

2 See Kittur DS, Hogan MM, Thukral VK, McGaw LJ, Alexander JW. Incentives for organ donation? *Lancet* 1991;338: 1441 who report that organ donation in Belgium has increased by 119% in the three years since opting-out legislation was introduced.

3 West R. *Organ transplantation.* London: Office of Health Economics, 1991:10.

4 For altruistic reasons some potential recipients may prefer to see donated organs go to younger people or to those with dependants and there are, of course, some religious groups who do not accept transplantation.

5 Although transplantation is obviously an expensive medical treatment, it has been noted that over a period of some years, renal transplantation is more economical than continued dialysis. See also reference 3: 25.

6 The presumed consent implicit in opting-out systems may also facilitate the speedier recovery of organs from deceased persons, reducing the demand for elective ventilation of cadavers with the additional ethical doubts that this procedure raises.

7 The use of the terms "generous" and "selfish" are of course, value-laden, and oversimplify the motives behind a decision to donate or to refrain from donation. These terms are intended here as a shorthand and to give the flavour of the moral argument.

8 In the hypothetical case of someone who has opted-out and then becomes aware that he/she needs a transplant it is, of course, possible for that person to "change his/her mind" but the changed circumstances will leave some doubt as to the aetiology of the decision. In any case, publicity of such cases may serve to discourage other potential opters-out.

9 Jarvis R. Join the club: a modest proposal to increase availability of donor organs. *Journal of Medical Ethics* 1995;21:199-204.

10 Only free-riders would be penalised on the perfectly implemented Jarvis proposal as those who refused to donate on, for example religious grounds, would presumably also refuse to accept organs in transplantation.

11 Gillon R. On giving preference to prior volunteers when allocating organs for transplant [editorial]. *Journal of Medical Ethics* 1995;21:195-6.

12 See Reference 11: 195.

13 Adams J. *Risk.* London: University College London Press, 1995.

[27]

The Moral Status of Preferences for Directed Donation: Who Should Decide Who Gets Transplantable Organs?

RACHEL A. ANKENY

Introduction

Bioethics has entered a new era: as many commentators have noted, the familiar mantra of autonomy, beneficence, nonmaleficence, and justice has proven to be an overly simplistic framework for understanding problems that arise in modern medicine, particularly at the intersection of public policy and individual preferences. A tradition of liberal pluralism grounds respect for individual preferences and affirmation of competing conceptions of the good. But we struggle to maintain (or at times explicitly reject) this tradition in the face of individual preferences that we find distasteful, suspect, or even repugnant, especially where the broader social good or respect for equality is at stake. Directed donation presents us with such a dilemma: can we uphold the right of self-determination through respect of individual preferences regarding disposition of transplantable organs[1] while at the same time maintaining an allocation system that reflects values of equity and justice claimed to underlie the socially negotiated practice of transplantation?[2] Or are some preferences simply to be deemed unethical and not respected, even if that leads to a reduction in the number of transplantable organs available and to an apparent disregard for the autonomous decisions of the recently deceased?

Directed donation occurs when a person requests that transplantable organs be given to a particular candidate or class of candidates after his or her death.[3] Informal reports indicate that such requests occur fairly infrequently, although increased public education about organ donation and protocols such as controlled nonheartbeating organ donation (NHBOD) could result in more consideration about who specifically might be benefited by a gift of transplantable organs.[4] More importantly, directed donation prompts reflection on the complex of principles underlying the policies inherent in the current organ-donation system and its historical development in the United States.

I present an argument against permitting most forms of directed donation, focusing on utilitarian justifications for policies on directed donation because these are the most common forms of argument utilized in this debate.[5] Based on a moral framework drawn from political philosophy and moral theory

Thanks to Lisa Parker, Joel Frader, audiences at the III World Congress of Bioethics, San Francisco, California, November 1996, and the Department of Philosophy at Macquarie University, Sydney, Australia, September 1999, and the editors of this special issue for comments on earlier versions of this paper. I am also grateful to members of the UPMC cardiopulmonary transplant team for numerous opportunities to discuss and examine ethical issues in transplantation. All responsibility for content is strictly my own.

Rachel A. Ankeny

regarding preferences, I provide a taxonomy of impermissible (and limited permissible) instances of directed donation given the current structure of the U.S. organ-allocation system overseen by the United Network for Organ Sharing (UNOS).[6] The implications of my argument for the existing organ-allocation system as overseen by UNOS also are briefly explored, particularly regarding prioritization of local candidates and the effects of geography on organ distribution.

Background

What are the general principles underlying UNOS policies regarding allocation of donated cadaveric organs? When a cadaveric organ is donated, it is offered first to the person who is listed at a transplant center in the local area who is a match based on biological characteristics and who fulfills some combination of other attributes (e.g., most amount of waiting time, urgency for some organ types, and so on), with an exception being perfectly matched kidneys.[7] If there is no one waiting in the local area, then the organ is offered based on the same matching principles in the region (which generally is defined historically by the existence of an organ procurement organization [OPO]), then nationally.[8] With regard specifically to directed donation, the UNOS board approved a statement in accordance with a recommendation by its ethics committee that "donation of organs in a manner which discriminates for or against a class of people based on race, national origin, religion, gender, or similar characteristics is unethical and may not ethically be accepted by UNOS members or transplant professionals."[9] However, it is difficult to determine whether such a recommendation is enforceable. Currently, OPOs respond differently to directed donation requests. A few states have prohibited directed donation, but most of these have not explicitly changed their donation laws, which reflect the Uniform Anatomical Gift Act (UAGA), which allows directed donation (section 4[c]). Although several states have deleted references to directed donation, their laws leave it unclear whether it is not permissible or simply not encouraged. Most importantly, particularly given the range of laws and public opinion on the subject, the moral reasoning underlying the UNOS policy has not been provided.

Many instances of directed donation intuitively seem unproblematic to us. Consider the following: "A daughter's last gift: A young woman killed in a car accident saves her father's life by donating her heart for a transplant."[10] Clearly tragic, but unethical? How about "Transplant of son's eye gives sight to mother"?[11] These donation decisions closely parallel the sorts of decisions made by living organ donors. Perhaps if all instances of directed donation were of this sort, our moral sensors would not go off.

Concerns are immediately raised by other sorts of requests regarding directed donation, especially where it seems that the media is involved in promoting the cause of a particular waiting transplant candidate or where a family aggressively seeks a donor by publicly stressing that their family member is particularly needy. For instance, an example of what might be called "media abetted" allocation occurred when a family directed donation of their son's heart to a teenager waiting in St. Louis about whom they read in their local paper. They reportedly selected him from among a group of young people in the same hospital waiting for heart transplants, because they were from the same town as the recipient.[12] In this class of cases, although the situations are indeed tragic

The Moral Status of Directed Donation

and there does not seem to be anything patently discriminatory about donors or their families directing donation of transplantable organs, it at least smacks of "gaming the system." It is also interesting to note that the rhetoric surrounding many such cases seems to imply that certain candidates are in some way more deserving that others, or are "ethically special" in some way that make a personal appeal for a directed donation appropriate.[13]

A third class of cases arises when donors or their families direct organ donations toward or away from certain groups. A Florida newspaper recounted the story of a family who agreed to donate their son's organs, but only if they went to people who were White like their son, reportedly in part because the man had been an active member of a White supremacist group.[14] This case led to a legislative ban in the state of Florida on directed donation to particular groups.[15] The article also recounts that a Nazi concentration camp survivor stipulated that none of her organs could go to people of German descent. These sorts of cases are more troubling to us and motivate an investigation of whether our moral intuitions can be grounded in a more adequate ethical framework through an examination of arguments regarding directed donation in the current bioethics literature.

Directed Donation Issues

Organs as Social Goods?

Eike-Hennner Kluge has argued that because organ donation must occur in a heavily institutionalized and social context, the gift of a donated cadaveric organ is "not complete within itself."[16] Thus, because the process requires people other than donors and recipients for the procedure to occur and for the gift to gain its meaning and significance, the organ that as bodily tissue was merely a private good becomes a social good when it is a donated organ. Although it is clear that organ donation has a social character and there is a symbolic change of meaning that occurs when mere flesh becomes donated organ,[17] this argument fails to capture some of the salient facets of the situation. As a result, it provides a weak justification for prohibition of most forms of directed donation, particularly against utilitarian arguments in favor of directed donation to be described later. First, note that the social nature of organ donation is a contingent phenomenon, reflecting our current allocation system. Some economists argue that whether goods are public or private depends on the empirical question of how they are best marketed, which leaves most goods (including transplantable organs, it could be argued) in the realm of "ambiguous goods."[18] Presumably, those in favor of a wholly or partially commercialized system for procurement and distribution of transplantable organs would agree.[19] More importantly, many undertakings are social—not only because they are socially embedded but also because they require others in order to attain completion—but do not necessarily result in the creation of social resources. An example is the bequest of material possessions after death via a socially recognized and enforced document such as a will. Directed blood donation is currently permitted (and encouraged) in many places. Although outsiders are required to draw, store, and transport the blood products, individuals' desires to have blood from members of their family or community and to donate blood directly to particular individuals in need are often respected.[20]

Rachel A. Ankeny

Although there may be other reasons not to allow directed blood donation (e.g., to reduce perpetuation of misconceptions about "clean blood" and blood-borne disease transmission, especially given the extra costs involved in directed donation), Kluge's argument based on the creation of social goods does not engage or address the most relevant ethical considerations.

Race-Based Allocation of Organs?

In light of evidence that Blacks on U.S. kidney waiting lists wait almost twice as long as Whites,[21] even when the data are controlled for medical and geographic factors, Wayne B. Arnason has argued in favor of a policy experiment that would match Black donor kidneys with Black recipients based on standardized UNOS criteria but without consideration of waiting time, except in cases of Black-Black recipient ties. He claims that "the prospect of a black donor's kidney finding its way into the body of a black recipient would *remove a disincentive* for black donors,"[22] while rejecting the idea that some form of "affirmative action" program for prospective Black recipients could be guaranteed to provide an incentive for increased donation given the currently available empirical evidence.[23]

Arnason's argument is questionable for several reasons. First, he claims that there are exceptions to the impartial, condition-specific allocation system, and he relies on these as precedents for using allocation principles other than the point system for allocation; his examples include the permissibility of live, emotionally related donation, and the prohibition of exportation of organs outside of the United States and Canada. The former consideration will be discussed below, but suffice to say that the paradigm of living donation circumscribes a very specific class of permissible instances of directed donation.[24] The latter consideration theoretically is not an instance of *who* receives the organs (i.e., whether a donation is directed away from or toward a particular individual or group) because foreign nationals can be put on the UNOS transplant waiting list so long as they are listed via a U.S. transplant center, but *where* the transplant occurs. Second, his policy experiment relies on an unexplicated notion of how "race" would be determined, particularly problematic because an adequate scientifically or socially based concept of race has proven notoriously difficult or impossible to define.

Motivating Donors through Directed Donation

Robert M. Sade recently has proposed a system for distribution of organs for transplantation, which he calls the Selection of Potential Recipients of Transplants (SPRT).[25] This system would allow donors or relatives of a medically suitable donor to choose a specific individual recipient or category of recipients to receive the donated organ(s), which he believes would reconnect the donor and the recipient, thus increasing donation by emphasizing the personal stake of the donor and/or the donor's family in the donation process. As he admits, whether SPRT actually would result in an increase in organ donation is an empirical question best answered through pilot studies. But the form of his argument is of most interest because it relies largely on a utilitarian justification. He claims that such a system would maximize benefits—in this case, defined as the number of organs available for transplant together with recog-

The Moral Status of Directed Donation

nition and advancement of "personal values" of recipients—while minimizing harms, among which he includes disincentives to organ donation, including distrust of the current system. Perhaps at best this proposal might help to reinstate a broader idea of community that seems currently lacking due to this distrust and places us on difficult moral ground for making judgments about an individual's willingness to donate. For as Richard Rorty has put it in a different context, "One cannot be irresponsible toward a community of which one does not think of oneself as a member."[26]

Karen A. Korzick and Peter B. Terry briefly criticize Sade's proposal against the background of various theories of distributive justice. However, they fail to provide an argument that the principle of justice should be the most relevant principle to consider when establishing policies for transplantation, particularly given Sade's concern about distrust and lack of a unified community.[27] They also claim that under a system of utilitarian distributive justice, there can be no claims to individual rights. However, preference utilitarians would assert that justice in distribution consists in maximizing the extent to which people have what they prefer or want, even if the preferences of some fail to be satisfied. Sade (and some utilitarians) also could respond by claiming that, although individual rights do not count qua individual rights, fostering a political atmosphere that supports such rights often contributes to an overall maximization of benefit as compared to harm. Sade's proposal leaves us with the currently unanswerable empirical question of what would happen under a directed donation scheme such as SPRT; in other words, whether benefit indeed would be maximized.

Of particular concern for making the judgment about degree of benefit is whether we consider these types of preferences to be personal (i.e., preferences focused on the individual's own enjoyment of a good or an opportunity, say to express his wishes or to be memorialized after death) or external (i.e., preferences for the assignment of goods or opportunities toward or away from others). As Ronald Dworkin has argued, this distinction is all important to the utilitarian argument because a truly utilitarian distribution is also egalitarian and observes strict impartiality; thus external preferences that rely on political theories that are contrary to utilitarianism corrupt it.[28] If such external preferences are allowed to be decisive in a policy decision (such as one about the permissibility of directed donation), Dworkin claims, the fact that the policy makes a community better off in the utilitarian sense is no longer an adequate justification for disadvantaging some who should be treated as equals. Thus Dworkin's argument is extremely useful in examining the case at hand, where utilitarian justifications are being used for policy decisions, complex preferences are at issue, and particular individuals (or classes of individuals) seem to be jumping the queue, violating basic principles of equity.[29] Therefore, the more interesting philosophical questions are how to understand people's preferences as expressions of their conceptions of the good and when such conceptions should be accommodated, particularly in cases where it is difficult to disentangle personal and external preferences.

Permissible Preferences and Political Theory

Returning to the main question: how should the organ allocation system be structured to accommodate (or rule out) preferences regarding the characteris-

Rachel A. Ankeny

tics or identity of an anticipated recipient of donated organs? To maintain or increase donation rates and public support for the transplantation process, it is essential to prioritize focus on the process that has established and oversees ongoing alterations in the rules governing the organ distribution system. An assumption underlying the UNOS policies is that persons may decline to donate if they perceive that the allocation system is not equitable or if persons in similar circumstances such as themselves may not be treated equitably in the allocation system. But how equity is to be defined is at least partially an empirical issue. Instances of partiality occur under the current system but are substantiated by largely, though not universally, shared principles concerning the appropriateness of such partiality. For example, all medical criteria for distributing donated cadaveric organs are in fact instances of partiality: they allow preference of one candidate over another based on factors that have been to a certain extent negotiated and codified in UNOS allocation policy.

Similarly, our moral intuitions suggest that donation to a particular emotionally or biologically related person is permissible, and even admirable. After all, when we permit living donation, we are in fact indirectly endorsing a form of directed donation. Therefore, it is inconsistent not to permit such donation following death, so long as there is a relationship between the individuals (along with criteria for assessing such a relationship, etc.).[30] To put it in utilitarian terms, the preference being expressed is a personal one, and it does not unduly corrupt the egalitarian basis of utilitarianism, because we in fact generally deem such a preference to be appropriate. In fact, we allow directed living donation precisely because of the partiality on the part of the donor for the recipient, which in turn engenders benefits to both parties because the donor serves his or her own interests (particularly if these interests are defined as including broader familial interests) by helping to save the life of a related other. Thus, cadaveric directed donations should be permissible provided that the recipient and donor are emotionally related.

Notice that merely coming to care about a potential recipient whom you see night after night on the local news does not count as a morally significant emotional relationship, or to put it in a slightly different way, does not provide grounds for appropriate partiality. Given that media access is not uniform, it is not appropriate to allow unequal access to publicity to result in unequal access to transplantable organs. The emotional appeal of those needing organ transplantation should be employed to prompt general interest in organ donation. To permit especially attractive (typically young, photogenic) potential recipients or VIPs to solicit or attract directed donors (and thus jump the queue) would unfairly disadvantage those who might be viewed in the glare of the cameras as less attractive candidates. In particular, it does not have the compensating ethical advantage that the emotionally related case does, because the emotionally related person's interests and preferences are directly and personally tied to the welfare of the potential recipient.

However, it is not so clear whether we should endorse living donation toward or away from certain groups. Our intuitions suggest that it is morally reprehensible, or at least suspect, to be willing to donate but refuse to allow the organ to go to members of a particular group, for example due to ageism, racism, sexism, religious or ethnic hatred, or because of perceptions about some diseases being self-induced. Dworkin's discussion of external preferences is particularly helpful here; suppose there is a situation where many individuals

The Moral Status of Directed Donation

who are racists express preferences that scarce medical resources be directed to a White man who needs them rather than to a Black man who needs them more (and that these individuals do not themselves need the resources, hence the preferences are not personal). As he states, "If utilitarianism counts these political preferences at face value, then it will be, from the standpoint of personal preferences, self-defeating, because the distribution of medicine will then not be, from that standpoint, utilitarian at all."[31]

It is less obvious how to articulate the moral ground for our different intuitions about honoring refusals of donation to members of a particular group versus honoring positive directed donations (e.g., choosing to donate to members of one's church or sorority, an extended family member, or someone in the local community), particularly when such preferences seem in part to be an expression of individual identity and a strong association with a particular group. It is at this point that political theory addressing mixed preferences (those that represent an intermingling of external and personal preferences) and respect for them within a broader sociopolitical structure becomes most relevant. In an article focused on the phenomenon of endogenous preferences, preferences that seem to adapt to a wide range of factors including sociopolitical and cultural context, legal and social rules, current information available, past choices, and so on, Cass R. Sunstein notes that "[i]t is one thing to affirm competing conceptions of the good; it is a quite another to suggest that political outcomes must generally be justified by or even should always respect, private preferences."[32] He argues that constraints on respecting preferences are appropriate even when the preferences reflect collective judgments (1) when the choice that would be eliminated by respecting the preference has some special character and especially if it is a part of deliberative democracy itself; (2) when the collective desires or preferences are objectionable or a product of unjust background conditions; and/or (3) if the collective preferences reflect a special weakness on the part of the majority. Thus directed donation to people who are not members of a particular group, for example, donation by a KKK member to "anyone but a Black or a Jew," should be impermissible. Such donations exhibit morally suspect or reprehensible value commitments and beliefs (what could be termed "inappropriate partiality") that could be argued to be objectionable in themselves, or at least a product of unjust background conditions. In themselves, such motivations exhibit a failure to respect individuals as equals, as worthy of equal respect and dignity, which it can be argued undermines the basis of utilitarianism. Permitting members of some groups to be passed over because of donor preferences and group affiliations would be unfair because it is not a case where personal or emotional ties or preferences trump our typical concerns about partiality, and hence the compensating ethical advantage discussed earlier is lacking. Such practices would likely exacerbate existing inequalities that could be viewed as part of the unjust background conditions against which these preferences have been formed, specifically in this case the late referral of members of minorities for healthcare and especially for transplantation.

So what are we to do about positive directed donation to members of a group, for example members of my faith, community, ethnic group, and so on? Respect for self-determination, individual values, expression of preferences, and partiality might suggest that such directed donation should be permissible.

Rachel A. Ankeny

However, for similar reasons to those suggesting it should be impermissible to allow directed donation away from certain people or classes of people, it should be impermissible to donate only to members of a particular group. If the ties of group relationship are sufficiently strong as to form the basis of friendship, love, or other emotional relation (i.e., appropriate partiality), then the prospective donor could presumably name the prospective recipient in his or her donor card. If the ties are not so strong and so personalized, then from the perspective of preserving a fair organ-allocation system and maintaining impartiality, donation to members of one group may be viewed merely as a surrogate for refusal of donation to another. In more formal philosophical terms, associational preferences are particularly dangerous, given that they often reflect personal preferences that are parasitic on external preferences, particularly in cases affected by prejudice.[33]

Geography and Organ Distribution

Against the background of this discussion, consider the general UNOS cadaveric organ allocation policies. Notice that any "locals first" policy relies, in part, on the beliefs that (1) it is permissible (in the sense of being morally appropriate) to prefer to donate to members of your local community, and (2) people in fact prefer to donate locally. This line of reasoning, among others, was cited by UNOS in their 1991 report on the (lack of) feasibility of a national waiting list.[34] Relatedly, the policy statement indicated that many transplant professionals believe that more organs are donated for transplantation when organs are kept locally, and it might be the case that retaining organs locally encourages professionals to request donation more frequently.[35] It is not clear what public opinion actually concerning this question is; at least one survey found that 66% of people who had not yet signed donor cards would be more strongly influenced to become a donor by a policy that favored national distribution, and an OPTN poll in 1990 showed that over 75% of respondents disagreed with the statement that "donor organs should go to someone in the area where the donor lived."[36] Furthermore, offering organs locally means offering organs to those listed at local programs who in fact are not necessarily residents of the local community, given that many individuals are listed at programs not proximate to their residences and larger transplant centers attract candidates from a wide geographical area.

Ironically, the insight that UNOS relies on to justify its local rule may be used to undermine it. Such a local rule can only be ethically justified if it is assumed that each locality will be inclined, and roughly equally inclined, to look after its own members; that is, to exhibit partiality toward those listed at a local transplant center. Otherwise, access to a resource would depend on where one is lucky or savvy enough to be listed as a transplant candidate. But it is clear that there are differential donation rates around the United States, and greatly divergent densities of populations of candidates awaiting transplant in various regions.[37] Thinking about directed donation in terms of partiality and permissible preferences leads to the conclusion that so long as preservation or ischemic time is not at issue, any form of a "locals first" policy is ethically flawed because it assumes preference of donation to a particular group (i.e., local candidates), a conclusion that is neither empirically justified nor ethically grounded in terms of permissible partiality.

The Moral Status of Directed Donation

Conclusions

Directed donation presents us with a classic dilemma—the clash of individual preferences and the right of self-determination with the values of equity and justice reflected in our public policies. I have provided an argument against permitting most forms of directed donation using a utilitarian justification, against a moral framework drawn from political philosophy and moral theory regarding preferences. However, suppose that not allowing directed donation leads to a decrease in the overall number of organs donated. Given that we are working within a utilitarian framework, we must consider the following question: what good can be supposed to arise from instituting and enforcing such a limiting policy? This question leads to a rather unexpected conclusion: not that we should consider allowing directed or otherwise restricted organ donations in all cases, but instead that the process surrounding policy development in transplantation must be more open for public scrutiny.[38] It is not enough to institute rules, however fair they may be. Morally adequate rationalizations for rules must also be formulated, debated, and well publicized. Such a process may have the compensating advantage of actually influencing and transforming people's preferences over the longer run, a goal that is claimed by some to be at the core of any political process:

> ... over time one will in fact come to be swayed by considerations about the common good ... one would have to invoke the power of reason to break down prejudice and selfishness. By speaking in the voice of reason, one also exposes oneself to reason. To sum up, then, the conceptual impossibility of expressing selfish arguments in public debate, and the psychological difficulty of expressing other-regarding preferences without coming to acquire them, jointly bring it about that public discussions lead to realization of the common good.[39]

And as much as it is a medical process, so too is transplantation a sociopolitical one that needs to reinstate the common good firmly at its core.

Notes

1. For a brief argument in favor of allowing directed donation to particular individuals on the basis of donor autonomy, see: Fox MD. When an organ donor names the recipient. *American Journal of Nursing* 1996;96:68.
2. United Network for Organ Sharing. The UNOS statement of principles and objective of equitable organ allocation. *UNOS Update* Aug 1994:20–38. A summary of UNOS policies is available at: http://www.unos.org
3. For the purposes of this paper, I assume that the desire to make a directed donation is articulated by the prospective donor prior to death on a donor card or in some other manner, or is expressed by his or her family based on good evidence that the directed donation reflects the decedent's prior preferences. Hence I focus on preferences that seem to be objectionable not because of their origin (i.e., not out of concern that they have arisen nonautonomously or under inappropriate coercive influences) but on the more controversial category of preferences that seem to be problematic because of their content. This taxonomy is clearly articulated by Jon Elster in his *Sour Grapes: Studies in the Subversion of Rationality*. London/New York: Cambridge University Press, 1983:22.
4. Thanks to Lisa Parker for making this point. On NHBOD, see: Arnold RM, Younger SY, Schapiro R, Spicer CM, eds. *Procuring Organs for Transplant: The Debate over Non-Heart-Beating*

Rachel A. Ankeny

Cadaver Protocols. Baltimore: Johns Hopkins University Press, 1995; Institute of Medicine. *Non-Heart-Beating Organ Transplantation: Medical and Ethical Issues in Procurement.* Washington, D.C.: National Academy Press, 1997.

5. I do not address the wide array of nonutilitarian arguments (e.g., libertarian or rights-based justifications) for directed donation because most literature in favor of directed donation takes utilitarianism as its main defense. I also do not address the responsibilities or moral authority of healthcare professionals or individual donors at stake in directed donation, taking policy as my primary level of focus, though fairly obvious implications for these follow from my argument.

6. This paper does not attempt to engage the issue of whether transplantation should in fact be a healthcare priority, and therefore the question of whether the current organ supply is indeed a "shortage" goes unexamined. For criticisms of this assumption, see: Fox RC. An ignoble form of cannibalism: reflections on the Pittsburgh protocol for procuring organs from non-heart-beating cadavers. *Kennedy Institute of Ethics Journal* 1993;3:231–40; Holmes HB. Closing the gaps: an imperative for feminist bioethics. In: Donchin A, Purdy LM, eds. *Embodying Bioethics: Recent Feminist Advances.* Lanham, Md.: Rowman & Littlefield, 1999:45–64.

7. UNOS Policies, section 3.3, May 1988. A long-debated rule of the Department of Health and Human Services (DHHS) became effective March 16, 2000, which mandates organ distribution based on medical urgency without regard to location of organs/candidates (see DHHS 42 CFR Part 121, *Federal Register* 22 Mar 2000;65:15252). Also see, for example: HHS amends organ donor rules in face of criticism. *Washington Post* 19 Oct 1999:A7. However the actual policies to be implemented continue to be negotiated by the DHHS together with representatives from UNOS and the Institute of Medicine (IOM). See also note 2, UNOS 1994.

8. This system is based the assumption that it is optimal not to transport cadaveric organs in order to reduce ischemic time and thus to reduce organ damage and waste. On debates surrounding appropriate ischemic time and their implications for transplant policy, see: Ankeny RA. Multiple listing: autonomy unbounded or a reasonable solution in light of organ scarcity? *Cambridge Quarterly of Healthcare Ethics* 1999;8:330–9.

9. See *UNOS Update* 1994,10:9. Also see note 2, UNOS 1994.

10. Hull JD. A daughter's last gift: C. Szuber receives heart of his daughter in a transplant operation. *Time Magazine* 5 Sep 1994:45; Father receives heart transplant from daughter. *New York Times* 26 Aug 1994:A14.

11. *New York Times* 26 Mar 1994:A27.

12. Sauerwein K. Family selects heart recipient, raises issues. *St. Louis Post-Dispatch* 1 May 1996:A1; Librach PB. Five youths here in need of heart transplants: "We've never had that many," doctor says. *St. Louis Post-Dispatch* 19 Apr 1996:A1. For an early article on the role of the media, see: Gunby P. Media-abetted liver transplants raise questions of "equity and decency." *JAMA* 1983;249:1973–82.

13. For difficulties presented by these types of cases, see: Kluge E-H. Designated organ donation: private choice in social context. *Hastings Center Report* 1989;19:10–6.

14. Testerman J. Should donors say who gets organs? *St. Petersburg Times* 9 Jan 1994:A1. Compare the case of a Palestinian family who donated their 9-year-old son's organs, after he was killed by a rubber-coated bullet in a West Bank protest, to needy candidates explicitly without regard to national origin or religion; Parents donate organs of son who was shot by Israeli soldier. *Buffalo News* 16 Nov 1997:A11.

15. In contrast, the law in the state of Louisiana recently was amended to explicitly allow directed donation, and it also requires that organs procured there to be given to recipients in the state unless the OPO cannot find a suitable in-state recipient, in which case organs can be sent to an out-of-state OPO with a reciprocal sharing arrangement (La. R.S. 17:2353, 1999); these laws seem to conflict with the DHHS' final rule mandating broader sharing of organs and accordingly several states requested injunctions against enforcement of the rule (see note 7). See also: Walters J. Whose organs are they? (legal battle over rights to donated organs). *Saturday Evening Post* 1998;270:70.

16. See note 13, Kluge 1989:10.

17. On the embeddedness of meaning in consumption and production of goods, see: Douglas M, Isherwood B. *The World of Goods*, rev. ed. London: Routledge, 1996. An extensive literature exists on the concept and related sociocultural dimensions of the body as property, which I do not explore here; in bioethics, see, for example: ten Have H, Welie J, eds. *Ownership of the Human Body: Philosophical Considerations on the Use of the Human Body and Its Parts in Healthcare.*

The Moral Status of Directed Donation

Dordrecht: Kluwer, 1998; Nelkin D, Andrews L. Homo economicus: commercialization of body tissue in the age of biotechnology. *Hastings Center Report* 1998;28:30–9; Marshall PA, Thomasma DC, Daar AS. Marketing human organs: the autonomy paradox. *Theoretical Medicine* 1996;17:1–18; Joralemon D. Organ wars: the battle for body parts. *Medical Anthropology Quarterly* 1995;9:335–56.

18. Head JG, Shoup CS. Public goods, private goods, and ambiguous goods. *Economic Journal* 1969;79:567–72. Cf. von Schubert H. Donated blood—gift or commodity? some economic and ethical considerations on voluntary vs. commercial donation of blood. *Social Science and Medicine* 1994;39:201–6, where it is argued that donated blood should be viewed as a "public good."

19. On this debate, see, for example: Hansman H. The economics and ethics of markets for human organs. *Journal of Health Politics, Policy, and Law* 1989;14:57–86; Peters D. A unified approach to organ donor recruitment, organ procurement, and distribution. *Journal of Law and Health* 1989;3:157–87; Barnett AH, Kaserman DL. The shortage of organs for transplantation: exploring the alternatives. *Issues in Law and Medicine* 1993;9:117–37.

20. Note that Kluge might also extend his argument to address directed blood donation and likely would allow donation within families, given that he does explicitly allow directed organ donation to a family member. On arguments for and against directed blood donation, see: Page PL. Controversies in transfusion medicine: directed blood donations (con). *Transfusion* 1989;29:65–8; Goldfinger D. Directed blood donations (pro). *Transfusion* 1989;29:70–4; Mayer K. The community: still the best source of blood. *Hastings Center Report* 1987;17:5–7; Goldfinger D. The case for directed blood donation. *Hastings Center Report* 1987;17:7–8; Reiss RF, Pindyck J. Reconciling patient wishes with public good. *Hastings Center Report* 1987;17:9–11. In the case of bone marrow donation, although there are often vigorous media campaigns on behalf of a particular waiting individual who has been unable to find an appropriate match within his or her family, volunteers typically have their typing information and willingness to donate recorded in a registry for future use, which could be claimed to negate most adverse effects of what began initially as a case of directed donation. Similarly, oftentimes not all blood designated for a particular recipient is used for his or her treatment and instead is redirected to other recipients in need.

21. For the most up-to-date report that shows roughly the same discrepancy, see: Department of Health and Human Services, Office of Inspector General. *Racial and Geographic Disparity in the Distribution of Organs for Transplantation.* Boston: Department of Health and Human Services, 1998.

22. Arnason WB. Directed donation: the relevance of race. *Hastings Center Report* 1991;21:13–9, 16. In the case of a tie based on medical criteria between a Black and a non-Black candidate, priority would be given to the Black candidate.

23. For a recent discussion of the continued barriers to organ donation and potential methods for increasing consent rates, see: Siminoff LA, Arnold RM. Increasing organ donation in the African-American community: altruism in the face of an untrustworthy system. *Annals of Internal Medicine* 1999;130:607–9.

24. For a literature review and discussion of factors involved in emotionally related donation, see, for example: Majeske RA, Parker LS, Frader J. In search of an ethical framework for consideration of decisions regarding live donation. In: B Spielman, ed. *Organ and Tissue Donation: Ethical, Legal, and Policy Issues.* Carbondale: Southern Illinois University Press, 1996:89–101. For a recent case that tests the limits of criteria for establishing relatedness occurred with families who met in the hospital waiting room, where one eventually directed donation of a family member's heart to a member of the other's family, see: Gilbert K. Hospital friendship and the gift of life. *Baltimore Sun* 10 Mar 1998;B1.

25. Sade RM. Cadaveric organ donation: rethinking donor motivation. *Archives of Internal Medicine* 1999;159:438–42.

26. Rorty R. Postmodernist bourgeois liberalism. *Journal of Philosophy* 1983;80:583–9, 583.

27. Korzick KA, Terry PB. Cadaveric organ donation: rethinking SPRT. *Archives of Internal Medicine* 1999;159:427–8.

28. Dworkin R. *Taking Rights Seriously.* London: Duckworth, 1977: 233–8. See also: Dworkin R. Liberalism. In: Hampshire S, ed. *Public and Private Morality.* London/New York: Cambridge University Press, 1978:113–43. Notice that by adopting this form of utilitarianism, I explicitly am rejecting forms of utilitarianism that do not assume a minimal amount of egalitarianism, and in turn reject what is commonly termed the "repugnant conclusion" (as coined by J. J. S.

Rachel A. Ankeny

Smart; e.g., see his contribution to *Utilitarianism: For and Against*. London/New York: Cambridge University Press, 1973). Furthermore, as Madison Powers has put it (Repugnant desires and the two-tier conception of utility. *Utilitas* 1994;6:171–6), it is clearly not the case that all other-regarding (external) preferences are morally repugnant or that all repugnant preferences are external preferences. My main focus here is on external preferences that can be determined to be repugnant because they rely on theories that are contrary to a form of utilitarianism that has equality at its core and that can be affected by policy (i.e., that public policy can be used to establish criteria to eliminate expression of such repugnant or morally suspect preferences).

29. Dworkin's utilitarianism is not the only form of argument that could be used against arguments in favor of directed donation, but it is used here because it is a prominent instance of a theory of utilitarianism that incorporates consideration of preferences; for instance, a relational conception of persons might be developed that could produce a similar taxonomy of permissible and impermissible instances of directed donation.

30. See note 24.

31. See note 28, Dworkin 1977:235.

32. Sunstein C. Preferences and politics. *Philosophy and Public Affairs* 1991;20:3–34, 5.

33. See note 28, Dworkin 1977:236.

34. United Network of Organ Sharing. *The Feasibility of Allocating Organs on the Basis of a Single National List*. Richmond, Va.: UNOS, 1991.

35. See note 34, UNOS 1991:33, n. 2.

36. For these data, see Gallup Organization, Inc. *The American Public's Attitudes Toward Organ Donation and Transplantation: A Survey*. Boston: Partnership for Organ Donation, 1993.

37. A recent report from the IOM of the National Academy of Sciences indicates the need to allocate available transplantable organs across wider geographic areas made up of larger numbers of people to enhance the prospects that organs will be allocated to patients with the most urgent medical needs: Committee on Organ Procurement and Transplantation Policy, Institute of Medicine. *Organ Procurement and Transplantation: Assessing Current Policies and the Potential Impact of the DHHS Final Rule*. Washington, D.C.: IOM, 1999. See also notes 7, 15.

38. For a discussion on this issue in the context of candidate selection, see: Ankeny RA. Transforming objectivity to promote equity in transplant candidate selection. *Theoretical Medicine* 1996;17:45–59; see also the special section of *Cambridge Quarterly of Healthcare Ethics* entitled Shaping policy and keeping public trust. 1999;8:269–350.

39. See note 3, Elster 1983:36.

Part VIII
Xenotransplantation

[28]

THE PIG, THE TRANSPLANT SURGEON AND THE NUFFIELD COUNCIL

WILL CARTWRIGHT*

As a treatment for organ failure transplantation has turned out to be much more successful and less expensive than many had originally supposed it would be. A major constraint upon it, however, is the shortage of available organs. Some suppose that this can be circumvented by the use of organs from other animals. Occasional attempts have been made since the beginning of the century to transplant animal organs and tissue into humans, but with little success. Now something altogether more serious and sustained is afoot, which raises the real prospect of xenotransplantation or xenografting, as it is known, becoming a viable procedure. The UK company Imutran Ltd. has said that it aims to conduct clinical trials in due course involving the transplantation of pig hearts into humans. In the light of these developments and the ethical issues thought to be raised by them, the Nuffield Council on Bioethics set up a working party in January 1995 to investigate and report upon the matter, and the government followed suit in September 1995. The Nuffield Council published its report in March 1996.[1]

The Report describes the current state of research into xenografting and explores a variety of more or less ethical questions raised by the practice. Recommendations are offered on these questions and on the appropriate legal and administrative framework for supervising the new treatment. The Report is at once informative, lucid and if one accepts the key moral position adopted by it, sensible in its conclusions. I shall describe the report, reflect upon the function of committees like this, and then focus on that key position.

I. THE NUFFIELD REPORT

The Report begins by exploring various ways of overcoming the shortage of organs.[2] It mentions a number of changes that would probably increase the supply of human organs to some extent, but remarks that some of the suggestions, such as a system of presumed rather than explicit consent to organ transplantation, are morally controversial

---

* Lecturer, Department of Philosophy, University of Essex.
[1] Report of the Nuffield Council on Bioethics, *Animal-to-Human Transplants. The Ethics of Xenotransplantation* (London 1996).
[2] *Ibid.* ch. 2.

and that, even if successful, such measures would fall a long way short
of meeting the demand. Artificial organs such as battery-powered
hearts have made advances recently, but still face major problems, and
are unlikely to be able to replace organs such as the liver which have
complex biochemical functions. Replacement organs of this sort are
more likely to be produced by tissue engineering techniques, in which
living cells are used to produce the substitute organs, but again this is
not possible at present. Hence attention has turned to xenografting
where the prospects of success are more immediate.

More immediate perhaps, but by no means certain. One of the key
problems is organ rejection by the host's immune system, as indeed it
is when human organs are used, but here it is more acute. The greater
the biological distance between the recipient and the source of the
organ the more severe is the immune system's response. This problem
has elicited two different strategies in the search for a solution. Some
in the USA wish to use primates such as baboons as source animals on
the ground of their biological closeness to human beings. The immune
response to a primate xenograft is not notably stronger than that to
a poorly matched human transplant. But the very proximity that
mitigates the rejection problem makes their use morally controversial,
and others have therefore looked elsewhere. They have selected the
pig, whose organs compare in size to human ones and which repro-
duces quickly and prolifically. The greater genetic distance from
humans is thought to alleviate the moral problem, but it renders the
rejection problem acute. The method of overcoming this which is
currently being explored is to inject human genetic material into the
pig so that its organs will be less susceptible to rejection by the recipient.
The proposed trials by Imutran Ltd., are to involve such transgenic
pigs. Even if the rejection problem can be overcome, however, it still
remains to be seen whether animal organs are capable of fulfilling the
functions of human organs.

In short, though significant progress has been made, it is not yet
clear whether xenografting will work. If it does, however, the benefit
will be considerable, since presumably a sufficiently large number of
transgenic pigs could be produced to meet the demand for organs. It is
not just that those presently on waiting lists would receive organs, but
also that those who, given their condition and the shortage, are not
now seriously considered for transplantation, could then be so considered. In principle transplantation could become a much more widely
available treatment.[3]

But even if xenografting works, is it right? The Report examines a
number of moral issues in this connection, the most fundamental

[3] *Ibid.* ch. 3.

of which is whether it is right to use animals in this way at all. In the pivotal chapter of the Report, the Working Party review the arguments about the use of animals for medical purposes in general.[4] It adopts the position that some use of animals for such purposes is "an undesirable but unavoidable necessity" and that

> in the absence of any scientifically and morally acceptable alternative, some use of animals in biomedical research can be justified as necessary to safeguard and improve the health and alleviate the suffering of human beings...[5]

I say that the Report adopts this position rather than reaches this conclusion, because the latter implies the presence of some developing argument for the view taken, and such an argument is scarcely discernible. Furthermore, the words quoted above are not those of the Working Party; it merely endorses them. They come originally from a report of a Working Party of the Institute of Medical Ethics.[6] For the moment I will say no more about this fundamental issue and the report's handling of it, since I propose to return to it in more detail later.

The Working Party interprets this general position on the use of animals for medical purposes as licensing xenografting. It considers that the use of primates for this purpose raises serious moral doubts, given their biological proximity to humans, but that since pigs appear to be a viable alternative and are more remote from us, their use is both morally preferable and acceptable. If the use of pig organs should prove to be a failure, members of the Working Party were divided on whether it would then be permissible to have recourse to primates as a source of organs. Furthermore, no serious moral objection is taken to the genetic modification of the pigs to lessen the chances of organ rejection. The number of human genes that is inserted into the pig is very small and cannot be said to alter the pig's essence.[7] Though endorsing the use of pigs in xenografting, the Report emphasises the moral need to ensure the animals' welfare during the process, and for this purpose recommends that the Home Office should require the animals to be protected under the Animals (Scientific Procedures) Act 1986.[8]

Xenotransplantation involves a risk that diseases will pass from the animal to the recipient and perhaps on into the general human population. The risk is hard to assess. There is evidence that it will be greater

---

[4] *Ibid.* ch. 4.
[5] *Ibid.* ch. 4, paras. 4.25 and 4.26.
[6] J. A. Smith and K. M. Boyd (eds.) *Lives in the Balance: The Ethics of Using Animals in Biomedical Research*, The Report of a Working Party of the Institute of Medical Ethics (Oxford 1991) at 310–11.
[7] *Op. cit.* ch. 4.
[8] *Ibid.* ch. 5.

if primates are used as the source of organs, which reinforces the case for using pigs. But at the worst, new diseases, which would be difficult to control, could be unleashed into the general population. The Working Party holds that this problem has not been adequately addressed so far, and that until it is, it will not be ethical to begin clinical trials with human subjects. The Report recommends that further research on this issue should be conducted, that a regulatory framework be devised to control the safety and quality of animal organs, and that mechanisms for monitoring xenograft recipients for disease transmission be developed. In view of the seriousness of these issues the Report recommends the establishment of an Advisory Committee on Xenotransplantation to implement these recommendations. Finally, the Report trenchantly insists that there must be a commitment to suspend or, if necessary, discontinue xenotransplantation if there are signs of new infectious diseases emerging.[9]

At present xenografting experiments are being conducted using animals as the recipients as well as the sources of the organs. A further ethical question, setting aside the disease transmission problem, is when will it be proper more generally to begin trials involving human subjects? This question is raised by any new treatment, but is particularly acute in this case, though again not uniquely, because a xenograft may be the only hope for some patients. The Report's test for deciding this question is that there must be a reasonable chance of success, and there is said to be little consensus among the transplantation community as to whether this threshold has been reached. Proposed clinical trials would have to be approved by local research ethics committees, and the Report recommends further that no such trials take place until the proposed Advisory Committee on Xenotransplantation has been established and has approved them. Though xenografting is regarded as a potential means of overcoming the particularly acute shortage of organs for babies and children, the Report takes the general view that therapeutic research, which this would be, should not be conducted on children if it can be conducted first and equally well on adults, who are capable, unlike children, of weighing the risks and benefits of the treatment and of giving consent. And so it recommends that the first xenotransplantation trials should involve adults.[10]

Xenografting involves the introduction of an organ or tissue from another species into the human body and this might affect how the recipients view their bodies and identities. The Report recommends research into this topic.[11] Finally there is the question of cost. The

---

[9] *Ibid.* ch. 6.
[10] *Ibid.* ch. 7.
[11] *Ibid.* ch. 9.

Report supposes that the major cost implications of xenografting becoming a successful procedure will be the larger number of transplants that will become possible. It recommends that xenografting should be introduced in a limited and controlled way under the aegis of the Supra Regional Services Advisory Group, which is an existing body responsible for the introduction and provision of specialist services.[12]

II. ETHICS AND COMMITTEES

The upshot of the Report is that the development of xenotransplantation should continue subject to rigorous regulation to protect the interests of both the animals and humans involved. If one accepts the Working Party's moral view on the use of animals for medical research, then its other positions and recommendations will seem very plausible. The status and credibility of that key moral view therefore warrant further inspection, but first some remarks on the function of reports like this one are necessary.

In common with other recent committees, like the Warnock Committee, this one was charged with investigating certain controversial ethical issues.[13] But how, some ask, can such issues be resolved by a committee? Given that the issues are controversial, the members of the committee are likely to have significantly different views and, if a report is to be forthcoming at all, some compromise needs to be arrived at. But there is no reason to think that a moral position arrived at by compromise is likely to be the most intellectually defensible, if it is coherent at all. Of course, so the argument goes, if the function of the committee were to work out a *policy* that would attract the widest support, that would be different—that would be politics, and compromise has a coherent and honourable place in that setting. But it has no place in a serious ethical enquiry. Quite what *that* would be is a further matter, of course, and those who share reservations about such ethical committees will entertain various views about the nature of such an enquiry. But for a significant party of opinion what is required is the construction of the most plausible ethical theory that we can contrive and its application to the practical moral issues in hand. A committee is hardly the setting in which to accomplish this.[14]

These suspicions of ethical committees might seem to be confirmed by a close scrutiny of the Working Party's discussion of the morality

---

[12] *Ibid.* ch. 8.

[13] M. Warnock, *A Question of Life. The Warnock Report on Human Fertilisation and Embryology* (Blackwell 1985).

[14] For an example of this sceptical view of ethical committees see P. Singer and D. Wells. *The Reproduction Revolution* (Oxford 1984), ch. 8.

of using animals for medical research.[15] Various arguments on the matter are rather neutrally considered and then a conclusion emerges, but how the former gives rise to the latter remains rather opaque, as I observed earlier. The discussion contains arguments, but they are not sorted and shaped into a convincing case for the conclusion. Such considerations might suggest to the sceptics about ethical committees that the real explanation for the conclusion is that it is a moral compromise forged between the committee members. Indeed the language used in the Report suggests this. It will be recalled that the Working Party adopts a formula used by a Working Party of the Institute of Medical Ethics (IME). It is apparent from the passages quoted in the Nuffield Report that the IME Working Party contained a variety of views on the moral status of animals and that their formula represented a "working agreement" between the members of the party.[16] Similarly the members of the Nuffield group say that they are "prepared to accept" the IME statement, though they differ among themselves in the detailed interpretation of the formula.[17] Thus the position seems to have represented a moral compromise for both working parties which would explain why in the Nuffield Report it seemed rather uncertainly related to the arguments discussed.

However, I suggest that this account of the shortcomings of ethical committees misconstrues their function. On a more plausible account their role is to arrive at a view on the issues in hand that is faithful to the underlying moral commitments of society, that is likely to command the widest possible moral assent, and that is intellectually defensible, even if not uniquely so. This is not doing moral philosophy in the way that the critics of committees seem to want, but nor is it just fixing a political compromise in the way that these critics suppose is the only alternative. It represents a genuine kind of collective moral thinking, in which a group of more or less representative individuals, who know or come to know about the issues, endeavour to forge a moral position on them that they and, they suppose, a large number of their fellow citizens can accept. Given this we can then see the Nuffield Working Party's position in a different light. Its view that the use of animals in medical research is "an undesirable but unavoidable necessity" may then be regarded as its attempt to capture a moral position on animals that would command the widest assent as well as being intellectually credible. This would explain the somewhat loose connection between the position and the arguments. On this view it is important that the position cohere at least with the arguments – which

---

[15] *Op. cit.* ch. 4.
[16] *Ibid.* ch. 4, para. 4.25.
[17] *Ibid.* ch. 4, para. 4.26.

it does – but not necessary that it follow from them in some logically compelling way – which it does not.

This way of understanding the Working Party's role and moral position is further confirmed by certain explicit remarks in its Report. To those, referred to above, who urge that serious ethical thought requires the application of a moral theory to the issues in hand, the Working Party responds that no single ethical theory can capture all the reasons and values that might be thought pertinent to xenotransplantation.[18] Furthermore, acknowledging the lack of a social consensus on the issues addressed in the Report, the Working Party say that the aim of the Report is to seek as much common ethical ground as possible.[19]

I have argued that ethical committees like the Nuffield Working Party have a coherent moral task to perform and are not to be criticised for failing to do moral philosophy. It might be said however that the moral task I have attributed to them is closer to doing moral philosophy than the view of the critics suggests. For according to an influential account, the task of moral philosophy is to seek that interpretation of our morality which most satisfactorily explains our deepest and most settled moral convictions, and then to use that account in resolving moral issues about which we are less certain.[20]

When the Nuffield Working Party propose that the use of animals in medical research is an undesirable but unavoidable necessity and therefore justifiable, it may be thought that they are endeavouring to articulate the principle that underlies a widely shared set of values in this area. And there is a deeper position that, I suggest, may plausibly be thought to underpin this principle, namely, that animals matter morally, which is why their use in medical research is undesirable, but they matter less than humans, which is why their use is nevertheless justified. Such excavations into the foundations of our considered moral views may be thought to constitute steps towards articulating that best interpretation of our morality which, according to this view, it is the task of moral philosophy to supply.

Whether or not the reflections of the Nuffield group are just an attempt to describe the most widely shared moral ground on this issue or can be represented as something more philosophical, I think the position that they take up *is* widely shared, as is the deeper position that I have just suggested underlies it. But this deeper position is not just widely shared; it is also, I am going to suggest in the next section,

---

[18] *Ibid.* ch. 1, para. 1.30.
[19] *Ibid.* ch. 1, para. 1.29; at 129, para. 13.
[20] J. Rawls, *A Theory of Justice* (Oxford 1971).

the most intellectually defensible.[21] In the course of showing this I shall, amongst other things, refer to the arguments sketched out in chapter 4 of the Report in order to propose that, when amplified and reshaped, they lend more support to the Working Party's conclusion, or at any rate what underlies it, than its own discussion suggests.

III. THE MORAL STATUS OF ANIMALS

The Report notices the tendency in recent times to assign a higher moral status to animals than has hitherto been the case, and refers to two distinct philosophical approaches that may be used to support this tendency. One holds that actions are right or wrong to the extent that they benefit or harm those affected. Animals, no less than humans, can be benefited and harmed, and their interests must thus be taken into account in determining how we should act. Indeed, if we take something like suffering, it is not clear on this view why the suffering of an animal should count for any less than the suffering of a human being. This is a utilitarian approach which strikingly appears to assign a more or less equal status to humans and other animals, and some contemporary zoophiles therefore embrace it.[22] But while animal interests must be taken into account equally with human ones, the theory allows that when the calculations are made as to where the balance of benefit and harm lies, the interests of animals may be outweighed by human ones, though equally, presumably, the reverse may happen. Thus despite the enhanced moral status assigned to animals by the theory, they nevertheless turn out to be less well protected than some would wish. What this reflects is not a particular bias against animals in the theory, but the fact that beings with interests, whether human or animal, are arguably insufficiently protected by it.

Some seek a more robust protection for animals in a theory of rights.[23] Human beings are widely agreed to have rights, and they have them by virtue of possessing certain characteristics. We now know that animals share in these characteristics to a significant degree and therefore, it is argued by some, they too should be credited with rights. Such rights protect their bearers, whether human or animal, from being sacrificed to the general interest. So, for example, the fact, if it is

---

[21] As I have argued elsewhere, in a rather different fashion: W. Cartwright, 'The Ethics of Xenografting in Man' in W. Land and J. B. Dossetor, (eds.) *Organ Replacement Therapy: Ethics, Justice and Commerce* (Springer-Verlag 1991).

[22] *Op. cit.* ch. 4, paras. 4.5 and 4.6; P. Singer, *Animal Liberation*, (2nd edn.) (London 1995), P. Singer, *Practical Ethics* (2nd edn.) (Cambridge 1993), ch. 3.

[23] The Nuffield Report, ch. 4, paras. 4.7 and 4.8; T. Regan, *The Case for Animal Rights* (Routledge and Kegan Paul 1983).

one, that using animals as a source of organs for xenotransplantation would produce more human benefit than animal harm does not make such use morally right, according to this view. Despite the contemporary prominence and importance of human rights, there is a range of philosophical questions about them which remain disturbingly hard to answer. One of these is the question of what a being has to be like in order to be coherently thought of as a bearer of rights. The intractability of this question means that the issue of whether or not animals have rights remains peculiarly controversial.

We have already noticed the Working Party's view that no single philosophical theory can do justice to the variety of considerations that bear upon the ethics of xenografting, and so having briefly explored the two theories it steps round them. It remarks that whether the argument is framed in terms of the interests or the rights of animals, the important point is the extent to which animals share the features supposed to be important to human interests and rights. The Working Party focus upon the feature of self-awareness which they suppose to be connected with the possession of a language. But this is a rather sophisticated characteristic, and I think that the comparison of humans and animals should begin, at least, at a more basic level where we may nevertheless find morally relevant features.

A. *Interests and Animal Mentality*

As already noted, a crucial question about rights is what a being has to be like to be a bearer of them. An attractive suggestion is that it must possess interests.[24] Rights presumably ensure that the subjects of them are not harmed in certain ways and are benefitted in others, and only beings that have interests can be harmed and benefitted. Thus arguably both the rights and the utilitarian approaches presuppose the same claim, that animals have interests. We must now ask what has to be true of a being for it to be coherently said to have interests. Something with interests can be harmed and benefited, and arguably it can only be thus affected if it has desires or aims, the satisfaction of which benefit it and the frustration of which harm it. Further, the possession of desires or aims seems to presuppose the possession of beliefs: one wants x because one believes it has property y Thus to have interests and hence moral importance seems to require the possession of desires, beliefs and cognitive awareness, in short a mental life of some degree.[25]

Common sense will think it rather evident that animals pass this

---

[24] J. Feinberg, 'The Rights of Animals and Unborn Generations' in his *Rights, Justice and the Bounds of Liberty*, (Princeton 1980).
[25] *Ibid.*

test. If common sense is right, then one moral view of animals that has
been explicitly articulated by thinkers past and present, and even more
commonly but implicitly expressed in much of our behaviour towards
them, is mistaken: namely, that animals do not matter morally and
that we can use them as we see fit.[26] Some argue, however, that the
response of common sense is just indicative of its anthropomorphism.
Many thinkers, both philosophical and scientific, both past and
present, think that animals are more accurately viewed as automata
who lack a mental life. A good example is Descartes, who thought the
inability of animals to use language was crucial, as have many
others.[27]

In order to assess Descartes' claim it is necessary to distinguish
between different aspects of mental life, between being conscious, on
the one hand, and possessing what philosophers call propositional
attitudes, on the other, such as wants and beliefs. There seems little
plausibility in the claim that the possession of language is necessary in
order to be conscious, but rather more in the idea that it is necessary
for the entertaining of propositional attitudes. Beliefs, and propositional attitudes in general, have a content which can be captured in a
particular proposition or sentence: one believes that *chickens lay eggs*,
for example. Having a belief may then be analysed as taking a certain
sentence to be true. But how can a being which lacks language entertain sentences and take them as true? This argument appears to show
that the possession of language is necessary for the having of beliefs,
and a parallel argument can be readily made for the possession of
desires and propositional attitudes generally. If killing is wrong principally because it frustrates the victim's desire to go on living, and
animals have no such desire because they have no desires, then killing
animals would not seem to be wrong.[28]

We should reject this argument. The entertaining of beliefs does not
require the possession of a language, I think, but the possession of
concepts. Thus one could not coherently attribute to an animal a belief
that it is in danger unless it is allowed to possess the concept of
danger. However it does not follow that it must be able to entertain
the sentence 'I am in danger' and in general to use a language. But, it

---

[26] The more humane exponents of this view acknowledge that we should not be cruel to
them, but only because those cruel to animals are more likely to be cruel to human
beings. Our duties to animals are thus indirect. See the selections from Aquinas and
Kant in T. Regan and P. Singer (eds.) *Animal Rights and Human Obligations* (2nd
edn.) (Prentice Hall 1989), part one; see also the extract from a Catholic Dictionary in
part four of the same.

[27] See *Ibid.* part one for extracts from Descartes.

[28] This argument is advanced by R. G. Frey in his 'Why animals lack beliefs and desires'
in T. Regan and P. Singer (eds.) *op. cit.* part two.

may be replied, do I not manifest my own possession of the concept of danger by using the word 'danger' appropriately? Certainly this is one manifestation but it is not the only one. My non-linguistic behaviour, such as my flight from a threat, testifies also to my possession of the concept, and such behaviour on the part of an animal may testify to its possession of the concept too. It may be true that the possession of more sophisticated concepts requires the possession of language, but if true that would only limit the range of beliefs and desires we could assign to animals rather than exclude such assignment entirely.

To deny propositional attitudes to animals is one thing; to deny in addition that they are conscious at all is another, for this rules out sensory experience as well as beliefs and desires. This seems to be the burden of Descartes' claim that animals are automata and that their behaviour consists of nothing more than a mechanical system of reflexes. Before this view is dismissed by common sense as quite outlandish, it would do well to remind itself that it is this view that came to dominate twentieth-century behaviourism, which saw no need to postulate cognitive structures between the stimulus and the behavioural response of the animal. And in any case common sense would do well not to be too smug about its own credentials. Nevertheless, with the rise of cognitive psychology and of ethology in recent times this view is in retreat, and there is now a wider disposition to credit animals with mental states of various kinds.[29]

But it might still be insisted that this does not settle the question of animal consciousness. Perhaps they, unlike us, have mental states without being conscious of them. We can readily make sense of this suggestion with respect to propositional attitudes, for human beings have many beliefs and desires of which they are not conscious. It is rather more difficult to get hold of it with respect to sensory experience, for such experience seems inseparable from consciousness. Without it there would seem to be no experience. But consider the phenomenon of blindsight. People who have suffered lesions in the striate cortex may lose all conscious experience in part of their visual field. They insist that they can see nothing in that area. Nevertheless, if asked to guess, they prove to be strikingly successful at describing and grasping objects presented to them in that area. The conclusion suggested by this phenomenon is that the subjects of it have visual experiences of which they are not conscious. Consciousness is apparently not inseparable from experience therefore. Perhaps the visual experiences of animals, and indeed their sensory experiences in general, are similar. Perhaps even their pains are non-conscious, in the

---

[29] *Ibid.* part two; C. Blakemore and S. Greenfield (eds.) *Mindwaves* (Blackwell 1987), Part 2.

sense that while the familiar repertoire of pain behaviour is present, nothing is felt. If correct, this would be a morally important conclusion, because pains that are not felt presumably cease to be objects of moral concern. Other things being equal there would seem to be no objection to causing pain to an animal if it feels nothing unpleasant.

This rather striking line of argument has been advanced by the philosopher Peter Carruthers.[30] But the most that has been shown so far is that animals *might* have non-conscious mental lives. Do we, however, have any reason to think that they *do* have such lives? The supposition that they do will strike many as postulating an implausibly sharp distinction between us and them. Carruthers however has an argument for thinking that their mental lives are as described, and it turns on the nature of consciousness, which perplexes philosophers. One might think that consciousness can be equated with a subjective inner feel, so that an experience such as an ache is conscious in so far as it is apprehended by the subject as having a certain distinctive inner quality. Though this seems plausible with respect to experiences, it does not with respect to most beliefs and many desires. Entertaining the conscious belief that chickens lay eggs does not feel like anything. What differentiates conscious from non-conscious beliefs must be something other than feel. Carruthers proposes that what makes a mental state, whether sensory experience or propositional attitude, conscious is that it is available to thought, which itself must be conscious. So a belief, *qua* dormant state, is conscious in so far as it is apt to emerge in a conscious thought with the same content. My belief that chickens lay eggs is conscious in so far as I am disposed in suitable circumstances to think to myself 'chickens lay eggs'. Similarly, though not exactly so, an experience is conscious whose existence and content are available to be consciously thought about. Carruthers insists that for a mental state to be conscious the thought it may issue in must itself be conscious. To hold otherwise, that the thought may be non-conscious, would yield the implausible result that a mental state is conscious by virtue of a connection with something non-conscious. But for the thought to be conscious means, applying Carruthers' account once again, that it must in turn be available to a further thought, presumably itself conscious. In short, a being that has a conscious mental life must be able to think about its own thoughts, and Carruthers now argues that it is very implausible to suppose that animals can do this, even chimpanzees. It follows from this that the pains of animals are non-conscious and therefore presumably cease to be objects of moral concern.

---

[30] P. Carruthers, *The Animals Issue* (Cambridge 1992), ch. 8.

I think that Carruthers' argument depends for its effectiveness upon a concealed equivocation about consciousness. It is initially plausible to suppose that for an experience like pain to be conscious is for it to be felt. As we have seen, Carruthers denies this and suggests that what makes experiences conscious is their availability for thought. Animal experiences are said not to be so available, and are therefore non-conscious. And a pain that is not conscious is of no moral account. I judge that the plausibility of this last moral point silently derives from the view of consciousness that Carruthers has rejected. The reason why one might think that a non-conscious pain is of no moral signifi-cance is because one supposes that it is not felt. But this is not, of course, what it means on Carruthers' account for the pain to be non-conscious. What is meant is only that it is not available for thought. Once one reminds oneself of this, it is not at all so obvious that a pain of which this is true is of no moral importance. Why should the fact that a pain is not available to further thought undercut its moral significance? What would have that effect is if the pain is not felt, and is non-conscious in that sense, but Carruthers has done nothing to show that this is true of animal pain. In short, Carruthers' claim that animals are not conscious depends on one account of consciousness, whereas the plausibility of his moral conclusion that their pains do not matter depends upon the silent invocation of another account of consciousness. Maybe Carruthers thinks that the two accounts are linked, that if a pain is not available to be thought about, then it is not felt. But he offers no argument for this inference, and it can scarcely be thought to be self-evident. Indeed it would seem entirely plausible to me that an experience could be felt without being available to be thought about. Perhaps in fact *this* is the condition of animal experi-ence rather than the one postulated by Carruthers.

The claim that very many animals have a conscious mental life of some degree or other seems to be defensible against the Cartesian tradition which has denied it. Given that they do, they can be credited with interests that make a moral claim on us. As we have seen, the resolution of this issue depends upon very fundamental questions in philosophy and science about the nature and extent of consciousness, and one cannot but be aware of the fragility of arguments and conclu-sions in this area. But moral life cannot wait for theory to make up its mind on these questions or on any others for that matter, a point which moral philosophers might do well to bear in mind. We have to decide what to do *now*. Given the uncertainty, the prudent thing to do presumably, indeed the moral thing to do, would be to give animals the benefit of the doubt on these questions. To treat creatures well, who turn out to have no claim to it, is no wrong; to continue to abuse creatures, who turn out to have such a claim, is.

B. Importance, Objectivity and the Human Point of View

I mentioned that the position of the Nuffield Working Party seemed to rest upon the view that animals matter morally, but less than humans. I take the recent discussion to show the first part of this view, that animals matter, to be defensible. What now about the second part? Most people no doubt accept it, but on what grounds? What entitles human beings to prefer their interests to those of animals? Some will say that human interests matter more just because they are human. Others have replied that this just amounts to a blank and unreasoned preference for our own species. It is like, and no better than, preferring the interests of whites and males to those of blacks and females just because they are white and male. These preferences we have come to regard as the prejudices of racism and sexism, and some think the preference for the human is a further, though less widely recognised, prejudice which they call speciesism. Mere species membership on this view carries no moral weight.[31] What might carry such weight, however, to turn to another line of argument, are other features associated with being human. Thus it has been variously supposed that it is our rationality, autonomy, complex self-awareness, and moral sense, to canvas just some of the possibilities, that either singly or in combination make human beings and their lives valuable, more valuable than those of animals.

However, this alternative way of justifying the assigning of greater weight to human interests faces its own difficulties. It can be argued that the valuable features just referred to are not peculiar to us, but are shared to some degree by some other animals. But this will only unsettle those who aspire to show, implausibly as I have argued, that animals have no moral value. Matters become rather more serious when it is added that some human beings lack these qualities and therefore value, either to some degree or maybe altogether. Putting these two points together, we get the result that some animals are morally more valuable than some humans, for example, the senile, the permanently unconscious and anencephalic babies. And this yields the rather unwelcome conclusion that it would be morally preferable, if it were feasible, to use anencephalic babies as a source of organs rather than pigs. Some of us, I suppose might learn to accommodate ourselves in due course to engaging proposals of this kind – there are earnest persons around who think we should – and we can comfort ourselves with the thought that this line of argument has at least shown that most human lives are more valuable than most animal lives. But there is a deeper difficulty about this argument that requires attention.

---

[31] See the works by P. Singer referred to in note 22.

The claim being considered is that human life is more valuable than animal life, that it matters more or is more important. There seems to be a distinction to be drawn between a relative and a non-relative kind of importance. Thus we can distinguish between something being important *to* someone and something being important *tout court*. It could be important to me, for example, to enlarge my collection of seventeenth-century oak furniture without it being true, or my having to suppose it true, that it is important. The kind of importance involved in the present discussion about human and animal life is rather evidently of the non-relative kind. Everyone can agree presumably that the life of an animal can be very important to someone, maybe even more important than many human lives. But our question here has to do with the importance *tout court* of animals and humans. However, on closer inspection this idea of non-relative importance begins to look rather suspect. To be important, one is tempted to say, is surely to be important *from some point of view*. Can anything really just be important if that means important from no particular point of view? Perhaps we can accommodate this point, while still retaining a notion of objective importance, by reinterpreting the notion of non-relative importance as importance from some ultimately objective point of view. But is there such a point of view? Whose point of view is that? Those who believe in a God perhaps have a subject to whom it can be attributed; for those who do not this point of view seems to be chimerical. What by contrast is perfectly real is the human point of view, and importance *tout court* is best understood as importance from that point of view. This still allows us to draw a robust distinction between this kind of importance and importance to a particular individual. We can say that though something is important to some individual, it is not important from some larger human perspective. If all this is correct, then when we ask whether human life is more important than animal life, we must be taken to be asking whether it is more important viewed from the human perspective. But this scarcely seems an impartial vantage point from which to answer this question in particular, and any answer given to it must seem necessarily to be biased. If no objective vantage point is available from which to answer the question, then human life cannot be said to be objectively more important or valuable than animal life, and the second part of the principle underlying the Nuffield position seemingly cannot be vindicated.

There are some well-known remarks of John Stuart Mill on this topic which might seem to reopen the possibility of objective judgments on the value of lives.[32] Mill's idea is roughly that a being that has

---

[32] J. S. Mill, *Utilitarianism* (1863), various editions, ch. II.

experience of different sorts of life is in a position to judge them impartially. He thinks that this is true with respect to human and animal life. Humans have acquaintance with animal life in so far as they share with animals certain physical desires, such as hunger and lust, and the satisfactions that still these desires. Human and animal life thus overlap. But humans also possess more elevated faculties of a moral and intellectual kind which yield their own kind of rewards. In Mill's estimation hardly any human being would consent to exchange human life for, say, porcine or any other animal life, even though promised the fullest allowance of the beast's pleasures, and even though aware of the dissatisfactions that attend the human lot. In the light of this Mill famously concludes that:

> ...it is better to be a human being dissatisfied than a pig satisfied...And if...the pig [is] of a different opinion, it is because [it] only know[s its] own side of the question. The other party to the comparison knows both sides.[33]

His position thus is that since the human judge is acquainted with both lives, an objective judgment can be made on the value of human and animal life.

But this will not do for two reasons. Granted that both humans and pigs experience lust, it does not follow that humans know what porcine lust is like. To put the point more generally, pigs have, as we might say, a point of view which humans cannot access, and the same is true for other animals. Since we cannot grasp their lives from the inside, we can scarcely claim to judge them impartially. But even if we could gain such access, there is a further problem. When we come to make the supposedly impartial judgment between their lives and ours, it appears to get made on Mill's account from the presumably partial human point of view. The problem explored above is thus still with us, apparently unaddressed in Mill's discussion. In order to solve this problem we should have to be able to assume a point of view that is neither animal nor human, from which we could judge the respective merits of the lives in question. Thus to carry through the enterprise of objectively assessing the importance of human and animal lives, we should have to be able to do two things: to enter their points of view and then to enter a neutral point of view that is neither ours nor theirs. Either way we should have to be able to abandon our own point of view. The possibility of doing any of these things may be seriously doubted. The impossibility is not merely practical, as though technology might one day allow us to grasp the world from the pig's point of view. It is, more deeply, an impossibility of a conceptual

---

[33] *Ibid.*

kind.[34] It is not clear that it makes sense to suppose that I might shed my human point of view and assume one of the other points of view referred to, whether animal or objective. For it might be reasonably supposed that I am defined by my humanity and its corresponding point of view, and that therefore I could not shed this point of view and assume another and still remain me.

We cannot then transcend the human point of view. Amongst other things it conditions what we can and do value. From within it human things understandably will be found to be important. This does not mean that we can only value the human, which is evidently false, but it does perhaps mean that we can only value something if we can trace intelligible steps from valuing the human to valuing it, to put it with deliberate vagueness. Those who believe in God value him above all else, and this extension in valuing beyond the human is readily intelligible because, in our tradition at least, God has been credited with a range of human qualities brought to perfection. In the other direction, so to speak, we value other animals. Once again the connection with the human is apparent. The anthropomorphic tendencies of common sense testify to our capacity to see the human in other animals, and the true nature and extent of their connection with the human is increasingly revealed by our science. The reason why animals are valued less than human beings and God is valued more is, we may suppose, that human qualities are found more, or more perfectly, in God, and less in animals, than they are in human beings.

Thus, though we cannot transcend the human point of view, we can and do come to value things from it that are not human, and sometimes to value them more. We might record these facts by saying that a measure of objectivity is to this extent possible within this point of view. Some will still argue that clutching at this straw of residual objectivity cannot alter the fact that the human point of view is unavoidably partial and the preference for ourselves over animals a prejudice like racism and sexism. However tactically astute the parallel with racism and sexism is as a persuasive device, it is a spurious one. Viewing the world from a white or a male point of view is not inevitable; such points of view, if that is what they are, can be, and rather commonly are, transcended. Of those who achieve this we say that they begin to view things as human beings rather than as whites or males. But the human point of view is different. As I have been at pains to stress, this cannot intelligibly be transcended nor in consequence, I think, can those who occupy it be regarded as thereby prejudiced. Before a point of view can coherently be regarded as prejudiced,

---

[34] The contrary view, that the difficulty is only practical and not conceptual, is argued by P. Singer in *Practical Ethics, supra* at 105–9.

there has to be another point of view which can be taken up and which is more objective. But there is no such further point of view in the human case. To see the world from the human point of view is a perfectly proper, because inevitable, thing for humans to do. From that point of view humans predictably but properly matter more than animals.

I suggested that the principle underlying the Nuffield Working Party's position was that animals matter, but less than humans. I take the recent argument to show that the second part of this principle can be defended, no less than the first. In their discussion of the issues the Working Party explores the charge of speciesism and its ramifications.[35] It thinks the charge should be treated with caution because the especial concern we have for our species is built deeply into our nature and it is probably not open to us to overcome it. It will be apparent that I concur with this conclusion if for somewhat different reasons. Furthermore, the Working Party draws an interesting distinction between our relationships with other animals and our relatedness to them.[36] The chimpanzee is closely related to humans in a genetic sense, and the Working Party and I seem to be in agreement that that relatedness grounds our assignment of value to it. Rather differently I might have a relationship with a domestic animal such as a dog and value its life, though it is much less closely related to me genetically than the chimpanzee. Perhaps this distinction connects up with another one that I marked earlier, between importance to me and importance *tout court*, later reinterpreted as importance from the human point of view. One might say that chimpanzees are important in view of their relatedness to us, but that a particular dog is important to me in view of my relationship to it, though I might concede that the life of a dog is less valuable than that of a chimpanzee. Nevertheless, the life of a dog has some value and this, together with its particular importance to me, might lead me to conclude that morally I ought to save it rather than the chimpanzee, if I had to choose between them in an emergency. Indeed, a whole society might have traditional relationships with certain animals such that they had a particular moral importance to it. This is reflected in the fact that in Britain special legal protection is assigned to dogs, cats and horses as well as to primates.[37]

---

[35] *Op. cit.* ch. 4, para. 4.13–4.15.
[36] *Ibid.* ch. 4, para. 4.16–4.18.
[37] Animals (Scientific Procedures) Act 1986, s. 10.

IV. CONCLUSION

The general moral principle underlying the Nuffield Report, that animals matter but less than humans, is implicit in the response of many to animals and is also, I have suggested, intellectually defensible. But it is a very general principle that leaves many questions unanswered. If animals matter, how much do they matter? Some presumably matter more than others, but how do we determine this? The answers will necessarily be rough, but our increasing understanding of animals together with reflection on our traditional relationships with them will permit broad answers, as indicated above. Rather differently, what constraints do the varying values of animals place on our behaviour towards them? Evidently the lesser value of animals permits us to save a human rather than an animal in an emergency where we cannot save both. But does it *require* us to do this, *whatever* our relationship to the animal? Much more importantly, are we permitted to interfere systematically in their lives to solve our problems and to gratify our whims? Here the implications are much more indeterminate, though we can at least say, presumably, that the greater the benefit to humans and the less the value of the animals, the more likely the practice is to be justified. As always in moral life, such abstractions require to be fleshed out with more determinate judgments. There is no reason to suppose that there is only one set of defensible determinate judgments here, and different moral communities will develop different moral consensuses on these matters.

What then about xenografting using pigs? The Working Party discerns wide acceptance in our society of the view that it is permissible to use animals for medical purposes, depending on the animal, and it also notes wide acceptance of the practice of eating pigs. The Working Party not unreasonably infers from these two things that the use of pigs for xenografting ought to command similarly wide acceptance. If it is permissible to kill pigs for gastronomic pleasure, then it looks as though it must be permissible to kill them to save human life.[38] But the principle underlying the Working Party's position implies a reservation. Though justifiable, xenografting has a moral cost because the lives of morally valuable creatures are sacrificed. The Working Party's position is that xenografting is undesirable but necessary. But this means that, if there are other ways that are morally less costly of increasing the supply of organs, then we should pursue them. So we should seek to increase the supply of human organs in morally acceptable ways, and continue to develop artificial and bioengineered organs, even if for the moment such approaches are not capable of

---

[38] *op. cit.* ch. 4, para. 4.42.

overcoming the shortage. The Working Party is aware of this implication and mentions it twice.[39] But the references are rather cursory and the point does not receive the emphasis that I think it deserves. Had it received it, the overall impression left by the Report would have been significantly altered. Readers would not have been left with the sense, which I think they will now receive from the Report, that xenografting is a practice with which we can be morally comfortable. Finally, if xenografting involving pigs is only legitimate because necessary in the sense explained, how can eating them, or other animals, be legitimate since it is not necessary? The Working Party's way of endorsing xenografting seems to make it hard to defend eating meat.

---

[39] *Ibid.* ch. 4, para. 4.40; ch. 10, para. 10.12.

[29]

ARE XENOTRANSPLANTATION SAFEGUARDS LEGALLY VIABLE?

By Patrik S. Florencio[†] and Erik D. Ramanathan[‡]

ABSTRACT

Scientists agree on the need for robust public health safeguards to accompany the imminent introduction of xenotransplantation—clinical transplantation of animal tissues into humans. To protect society in the event of emerging infectious diseases, governments must devise a legally effective means of ensuring compliance with such safeguards.

Neither consent law, the law of contracts, nor existing public health legislation can adequately enforce such compliance. Consent law serves as a mechanism of communicating the momentary waiver of legal rights, not as a durable enforcement doctrine. Because it would be essential for recipients personally to comply with public safety measures, the law of contracts would also be unable to compel compliance. Existing public health legislation would also likely be ineffective because it would need to be substantially amended to incorporate the heightened powers necessary for the periodic examination of asymptomatic xenotransplant recipients.

Xenotransplantation-specific legislation would be a legally effective means of enforcing public health safeguards since it could require conforming behaviors and could impose monetary fines on those recipients who, having benefited from life-saving intervention, fail to comply. This Article argues that legislation implementing a post-xenotransplantation surveillance system should withstand constitutional scrutiny because it would not be discriminatory and because, although it would violate fundamental rights of recipients, such violations would be justified under existing constitutional doctrines.

[†]   Associate, Proskauer Rose LLP, New York; LL.B., B.C.L., McGill Law School; B.Sc., McGill University. Contact (212) 969-3000 or pflorencio@proskauer.com.

[‡]   Director, Legal Department, ImClone Systems Inc., New York; J.D., Harvard Law School; B.A., The Johns Hopkins University. Contact (212) 645-1405 or erikr@imclone.com.

TABLE OF CONTENTS

I.   INTRODUCTION

Xenotransplantation is an innovative medical procedure in which materials such as cells, tissues, or organs are procured from animal sources and subsequently transplanted into humans. Scientists have already managed successfully to transplant animal cells and tissues into humans;[1] all attempts at animal-to-human whole organ transplantation, however, have failed because of immunological rejection.[2] Nonetheless, scientists have

---

1. Terrence Deacon et al., *Histological Evidence of Fetal Pig Neural Cell Survival After Transplantation into a Patient with Parkinson's Disease*, 3 NATURE MED. 350 (1997); C.G. Groth et al., *Transplantation of Porcine Fetal Pancreas to Diabetic Patients*, 344 LANCET 1402 (1994); Ole Isacson & Xandra O. Breakefield, *Benefits and Risks of Hosting Animal Cells in the Human Brain*, 3 NATURE MED. 964 (1997); Rachel Nowak, *Xenotransplants Set to Resume*, 266 SCI. 1148 (1994); Joseph Palca, *Animal Organs for Human Patients?*, 25 HASTINGS CENT. REP. 4 (1995).

2. Leonard L. Bailey et al., *Baboon-to-Human Cardiac Xenotransplantation in a Neonate*, 254 JAMA 3321 (1985); Keith Reemtsma, *Renal Heterotransplantation from Non-Human Primate to Man*, 162 ANNALS. N.Y. ACAD. SCI. 412 (1969); T.E. Starzl et

recently achieved significant experimental progress in overcoming the immunological and physiological barriers to whole organ xenotransplantations, and expect this biotechnology to become a clinical reality in the near future.[3]

By offering a potentially limitless source of animal materials for transplantation,[4] xenotransplantation biotechnology—or xenobiotechnology for short—promises substantial future medical benefits, and may put an end to the current worldwide shortage of replacement organs.[5] Yet xenobiotechnology also carries with it a serious risk of introducing and spreading new infectious diseases into the world's human population.[6] Specifically, infectious animal agents residing in the source material could infect the xenotransplant recipient who could then pass this infection on to the community, causing morbidity and mortality if pathogenic. There is, consequently, a foreseeable yet unquantifiable possibility that xenobiotechnology might give rise to a human epidemic with effects comparable to those of HIV/AIDS or worse.[7]

In light of these foreseeable risks of harm, some commentators have advocated a precautionary approach to clinical xenotransplantation on the basis that a number of scientific, ethical, legal, and public health issues need to be addressed before proceeding with xenobiotechnology.[8] In con-

---

al., *Baboon-to-Human Liver Transplantation*, 341 LANCET 65 (1993); T.E. Starzl et al., *Renal Heterotransplantation from Baboon to Man: Experience with Six Cases*, 2 TRANSPLANTATION 752 (1964).

3. Jeffrey L. Platt, *New Directions for Organ Transplantation*, 392 NATURE 11 (1998); Thomas E. Starzl et al., *Will Xenotransplantation Ever Be Feasible?*, 186 J. AM. C. SURGEONS 383 (1998).

4. Robert P. Lanza et al., *Xenotransplantation*, 277 SCI. AM. 54 (1997).

5. According to recent Canadian statistics, the shortage of human donor organs is such that each year only 16% of Canadians waiting to receive a heart transplant and 2.7% of Canadians waiting for a kidney transplant actually obtain one. Comparable statistics apply to potential liver and lung transplant patients. *See The Canadian Organ Replacement Register Annual Report: Organ Donation and Transplantation*, 2 CANADIAN INST. FOR HEALTH INFO. (1997).

6. Jonathan S. Allan, *Xenotransplantation at a Crossroads: Prevention Versus Progress*, 2 NATURE MED. 18 (1996); Louisa E. Chapman et al., *Xenotransplantation and Xenogeneic Infections*, 333 NEW ENG. J. MED. 1498 (1995); Jay A. Fishman, *The Risk of Infection in Xenotransplantation*, 862 ANNALS N.Y. ACAD. SCI. 45 (1998); Clive Patience et al., *Zoonosis in Xenotransplantation*, 10 CURRENT OPINION IMMUNOLOGY 539 (1998); Robin A. Weiss, *Transgenic Pigs and Virus Adaptation*, 391 NATURE 327 (1998).

7. *Id.* For a good summary of the risks and benefits associated with xenotransplantation, see Declan Butler et al., *Last Chance to Stop and Think on Risks of Xenotransplantation*, 391 NATURE 320 (1998).

8. *See, e.g.*, Jonathan S. Allan, *Nonhuman Primates as Organ Donors?*, 77 BULL. WORLD HEALTH ORG. 62 (1999); F.H. Bach et al., *Uncertainty in Xenotransplantation:*

trast, other commentators have stressed that progress should not be im-
peded, as the potential benefits to patients could be great and the associated risk to the community remains unquantifiable.[9] Given the recent international flurry of activity preparing for the arrival of xenotransplantation, the latter view seems to be prevailing.[10]

The critical question no longer revolves around whether we have the
scientific knowledge and ability to introduce clinical xenotransplantation,
but is instead directed at the circumstances under which it would be acceptable to proceed. Importantly, despite the divergence of opinion as to
whether further scientific, ethical, and legal analyses are required prior to
introducing clinical xenotransplantation, everyone has agreed that should
xenotransplantation proceed in the near future, the government must also
implement robust public safety measures.[11] The debate now encompasses
an important legal component: to what extent, if at all, will the law be capable of enforcing those public health safeguards that the scientific community deems necessary?

This Article will argue that the legal authority to enforce the most important public health safeguard associated with post-xenotransplantation
surveillance—the periodic collection of bodily specimens such as serum
samples from xenotransplant recipients—could exist, but that its subsis-
tence would ultimately depend on its ability to withstand constitutional
challenges. Although the medical community could not physically compel

---

Individual Benefit Versus Collective Risk, 4 NATURE MED. 141 (1998); Patrik S. Floren-
cio & Timothy Caulfield, *Xenotransplantation and Public Health: Identifying the Legal
Issues*, 90 CAN. J. PUB. HEALTH 282 (1999); Jonathan Hughes, *Xenografting: Ethical
Issues*, 24 J. MED. ETHICS 18 (1998).

    9. *See, e.g.*, David H. Sachs et al., *Xenotransplantation—Caution, But No Morato-
rium*, 4 NATURE MED. 372 (1998); Daniel R. Salomon et al., *Xenotransplants: Proceed
with Caution*, 392 NATURE 11 (1998); Thomas E. Starzl et al., *Will Xenotransplantation
Ever Be Feasible?*, 186 J. AM. C. SURGEONS 383 (1998).

    10. *See, e.g.*, Xavier Bosch, *Spanish Researchers Reject Xeno Moratorium While
Canada Faces the Issue Head-On*, 5 NATURE MED. 361 (1999); Declan Butler, *US Decides Close Tabs Must Be Kept on Xenotransplants and Sets Up a Body To Oversee Trials*, 405 NATURE 606 (2000); Rebecca Currie, *UK Moves Ahead on the Xenotransplantation Issue*, 4 NATURE MED. 988 (1998); Gretchen Vogel, *No Moratorium on Clinical
Trials*, 279 SCI. 648 (1998). *But see* Declan Butler, *Europe is Urged to Hold Back on
Xenotransplant Clinical Trials*, 397 NATURE 281 (1999).

    11. *See generally supra* notes 6, 8 and 9. *See also* L.E. Chapman et al., *Xenotrans-
plantation: The Potential for Xenogeneic Infections*, 31 TRANSPLANTATION PROC. 909
(1999); Jay A. Fishman, *Infection and Xenotransplantation: Developing Strategies to
Minimize Risk*, 862 ANNALS N.Y. ACAD. SCI. 52 (1998); Frederick A. Murphy, *The Public Health Risk of Animal Organ and Tissue Transplantation into Humans*, 273 SCI. 746
(1996); Robin A. Weiss, *Xenografts and Retroviruses*, 285 SCI. 1221 (1999).

recipients to provide serum samples, the government could enact legislation to fine recipients who, having benefited from the life saving intervention, refused to accept responsibility for conforming to the public safety measures.

This Article begins by explaining why the scientific community agrees that xenotransplantation requires robust public safety measures. The Article will demonstrate that the importance of the safeguards lies not in their ability to prevent the emergence of infectious diseases—because they are incapable of doing so—but in their ability to provide the foundation for a rapid response to emerging infectious diseases. The Article then summarizes the nature and scope of the public safety measures proposed by the health authorities in the various countries now contemplating the introduction of clinical xenotransplantation.

The Article goes on to examine the various sources of legal authority that authorities might use to enforce compliance with the safeguards. In this discussion, the Article focuses on the laws of both the United States and Canada for two reasons. First, a comparative review of their laws allows one to draw upon the best practices of two legal traditions in analyzing existing and proposed legal safeguards. Second, the public health systems of these neighboring nations are inextricably intertwined and, although they cannot insulate themselves from the world's public health crises in an age of global travel and migration, coordination of multinational public health efforts would be an excellent start to addressing the problem globally. The final section of the Article comments on the constitutional dimension of the problem in both countries. The Article concludes that restrictions on the rights of recipients that would necessarily result from the enactment of xenotransplantation legislation would be in accordance with the principles of fundamental justice and would thus be demonstrably justified in a free and democratic society.

II. LEGAL REGULATION OF XENOTRANSPLANTATION

A. Public Safety Measures

1. The Need for Public Safety Measures

It is probably fair to state that we are not yet, nor are we likely to become in the near future, masters of the microbial world.[12] Even though

---

12. The microbial world is thought by many to pose one of the biggest threats to the future existence of humankind:

Ingenuity, knowledge, and organization alter but cannot cancel humanity's vulnerability to invasion by parasitic forms of life. Infectious dis-

infectious diseases have always plagued humans, our science is still young and has not yet matured to a level where it might be acceptable to ignore the potential harms that infectious diseases can cause. One need only to look at the devastation wrought by the periodic emergence of yellow fever in European and American cities during the eighteenth and nineteenth centuries to see the damage that infectious disease can cause.[13] Recent examples, such as the 1995 epidemic of Ebola hemorrhagic fever in the Democratic Republic of Congo, demonstrate that our vulnerability to infectious diseases is not a historical relic.[14] The resurgence of diseases such as tuberculosis[15] and the spread of HIV[16] remind us that infectious illnesses can also have a dramatic impact on the modern western world. Today, infectious diseases are the third leading cause of death in the United States, and the leading cause worldwide.[17]

It is because of our physiological vulnerability to infectious microbes that we must proceed prudently and conscientiously when engaging in activities that raise the specter of emerging infectious illnesses, especially when the etiology of disease is our own behavior. Indeed, human behavior

---

ease which antedated the emergence of humankind and will last as long as humanity itself, and will surely remain, as it has been hitherto, one of the fundamental parameters and determinants of human history.

WILLIAM H. MCNEILL, PLAGUES AND PEOPLES 291 (1976). *See also* Joshua Lederberg, *Medical Science, Infectious Diseases, and the Unity of Humankind,* 260 JAMA 684 (1988).

13. For instance, the yellow fever epidemic that hit Memphis in 1878 is recorded to have led to the death of a quarter of its population. J.M. KEATING, HISTORY OF THE YELLOW FEVER EPIDEMIC OF 1878 IN MEMPHIS, TENNESSEE 116 (Cincinnati, Wrightson & Co. 1879).

14. Barbara Kerstiëns & Francine Matthys, *Interventions to Control Virus Transmission during an Outbreak of Ebola Hemorrhagic Fever: Experience from Kikwit, Democratic Republic of the Congo, 1995,* 179 J. INFECTIOUS DISEASES 263 (Supp. 1999). *See also* MICHAEL B.A. OLDSTONE, VIRUSES, PLAGUES, AND HISTORY 130-35 (1998).

15. Christopher Dye et al., *Global Burden of Tuberculosis: Estimated Incidence, Prevalence, and Mortality by Country,* 282 JAMA 677 (1999); Thomas R. Frieden et al., *The Emergence of Drug-Resistant Tuberculosis in New York City,* 328 NEW ENG. J. MED. 52 (1993).

16. Jonathan M. Mann & Daniel J.M. Tarantola, *HIV 1998: The Global Picture,* 279 SCI. AM. 82, 82 (1998) ("Since the early 1980s more than 40 million individuals have contracted HIV, and almost 12 million have died . . . . In 1997 alone, nearly six million people—close to 16,000 a day—acquired HIV, and some 2.3 million perished from it, including 460,000 children.").

17. Gregory L. Armstrong et al., *Trends in Infectious Disease Mortality in the United States During the 20th Century,* 281 JAMA 61 (1999); Sue Binder et al., *Emerging Infectious Diseases: Public Health Issues for the 21st Century,* 284 SCI. 1311 (1999); Robert W. Pinner et al., *Trends in Infectious Diseases Mortality in the United States,* 275 JAMA 189 (1996).

is the leading cause of emerging infectious diseases.[18] For example, the immense volume of global travel has made us more vulnerable to the effects of infectious diseases today than we have ever been in the past.[19] If we are not careful, xenotransplantation could become the next example of human behavior that results in the introduction of new infectious microbes into the human population.[20]

The foregoing commentary means to provide the reader with an awareness of why the scientific community agrees that robust public safety measures must accompany the introduction of xenotransplantation. The following passage embodies the quintessence of this commentary: "[h]istory has shown us repeatedly, in terms of both human suffering and economic loss, that the costs of preparedness through vigilance are far lower than those needed to respond to unanticipated public health crises."[21] In the context of xenotransplantation, preparedness means public health safeguards.

---

18. David M. Forrest, *Control of Imported Communicable Diseases: Preparation and Response*, 87 CAN. J. PUB. HEALTH 368, 368-69 (1996):

> A number of factors, both singly and interactively, facilitate the emergence of new diseases. These include environmental and geoclimatic conditions, fluctuating reservoir and vector characteristics, microbial conditions, and especially, human factors. Human factors include anthropogenic ecological change, alterations in demographics and behaviours, international travel and commerce, and deficiencies in public health structure.

See also Stephen S. Morse & Ann Schluederberg, *Emerging Viruses: The Evolution of Viruses and Viral Diseases*, 162 J. INFECTIOUS DISEASES 7 (1990).

19. Stephen S. Morse, *Factors in the Emergence of Infectious Diseases*, 1 EMERGING INFECTIOUS DISEASES 1, 10 (1995).

> The history of infectious diseases has been a history of microbes on the march, often in our wake, and of microbes that have taken advantage of the rich opportunities offered them to thrive, prosper, and spread. And yet the historical processes that have given rise to the emergence of new infections throughout history continue today with unabated force; in fact, they are accelerating, because the conditions of modern life ensure that the factors responsible for disease emergence are more prevalent than ever before.

See generally MARY E. WILSON, A WORLD GUIDE TO INFECTIONS: DISEASES, DISTRIBUTION, DIAGNOSIS (1991).

20. Patrik S. Florencio & Nathalie Weizmann, *Xenotransplantation and the Role of Human Behaviour in the Emergence of Infectious Disease*, 7 HEALTH L. REV. 20 (1998).

21. Ruth L. Berkelman et al., *Infectious Disease Surveillance: A Crumbling Foundation*, 264 SCI. 368, 370 (1994).

Public safety measures would establish a surveillance system[22] that should permit the early detection of—and a rapid response to—any emerging epidemics.[23] Commentators have often described surveillance as the cornerstone of infectious disease control,[24] and as "essential to minimize illness, disability, death, and economic losses."[25] However, it must be made absolutely clear that any surveillance system would be incapable of preventing the emergence of infectious illnesses. As one group of commentators stated: "surveillance is not the same as prevention. New infectious agents may spread and cause disease among human populations before surveillance techniques have permitted their detection and isolation. Further, detection and isolation of infectious agents does not equate to the containment of their propagation at the human level."[26]

The importance of surveillance is problematic, because, in general, our public health infrastructure is "geared to crisis response, but seems inadequately prepared for proaction, crisis anticipation, and prevention."[27] Prevention means avoiding a public health crisis through instrumentalities such as vaccines and, in the case of xenotransplantation, the imposition of a moratorium until we know more about the associated infectious disease risks. As noted above, however, the current international trend has been to reject the precautionary approach and to prepare for the arrival of clinical xenotransplantation. Further, even if governments implement preventative measures, infectious microbes could still emerge from xenotransplantation and could result in severe morbidity and mortality if pathogenic in human populations. Appropriate safeguards would nevertheless represent an essential precaution to such consequences, as they would ideally enable offi-

---

22. The United Kingdom Xenotransplantation Interim Regulatory Authority (UKXIRA), the regulatory authority in charge of overseeing xenobiotechnology in England, defines surveillance as the "on-going systematic collection, analysis, and interpretation of relevant data, closely integrated with the timely dissemination of these data to those responsible for control and prevention" and state that surveillance is a "critical step in the pathway of identification and prevention of infectious diseases and xenogeneic infections." *See* U.K. XENOTRANSPLANTATION INTERIM REGULATORY AUTH., DRAFT REPORT OF THE INFECTION SURVEILLANCE STEERING GROUP OF THE UKXIRA 6, 17 (May 1999), *at* http://www.doh.gov.uk/pub/docs/doh/surveil.pdf [hereinafter UKXIRA].

23. James M. Hughes & John R. La Montagne, *Emerging Infectious Diseases* 170 J. INFECTIOUS DISEASES 263 (1994).

24. Donald A. Henderson, *Surveillance Systems and Intergovernmental Cooperation, in* EMERGING VIRUSES 283 (Stephen S. Morse ed., 1993). *See also* Ruth L. Berkelman & James M. Hughes, *The Conquest of Infectious Diseases: Who Are We Kidding?* 119 ANNALS INTERNAL MED. 426 (1993).

25. Binder et al., *supra* note 17, at 1311.

26. Florencio & Caulfield, *supra* note 8, at 283-84.

27. Forrest, *supra* note 18, at 368.

cials to respond quickly to emerging infectious diseases through the rapid detection and isolation of the microbes responsible for causing sickness and the subsequent development of treatments.

2. *Proposed Public Safety Measures in the Case of Xenotransplantation*

Recognizing the need for public safety measures to accompany the clinical introduction of xenotransplantation, the health departments of various governments—including those of the United States,[28] the United Kingdom,[29] and Canada[30]—have drafted guidelines proposing public health safeguards that are intended to form the foundation of infectious disease surveillance. Although each country's guidelines differ in many respects, each imposes similar requirements on xenotransplant recipients. In light of this similarity, and to avoid repetition, this Article will use the recently drafted guidelines from the United Kingdom to exemplify the nature of the safeguards proposed in all three jurisdictions.[31]

According to the United Kingdom's guidelines, its surveillance system intends to enable the prompt recognition, investigation and management of infectious illnesses that might emerge as a result of xenobiotechnology.[32] In order to have access to clinical xenotransplantation, recipients would need to agree to: 1) the periodic provision of bodily samples that would then be archived for epidemiological purposes;[33] 2) post-mortem analysis in case of death, the storage of samples post-mortem, and the disclosure of this agreement to their family; 3) refrain from donating blood, tissue or organs; 4) the use of barrier contraception when engaging in sexual intercourse; 5) keep both name and current address on register and to notify the

---

28. *See* U.S. DEP'T OF HEALTH AND HUMAN SERVS., PHS GUIDELINE ON INFECTIOUS DISEASE ISSUES IN XENOTRANSPLANTATION, *at* http://www.fda.gov/cber/gdlns/xenophs0101.pdf (January 19, 2001) [hereinafter U.S. DEP'T OF HEALTH AND HUMAN SERVS.].

29. *See* UKXIRA, *supra* note 22.

30. *See* HEALTH CANADA, PROPOSED CANADIAN STANDARD FOR XENOTRANSPLANTATION, *at* http://www.hc-sc.gc.ca/hpb-dgps/therapeut/zfiles/english/btox/standards/xeno_std_e.html (July 1999) [hereinafter HEALTH CANADA].

31. Although we have chosen to focus on American and Canadian law in this Article, we believe that the xenotransplantation guidelines issued by the United Kingdom are the most comprehensive to date, and are therefore the best model for the discussion of Western governments' preliminary thinking about xenotransplantation safeguards.

32. *See* UKXIRA, *supra* note 22, at 8.

33. *Id.* at 29. The guidelines, which are subject to review on the basis of emerging scientific information, call for baseline sampling pre-xenotransplantation and for sampling at 0-2 days; 2, 4 and 6 weeks; 3 and 6 months; 1 and 2 years post-xenotransplantation.

relevant health authorities when moving abroad; and 6) divulge confidential information, including one's status as a xenotransplant recipient, to researchers, all health care professionals from whom one seeks professional services, and close contacts such as current and future sexual partners.[34] The recipient would have to adhere to these obligations consistently for the recipient's lifetime, or until the government determines that there is no longer a need for public health safeguards.[35]

By far the most important of these public health safeguards, and the only safeguard that will be receiving attention throughout this article, is the collection and archiving of bodily specimens that are needed for epidemiological purposes. Regarding this essential safeguard, the United Kingdom's guidelines state that:

> Surveillance of potential xenogeneic infections in humans *requires* access to human and animal data . . . . Effective public health response to an incident [of infectious disease] is *dependent* on both maintenance of records and of archived specimens both at the time of xenotransplantation and for the future. Animal and human specimens need to be held for public purposes. Access by the relevant authorities to appropriate information and samples from locally held records and archives *must be a precondition to approval for a clinical trial.*[36]

Even outside of the context of xenobiotechnology, scientists have been calling for "well-controlled epidemiology, careful clinical and histologic observations, and increased attention to specimen collection and processing."[37] Without the enforcement of this safeguard in connection with

---

34. *Id.* at 29-30.

35. *Id.* at 11, 21.

36. *Id.* at 10-13 (emphasis added). Similarly, the Canadian guidelines stipulate that the "patient will *need* to comply with long term surveillance *necessitating* routine physical evaluations with archiving of tissues and/or serum specimens from the recipient" and that "[c]onsent should indicate that the patient is *obligated* to follow all of the requirements of the program." HEALTH CANADA, *supra* note 30 (emphasis added). Moreover, the United States guidelines state for example that "[p]ost-xenotransplantation clinical and laboratory surveillance of xenotransplantation recipients is *critical, as it provides the means of monitoring for any* introduction and propagation of xenogeneic infectious agents in the xenotransplantation product recipient." DEP'T OF HEALTH AND HUMAN SERVS., *supra* note 28, at 35 (emphasis added).

37. David A. Relman, *The Search for Unrecognized Pathogens,* 284 SCI. 1308, 1310 (1999). *See also* K.F. Gensheimer et al., *Preparing for Pandemic Influenza: The Need for Enhanced Surveillance,* 5 EMERGING INFECTIOUS DISEASES 297, 297 (1999) ("Because it establishes the scientific foundation for a public health response, surveillance is the single most important tool for identifying new or re-emerging infectious diseases with potential to cause serious public health problems.").

xenotransplantation, scientists would be handicapped in detecting and isolating the infectious microbes causing any resulting illness. Such a handicap could prove to be fatal because until doctors identify the illness-causing microbes, treatment strategies may be no more sophisticated than a game of trial and error.

B. Enforcing Public Safety Measures

Although the scientific community almost universally agrees that public health safeguards must be a prerequisite to the introduction of clinical xenotransplantation, and although extensive work has gone into the development of comprehensive safeguards, little thought has been given to how to enforce these safeguards. The relevant scientific literature often appears to assume that the law will be able to accommodate and enforce whatever measures scientists deem necessary.[38] The reality is that there are limits to the enforcement measures that the law can currently accommodate.

The remaining sections of this Article discuss whether officials could use existing or novel legal frameworks to enforce the proposed public safety measures. Possibilities among existing law include consent law, the law of contracts, and existing public health legislation. Because the law is not immutable, it can be adapted to reflect changing social and scientific realities. Thus, even if the public safety measures prove unenforceable under existing law, legislatures could enact new statutes or executive agencies could adopt new regulations that would render lawful the required enforcement mechanisms.

Regardless of the approved legal standards, the judiciary could declare these new enactments illegal if they transgress constitutionally protected rights and freedoms. If the courts strike down such legislation on constitutional grounds, xenotransplant recipients in the relevant jurisdiction would not be legally obligated to comply with the public health safeguards. As a result, the ability of scientists to gather epidemiological data in that jurisdiction, and hence the capacity of the public safety measures to perform their protective function, would depend entirely on the willingness of recipients to comply voluntarily with the invasive measures. In the absence of such willingness, the surveillance system would crumble, leaving society defenseless in the advent of an epidemic. Part III of this Article examines the constitutional limitations that courts might impose on public safety legislation.

---

38. *See, e.g.*, Michele L. Pearson, M.D. et al., *Xenotransplantation: Is the Future Upon Us?*, 19 INFECTION CONTROL AND HOSP. EPIDEMIOLOGY (1998). Other scientific articles recognize that enforcement may be an issue but defer discussion of enforcement to other commentators. *See, e.g.*, Bach et al., *supra* note 8, at 144.

1. From Informed Consent to Binding Contract?

a) Informed Consent is Not a Promise to Undertake Future Obligations

Mandatory compliance with public safety measures has rarely, if ever, served as a prerequisite to having access to innovative medical interventions. Indeed, the case of xenotransplantation would be exceptional in this regard; all that is normally required before doctors provide medical treatment is the patient's informed consent.[39] Lawmakers designed informed consent to correct the imbalance in knowledge, and hence power, between health care providers and patients.[40] It is premised on the patient's right to self-determination[41] and requires the physician to disclose "the nature of the proposed operation, its gravity, any material risks and any special or unusual risks attendant upon the performance of the operation."[42] The level of disclosure required varies depending on the nature of the intervention.[43] In the case of experimental procedures such as xenotransplantation, the degree of disclosure would be higher than that necessary for conventional medical treatments.[44]

In addition to the right to know, the patient's right to self-determination encompasses the right to accept or reject treatment.[45] It is ultimately the patient, and not the health care provider, who decides whether or not the intervention will be performed. Moreover, health care providers cannot interfere with the patient's decision to refuse treatment, no matter how foolish or medically unsound they believe it to be.[46]

---

39. ELLEN T. PICARD & GERALD B. ROBERTSON, LEGAL LIABILITY OF DOCTORS AND HOSPITALS IN CANADA 84-85 (3d ed. 1996).

40. Dow Corning Corp. v. Hollis, [1995] 4 S.C.R. 634, 656 ("The doctrine of 'informed consent' was developed as a judicial attempt to redress the inequality of information that characterizes a doctor-patient relationship.").

41. For an early source making reference to this right, see Schloendorff v. Soc'y of N.Y. Hosps., 105 N.E. 92, 93 (N.Y. Ct. App. 1914) ("Every human being of adult years and sound mind has a right to determine what shall be done with his own body."). *See generally* Tom L. Beauchamp, *Informed Consent, in* MEDICAL ETHICS 185-208 (Robert M. Veatch ed., 1997).

42. Hopp v. Lepp, [1980] 2 S.C.R. 192, 210. *See also* Canterbury v. Spence, 464 F.2d 772 (D.C. Cir. 1972); Salgo v. Leland Stanford Jr. Univ. Bd. of Trs., 317 P.2d 170 (1957); Reibl v. Hughes, [1980] 2 S.C.R. 880.

43. Margaret A. Somerville, *Structuring the Issues in Informed Consent,* 26 MCGILL L.J. 740 (1981).

44. Weiss v. Solomon, [1989] 48 C.C.L.T. 280, 282 (Que. S.C.); Halushka v. Univ. of Sask., [1965] 53 D.L.R. (2d) 436, 443-44 (Sask. C.A.).

45. Hopp, 2 S.C.R. at 192.

46. *See* Fleming v. Reid, [1991] 4 O.R. (3d) 74, 85 (C.A.):

Although the doctrine of informed consent protects the patient's right to know the risks of a medical procedure, it does not bind the patient to a contractual agreement. Importantly, consent speaks not to the patient's promise to undertake future obligations in consideration of having access to medical care, but to the patient's initial acquiescence to a particular intervention. In the case of xenotransplantation, the recipient's consent to the intervention, even with full understanding of the accompanying public health safeguards, would not legally bind the recipient to comply with the safeguards. This is because the recipient's right to self-determination continues after she gives her initial consent and begins treatment. Recipients could withdraw their consent, written or otherwise, at any time.[47]

Because the recipient's consent is insufficient to guarantee adherence to public safety measures, some other legal mechanism is required. This alternative mechanism will necessarily conflict with the now-entrenched patient autonomy model of medical decision making. As such, officials would need to find a distinct source of legal authority that might be used to trump or pre-empt the application of the right to self-determination. What we must therefore determine is the nature of the legal authority that might accomplish this task.

b) Contract Law Is Not a Viable Enforcement Mechanism

Medical commentators have emphasized that the law of contracts may provide a means of legally enforcing a patient's compliance with the safeguards. For instance, according to one commentator, "[t]he fact that the patient is going to be *required* to comply with postoperative monitoring alters the nature of 'consent' to something more binding and contrac-

---

The fact that serious risks or consequences may result from a refusal of medical treatment does not vitiate the right of medical self-determination. The doctrine of informed consent ensures the freedom of individuals to make choices about their medical care. It is the patient, not the doctor, who ultimately must decide if treatment—any treatment—is to be administered.

See also Walker v. Region 2 Hospital Corp., [1994] 116 D.L.R. (4th) 477 (N.B.C.A.); Malette v. Shulman, [1990] 67 D.L.R. (4th) 321 (Ont. C.A.).

47. *See* Ciarlariello v. Schacter, [1993] 2 S.C.R. 119, 136 (holding that a "patient's right to bodily integrity provides the basis for the withdrawal of a consent to a medical procedure even while it is underway."). The right to withdraw consent exists even in the context of life sustaining interventions. *See* Cruzan v. Dir., Miss. Dept. of Health, 497 U.S. 261 (1990) (holding that vegetative patient's wishes to not have life sustaining interventions must be honored if they are proven with clear and convincing evidence); Nancy B v. Hotel-Dieu de Québec, [1992] 86 D.L.R. (4th) 385 (Que. S.C.).

950 BERKELEY TECHNOLOGY LAW JOURNAL [Vol. 16:937

tual."[48] According to another commentator, recipients and their close contacts:

> would not only have to agree to the risks attendant to a transplant procedure, but also to a contract binding the patient and others to carry out future obligations, including the patient's possible quarantine, as well as modification of the guarantees of confidentiality and surrender of the right to 'drop out' of the study.[49]

As currently formulated, the law of contracts would most likely be unable to ensure that recipients comply with the public health safeguards. At first blush, one might employ the common law theories of promise[50] or reliance[51] to validate the contract. The theory here would be that since the recipient promises to comply with the safeguards and society relies upon that promise, society should be able to enforce the promise. Indeed, one might view compliance with the safeguards as the consideration that is required in order to have access to the innovative biotechnology. Similarly, under the Civil Code of Quebec, all that is theoretically required for the existence of a valid contract is a meeting of the minds between persons having the capacity to contract.[52] Yet, there are a number of reasons for believing that the law of contracts would be incapable of serving as an effective source of legal enforcement.

There are two threshold challenges to using the law of contracts as a source of legal authority. One must first identify the legal entity with

---

48. A.S. Daar, *Ethics of Xenotransplantation: Animal Issues, Consent, and Likely Transformation of Transplant Ethics*, 21 WORLD J. SURGERY 975, 977 (1997). *See also* A.S. Daar, *Animal-to-Human Organ Transplantation—A Solution or a New Problem?*, 77 BULL. WORLD HEALTH ORG. 54, 58 (1999).

49. Bach et al., *supra* note 8, at 144. *See also* DAVID K.C. COOPER & ROBERT P. LANZA, XENO: THE PROMISE OF TRANSPLANTING ANIMAL ORGANS INTO HUMANS 218 (2000):

> What is being envisaged is no longer a simple matter of the patient's signing a consent form after being provided with the necessary information. In view of the perceived potential risk to the community from infection passed from the patient to his or her contacts, the patient will be expected to enter into what can be considered a 'contract' with the surgical team and transplant center. Some have suggested that this might have to be a binding legal contract. The patient—and possibly even members of the patient's family—will agree to lifelong monitoring in return for the potential benefits that might result from undergoing the xenotransplant.

50. *See generally* CHARLES FRIED, CONTRACTS AS PROMISE (1981).

51. *See generally* P.S. ATIYAH, THE RISE AND FALL OF FREEDOM OF CONTRACT (1979).

52. *See* Arts. 1378, 1385 C.C.Q. (Can.).

whom the recipients would be contracting and determine whether that entity would have the legal capacity to enter into and enforce such contractual undertakings. Stated differently, who would be the creditor of the recipient's obligation of complying with the safeguards? The surgical team or institution performing the operation? The federal or provincial/state government(s)? Society? Moreover, could any of these "creditors" enforce the obligation?

Assuming that one could answer these threshold queries, a court could nevertheless strike down the contract, or at least render it unenforceable, as being against public policy.[53] Compulsory compliance with the safeguards would require the relinquishment of certain civil liberties, and, as a matter of public policy or human rights, it is highly unlikely that these could be contracted away.[54] Recipients may initially agree to bind themselves to contracts calling for, among other things, the periodic provision of bodily samples. If they later withdraw their consent, however, the specific performance of these contracts would be incompatible with legislation upholding civil liberties such as the inviolability of the body.[55] To be lawful, an invasion of civil liberties would have to be expressly authorized by legislation and the legislation would itself be subject to constitutional scrutiny.

Even after surmounting these hurdles, courts could nonetheless consider the contracts to be illicit. This is true because, unlike most contracts, under which there is no requirement that the debtor personally perform the obligation(s),[56] the nature of the contractual undertaking in the case of xenotransplantation requires the recipient to comply with the safeguards himself or herself.

The civil law of Quebec refers to such contracts as *intuitu personae* and generally refuses to enforce them.[57] Simply put, enforcement of such

---

53. *See* RESTATEMENT (SECOND) OF CONTRACTS § 178 (1981).

54. *See, e.g.,* Arts. 3(2), 8 C.C.Q. (Can.).

55. *See, e.g.,* Arts. 3(1), 10 C.C.Q. (Can.); *see also Quebec Charter of Human Rights and Freedoms*, R.S.Q., ch. C-12, § 1, pmbl. (1985) (Can.). The specific performance of these contracts would also engage constitutional protections such as the rights to liberty and security of the person. *See* CAN. CONST. (Constitution Act 1982), pt. I (Canadian Charter of Rights and Freedoms), cl. 11 § 7; *see also* U.S. CONST. amend. XIII (outlawing involuntary servitude).

56. In general, the debtor of the obligation(s) under a contract always has the option of delegating the performance of the obligations to a third party such as an agent or an employee.

57. Specific performance of the contract can be enforced so long as there is no requirement that the contract's prestation be carried out by the debtor in person. *See* Rosa-

952   BERKELEY TECHNOLOGY LAW JOURNAL   [Vol. 16:937]

contracts would lead to a conflict between two competing legal values—those of holding the debtor to her word, and respect for individual liberty.[58] In light of this conflict, the State may not use its power to force the debtor personally to execute the contract's obligations.[59]

In the common law, the remedy of specific performance best approximates the idea behind *intuitu personae* contracts. The traditional rule has been that equitable relief clauses, requiring the specific performance of contractual obligations, will only be awarded when monetary damages are inadequate.[60] Such is the case where the contractual obligation involves the transfer of a "unique" parcel of land.[61] Given that the viability of the public health safeguards depend on the execution of the contractual undertakings by the recipients personally, the circumstances of xenotransplantation arguably present another occasion where a court may consider monetary damages inadequate. Yet, similarly to Quebec civil law, Canadian[62] and American[63] common law seldom enforce the specific performance of personal service contracts.

It is also unlikely that the law of contracts could furnish an alternative remedy to specific performance, such as monetary damages that might be

---

lie Jukier, *The Emergence of Specific Performance as a Major Remedy in Quebec Law*, 47 REVUE DU BARREAU 47 (1987).

58. JEAN-LOUIS BAUDOUIN, LES OBLIGATIONS 413 (4th ed. 1993):

L'exécution en nature d'une obligation de faire, par le débiteur lui-même, pose clairement le conflit entre deux principes juridiques fondamentaux: le respect de la parole donnée, qui exige que la loi fasse tout pour obliger le débiteur à l'exécution, et le respect de la liberté individuelle, selon lequel la loi ne doit pas, dans des circonstances ordinaires, aller jusqu'à priver de sa liberté celui qui ne respecte pas son engagement.

59. *Id.*

60. *See* Harnett v. Yielding, [1805] 2 Sch. & Lef. 549, 553; *see also* George T. Washington, *Damages in Contract at Common Law*, 47 L.Q. REV. 345 (1931).

61. Semelhago v. Paramadevan, [1996] 2 S.C.R. 415, 424-25.

62. *See* Warner Bros. Pictures Inc. v. Nelson, [1937] 1 K.B. 209; Emerald Resources Ltd. v. Sterling Oil Props. Mgmt. Ltd., [1969] 3 D.L.R. (3d) 630, 647 (Alta. C.A.) ("An example of a contract of which the Court will not compel specific performance is a contract of personal service . . . . [T]his seems to be based on the grounds of public policy; that it would be improper to make one man serve another against his will."), *aff'd*, [1970] 15 D.L.R. (3d) 256 (S.C.C.). *See generally*, ROBERT J. SHARPE, INJUNCTIONS AND SPECIFIC PERFORMANCE 7.540-7.630 (2000) (looseleaf ed.).

63. *See* Fitzpatrick v. Michael, 9A.2d 639 (Md. 1939); American Broadcasting Companies, Inc. v. Warner Wolf, 420 N.E.2d 363 (N.Y. Ct. App. 1981). Judicial compulsion of performance may even run afoul of the Thirteenth Amendment to the United States Constitution that prohibits involuntary servitude. *See* Arthur v. Oakes, 63 F. 310, 318 (7th Cir. 1894).

used indirectly to coerce the recipient into compliance. This is because the most logical creditor of the obligation (the surgical team or transplant center) would suffer no loss as a result of a breach of contract. The loss would instead be borne by the public, the third-party beneficiary to the contract. Yet, the public similarly would be incapable of obtaining an award in damages following a breach of contract. The common laws of the United States[64] and Canada,[65] as well as the civil law of Quebec,[66] require that one could identify third-party beneficiaries at the time the promise is to be performed. The 'public,' however, is not an identifiable beneficiary. As a result, the most vital safeguard—the collection and archiving of bodily samples from recipients for epidemiological purposes—would remain unenforceable under contract law.[67]

2. Current Public Health Legislation

a) Current Public Health Legislation is Designed to Curb the Spread of Infectious Disease by Authorizing Examination of Individuals and Penalties for Non-compliance

The federal governments of both the United States and Canada have enacted legislation designed to curb the spread of communicable disease.[68] While the American federal government, acting primarily through the Centers for Disease Control and Prevention,[69] has been active in commu-

---

64. E. ALLAN FARNSWORTH, CONTRACTS § 10.3 (3rd ed. 1999).

65. In common law Canada, the doctrine of privity has not been relaxed to the extent that it has in other jurisdictions such as Quebec and the United States. As a result, third-party beneficiaries can only derive rights from a contract in very narrow circumstances. *See* Fraser River Pile & Dredge v. Can-Dive Servs. Ltd., [1999] 3 S.C.R. 108; London Drugs Ltd. v. Nagel Int'l Ltd., [1992] 3 S.C.R. 299. The public would not be recognized as a third-party beneficiary in common law Canada.

66. Arts. 1444-1445 C.C.Q. (Can.).

67. Even if this third party beneficiary problem were solved, the courts could construe any damages specified in a contract with a xenotransplant recipient as punitive penalties rather than liquidated damages. Such categorization would render such measures unenforceable, however, as it is a fundamental precept of contract law that damages for breach of contract must be an estimation of actual damages resulting from the breach, not a coercive mechanism to obtain performance. *See* RESTATEMENT (SECOND) OF CONTRACTS § 356 (1981). The same rule applies in Canada. *See* G.H.L. FRIDMAN, THE LAW OF CONTRACT IN CANADA 811-17(4th ed. 1999).

68. *See, e.g.,* 42 U.S.C. § 264 (1994) (U.S. Public Health Service Authority); 21 C.F.R. § 1240 (2001) (U.S. Food and Drug Administration Authority); Quarantine Act, R.S.C., ch. Q-1 (2000) (Can.).

69. The Centers for Disease Control and Prevention is an agency of the United States Department of Health and Human Services. For a description of the U.S. Centers for Disease Control's active role in public health matters, see Centers for Disease Control

nicable disease control, the Canadian federal government's participation has largely been limited to the management of communicable disease in the context of people crossing the Canadian border.[70]

In addition to this central regulation through their federal governments, each U.S. state[71] as well as every Canadian province and territory[72] has enacted public health legislation specifically addressing communicable disease control. In Canada, although some provinces such as British Columbia and Saskatchewan have enacted specific venereal disease legislation,[73] most provinces deal with all communicable diseases by way of a single statute.[74] In the United States, the public health laws of most states are much more disease specific.[75] For instance, in addition to having a number of provisions that apply to communicable diseases generally, New York's public health law also has separate provisions dealing specifically with typhoid fever, poliomyelitis, tuberculosis, HIV, and others.[76]

In both the United States and Canada, public health legislation affords wide powers to public health officials. These include the powers to examine, detain, and isolate individuals, and to enter and close places.[77] Given that the collection and archiving of bodily samples is vital to effective post-xenotransplantation surveillance, the most significant power con-

---

and Prevention, About CDC, *at* http://www.cdc.gov/aboutCDC.htm (last modified July 28, 2001).

70. *See* Immigration Act, R.S.C., ch. I-2, § 91 (2000) (Can.); Quarantine Act, R.S.C., ch. Q-1 (2000) (Can.).

71. *See, e.g.,* DEL. CODE ANN. tit. 16 §§ 501-508 (2001); D.C. CODE ANN. § 6-117 (1999); KAN. STAT. ANN. § 65-118 (2000); KAN. STAT. ANN. §§ 65-116(a)-(m), 119, 122, 123, 126-129 (1992).

72. Public Health Act, R.S.A. 1984, ch. P-27.1 (2001) (Can.); Public Health Act, R.S.M., ch. P210 (2001) (Can.); Health Protection and Promotion Act, R.S.O. 1990, ch. H-7 (2001) (Can.).

73. *See* Venereal Disease Act, R.S.B.C. 1996, ch. 475 (2001) (Can.); Venereal Disease Prevention Act, R.S.S. 1978, ch. V-4 (2000) (Can.).

74. *See* Public Health Act, R.S.A. 1984, ch. P-27.1 (2001) (Can.); Public Health Act, R.S.M., ch. P210 (2001) (Can.); Health Protection and Promotion Act, R.S.O. 1990, ch. H-7 (2001) (Can.).

75. *See, e.g.,* COLO. REV. STAT. § 25-4-1201 (2000) (streptococcus); DEL. CODE ANN. tit. 16 § 507 (2001) (diphtheria immunization); FLA. STAT. § 392.51 (2000) (tuberculosis); MD. CODE ANN. HEALTH-GEN. I § 18-324 (2001) (tuberculosis).

76. N.Y. PUB. HEALTH LAW § 2120 (McKinney 2001) (typhoid fever); N.Y. PUB. HEALTH LAW § 2164 (poliomyelitis, mumps, vaccinations); N.Y. PUB. HEALTH LAW § 2200 (McKinney 2001) (tuberculosis); N.Y. PUB. HEALTH LAW § 2781 (McKinney 2001) (HIV testing).

77. *See, e.g.,* DEL. CODE ANN. tit. 16 §§ 501-508 (2001); MD. CODE ANN. HEALTH-GEN. I § 18-324 (2001); Public Health Act, R.S.A. 1984, ch. P-27.1 §§ 30, 39, 40 (2001) (Can.); Health Protection and Promotion Act, R.S.O. 1990, ch. H-7 § 22(4) (2001) (Can.).

tained in public health legislation will be the authority to examine individuals. The nature and extent of the power to examine, however, varies from jurisdiction to jurisdiction. In the province of Ontario, for example, the medical officer of health can direct a person—under the authority of the Health Protection and Promotion Act—to submit "to an examination by a physician."[78] Unfortunately, because the Act does not define the term "examination," it is unclear whether this includes the power to collect bodily specimens.

The legislation in Quebec, although equally ambiguous, appears to grant relatively broad powers of examination.[79] The legislation specifies that the Minister of Health and Social Services has the duty to "establish and maintain a system for gathering . . . medical and epidemiological data . . . ."[80] Further, the provincial government, in consultation with the Bureau of Quebec Physicians, has the authority to "take the steps necessary" to examine persons coming under the jurisdiction of the relevant act.[81] Similarly, the California Health and Safety Code authorizes the State Department of Health, upon being informed by a health officer of any contagious, infectious, or communicable disease, to "take measures as are necessary to ascertain the nature of the disease and prevent its spread."[82] If the language of necessity in the Quebec and California statutes is meant to authorize a particular mode of examination so long as it can qualify as "necessary" to the determination of whether an individual is infected with a communicable disease, then these laws could be used to sanction the collection of bodily specimens.[83]

Some legislation, however, unambiguously provides for the collection of bodily samples. For instance, British Columbia's legislation specifically authorizes the collection of "blood, sputum or other excreta" and the per-

---

78. Health Protection and Promotion Act, R.S.O. 1990, ch. H.7, § 22(4)(f) (2001) (Can.).

79. *See* Public Health Protection Act, R.S.Q. 1977, ch. P-35 (2001) (Can.).

80. *Id.* § 2(d).

81. *Id.* §§ 10, 11.

82. CAL. HEALTH & SAFETY CODE § 120,140 (West 2000). *See also id.* § 120,175.

83. Alberta's public health legislation also uses the language of necessity and, although equally as broad, is somewhat less vague than the legislation in Quebec and California. The Alberta legislation would almost certainly authorize the collection of bodily specimens since it provides that individuals coming under the purview of the Act must "submit to *any examinations necessary* to determine whether the person is infected with the disease." Public Health Act, R.S.A. 1984, ch. P-27.1, § 41 (2001) (Can.) (emphasis added).

formance of X-ray examinations.[84] Likewise, New York's public health law provides that the commissioner of health can set forth in the sanitary code of the state of New York "the diseases for which specimens shall be submitted for examination to a laboratory approved by the department."[85]

In sum, the power to collect bodily samples for the purposes of examination probably exists in most jurisdictions. While the legislation in some jurisdictions expressly and unambiguously provides for the collection of bodily specimens, the legislation in other jurisdictions uses language that is sufficiently broad to infer the existence of the power to take samples.

On balance, public health law provides a more satisfactory legal mechanism to enforce xenotransplantation precautions than contract law. Unlike the law of contracts, public health law encompasses the authority to demand the performance of human conduct that officials deem necessary to protect society from the spread of infectious diseases.[86] Moreover, the enforcement provisions of public health legislation have greater coercive effect than those of contract law since courts can levy severe penalties for non-compliance with an order given pursuant to legislation. The nature and extent of these penalties vary greatly among jurisdictions. For instance, although every jurisdiction empowers officials to impose a monetary fine in the case of non-compliance, the maximum fine that they can issue varies greatly.[87] In addition, while the legislation in some jurisdictions provides only for the imposition of monetary fines,[88] the legislation

---

84. Health Act, R.S.B.C. 1996, ch. 179, § 65(3) (2001) (Can.). Similarly, Saskatchewan public health legislation authorizes the taking of "specimens of blood or body discharge." Venereal Disease Prevention Act, R.S.S. 1978, ch. V-4, § 15(2) (2000) (Can.).

85. N.Y. PUB. HEALTH LAW § 225(5)(g) (McKinney 2001). *See also id.* § 201 (requiring the New York state department of health to "conduct laboratory examinations for the diagnosis and control of disease"); *id.* § 2100 (requiring local boards of health to exercise "proper and vigilant medical examination and control of all persons . . . infected with or exposed to [communicable diseases].").

86. *See supra* note 77 and accompanying text.

87. In Quebec, public health law authorizes the imposition of monetary fines up to a maximum of $1000 for each day that the offense continues. Public Health Protection Act, R.S.Q. 1977, ch. P-35, § 71 (2001) (Can.). In Ontario, the maximum is $5000 for each day or part day that the offense continues. Health Protection and Promotion Act, R.S.O. 1990, ch. H.7, § 101(1) (2001) (Can.). In contrast to these elevated penalties, Alberta's legislation provides for a fine of not more than $100 for each day that the offense continues. Public Health Act, R.S.A. 1984, ch. P-27.1, § 81(2) (2001) (Can.).

88. *See, e.g., id.*

in other jurisdictions also permits the temporary incarceration of non-compliant individuals.[89]

In short, current public health legislation may offer a source of legal authority from which to guarantee compliance with post-xenotransplantation public safety measures. Unlike contract law, existing public health legislation in some jurisdictions can require the performance of conduct such as the collection of bodily specimens. In addition, because of its strong enforcement provisions, public health law has coercive tools that contract law does not. What remains to be determined, however, is whether there are any impediments that might frustrate or disqualify the use of current public health legislation as a means of regulating xenotransplantation.

b) Current Public Health Legislation is Nevertheless Incapable of Adequately Regulating Xenotransplantation

One possible impediment to the use of current public health legislation is the common law right to self-determination. This right grants individuals the authority to accept, reject and/or withdraw their consent to medical treatments. The right to self-determination may not, however, hinder the application and enforcement of public health legislation, because statutes take precedence over such common law doctrines. Moreover, should a separate statute protect the right to self-determination, as it does in Ontario,[90] the public health legislation typically pre-empts the application of a conflicting statute.[91]

Nevertheless, there are a number of other reasons why current public health legislation cannot regulate xenotransplantation. One reason is that in the case of xenotransplantation, officials probably could not satisfy the legislation's conditions precedent. Typical conditions include the presence of a certain level of proof that the individual in question has in fact contracted an infectious disease and poses a risk to the public health. In Quebec, for example, officials have the power to examine only a "person who apparently has a disease" contemplated by the legislation.[92] In Ontario, officials must have "reasonable and probable" grounds for believing that a

---

89. In New York, violations of the sanitary code can result in both monetary penalties as well as imprisonment. A first offense is punishable by a fine not exceeding $250 or by imprisonment for a time not exceeding 15 days, or both. N.Y. PUB. HEALTH LAW § 229 (McKinney 2001). A subsequent offense is punishable by a fine not exceeding $500 or by imprisonment for a time not exceeding 15 days, or both. *Id.*

90. *See* Health Care Consent Act, S.O. 1996, ch. 2 (2001) (Can.).

91. *See, e.g.,* Health Protection and Promotion Act, R.S.O. 1990, ch. H-7, §22(5.1) (2001) (Can.).

92. Public Health Protection Act, R.S.Q. 1977, ch. P-35 § 11 (2001) (Can.).

communicable disease "exists or may exist or that there is an immediate risk of an outbreak"; that the disease "presents a risk to the health of persons"; and that "the requirements specified in the order are necessary in order to decrease or eliminate the risk to health presented by the communicable disease."[93]

In general, satisfaction of the required level of proof will depend on the extent to which an individual *appears* to be sick. Thus, if an individual exhibits symptoms of infection officials may have grounds for invoking the legislation. In contrast, if an individual is asymptomatic officials will normally not have prima facie grounds justifying the application of the intrusive legislation. There are, however, exceptions to this general rule. Tuberculosis legislation in California provides one such exception. The legislation allows officials to examine those who are in close contact with individuals infected with active tuberculosis and anyone else officials have "reasonable grounds to determine are at heightened risk of tuberculosis exposure."[94] Such exceptions are present only in legislation that applies only to specific diseases and are therefore not generally applicable.

Because the infectious disease risks associated with xenotransplantation, even if foreseeable, are theoretical both in nature and in severity, there would probably be insufficient grounds for invoking and applying general public health law provisions to recipients for as long as they remained asymptomatic.[95] Yet, the viability of a post-xenotransplantation surveillance system depends upon its ability to collect epidemiological data whether the recipients appear to be symptomatic or not. Similarly, existing public health legislation would be inapplicable to xenotransplantation because it applies only to infectious diseases that legislators can list in the legislation or corresponding regulations. For instance, New York's officials can only enforce their public health legislation against individuals infected by or exposed to a communicable disease that the sanitary code expressly designates.[96]

---

93. Health Protection and Promotion Act, R.S.O. 1990, ch. H.7, § 22(2) (2001) (Can.).

94. CAL. HEALTH & SAFETY CODE § 120,142 (West 2000). *See also id.* §§ 121,363, 121,364.

95. As one group of commentators put it: "existing legislation would require modification in order to compel the continued surveillance of asymptomatic individuals. In general, Canadian public health laws are designed to allow a response when an individual has a known infectious disease. There are no 'monitoring' provisions." Florencio & Caulfield, *supra* note 8, at 283.

96. N.Y. PUB. HEALTH LAW § 2100 (McKinney 2001). Similarly, Ontario's public health legislation only applies to communicable and virulent diseases, the former being defined as "a disease specified as a communicable disease by regulation made by the

The degree of specificity that the application of public health legislation currently requires is unattainable for xenotransplantation. Commentators have described xenotransplantation as presenting an unquantifiable yet undeniable risk to the public health.[97] The risk is undeniable because our science base enables us to appreciate the theoretical threats associated with xenotransplantation. More importantly, the risk remains unquantifiable because we have a limited ability to predict the nature and extent of the harms that might arise. Scientists have already discovered the identity of one potential disease threat that is capable of replicating in human cells in vitro[98] and in mice in vivo,[99] but does not appear to lead to illness in recipients.[100] There could exist countless other infectious agents residing in xenografts that have not yet been identified. These infectious agents could cause disease in their natural state or could recombine with innocuous human retroviruses to form new chimeric agents.[101] It is unclear which infectious agents present in xenografts would be communicable and pathogenic in human populations.[102]

Minister" and the later being defined as including those illnesses enumerated in the legislation such as ebola, plague, Lassa fever, leprosy, smallpox, syphilis, and tuberculosis as well as any diseases specified by regulation. *See* Health Protection and Promotion Act, R.S.O. 1990, ch. H.7, § 1(1) (2001) (Can.).

97. *See* Chapman et al., *supra* note 6. *See generally supra* notes 6-8 and accompanying text.

98. Paul Le Tissier et al., *Two Sets of Human-Tropic Pig Retrovirus,* 389 NATURE 681 (1997); Ulrich Martin et al., *Expression of Pig Endogenous Retrovirus by Primary Porcine Endothelial Cells and Infection of Human Cells,* 352 LANCET 692 (1998); Clive Patience et al., *Infection of Human Cells by an Endogenous Retrovirus of Pigs,* 3 NATURE MED. 282 (1997).

99. Luc J.W. van der Laan et al., *Infection by Porcine Endogenous Retrovirus After Islet Xenotransplantation in SCID Mice,* 407 NATURE 501 (2000).

100. Walid Heneine et al., *No Evidence of Infection with Porcine Endogenous Retrovirus in Recipients of Porcine Islet-Cell Xenografts,* 352 LANCET 695 (1998); Khazal Paradis et al., *Search for Cross-Species Transmission of Porcine Endogenous Retrovirus in Patients Treated with Living Pig Tissue,* 285 SCIENCE 1236 (1999).

101. Jon Allan, *Silk Purse or Sow's Ear,* 3 NATURE MED. 275 (1997); Douglas M. Smith, *Endogenous Retrovirus in Xenografts,* 328 NEW ENG. J. MED. 142 (1993). Such recombination is a course of events not uncommon in cells infected with retroviruses. M.A. McClure et al., *Sequence Comparisons of Retroviral Proteins: Relative Rates of Change and General Phylogeny,* 85 PROC. NAT'L ACAD. SCI. U.S.A. 2469 (1988). This latter mechanism is thought to account for the pandemics caused by the modified influenza viruses in 1957 (subtype H2N2) and 1968 (subtype H3N2). C. Scholtissek et al., *On the Origin of the Human Influenza Virus Subtypes H2N2 and H3N2,* 87 VIROLOGY 13 (1978).

102. Although some agents might not be pathogenic, others, like the deadly human influenza virus which in 1918 is estimated to have killed between 20 to 40 million people in less than a year, might result in considerable morbidity and mortality. *See* Elizabeth

In sum, current public health law provisions cannot be used to enforce post-xenotransplantation surveillance because the nature and communicability of the pathogen and severity of the resultant disease are not yet determined. Furthermore, most current public health legislation would fail because symptoms or other indices of disease are required before official intervention, even though adequate prevention of epidemics relies on the ability to identify infected but asymptomatic individuals. This is problematic given that public health law has the unique ability to enforce performance of human conduct such as the collection of bodily specimens. It is this ability that renders public health law the most effective, if not the only, legal mechanism for ensuring compliance with the public safety measures.

There are, however, two solutions that may allow officials to apply public health legislation to xenotransplantation. Officials could either amend the general provisions in public health legislation so that they apply to xenotransplantation, or enact xenotransplantation-specific legislation. The latter represents the better solution because existing general public health provisions are ill-suited to cope with the exceptional difficulties posed by xenotransplantation, and because amendment to incorporate the necessary powers might overtax and confuse these provisions.

3. Proposal for New Xenotransplantation Legislation

The main function of xenotransplantation legislation would be to provide legal authority for the monitoring requirements of the public health safeguards—especially the periodic collection of bodily specimens from recipients regardless of whether or not they appear to be symptomatic, and the power to conduct post-mortem analyses. In this regard, the legislation would only apply to those individuals who undergo an animal-to-human organ, tissue, or cellxenotransplantation procedure. Pre-xenotransplanta tion baseline sampling would not fall under the aegis of the legislation but would instead be a prerequisite to undergoing the operation. In addition to authorizing monitoring of recipients, xenotransplantation legislation could provide a contingency plan in the event that recipients become infected with communicable agents as a result of the operation. If so, the legislation would need to grant public health officials the powers to treat and to detain and isolate the recipient if necessary. Alternatively, control of any emerging communicable illnesses, once detected through surveillance authorized by xenotransplantation-specific legislation, could be handled by existing public health legislation.

Pennisi, *Virology: First Genes Isolated From the Deadly 1918 Flu Virus,* 275 SCIENCE 1739 (1997).

If enacted, the monitoring provisions of xenotransplantation legislation would grant health authorities greater power than that found in existing public health legislation. In existing legislation, the officials' power to examine functions only to assess whether an individual is infected with a specific and identifiable agent. Such an examination will normally lead to treatment or other intervention only if the examination results are positive. In the case of xenotransplantation monitoring provisions, however, the officials' power to examine must be expanded because monitoring will need to be an ongoing process as opposed to a single event. This is necessary to monitor recipients for signs of infection and to collect epidemiological data because those carrying out the monitoring will be looking not for a specific agent but for any and all signs of infection that might arise over time. Ongoing monitoring will also be critical for the identification of novel infectious agents through epidemiological strategies that require large data bases, as well as data points collected at different moments in time.

In implementing xenotransplantation legislation, officials must also consider the appropriate penalties for violations of the monitoring provisions. In general, loss of liberty would be too onerous an enforcement mechanism to impose on recipients given the theoretical nature of the risks to the public health. As long as recipients remain asymptomatic and there is no evidence of further transmissibility, officials would not have sufficient grounds to justify imprisonment. If diligently enforced, monetary fines could be a sufficiently persuasive means of enforcement. Officials should, however, ultimately be empowered to isolate and detain individuals to prevent or quell the spread of disease should recipients become infected with a communicable agent posing a threat to the public health. Officials need to direct more thought toward devising the fairest enforcement model possible in light of the current social and scientific knowledge that has been gathered on xenotransplantation.

Another issue requiring further reflection is what level of government should have the power to enact and enforce the legislation. To be most effective, the public health safeguards would need to be uniformly applicable worldwide. Assuming that global implementation will not be feasible in the near future due to the novelty of the issue, uncertainty of the potential harm, and disparities in governmental and economic resources available to implement public health measures, legislation should at least extend to the largest areas with border controls—typically nations.[103] If it is

---

103. In areas such as the European Union with no national border controls, implementation across the included territory would be advisable.

not, then recipients receiving a xenotransplant in a jurisdiction with adequate safeguards could move to a jurisdiction having less onerous and possibly substandard safeguards. Such a state of affairs would erode the surveillance system and would therefore be unacceptable.

There are two ways of ensuring legislative uniformity within national borders. Legislators could prepare a single set of minimum safeguards that would be ratified at the local level by each of the provinces/states in every nation hosting clinical xenotransplantation. Another possibility would be to have the central governments of each nation enact the legislation. Although this latter option would pose little problem in countries where the federal government has played an active role in communicable disease control (for example, the United States),[104] it may pose problems in other countries where the involvement of the central government in public health matters has thus far been limited (for example, Canada).[105] Nevertheless, the problem is likely solvable given the national scope of the potential health problem.[106]

Although xenotransplantation legislation would impose onerous obligations on recipients, it nevertheless represents a fair compromise between outright prohibition of clinical xenotransplantation and unduly jeopardizing the public's health through non-existent, inadequate or ineffective regulation. In exchange for the opportunity to save and prolong their lives, xenotransplant recipients would provide society with the minimum level of epidemiological data that it requires to protect itself. When comparing the advantages of xenotransplantation with the disadvantages of the public

---

104. *See* Lawrence O. Gostin, *Public Health Law in a New Century—Part II: Public Health Powers and Limits*, 283 JAMA 2979, 2979-80 (2000). In addition to direct intervention through the U.S. Centers for Disease Control and other divisions of the U.S. Department of Health and Human Services, the federal government often uses its constitutional spending power to make crucial federal public health funds contingent on state conformance with uniform federal standards. *See id.* at 2980.

105. *See supra*, note 70 and accompanying text.

106. For example, given its dual jurisdiction over matters of health, the Canadian parliament likely possesses the authority to enact xenotransplantation legislation:

> Legislation dealing with health matters has been found within the provincial power where the approach in the legislation is to an aspect of health, local in nature . . . . On the other hand, federal legislation in relation to 'health' can be supported where the dimension of the problem is national rather than local in nature . . . . In sum 'health' is not a matter which is subject to specific constitutional assignment but instead is an amorphous topic which can be addressed by valid federal or provincial legislation, depending in the circumstances of each case on the nature or scope of the health problem in question.

Schneider v. The Queen, [1982] 2 S.C.R. 112, 141-142.

health legislation, the advantage of saving one's life through xenotransplantation should greatly outweigh the drawback of having to provide periodic serum samples. Moreover, in light of the public health risks associated with xenotransplantation, the monitoring provisions would not represent an excessive safety measure. Rather, they would be a minimum precaution based on sound scientific principles. Thus, judicial review of xenotransplantation legislation should be reluctant to dismiss the scientific underpinnings upon which it is founded.[107]

III. CONSTITUTIONAL DIMENSION: BALANCING THE RIGHTS OF THE COLLECTIVE AND THE DUTY OF THE STATE TO PROTECT THE PUBLIC HEALTH WITH THE RIGHTS OF THE INDIVIDUAL

The use of coercive measures such as monetary fines to attain public health goals raises difficult issues concerning an individual's responsibility to protect other members of society as well as society's obligation to respect the civil rights and liberties of its individual citizens.[108] Should

---

107. Lawrence O. Gostin, *Public Health Law in a New Century—Part III: Public Health Regulation: A Systematic Evaluation*, 283 JAMA 3118, 3120 (2000):

> [T]o the extent possible, risk assessments should be based on objective and reliable scientific evidence provided by the multiple disciplines of public health, including medicine, virology, bacteriology, and epidemiology. Science-based risk assessments provide a more secure ground for decision making and avoid reflexive actions based on irrational fears, speculation, stereotypes, or pernicious mythologies.

See also Lawrence O. Gostin, *The Future of Public Health Law*, 12 AM. J. LAW & MED. 461, 464 (1988) [hereinafter Gostin, *The Future of Public Health Law*]:

> Science has a more precise understanding of the etiological agents of infectious disease, the most likely harborers of the agent, the most efficient modes of its transmission, and the methods of modifying behaviors or environments in order to interrupt its spread. Accordingly, modern measures for reducing the spread of disease are predominantly based upon research, education, and counselling, specifically targeted to groups at risk of spreading or contracting the disease. Public health statutes and judicial review of public health action should reflect these new scientific understandings by requiring that the goals of public health measures be limited to the interruption of the most efficient modes of disease transmission.

108. As stated by one commentator:

> [T]here is a fundamental conflict of interest between providing medical care to individuals and providing public health services to a community. The patient-autonomy model that underlies personal health care is incompatible with the subrogation of individual interests that is neces-

xenotransplantation legislation be enacted and subsequently challenged,[109] courts will be seized with the delicate task of striking the right balance between individual and societal rights and responsibilities. The purpose of this section is not to provide an exhaustive discussion of the constitutional dimension of the problem but simply to offer some preliminary thoughts on some of the issues that are likely to be raised.

A. Individual Rights and Freedoms

1. *Personal Rights and Liberties*

Section 7 of the Canadian *Charter* guarantees an individual's right not to be deprived of life, liberty, or security of the person except in accordance with the principles of fundamental justice.[110] Xenotransplantation safeguards do not, however, involve literal intrusion upon the physical integrity of nonconsenting recipients since the monitoring provisions would provide for monetary sanctions, rather than physical force, as a means of enforcing the collection of bodily samples. This is important because physical intrusion would clearly violate the *Charter's* provisions.[111] Notwithstanding the non-physical nature of the coercion involved, xenotransplantation legislation could infringe a transplant recipient's constitutional rights. For instance, the legislation would infringe the recipient's right to personal autonomy and self-determination by removing the option of withdrawing his or her participation from public health safeguards[112] Ad-

---

sary for effective public health .... Public health rejects the patient's
right to have sole control of his/her treatment.
Edward P. Richards & Katharine C. Rathbun, *The Role of the Police Power in 21st Century Public Health*, 26 SEXUALLY TRANSMITTED DISEASES 350, 354-55 (1999).

109. Florencio & Caulfield, *supra* note 8, at 284 ("Although xenotransplant candidates would have to agree to participate in all public health measures to be eligible for the transplant procedure, once the procedure has taken place and their health has improved, patients may feel that the restrictions on their rights are too onerous.").

110. CAN. CONST. (Constitution Act 1982), pt. I (Canadian Charter of Rights and Freedoms), cl. 11 § 7.

111. CAN. CONST. (Constitution Act 1982), pt. I (Canadian Charter of Rights and Freedoms), cl. 11 § 7-8. If an individual is symptomatic, he will be isolated and detained in accordance with regular public health legislation and thus, there would be no violation of the Charter's provisions.

112. The right to autonomy derives from the common law but it is arguably also protected by the Charter. *See* Rodriguez v. B.C.(A.G.), [1993] 3 S.C.R. 519, 588:

There is no question, then, that personal autonomy, at least with respect to the right to make choices concerning one's own body, control over one's physical and psychological integrity, and basic human dignity are encompassed within security of the person, at least to the extent of freedom from criminal prohibitions which interfere with these.

ditionally, by tying weighty penal consequences to non-compliant behavior, the legislation might also be contravening the recipient's interest in personal security by inflicting serious psychological stress upon him.[113] Determining the viability of xenotransplantation legislation under section 7 of the Charter would involve a two-step process. First, a court would decide if there had been a breach of the right to life, liberty or security of the person. If there was no breach, the legislation would be upheld as valid. If there was a breach, a court would next determine whether such a breach was in accordance with the principles of fundamental justice.

The Supreme Court of Canada has been using two different approaches to determine whether fundamental justice justifies a violation of personal rights and liberties. According to the first approach, the contravention of an individual's section 7 rights will be in accordance with the principles of fundamental justice so long as the societal or state interest outweighs the individual's right to life, liberty and/or security of the person.[114] The second approach is to perform an analysis under section 1 of

---

Given the quasi-criminal and penal nature of public health legislation, it is highly probable that the right to personal autonomy would enjoy as much protection in a public health context as it does in a criminal context. *See also* Fleming v. Reid, [1991] 4 O.R. (3d) 74, 88 (C.A.) ("[T]he common law right to determine what shall be done with one's own body and the constitutional right to security of the person, both of which are founded on the belief in the dignity and autonomy of each individual, can be treated as coextensive.").

113. *See* R. v. Morgentaler, [1988] 1 S.C.R. 30, 56 ("[S]tate interference with bodily integrity and serious state-imposed psychological stress, at least in the criminal law context, constitutes a breach of security of the person."). It is noteworthy that the minority in *Morgentaler* chose to set forth a more stringent test as to when state-imposed psychological stress would result in a violation of the security of the person interest:

As to an asserted right to be free from any state interference with bodily integrity and serious state-imposed psychological stress, I would say that to be accepted, as a constitutional right, it would have to be based on something more than the mere imposition, by the State, of such stress and anxiety .... A breach of the right would have to be based upon an infringement of some interest which would be of such nature and such importance as to warrant constitutional protection. This, it would seem to me, would be limited to cases where the state-action complained of, in addition to imposing stress and strain, also infringed another right, freedom or interest which was deserving of protection under the concept of security of the person.

Id. at 146-147. Interestingly, because the monitoring provisions would both impinge upon the personal autonomy of recipients and impose psychological stress upon them, counsel for the recipients might contend that even the requirements of the minority's test would be satisfied in the circumstances.

114. *See, e.g.,* Thomson Newspapers v. Canada (Dir. of Investigation and Research, Restrictive Trade Practices Comm'n), [1990] 1 S.C.R. 425, 583 ("Fundamental justice in

the Charter which states that the rights and freedoms guaranteed by the Charter are subject to "such reasonable limits prescribed by law as can be demonstrably justified in a free and democratic society."[115] This Article argues that the second approach would be superior to the first in determining whether xenotransplantation legislation is justified by the principles of fundamental justice.

The first approach, or the 'balancing' approach, to fundamental justice is problematic in several regards. First, courts consider the societal interest under section 7, where the burden of proof lies with the *Charter* claimant, instead of under section 1, where the burden of proof lies with the state. Second, unlike section 1, section 7 does not provide an analytical framework capable of structuring judicial discretion during the performance of the balancing test. Third, the fact that courts consider the interests of the state along with those of the individual directly within section 7 of the *Charter* weakens the ability of the *Charter* to operate as a rights-based, counter-majoritarian instrument.[116]

The second approach defines the principles of fundamental justice as being located within the basic tenets of the Canadian legal system.[117] Under this approach, courts only consider the interests of the state under section 1 of the *Charter*.[118] This second approach does not suffer from the

---

our Canadian legal tradition . . . is primarily designed to ensure that a fair balance be struck between the interests of society and those of its citizens"); *see also* R. v. Beare, [1988] 2 S.C.R. 387, 415 (holding that fingerprinting a person charged with but not convicted of an indictable offense does not infringe upon rights guaranteed in section 7 of the Canadian Charter of Rights and Freedoms); R. v. Lyons, [1987] 2 S.C.R. 309 (examining whether the dangerous offenders provisions of the criminal code contravened the right to liberty guaranteed under the Charter); R v. Jones, [1986] 2 S.C.R. 284 (balancing the compelling state interest in compulsory education against right to liberty under Section 7 of the Charter).

115. CAN. CONST. (Constitution Act 1982), pt. I (Canadian Charter of Rights and Freedoms), cl. 11 § 1.

116. *See* Patrik S. Florencio & Robert H. Keller, *End-of-Life Decision Making: Rethinking the Principles of Fundamental Justice in the Context of Emerging Empirical Data*, 7 HEALTH L. J. 233, 247 (1999).

117. *See* Reference Re Section 94(2) of the *Motor Vehicle Act*, R.S.B.C. 1979, [1985] 2 S.C.R. 486, 503 ("The principles of fundamental justice are to be found in the basic tenets of our legal system. They do not lie in the realm of general public policy but in the inherent domain of the judiciary as guardian of the justice system.").

118. For example, legislation depriving individuals of life, liberty, and security of the person must not be substantively or procedurally arbitrary lest it violate the principles of fundamental justice. *See* B.(R.) v. Children's Aid Soc'y of Metro. Toronto, [1995] 1 S.C.R. 315, 374 ("The protection of a child's right to life and to health, when it becomes necessary to do so, is a basic tenet of our legal system, and legislation to that end accords with the principles of fundamental justice . . . ."); R. v. Swain, [1991] 1 S.C.R. 933, 977

infirmities enumerated above and is hence both analytically superior and more just in its result than its balancing counterpart.[119]

According to either the first or the second approach, however, the xenotransplantation legislation meets the requirements of fundamental justice, although the second approach requires that the legislation meet a stricter test. Indeed, given that the monitoring provisions would not be arbitrary—they would be based on *sound* scientific principles for the *legitimate* objective of protecting the public health and would apply *only* to individuals having received a xenotransplantation—officials could forcefully maintain that the legislation would not be in violation of the principles of fundamental justice. Thus, notwithstanding the breaches to the personal security interest of recipients, the monitoring legislation would not contravene section 7 of the *Charter* since the breaches would be in accordance with fundamental justice.

The U.S. Constitution also limits the extent to which public health legislation may impinge upon the fundamental rights of privacy and bodily integrity. The concept of privacy is most directly embodied in the Fourth Amendment to the Constitution, which provides that the government shall not violate "[t]he right of the people to be secure in their persons, houses, papers, and effects, against unreasonable searches and seizures . . . ."[120] The Supreme Court has consistently held that state-compelled collection and testing of bodily fluids such as blood or urine, such as would be required of xenotransplant recipients, is a "search" subject to the Fourth Amendment.[121] Whether a search or seizure passes constitutional scrutiny under the Fourth Amendment would depend upon whether that search or seizure is reasonable in light of the balance between the intrusion on the

---

(holding that the "common law rule which allows the Crown to raise evidence of insanity over and above the accused's wishes is a denial of liberty which is not in accordance with the principles of fundamental justice"); Singh v. Minister of Employment and Immigration, [1985] 1 S.C.R. 177, 220 (holding that procedures under the 1976 Immigration Act did not meet the requirements of fundamental justice under section 7 of the Charter and that such procedures did not constitute a reasonable limit on the rights of persons claiming refugee status within the meaning of section 1 of the Charter).

119. *See* Florencio & Keller, *supra* note 116, at 247-248, for a more detailed discussion of why the second approach is superior to the first approach.

120. U.S. CONST. amend. IV.

121. *See, e.g.*, Vernonia School District 47J v. Acton, 515 U.S. 646, 652 (1995); Skinner v. Railway Labor Executives' Ass'n, 489 U.S. 602, 617 (1989); Schmerber v. Cal., 384 U.S. 757, 767-68 (1966). Courts would consider a search that is authorized or required by xenotransplantation legislation to be state-compelled even if private transplant centers or physicians conduct it. *See Skinner*, 489 U.S. at 614-15. Courts may also view sampling of bodily fluids as a "seizure" because it interferes with a xenotransplant recipient's possessory interest in her bodily fluids. *See id.* at 617, n.4.

individual's legitimate privacy interests and the government's legitimate interest in protecting the public health.[122]

Courts are likely to find that the intrusion on a transplant recipient's privacy is minimal for several reasons. First, a reasonable expectation of the privacy of her bodily fluids is substantially reduced because ongoing surveillance of those bodily fluids would follow a recipient's voluntary and extensive experience with the high degree of intrusion involved in transplant surgery and the large number of related medical examinations that are conducted before and after surgery.[123] Second, several factors would make the character of the intrusion less compromising of privacy. Two such factors are that officials would likely take blood samples rather than excretory fluids[124] and that officials would draw these samples in a medical establishment rather than in a more public setting.[125] A final consideration which should inform the drafting of xenotransplantation legislation, is that courts will be more likely to consider a search or seizure reasonable if the results are disclosed only to those who need to know the results—i.e., the recipient's physicians and relevant public health authorities.[126]

Privacy and bodily integrity are also protected by the "substantive due process" conception of implied fundamental liberty rights embodied in the Due Process Clause of the Fourteenth Amendment.[127] Courts generally

---

122. *See Vernonia*, 515 U.S. at 652-53. Although we believe that the risks posed by xenotransplantation without surveillance make the government's interest in surveillance compelling, the U.S. Supreme Court requires only that the governmental interest be more important than the legitimate expectation of privacy that testing would intrude upon. *See id.* at 660-61. However, it is particularly important that the governmental interest in surveillance clearly outweighs the privacy interest because xenotransplant recipients would be tested without individual suspicion of infection. *See Skinner*, 489 U.S. at 624 (holding that a search may be reasonable despite the absence of individualized suspicion if the important governmental interest furthered by the search would be jeopardized by a requirement of individualized suspicion).

123. *See Vernonia*, 515 U.S. at 656-57 (holding that student athletes have a reduced expectation of privacy because they voluntarily "go out for the team" and because public school students already are subject to medical examination and vaccination).

124. *See Skinner*, 489 U.S. at 617, 626 (distinguishing blood tests from urinalysis and other tests taken in a manner that compromises traditional expectations of privacy).

125. *See Schmerber*, 384 U.S. at 771 (holding that blood tests are more reasonable when taken by a physician in a hospital environment according to accepted medical practices).

126. *See Vernonia*, 796 F. Supp. at 1364.

127. *See, e.g.*, Cruzan v. Dir., Miss. Dept. of Health, 497 U.S. 261, 262 (1990) (discussing the right to bodily integrity); Roe v. Wade, 410 U.S. 113, 153 (1973) (recognizing that the right to privacy encompasses the abortion decision); Eisenstadt v. Baird, 405 U.S. 438, 438 (1972) (recognizing a fundamental right to privacy including the decision

subject laws that burden a fundamental right to "strict scrutiny."[128] Under strict scrutiny, when an individual's liberty interest is balanced against the government's interest in enforcing a restriction on liberty, the restriction must be narrowly drawn to achieve a compelling state interest, rather than merely having a rational relation to a governmental interest.

Even if we assume that a court would apply strict scrutiny, xenotransplantation legislation is likely to pass constitutional muster. For decades the Supreme Court has been highly deferential to the government with respect to public health legislation, rarely questioning its compelling nature.[129] This is particularly true when legislation calls for intrusions of limited duration and severity,[130] and when it protects the health of the individual whose rights are being intruded upon, as well as the rights of the populace.[131] Although monitoring of a xenotransplant recipient could go on for an indefinite duration, perhaps for many years, the severity of the intrusions necessary for surveillance should be minimal and the health of the recipient is protected by such surveillance. Thus, carefully drawn xenotransplantation legislation should withstand a substantive due process challenge.

2. Finding the Right Balance

This section has argued that although the monitoring provisions in xenotransplantation legislation would constitute a violation of the rights of recipients to liberty and/or to the security of their persons, this violation would be in accordance with the principles of fundamental justice and therefore inherently justified. Lest this reasoning be amiss, it is also important to inquire whether the proposed legislation might be justified on

---

whether or not to use contraception). *But see,* Bowers v. Hardwick, 478 U.S. 186, 191 (1986) (failing to extend the right of privacy to acts of sodomy). The Fourteenth Amendment provides that no state shall "deprive any person of life, liberty, or property, without due process of law." U.S. CONST. amend. XIV.

128. *See, e.g.,* Planned Parenthood of Southeastern Pa. v. Casey, 505 U.S. 833, 871 (1992).

129. *See, e.g.,* Washington v. Harper, 494 U.S. 210, 222 (1990) (finding that forced treatment of a prisoner with antipsychotic medication was justified by potential harm to the prisoner and others); Whalen v. Roe, 429 U.S. 589, 603-604 (1977) (upholding prescription reporting legislation for controlled substances); Buck v. Bell, 274 U.S. 200, 207 (1927) (allowing sexual sterilization of a mentally retarded prisoner on public health grounds); Jacobson v. Mass., 197 U.S. 11, 31 (1905) (upholding compulsory vaccination of the general public).

130. *See, e.g., Jacobson,* 197 U.S. at 24-30.

131. *See, e.g., id.; Washington,* 494 U.S. at 222.

the less fundamental ground that it imposes reasonable limitations that can be demonstrably justified in a free and democratic society.[132]

In his book "The Plague," Camus expressed the idea that the consequences of an epidemic are not experienced by citizens individually, but by society as a whole in the form of a collective history.[133] It is exactly this characteristic—the collective nature of the health ramifications that can result from infectious diseases—that makes public health legislation so important. Public health law seeks to reduce the incidence of morbidity and mortality by preventing or curbing the spread of infectious diseases. Society has long considered the protection and preservation of the public health to be a value of fundamental importance and this sentiment persists to this day.[134] The state would clearly have a compelling interest in enforcing a surveillance system that aims to acquire epidemiological data that would permit health authorities rapidly to identify and contain infectious agents that could arise from xenotransplantation.

Yet, even when the state sets out to accomplish an important end point, the means by which it attempts to do so must be rationally related to the purpose of the legislation. In the case of public health legislation, the

---

132. The answer to this question should inform any constitutional analysis of xenotransplantation legislation, but is specifically required under section 1 of the *Charter*. *See* CAN. CONST. (Constitution Act 1982), pt. I (Canadian Charter of Rights and Freedoms), cl. 11 § 1. For the leading case on balancing under section 1 of the Charter, see R. v. Oakes, [1986] 1 S.C.R. 103.

133. *See* ALBERT CAMUS, THE PLAGUE 167 (Stuart Gilbert trans., Vintage Int'l 1991):

> Thus week by week the prisoners of plague put up what fight they could. Some ... even contrived to fancy they were still behaving as free men and had the power of choice. But actually it would have been truer to say that by this time ... the plague had swallowed up everything and everyone. No longer were there individual destinies; only a collective destiny, made of plague and the emotions shared by all.

134. *See*, Gostin, *The Future of Public Health Law*, *supra* note 107, at 483:

> Ultimately, the right of the state to take measures which avoid a probable and grave harm must be respected, even at the cost of individual civil liberties. It does no service to groups at risk for disease to fail to implement effective public health measures in the name of protection of their liberty. The health of the community is perhaps the most important human and societal value.

The Latin maxim *salus populi suprema lex*, meaning that the welfare or health of the people is the supreme law of the land, frequently appeared in nineteenth century cases such as *Haverty v. Bass*, 66 Me. 71 (1876). *See* WILLIAM J. NOVAK, THE PEOPLE'S WELFARE: LAW AND REGULATION IN NINETEENTH-CENTURY AMERICA (1996). *See also* Elmer E. Smead, Sic utere tuo ut alienum non laedas: *A Basis of the State Police Power*, 21 CORNELL L.Q. 276 (1936).

means, or the specific powers that the legislation grants, must be premised on the biological characteristics of the particular infectious disease threats from which the legislation seeks to shield society. For instance, although restrictions on the rights to liberty and association may be a valid policy in the case of airborne pathogens, they are not justified in the case of blood-borne pathogens such as HIV, whose transmissibility is limited to activities such as blood transfusions, sexual relations and/or needle-sharing.[135]

The biological reality of xenotransplantation is that animal agents residing in xenografts could infect xenotransplant recipients who could then pass the agents to the community at large. Although this infectious disease threat is foreseeable, the identity of the agents that are likely to infect recipients as a result of xenotransplantation, and the method of their transmission, remain unknown. Given this reality, the government's implementation of a surveillance system to collect data that will hopefully enable scientists to identify and track down infectious agents that might arise as a result of xenobiotechnology is unquestionably a rational means of protecting the public health. Moreover, requiring xenotransplant recipients to engage in conforming behavior would be central to the state's interest in having an effective surveillance system given that "[i]ncomplete and unreliable data [would] greatly reduce our power to detect and contain outbreaks of infectious disease."[136]

Such a surveillance system would also constitute the most equitable means of protecting the public health from the infectious disease risks associated with xenotransplantation. The government could take other approaches to fulfill this important objective such as isolating recipients or forbidding clinical xenotransplantations until more is known about the infectious disease risks. These approaches would be better suited to the task of protecting the public health but would involve far greater restrictions to the liberty and security interests of recipients. A surveillance system has the distinct advantage of offering an important means of protecting the public health while allowing recipients both to take advantage of xenobiotechnology and to retain their freedoms of movement and association within society. Thus, a surveillance system represents the best of the possible options.

It is important, however, not to make light of the fact that xenotransplantation legislation—by authorizing the periodic examination of asymptomatic xenotransplant recipients—would grant health authorities greater

---

135. L.O. Gostin, *The Resurgent Tuberculosis Epidemic in the Era of AIDS: Reflections on Public Health, Law, and Society*, 54 MARYLAND L. REV. 1, 8 (1995).

136. Florencio & Caulfield, *supra* note 8, at 284.

power than that provided by traditional public health legislation. It would, in other words, represent an extensive change to our existing law and would need to be rigorously justified by public policy. Policy matters involving extensive changes to the existing law are better left, in a constitutional democracy, to the legislative branch of government.[137] Correspondingly, when asked to review legislative solutions to complex matters of policy, the judiciary should extend to the legislature a sufficient degree of deference.[138] This is especially true when the policy matter relates to the protection of the public health.[139] If a court struck down xenotransplanta-

---

137. *See, e.g.,* Dobson (Litig. Guardian of) v. Dobson, [1999] 2 S.C.R. 753, 766 ("Matters of public policy are concerned with sensitive issues that involve far-reaching and unpredictable implications for Canadian society. It follows that the legislature is the more appropriate forum for the consideration of such problems and the implementation of legislative solutions to them."); *see also* Winnipeg Child and Family Servs. v. G.(D.F.), [1997] 3 S.C.R. 925, 960-961 (holding that it is not appropriate for a court to extend its power to order the detention of a pregnant woman for the purpose of preventing harm to her unborn child); Watkins v. Olafson, [1989] 2 S.C.R. 750, 764 (holding that in the absence of enabling legislation or the consent of all parties, a court cannot order that a plaintiff forego his traditional right to a lump-sum judgment for a series of period payments).

138. *See, e.g.,* McKinney v. Univ. of Guelph, [1990] 3 S.C.R. 229, 315:

> [H]aving accepted the importance of the legislative objective, one must . . . recognize that if the legislative goal is to be achieved, it will inevitably be achieved to the detriment of some. Moreover, attempts to protect the rights of one group will also inevitably impose burdens on the rights of other groups. There is no perfect scenario in which the rights of all can be equally protected.

See also Irwin Toy Ltd. v. Quebec (A.G.), [1989] 1 S.C.R. 927, 933 (sustaining the reasonableness of a legislative conclusion that a "ban on commercial advertising directed to children was the minimal impairment of free expression consistent with the pressing and substantial goal of protecting children against manipulation through advertising"); R. v. Edwards Books and Art, [1986] 2 S.C.R. 713, 787 (upholding the constitutionality of the Retail Business Holidays Act based on the stated legislative purpose). American case law also expresses the view that a degree of deference must be extended to the legislature. *See, e.g.,* Williams v. Mayor of Baltimore, 289 U.S. 36, 42 (1933) ("The judicial function is exhausted with the discovery that the relation between means and end is not wholly vain and fanciful, an illusory pretense. Within the field where men of reason may reasonably differ, the legislature must have its way.").

139. *See supra* note 129; *see also* Arizona ex rel. Conway v. Southern Pac. Co., 145 P.2d 530, 532 (Ariz. 1943) ("where the police power is set in motion in its proper sphere, the courts have no jurisdiction to stay the arm of the legislative branch") (quoting State v. Superior Court, 174 P.973, 976 (Wash. 1918).). *See generally* Lawrence O. Gostin, *The Americans with Disabilities Act and the Corpus of AntiDiscimination Law: A Force for Change in the Future of Public Health Regulation*, 3 HEALTH MATRIX 89 (1993) (arguing that the standard judicial review of the constitutionality of public health statutes is being replaced by disability law which is applicable to protect people with infectious conditions).

tion legislation on constitutional grounds, the capacity of the surveillance system to generate the data required for the protection of the public health would depend entirely on the willingness of recipients voluntarily to comply with the safeguards. In the absence of such willingness, the surveillance system would collapse and society could be left defenseless in the wake of an epidemic.

B. Freedom From Discrimination

Since xenotransplantation legislation would only apply to individuals who underwent a xenotransplant operation, one might ask whether the legislation violates section 15 of the *Charter* by infringing an individual's right to be free from discrimination.[140] In *Law v. Canada (Minister of Employment and Immigration)*, the Supreme Court of Canada recently restated the appropriate approach to conducting equality analyses.[141] The Court stated that a court making a discrimination inquiry should make the following inquiries:

> First, does the impugned law (a) draw a formal distinction between the claimant and others on the basis of one or more personal characteristics, or (b) fail to take into account the claimant's already disadvantaged position within Canadian society. . . .? Second, was the claimant subject to differential treatment on the basis of one or more of the enumerated and analogous grounds? And third, does the differential treatment discriminate in a substantive sense, bringing into play the purpose of s. 15(1) of the Charter in remedying such ills as prejudice, stereotyping, and historical disadvantage?[142]

A court making the above inquiry would not hold that xenotransplantation violates an individual's right to be free from discrimination. Xenotransplantation legislation would draw a formal distinction on the basis of whether or not individuals are recipients of animal cells, tissues and/or organs and would impose the burden of complying with the public health safeguards upon those who are recipients. This distinction, however, would not be based on an enumerated or analogous ground.[143] More-

---

140. CAN. CONST. (Constitution Act 1982), pt. I (Canadian Charter of Rights and Freedoms), cl. 11 § 15.

141. *See* Law v. Canada (Minister of Employment and Immigration), [1999] 1 S.C.R. 497, 524.

142. *Id.*

143. Some may argue that xenotransplantation legislation would distinguish individuals on the basis of physical disability which is an enumerated ground. Yet, the mere fact of having undergone a xenotransplantation and consequently of being a carrier of

over, even if one could persuasively argue that the legislation did distinguish on the basis of an enumerated or analogous ground, the legislation would not be discriminatory because it would not be based on stereotyping, historical disadvantage, or political and social prejudice in Canadian society. It would be based, rather, on sound scientific principles and the need to safeguard the health of society.

The corresponding analysis under the Equal Protection Clause of the Fourteenth Amendment to the U.S. Constitution is similar.[144] The law does not allow public health authorities to exercise their police powers in ways that discriminate based upon race or other suspect classes without a compelling state interest.[145] Governmental regulation of the public health, however, would not violate the Equal Protection Clause merely because it applies only to xenotransplant recipients and is, therefore, not all-encompassing.[146] Xenotransplantation legislation would apply uniformly to all xenotransplant recipients and therefore would only need to be rationally related to a legitimate government interest to survive constitu-

---

animal cells, tissues and/or organs does not render recipients physically disabled. There is no disability per se. If it were otherwise, then all individuals having undergone some form of surgery, or at least those having undertaken an allotransplantation, would be subject to the characterization of being physically disabled and would be deserving of constitutional protection. Interestingly, Professor Hogg has contended that legislative distinctions that are based on personal characteristics arising as a result of voluntary choices, such as the choice to undergo a xenotransplantation, are not deserving of constitutional protection. *See* PETER W. HOGG, CONSTITUTIONAL LAW OF CANADA 914-15 (4th ed. 1996):

> Another way of looking at immutability as the common element of the listed personal characteristics is to notice that the characteristics are inherent, rather than acquired. They do not reflect a voluntary choice by anyone, but rather an involuntary inheritance .... It is true that individuals may claim to be treated unfairly by the law for conditions that are their own responsibility, but this kind of claim even if fully justified does not warrant a constitutional remedy.

144. The Equal Protection Clause provides that the government may not deprive any person of life, liberty or property "without equal protection of the laws." U.S. CONST. amend. XIV.

145. *See, e.g.*, City of Cleburne v. Cleburne Living Ctr., 473 U.S. 432, 442-46 (1985) (declining to recognize the mentally retarded as a quasi-suspect class, and suggesting similar treatment for "the disabled, the mentally ill, and the infirm"); Coolbaugh v. State of La., 136 F.3d 430, 433-34 (5th Cir. 1998) (surveying federal case law denying heightened scrutiny for various forms of physical disability); Jew Ho v. Williamson, 103 F. 10 (N.D. Cal. 1900) (striking down a bubonic plague quarantine that affected only the Chinese population).

146. *See* Zucht v. King, 260 U.S. 174, 176-77 (1922).

tional scrutiny.[147] In light of the sound public health rationale for enacting xenotransplantation safeguards and the lack of any history of discrimination against xenotransplant recipients, narrowly drawn xenotransplantation legislation would survive challenge under the Equal Protection Clause.[148]

Although some may worry that officials may enforce xenotransplantation legislation in a discriminatory manner—namely, in a manner that is influenced by social characteristics instead of in a manner that is neutral and uniform—this risk does not speak to the constitutionality of the legislation itself. Should such difficulties arise, agencies such as human rights commissions[149] and/or ombudspersons[150] could remedy them. Interestingly, similar fears were raised [151] when the New York City Department of Health updated its Health Code to permit compulsory actions, such as the detention for treatment of persistently non-compliant tuberculosis infected individuals.[152] The anticipated discriminatory practices, however, never materialized.[153] Indeed, a recent follow-up study found that the Health Code was not enforced in a discriminatory fashion since patients were detained on the basis of their history of compliance, rather than on the basis of their social characteristics.[154]

---

147. *See, e.g., City of Cleburne*, 473 U.S. at 442 (1985) (zoning regulations barring group home for the mentally disabled subject only to the rational basis test, not heightened scrutiny).

148. Indeed, it has been suggested that even legislation quarantining all HIV-infected individuals—a concept far more restrictive than most alternative strategies now in place to control the spread of HIV—would likely pass muster under the Equal Protection Clause. *See* 7 Deborah Jones Merritt, *Communicable Disease and Constitutional Law: Controlling AIDS*, 61 N.Y.U. LAW REV. 739 (1986).

149. *See, e.g.,* Human Rights Code, S.O. 1993, ch. H.19 (2001) (Can.).

150. *See, e.g.,* Ombudsman Act, R.S.O. 1990, ch. O.6 (2001) (Can.).

151. George J. Annas, *Control of Tuberculosis—The Law and the Public's Health* 328 NEW ENGL. J. MED. 585 (1993) (raising the concern that the tuberculosis regulations might be enforced in a discriminatory manner—i.e., that patients with a history of drug abuse or homelessness could be singled out for legal action).

152. N.Y. CITY HEALTH CODE § 11.47(d) (1994).

153. For an excellent discussion of the legal and policy issues surrounding the tuberculosis control measures that were adopted by the New York City Department of Health, see Carlos A. Ball & Mark Barnes, *Public Health and Individual Rights: Tuberculosis Control and Detention Procedures in New York City*, 12 YALE LAW & POLICY REVIEW 38 (1994).

154. M. Rose Gasner et al., *The Use of Legal Action in New York City to Ensure Treatment of Tuberculosis*, 340 NEW ENGL. J. MED. 359, 365 (1999).

IV. CONCLUSION

Given the significant risks of harm associated with xenobiotechnology, the scientific community agrees that robust public safety measures need to accompany the introduction of clinical xenotransplantation. There is a need to devise a legally effective means of ensuring adherence to such public safety measures because a recipient's refusal to comply voluntarily with the safeguards would leave society without any means of protecting itself in the event of emerging infectious diseases. This Article has argued that xenotransplantation-specific public health legislation presents the most effective means of enacting and enforcing the appropriate public health safeguards.

Neither consent law nor the law of contracts would be capable of accomplishing this important objective. Consent law is ill suited to enforce the specific performance of promises because lawmakers designed it to serve as a mechanism of communicating the waiver of legal rights on the part of the consenting party, thereby obviating liability on the part of the party who received the consent. In the case of xenobiotechnology, the consent of recipients to the xenotransplant procedure and to its accompanying safeguards, such as the periodic collection of bodily specimens, would merely indicate the acquiescence of recipients to having the interventions performed on their person. Importantly however, the recipients' consent would not legally bind them, because they could unilaterally withdraw their consent to the public health safeguards at any time after having received the xenotransplant.

Contract law would be similarly ineffective. Because it would be essential for recipients to comply personally with the public safety measures, the law of contracts would be unable to use state power to force the personal execution of contractual obligations. Moreover, because specific performance of these contracts would be incompatible with competing legal principles, including the inviolability of the human body, an invasion of civil liberties would need to be expressly authorized by legislation.

In addition, existing public health legislation is not capable of enforcing the necessary public health safeguards. Although existing public health legislation might be amended to incorporate the powers necessary for the periodic examination of asymptomatic xenotransplant recipients, such amendments might overburden and confuse the existing statutes. The better solution would be to enact new legislation specific to the underlying science and particular risks of harm associated with xenotransplantation.

Xenotransplantation legislation would be a legally effective means of compelling compliance with the safeguards. Such legislation could require the performance of conforming behaviors and could authorize the issuance of monetary fines against recipients who, having benefited from the life saving intervention, refuse to honor their obligations under the legislation. Ultimately however, the ability of xenotransplantation legislation to guarantee the generation of the epidemiological data necessary to protect the public health will depend on its ability to withstand constitutional attack.

This Article has argued that the post-xenotransplantation surveillance system would survive a constitutional attack. The legislation would not be discriminatory and although the monitoring provisions of the legislation would constitute a violation of the rights of recipients to liberty and/or to the security of their person, this violation would be in accordance with the principles of fundamental justice and therefore would pass constitutional muster. If the constitutionality of the legislation ultimately depends on a court's balancing of the competing interests, the judiciary should be reluctant to dismiss the exceptional nature of the risks of harm associated with xenobiotechnology and therefore should take a deferential approach to the proposed legislative solutions.

Name Index